MW00823842

# A Mechanical Translation of the Book of Genesis

## The Hebrew text literally translated word for word

~~~~~~~~~~~~~~~~~~~~~~~~~~~~~~~~~~~~~~~~~~~~~~~

**Jeff A. Benner**

Cover design by Jeff A. Benner.

"A Mechanical Translation of the Book of Genesis," by Jeff Benner. ISBN 978-1-60264-033-7.

Library of Congress Control Number: 2007930400.

Manufactured in the United States of America.

# Table of Contents

ACKNOWLEDGEMENTS ............................................................... 1
INTRODUCTION ....................................................................... 3
    *Contents* ........................................................................ 3
    *The project* ..................................................................... 4
    *The Translation* ............................................................... 5
    *The Hebrew Language* ....................................................... 5
    *Hebrew Names* ................................................................. 7
    *The Names of God* ............................................................ 8
    *Hebrew words* .................................................................. 9
    *Hebrew Verbs* ................................................................ 10
    *Hebrew gender* ............................................................... 12
    *Hebrew numbers* ............................................................. 13
THE MECHANICAL TRANSLATION OF GENESIS ......................... 15
    *Chapter 1* ...................................................................... 15
    *Chapter 2* ...................................................................... 20
    *Chapter 3* ...................................................................... 25
    *Chapter 4* ...................................................................... 29
    *Chapter 5* ...................................................................... 34
    *Chapter 6* ...................................................................... 39
    *Chapter 7* ...................................................................... 43
    *Chapter 8* ...................................................................... 47
    *Chapter 9* ...................................................................... 51
    *Chapter 10* ..................................................................... 56
    *Chapter 11* ..................................................................... 61
    *Chapter 12* ..................................................................... 66
    *Chapter 13* ..................................................................... 70
    *Chapter 14* ..................................................................... 74
    *Chapter 15* ..................................................................... 79
    *Chapter 16* ..................................................................... 82
    *Chapter 17* ..................................................................... 85
    *Chapter 18* ..................................................................... 90
    *Chapter 19* ..................................................................... 96
    *Chapter 20* ................................................................... 104
    *Chapter 21* ................................................................... 108
    *Chapter 22* ................................................................... 114
    *Chapter 23* ................................................................... 119
    *Chapter 24* ................................................................... 123
    *Chapter 25* ................................................................... 135
    *Chapter 26* ................................................................... 141
    *Chapter 27* ................................................................... 148
    *Chapter 28* ................................................................... 156
    *Chapter 29* ................................................................... 161
    *Chapter 30* ................................................................... 167

Chapter 31 ........................................................................... 175
Chapter 32 ........................................................................... 185
Chapter 33 ........................................................................... 191
Chapter 34 ........................................................................... 195
Chapter 35 ........................................................................... 201
Chapter 36 ........................................................................... 206
Chapter 37 ........................................................................... 214
Chapter 38 ........................................................................... 221
Chapter 39 ........................................................................... 227
Chapter 40 ........................................................................... 231
Chapter 41 ........................................................................... 235
Chapter 42 ........................................................................... 246
Chapter 43 ........................................................................... 253
Chapter 44 ........................................................................... 259
Chapter 45 ........................................................................... 265
Chapter 46 ........................................................................... 271
Chapter 47 ........................................................................... 278
Chapter 48 ........................................................................... 284
Chapter 49 ........................................................................... 289
Chapter 50 ........................................................................... 295
DICTIONARY OF WORDS AND NAMES ........................................ 301
  Words .............................................................................. 301
  Prefixes, Suffixes and Conjugations ...................................... 369
  Names .............................................................................. 371
CONCORDANCE OF WORDS AND NAMES ...................................... 381
  Words .............................................................................. 381
  Prefixes, Suffixes and Conjugations ...................................... 413
  Name ............................................................................... 414
APPENDIXES ......................................................................... 422
  Appendix A: Verb Translations ............................................. 422
  Appendix B: Phrase Translations .......................................... 423
  Appendix C: Alternative Translations ..................................... 425
  Appendix D: Idioms ............................................................ 427
  Appendix E: Pronunciations for transliterated words and names ...... 428
  Appendix F: Verse Notes ..................................................... 429
BIBLIOGRAPHY ...................................................................... 439
NOTES ................................................................................. 440

# _Acknowledgements_

I am especially thankful to my wife Denise and my children Josiah, Jeremiah and Jedidiah for allowing me the time to dedicate to this project as well as their continued support.

A special thanks goes to Rob Black, Doris Dippel, Myhrrhleine Hunter, Jeanne M. Irons and Frances Stolz for their careful and extensive review, editing and content suggestions of the manuscript. Without their assistance this book would not have been the quality that it is.

I would also like to thank the following individuals who assisted with the editing of the manuscript and provided valuable suggestions for content and corrections;

| | | |
|---|---|---|
| Lance Beard | Janice Gonzalez | John Neff |
| Donnie Blankenship | Rose Holiday | Josh Nielson |
| Cheryl Bruno | Sandra S. Keller | Peter Roy |
| LuAna Craig | Frank R. Krueger | Mary Sellmar |
| Robert Fier | Jerry R Lambert | Yvonne Todd |
| Ken Finn | Duncan Law | Steve Wu |
| Steven M. Foisy | Bridgett Magee | Janet Wyckoff |

# _Introduction_

Have you ever read a translation of the Bible and wanted to know what the original Hebrew behind that translation really said, but didn't know Hebrew? Well now you can. This translation reveals the Hebrew in a very mechanical and literal way as never before allowing you to see the Hebrew text behind the English without knowing Hebrew.

## Contents

This book will include two translations. The first is the Mechanical Translation (MT), located in the left column, where every Hebrew word, prefix and suffix is translated exactly the same way every time they occur and in the same order as it is found in the Hebrew text. The second is the Revised Mechanical Translation (RMT), located in the right column, which re-arranges the words so that they can be understood through standard English grammar. Included with each verse is the Hebrew text (_Biblia Hebraica Leningradensia_) for those who know, or are learning, Hebrew and is located above the MT and RMT.

Because the meaning of a Hebrew word cannot be conveyed completely through one or two English words, each word found in the MT will be included in the dictionary located at the back of this book. This dictionary will more accurately define each word within the context of the Ancient Hebrew language and culture.

Also included at the back of this book is a concordance allowing the reader to search for each occurrence of a word within the book of Genesis.

3

# The project

This book is the beginning of a series of translations of the books of the Bible which will, for the first time, translate the Hebrew text of the Bible literally into English without inserting a translators interpretation of the text.

The foundation to this translation is the *Ancient Hebrew Lexicon of the Bible* which defines each Hebrew word within the context of its etymological roots and the cultural background behind each word.

The MT was created by examining each Hebrew word (which will often include one or more prefixes and suffixes) and translating it into English. For instance, the first word of the Bible is בראשית *bereshiyt* (The Hebrew text is read from right to left while the transliteration, in italics, is read from left to right) includes the prefix ב *b* and the word ראשית *reshiyt*. Every place the prefix ב *b* is found, it is translated as "in~" and every occurrence of the word ראשית *reshiyt* is translated as Summit hence, the complete translation of this word would be in~Summit.

Once the MT was completed, work on the RMT began which translates each verse as accurately as possible to retain the literal meaning of the text yet allow one who does not know Hebrew sentence structure to be able to read and understand the text.

It is not the intention of this book to replace all existing translations and dictionaries but instead to be a study guide to assist the reader to see the text from its raw Hebraic perspective.

This translation may also be used by those learning Hebrew as a tool for identifying words, prefixes and suffixes and verb conjugations as well as Hebrew sentence structures and how to properly translate and interpret the text.

Accompanying this book is the Mechanical Translation Website (http://mthb.ancient-hebrew.org) which will include additional

4

information for this book, as well as updates and corrections and the progress of additional volumes.

## The Translation

A word in the MT beginning with an uppercase letter represents a Hebrew word while a word beginning with a lower case letter represents a prefix, suffix or verb tense. As an example, the first word of the Hebrew Bible is "in~Summit" where the word "in~" is a prefix to the word "Summit."

Some words will be added in the RMT to clarify the text. The most common of these will be the various conjugations of the verb "to be" (is, are, was, were, etc.), "of," "a," "an," "the" or "it."

The word "one" or "thing" is occasionally added to a noun for clarification. For instance, in 24:2 the servant of Avraham is called a "beard" but is best translated as a "bearded one" meaning an elder (see the dictionary entry for this word).

Some verses may be translated more than one way or will have grammatical or textual errors within the Hebrew text. Such verses will be identified by an asterisk behind the verse number and an explanation for this verse will be found in Appendix F.

## The Hebrew Language

The language of the Ancient Hebrews is closely related to their agricultural and nomadic lifestyle. Each word must be understood through this culture rather than from our own modern western Greco-Roman culture. As an example, the Hebrew word מצוה mitsvah is usually translated as a command or commandment in most other translations but Hebraicly means the directions given to guide one on the journey. Hence, this word will be translated in the MT as "direction."

Hebraic thought differs from our own process of thinking in that the Hebrews were concrete thinkers in contrast to our own abstract way of thinking. Concrete thought relates all words, concepts and ideas to something that can be sensed by the five senses. For instance, the Hebrew word אף *aph* is the nose, or nostrils, but is the same word for anger since one who is angry will flare the nostrils.

At times you are going to come across a word in this translation that seems to make absolutely no sense. This is mostly due to the differences between our modern Greco-Roman perspective of thought and the ancient Hebrew's perspective of thought. Also keep in mind that each Hebrew word is translated exactly the same way every time, so there will be instances when the word seems out of context. What you will need to do is study that word and the context which it is used in, so you can better understand its Hebraic meaning. Once this has been done the word, and the verse itself, will come to life in ways never before perceived. A good example of this is found in the very first verse of Genesis where most translations will have "In the beginning God created." The Revised Mechanical Translation reads "In the summit Elohiym fattened." The Hebrew word ראשית *reshiyt* literally means the head or top of a place or time, what is prominent. The Hebrew word ברא *bara* literally means to fatten but with the extended idea of filling up. In context, the first chapter of Genesis is about importance of the filling up of the heavens and the earth, not its creation within a span of time (an abstract idea that is foreign to Hebraic thinking).

Hebrew words, verbs, nouns, adjectives, etc., are best defined through a visual action. The Hebrew root עקב is used for the noun *eqev* meaning the heel, the verb *aqav* meaning to restrain in the sense of grabbing the heel to hold one back and the adjective *eyqev* meaning because, or since, through the concept of one idea in a sentence on the heel of another idea within the sentence.

The Hebrew word את *et* (translated as "At" in the MT) is frequently found in the Hebrew text to identify the direct object of a verb by preceding it. Since there is no English equivalent for this grammatical tool this word will not be translated in the RMT.

However, this word is used in the text on occasion to mean "with" or "at."

Because the original Hebrew text does not include any punctuation such as periods and quotations, the MT will not include these either. The only exception to this is the use of the comma which will be used in the RMT to separate phrases where the grammar of the sentence requires a separation as well as at the end of a thought.

A combination of Hebrew words, prefixes and/or suffixes are occasionally used to convey one idea. The Hebrew phrase על כן *al ken* literally means "upon so" but is translated in the RMT as "therefore." A list of these types of phrases are found in appendix B.

Some Hebrew idioms are found in the Bible. An idiom is a word, or phrase used in a sense that is not meant to be taken literally. An example of a Hebrew idiom is the phrase "bone of the day" (7:13), an idiom meaning "noontime." A list of idioms is found in appendix D.

## Hebrew Names

In our western culture we are comfortable using names, such as Noah or Adam, as simple identifiers with no actual meaning attached to the name. But, this is not the case with Hebrew names where each name is a word, or a combination of words, with a meaning. For instance, the name עבר *ever* (see 10:21) is usually transliterated as Ever or Eber but, is a Hebrew word meaning "cross over." The MT and the RMT will represent this name as "Ever [*cross over*]".

An individual descended from Ever is identified as עברי *eevriy* (see 14:13) where the suffix י *iy* means "one of." The MT will translate this name as "'Ever [*cross over*]"~of' and the RMT as 'one of "Ever [*cross over*]".' A people descended from Ever is identified as עברים *eevriym* (see 40:15) where the suffix ים *iym* identifies the name as a plural meaning "ones of." The MT will translate this name as '"Ever [*cross over*]"~s' and the RMT as 'ones of "Ever [*cross over*]".'

The common pronunciation of the word Pharoah comes from the Greek translation called the Septuagint. In the Hebrew text this is pronounced Paroh (pah-roh).

Appendix E includes a guide for pronouncing transliterated Hebrew names.

## The Names of God

The name Jehovah/Yahweh is written in Hebrew with four letters - יהוה *yhwh*. These four letters, as a Hebrew word, is the third person, masculine, singular, imperfect tense of the verb הוה *hawah* and literally means "he exists" and would be transliterated as "yihweh" or "yehuwh." However, because of the strong controversy over the actual pronunciation of the name this translation will represent this name as "YHWH [*he exists*]".'

The Hebrew word אלהים *elohiym*, commonly translated as "God" in most modern translations, is a masculine plural word meaning "powers." This word is used in 1:1 as the subject of the verb ברא *bara* meaning "he fattened" where the "he" identifies the subject of the verb as a masculine singular. Because of this conflict of number where the verb identifies the subject as a singular but the subject being a plural word, it is apparent that the word אלהים *elohiym* is a proper name and not a noun and is therefore translated as "Elohiym [*Powers*]". However, when this word is written in the Hebrew as אלהי *elohey* (identified as a construct due to the missing ם), such as in 9:26, it is apparently being used as a noun rather than a proper name and will be translated as "powers of..."

The Hebrew words אדני *adonai* (meaning "my lords", see 15:2) and שדי *shaddai* (meaning "my breasts", see 17:1) are frequently used for God and will also be treated as proper names.

# Hebrew words

Some Hebrew words are always written in the plural (e.g. faces and waters). This idiomatic form does not always imply that the word is plural and will usually be translated in the singular in the RMT.

Some words have various nuances of meaning. In most cases the context will help define the nuance, but in some cases the nuance cannot be determined. For instance, in 4:26 the word "pierced" can be interpreted as "begin" or "profane;" but, the context does not make clear which nuance is intended.

In the MT, words written with a period between them represent one Hebrew word. For instance, the Hebrew word תהום *tehom* (1:2) means a deep sea and will be represented by "Deep.sea" in the MT but will be written as "deep sea" in the RMT.

The English translation chosen for each Hebrew word was chosen based on two criteria. First the translation had to be close in meaning to the Hebrew (although keep in mind the dictionary will more precisely define this word) and secondly it was to be a unique word that was not used for any other word. As an example, the Hebrew words קום *qum* and רום *rum* both mean to "raise" so the meaning of "rise" has been assigned to קום *qum* and "raise" to רום *rum*.

Most Hebrew words can be used in a literal or figurative application which will usually be defined by the context it is used. For instance, the word hand can literally refer to the hand as in 22:6. But, this same word is used in 9:2 figuratively to mean "at hand" or "in possession."

While the RMT strives to translate each Hebrew word exactly the same way each time it appears, there will be times where the context of the passage or English sentence structure will require the word to be translated differently. For instance, in 4:25 the MT has the phrase "Seed Other Under." The word "Other" can also be translated as "another" and the word "Under" can also be translated as "in place of." Therefore this phrase is translated in the RMT as "another seed in place of." A complete list of words with their alternate translations are available in Appendix C.

Intensity of a word can be expressed by repeating a word in the Hebrew text. For instance, in 7:19 the word "many" is repeated to express a "great many." In these cases the RMT will translate the two words only once and add the word "great" or other adjective to express this intensity.

Questions are usually formed in the text by using such words as "what," "where," "if," etc but, the Hebrew language can also form the text into a question by using the "interrogative hey" (in the Hebrew this is represented by the letter ה *h* as a prefix and will be translated in the MT as "?~"). For instance, the phrase "Not He he~did~say" would be translated in the RMT as "he did not say" but in 20:5 this phrase is written as "?~Not He he~did~say" and is translated as "did he not say" in the RMT.

A noun followed by a pronoun such as the "Hand~him" in 3:22 would literally be translated as "hand of him" but the RMT will translate this as "his hand."

## Hebrew Verbs

Hebrew verbs can be easily identified by their prefixes or suffixes attached to the verb. Each verb will be preceded by did~, will~, had~, !~ or >~ or followed by ~ing or ~ed.

Hebrew verbs have two tenses, perfect (a completed action, identified in the MT with the prefix "did~") and imperfect (an incomplete action, identified in the MT with the prefix "will~"). In addition, most Hebrew verbs will identify the number and gender of the subject of the verb. As an example, the Hebrew verb אמר *amar* is a verb meaning "to say" and is in the perfect tense and identifies the subject of the verb as first person, masculine singular. The MT will translate this verb as "he~did~say" and the RMT will translate it as "he said." The Hebrew verb תאמר *tomer* is again the verb meaning "to say" but is in the imperfect tense and identifies the subject of the verb as second person, masculine singular. The MT will translate this verb as "you~will~say" and the RMT will translate it as "you will say."

Hebrew verbs, whose tenses are related to action (completed and incomplete), must be converted to English verbs related to time (past, present and future) when being translated. In most cases the perfect tense (completed action) is translated into the past tense English verbs and imperfect tense (incomplete action) is translated into present or future tense English verbs. However, in some cases this style of translating will not accurately convey the meaning of the Hebrew. For instance, in 22:2 the word "you(ms)~did~Love" is written in the perfect tense meaning a completed action but, if translated into English as "you loved" (past tense), it would imply that he was no longer loved. Therefore, in this instance, the verb will be translated as "you love" (present tense). Also see 29:5, 37:3 and 48:19 for other examples of this.

When the prefix "and~" is added to a verb the tense is usually reversed. For instance, the verb "he~will~Say" would be translated in the RMT as "he will say" but the verb "and~he~will~Say" will be translated in the RMT as "and he said."

The subject of the verb will usually follow the verb. For instance, אמר אב *amar av* will be written in the MT as "he~did~say Father" and translated as "father said" in the RMT. In some cases the subject of the verb will precede the verb instead. This is the past perfect tense of the verb (see 3:13). When this occurs, the MT will use the prefix "had~" instead of "did~."

Emphasis is often placed on a Hebrew verb by writing it twice. The RMT will translate this verb once and add an adverb such as quickly, greatly, completely or surely before it.

The Piel form of verbs, identified in the MT with the prefix "much~," is an intensive form of the verb and is usually translated in the RMT with an adverb.

Verb participles, identified by "~ing" in the MT, identifies an action or one of action. As an example, the participle "Feed-ing" may be translated in the RMT as "feeding" (see 37:2) or "feeder" (one who feeds, a shepherd or herdsman, see 13:7).

Each Hebrew verb can be written with different moods and voices. For example, The active voice of the verb ראה *ra'ah* means to "see" but, the passive voice, identified by the prefix "be~", means "be seen" but is translated as "appeared" in the RMT. As another example, the simple mood of the verb בוא *bo* means to "come" but, the causative mood, identified by the prefix "make~", means "make come" but, is translated as "bring" in the RMT. A complete list of these verb translational variations are listed in appendix A.

## Hebrew gender

All Hebrew nouns are either masculine or feminine. The dictionary will identify masculine nouns with [masc] and feminine nouns as [fem]. Some nouns can be either masculine or feminine, called common nouns and will be identified with [com].

All Hebrew pronouns will be translated as "he" or "she." This may appear strange at first as a word like "ground," a feminine word, will be identified as a "she" (see 4:12). This is an important issue as knowing the correct gender of a pronoun can influence interpretation. A classic example is found in 4:7 where most translations read "...sin is crouching at the door; its desire is for you." It is usually assumed the word "its" is referring to the word "sin" but, knowing that the word "sin" is a feminine word and "its" is a masculine pronoun we discover that the word "its" cannot be referring to the "sin."

# Introduction

Hebrew genders should not be viewed in the same manner we view gender. For instance the word "beast" is a feminine word and any pronoun associated with this word will be a "she" with no regard to the actual gender of the beast.

Hebrew grammar uses the masculine form of nouns and pronouns for a group of mixed genders. For instance, in 36:25 the "sons" (masculine plural) of Anah are identified as Dishon (a male) and Ahalivamah (a female).

## Hebrew numbers

There are two different types of plurals in Hebrew, simple plural and double plural. The word "Hundred" is a singular word and refers to "one hundred." The simple plural "Hundred~s" refers to a number of hundreds such as in the phrase "Three Hundred~s" (this would be translated as "three hundred" in the RMT). When the same word is written in the double plural "Hundred~s2," its translation would be "two hundred."

When a Hebrew number is written in the simple plural form it is multiplied by ten. For instance, the word "Three~s" would mean thirty. The only exception is the plural form of ten ("Ten~s") which means twenty.

# The Mechanical Translation of Genesis

## Chapter 1

**1:1** בְּרֵאשִׁית בָּרָא אֱלֹהִים אֵת הַשָּׁמַיִם וְאֵת הָאָרֶץ

in~Summit he~did~Fatten "Elohiym [*Powers*]" At the~Sky~s2 and~At the~Land

in the summit "Elohiym [*Powers*]" fattened the sky and the land,

**1:2** וְהָאָרֶץ הָיְתָה תֹהוּ וָבֹהוּ וְחֹשֶׁךְ עַל פְּנֵי תְהוֹם וְרוּחַ אֱלֹהִים מְרַחֶפֶת עַל פְּנֵי הַמָּיִם

and~the~Land she~had~Exist Confusion and~Unfilled and~Darkness Upon Face~s Deep.sea and~Wind "Elohiym [*Powers*]" much~Flutter~ing(fs) Upon Face~s the~Water~s2

and the land had existed in confusion and was unfilled and darkness was upon the face of the deep sea and the wind of "Elohiym [*Powers*]" was much fluttering upon the face of the water,

**1:3\*** וַיֹּאמֶר אֱלֹהִים יְהִי אוֹר וַיְהִי אוֹר

and~he~will~Say "Elohiym [*Powers*]" he~will~Exist Light and~he~will~Exist Light

and "Elohiym [*Powers*]" said, light exist and light existed,

**1:4** וַיַּרְא אֱלֹהִים אֵת הָאוֹר כִּי טוֹב וַיַּבְדֵּל אֱלֹהִים בֵּין הָאוֹר וּבֵין הַחֹשֶׁךְ

and~he~will~See "Elohiym [*Powers*]" At the~Light Given.that Functional and~he~will~make~Separate "Elohiym [*Powers*]" Between the~Light and~Between the~Darkness

and "Elohiym [*Powers*]" saw the light given that it was functional and "Elohiym [*Powers*]" made a separation between the light and the darkness,

**1:5** וַיִּקְרָא אֱלֹהִים לָאוֹר יוֹם וְלַחֹשֶׁךְ קָרָא לָיְלָה וַיְהִי עֶרֶב וַיְהִי בֹקֶר יוֹם אֶחָד

and~he~will~Call.out "Elohiym [*Powers*]" to~Light Day and~to~Darkness he~did~Call.out Night and~he~will~Exist Evening and~he~will~Exist Morning Day Unit

and "Elohiym [*Powers*]" called out to the light day and to the darkness he called out night and evening existed and morning existed one day,

**1:6** וַיֹּאמֶר אֱלֹהִים יְהִי רָקִיעַ בְּתוֹךְ הַמָּיִם וִיהִי מַבְדִּיל בֵּין מַיִם לָמָיִם

and~he~will~Say "Elohiym [*Powers*]"

and "Elohiym [*Powers*]" said, a

he~will~Exist Sheet in~Midst the~
Water~s2 and~he~will~Exist make~
Separate~ing(ms) Between Water~s2
to~Water~s2

sheet will exist in the midst of the
water and he existed making a
separation between water to water,

**1:7** וַיַּעַשׂ אֱלֹהִים אֶת הָרָקִיעַ וַיַּבְדֵּל בֵּין הַמַּיִם אֲשֶׁר מִתַּחַת לָרָקִיעַ
וּבֵין הַמַּיִם אֲשֶׁר מֵעַל לָרָקִיעַ וַיְהִי כֵן

and~he~will~Do "Elohiym [*Powers*]"
At the~Sheet and~he~will~make~
Separate Between the~Water~s2
Which from~Under to~Sheet and~
Between the~Water~s2 Which from~
Upon to~Sheet and~he~will~Exist So

and "Elohiym [*Powers*]" made the
sheet and he made a separation
between the water which is under
the sheet and the water which is
upon the sheet and he existed so,

**1:8** וַיִּקְרָא אֱלֹהִים לָרָקִיעַ שָׁמָיִם וַיְהִי עֶרֶב וַיְהִי בֹקֶר יוֹם שֵׁנִי

and~he~will~Call.out "Elohiym
[*Powers*]" to~Sheet Sky~s2 and~he~
will~Exist Evening and~he~will~Exist
Morning Day Second

and "Elohiym [*Powers*]" called out
to the sheet, sky, and evening
existed and morning existed a
second day,

**1:9** וַיֹּאמֶר אֱלֹהִים יִקָּווּ הַמַּיִם מִתַּחַת הַשָּׁמַיִם אֶל מָקוֹם אֶחָד
וְתֵרָאֶה הַיַּבָּשָׁה וַיְהִי כֵן

and~he~will~Say "Elohiym [*Powers*]"
he~will~be~Bound.up the~Water~s2
from~Under the~Sky~s2 To Place
Unit and~she~be~See the~Dry.ground
and~he~will~Exist So

and "Elohiym [*Powers*]" said, the
water will be bound up from under
the sky to one place and dry ground
appeared and he existed so,

**1:10** וַיִּקְרָא אֱלֹהִים לַיַּבָּשָׁה אֶרֶץ וּלְמִקְוֵה הַמַּיִם קָרָא יַמִּים וַיַּרְא
אֱלֹהִים כִּי טוֹב

and~he~will~Call.out "Elohiym
[*Powers*]" to~Dry.ground Land and~
to~Collection the~Water~s2 he~did~
Call.out Sea~s and~he~will~See
"Elohiym [*Powers*]" Given.that
Functional

and "Elohiym [*Powers*]" called out
to the dry ground, land, and the
collection of the water he called
out, seas, and "Elohiym [*Powers*]"
saw that it was functional,

**1:11** וַיֹּאמֶר אֱלֹהִים תַּדְשֵׁא הָאָרֶץ דֶּשֶׁא עֵשֶׂב מַזְרִיעַ זֶרַע עֵץ פְּרִי
עֹשֶׂה פְּרִי לְמִינוֹ אֲשֶׁר זַרְעוֹ בוֹ עַל הָאָרֶץ וַיְהִי כֵן

and~he~will~Say "Elohiym [*Powers*]"
she~will~make~Sprout the~Land Grass
Herb make~Sow~ing(ms) Seed Tree
Produce Do~ing(ms) Produce to~
Kind~him Which Seed~him in~him
Upon the~Land and~he~will~Exist So

and "Elohiym [*Powers*]" said, the
land will make grass sprout, herbs
making a sowing of seeds, trees of
produce making produce to his kind
which his seed is in him upon the
land, and he existed so,

**1:12** וַתּוֹצֵא הָאָרֶץ דֶּשֶׁא עֵשֶׂב מַזְרִיעַ זֶרַע לְמִינֵהוּ וְעֵץ עֹשֶׂה פְּרִי

אֲשֶׁר זַרְעוֹ בוֹ לְמִינֵהוּ וַיַּרְא אֱלֹהִים כִּי טוֹב

and~she~will~make~Go.out the~Land
Grass Herb make~Sow~ing(ms) Seed
to~Kind~him and~Tree Do~ing(ms)
Produce Which Seed~him in~him
to~Kind~him and~he~will~See
"Elohiym [*Powers*]" Given.that
Functional

and the land brought grass out,
herbs making a sowing of seeds to
his kind and trees making produce
which has his seed in him to his
kind and "Elohiym [*Powers*]" saw
that it was functional,

**1:13**

וַיְהִי עֶרֶב וַיְהִי בֹקֶר יוֹם שְׁלִישִׁי

and~he~will~Exist Evening and~he~
will~Exist Morning Day Third

and evening existed and morning
existed a third day,

**1:14** וַיֹּאמֶר אֱלֹהִים יְהִי מְאֹרֹת בִּרְקִיעַ הַשָּׁמַיִם לְהַבְדִּיל בֵּין הַיּוֹם
וּבֵין הַלָּיְלָה וְהָיוּ לְאֹתֹת וּלְמוֹעֲדִים וּלְיָמִים וְשָׁנִים

and~he~will~Say "Elohiym [*Powers*]"
he~will~Exist Luminary~s in~Sheet
the~Sky~s2 to~>~make~Separate
Between the~Day and~Between the~
Night and~they~did~Exist to~Sign~s
and~to~Appointed~s and~to~Day~s
and~Year~s

and "Elohiym [*Powers*]" said, the
luminaries will exist in the sheet of
the sky to make a separation
between the day and the night and
they exist for signs and for
appointed times and for days and
years,

**1:15** וְהָיוּ לִמְאוֹרֹת בִּרְקִיעַ הַשָּׁמַיִם לְהָאִיר עַל הָאָרֶץ וַיְהִי כֵן

and~they~did~Exist to~Luminary~s in~
Sheet the~Sky~s2 to~>~make~Glow
Upon the~Land and~he~will~Exist So

and they exist for luminaries in the
sheet of the sky to make glow upon
the land and he existed so,

**1:16** וַיַּעַשׂ אֱלֹהִים אֶת שְׁנֵי הַמְּאֹרֹת הַגְּדֹלִים אֶת הַמָּאוֹר הַגָּדֹל
לְמֶמְשֶׁלֶת הַיּוֹם וְאֶת הַמָּאוֹר הַקָּטֹן לְמֶמְשֶׁלֶת הַלַּיְלָה וְאֵת
הַכּוֹכָבִים

and~he~will~Do "Elohiym [*Powers*]"
At Two the~Luminary~s the~
Magnificent~s At the~Luminary the~
Magnificent to~Regulation the~Day
and~At the~Luminary the~Small to~
Regulation the~Night and~At the~
Star~s

and "Elohiym [*Powers*]" made two
of the magnificent luminaries, the
magnificent luminary to regulate
the day and the small luminary to
regulate the night and the stars,

**1:17** וַיִּתֵּן אֹתָם אֱלֹהִים בִּרְקִיעַ הַשָּׁמָיִם לְהָאִיר עַל הָאָרֶץ

and~he~will~Give At~them(m)
"Elohiym [*Powers*]" in~Sheet the~
Sky~s2 to~>~make~Glow Upon the~
Land

and "Elohiym [*Powers*]" gave them
in the sheet of the sky to make a
glow upon the land,

**1:18** וְלִמְשֹׁל בַּיּוֹם וּבַלַּיְלָה וּלְהַבְדִּיל בֵּין הָאוֹר וּבֵין הַחֹשֶׁךְ וַיַּרְא

אֱלֹהִים כִּי טוֹב

| | |
|---|---|
| and~to~>~Regulate in~Day and~in~ Night and~to~>~make~Separate Between the~Light and~Between the~ Darkness and~he~will~See "Elohiym [*Powers*]" Given.that Functional | and to regulate in the day and in the night and to make a separation between the light and the darkness and "Elohiym [*Powers*]" saw that it was functional, |

**1:19**

וַיְהִי עֶרֶב וַיְהִי בֹקֶר יוֹם רְבִיעִי

| | |
|---|---|
| and~he~will~Exist Evening and~he~ will~Exist Morning Day Fourth | and evening existed and morning existed a fourth day, |

**1:20** וַיֹּאמֶר אֱלֹהִים יִשְׁרְצוּ הַמַּיִם שֶׁרֶץ נֶפֶשׁ חַיָּה וְעוֹף יְעוֹפֵף עַל הָאָרֶץ עַל פְּנֵי רְקִיעַ הַשָּׁמָיִם

| | |
|---|---|
| and~he~will~Say "Elohiym [*Powers*]" they(m)~will~Swarm the~Water~s2 Swarmer Being Life and~Flyer he~ will~much~Fly Upon the~Land Upon Face~s Sheet the~Sky~s2 | and "Elohiym [*Powers*]" said, the water will swarm, swarmers of beings of life and flyers will fly upon the land upon the face of the sheet of the sky, |

**1:21** וַיִּבְרָא אֱלֹהִים אֶת הַתַּנִּינִם הַגְּדֹלִים וְאֵת כָּל נֶפֶשׁ הַחַיָּה הָרֹמֶשֶׂת אֲשֶׁר שָׁרְצוּ הַמַּיִם לְמִינֵהֶם וְאֵת כָּל עוֹף כָּנָף לְמִינֵהוּ וַיַּרְא אֱלֹהִים כִּי טוֹב

| | |
|---|---|
| and~he~will~Fatten "Elohiym [*Powers*]" At the~Taniyn~s the~ Magnificent~s and~At All Being the~Life the~Tread~ing(fs) Which they(m)~did~Swarm the~Water~s2 to~ Kind~them(m) and~At All Flyer Wing to~Kind~him and~he~will~See "Elohiym [*Powers*]" Given.that Functional | and "Elohiym [*Powers*]" fattened the magnificent taniyns and all of the beings of the life, the treading ones which swarm the water to their kind and all of the flyers of the wing to his kind and "Elohiym [*Powers*]" saw that it was functional, |

**1:22** וַיְבָרֶךְ אֹתָם אֱלֹהִים לֵאמֹר פְּרוּ וּרְבוּ וּמִלְאוּ אֶת הַמַּיִם בַּיַּמִּים וְהָעוֹף יִרֶב בָּאָרֶץ

| | |
|---|---|
| and~he~will~much~Kneel At~them(m) "Elohiym [*Powers*]" to~>~Say !(mp)~ Reproduce and~!(mp)~Increase and~ !(mp)~Fill At the~Water~s2 in~the~ Sea~s and~the~Flyer he~did~Increase in~the~Land | and "Elohiym [*Powers*]" respected them saying, reproduce and increase and fill the water in the seas and the flyers increased in the land, |

**1:23**

וַיְהִי עֶרֶב וַיְהִי בֹקֶר יוֹם חֲמִישִׁי

| | |
|---|---|
| and~he~will~Exist Evening and~he~ will~Exist Morning Day Fifth | and evening existed and morning existed a fifth day, |

**1:24** וַיֹּאמֶר אֱלֹהִים תּוֹצֵא הָאָרֶץ נֶפֶשׁ חַיָּה לְמִינָהּ בְּהֵמָה וָרֶמֶשׂ

וְחַיְתוֹ אֶרֶץ לְמִינָהּ וַיְהִי כֵן

and~he~will~Say "Elohiym [*Powers*]"
she~will~make~Go.out the~Land Being
Life to~Kind~her Beast and~Treader
and~Life~him Land to~Kind~her and~
he~will~Exist So

and "Elohiym [*Powers*]" said, the
land will bring out beings of life to
her kind, beasts and treaders and his
living ones of the land to her kind
and he existed so,

**1:25** וַיַּעַשׂ אֱלֹהִים אֶת חַיַּת הָאָרֶץ לְמִינָהּ וְאֶת הַבְּהֵמָה לְמִינָהּ וְאֵת
כָּל רֶמֶשׂ הָאֲדָמָה לְמִינֵהוּ וַיַּרְא אֱלֹהִים כִּי טוֹב

and~he~will~Do "Elohiym [*Powers*]"
At Life the~Land to~Kind~her and~
At the~Beast to~Kind~her and~At
All Treader the~Ground to~Kind~him
and~he~will~See "Elohiym [*Powers*]"
Given.that Functional

and "Elohiym [*Powers*]" made
living ones of the land to her kind
and the beast to her kind and all of
the treaders of the ground to his
kind and "Elohiym [*Powers*]" saw
that it was functional,

**1:26** וַיֹּאמֶר אֱלֹהִים נַעֲשֶׂה אָדָם בְּצַלְמֵנוּ כִּדְמוּתֵנוּ וְיִרְדּוּ בִדְגַת הַיָּם
וּבְעוֹף הַשָּׁמַיִם וּבַבְּהֵמָה וּבְכָל הָאָרֶץ וּבְכָל הָרֶמֶשׂ הָרֹמֵשׂ עַל
הָאָרֶץ

and~he~will~Say "Elohiym [*Powers*]"
we~will~Do Human in~Image~us
like~Likeness~us and~he~did~Rule in~
Swimmer the~Sea~s and~in~Flyer
the~Sky~s2 and~in~Beast and~in~All
the~Land and~in~All the~Treader
the~Tread~ing(ms) Upon the~Land

and "Elohiym [*Powers*]" said, we
will make a human in our image
like our likeness and he will rule in
the swimmers of the seas and in the
flyers of the sky and in the beast
and in all of the land and in all of
the treaders treading upon the land,

**1:27** וַיִּבְרָא אֱלֹהִים אֶת הָאָדָם בְּצַלְמוֹ בְּצֶלֶם אֱלֹהִים בָּרָא אֹתוֹ
זָכָר וּנְקֵבָה בָּרָא אֹתָם

and~he~will~Fatten "Elohiym
[*Powers*]" At the~Human in~Image~
him in~Image "Elohiym [*Powers*]"
he~did~Fatten At~him Male and~
Female and~he~will~Fatten At~
them(m)

and "Elohiym [*Powers*]" fattened
the human in his image, in the
image of "Elohiym [*Powers*]" he
fattened him, male and female he
fattened them,

**1:28** וַיְבָרֶךְ אֹתָם אֱלֹהִים וַיֹּאמֶר לָהֶם אֱלֹהִים פְּרוּ וּרְבוּ וּמִלְאוּ אֶת
הָאָרֶץ וְכִבְשֻׁהָ וּרְדוּ בִדְגַת הַיָּם וּבְעוֹף הַשָּׁמַיִם וּבְכָל חַיָּה
הָרֹמֶשֶׂת עַל הָאָרֶץ

and~he~will~much~Kneel At~them(m)
"Elohiym [*Powers*]" and~he~will~Say
to~them(m) "Elohiym [*Powers*]"
!(mp)~Reproduce and~!(mp)~Increase
and~!(mp)~Fill At the~Land and~
!(mp)~Subdue~her and~!(mp)~Rule in~

and "Elohiym [*Powers*]" respected
them and "Elohiym [*Powers*]" said
to them, reproduce and increase and
fill the land and subdue her and rule
in the swimmers of the seas and in
all the living ones treading upon the

**19**

Swimmer the~Sea~s and~in~Flyer
the~Sky~s2 and~in~All Life the~
Tread~ing(fs) Upon the~Land

land,

**1:29** וַיֹּאמֶר אֱלֹהִים הִנֵּה נָתַתִּי לָכֶם אֶת כָּל עֵשֶׂב זֹרֵעַ זֶרַע אֲשֶׁר עַל פְּנֵי כָל הָאָרֶץ וְאֶת כָּל הָעֵץ אֲשֶׁר בּוֹ פְרִי עֵץ זֹרֵעַ זָרַע לָכֶם יִהְיֶה לְאָכְלָה

and~he~will~Say "Elohiym [*Powers*]"
Look i~did~Give to~you(mp) At All
Herb Sow~ing(ms) Seed Which
Upon Face~s All the~Land and~At
All the~Tree Which in~him Produce
Tree Sow~ing(ms) Seed to~you(mp)
he~will~Exist to~Food

and "Elohiym [*Powers*]" said, look,
I gave to you all of the herbs
sowing seed which are upon the
face of the land and all of the trees
which are in him, produce of the
trees sowing seed for you will exist
for food,

**1:30** וּלְכָל חַיַּת הָאָרֶץ וּלְכָל עוֹף הַשָּׁמַיִם וּלְכֹל רוֹמֵשׂ עַל הָאָרֶץ אֲשֶׁר בּוֹ נֶפֶשׁ חַיָּה אֶת כָּל יֶרֶק עֵשֶׂב לְאָכְלָה וַיְהִי כֵן

and~to~All Life the~Land and~to~All
Flyer the~Sky~s2 and~to~All Tread~
ing(ms) Upon the~Land Which in~
him Being Life At All Green Herb
to~Food and~he~will~Exist So

and to all of the living ones of the
land and to all of the flyers of the
sky and to all of the treading ones
upon the land which is in him a
being of life, all of the green herbs
for food and he existed so,

**1:31** וַיַּרְא אֱלֹהִים אֶת כָּל אֲשֶׁר עָשָׂה וְהִנֵּה טוֹב מְאֹד וַיְהִי עֶרֶב וַיְהִי בֹקֶר יוֹם הַשִּׁשִּׁי

and~he~will~See "Elohiym [*Powers*]"
At All Which he~did~Do and~Look
Functional Many and~he~will~Exist
Evening and~he~will~Exist Morning
Day the~Sixth

and "Elohiym [*Powers*]" saw all of
which he made and look, it is much
functional and evening existed and
morning existed a sixth day,

# Chapter 2

**2:1** וַיְכֻלּוּ הַשָּׁמַיִם וְהָאָרֶץ וְכָל צְבָאָם

and~they(m)~will~be~Finish the~Sky~s2
and~the~Land and~All Army~them(m)

and the sky and the land and all of
their armies were finished,

**2:2** וַיְכַל אֱלֹהִים בַּיּוֹם הַשְּׁבִיעִי מְלַאכְתּוֹ אֲשֶׁר עָשָׂה וַיִּשְׁבֹּת בַּיּוֹם הַשְּׁבִיעִי מִכָּל מְלַאכְתּוֹ אֲשֶׁר עָשָׂה

and~he~will~Finish "Elohiym
[*Powers*]" in~the~Day the~Seventh
Occupation~him Which he~did~Do
and~he~will~Cease in~the~Day the~

and "Elohiym [*Powers*]" finished in
the seventh day his occupation
which he did and he ceased in the
seventh day from all of his

Seventh from~All Occupation~him
Which he~did~Do

occupation which he did,

**2:3** וַיְבָרֶךְ אֱלֹהִים אֶת יוֹם הַשְּׁבִיעִי וַיְקַדֵּשׁ אֹתוֹ כִּי בוֹ שָׁבַת מִכָּל
מְלַאכְתּוֹ אֲשֶׁר בָּרָא אֱלֹהִים לַעֲשׂוֹת

and~he~will~much~Kneel "Elohiym
[Powers]" At Day the~Seventh and~
he~will~Set.apart At~him Given.that
in~him he~did~Cease from~All
Occupation~him Which he~did~Fatten
"Elohiym [Powers]" to~>~Do

and "Elohiym [Powers]" respected
the seventh day and he set him
apart given that in him he ceased
from all of his occupation which
"Elohiym [Powers]" fattened to
make,

**2:4** אֵלֶּה תוֹלְדוֹת הַשָּׁמַיִם וְהָאָרֶץ בְּהִבָּרְאָם בְּיוֹם עֲשׂוֹת יְהֹוָה
אֱלֹהִים אֶרֶץ וְשָׁמָיִם

These Birthing~s Sky~s2 and~the~
Land in~>~be~Fatten~them(m) in~Day
>~Do "YHWH [He exists]"
"Elohiym [Powers]" Land and~Sky~s2

these are the birthings of the sky
and the land in their being fattened
in the day "YHWH [He exists]" of
"Elohiym [Powers]" made land and
sky,

**2:5** וְכֹל שִׂיחַ הַשָּׂדֶה טֶרֶם יִהְיֶה בָאָרֶץ וְכָל עֵשֶׂב הַשָּׂדֶה טֶרֶם יִצְמָח
כִּי לֹא הִמְטִיר יְהֹוָה אֱלֹהִים עַל הָאָרֶץ וְאָדָם אַיִן לַעֲבֹד אֶת
הָאֲדָמָה

and~All Shrub the~Field Before he~
will~Exist in~the~Land and~All Herb
the~Field Before he~will~Spring.up
Given.that Not he~did~make~
Precipitate "YHWH [He exists]"
"Elohiym [Powers]" Upon the~Land
and~Human Without to~>~Serve At
the~Ground

and all of the shrubs of the field
before existing in the land and all of
the herbs of the field before
springing up given that "YHWH
[He exists]" of "Elohiym [Powers]"
did not make it precipitate upon the
land and without a human to serve
the ground,

**2:6** וְאֵד יַעֲלֶה מִן הָאָרֶץ וְהִשְׁקָה אֶת כָּל פְּנֵי הָאֲדָמָה

and~Mist he~will~Go.up From the~
Land and~he~did~make~Drink At All
Face~s the~Ground

and a mist will go up from the land
and he made all of the face of the
ground drink,

**2:7** וַיִּיצֶר יְהֹוָה אֱלֹהִים אֶת הָאָדָם עָפָר מִן הָאֲדָמָה וַיִּפַּח בְּאַפָּיו
נִשְׁמַת חַיִּים וַיְהִי הָאָדָם לְנֶפֶשׁ חַיָּה

and~he~will~Mold "YHWH [He
exists]" "Elohiym [Powers]" At the~
Human Powder From the~Ground
and~he~will~Exhale in~Nose~s2~him
Breath Life~s and~he~will~Exist the~
Human to~Being Life

and "YHWH [He exists]" of
"Elohiym [Powers]" molded the
human of powder from the ground
and he exhaled in his nostrils a
breath of life and the human existed
for a being of life,

**2:8**     וַיִּטַּע יְהוָה אֱלֹהִים גַּן בְּעֵדֶן מִקֶּדֶם וַיָּשֶׂם שָׁם אֶת הָאָדָם אֲשֶׁר יָצָר

and~he~will~Plant "YHWH [*He exists*]" "Elohiym [*Powers*]" Garden in~"Eden [*Pleasure*]" from~East and~he~will~Set.in.place There At the~Human Which he~did~Mold

and "YHWH [*He exists*]" of "Elohiym [*Powers*]" planted a garden in "Eden [*Pleasure*]" from the east and set in place there the human which he molded,

**2:9\***     וַיַּצְמַח יְהוָה אֱלֹהִים מִן הָאֲדָמָה כָּל עֵץ נֶחְמָד לְמַרְאֶה וְטוֹב לְמַאֲכָל וְעֵץ הַחַיִּים בְּתוֹךְ הַגָּן וְעֵץ הַדַּעַת טוֹב וָרָע

and~he~will~make~Spring.up "YHWH [*He exists*]" "Elohiym [*Powers*]" From the~Ground All Tree be~Crave~ing(ms) to~Appearance and~Functional to~Nourishment and~Tree the~Life~s in~Midst the~Garden and~Tree the~Discernment Functional and~Dysfunctional

and "YHWH [*He exists*]" of "Elohiym [*Powers*]" made all of the trees spring up from the ground being a craving to appearance and functional for nourishment and a tree of the life in the midst of the garden and a tree of the discernment of function and dysfunction,

**2:10**     וְנָהָר יֹצֵא מֵעֵדֶן לְהַשְׁקוֹת אֶת הַגָּן וּמִשָּׁם יִפָּרֵד וְהָיָה לְאַרְבָּעָה רָאשִׁים

and~River Go.out~ing(ms) from~"Eden [*Pleasure*]" to~>~make~Drink At the~Garden and~from~There he~will~be~Divide.apart and~he~did~Exist to~Four Head~s

and a river going out from "Eden [*Pleasure*]" to make the garden drink and from there he will be divided apart existing to four heads,

**2:11**     שֵׁם הָאֶחָד פִּישׁוֹן הוּא הַסֹּבֵב אֵת כָּל אֶרֶץ הַחֲוִילָה אֲשֶׁר שָׁם הַזָּהָב

Title the~Unit "Pishon [*Scatter*]" He the~Go.around~ing(ms) At All Land the~"Hhawilah [*Twisting*]" Which There the~Gold

the title of the one is "Pishon [*Scatter*]", the one going around all of the land of the "Hhawilah [*Twisting*]" where there is the gold,

**2:12**     וּזְהַב הָאָרֶץ הַהִוא טוֹב שָׁם הַבְּדֹלַח וְאֶבֶן הַשֹּׁהַם

and~Gold the~Land the~She Functional There the~Amber and~Stone the~Shoham

and the gold of that land is functional, there is the amber and the stone of the shoham,

**2:13**     וְשֵׁם הַנָּהָר הַשֵּׁנִי גִּיחוֹן הוּא הַסּוֹבֵב אֵת כָּל אֶרֶץ כּוּשׁ

and~Title the~River the~Second "Giyhhon [*Burst*]" He the~Go.around~ing(ms) At All Land "Kush [*Black*]"

and the title of the second river is "Giyhhon [*Burst*]", he is the one going around all of the land of "Kush [*Black*]",

**2:14**     וְשֵׁם הַנָּהָר הַשְּׁלִישִׁי חִדֶּקֶל הוּא הַהֹלֵךְ קִדְמַת אַשּׁוּר וְהַנָּהָר

הָרְבִיעִי הוּא פְרָת

and~Title the~River the~Third "Hhideqel [*Rapid*]" He the~Walk~ing(ms) Eastward "Ashur [*Step*]" and~the~River the~Fourth He "Perat [*Break*]"

and the title of the third river is "Hhideqel [*Rapid*]", he is the one walking eastward of "Ashur [*Step*]" and the fourth river he is "Perat [*Break*]",

**2:15** וַיִּקַּח יְהֹוָה אֱלֹהִים אֶת הָאָדָם וַיַּנִּחֵהוּ בְגַן עֵדֶן לְעָבְדָהּ וּלְשָׁמְרָהּ

and~he~will~Take "YHWH [*He exists*]" "Elohiym [*Powers*]" At the~Human and~he~will~make~Deposit~him in~Garden "Eden [*Pleasure*]" to~>~Serve~her and~to~>~Guard~her

and "YHWH [*He exists*]" of "Elohiym [*Powers*]" took the human and he caused him to be deposited in the garden of "Eden [*Pleasure*]" to serve her and to guard her,

**2:16** וַיְצַו יְהֹוָה אֱלֹהִים עַל הָאָדָם לֵאמֹר מִכֹּל עֵץ הַגָּן אָכֹל תֹּאכֵל

and~he~will~much~Direct "YHWH [*He exists*]" "Elohiym [*Powers*]" Upon the~Human to~>~Say from~All Tree the~Garden >~Eat you(ms)~will~Eat

and "YHWH [*He exists*]" of "Elohiym [*Powers*]" directed upon the human saying, from all of the trees of the garden an eating you will eat,

**2:17** וּמֵעֵץ הַדַּעַת טוֹב וָרָע לֹא תֹאכַל מִמֶּנּוּ כִּי בְּיוֹם אֲכָלְךָ מִמֶּנּוּ מוֹת תָּמוּת

and~from~Tree the~Discernment Functional and~Dysfunctional Not you(ms)~will~Eat From~him Given.that in~Day you(ms)~>~Eat From~him >~Die you(ms)~will~Die

and from the tree of the discernment of function and dysfunction you will not eat from him given that in the day you eat from him a dying you will die,

**2:18** וַיֹּאמֶר יְהֹוָה אֱלֹהִים לֹא טוֹב הֱיוֹת הָאָדָם לְבַדּוֹ אֶעֱשֶׂה לּוֹ עֵזֶר כְּנֶגְדּוֹ

and~he~will~Say "YHWH [*He exists*]" "Elohiym [*Powers*]" Not Functional >~Exist the~Human to~Separated.thing~him i~will~Do to~him Helper like~Opposite~him

and "YHWH [*He exists*]" of "Elohiym [*Powers*]" said, it is not functional for the human existing by himself, I will make for him a helper such as his opposite,

**2:19** וַיִּצֶר יְהֹוָה אֱלֹהִים מִן הָאֲדָמָה כָּל חַיַּת הַשָּׂדֶה וְאֵת כָּל עוֹף הַשָּׁמַיִם וַיָּבֵא אֶל הָאָדָם לִרְאוֹת מַה יִּקְרָא לוֹ וְכֹל אֲשֶׁר יִקְרָא לוֹ הָאָדָם נֶפֶשׁ חַיָּה הוּא שְׁמוֹ

and~he~will~Mold "YHWH [*He exists*]" "Elohiym [*Powers*]" From the~Ground All Life the~Field and~At All Flyer the~Sky~s2 and~he~

and "YHWH [*He exists*]" of "Elohiym [*Powers*]" molded from the ground all of the living ones of the field and all of the flyers of the

will~make~Come To the~Human to~
>~See What he~will~Call.out to~him
and~All Which he~will~Call.out to~
him the~Human Being Life He
Title~him

sky and he brought to the human to
see what he will call out for him
and all of which the human will call
out to him a being of life he was his
title,

**2:20** וַיִּקְרָא הָאָדָם שֵׁמוֹת לְכָל הַבְּהֵמָה וּלְעוֹף הַשָּׁמַיִם וּלְכֹל חַיַּת
הַשָּׂדֶה וּלְאָדָם לֹא מָצָא עֵזֶר כְּנֶגְדּוֹ

and~he~will~Call.out the~Human Title~
s to~All the~Beast and~to~Flyer
the~Sky~s2 and~to~All Life the~Field
and~to~Human Not he~did~Find
Helper like~Opposite~him

and the human called out the titles
to all of the beasts and for the flyers
of the sky and for all of the living
ones of the field and for the human
he did not find a helper such as
opposite him,

**2:21** וַיַּפֵּל יְהוָה אֱלֹהִים תַּרְדֵּמָה עַל הָאָדָם וַיִּישָׁן וַיִּקַּח אַחַת
מִצַּלְעֹתָיו וַיִּסְגֹּר בָּשָׂר תַּחְתֶּנָּה

and~he~will~make~Fall "YHWH [*He
exists*]" "Elohiym [*Powers*]" Trance
Upon the~Human and~he~will~Sleep
and~he~will~Take Unit from~Rib~s~
him and~he~will~Shut Flesh Under~
her

and "YHWH [*He exists*]" of
"Elohiym [*Powers*]" made a trance
fall upon the human and he slept and
he took a unit from his ribs and he
shut the flesh under her,

**2:22** וַיִּבֶן יְהוָה אֱלֹהִים אֶת הַצֵּלָע אֲשֶׁר לָקַח מִן הָאָדָם לְאִשָּׁה
וַיְבִאֶהָ אֶל הָאָדָם

and~he~will~Build "YHWH [*He
exists*]" "Elohiym [*Powers*]" At the~
Rib Which he~did~Take From the~
Human to~Woman and~he~will~make~
Come~her To the~Human

and "YHWH [*He exists*]" of
"Elohiym [*Powers*]" built the rib
which he took from the human for a
woman and he made her come to
the human,

**2:23** וַיֹּאמֶר הָאָדָם זֹאת הַפַּעַם עֶצֶם מֵעֲצָמַי וּבָשָׂר מִבְּשָׂרִי לְזֹאת
יִקָּרֵא אִשָּׁה כִּי מֵאִישׁ לֻקֳחָה זֹּאת

and~he~will~Say the~Human This
the~Stroke.of.time Bone from~Bone~s~
me and~Flesh from~Flesh~me to~This
he~will~be~Call.out Woman Given.that
from~Man she~did~much.be~Take This

and the human said this time is
bone from my bones and flesh from
my flesh for this she will be called
out woman given that from man
this was taken,

**2:24** עַל כֵּן יַעֲזָב אִישׁ אֶת אָבִיו וְאֶת אִמּוֹ וְדָבַק בְּאִשְׁתּוֹ וְהָיוּ לְבָשָׂר
אֶחָד

Upon So he~will~Leave Man At
Father~him and~At Mother~him and~
he~did~Adhere in~Woman~him and~
they~did~Exist to~Flesh Unit

therefore a man will leave his father
and his mother and he will adhere
with his woman and they will exist
a flesh unit,

**2:25** וַיִּהְיוּ שְׁנֵיהֶם עֲרוּמִּים הָאָדָם וְאִשְׁתּוֹ וְלֹא יִתְבֹּשָׁשׁוּ

| | |
|---|---|
| and~they~will~Exist Two~them(m) Nude~s the~Human and~Woman~him and~Not they(m)~will~self~Ashamed | and the two of them, the human and his woman, existed nude and they were not ashamed of themselves, |

# Chapter 3

**3:1** וְהַנָּחָשׁ הָיָה עָרוּם מִכֹּל חַיַּת הַשָּׂדֶה אֲשֶׁר עָשָׂה יְהֹוָה אֱלֹהִים וַיֹּאמֶר אֶל הָאִשָּׁה אַף כִּי אָמַר אֱלֹהִים לֹא תֹאכְלוּ מִכֹּל עֵץ הַגָּן

| | |
|---|---|
| and~the~Serpent he~had~Exist Subtle from~All Life the~Field Which he~ did~Do "YHWH [*He exists*]" "Elohiym [*Powers*]" and~he~will~Say To the~Woman Moreover Given.that he~did~Say "Elohiym [*Powers*]" Not you(mp)~will~Eat from~All Tree the~ Garden | and the serpent had existed as a subtle one from all of the living ones of the field which "YHWH [*He exists*]" of "Elohiym [*Powers*]" made and he said to the woman, did "Elohiym [*Powers*]" really say you will not eat from all of the trees of the garden, |

**3:2** וַתֹּאמֶר הָאִשָּׁה אֶל הַנָּחָשׁ מִפְּרִי עֵץ הַגָּן נֹאכֵל

| | |
|---|---|
| and~she~will~Say the~Woman To the~Serpent from~Produce Tree the~ Garden we~will~Eat | and the woman said to the serpent, from the produce of the tree of the garden we eat, |

**3:3** וּמִפְּרִי הָעֵץ אֲשֶׁר בְּתוֹךְ הַגָּן אָמַר אֱלֹהִים לֹא תֹאכְלוּ מִמֶּנּוּ וְלֹא תִגְּעוּ בּוֹ פֶּן תְּמֻתוּן

| | |
|---|---|
| and~from~Produce the~Tree Which in~Midst the~Garden he~did~Say "Elohiym [*Powers*]" Not you(mp)~ will~Eat From~him and~Not you(mp)~will~Touch in~him Otherwise you(mp)~will~Die | and from the produce of the tree which is in the midst of the garden "Elohiym [*Powers*]" said, you will not eat from him and you will not touch in him otherwise you will die, |

**3:4** וַיֹּאמֶר הַנָּחָשׁ אֶל הָאִשָּׁה לֹא מוֹת תְּמֻתוּן

| | |
|---|---|
| and~he~will~Say the~Serpent To the~ Woman Not >~Die you(mp)~will~Die | and the serpent said to the woman, a dying you will not die, |

**3:5** כִּי יֹדֵעַ אֱלֹהִים כִּי בְּיוֹם אֲכָלְכֶם מִמֶּנּוּ וְנִפְקְחוּ עֵינֵיכֶם וִהְיִיתֶם כֵּאלֹהִים יֹדְעֵי טוֹב וָרָע

| | |
|---|---|
| Given.that Know~ing(ms) "Elohiym [*Powers*]" Given.that in~Day >~Eat~ you(mp) From~him and~they(f)~did~ be~Open.up Eye~s2~you(mp) and~ you(mp)~did~Exist like~"Elohiym | given that "Elohiym [*Powers*]" is knowing that in the day you eat from him then your eyes will be opened up and you will exist like "Elohiym [*Powers*]" knowing |

[*Powers*]" Know~ing(mp) Functional and~Dysfunctional

function and dysfunction,

**3:6** וַתֵּרֶא הָאִשָּׁה כִּי טוֹב הָעֵץ לְמַאֲכָל וְכִי תַאֲוָה הוּא לָעֵינַיִם וְנֶחְמָד הָעֵץ לְהַשְׂכִּיל וַתִּקַּח מִפִּרְיוֹ וַתֹּאכַל וַתִּתֵּן גַּם לְאִישָׁהּ עִמָּהּ וַיֹּאכַל

and~she~will~See the~Woman Given.that Functional the~Tree to~Nourishment and~Given.that Yearning He to~Eye~s2 and~be~Crave~ing(ms) the~Tree to~>~make~Calculate and~she~will~Take from~Produce~him and~she~will~Eat and~she~will~Give Also to~Man~her With~her and~he~will~Eat

and the woman saw that the function of the tree is for nourishment and that he is yearning to the eyes and the tree was a craving to make calculations and she took from his produce and she ate and she gave also to the man with her and he ate,

**3:7** וַתִּפָּקַחְנָה עֵינֵי שְׁנֵיהֶם וַיֵּדְעוּ כִּי עֵירֻמִּם הֵם וַיִּתְפְּרוּ עֲלֵה תְאֵנָה וַיַּעֲשׂוּ לָהֶם חֲגֹרֹת

and~they(f)~will~be~Open.up Eye~s2 Two~them(m) and~they(m)~will~Know Given.that Naked~s They(m) and~they(m)~will~Sew.together Leaf Fig and~they(m)~will~Do to~them(m) Loin.covering~s

and the eyes of the two of them were opened up and they knew that they were naked and they sewed together leaves of the fig and they did for them loin coverings,

**3:8** וַיִּשְׁמְעוּ אֶת קוֹל יְהוָה אֱלֹהִים מִתְהַלֵּךְ בַּגָּן לְרוּחַ הַיּוֹם וַיִּתְחַבֵּא הָאָדָם וְאִשְׁתּוֹ מִפְּנֵי יְהוָה אֱלֹהִים בְּתוֹךְ עֵץ הַגָּן

and~they(m)~will~Hear At Voice "YHWH [*He exists*]" "Elohiym [*Powers*]" self~Walk~ing(ms) in~Garden to~Wind the~Day and~he~will~self~Withdraw the~Human and~Woman~him from~Face~s "YHWH [*He exists*]" "Elohiym [*Powers*]" in~Midst Tree the~Garden

and they heard the voice of "YHWH [*He exists*]" of "Elohiym [*Powers*]" walking himself in the garden for the wind of the day and the human and his woman withdrew themselves from the face of "YHWH [*He exists*]" of "Elohiym [*Powers*]" in the midst of the tree of the garden,

**3:9** וַיִּקְרָא יְהוָה אֱלֹהִים אֶל הָאָדָם וַיֹּאמֶר לוֹ אַיֶּכָּה

and~he~will~Call.out "YHWH [*He exists*]" "Elohiym [*Powers*]" To the~Human and~he~will~Say to~him Where~you(ms)

and "YHWH [*He exists*]" of "Elohiym [*Powers*]" called out to the human and he said to him, where are you,

**3:10** וַיֹּאמֶר אֶת קֹלְךָ שָׁמַעְתִּי בַּגָּן וָאִירָא כִּי עֵירֹם אָנֹכִי וָאֵחָבֵא

and~he~will~Say At Voice~you(ms) i~did~Hear in~Garden and~i~will~Fear Given.that Naked I and~i~will~

and he said, I heard your voice in the garden and feared given that I was naked and I withdrew,

Withdraw

**3:11** וַיֹּאמֶר מִי הִגִּיד לְךָ כִּי עֵירֹם אָתָּה הֲמִן הָעֵץ אֲשֶׁר צִוִּיתִיךָ לְבִלְתִּי אֲכָל מִמֶּנּוּ אָכָלְתָּ

and~he~will~Say Who he~did~make~
Be.face.to.face to~you(ms) Given.that
Naked You(ms) the~From the~Tree
Which i~did~much~Direct~you(ms) to~
Except >~Eat From~him you(ms)~
will~Eat

and he said, who told to you that
you were naked, are you eating
from the tree which I directed you
to not eat from,

**3:12** וַיֹּאמֶר הָאָדָם הָאִשָּׁה אֲשֶׁר נָתַתָּה עִמָּדִי הִוא נָתְנָה לִי מִן הָעֵץ וָאֹכֵל

and~he~will~Say the~Human the~
Woman Which you(ms)~did~Give
By~me She she~did~Give to~me
From the~Tree and~i~will~Eat

and the human said, the woman
which you gave by me, she gave to
me from the tree and I ate,

**3:13** וַיֹּאמֶר יְהוָה אֱלֹהִים לָאִשָּׁה מַה זֹּאת עָשִׂית וַתֹּאמֶר הָאִשָּׁה הַנָּחָשׁ הִשִּׁיאַנִי וָאֹכֵל

and~he~will~Say "YHWH [He
exists]" "Elohiym [Powers]" to~
Woman What This you(fs)~did~Do
and~she~will~Say the~Woman the~
Serpent he~had~make~Deceive~me
and~i~will~Eat

and "YHWH [He exists]" of
"Elohiym [Powers]" said to the
woman, what is this you did and the
woman said, the serpent had
deceived me and I ate,

**3:14** וַיֹּאמֶר יְהוָה אֱלֹהִים אֶל הַנָּחָשׁ כִּי עָשִׂיתָ זֹּאת אָרוּר אַתָּה מִכָּל הַבְּהֵמָה וּמִכֹּל חַיַּת הַשָּׂדֶה עַל גְּחֹנְךָ תֵלֵךְ וְעָפָר תֹּאכַל כָּל יְמֵי חַיֶּיךָ

and~he~will~Say "YHWH [He
exists]" "Elohiym [Powers]" To the~
Serpent Given.that you(mp)~did~Do
This Spit.upon~ed(ms) You(ms) from~
All the~Beast and~from~All Life
the~Field Upon Belly you(ms)~will~
Walk and~Powder you(ms)~will~Eat
All Day~s Life~s~you(ms)

and "YHWH [He exists]" of
"Elohiym [Powers]" said to the
serpent, given that you did this,
spitted upon are you from all of the
beasts and from all of the living
ones of the field, upon the belly you
will walk and powder you will eat
all of the days of your life,

**3:15** וְאֵיבָה אָשִׁית בֵּינְךָ וּבֵין הָאִשָּׁה וּבֵין זַרְעֲךָ וּבֵין זַרְעָהּ הוּא יְשׁוּפְךָ רֹאשׁ וְאַתָּה תְּשׁוּפֶנּוּ עָקֵב

and~Hostility i~did~Set.down Between~
you(ms) and~Between the~Woman
and~Between Seed~you(ms) and~
Between Seed~her He he~will~
Fall.upon~you(ms) Head and~You(ms)

and hostility I sat down between
you and the woman and between
your seed and her seed, he will fall
upon you a head and you will fall
upon him a heel,

you(ms)~will~Fall.upon~him   Heel

**3:16**  אֶל הָאִשָּׁה אָמַר הַרְבָּה אַרְבֶּה עִצְּבוֹנֵךְ וְהֵרֹנֵךְ בְּעֶצֶב תֵּלְדִי בָנִים וְאֶל אִישֵׁךְ תְּשׁוּקָתֵךְ וְהוּא יִמְשָׁל בָּךְ

To the~Woman he~did~Say >~make~ Increase i~will~make~Increase Hardship~you(fs) and~Pregnancy~you(fs) in~Distressing.pain you(fs)~will~ Bring.forth Son~s and~To Man~ you(fs) Following~you(fs) and~He he~ will~Regulate in~you(fs)

To the woman he said, I will make a great increase of your hardship and your pregnancy, in distressing pain you will bring forth sons and to your man is your following and he will regulate in you,

**3:17**  וּלְאָדָם אָמַר כִּי שָׁמַעְתָּ לְקוֹל אִשְׁתֶּךָ וַתֹּאכַל מִן הָעֵץ אֲשֶׁר צִוִּיתִיךָ לֵאמֹר לֹא תֹאכַל מִמֶּנּוּ אֲרוּרָה הָאֲדָמָה בַּעֲבוּרֶךָ בְּעִצָּבוֹן תֹּאכְלֶנָּה כֹּל יְמֵי חַיֶּיךָ

and~to~Human he~did~Say Given.that you(ms)~did~Hear to~Voice Woman~ you(ms) and~you(ms)~will~Eat From the~Tree Which i~did~much~Direct~ you(ms) to~>~Say Not you(ms)~will~ Eat From~him Spit.upon~ed(ms) the~ Ground On.account.of~you(ms) in~ Hardship~you(ms) you(ms)~will~Eat~her All Day~s Life~s~you(ms)

and to the human he said, given that you heard the voice of your woman and you ate from the tree which I directed you saying, you will not eat from him, spitted upon is the ground on account of you, in your hardship you will eat of her all of the days of your life,

**3:18**  וְקוֹץ וְדַרְדַּר תַּצְמִיחַ לָךְ וְאָכַלְתָּ אֶת עֵשֶׂב הַשָּׂדֶה

and~Bramble and~Thistle she~will~ make~Spring.up to~you(fs) and~ you(ms)~did~Eat At Herb the~Field

and brambles and thistles she will make spring up for you and you will eat the herbs of the field,

**3:19**  בְּזֵעַת אַפֶּיךָ תֹּאכַל לֶחֶם עַד שׁוּבְךָ אֶל הָאֲדָמָה כִּי מִמֶּנָּה לֻקָּחְתָּ כִּי עָפָר אַתָּה וְאֶל עָפָר תָּשׁוּב

in~Sweat Nose~s~you(ms) you(ms)~ will~Eat Bread Until >~Turn.back~ you(ms) To the~Ground Given.that From~her you(ms)~did~be~Take Given.that Powder You(ms) and~To Powder you(ms)~will~Turn.back

in the sweat of your nostrils you will eat bread, until you turn back to the ground given that from her you were taken, given that you are powder and to powder you will turn back,

**3:20**  וַיִּקְרָא הָאָדָם שֵׁם אִשְׁתּוֹ חַוָּה כִּי הִוא הָיְתָה אֵם כָּל חָי

and~he~will~Call.out the~Human Title Woman~him "Hhawah [*Living*]" Given.that She she~did~Exist Mother All Life

and the human called out the title of his woman "Hhawah [*Living*]" given that she existed a mother of all of the life,

**3:21**  וַיַּעַשׂ יְהֹוָה אֱלֹהִים לְאָדָם וּלְאִשְׁתּוֹ כָּתְנוֹת עוֹר וַיַּלְבִּשֵׁם

and~he~will~Do "YHWH [*He exists*]"   and "YHWH [*He exists*]" of

"Elohiym [*Powers*]" to~Human and~ to~Woman~him Tunic~s Skin and~ he~will~Clothe~them(m)

"Elohiym [*Powers*]" made for the man and for his woman tunics of skin and he clothed them,

**3:22** וַיֹּאמֶר יְהוָה אֱלֹהִים הֵן הָאָדָם הָיָה כְּאַחַד מִמֶּנּוּ לָדַעַת טוֹב וָרָע וְעַתָּה פֶּן יִשְׁלַח יָדוֹ וְלָקַח גַּם מֵעֵץ הַחַיִּים וְאָכַל וָחַי לְעֹלָם

and~he~will~Say "YHWH [*He exists*]" "Elohiym [*Powers*]" Though the~Human he~had~Exist like~Unit From~us to~>~Discernment Functional and~Dysfunctional and~Now Otherwise he~will~Send Hand~him and~he~did~ Take Also from~Tree the~Life~s and~he~did~Eat and~he~did~Live to~ Distant.time

and "YHWH [*He exists*]" of "Elohiym [*Powers*]" said, though the human had existed like a unit from us to discern function and dysfunction and now otherwise he will send his hand and he will take also from the tree of the life and he will eat and he will live to a distant time,

**3:23** וַיְשַׁלְּחֵהוּ יְהוָה אֱלֹהִים מִגַּן עֵדֶן לַעֲבֹד אֶת הָאֲדָמָה אֲשֶׁר לֻקַּח מִשָּׁם

and~he~will~Send~him "YHWH [*He exists*]" "Elohiym [*Powers*]" from~ Garden "Eden [*Pleasure*]" to~>~Serve At the~Ground Which he~did~be~ Take from~There

and "YHWH [*He exists*]" of "Elohiym [*Powers*]" sent him from the garden of "Eden [*Pleasure*]" to serve the ground which from there he was taken,

**3:24** וַיְגָרֶשׁ אֶת הָאָדָם וַיַּשְׁכֵּן מִקֶּדֶם לְגַן עֵדֶן אֶת הַכְּרֻבִים וְאֵת לַהַט הַחֶרֶב הַמִּתְהַפֶּכֶת לִשְׁמֹר אֶת דֶּרֶךְ עֵץ הַחַיִּים

and~he~will~Cast.out At the~Human and~he~will~Dwell from~East to~ Garden "Eden [*Pleasure*]" At "Keruv [*Sword*]" and~At Blazing the~Sword the~self~Overturn~ing(fs) to~>~Guard At Road Tree the~Life~s

and he cast out the human, and the "Keruv [*Sword*]" and a blazing one dwelt from the east to the garden of "Eden [*Pleasure*]", the sword overturning herself to guard the road of the tree of the life,

# Chapter 4

**4:1** וְהָאָדָם יָדַע אֶת חַנָּה אִשְׁתּוֹ וַתַּהַר וַתֵּלֶד אֶת קַיִן וַתֹּאמֶר קָנִיתִי אִישׁ אֶת יְהוָה

and~the~Human he~had~Know At "Hhawah [*Living*]" Woman~him and~ she~will~Conceive and~she~will~ Bring.forth At "Qayin [*Acquired*]" and~she~will~Say i~did~Purchase Man At "YHWH [*He exists*]"

and the human had known "Hhawah [*Living*]" his woman and she conceived and she brought forth "Qayin [*Acquired*]" and she said, I purchased a man with "YHWH [*He exists*]",

**4:2** וַתֹּסֶף לָלֶדֶת אֶת אָחִיו אֶת הָבֶל וַיְהִי הֶבֶל רֹעֵה צֹאן וְקַיִן הָיָה עֹבֵד אֲדָמָה

and~she~did~make~Add to~>~
Bring.forth At Brother~him At
"Hevel [*Empty*]" and~he~will~Exist
"Hevel [*Empty*]" Feed~ing(ms) Flocks
and~"Qayin [*Acquired*]" he~did~Exist
Serve~ing(ms) Ground

and she again brought forth his
brother "Hevel [*Empty*]" and
"Hevel [*Empty*]" existed as a feeder
of the flocks and "Qayin
[*Acquired*]" existed as a server of
the ground,

**4:3\*** וַיְהִי מִקֵּץ יָמִים וַיָּבֵא קַיִן מִפְּרִי הָאֲדָמָה מִנְחָה לַיהוָה

and~he~will~Exist from~Conclusion
Day~s and~he~will~make~Come
"Qayin [*Acquired*]" from~Produce
the~Ground Donation to~"YHWH [*He
exists*]"

and it came to pass at the
conclusion of days, "Qayin
[*Acquired*]" brought from the
produce of the ground, a donation
to "YHWH [*He exists*]",

**4:4** וְהֶבֶל הֵבִיא גַם הוּא מִבְּכֹרוֹת צֹאנוֹ וּמֵחֶלְבֵהֶן וַיִּשַׁע יְהוָה אֶל הֶבֶל וְאֶל מִנְחָתוֹ

and~"Hevel [*Empty*]" he~had~make~
Come Also He from~
Firstborn.female~s Flocks~him and~
from~Fat~them(f) and~he~will~
Look.with.respect "YHWH [*He
exists*]" To "Hevel [*Empty*]" and~To
Donation~him

and "Hevel [*Empty*]", he also, had
brought from the firstborn females
of his flocks and from their fat and
"YHWH [*He exists*]" looked with
respect to "Hevel [*Empty*]" and to
his donation,

**4:5** וְאֶל קַיִן וְאֶל מִנְחָתוֹ לֹא שָׁעָה וַיִּחַר לְקַיִן מְאֹד וַיִּפְּלוּ פָּנָיו

and~To "Qayin [*Acquired*]" and~To
Donation~him Not he~did~
Look.with.respect and~he~will~Flare.up
to~"Qayin [*Acquired*]" Many and~
they(m)~will~Fall Face~s~him

and to "Qayin [*Acquired*]" and to
his donation he did not look with
respect and "Qayin [*Acquired*]"
was much flared up and his face
fell,

**4:6** וַיֹּאמֶר יְהוָה אֶל קַיִן לָמָּה חָרָה לָךְ וְלָמָּה נָפְלוּ פָנֶיךָ

and~he~will~Say "YHWH [*He
exists*]" To "Qayin [*Acquired*]" to~
What he~did~Flare.up to~you(fs) and~
to~What they~did~Fall Face~s~you(ms)

and "YHWH [*He exists*]" said to
"Qayin [*Acquired*]", why were you
flared up and why is your face
fallen,

**4:7** הֲלוֹא אִם תֵּיטִיב שְׂאֵת וְאִם לֹא תֵיטִיב לַפֶּתַח חַטָּאת רֹבֵץ וְאֵלֶיךָ תְּשׁוּקָתוֹ וְאַתָּה תִּמְשָׁל בּוֹ

?~Not If you(ms)~will~make~Do.well
>~Lift.up and~If Not you(ms)~will~
make~Do.well to~Opening Error
Stretch.out~ing(ms) and~To~you(ms)
Following~him and~You(ms) you(ms)~

if you cause it to be done well, will
it not be lifted up and if you do not
cause it to be done well, an opening
of error is stretching out and to you
is his following and you will

will~Regulate in~him | regulate in him,

**4:8\*** וַיֹּאמֶר קַיִן אֶל הֶבֶל אָחִיו וַיְהִי בִּהְיוֹתָם בַּשָּׂדֶה וַיָּקָם קַיִן אֶל הֶבֶל אָחִיו וַיַּהַרְגֵהוּ

and~he~will~Say "Qayin [Acquired]" To "Hevel [Empty]" Brother~him and~he~will~Exist in~>~Exist~them(m) in~Field and~he~will~Rise "Qayin [Acquired]" To "Hevel [Empty]" Brother~him and~he~will~Kill~him

and "Qayin [Acquired]" said to "Hevel [Empty]" his brother, let us go out into the field, and it came to pass in their existing in the field and "Qayin [Acquired]" rose to "Hevel [Empty]" his brother and he killed him,

**4:9** וַיֹּאמֶר יְהוָה אֶל קַיִן אֵי הֶבֶל אָחִיךָ וַיֹּאמֶר לֹא יָדַעְתִּי הֲשֹׁמֵר אָחִי אָנֹכִי

and~he~will~Say "YHWH [He exists]" To "Qayin [Acquired]" Where "Hevel [Empty]" Brother~ you(ms) and~he~will~Say Not i~will~ Know ?~Guard~ing(ms) Brother~me I

and "YHWH [He exists]" said to "Qayin [Acquired]", where is "Hevel [Empty]" your brother, and he said, I do not know, am I the guard of my brother,

**4:10** וַיֹּאמֶר מֶה עָשִׂיתָ קוֹל דְּמֵי אָחִיךָ צֹעֲקִים אֵלַי מִן הָאֲדָמָה

and~he~will~Say What you(ms)~did~ Do Voice Blood~s Brother~you(ms) Cry.out~ing(mp) To~me From the~ Ground

and he said, what did you do, the voice of the blood of your brother is crying out to me from the ground,

**4:11** וְעַתָּה אָרוּר אָתָּה מִן הָאֲדָמָה אֲשֶׁר פָּצְתָה אֶת פִּיהָ לָקַחַת אֶת דְּמֵי אָחִיךָ מִיָּדֶךָ

and~Now Spit.upon~ed(ms) You(ms) From the~Ground Which she~did~Part At Mouth~her to~>~Take At Blood~ s Brother~you(ms) from~Hand~you(ms)

and now you are spitted upon from the ground which parted her mouth to take the blood of your brother from your hand,

**4:12** כִּי תַעֲבֹד אֶת הָאֲדָמָה לֹא תֹסֵף תֵּת כֹּחָהּ לָךְ נָע וָנָד תִּהְיֶה בָאָרֶץ

Given.that you(ms)~will~Serve At the~Ground Not she~will~make~Add >~Give Strength~her to~you(fs) Stagger~ing(ms) and~Nod~ing(ms) you(ms)~will~Exist in~the~Land

given that you will serve the ground, she will not again give her strength to you, you will exist in the land, staggering and nodding,

**4:13** וַיֹּאמֶר קַיִן אֶל יְהוָה גָּדוֹל עֲוֹנִי מִנְּשֹׂא

and~he~will~Say "Qayin [Acquired]" To "YHWH [He exists]" Magnificent Iniquity~me from~>~Lift.up

and "Qayin [Acquired]" said to "YHWH [He exists]", my iniquity is too magnificent to lift up,

**4:14** הֵן גֵּרַשְׁתָּ אֹתִי הַיּוֹם מֵעַל פְּנֵי הָאֲדָמָה וּמִפָּנֶיךָ אֶסָּתֵר וְהָיִיתִי

נָע וָנָד בָּאָרֶץ וְהָיָה כָל מֹצְאִי יַהַרְגֵנִי

Though you(ms)~did~much~Cast.out At~me the~Day from~Upon Face~s the~Ground and~from~Face~s~you(ms) i~will~be~Hide and~i~did~Exist Stagger~ing(ms) and~Nod~ing(ms) in~ the~Land and~he~did~Exist All Find~ ing(ms)~me he~will~Kill~me

though you cast me out today from upon the face of the ground and I will be hidden from your face and I will exist in the land, staggering and nodding and it will come to pass all of the ones finding me will kill me,

**4:15** וַיֹּאמֶר לוֹ יְהוָה לָכֵן כָּל הֹרֵג קַיִן שִׁבְעָתַיִם יֻקָּם וַיָּשֶׂם יְהוָה לְקַיִן אוֹת לְבִלְתִּי הַכּוֹת אֹתוֹ כָּל מֹצְאוֹ

and~he~will~Say to~him "YHWH [He exists]" to~So All Kill~ing(ms) "Qayin [Acquired]" Seventh.time~s2 he~will~make.be~Avenge and~he~will~ Set.in.place "YHWH [He exists]" to~ "Qayin [Acquired]" Sign to~Except >~make~Hit At~him All Find~ ing(ms)~him

and "YHWH [He exists]" said to him, because of this, all of the ones killing "Qayin [Acquired]" will be made avenged sevenfold and "YHWH [He exists]" set in place to "Qayin [Acquired]" a sign for all of the ones finding him to not hit him,

**4:16** וַיֵּצֵא קַיִן מִלִּפְנֵי יְהוָה וַיֵּשֶׁב בְּאֶרֶץ נוֹד קִדְמַת עֵדֶן

and~he~will~Go.out "Qayin [Acquired]" from~to~Face~s "YHWH [He exists]" and~he~will~Settle in~ Land "Nod [Wander]" Eastward "Eden [Pleasure]"

and "Qayin [Acquired]" went out from before "YHWH [He exists]" and he settled in the land of "Nod [Wander]", eastward of "Eden [Pleasure]",

**4:17** וַיֵּדַע קַיִן אֶת אִשְׁתּוֹ וַתַּהַר וַתֵּלֶד אֶת חֲנוֹךְ וַיְהִי בֹּנֶה עִיר וַיִּקְרָא שֵׁם הָעִיר כְּשֵׁם בְּנוֹ חֲנוֹךְ

and~he~will~Know "Qayin [Acquired]" At Woman~him and~she~will~ Conceive and~she~will~Bring.forth At "Hhanokh [Dedicated]" and~he~will~ Exist Build~ing(ms) City and~he~ will~Call.out Title the~City like~Title Son~him "Hhanokh [Dedicated]"

and "Qayin [Acquired]" knew his woman and she conceived and she brought forth "Hhanokh [Dedicated]" and he existed a builder of a city and called out the title of the city "Hhanokh [Dedicated]" like the title of his son,

**4:18** וַיִּוָּלֵד לַחֲנוֹךְ אֶת עִירָד וְעִירָד יָלַד אֶת מְחוּיָאֵל וּמְחִיָּיאֵל יָלַד אֶת מְתוּשָׁאֵל וּמְתוּשָׁאֵל יָלַד אֶת לָמֶךְ

and~he~will~be~Bring.forth to~ "Hhanokh [Dedicated]" At "Irad [Wild donkey]" and~"Irad [Wild donkey]" he~had~Bring.forth At "Mehhuya'el [Who proclaims El]" and~"Mehhuya'el [Who proclaims El]"

and "Irad [Wild donkey]" was brought forth to "Hhanokh [Dedicated]" and "Irad [Wild donkey]" had brought forth "Mehhuya'el [Who proclaims El]" and "Mehhuya'el [Who proclaims

he~had~Bring.forth  At  "Metusha'el [His death asks]" and~"Metusha'el [His death asks]" he~had~Bring.forth At "Lamekh [Powerful]"

*El*]" had brought forth "Metusha'el [*His death asks*]" and "Metusha'el [*His death asks*]" had brought forth "Lamekh [*Powerful*]",

**4:19** וַיִּקַּח לוֹ לֶמֶךְ שְׁתֵּי נָשִׁים שֵׁם הָאַחַת עָדָה וְשֵׁם הַשֵּׁנִית צִלָּה

and~he~will~Take  to~him  "Lamekh [*Powerful*]" Two Woman~s Title the~Unit "Adah [*Ornament*]" and~ Title the~Second "Tsilah [*Shadow*]"

and "Lamekh [*Powerful*]" took to him two women, the title of the one is "Adah [*Ornament*]" and the title of the second is "Tsilah [*Shadow*]",

**4:20** וַתֵּלֶד עָדָה אֶת יָבָל הוּא הָיָה אֲבִי יֹשֵׁב אֹהֶל וּמִקְנֶה

and~she~will~Bring.forth  "Adah [*Ornament*]" At "Yaval [*Watercourse*]" He he~did~Exist Father~of Settle~ing(ms) Tent and~ Livestock

and "Adah [*Ornament*]" brought forth "Yaval [*Watercourse*]", he existed as father of tent and livestock settlers,

**4:21** וְשֵׁם אָחִיו יוּבָל הוּא הָיָה אֲבִי כָּל תֹּפֵשׂ כִּנּוֹר וְעוּגָב

and~Title  Brother~him  "Yuval [*Creek*]" He he~did~Exist Father~of All Seize.hold~ing(ms) Harp and~ Reed-pipes

and the title of his brother is "Yuval [*Creek*]", he existed as father of all of the ones seizing hold of the harp and reed-pipe,

**4:22** וְצִלָּה גַם הִוא יָלְדָה אֶת תּוּבַל קַיִן לֹטֵשׁ כָּל חֹרֵשׁ נְחֹשֶׁת וּבַרְזֶל וַאֲחוֹת תּוּבַל קַיִן נַעֲמָה

and~"Tsilah [*Shadow*]" Also She she~had~Bring.forth At "Tuval-Qayin [*Flow of acquiring*]" Sharpen~ing(ms) All Scratch~ing(ms) Bronze and~Iron and~Sister "Tuval-Qayin [*Flow of acquiring*]" "Na'amah [*Sweet*]"

and "Tsilah [*Shadow*]" also had brought forth "Tuval-Qayin [*Flow of acquiring*]" a sharpener of all of the ones scratching of bronze and iron and the sister of "Tuval-Qayin [*Flow of acquiring*]" is "Na'amah [*Sweet*]",

**4:23** וַיֹּאמֶר לֶמֶךְ לְנָשָׁיו עָדָה וְצִלָּה שְׁמַעַן קוֹלִי נְשֵׁי לֶמֶךְ הַאֲזֵנָּה אִמְרָתִי כִּי אִישׁ הָרַגְתִּי לְפִצְעִי וְיֶלֶד לְחַבֻּרָתִי

and~he~will~Say  "Lamekh [*Powerful*]" to~Woman~s~him "Adah [*Ornament*]" and~"Tsilah [*Shadow*]" !(fp)~Hear Voice~me Woman~s "Lamekh [*Powerful*]" !(fp)~make~Listen Speech~ me Given.that Man i~did~Kill to~ Bruise~me and~Boy to~Striped.bruise~ me

and "Lamekh [*Powerful*]" said to his women, "Adah [*Ornament*]" and "Tsilah [*Shadow*]", listen to my voice, women of "Lamekh [*Powerful*]", give an ear to my speech, given that I killed a man for my bruise and a boy for my striped bruise,

**4:24** כִּי שִׁבְעָתַיִם יֻקַּם קָיִן וְלֶמֶךְ שִׁבְעִים וְשִׁבְעָה

Given.that  Seventh.time~s2  he~will~

given that "Qayin [*Acquired*]" will

make.be~Avenge "Qayin [*Acquired*]" and~"Lamekh [*Powerful*]" Seven~s and~Seven

be avenged sevenfold then "Lamekh [*Powerful*]" seventy and seven,

**4:25** וַיֵּדַע אָדָם עוֹד אֶת אִשְׁתּוֹ וַתֵּלֶד בֵּן וַתִּקְרָא אֶת שְׁמוֹ שֵׁת כִּי שָׁת לִי אֱלֹהִים זֶרַע אַחֵר תַּחַת הֶבֶל כִּי הֲרָגוֹ קָיִן

and~he~will~Know Human Yet.again At Woman~him and~she~will~Bring.forth Son and~she~will~Call.out At Title~him "Shet [*Buttocks*]" Given.that he~did~Set.down to~me "Elohiym [*Powers*]" Seed Other Under "Hevel [*Empty*]" Given.that he~did~Kill~him "Qayin [*Acquired*]"

and the human knew yet again his woman and she brought forth a son and she called out his title "Shet [*Buttocks*]" given that "Elohiym [*Powers*]" set down for me another seed in place of "Hevel [*Empty*]" given that "Qayin [*Acquired*]" killed him,

**4:26\*** וּלְשֵׁת גַּם הוּא יֻלַּד בֵּן וַיִּקְרָא אֶת שְׁמוֹ אֱנוֹשׁ אָז הוּחַל לִקְרֹא בְּשֵׁם יְהוָה

and~to~"Shet [*Buttocks*]" Also He he~had~much.be~Bring.forth Son and~he~will~Call.out At Title~him "Enosh [*Man*]" At.that.time he~did~Pierce to~>~Call.out in~Title "YHWH [*He exists*]"

and "Shet [*Buttocks*]" also had been brought forth a son and he called out his title "Enosh [*Man*]", at that time they pierced to call out in the title of "YHWH [*He exists*]",

# Chapter 5

**5:1** זֶה סֵפֶר תּוֹלְדֹת אָדָם בְּיוֹם בְּרֹא אֱלֹהִים אָדָם בִּדְמוּת אֱלֹהִים עָשָׂה אֹתוֹ

This Scroll Birthing~s Human in~Day >~Fatten "Elohiym [*Powers*]" Human in~Likeness "Elohiym [*Powers*]" he~did~Do At~him

this is the scroll of the birthings of the human in the day "Elohiym [*Powers*]" fattened the human, in the likeness of "Elohiym [*Powers*]" he did him,

**5:2** זָכָר וּנְקֵבָה בְּרָאָם וַיְבָרֶךְ אֹתָם וַיִּקְרָא אֶת שְׁמָם אָדָם בְּיוֹם הִבָּרְאָם

Male and~Female he~did~Fatten~them(m) and~he~will~much~Kneel At~them(m) and~he~will~Call.out At Title~them(m) Human in~Day >~be~Fatten~them(m)

male and female he fattened them and he respected them and he called out their title human in the day he fattened them,

**5:3** וַיְחִי אָדָם שְׁלֹשִׁים וּמְאַת שָׁנָה וַיּוֹלֶד בִּדְמוּתוֹ כְּצַלְמוֹ וַיִּקְרָא אֶת שְׁמוֹ שֵׁת

and~he~will~Live Human Three~s and~Hundred Year and~he~will~make~Bring.forth in~Likeness~him like~Image~him and~he~will~Call.out At Title~him "Shet [*Buttocks*]"

and the human lived a hundred and thirty years and he caused to bring forth in his likeness, like his image and he called out his title "Shet [*Buttocks*]",

**5:4** וַיִּהְיוּ יְמֵי אָדָם אַחֲרֵי הוֹלִידוֹ אֶת שֵׁת שְׁמֹנֶה מֵאֹת שָׁנָה וַיּוֹלֶד בָּנִים וּבָנוֹת

and~they(m)~will~Exist Day~s Human After >~make~Bring.forth~him At "Shet [*Buttocks*]" Eight Hundred~s Year and~he~will~make~Bring.forth Son~s and~Daughter~s

and the days of the human existed after his causing to bring forth were eight hundred years and he caused to bring forth sons and daughters,

**5:5** וַיִּהְיוּ כָּל יְמֵי אָדָם אֲשֶׁר חַי תְּשַׁע מֵאוֹת שָׁנָה וּשְׁלֹשִׁים שָׁנָה וַיָּמֹת

and~they(m)~will~Exist All Day~s Human Which he~did~Live Nine Hundred~s Year Three~s Year and~he~will~Die

and all of the days of the human existed which he lived were nine hundred and thirty years and he died,

**5:6** וַיְחִי שֵׁת חָמֵשׁ שָׁנִים וּמְאַת שָׁנָה וַיּוֹלֶד אֶת אֱנוֹשׁ

and~he~will~Live "Shet [*Buttocks*]" Five Year~s and~Hundred Year and~he~will~make~Bring.forth At "Enosh [*Man*]"

and "Shet [*Buttocks*]" lived a hundred and five years and he caused to bring forth "Enosh [*Man*]",

**5:7** וַיְחִי שֵׁת אַחֲרֵי הוֹלִידוֹ אֶת אֱנוֹשׁ שֶׁבַע שָׁנִים וּשְׁמֹנֶה מֵאוֹת שָׁנָה וַיּוֹלֶד בָּנִים וּבָנוֹת

and~he~will~Live "Shet [*Buttocks*]" After >~make~Bring.forth~him At "Enosh [*Man*]" Seven Year~s and~Eight Hundred~s Year and~he~will~make~Bring.forth Son~s and~Daughter~s

and "Shet [*Buttocks*]" lived after his causing to bring forth "Enosh [*Man*]" eight hundred and seven years and he caused to bring forth sons and daughters,

**5:8** וַיִּהְיוּ כָּל יְמֵי שֵׁת שְׁתֵּים עֶשְׂרֵה שָׁנָה וּתְשַׁע מֵאוֹת שָׁנָה וַיָּמֹת

and~they(m)~will~Exist All Day~s "Shet [*Buttocks*]" Two Ten Year and~Nine Hundred~s Year and~he~will~Die

and all of the days of "Shet [*Buttocks*]" existed nine hundred and twelve years and he died,

**5:9** וַיְחִי אֱנוֹשׁ תִּשְׁעִים שָׁנָה וַיּוֹלֶד אֶת קֵינָן

and~he~will~Live "Enosh [*Man*]" Nine~s Year and~he~will~make~Bring.forth At "Qeynan [*Possession*]"

and "Enosh [*Man*]" lived ninety years and he caused to bring forth "Qeynan [*Possession*]",

**5:10** וַיְחִי אֱנוֹשׁ אַחֲרֵי הוֹלִידוֹ אֶת קֵינָן חֲמֵשׁ עֶשְׂרֵה שָׁנָה וּשְׁמֹנֶה מֵאוֹת שָׁנָה וַיּוֹלֶד בָּנִים וּבָנוֹת

and~he~will~Live "Enosh [*Man*]" After >~make~Bring.forth~him At "Qeynan [*Possession*]" Five Ten Year and~Eight Hundred~s Year and~he~will~make~Bring.forth Son~s and~Daughter~s

and "Enosh [*Man*]" lived after causing to bring forth "Qeynan [*Possession*]" eight hundred and fifteen years and he caused to bring forth sons and daughters,

**5:11** וַיִּהְיוּ כָּל יְמֵי אֱנוֹשׁ חָמֵשׁ שָׁנִים וּתְשַׁע מֵאוֹת שָׁנָה וַיָּמֹת

and~they(m)~will~Exist All Day~s "Enosh [*Man*]" Five Year~s and~Nine Hundred~s Year and~he~will~Die

and all of the days of "Enosh [*Man*]" existed nine hundred and five years and he died,

**5:12** וַיְחִי קֵינָן שִׁבְעִים שָׁנָה וַיּוֹלֶד אֶת מַהֲלַלְאֵל

and~he~will~Live "Qeynan [*Possession*]" Seven~s Year and~he~will~make~Bring.forth At "Mahalalel [*Praise of El*]"

and "Qeynan [*Possession*]" lived seventy years and he caused to bring forth "Mahalalel [*Praise of El*]",

**5:13** וַיְחִי קֵינָן אַחֲרֵי הוֹלִידוֹ אֶת מַהֲלַלְאֵל אַרְבָּעִים שָׁנָה וּשְׁמֹנֶה מֵאוֹת שָׁנָה וַיּוֹלֶד בָּנִים וּבָנוֹת

and~he~will~Live "Qeynan [*Possession*]" After >~make~Bring.forth~him At "Mahalalel [*Praise of El*]" Four~s Year and~Eight Hundred~s Year and~he~will~make~Bring.forth Son~s and~Daughter~s

and "Qeynan [*Possession*]" lived after his causing to bring forth "Mahalalel [*Praise of El*]" eight hundred and forty years and he caused to bring forth sons and daughters,

**5:14** וַיִּהְיוּ כָּל יְמֵי קֵינָן עֶשֶׂר שָׁנִים וּתְשַׁע מֵאוֹת שָׁנָה וַיָּמֹת

and~they(m)~will~Exist All Day~s "Qeynan [*Possession*]" Ten Year~s and~Nine Hundred~s Year and~he~will~Die

and all of the days of "Qeynan [*Possession*]" existed nine hundred and ten years and he died,

**5:15** וַיְחִי מַהֲלַלְאֵל חָמֵשׁ שָׁנִים וְשִׁשִּׁים שָׁנָה וַיּוֹלֶד אֶת יָרֶד

and~he~will~Live "Mahalalel [*Praise of El*]" Five Year~s and~Six~s Year and~he~will~make~Bring.forth At "Yared [*Descend*]"

and "Mahalalel [*Praise of El*]" lived sixty-five years and he caused to bring forth "Yared [*Descend*]",

**5:16** וַיְחִי מַהֲלַלְאֵל אַחֲרֵי הוֹלִידוֹ אֶת יֶרֶד שְׁלֹשִׁים שָׁנָה וּשְׁמֹנֶה מֵאוֹת שָׁנָה וַיּוֹלֶד בָּנִים וּבָנוֹת

and~he~will~Live "Mahalalel [*Praise of El*]" After >~make~Bring.forth~him

and "Mahalalel [*Praise of El*]" lived after his causing to bring forth

At "Yared [*Descend*]" Three~s Year and~Eight Hundred~s Year and~he~will~make~Bring.forth Son~s and~Daughter~s

"Yared [*Descend*]" eight hundred and thirty years and he caused to bring forth sons and daughters,

**5:17** וַיִּהְיוּ כָּל יְמֵי מַהֲלַלְאֵל חָמֵשׁ וְתִשְׁעִים שָׁנָה וּשְׁמֹנֶה מֵאוֹת שָׁנָה וַיָּמֹת

and~they(m)~will~Exist All Day~s "Mahalalel [*Praise of El*]" Five and~Nine~s Year Eight Hundred~s Year and~he~will~Die

and all of the days of "Mahalalel [*Praise of El*]" existed eight hundred and ninety-five years and he died,

**5:18** וַיְחִי יֶרֶד שְׁתַּיִם וְשִׁשִּׁים שָׁנָה וּמְאַת שָׁנָה וַיּוֹלֶד אֶת חֲנוֹךְ

and~he~will~Live "Yared [*Descend*]" Two and~Six~s Year and~Hundred Year and~he~will~make~Bring.forth At "Hhanokh [*Dedicated*]"

and "Yared [*Descend*]" lived a hundred and sixty-two years and he caused to bring forth "Hhanokh [*Dedicated*]",

**5:19** וַיְחִי יֶרֶד אַחֲרֵי הוֹלִידוֹ אֶת חֲנוֹךְ שְׁמֹנֶה מֵאוֹת שָׁנָה וַיּוֹלֶד בָּנִים וּבָנוֹת

and~he~will~Live "Yared [*Descend*]" After >~make~Bring.forth~him At "Hhanokh [*Dedicated*]" Eight Hundred~s Year and~he~will~make~Bring.forth Son~s and~Daughter~s

and "Yared [*Descend*]" lived after his causing to bring forth "Hhanokh [*Dedicated*]" eight hundred years and he caused to bring forth sons and daughters,

**5:20** וַיִּהְיוּ כָּל יְמֵי יֶרֶד שְׁתַּיִם וְשִׁשִּׁים שָׁנָה וּתְשַׁע מֵאוֹת שָׁנָה וַיָּמֹת

and~they(m)~will~Exist All Day~s "Yared [*Descend*]" Two and~Six~s Year and~Nine Hundred~s Year and~he~will~Die

and all of the days of "Yared [*Descend*]" existed nine hundred and sixty-two years and he died,

**5:21** וַיְחִי חֲנוֹךְ חָמֵשׁ וְשִׁשִּׁים שָׁנָה וַיּוֹלֶד אֶת מְתוּשָׁלַח

and~he~will~Live "Hhanokh [*Dedicated*]" Five and~Six~s Year and~he~will~make~Bring.forth At "Metushelahh [*His death sends*]"

and "Hhanokh [*Dedicated*]" lived sixty-five years and he caused to bring forth "Metushelahh [*His death sends*]",

**5:22** וַיִּתְהַלֵּךְ חֲנוֹךְ אֶת הָאֱלֹהִים אַחֲרֵי הוֹלִידוֹ אֶת מְתוּשֶׁלַח שְׁלֹשׁ מֵאוֹת שָׁנָה וַיּוֹלֶד בָּנִים וּבָנוֹת

and~he~will~self~Walk "Hhanokh [*Dedicated*]" At the~"Elohiym [*Powers*]" After >~make~Bring.forth~him At "Metushelahh [*His death sends*]" Three Hundred~s Year and~he~will~make~Bring.forth Son~s and~Daughter~s

and "Hhanokh [*Dedicated*]" walked himself with the "Elohiym [*Powers*]" after his causing to bring forth "Metushelahh [*His death sends*]" three hundred years and he caused to bring forth sons and daughters,

**5:23**

וַיְהִי כָּל יְמֵי חֲנוֹךְ חָמֵשׁ וְשִׁשִּׁים שָׁנָה וּשְׁלֹשׁ מֵאוֹת שָׁנָה

and~he~will~Exist All Day~s "Hhanokh [*Dedicated*]" Five and~Six~s Year and~Three Hundred~s Year

and all of the days of "Hhanokh [*Dedicated*]" existed three hundred and sixty-five years,

**5:24**

וַיִּתְהַלֵּךְ חֲנוֹךְ אֶת הָאֱלֹהִים וְאֵינֶנּוּ כִּי לָקַח אֹתוֹ אֱלֹהִים

and~he~will~self~Walk "Hhanokh [*Dedicated*]" At the~"Elohiym [*Powers*]" and~Without~him Given.that he~did~Take At~him "Elohiym [*Powers*]"

and "Hhanokh [*Dedicated*]" walked himself with the "Elohiym [*Powers*]" and without him given that "Elohiym [*Powers*]" took him,

**5:25**

וַיְחִי מְתוּשֶׁלַח שֶׁבַע וּשְׁמֹנִים שָׁנָה וּמְאַת שָׁנָה וַיּוֹלֶד אֶת לָמֶךְ

and~he~will~Live "Metushelahh [*His death sends*]" Seven and~Eight~s Year and~Hundred Year and~he~will~make~Bring.forth At "Lamekh [*Powerful*]"

and "Metushelahh [*His death sends*]" lived a hundred and eighty-seven years and he caused to bring forth "Lamekh [*Powerful*]",

**5:26**

וַיְחִי מְתוּשֶׁלַח אַחֲרֵי הוֹלִידוֹ אֶת לֶמֶךְ שְׁתַּיִם וּשְׁמוֹנִים שָׁנָה וּשְׁבַע מֵאוֹת שָׁנָה וַיּוֹלֶד בָּנִים וּבָנוֹת

and~he~will~Live "Metushelahh [*His death sends*]" After >~make~Bring.forth~him At "Lamekh [*Powerful*]" Two and~Eight~s Year and~Seven Hundred~s Year and~he~will~make~Bring.forth Son~s and~Daughter~s

and "Metushelahh [*His death sends*]" lived after his causing to bring forth "Lamekh [*Powerful*]" seven hundred and eighty-two years and he caused to bring forth sons and daughters,

**5:27**

וַיִּהְיוּ כָּל יְמֵי מְתוּשֶׁלַח תֵּשַׁע וְשִׁשִּׁים שָׁנָה וּתְשַׁע מֵאוֹת שָׁנָה וַיָּמֹת

and~they(m)~will~Exist All Day~s "Metushelahh [*His death sends*]" Nine and~Six~s Year and~Nine Hundred~s Year and~he~will~Die

and all of the days of "Metushelahh [*His death sends*]" existed nine hundred and sixty-nine years and he died,

**5:28**

וַיְחִי לֶמֶךְ שְׁתַּיִם וּשְׁמֹנִים שָׁנָה וּמְאַת שָׁנָה וַיּוֹלֶד בֵּן

and~he~will~Live "Lamekh [*Powerful*]" Two and~Eight~s Year and~Hundred Year and~he~will~make~Bring.forth Son

and "Lamekh [*Powerful*]" lived a hundred and eighty-two years and he caused to bring forth a son,

**5:29**

וַיִּקְרָא אֶת שְׁמוֹ נֹחַ לֵאמֹר זֶה יְנַחֲמֵנוּ מִמַּעֲשֵׂנוּ וּמֵעִצְּבוֹן יָדֵינוּ מִן הָאֲדָמָה אֲשֶׁר אֵרְרָהּ יְהוָה

and~he~will~Call.out At Title~him "No'ahh [*Rest*]" >~Say This he~will~

and he called out his title "No'ahh [*Rest*]" saying, this one will much

much~Comfort~us from~Work~us and~ from~Hardship Hand~s2~us From the~Ground Which he~did~much~Spit.upon "YHWH [*He exists*]"

comfort us from our work and from the hardship of our hands, from the ground which "YHWH [*He exists*]" much cursed,

**5:30** וַיְחִי לֶמֶךְ אַחֲרֵי הוֹלִידוֹ אֶת נֹחַ חָמֵשׁ וְתִשְׁעִים שָׁנָה וַחֲמֵשׁ מֵאֹת שָׁנָה וַיּוֹלֶד בָּנִים וּבָנוֹת

and~he~will~Live "Lamekh [*Powerful*]" After >~make~Bring.forth~him At "No'ahh [*Rest*]" Five and~Nine~s Year and~Five Hundred~s Year and~he~will~make~Bring.forth Son~s and~Daughter~s

and "Lamekh [*Powerful*]" lived after causing to bring forth "No'ahh [*Rest*]" five hundred and ninety five years and he caused to bring forth sons and daughters,

**5:31** וַיִּהְיוּ כָּל יְמֵי לֶמֶךְ שֶׁבַע וְשִׁבְעִים שָׁנָה וּשְׁבַע מֵאוֹת שָׁנָה וַיָּמֹת

and~he~will~Exist All Day~s "Lamekh [*Powerful*]" Seven and~Seven~s Year and~Seven Hundred~s Year and~he~will~Die

and all of the days of "Lamekh [*Powerful*]" existed seven hundred and seventy-seven years and he died,

**5:32** וַיְהִי נֹחַ בֶּן חֲמֵשׁ מֵאוֹת שָׁנָה וַיּוֹלֶד נֹחַ אֶת שֵׁם אֶת חָם וְאֶת יָפֶת

and~he~will~Exist "No'ahh [*Rest*]" Son Five Hundred~s Year and~he~will~make~Bring.forth "No'ahh [*Rest*]" At "Shem [*Character*]" At "Hham [*Hot*]" and~At "Yaphet [*Wonder*]"

and "No'ahh [*Rest*]" existed a son of five hundred years and "No'ahh [*Rest*]" caused to bring forth "Shem [*Character*]", "Hham [*Hot*]" and "Yaphet [*Wonder*]",

# Chapter 6

**6:1** וַיְהִי כִּי הֵחֵל הָאָדָם לָרֹב עַל פְּנֵי הָאֲדָמָה וּבָנוֹת יֻלְּדוּ לָהֶם

and~he~will~Exist Given.that he~did~make~Pierce the~Human to~>~Increase.in.number Upon Face~s the~Ground and~Daughter~s they~did~much~Bring.forth to~them(m)

and it came to pass that the human began to increase in number upon the face of the ground and caused to bring forth daughters for them,

**6:2** וַיִּרְאוּ בְנֵי הָאֱלֹהִים אֶת בְּנוֹת הָאָדָם כִּי טֹבֹת הֵנָּה וַיִּקְחוּ לָהֶם נָשִׁים מִכֹּל אֲשֶׁר בָּחָרוּ

and~they(m)~will~See Son~s the~"Elohiym [*Powers*]" At Daughter~s the~Human Given.that Functional~s They(f) and~they(m)~will~Take to~them(m) Woman~s from~All Which they~did~Choose

and the sons of the "Elohiym [*Powers*]" saw the daughters of the human that they were functional and took for them the women from which they chose,

**6:3** וַיֹּאמֶר יְהוָה לֹא יָדוֹן רוּחִי בָאָדָם לְעֹלָם בְּשַׁגַּם הוּא בָשָׂר וְהָיוּ יָמָיו מֵאָה וְעֶשְׂרִים שָׁנָה

and~he~will~Say "YHWH [*He exists*]" Not he~will~Moderate Wind~me in~the~Human to~Distant.time in~which~Also He Flesh and~they~did~Exist Day~s~him Hundred and~Ten~s Year

and "YHWH [*He exists*]" said my wind will not moderate in the human to a distant time whereas he is flesh and his days will exist a hundred and ten years,

**6:4** הַנְּפִלִים הָיוּ בָאָרֶץ בַּיָּמִים הָהֵם וְגַם אַחֲרֵי כֵן אֲשֶׁר יָבֹאוּ בְּנֵי הָאֱלֹהִים אֶל בְּנוֹת הָאָדָם וְיָלְדוּ לָהֶם הֵמָּה הַגִּבֹּרִים אֲשֶׁר מֵעוֹלָם אַנְשֵׁי הַשֵּׁם

the~"Nephilim [*Fallen ones*]" they~did~Exist in~the~Land in~the~Day~s the~them(m) and~Also After So Which they(m)~will~Come Son~s the~"Elohiym [*Powers*]" To Daughter~s the~Human and~they(m)~will~Bring.forth to~them(m) They(m) the~Courageous~s Which from~Distant.time Man~s the~Title

the "Nephilim [*Fallen ones*]" existed in the land in the days of them and also afterward, when the sons of the "Elohiym [*Powers*]" come to the daughters of the human and they brought forth to them, they are the courageous ones which are from a distant time, men of the title,

**6:5** וַיַּרְא יְהוָה כִּי רַבָּה רָעַת הָאָדָם בָּאָרֶץ וְכָל יֵצֶר מַחְשְׁבֹת לִבּוֹ רַק רַע כָּל הַיּוֹם

and~he~will~See "YHWH [*He exists*]" Given.that Abundant Dysfunctional the~Human in~the~Land and~All Thought Invention~s Heart~him Only Dysfunctional All the~Day

and "YHWH [*He exists*]" saw that the dysfunctions of the human in the land was abundant and all of the thought of inventions of his heart was only dysfunctional all of the day,

**6:6** וַיִּנָּחֶם יְהוָה כִּי עָשָׂה אֶת הָאָדָם בָּאָרֶץ וַיִּתְעַצֵּב אֶל לִבּוֹ

and~he~will~be~Comfort "YHWH [*He exists*]" Given.that he~did~Do At the~Human in~the~Land and~he~will~self~Distress To Heart~him

and "YHWH [*He exists*]" was comforted given that he made the human in the land and he distressed himself to his heart,

**6:7** וַיֹּאמֶר יְהוָה אֶמְחֶה אֶת הָאָדָם אֲשֶׁר בָּרָאתִי מֵעַל פְּנֵי הָאֲדָמָה מֵאָדָם עַד בְּהֵמָה עַד רֶמֶשׂ וְעַד עוֹף הַשָּׁמָיִם כִּי נִחַמְתִּי כִּי עֲשִׂיתִם

and~he~will~Say "YHWH [*He exists*]" i~will~Wipe.away At the~Human Which i~did~Fatten from~Upon Face~s the~Ground from~Human Until Beast Until Treader

and "YHWH [*He exists*]" said, I will wipe away the human which I fattened from upon the face of the ground, from the human as well as the beast as well as the treader and

and~Until Flyer the~Sky~s2
Given.that i~did~be~Comfort Given.that
i~did~Do~them(m)

also the flyer of the sky given that I
was comforted given that I made
them,

**6:8**

וְנֹחַ מָצָא חֵן בְּעֵינֵי יְהוָה

and~"No'ahh [*Rest*]" he~did~Find
Beauty in~Eye~s2 "YHWH [*He
exists*]"

and "No'ahh [*Rest*]" found beauty
in the eyes of "YHWH [*He exists*]",

**6:9** אֵלֶּה תּוֹלְדֹת נֹחַ נֹחַ אִישׁ צַדִּיק תָּמִים הָיָה בְּדֹרֹתָיו אֶת
הָאֱלֹהִים הִתְהַלֶּךְ נֹחַ

These Birthing~s "No'ahh [*Rest*]"
"No'ahh [*Rest*]" Man Correct Mature
he~did~Exist in~Generation~s~him At
the~"Elohiym [*Powers*]" he~did~self~
Walk "No'ahh [*Rest*]"

these are the birthings of "No'ahh
[*Rest*]", "No'ahh [*Rest*]" existed a
correct and mature man in his
generations, "No'ahh [*Rest*]"
walked himself with the "Elohiym
[*Powers*]",

**6:10** וַיּוֹלֶד נֹחַ שְׁלֹשָׁה בָנִים אֶת שֵׁם אֶת חָם וְאֶת יָפֶת

and~he~will~make~Bring.forth "No'ahh
[*Rest*]" Three Son~s At "Shem
[*Character*]" At "Hham [*Hot*]" and~
At "Yaphet [*Wonder*]"

and "No'ahh [*Rest*]" caused to bring
forth three sons, "Shem
[*Character*]", "Hham [*Hot*]" and
"Yaphet [*Wonder*]",

**6:11*** וַתִּשָּׁחֵת הָאָרֶץ לִפְנֵי הָאֱלֹהִים וַתִּמָּלֵא הָאָרֶץ חָמָס

and~she~will~be~Damage the~Land
to~Face~s the~"Elohiym [*Powers*]"
and~she~will~be~Fill the~Land
Violence

and the land was damaged to the
face of the "Elohiym [*Powers*]" and
the land of violence was filled,

**6:12** וַיַּרְא אֱלֹהִים אֶת הָאָרֶץ וְהִנֵּה נִשְׁחָתָה כִּי הִשְׁחִית כָּל בָּשָׂר אֶת
דַּרְכּוֹ עַל הָאָרֶץ

and~he~will~See "Elohiym [*Powers*]"
At the~Land and~Look she~did~be~
Damage Given.that he~did~make~
Damage All Flesh At Road~him
Upon the~Land

and "Elohiym [*Powers*]" saw the
land and look, she was damaged
given that all of the flesh destroyed
his road upon the land,

**6:13** וַיֹּאמֶר אֱלֹהִים לְנֹחַ קֵץ כָּל בָּשָׂר בָּא לְפָנַי כִּי מָלְאָה הָאָרֶץ
חָמָס מִפְּנֵיהֶם וְהִנְנִי מַשְׁחִיתָם אֶת הָאָרֶץ

and~he~will~Say "Elohiym [*Powers*]"
to~"No'ahh [*Rest*]" Conclusion All
Flesh he~did~Come to~Face~s~me
Given.that she~did~Fill the~Land
Violence from~Face~s~them(m) and~
Look~me make~Damage~ing(ms) At
the~Land

and "Elohiym [*Powers*]" said to
"No'ahh [*Rest*]", a conclusion of all
of the flesh came to my face given
that the land of violence was filled
from their face and here am I
destroying the land,

**6:14** עֲשֵׂה לְךָ תֵּבַת עֲצֵי גֹפֶר קִנִּים תַּעֲשֶׂה אֶת הַתֵּבָה וְכָפַרְתָּ אֹתָהּ מִבַּיִת וּמִחוּץ בַּכֹּפֶר

!(ms)~Do to~you(ms) Vessel Tree~s Gopher Nest~s you(ms)~will~Do At the~Vessel and~you(ms)~did~Cover At~her from~House and~from~Outside in~the~Covering

make for you a vessel of trees of gopher, nests you will make for the vessel and cover her from the house and from the outside with the covering,

**6:15** וְזֶה אֲשֶׁר תַּעֲשֶׂה אֹתָהּ שְׁלֹשׁ מֵאוֹת אַמָּה אֹרֶךְ הַתֵּבָה חֲמִשִּׁים אַמָּה רָחְבָּהּ וּשְׁלֹשִׁים אַמָּה קוֹמָתָהּ

and~This Which you(ms)~will~Do At~her Three Hundred~s Forearm Length the~Vessel Five~s Forearm Width~her and~Three~s Forearm Height~her

and this is how you will make her, three hundred forearms is the length of the vessel, fifty forearms is her width and thirty forearms is her height,

**6:16** צֹהַר תַּעֲשֶׂה לַתֵּבָה וְאֶל אַמָּה תְּכַלֶּנָּה מִלְמַעְלָה וּפֶתַח הַתֵּבָה בְּצִדָּהּ תָּשִׂים תַּחְתִּיִּם שְׁנִיִּם וּשְׁלִשִׁים תַּעֲשֶׂהָ

Shining you(ms)~will~Do to~the~Vessel and~To Forearm you(ms)~will~much~Finish~her from~to~Upward~her and~Opening the~Vessel in~Side~her you(ms)~will~Set.in.place Under~s Second~s and~Third~s you(ms)~will~Do~her

you will make a shining to the vessel and to a forearm you will much finish her from her upward one and you will set in place an opening of the vessel in her side, under ones, second ones and third ones you will make for her,

**6:17** וַאֲנִי הִנְנִי מֵבִיא אֶת הַמַּבּוּל מַיִם עַל הָאָרֶץ לְשַׁחֵת כָּל בָּשָׂר אֲשֶׁר בּוֹ רוּחַ חַיִּים מִתַּחַת הַשָּׁמָיִם כֹּל אֲשֶׁר בָּאָרֶץ יִגְוָע

and~I Look~me make~Come~ing(ms) At the~Flood Water~s2 Upon the~Land to~>~much~Damage All Flesh Which in~him Wind Life~s from~Under the~Sky~s2 All Which in~the~Land he~will~Expire

and here am I, I am making the flood of water come upon the land to do much damage to all of the flesh which has in him the wind of life from under the sky, all of the ones which are in the land will expire,

**6:18** וַהֲקִמֹתִי אֶת בְּרִיתִי אִתָּךְ וּבָאתָ אֶל הַתֵּבָה אַתָּה וּבָנֶיךָ וְאִשְׁתְּךָ וּנְשֵׁי בָנֶיךָ אִתָּךְ

and~i~will~make~Rise At Covenant~me At~you(ms) and~you(ms)~did~Come To the~Vessel You(ms) and~Son~s~you(ms) and~Woman~you(ms) and~Woman~s Son~s~you(ms) At~you(ms)

and I will make my covenant rise with you and you will come to the vessel, you and your sons and your woman and the women of your sons with you,

**6:19** וּמִכָּל הָחַי מִכָּל בָּשָׂר שְׁנַיִם מִכֹּל תָּבִיא אֶל הַתֵּבָה לְהַחֲיֹת אִתָּךְ זָכָר וּנְקֵבָה יִהְיוּ

and~from~All the~Life from~All Flesh Two from~All you(ms)~will~make~Come To the~Vessel to~>~make~Live At~you(ms) Male and~Female they(m)~will~Exist

and from all of the living ones, from all of the flesh, two from all of the ones you will bring to the vessel to live with you, male and female will exist,

**6:20** מֵהָעוֹף לְמִינֵהוּ וּמִן הַבְּהֵמָה לְמִינָהּ מִכֹּל רֶמֶשׂ הָאֲדָמָה לְמִינֵהוּ שְׁנַיִם מִכֹּל יָבֹאוּ אֵלֶיךָ לְהַחֲיוֹת

from~the~Flyer to~Kind~him and~From the~Beast to~Kind~her from~All Treader the~Ground to~Kind~him Two from~All they(m)~will~Come To~you(ms) to~>~make~Live

from the flyer to his kind and from the beast to her kind, from all of the treaders of the ground to his kind, two from all will come to you to live,

**6:21** וְאַתָּה קַח לְךָ מִכָּל מַאֲכָל אֲשֶׁר יֵאָכֵל וְאָסַפְתָּ אֵלֶיךָ וְהָיָה לְךָ וְלָהֶם לְאָכְלָה

and~You(ms) !(ms)~Take to~you(ms) from~All Nourishment Which he~will~be~Eat and~you(ms)~did~Gather To~you(ms) and~he~did~Exist to~you(ms) and~to~them(m) to~Food

and you take for you from all of the nourishment which will be eaten and you will gather for you and he will exist for you and for them for food,

**6:22** וַיַּעַשׂ נֹחַ כְּכֹל אֲשֶׁר צִוָּה אֹתוֹ אֱלֹהִים כֵּן עָשָׂה

and~he~will~Do "No'ahh [Rest]" like~All Which he~did~much~Direct At~him "Elohiym [Powers]" So he~did~Do

and "No'ahh [Rest]" did just as "Elohiym [Powers]" directed him, so he did,

# Chapter 7

**7:1** וַיֹּאמֶר יְהוָה לְנֹחַ בֹּא אַתָּה וְכָל בֵּיתְךָ אֶל הַתֵּבָה כִּי אֹתְךָ רָאִיתִי צַדִּיק לְפָנַי בַּדּוֹר הַזֶּה

and~he~will~Say "YHWH [He exists]" to~"No'ahh [Rest]" !(ms)~Come You(ms) and~All House~you(ms) To the~Vessel Given.that At~you(ms) i~did~See Correct to~Face~s~me in~the~Generation the~This

and "YHWH [He exists]" said to "No'ahh [Rest]", come, you and all of your house to the vessel given that I saw you are a correct one to my face in this generation,

**7:2** מִכֹּל הַבְּהֵמָה הַטְּהוֹרָה תִּקַּח לְךָ שִׁבְעָה שִׁבְעָה אִישׁ וְאִשְׁתּוֹ וּמִן הַבְּהֵמָה אֲשֶׁר לֹא טְהֹרָה הִוא שְׁנַיִם אִישׁ וְאִשְׁתּוֹ

from~All the~Beast the~Pure you(ms)~will~Take to~you(ms) Seven Seven Man and~Woman~him and~From the~Beast Which Not Pure She Two Man and~Woman~him

from all of the pure beasts you will take to you seven, seven of the man and his woman and from the beast which is not pure, she is two of the man and his woman,

**7:3** גַּם מֵעוֹף הַשָּׁמַיִם שִׁבְעָה שִׁבְעָה זָכָר וּנְקֵבָה לְחַיּוֹת זֶרַע עַל פְּנֵי כָל הָאָרֶץ

Also from~Flyer the~Sky~s2 Seven Seven Male and~Female to~>~much~Live Seed Upon Face~s All the~Land

also from the flyer of the sky seven, seven of the male and female to keep alive the seed upon the face of all of the land,

**7:4** כִּי לְיָמִים עוֹד שִׁבְעָה אָנֹכִי מַמְטִיר עַל הָאָרֶץ אַרְבָּעִים יוֹם וְאַרְבָּעִים לָיְלָה וּמָחִיתִי אֶת כָּל הַיְקוּם אֲשֶׁר עָשִׂיתִי מֵעַל פְּנֵי הָאֲדָמָה

Given.that to~Day~s Yet.again Seven I make~Precipitate~ing(ms) Upon the~Land Four~s Day and~Four~s Night and~i~did~Wipe.away At All the~Substance Which i~did~Do from~Upon Face~s the~Ground

given that for yet again seven days I will make a precipitating upon the land forty days and forty nights and I will wipe away all of the substance I made from upon the face of the ground,

**7:5** וַיַּעַשׂ נֹחַ כְּכֹל אֲשֶׁר צִוָּהוּ יְהוָה

and~he~will~Do "No'ahh [*Rest*]" like~All Which he~did~much~Direct~him "YHWH [*He exists*]"

and "No'ahh [*Rest*]" did just as all that "YHWH [*He exists*]" directed him,

**7:6** וְנֹחַ בֶּן שֵׁשׁ מֵאוֹת שָׁנָה וְהַמַּבּוּל הָיָה מַיִם עַל הָאָרֶץ

and~"No'ahh [*Rest*]" Son Six Hundred~s Year and~the~Flood he~had~Exist Water~s2 Upon the~Land

and "No'ahh [*Rest*]" was a son of six hundred years and the flood had existed, water upon the land,

**7:7** וַיָּבֹא נֹחַ וּבָנָיו וְאִשְׁתּוֹ וּנְשֵׁי בָנָיו אִתּוֹ אֶל הַתֵּבָה מִפְּנֵי מֵי הַמַּבּוּל

and~he~will~Come "No'ahh [*Rest*]" and~Son~s~him and~Woman~him and~Woman~s Son~s~him At~him To the~Vessel from~Face~s Water~s2 the~Flood

and "No'ahh [*Rest*]" and his sons and his woman and the women of his sons with him came to the vessel from the face of the water of the flood,

**7:8** מִן הַבְּהֵמָה הַטְּהוֹרָה וּמִן הַבְּהֵמָה אֲשֶׁר אֵינֶנָּה טְהֹרָה וּמִן הָעוֹף וְכֹל אֲשֶׁר רֹמֵשׂ עַל הָאֲדָמָה

From the~Beast the~Pure and~From the~Beast Which Without~her Pure and~From the~Flyer and~All Which

from the pure beasts and from the beast that is not pure and from the flyer and all that are treading upon

Tread~ing(ms)  Upon  the~Ground | the ground,

**7:9** שְׁנַיִם שְׁנַיִם בָּאוּ אֶל נֹחַ אֶל הַתֵּבָה זָכָר וּנְקֵבָה כַּאֲשֶׁר צִוָּה אֱלֹהִים אֶת נֹחַ

Two  Two  they~did~Come  To "No'ahh [*Rest*]"  To  the~Vessel  Male and~Female  like~Which  he~did~much~ Direct  "Elohiym [*Powers*]"  At "No'ahh  [*Rest*]"

two of two they came to "No'ahh [*Rest*]", to the vessel, male and female just as "Elohiym [*Powers*]" directed "No'ahh [*Rest*]",

**7:10** וַיְהִי לְשִׁבְעַת הַיָּמִים וּמֵי הַמַּבּוּל הָיוּ עַל הָאָרֶץ

and~he~will~Exist  to~Seven  the~Day~s and~Water~s2  the~Flood  they~did~ Exist  Upon  the~Land

and it came to pass to the seven of the days and the water of the flood existed upon the land,

**7:11** בִּשְׁנַת שֵׁשׁ מֵאוֹת שָׁנָה לְחַיֵּי נֹחַ בַּחֹדֶשׁ הַשֵּׁנִי בְּשִׁבְעָה עָשָׂר יוֹם לַחֹדֶשׁ בַּיּוֹם הַזֶּה נִבְקְעוּ כָּל מַעְיְנֹת תְּהוֹם רַבָּה וַאֲרֻבֹּת הַשָּׁמַיִם נִפְתָּחוּ

in~Year  Six  Hundred~s  Year  to~ Life~s  "No'ahh [*Rest*]"  in~the~ New.moon  the~Second  in~Seven  Ten Day  to~the~New.moon  in~the~Day the~This  they~did~be~Cleave  All Spring~s  Deep.sea  Abundant  and~ Chimney~s  the~Sky~s2  they~had~be~ Open

in the year of six hundred years to the life of "No'ahh [*Rest*]", in the second new moon, in the seventeenth day to the new moon, in this day all of the springs of the deep sea cleaved abundantly and the chimneys of the sky had been opened,

**7:12** וַיְהִי הַגֶּשֶׁם עַל הָאָרֶץ אַרְבָּעִים יוֹם וְאַרְבָּעִים לָיְלָה

and~he~will~Exist  the~Rain.shower Upon  the~Land  Four~s  Day  and~ Four~s  Night

and the rain showers existed upon the land forty days and forty nights,

**7:13** בְּעֶצֶם הַיּוֹם הַזֶּה בָּא נֹחַ וְשֵׁם וְחָם וָיֶפֶת בְּנֵי נֹחַ וְאֵשֶׁת נֹחַ וּשְׁלֹשֶׁת נְשֵׁי בָנָיו אִתָּם אֶל הַתֵּבָה

in~Bone  the~Day  the~This  he~did~ Come  "No'ahh [*Rest*]"  and~"Shem [*Character*]"  and~"Hham [*Hot*]"  and~ "Yaphet [*Wonder*]"  Son~s  "No'ahh [*Rest*]"  and~Woman  "No'ahh [*Rest*]" and~Three  Woman~s  Son~s~him  At~ them(m)  To  the~Vessel

in the bone of this day "No'ahh [*Rest*]" and "Shem [*Character*]" and "Hham [*Hot*]" and "Yaphet [*Wonder*]", the sons of "No'ahh [*Rest*]" and the woman of "No'ahh [*Rest*]" and the three women of his sons with them came to the vessel,

**7:14** הֵמָּה וְכָל הַחַיָּה לְמִינָהּ וְכָל הַבְּהֵמָה לְמִינָהּ וְכָל הָרֶמֶשׂ הָרֹמֵשׂ עַל הָאָרֶץ לְמִינֵהוּ וְכָל הָעוֹף לְמִינֵהוּ כֹּל צִפּוֹר כָּל כָּנָף

They(m)  and~All  the~Life  to~Kind~ her  and~All  the~Beast  to~Kind~her

they and all of the living ones to her kind and all of the beast to her kind and~All the~Treader the~Tread~ing(ms) Upon the~Land to~Kind~him and~All the~Flyer to~Kind~him All Bird All Wing

and all of the treaders treading upon the land to his kind and all of the flyer to his kind, all of the birds of all of the wings,

**7:15**  וַיָּבֹאוּ אֶל נֹחַ אֶל הַתֵּבָה שְׁנַיִם שְׁנַיִם מִכָּל הַבָּשָׂר אֲשֶׁר בּוֹ רוּחַ חַיִּים

and~they(m)~will~Come To "No'ahh [Rest]" To the~Vessel Two Two from~All the~Flesh Which in~him Wind Life~s

and they came to "No'ahh [Rest]", to the vessel, two of two from all of the flesh which in him is the wind of life,

**7:16**  וְהַבָּאִים זָכָר וּנְקֵבָה מִכָּל בָּשָׂר בָּאוּ כַּאֲשֶׁר צִוָּה אֹתוֹ אֱלֹהִים וַיִּסְגֹּר יְהוָה בַּעֲדוֹ

and~the~Come~ing(mp) Male and~Female from~All Flesh they~did~Come like~Which he~did~much~Direct At~him "Elohiym [Powers]" and~he~will~Shut "YHWH [He exists]" Round.about~him

and the coming of the males and females from all of the flesh came just as "Elohiym [Powers]" directed him and "YHWH [He exists]" shut round about him,

**7:17**  וַיְהִי הַמַּבּוּל אַרְבָּעִים יוֹם עַל הָאָרֶץ וַיִּרְבּוּ הַמַּיִם וַיִּשְׂאוּ אֶת הַתֵּבָה וַתָּרָם מֵעַל הָאָרֶץ

and~he~will~Exist the~Flood Four~s Day Upon the~Land and~they(m)~will~Increase the~Water~s2 and~they(m)~will~Lift.up At the~Vessel and~she~will~Raise from~Upon the~Land

and the flood existed forty days upon the land and the water increased and lifted up the vessel and she rose from upon the land,

**7:18**  וַיִּגְבְּרוּ הַמַּיִם וַיִּרְבּוּ מְאֹד עַל הָאָרֶץ וַתֵּלֶךְ הַתֵּבָה עַל פְּנֵי הַמָּיִם

and~they(m)~will~Overcome the~Water~s2 and~they(m)~will~Increase Many Upon the~Land and~she~will~Walk the~Vessel Upon Face~s the~Water~s2

and the water overcame and increased much upon the land and the vessel walked upon the face of the water,

**7:19**  וְהַמַּיִם גָּבְרוּ מְאֹד מְאֹד עַל הָאָרֶץ וַיְכֻסּוּ כָּל הֶהָרִים הַגְּבֹהִים אֲשֶׁר תַּחַת כָּל הַשָּׁמָיִם

and~the~Water~s2 they~had~Overcome Many Many Upon the~Land and~they(m)~will~much~Conceal All the~Hill~s the~High~s Which Under All the~Sky~s2

and the water had overcome a great many upon the land and concealed all of the high hills which are under all of the sky,

**7:20**  חֲמֵשׁ עֶשְׂרֵה אַמָּה מִלְמַעְלָה גָּבְרוּ הַמָּיִם וַיְכֻסּוּ הֶהָרִים

Five Ten Forearm from~to~Upward

fifteen forearms upward the water

they~did~Overcome the~Water~s2 and~ they(m)~will~much~Conceal the~Hill~s

overcame and much concealed the hills,

**7:21** וַיִּגְוַע כָּל בָּשָׂר הָרֹמֵשׂ עַל הָאָרֶץ בָּעוֹף וּבַבְּהֵמָה וּבַחַיָּה וּבְכָל הַשֶּׁרֶץ הַשֹּׁרֵץ עַל הָאָרֶץ וְכֹל הָאָדָם

and~he~will~Expire All Flesh the~ Tread~ing(ms) Upon the~Land in~ the~Flyer and~in~the~Beast and~in~ the~Life and~in~All the~Swarmer the~Swarm~ing(ms) Upon the~Land and~All the~Human

and all of the flesh expired, the treading ones upon the land with the flyer and with the beast and with the living ones and with all of the swarming swarmers upon the land and all of the humans,

**7:22** כֹּל אֲשֶׁר נִשְׁמַת רוּחַ חַיִּים בְּאַפָּיו מִכֹּל אֲשֶׁר בֶּחָרָבָה מֵתוּ

All Which Breath Wind Life~s in~ Nose~s2~him from~All Which in~ the~Wasteland they~did~Die

all of the ones which have the breath of the wind of the life in his nostrils, from all of the ones which were in the wasteland died,

**7:23** וַיִּמַח אֶת כָּל הַיְקוּם אֲשֶׁר עַל פְּנֵי הָאֲדָמָה מֵאָדָם עַד בְּהֵמָה עַד רֶמֶשׂ וְעַד עוֹף הַשָּׁמַיִם וַיִּמָּחוּ מִן הָאָרֶץ וַיִּשָּׁאֶר אַךְ נֹחַ וַאֲשֶׁר אִתּוֹ בַּתֵּבָה

and~he~will~Wipe.away At All the~ Substance Which Upon Face~s the~ Ground from~Human Until Beast Until Treader and~Until Flyer the~ Sky~s2 and~they(m)~will~be~Wipe.away From the~Land and~he~will~be~ Remain Surely "No'ahh [*Rest*]" and~ Which At~him in~the~Vessel

and he wiped away all of the substance which was upon the face of the ground, from the human, as well as the beast, as well as, the treader and also the flyer of the sky and they were wiped away from the land and only "No'ahh [*Rest*]" remained and who were with him in the vessel,

**7:24** וַיִּגְבְּרוּ הַמַּיִם עַל הָאָרֶץ חֲמִשִּׁים וּמְאַת יוֹם

and~they(m)~will~Overcome the~Water~ s2 Upon the~Land Five~s and~ Hundred Day

and the water overcame upon the land a hundred and fifty days,

# Chapter 8

**8:1** וַיִּזְכֹּר אֱלֹהִים אֶת נֹחַ וְאֵת כָּל הַחַיָּה וְאֶת כָּל הַבְּהֵמָה אֲשֶׁר אִתּוֹ בַּתֵּבָה וַיַּעֲבֵר אֱלֹהִים רוּחַ עַל הָאָרֶץ וַיָּשֹׁכּוּ הַמָּיִם

and~he~will~Remember "Elohiym [*Powers*]" At "No'ahh [*Rest*]" and~ At All the~Life and~At All the~ Beast Which At~him in~the~Vessel

and "Elohiym [*Powers*]" remembered "No'ahh [*Rest*]" and all of the living ones and all of the beasts which were with him in the

and~he~will~make~Cross.over "Elohiym [*Powers*]" Wind Upon the~Land and~they(m)~will~Subside the~Water~s2

vessel and "Elohiym [*Powers*]" caused a wind to cross over upon the land and the water subsided,

**8:2** וַיִּסָּכְרוּ מַעְיְנֹת תְּהוֹם וַאֲרֻבֹּת הַשָּׁמָיִם וַיִּכָּלֵא הַגֶּשֶׁם מִן הַשָּׁמָיִם

and~they(m)~will~be~Shut Spring~s Deep.sea and~Chimney~s the~Sky~s2 and~he~will~be~Restrict the~Rain.shower From the~Sky~s2

and the springs of the deep sea and the chimneys of the sky were shut and the rain shower was restricted from the sky,

**8:3** וַיָּשֻׁבוּ הַמַּיִם מֵעַל הָאָרֶץ הָלוֹךְ וָשׁוֹב וַיַּחְסְרוּ הַמַּיִם מִקְצֵה חֲמִשִּׁים וּמְאַת יוֹם

and~they(m)~will~Turn.back the~Water~s2 from~Upon the~Land >~Walk and~>~Turn.back and~they(m)~will~Diminish the~Water~s2 from~Far.end Five~s and~Hundred Day

and the water will turn back from upon the land, walking and turning back, and the water diminished from the far end of a hundred and fifty days,

**8:4** וַתָּנַח הַתֵּבָה בַּחֹדֶשׁ הַשְּׁבִיעִי בְּשִׁבְעָה עָשָׂר יוֹם לַחֹדֶשׁ עַל הָרֵי אֲרָרָט

and~she~will~Rest the~Vessel in~the~New.moon the~Seventh in~Seven Ten Day to~the~New.moon Upon Hill~s "Ararat [*Curse*]"

and the vessel rested in the seventh new moon in the seventeenth day to the new moon upon the hills of "Ararat [*Curse*]",

**8:5** וְהַמַּיִם הָיוּ הָלוֹךְ וְחָסוֹר עַד הַחֹדֶשׁ הָעֲשִׂירִי בָּעֲשִׂירִי לַחֹדֶשׁ נִרְאוּ רָאשֵׁי הֶהָרִים

and~the~Water~s2 they~had~Exist >~Walk and~>~Diminish Until the~New.moon the~Tenth in~the~Tenth in~Unit to~the~New.moon they~did~be~See Head~s the~Hill~s

and the water had existed, walking and diminishing until the tenth new moon in the unit to the new moon, the heads of the hills appeared,

**8:6** וַיְהִי מִקֵּץ אַרְבָּעִים יוֹם וַיִּפְתַּח נֹחַ אֶת חַלּוֹן הַתֵּבָה אֲשֶׁר עָשָׂה

and~he~will~Exist from~Conclusion Four~s Day and~he~will~Open "No'ahh [*Rest*]" At Window the~Vessel Which he~did~Do

and it came to pass at the conclusion of the forty days and "No'ahh [*Rest*]" opened the window of the vessel which he made,

**8:7** וַיְשַׁלַּח אֶת הָעֹרֵב וַיֵּצֵא יָצוֹא וָשׁוֹב עַד יְבֹשֶׁת הַמַּיִם מֵעַל הָאָרֶץ

and~he~will~Send At the~Raven and~he~will~Go.out >~Go.out and~Turn.back Until >~Dry.out the~Water~s2 from~Upon the~Land

and he sent the raven and he went out, going out and turning back, until the drying out of the waters from upon the land,

**8:8** וַיְשַׁלַּח אֶת הַיּוֹנָה מֵאִתּוֹ לִרְאוֹת הֲקַלּוּ הַמַּיִם מֵעַל פְּנֵי הָאֲדָמָה

| | |
|---|---|
| and~he~will~Send At the~Dove from~ At~him to~>~See the~they~did~ Be.insubstantial the~Water~s2 from~ Upon Face~s the~Ground | and he sent the dove from him to see if the water was insubstantial from upon the face of the ground, |

**8:9** וְלֹא מָצְאָה הַיּוֹנָה מָנוֹחַ לְכַף רַגְלָהּ וַתָּשָׁב אֵלָיו אֶל הַתֵּבָה כִּי מַיִם עַל פְּנֵי כָל הָאָרֶץ וַיִּשְׁלַח יָדוֹ וַיִּקָּחֶהָ וַיָּבֵא אֹתָהּ אֵלָיו אֶל הַתֵּבָה

| | |
|---|---|
| and~Not she~did~Find the~Dove Resting.place to~Palm Foot~her and~ she~will~Turn.back To~him To the~ Vessel Given.that Water~s2 Upon Face~s All the~Land and~he~will~ Send Hand~him and~he~will~Take~her and~he~will~make~Come At~her To~ him To the~Vessel | and the dove did not find a resting place for the palm of her foot and she turned back to him to the vessel given that the water was upon the face of the land and he sent his hand and he took her and he brought her to him to the vessel, |

**8:10** וַיָּחֶל עוֹד שִׁבְעַת יָמִים אֲחֵרִים וַיֹּסֶף שַׁלַּח אֶת הַיּוֹנָה מִן הַתֵּבָה

| | |
|---|---|
| and~he~will~Twist Yet.again Seven Day~s Other~s and~he~will~make~Add >~much~Send At the~Dove From the~Vessel | and he twisted yet again another seven days and he again sent off the dove from the vessel, |

**8:11** וַתָּבֹא אֵלָיו הַיּוֹנָה לְעֵת עֶרֶב וְהִנֵּה עָלֵה זַיִת טָרָף בְּפִיהָ וַיֵּדַע נֹחַ כִּי קַלּוּ הַמַּיִם מֵעַל הָאָרֶץ

| | |
|---|---|
| and~she~will~Come To~him the~Dove to~Appointed.time Evening and~Look Leaf Olive Prey in~Mouth~her and~ he~will~Know "No'ahh [Rest]" Given.that they~did~Be.insubstantial the~Water~s2 from~Upon the~Land | and the dove came to him at the appointed time of the evening and look, a leaf of olive, a prey in her mouth and "No'ahh [Rest]" knew that the water was insubstantial from upon the land, |

**8:12** וַיִּיָּחֶל עוֹד שִׁבְעַת יָמִים אֲחֵרִים וַיְשַׁלַּח אֶת הַיּוֹנָה וְלֹא יָסְפָה שׁוּב אֵלָיו עוֹד

| | |
|---|---|
| and~he~will~Twist Yet.again Seven Day~s Other~s and~he~will~make~ Send At the~Dove and~Not she~did~ Add >~Turn.back To~him Yet.again | and he twisted yet again another seven days and he caused the dove to be sent and she did not add a turning back to him yet again, |

**8:13** וַיְהִי בְּאַחַת וְשֵׁשׁ מֵאוֹת שָׁנָה בָּרִאשׁוֹן בְּאֶחָד לַחֹדֶשׁ חָרְבוּ הַמַּיִם מֵעַל הָאָרֶץ וַיָּסַר נֹחַ אֶת מִכְסֵה הַתֵּבָה וַיַּרְא וְהִנֵּה חָרְבוּ פְּנֵי הָאֲדָמָה

| | |
|---|---|
| and~he~will~Exist in~Unit and~Six Hundred~s Year in~the~First in~Unit | and it came to pass in the unit and six hundred years in the first in the |

to~the~New.moon they~did~Dry.up the~Water~s2 from~Upon the~Land and~he~will~make~Turn.aside "No'ahh [*Rest*]" At Roof.covering the~Vessel and~he~will~See and~Look they~did~Dry.up Face~s the~Ground

unit to the new moon the water dried up from upon the land and "No'ahh [*Rest*]" removed the roof covering of the vessel and he saw and look, the face of the ground dried up,

**8:14**

וּבַחֹדֶשׁ הַשֵּׁנִי בְּשִׁבְעָה וְעֶשְׂרִים יוֹם לַחֹדֶשׁ יָבְשָׁה הָאָרֶץ

and~in~the~New.moon the~Second in~Seven and~Ten~s Day to~the~New.moon she~did~Dry.out the~Land

and in the second new moon in the seventeenth day to the new moon the land was dried out,

**8:15**

וַיְדַבֵּר אֱלֹהִים אֶל נֹחַ לֵאמֹר

and~he~will~Speak "Elohiym [*Powers*]" To "No'ahh [*Rest*]" to~>~Say

and "Elohiym [*Powers*]" spoke to "No'ahh [*Rest*]" saying,

**8:16**

צֵא מִן הַתֵּבָה אַתָּה וְאִשְׁתְּךָ וּבָנֶיךָ וּנְשֵׁי בָנֶיךָ אִתָּךְ

!(ms)~Go.out From the~Vessel You(ms) and~Woman~you(ms) and~Son~s~you(ms) and~Woman~s Son~s~you(ms) At~you(ms)

go out from the vessel, you and your woman and your sons and the women of your sons with you,

**8:17**

כָּל הַחַיָּה אֲשֶׁר אִתְּךָ מִכָּל בָּשָׂר בָּעוֹף וּבַבְּהֵמָה וּבְכָל הָרֶמֶשׂ הָרֹמֵשׂ עַל הָאָרֶץ הוֹצֵא (הַיְצֵא) אִתָּךְ וְשָׁרְצוּ בָאָרֶץ וּפָרוּ וְרָבוּ עַל הָאָרֶץ

All the~Life Which At~you(ms) from~All Flesh in~the~Flyer and~in~the~Beast and~in~All the~Treader the~Tread~ing(ms) Upon the~Land !(mp)~make~Go.out At~you(ms) and~they~did~Swarm in~the~Land and~they~did~Reproduce and~they~did~Increase Upon the~Land

all of the living ones which are with you from all of the flesh in the flyers and in the beast and in all of the treaders treading upon the land, bring out with you and they swarmed in the land and they reproduced and they increased upon the land,

**8:18**

וַיֵּצֵא נֹחַ וּבָנָיו וְאִשְׁתּוֹ וּנְשֵׁי בָנָיו אִתּוֹ

and~he~will~Go.out "No'ahh [*Rest*]" and~Son~s~him and~Woman~him and~Woman~s Son~s~him At~him

and "No'ahh [*Rest*]" went out and his sons and his woman and the women of his sons with him,

**8:19**

כָּל הַחַיָּה כָּל הָרֶמֶשׂ וְכָל הָעוֹף כֹּל רוֹמֵשׂ עַל הָאָרֶץ לְמִשְׁפְּחֹתֵיהֶם יָצְאוּ מִן הַתֵּבָה

All the~Life All the~Treader and~All the~Flyer All the~Tread~ing(ms) Upon the~Land to~Family~them(m) they~did~Go.out From the~Vessel

all of the living ones, all of the treaders and all of the flyers, all of the treading ones upon the land to their family went out from the vessel,

**8:20** וַיִּבֶן נֹחַ מִזְבֵּחַ לַיהוָה וַיִּקַּח מִכֹּל הַבְּהֵמָה הַטְּהֹרָה וּמִכֹּל הָעוֹף הַטָּהוֹר וַיַּעַל עֹלֹת בַּמִּזְבֵּחַ

and~he~will~Build "No'ahh [*Rest*]" Altar to~"YHWH [*He exists*]" and~he~will~Take from~All the~Beast the~Pure and~from~All the~Flyer the~Pure and~he~will~make~Go.up Rising~s in~the~Altar

and "No'ahh [*Rest*]" built an altar to "YHWH [*He exists*]" and he took from all of the pure beasts and from all of the pure flyers and he brought up a rising in the altar,

**8:21** וַיָּרַח יְהוָה אֶת רֵיחַ הַנִּיחֹחַ וַיֹּאמֶר יְהוָה אֶל לִבּוֹ לֹא אֹסִף לְקַלֵּל עוֹד אֶת הָאֲדָמָה בַּעֲבוּר הָאָדָם כִּי יֵצֶר לֵב הָאָדָם רַע מִנְּעֻרָיו וְלֹא אֹסִף עוֹד לְהַכּוֹת אֶת כָּל חַי כַּאֲשֶׁר עָשִׂיתִי

and~he~will~make~Smell "YHWH [*He exists*]" At Aroma the~Sweet and~he~will~Say "YHWH [*He exists*]" To Heart~him Not i~will~make~Add to~>~much~Be.insubstantial Yet.again At the~Ground in~the~On.account.of the~Human Given.that Thought Heart the~Human Dysfunctional from~Young.age~s~him and~Not i~will~make~Add Yet.again to~>~Hit At All Life like~Which i~did~Do

and "YHWH [*He exists*]" smelled the aroma of the sweet one and "YHWH [*He exists*]" said to his heart, I will not again make the ground be insubstantial on account of the human given that the thoughts of the heart of the human is dysfunctional from his young age and I will not continue to hit all of the living ones which I made,

**8:22** עֹד כָּל יְמֵי הָאָרֶץ זֶרַע וְקָצִיר וְקֹר וָחֹם וְקַיִץ וָחֹרֶף וְיוֹם וָלַיְלָה לֹא יִשְׁבֹּתוּ

Yet.again All Day~s the~Land Seed and~Harvest and~Cold and~Hot and~Summer and~Winter and~Day and~Night Not they(m)~will~Cease

Yet again are all of the days of the land, seed and harvest and cold and hot and summer and winter and day and night, they will not cease,

# Chapter 9

**9:1** וַיְבָרֶךְ אֱלֹהִים אֶת נֹחַ וְאֶת בָּנָיו וַיֹּאמֶר לָהֶם פְּרוּ וּרְבוּ וּמִלְאוּ אֶת הָאָרֶץ

and~he~will~much~Kneel "Elohiym [*Powers*]" At "No'ahh [*Rest*]" and~At Son~s~him and~he~will~Say to~them(m) !(mp)~Reproduce and~!(mp)~Increase and~!(mp)~Fill At the~Land

and "Elohiym [*Powers*]" respected "No'ahh [*Rest*]" and his sons and said to them reproduce and increase and fill the land,

**9:2\*** וּמוֹרַאֲכֶם וְחִתְּכֶם יִהְיֶה עַל כָּל חַיַּת הָאָרֶץ וְעַל כָּל עוֹף הַשָּׁמָיִם בְּכֹל אֲשֶׁר תִּרְמֹשׂ הָאֲדָמָה וּבְכָל דְּגֵי הַיָּם בְּיֶדְכֶם נִתָּנוּ

and~Fearing~you(mp) and~
Trembling.in.fear~you(mp) he~will~Exist
Upon All Life the~Land and~Upon
All Flyer the~Sky~s2 in~All Which
she~will~Tread the~Ground and~in~All
Fish~s the~Sea in~Hand~you(mp)
they~had~be~Give

and a fearing of you and a
trembling in fear of you will exist
upon all of the living ones of the
land and upon all of the flyers of
the sky, in all of the ones which the
ground will tread and in all of the
fish of the sea, in your hand, they
have been given,

**9:3** כָּל רֶמֶשׂ אֲשֶׁר הוּא חַי לָכֶם יִהְיֶה לְאָכְלָה כְּיֶרֶק עֵשֶׂב נָתַתִּי לָכֶם אֶת כֹּל

All Treader Which He Life to~
you(mp) he~will~Exist to~Food like~
Green Herb i~did~Give to~you(mp)
At All

all treaders which is living, he will
exist for you for food like the green
herbs I gave all to you,

**9:4** אַךְ בָּשָׂר בְּנַפְשׁוֹ דָמוֹ לֹא תֹאכֵלוּ

Surely Flesh in~Being~him Blood~
him Not you(mp)~will~Eat

surely the flesh is in his being, you
will not eat his blood,

**9:5** וְאַךְ אֶת דִּמְכֶם לְנַפְשֹׁתֵיכֶם אֶדְרֹשׁ מִיַּד כָּל חַיָּה אֶדְרְשֶׁנּוּ וּמִיַּד הָאָדָם מִיַּד אִישׁ אָחִיו אֶדְרֹשׁ אֶת נֶפֶשׁ הָאָדָם

and~Surely At Blood~you(mp) to~
Being~s~you(mp) i~will~Seek from~
Hand All Life i~will~Seek~him and~
from~Hand the~Human from~Hand
Man Brother~him i~will~Seek At
Being the~Human

and surely your blood for your
being I will seek, from the hand of
all of the living ones I will seek him
and from the hand of the human,
from the hand of the man of his
brother I will seek the being of the
human,

**9:6** שֹׁפֵךְ דַּם הָאָדָם בָּאָדָם דָּמוֹ יִשָּׁפֵךְ כִּי בְּצֶלֶם אֱלֹהִים עָשָׂה אֶת הָאָדָם

Pour.out~ing(ms) Blood the~Human
in~the~Human Blood~him he~will~be~
Pour.out Given.that in~Image
"Elohiym [*Powers*]" he~did~Do At
the~Human

pouring out the blood of the human,
in the human is his blood, he will
be poured out given that in the
image of "Elohiym [*Powers*]" he
made the human,

**9:7** וְאַתֶּם פְּרוּ וּרְבוּ שִׁרְצוּ בָאָרֶץ וּרְבוּ בָהּ

and~You(ms) !(mp)~Reproduce and~
!(mp)~Increase !(mp)~Swarm in~the~
Land and~!(mp)~Increase in~her

and you, reproduce and increase,
swarm in the land and increase in
her,

**9:8** וַיֹּאמֶר אֱלֹהִים אֶל נֹחַ וְאֶל בָּנָיו אִתּוֹ לֵאמֹר

and~he~will~Say "Elohiym [*Powers*]"
To "No'ahh [*Rest*]" and~To Son~s~
him At~him to~>~Say

and "Elohiym [*Powers*]" said to
"No'ahh [*Rest*]" and to his sons
with him saying,

**9:9**

וַאֲנִי הִנְנִי מֵקִים אֶת בְּרִיתִי אִתְּכֶם וְאֶת זַרְעֲכֶם אַחֲרֵיכֶם

and~I  Look~me  make~Rise~ing(ms)
At  Covenant~me  At~you(mp)  and~At
Seed~you(mp)  After~you(mp)

and here am I, making a rising of my covenant to you and your seed after you,

**9:10**

וְאֵת כָּל נֶפֶשׁ הַחַיָּה אֲשֶׁר אִתְּכֶם בָּעוֹף בַּבְּהֵמָה וּבְכָל חַיַּת הָאָרֶץ אִתְּכֶם מִכֹּל יֹצְאֵי הַתֵּבָה לְכֹל חַיַּת הָאָרֶץ

and~At  All  Being  the~Life  Which
At~you(mp)  in~the~Flyer  in~the~Beast
and~in~All  Life  the~Land  At~
you(mp)  from~All  Go.out~ing(mp)
the~Vessel  to~All  Life  the~Land

and with all of the beings of the living ones which are with you, with the flyer, with the beast and with all of the living ones of the land with you, from all going out of the vessel to all of the living ones of the land,

**9:11**

וַהֲקִמֹתִי אֶת בְּרִיתִי אִתְּכֶם וְלֹא יִכָּרֵת כָּל בָּשָׂר עוֹד מִמֵּי הַמַּבּוּל וְלֹא יִהְיֶה עוֹד מַבּוּל לְשַׁחֵת הָאָרֶץ

and~i~did~make~Rise  At  Covenant~me
At~you(mp)  and~Not  he~will~be~Cut
All  Flesh  Yet.again  from~Water~s2
the~Flood  and~Not  he~will~Exist
Yet.again  Flood  to~>~much~Damage
the~Land

and I made rise my covenant with you and all of the flesh will not be cut again from the water of the flood, the flood will not exist again to do much damage to the land,

**9:12**

וַיֹּאמֶר אֱלֹהִים זֹאת אוֹת הַבְּרִית אֲשֶׁר אֲנִי נֹתֵן בֵּינִי וּבֵינֵיכֶם וּבֵין כָּל נֶפֶשׁ חַיָּה אֲשֶׁר אִתְּכֶם לְדֹרֹת עוֹלָם

and~he~will~Say  "Elohiym  [*Powers*]"
This  Sign  the~Covenant  Which  I
Give~ing(ms)  Between~me  and~
Between~you(mp)  and~Between  All
Being  Life  Which  At~you(mp)  to~
Generation~s  Distant.time

and "Elohiym [*Powers*]" said, this is the sign of the covenant which I am giving between me and you and all of the beings of life which are with you for generations of a distant time,

**9:13**

אֶת קַשְׁתִּי נָתַתִּי בֶּעָנָן וְהָיְתָה לְאוֹת בְּרִית בֵּינִי וּבֵין הָאָרֶץ

At  Bow~me  i~did~Give  in~the~Cloud
and~she~did~Exist  to~Sign  Covenant
Between~me  and~Between  the~Land

I gave my bow in the cloud, and she will exist for a sign of the covenant between me and the land,

**9:14**

וְהָיָה בְּעַנְנִי עָנָן עַל הָאָרֶץ וְנִרְאֲתָה הַקֶּשֶׁת בֶּעָנָן

and~he~did~Exist  in~Cloud~me  >~
much~Watch  Upon  the~Land  and~
she~did~be~See  the~Bow  in~the~Cloud

and he will exist in my cloud, much watching upon the land and the bow appeared in the cloud,

**9:15**

וְזָכַרְתִּי אֶת בְּרִיתִי אֲשֶׁר בֵּינִי וּבֵינֵיכֶם וּבֵין כָּל נֶפֶשׁ חַיָּה בְּכָל בָּשָׂר וְלֹא יִהְיֶה עוֹד הַמַּיִם לְמַבּוּל לְשַׁחֵת כָּל בָּשָׂר

and~i~did~Remember  At  Covenant~me

and I will remember my covenant

Which Between~me and~Between~you(mp) and~Between All Being Life in~All Flesh and~Not he~will~Exist Yet.again the~Water~s2 to~Flood to~>~much~Damage All Flesh

which is between me and you and all of the beings of life with all of the flesh and the water for a flood will not again exist to do much damage to all of the flesh,

**9:16** וְהָיְתָה הַקֶּשֶׁת בֶּעָנָן וּרְאִיתִיהָ לִזְכֹּר בְּרִית עוֹלָם בֵּין אֱלֹהִים וּבֵין כָּל נֶפֶשׁ חַיָּה בְּכָל בָּשָׂר אֲשֶׁר עַל הָאָרֶץ

and~she~did~Exist the~Bow in~the~Cloud and~i~did~See~her to~>~Remember Covenant Distant.time Between "Elohiym [*Powers*]" and~Between All Being Life in~All Flesh Which Upon the~Land

and the bow will exist in the cloud and I will see her to remember the covenant of a distant time between "Elohiym [*Powers*]" and all of the beings of life in all of the flesh which is upon the land,

**9:17** וַיֹּאמֶר אֱלֹהִים אֶל נֹחַ זֹאת אוֹת הַבְּרִית אֲשֶׁר הֲקִמֹתִי בֵּינִי וּבֵין כָּל בָּשָׂר אֲשֶׁר עַל הָאָרֶץ

and~he~will~Say "Elohiym [*Powers*]" To "No'ahh [*Rest*]" This Sign the~Covenant Which i~did~make~Rise Between~me and~Between All Flesh Which Upon the~Land

and "Elohiym [*Powers*]" said to "No'ahh [*Rest*]", this is the sign of the covenant which I made rise between me and all of the flesh which is upon the land,

**9:18** וַיִּהְיוּ בְנֵי נֹחַ הַיֹּצְאִים מִן הַתֵּבָה שֵׁם וְחָם וָיָפֶת וְחָם הוּא אֲבִי כְנָעַן

and~they(m)~will~Exist Son~s "No'ahh [*Rest*]" the~Go.out~ing(mp) From the~Vessel "Shem [*Character*]" and~"Hham [*Hot*]" and~"Yaphet [*Wonder*]" and~"Hham [*Hot*]" He Father~of "Kena'an [*Lowered*]"

and the sons of "No'ahh [*Rest*]", the ones going out from the vessel were "Shem [*Character*]" and "Hham [*Hot*]" and "Yaphet [*Wonder*]" and "Hham [*Hot*]", he was the father of "Kena'an [*Lowered*]",

**9:19** שְׁלֹשָׁה אֵלֶּה בְּנֵי נֹחַ וּמֵאֵלֶּה נָפְצָה כָל הָאָרֶץ

Three These Son~s "No'ahh [*Rest*]" and~from~These she~did~Scatter All the~Land

these three are the sons of "No'ahh [*Rest*]" and from these all of the land scattered,

**9:20** וַיָּחֶל נֹחַ אִישׁ הָאֲדָמָה וַיִּטַּע כָּרֶם

and~he~will~Pierce "No'ahh [*Rest*]" Man the~Ground and~he~will~Plant Vineyard

and "No'ahh [*Rest*]", a man of the ground, pierced and he planted a vineyard,

**9:21\*** וַיֵּשְׁתְּ מִן הַיַּיִן וַיִּשְׁכָּר וַיִּתְגַּל בְּתוֹךְ אָהֳלֹה

and~he~will~Gulp From the~Wine and~he~will~Be.drunk and~he~will~make~self~Remove.the.cover in~Midst Tent~her

and he gulped from the wine and he became drunk and removed his cover in the midst of her tent,

**9:22*** וַיַּרְא חָם אֲבִי כְנַעַן אֵת עֶרְוַת אָבִיו וַיַּגֵּד לִשְׁנֵי אֶחָיו בַּחוּץ

and~he~will~See "Hham [*Hot*]" Father~of "Kena'an [*Lowered*]" At Nakedness Father~him and~he~will~make~Be.face.to.face to~Two Brother~s~him in~the~Outside

and "Hham [*Hot*]", the father of "Kena'an [*Lowered*]", saw the nakedness of his father and he told his two brothers in the outside,

**9:23** וַיִּקַּח שֵׁם וָיֶפֶת אֶת הַשִּׂמְלָה וַיָּשִׂימוּ עַל שְׁכֶם שְׁנֵיהֶם וַיֵּלְכוּ אֲחֹרַנִּית וַיְכַסּוּ אֵת עֶרְוַת אֲבִיהֶם וּפְנֵיהֶם אֲחֹרַנִּית וְעֶרְוַת אֲבִיהֶם לֹא רָאוּ

and~he~will~Take "Shem [*Character*]" and~"Yaphet [*Wonder*]" At the~Apparel and~they(m)~will~Set.in.place Upon Shoulder Two~them(m) and~they(m)~will~Walk Backward and~they(m)~will~Conceal At Nakedness Father~them(m) and~Face~s~them(m) Backward and~Nakedness Father~them(m) Not they~did~See

and "Shem [*Character*]" and "Yaphet [*Wonder*]" took the apparel and they set it in place upon the shoulder of the two of them and they walked backward and they concealed the nakedness of their father and their faces were backward and the nakedness of their father they did not see,

**9:24** וַיִּיקֶץ נֹחַ מִיֵּינוֹ וַיֵּדַע אֵת אֲשֶׁר עָשָׂה לוֹ בְּנוֹ הַקָּטָן

and~he~will~Awake "No'ahh [*Rest*]" from~Wine~him and~he~will~Know At Which he~did~Do to~him Son~him the~Small

and "No'ahh [*Rest*]" awoke from his wine and he knew what his small son did to him,

**9:25** וַיֹּאמֶר אָרוּר כְּנָעַן עֶבֶד עֲבָדִים יִהְיֶה לְאֶחָיו

and~he~will~Say Spit.upon~ed(ms) "Kena'an [*Lowered*]" Servant Servant~s he~will~Exist to~Brother~s~him

and he said, spitted upon is "Kena'an [*Lowered*]", he will exist as a servant of servants to his brothers,

**9:26** וַיֹּאמֶר בָּרוּךְ יְהֹוָה אֱלֹהֵי שֵׁם וִיהִי כְנַעַן עֶבֶד לָמוֹ

and~he~will~Say Kneel~ed(ms) "YHWH [*He exists*]" Power~s "Shem [*Character*]" and~he~will~Exist "Kena'an [*Lowered*]" Servant to~That.one

and he said, "YHWH [*He exists*]" of the powers of "Shem [*Character*]" is respected and "Kena'an [*Lowered*]" will exist a servant to that one,

**9:27** יַפְתְּ אֱלֹהִים לְיֶפֶת וְיִשְׁכֹּן בְּאָהֳלֵי שֵׁם וִיהִי כְנַעַן עֶבֶד לָמוֹ

he~will~make~Spread.wide "Elohiym [*Powers*]" to~"Yaphet [*Wonder*]" and~he~will~Dwell in~Tent~s "Shem [*Character*]" and~he~will~Exist "Kena'an [*Lowered*]" Servant to~That.one

"Elohiym [*Powers*]" will make "Yaphet [*Wonder*]" spread wide and he will dwell in the tents of "Shem [*Character*]" and "Kena'an [*Lowered*]" will exist a servant to that one,

**9:28**

וַיְחִי נֹחַ אַחַר הַמַּבּוּל שְׁלֹשׁ מֵאוֹת שָׁנָה וַחֲמִשִּׁים שָׁנָה

and~he~will~Exist "No'ahh [*Rest*]" After the~Flood Three Hundred~s Year and~Five~s Year

and "No'ahh [*Rest*]" existed after the flood three hundred and fifty years,

**9:29**

וַיִּהְיוּ כָּל יְמֵי נֹחַ תְּשַׁע מֵאוֹת שָׁנָה וַחֲמִשִּׁים שָׁנָה וַיָּמֹת

and~they(m)~will~Exist All Day~s "No'ahh [*Rest*]" Nine Hundred~s Year and~Five~s Year and~he~will~Die

and all of the days of "No'ahh [*Rest*]" existed nine hundred and fifty years and he died,

# Chapter 10

**10:1**

וְאֵלֶּה תּוֹלְדֹת בְּנֵי נֹחַ שֵׁם חָם וָיָפֶת וַיִּוָּלְדוּ לָהֶם בָּנִים אַחַר הַמַּבּוּל

and~These Birthing~s Son~s "No'ahh [*Rest*]" "Shem [*Character*]" "Hham [*Hot*]" and~"Yaphet [*Wonder*]" and~they(m)~will~be~Bring.forth to~them(m) Son~s After the~Flood

and these are the birthings of the sons of "No'ahh [*Rest*]", "Shem [*Character*]", "Hham [*Hot*]" and "Yaphet [*Wonder*]" and sons were brought forth to them after the flood,

**10:2**

בְּנֵי יֶפֶת גֹּמֶר וּמָגוֹג וּמָדַי וְיָוָן וְתֻבָל וּמֶשֶׁךְ וְתִירָס

Son~s "Yaphet [*Wonder*]" "Gomer [*Complete*]" and~"Magog [*Roof*]" and~"Maday [*Measure*]" and~"Yawan [*Wine*]" and~"Tuval [*Flow*]" and~"Meshek [*Draw out*]" and~"Tiras [*Breaking*]"

the sons of "Yaphet [*Wonder*]", "Gomer [*Complete*]" and "Magog [*Roof*]" and "Maday [*Measure*]" and "Yawan [*Wine*]" and "Tuval [*Flow*]" and "Meshek [*Draw out*]" and "Tiras [*Breaking*]",

**10:3**

וּבְנֵי גֹּמֶר אַשְׁכְּנַז וְרִיפַת וְתֹגַרְמָה

and~Son~s "Gomer [*Complete*]" "Ashkanaz [*Fire spread*]" and~"Riphat [*Health*]" and~"Togarmah [*Gnaw a bone*]"

and the sons of "Gomer [*Complete*]", "Ashkanaz [*Fire spread*]" and "Riphat [*Health*]" and "Togarmah [*Gnaw a bone*]",

**10:4**

וּבְנֵי יָוָן אֱלִישָׁה וְתַרְשִׁישׁ כִּתִּים וְדֹדָנִים

and~Son~s "Yawan [*Wine*]" "Elishah [*El of help*]" and~"Tarshish [*Contemplate*]" "Kit [*Bruiser*]"~s and~"Dodan [*Passion*]"~s

and sons of "Yawan [*Wine*]", "Elishah [*El of help*]" and "Tarshish [*Contemplate*]" and the ones of "Kit [*Bruiser*]" and the ones of "Dodan [*Passion*]",

**10:5**

מֵאֵלֶּה נִפְרְדוּ אִיֵּי הַגּוֹיִם בְּאַרְצֹתָם אִישׁ לִלְשֹׁנוֹ לְמִשְׁפְּחֹתָם

בְּגוֹיֵהֶם

from~These   they~did~be~Divide.apart
Island~s   the~Nation~s   in~Land~s~
them(m)   Man   to~Tongue~him   to~
Family~s~them(m)   in~Nation~s~them(m)

from these the islands of the nations were divided apart in their lands, each to his tongue, to their families in their nations,

**10:6**

וּבְנֵי חָם כּוּשׁ וּמִצְרַיִם וּפוּט וּכְנָעַן

and~Son~s "Hham [*Hot*]" "Kush [*Black*]" and~"Mitsrayim [*Troubles*]" and~"Puth [*Bow*]" and~"Kena'an [*Lowered*]"

and the sons of "Hham [*Hot*]", "Kush [*Black*]" and "Mitsrayim [*Troubles*]" and "Puth [*Bow*]" and "Kena'an [*Lowered*]",

**10:7**   וּבְנֵי כוּשׁ סְבָא וַחֲוִילָה וְסַבְתָּה וְרַעְמָה וּבְנֵי רַעְמָה שְׁבָא וּדְדָן

and~Son~s "Kush [*Black*]" "Seva [*Drunkard*]" and~"Hhawilah [*Twisting*]" and~"Savtah [*Go about*]" and~"Ramah [*Mane of a horse*]" and~"Savteka [*Lead around*]" and~Son~s "Ramah [*Mane of a horse*]" "Sheva [*Seven*]" and~"Dedan [*Friendship*]"

and the sons of "Kush [*Black*]", "Seva [*Drunkard*]" and "Hhawilah [*Twisting*]" and "Savtah [*Go about*]" and "Ramah [*Mane of a horse*]" and "Savteka [*Lead around*]" and the sons of "Ramah [*Mane of a horse*]", "Sheva [*Seven*]" and "Dedan [*Friendship*]",

**10:8**   וְכוּשׁ יָלַד אֶת נִמְרֹד הוּא הֵחֵל לִהְיוֹת גִּבֹּר בָּאָרֶץ

and~"Kush [*Black*]" he~had~Bring.forth At "Nimrod [*Rebellion*]" He he~did~ make~Pierce to~>~Exist Courageous in~the~Land

and "Kush [*Black*]" had brought forth "Nimrod [*Rebellion*]", he began to exist as a courageous one in the land,

**10:9**   הוּא הָיָה גִבֹּר צַיִד לִפְנֵי יְהֹוָה עַל כֵּן יֵאָמַר כְּנִמְרֹד גִּבּוֹר צַיִד לִפְנֵי יְהֹוָה

He he~did~Exist Courageous Hunter to~Face~s "YHWH [*He exists*]" Upon So he~will~be~Say like~ "Nimrod [*Rebellion*]" Courageous Hunter to~Face~s "YHWH [*He exists*]"

he existed as a courageous hunter to the face of "YHWH [*He exists*]" therefore, it will be said, like "Nimrod [*Rebellion*]" a courageous hunter to the face of "YHWH [*He exists*]",

**10:10**   וַתְּהִי רֵאשִׁית מַמְלַכְתּוֹ בָּבֶל וְאֶרֶךְ וְאַכַּד וְכַלְנֵה בְּאֶרֶץ שִׁנְעָר

and~she~will~Exist Summit Kingdom.place~him "Bavel [*Confusion*]" and~"Erekh [*long*]" and~ "Akad [*Jar*]" and~"Kalneh [*Consummation*]" in~Land "Shinar [*Country of two rivers*]"

and the summit of his kingdom place existed as "Bavel [*Confusion*]" and "Erekh [*long*]" and "Akad [*Jar*]" and "Kalneh [*Consummation*]", in the land of "Shinar [*Country of two rivers*]",

**10:11***   מִן הָאָרֶץ הַהוּא יָצָא אַשּׁוּר וַיִּבֶן אֶת נִינְוֵה וְאֶת רְחֹבֹת עִיר

57

וְאֵת כָּלַח

From the~Land the~She he~did~
Go.out "Ashur [*Step*]" and~he~will~
Build At "Ninweh [*Agreeable*]" and~
At "Rehhovot-Ghir [*Wide streets of
the city*]" and~At "Kalahh [*Old
age*]"

from that land, "Ashur [*Step*]" went
out and he built "Ninweh
[*Agreeable*]" and "Rehhovot-Ghir
[*Wide streets of the city*]" and
"Kalahh [*Old age*]",

**10:12**  וְאֵת רֶסֶן בֵּין נִינְוֵה וּבֵין כָּלַח הוּא הָעִיר הַגְּדֹלָה

and~At "Resen [*Halter*]" Between
"Ninweh [*Agreeable*]" and~Between
"Kalahh [*Old age*]" She the~City
the~Magnificent

and "Resen [*Halter*]" between
"Ninweh [*Agreeable*]" and "Kalahh
[*Old age*]", she is the magnificent
city,

**10:13**  וּמִצְרַיִם יָלַד אֶת לוּדִים וְאֶת עֲנָמִים וְאֶת לְהָבִים וְאֶת נַפְתֻּחִים

and~"Mitsrayim [*Troubles*]" he~had~
Bring.forth At "Lud [*Birth*]"~s and~
At "Anam [*Affliction of water*]"
and~At "Lehav [*Flame*]"~s and~At
"Naphtuhh [*Opening*]"~s

and "Mitsrayim [*Troubles*]" had
brought forth the ones of "Lud
[*Birth*]" and the ones of "Anam
[*Affliction of water*]" and the ones
of "Lehav [*Flame*]" and the ones of
"Naphtuhh [*Opening*]",

**10:14**  וְאֵת פַּתְרֻסִים וְאֶת כַּסְלֻחִים אֲשֶׁר יָצְאוּ מִשָּׁם פְּלִשְׁתִּים וְאֶת
כַּפְתֹּרִים

and~At "Patros [*Mouthful of
dough*]"~s and~At "Kasluhh
[*Fortified*]"~s Which they~did~Go.out
from~There "Peleshet [*Immigrant*]"~s
and~At "Kaphtor [*Knob*]"~s

and the ones of "Patros [*Mouthful
of dough*]" and the ones of
"Kasluhh [*Fortified*]", which the
ones of "Peleshet [*Immigrant*]"
went out from there, and the ones
of "Kaphtor [*Knob*]",

**10:15**  וּכְנַעַן יָלַד אֶת צִידֹן בְּכֹרוֹ וְאֶת חֵת

and~"Kena'an [*Lowered*]" he~had~
Bring.forth At "Tsidon [*Hunting*]"
Firstborn~him and~At "Hhet
[*Shattered*]"

and "Kena'an [*Lowered*]" had
brought forth "Tsidon [*Hunting*]"
his firstborn and "Hhet
[*Shattered*]",

**10:16**  וְאֶת הַיְבוּסִי וְאֶת הָאֱמֹרִי וְאֵת הַגִּרְגָּשִׁי

and~At the~"Yevus [*He threshes*]"~of
and~At the~"Emor [*Sayer*]"~of and~
At the~"Girgash [*Stranger on
clods*]"~of

and the one of "Yevus [*He
threshes*]" and the one of "Emor
[*Sayer*]" and the one of "Girgash
[*Stranger on clods*]",

**10:17**  וְאֶת הַחִוִּי וְאֶת הַעַרְקִי וְאֶת הַסִּינִי

and~At the~"Hhiw [*Village*]"~of and~
At the~"Araq [*Gnawing*]"~of and~At
the~"Sin [*Thorn*]"~of

and the one of "Hhiw [*Village*]"
and the one of "Araq [*Gnawing*]"
and the one of "Sin [*Thorn*]",

**10:18** וְאֶת־הָאַרְוָדִי וְאֶת־הַצְּמָרִי וְאֶת־הַחֲמָתִי וְאַחַר נָפֹצוּ מִשְׁפְּחוֹת הַכְּנַעֲנִי

and~At the~"Arwad [*I will preside over*]"~of and~At the~"Tsemar [*Woolen*]"~of and~At the~"Hhamat [*Fortress*]"~of and~After they~did~be~ Scatter.abroad Family~s "Kena'an [*Lowered*]"~of

and the one of "Arwad [*I will preside over*]" and the one of "Tsemar [*Woolen*]" and the one of "Hhamat [*Fortress*]" and after the families of the one of "Kena'an [*Lowered*]" were scattered abroad,

**10:19** וַיְהִי גְּבוּל הַכְּנַעֲנִי מִצִּידֹן בֹּאֲכָה גְרָרָה עַד עַזָּה בֹּאֲכָה סְדֹמָה וַעֲמֹרָה וְאַדְמָה וּצְבֹיִם עַד לָשַׁע

and~he~will~Exist Border the~"Kena'an [*Lowered*]"~of from~"Tsidon [*Hunting*] >~Come~you(ms) "Gerar [*Chew*]"~unto Until "Ghaza [*Strong*]" >~Come~you(ms) "Sedom [*Secret*]"~ unto and~"Ghamorah [*Rebellion*]" and~"Admah [*Red ground*]" and~ "Tseviim [*Gazzells*]" Until "Lesha [*Fissure*]"

and the border of the one of "Kena'an [*Lowered*]" existed from "Tsidon [*Hunting*]" as you come unto "Gerar [*Chew*]" as far as "Ghaza [*Strong*]", as your coming unto "Sedom [*Secret*]" and "Ghamorah [*Rebellion*]" and "Admah [*Red ground*]" and "Tseviim [*Gazzells*]", as far as "Lesha [*Fissure*]",

**10:20** אֵלֶּה בְנֵי חָם לְמִשְׁפְּחֹתָם לִלְשֹׁנֹתָם בְּאַרְצֹתָם בְּגוֹיֵהֶם

These Son~s "Hham [*Hot*]" to~ Family~s~them(m) to~Tongue~s~ them(m) in~Land~s~them(m) in~ Nation~s~them(m)

these are the sons of "Hham [*Hot*]", to their families to their tongues, in their lands, in their nations,

**10:21** וּלְשֵׁם יֻלַּד גַּם הוּא אֲבִי כָּל בְּנֵי עֵבֶר אֲחִי יֶפֶת הַגָּדוֹל

and~to~"Shem [*Character*]" he~did~ much.be~Bring.forth Also He Father~ of All Son~s "Ever [*Cross over*]" Brother~of "Yaphet [*Wonder*]" the~ Magnificent

and to "Shem [*Character*]" was also brought forth, he is the father of all of the sons of "Ever [*Cross over*]", the brother of "Yaphet [*Wonder*]" the magnificent,

**10:22** בְּנֵי שֵׁם עֵילָם וְאַשּׁוּר וְאַרְפַּכְשַׁד וְלוּד וַאֲרָם

Son~s "Shem [*Character*]" "Elam [*Ancient*]" and~"Ashur [*Step*]" and~ "Arpakhshad [*I will fail the breast*]" and~"Lud [*Birth*]" and~"Aram [*Palace*]"

the sons of "Shem [*Character*]", "Elam [*Ancient*]" and "Ashur [*Step*]" and "Arpakhshad [*I will fail the breast*]" and "Lud [*Birth*]" and "Aram [*Palace*]",

**10:23** וּבְנֵי אֲרָם עוּץ וְחוּל וְגֶתֶר וָמַשׁ

and~Son~s "Aram [*Palace*]" "Uts [*Counsel*]" and~"Hhul [*Twist*]" and~ "Getar [*Fear*]" and~"Mash [*Drawn

and the sons of "Aram [*Palace*]", "Uts [*Counsel*]" and "Hhul [*Twist*]" and "Getar [*Fear*]" and "Mash out]"

[*Drawn out*]",

**10:24**

וְאַרְפַּכְשַׁד יָלַד אֶת שָׁלַח וְשֶׁלַח יָלַד אֶת עֵבֶר

and~"Arpakhshad [*I will fail the breast*]" he~had~Bring.forth At "Shelahh [*Sent*]" and~"Shelahh [*Sent*]" he~had~Bring.forth At "Ever [*Cross over*]"

and "Arpakhshad [*I will fail the breast*]" had brought forth "Shelahh [*Sent*]" and "Shelahh [*Sent*]" had brought forth "Ever [*Cross over*]",

**10:25**

וּלְעֵבֶר יֻלַּד שְׁנֵי בָנִים שֵׁם הָאֶחָד פֶּלֶג כִּי בְיָמָיו נִפְלְגָה הָאָרֶץ וְשֵׁם אָחִיו יָקְטָן

and~to~"Ever [*Cross over*]" he~did~much.be~Bring.forth Two Son~s Title the~Unit "Peleg [*Half*]" Given.that in~Day~s~him she~did~be~Split the~Land and~Title Brother~him "Yaqthan [*He is small*]"

and to "Ever [*Cross over*]" were brought forth two sons, the title of the one was "Peleg [*Half*]" given that in his day the land was split and the title of his brother was "Yaqthan [*He is small*]",

**10:26**

וְיָקְטָן יָלַד אֶת אַלְמוֹדָד וְאֶת שָׁלֶף וְאֶת חֲצַרְמָוֶת וְאֶת יָרַח

and~"Yaqthan [*He is small*]" he~had~Bring.forth At "Almodad [*El of measure*]" and~At "Sheleph [*Pull*]" and~At "Hhatsarmawet [*Yard of death*]" and~At "Yerahh [*Moon*]"

and "Yaqthan [*He is small*]" had brought forth "Almodad [*El of measure*]" and "Sheleph [*Pull*]" and "Hhatsarmawet [*Yard of death*]" and "Yerahh [*Moon*]",

**10:27**

וְאֶת הֲדוֹרָם וְאֶת אוּזָל וְאֶת דִּקְלָה

and~At "Hadoram [*Honor*]" and~At "Uzal [*Waver*]" and~At "Diqlah [*Palm grove*]"

and "Hadoram [*Honor*]" and "Uzal [*Waver*]" and "Diqlah [*Palm grove*]",

**10:28**

וְאֶת עוֹבָל וְאֶת אֲבִימָאֵל וְאֶת שְׁבָא

and~At "Uval [*Round*]" and~At "Aviyma'el [*My father is from El*]" and~At "Sheva [*Seven*]"

and "Uval [*Round*]" and "Aviyma'el [*My father is from El*]" and "Sheva [*Seven*]",

**10:29**

וְאֶת אוֹפִר וְאֶת חֲוִילָה וְאֶת יוֹבָב כָּל אֵלֶּה בְּנֵי יָקְטָן

and~At "Ophir [*Reduced to ashes*]" and~At "Hhawilah [*Twisting*]" and~At "Yovav [*Howler*]" All These Son~s "Yaqthan [*He is small*]"

and "Ophir [*Reduced to ashes*]" and "Hhawilah [*Twisting*]" and "Yovav [*Howler*]", all of these are the sons of "Yaqthan [*He is small*]",

**10:30**

וַיְהִי מוֹשָׁבָם מִמֵּשָׁא בֹּאֲכָה סְפָרָה הַר הַקֶּדֶם

and~he~will~Exist Settling~them(m) from~"Mesha [*Storm*]" >~Come~you(ms) "Sephar [*Numbering*]"~unto Hill the~East

and their settling existed from "Mesha [*Storm*]" as you come unto "Sephar [*Numbering*]", the hill of the east,

**10:31**

אֵלֶּה בְנֵי שֵׁם לְמִשְׁפְּחֹתָם לִלְשֹׁנֹתָם בְּאַרְצֹתָם לְגוֹיֵהֶם

These Son~s "Shem [*Character*]" to~ Family~s~them(m) to~Tongue~s~ them(m) in~Land~s~them(m) to~ Nation~s~them(m)

these are the sons of "Shem [*Character*]", to their families, to their tongue, in their lands, to their nations,

**10:32** אֵלֶּה מִשְׁפְּחֹת בְּנֵי־נֹחַ לְתוֹלְדֹתָם בְּגוֹיֵהֶם וּמֵאֵלֶּה נִפְרְדוּ הַגּוֹיִם בָּאָרֶץ אַחַר הַמַּבּוּל

These Family~s Son~s "No'ahh [*Rest*]" to~Birthing~s~them(m) in~ Nation~s~them(m) and~from~These they~did~be~Divide.apart the~Nation~s in~the~Land After the~Flood

these are the families of the sons of "No'ahh [*Rest*]", to their birthings, in their nations and from these the nations were divided apart in the land after the flood,

# Chapter 11

**11:1** וַיְהִי כָל־הָאָרֶץ שָׂפָה אֶחָת וּדְבָרִים אֲחָדִים

and~he~will~Exist All the~Land Lip Unit and~Word~s Unit~s

and all of the land existed as one lip and units of words,

**11:2** וַיְהִי בְּנָסְעָם מִקֶּדֶם וַיִּמְצְאוּ בִקְעָה בְּאֶרֶץ שִׁנְעָר וַיֵּשְׁבוּ שָׁם

and~he~will~Exist in~>~Journey~ them(m) from~East and~they(m)~will~ Find Level.valley in~Land "Shinar [*Country of two rivers*]" and~ they(m)~will~Settle There

and it came to pass in their journey from the east that they found a level valley in the land of "Shinar [*Country of two rivers*]" and they settled there,

**11:3** וַיֹּאמְרוּ אִישׁ אֶל־רֵעֵהוּ הָבָה נִלְבְּנָה לְבֵנִים וְנִשְׂרְפָה לִשְׂרֵפָה וַתְּהִי לָהֶם הַלְּבֵנָה לְאָבֶן וְהַחֵמָר הָיָה לָהֶם לַחֹמֶר

and~they(m)~will~Say Man To Companion~him !(ms)~Provide we~ will~Make.bricks Brick~s and~we~ will~Cremate~^ to~Cremating and~she~ will~Exist to~them(m) the~Brick to~ Stone and~the~Tar he~did~Exist to~ them(m) to~Mortar

and they said each to his companion, provide, we will make bricks and we will greatly cremate and the brick existed to them for stone and the tar was to them for mortar,

**11:4** וַיֹּאמְרוּ הָבָה נִבְנֶה־לָּנוּ עִיר וּמִגְדָּל וְרֹאשׁוֹ בַשָּׁמַיִם וְנַעֲשֶׂה־לָּנוּ שֵׁם פֶּן־נָפוּץ עַל־פְּנֵי כָל־הָאָרֶץ

and~they(m)~will~Say !(ms)~Provide we~will~Build to~us City and~Tower and~Head~him in~the~Sky~s2 and~ we~will~Do to~us Title Otherwise we~will~Scatter.abroad Upon Face~s All the~Land

and they said, provide, we will build for us a city and a tower and his head will be in the sky and we will make for us a title otherwise we will scatter abroad upon the face of all of the land,

**11:5** וַיֵּרֶד יְהוָה לִרְאֹת אֶת הָעִיר וְאֶת הַמִּגְדָּל אֲשֶׁר בָּנוּ בְּנֵי הָאָדָם

and~he~will~Go.down "YHWH [He exists]" to~>~See At the~City and~At the~Tower Which they~did~Build Son~s the~Human

and "YHWH [He exists]" went down to see the city and the tower which the sons of the human built,

**11:6** וַיֹּאמֶר יְהוָה הֵן עַם אֶחָד וְשָׂפָה אַחַת לְכֻלָּם וְזֶה הַחִלָּם לַעֲשׂוֹת וְעַתָּה לֹא יִבָּצֵר מֵהֶם כֹּל אֲשֶׁר יָזְמוּ לַעֲשׂוֹת

and~he~will~Say "YHWH [He exists]" Though People Unit and~Lip Unit to~All~them(m) and~This >~make~Pierce~them(m) to~>~Do and~Now Not he~will~be~Fence.in from~them(m) All Which they(m)~will~Plot to~>~Do

and "YHWH [He exists]" said, though the people are a unit and one lip for all of them and this is what they will begin to do and now nothing will be fenced in from them, all which they will plot to do,

**11:7** הָבָה נֵרְדָה וְנָבְלָה שָׁם שְׂפָתָם אֲשֶׁר לֹא יִשְׁמְעוּ אִישׁ שְׂפַת רֵעֵהוּ

!(ms)~Provide~^ we~will~Go.down~^ and~we~will~Mix~^ There Lip~them(m) Which Not they(m)~will~Hear Man Lip Companion~him

provide, we will go down and we will mix there their lip that they will not hear each lip of his companion,

**11:8** וַיָּפֶץ יְהוָה אֹתָם מִשָּׁם עַל פְּנֵי כָל הָאָרֶץ וַיַּחְדְּלוּ לִבְנֹת הָעִיר

and~he~will~Scatter.abroad "YHWH [He exists]" At~them(m) from~There Upon Face~s All the~Land and~they(m)~will~Terminate to~>~Build the~City

and "YHWH [He exists]" scattered them abroad from there upon the face of all of the land and they terminated to build the city,

**11:9** עַל כֵּן קָרָא שְׁמָהּ בָּבֶל כִּי שָׁם בָּלַל יְהוָה שְׂפַת כָּל הָאָרֶץ וּמִשָּׁם הֱפִיצָם יְהוָה עַל פְּנֵי כָּל הָאָרֶץ

Upon So he~did~Call.out Title~her "Bavel [Confusion]" Given.that There he~did~Mix "YHWH [He exists]" Lip All the~Land and~from~There he~did~make~Scatter.abroad~them(m) "YHWH [He exists]" Upon Face~s All the~Land

therefore he called out her title "Bavel [Confusion]" given that there "YHWH [He exists]" mixed the lip of all of the land and from there "YHWH [He exists]" made them scatter abroad upon the face of all of the land,

**11:10** אֵלֶּה תּוֹלְדֹת שֵׁם שֵׁם בֶּן מְאַת שָׁנָה וַיּוֹלֶד אֶת אַרְפַּכְשָׁד שְׁנָתַיִם אַחַר הַמַּבּוּל

These Birthing~s "Shem [Character]" "Shem [Character]" Son Hundred Year and~he~will~make~Bring.forth At "Arpakhshad [I will fail the breast]" Year~s2 After the~Flood

these are the birthings of "Shem [Character]", "Shem [Character]" was a son of a hundred years and he caused to bring forth "Arpakhshad [I will fail the breast]" two years after the flood,

**11:11** וַיְחִי שֵׁם אַחֲרֵי הוֹלִידוֹ אֶת אַרְפַּכְשָׁד חֲמֵשׁ מֵאוֹת שָׁנָה וַיּוֹלֶד בָּנִים וּבָנוֹת

and~he~will~Exist "Shem [*Character*]" After >~make~Bring.forth~him At "Arpakhshad [*I will fail the breast*]" Five Hundred~s Year and~he~will~make~Bring.forth Son~s and~Daughter~s

and "Shem [*Character*]" existed five hundred years after his causing to bring forth "Arpakhshad [*I will fail the breast*]" and he caused to bring forth sons and daughters,

**11:12** וְאַרְפַּכְשַׁד חַי חָמֵשׁ וּשְׁלֹשִׁים שָׁנָה וַיּוֹלֶד אֶת שָׁלַח

and~"Arpakhshad [*I will fail the breast*]" he~did~Live Five and~Three~s Year and~he~will~make~Bring.forth At "Shelahh [*Sent*]"

and "Arpakhshad [*I will fail the breast*]" lived thirty-five years and he caused to bring forth "Shelahh [*Sent*]",

**11:13** וַיְחִי אַרְפַּכְשַׁד אַחֲרֵי הוֹלִידוֹ אֶת שֶׁלַח שָׁלֹשׁ שָׁנִים וְאַרְבַּע מֵאוֹת שָׁנָה וַיּוֹלֶד בָּנִים וּבָנוֹת

and~he~will~Live "Arpakhshad [*I will fail the breast*]" After >~make~Bring.forth~him At "Shelahh [*Sent*]" Three Year~s and~Four Hundred~s Year and~he~will~make~Bring.forth Son~s and~Daughter~s

and "Arpakhshad [*I will fail the breast*]" lived four hundred and three years after his causing to bring forth "Shelahh [*Sent*]" and he caused to bring forth sons and daughters,

**11:14** וְשֶׁלַח חַי שְׁלֹשִׁים שָׁנָה וַיּוֹלֶד אֶת עֵבֶר

and~"Shelahh [*Sent*]" he~did~Live Three~s Year and~he~will~make~Bring.forth At "Ever [*Cross over*]"

and "Shelahh [*Sent*]" lived thirty years and he caused to bring forth "Ever [*Cross over*]",

**11:15** וַיְחִי שֶׁלַח אַחֲרֵי הוֹלִידוֹ אֶת עֵבֶר שָׁלֹשׁ שָׁנִים וְאַרְבַּע מֵאוֹת שָׁנָה וַיּוֹלֶד בָּנִים וּבָנוֹת

and~he~will~Live "Shelahh [*Sent*]" After >~make~Bring.forth~him At "Ever [*Cross over*]" Three Year~s and~Four Hundred~s Year and~he~will~make~Bring.forth Son~s and~Daughter~s

and "Shelahh [*Sent*]" lived four hundred and three years after his causing to bring forth "Ever [*Cross over*]" and he caused to bring forth sons and daughters,

**11:16** וַיְחִי עֵבֶר אַרְבַּע וּשְׁלֹשִׁים שָׁנָה וַיּוֹלֶד אֶת פָּלֶג

and~he~will~Live "Ever [*Cross over*]" Four and~Three~s Year and~he~will~make~Bring.forth At "Peleg [*Half*]"

and "Ever [*Cross over*]" lived thirty-four years and he caused to bring forth "Peleg [*Half*]",

**11:17** וַיְחִי עֵבֶר אַחֲרֵי הוֹלִידוֹ אֶת פֶּלֶג שְׁלֹשִׁים שָׁנָה וְאַרְבַּע מֵאוֹת שָׁנָה וַיּוֹלֶד בָּנִים וּבָנוֹת

and~he~will~Live "Ever [*Cross over*]"
After >~make~Bring.forth~him At
"Peleg [*Half*]" Three~s Year and~
Four Hundred~s Year and~he~will~
make~Bring.forth Son~s and~Daughter~
s

and "Ever [*Cross over*]" lived four
hundred and thirty years after his
causing to bring forth "Peleg
[*Half*]" and he caused to bring forth
sons and daughters,

**11:18**　　　　וַיְחִי פֶלֶג שְׁלֹשִׁים שָׁנָה וַיּוֹלֶד אֶת רְעוּ

and~he~will~Live "Peleg [*Half*]"
Three~s Year and~he~will~make~
Bring.forth At "Re'u [*Companion*]"

and "Peleg [*Half*]" lived thirty
years and he caused to bring forth
"Re'u [*Companion*]",

**11:19**　　וַיְחִי פֶלֶג אַחֲרֵי הוֹלִידוֹ אֶת רְעוּ תֵּשַׁע שָׁנִים וּמָאתַיִם שָׁנָה
וַיּוֹלֶד בָּנִים וּבָנוֹת

and~he~will~Live "Peleg [*Half*]"
After >~make~Bring.forth~him At
"Re'u [*Companion*]" Nine Year~s
and~Hundred~s2 Year and~he~will~
make~Bring.forth Son~s and~Daughter~
s

and "Peleg [*Half*]" lived two
hundred and nine years after his
causing to bring forth "Re'u
[*Companion*]" and he caused to
bring forth sons and daughters,

**11:20**　　　　וַיְחִי רְעוּ שְׁתַּיִם וּשְׁלֹשִׁים שָׁנָה וַיּוֹלֶד אֶת שְׂרוּג

and~he~will~Live "Re'u [*Companion*]"
Two and~Three~s Year he~will~
make~Bring.forth At "Serug [*Branch*]"

and "Re'u [*Companion*]" lived
thirty-two years and he caused to
bring forth "Serug [*Branch*]",

**11:21**　　וַיְחִי רְעוּ אַחֲרֵי הוֹלִידוֹ אֶת שְׂרוּג שֶׁבַע שָׁנִים וּמָאתַיִם שָׁנָה
וַיּוֹלֶד בָּנִים וּבָנוֹת

and~he~will~Live "Re'u [*Companion*]"
After >~make~Bring.forth~him At
"Serug [*Branch*]" Seven Year~s and~
Hundred~s2 Year and~he~will~make~
Bring.forth Son~s and~Daughter~s

and "Re'u [*Companion*]" lived two
hundred and seven years after his
causing to bring forth "Serug
[*Branch*]" and he caused to bring
forth sons and daughters,

**11:22**　　　　וַיְחִי שְׂרוּג שְׁלֹשִׁים שָׁנָה וַיּוֹלֶד אֶת נָחוֹר

and~he~will~Live "Serug [*Branch*]"
Three~s Year and~he~will~make~
Bring.forth At "Nahhor [*Snorting*]"

and "Serug [*Branch*]" lived thirty
years and he caused to bring forth
"Nahhor [*Snorting*]",

**11:23**　　וַיְחִי שְׂרוּג אַחֲרֵי הוֹלִידוֹ אֶת נָחוֹר מָאתַיִם שָׁנָה וַיּוֹלֶד בָּנִים
וּבָנוֹת

and~he~will~Live "Serug [*Branch*]"
After >~make~Bring.forth~him At
"Nahhor [*Snorting*]" Hundred~s2 Year
and~he~will~make~Bring.forth Son~s
and~Daughter~s

and "Serug [*Branch*]" lived two
hundred years after his causing to
bring forth "Nahhor [*Snorting*]"
and he caused to bring forth sons
and daughters,

**11:24**

וַיְחִי נָחוֹר תֵּשַׁע וְעֶשְׂרִים שָׁנָה וַיּוֹלֶד אֶת תֶּרַח

and~he~will~Live "Nahhor [*Snorting*]" Nine and~Ten~s Year and~he~will~make~Bring.forth At "Terahh [*Station*]"

and "Nahhor [*Snorting*]" lived twenty-nine years and he caused to bring forth "Terahh [*Station*]",

**11:25**

וַיְחִי נָחוֹר אַחֲרֵי הוֹלִידוֹ אֶת תֶּרַח תְּשַׁע עֶשְׂרֵה שָׁנָה וּמְאַת שָׁנָה וַיּוֹלֶד בָּנִים וּבָנוֹת

and~he~will~Live "Nahhor [*Snorting*]" After >~make~Bring.forth~him At "Terahh [*Station*]" Nine Ten Year and~Hundred Year and~he~will~make~Bring.forth Son~s and~Daughter~s

and "Nahhor [*Snorting*]" lived a hundred and nineteen years after his causing to bring forth "Terahh [*Station*]" and he caused to bring forth sons and daughters,

**11:26**

וַיְחִי תֶרַח שִׁבְעִים שָׁנָה וַיּוֹלֶד אֶת אַבְרָם אֶת נָחוֹר וְאֶת הָרָן

and~he~will~Live "Terahh [*Station*]" Seven~s Year and~he~will~make~Bring.forth At "Avram [*Father raised*]" At "Nahhor [*Snorting*]" At "Haran [*Hill country*]"

and "Terahh [*Station*]" lived seventy years and he caused to bring forth "Avram [*Father raised*]", "Nahhor [*Snorting*]", "Haran [*Hill country*]",

**11:27**

וְאֵלֶּה תּוֹלְדֹת תֶּרַח תֶּרַח הוֹלִיד אֶת אַבְרָם אֶת נָחוֹר וְאֶת הָרָן וְהָרָן הוֹלִיד אֶת לוֹט

and~These Birthing~s "Terahh [*Station*]" "Terahh [*Station*]" he~had~make~Bring.forth At "Avram [*Father raised*]" At "Nahhor [*Snorting*]" and~At "Haran [*Hill country*]" and~"Haran [*Hill country*]" he~had~make~Bring.forth At "Loth [*Covering*]"

and these are the birthings of "Terahh [*Station*]", "Terahh [*Station*]" had caused to bring forth "Avram [*Father raised*]", "Nahhor [*Snorting*]" and "Haran [*Hill country*]" and "Haran [*Hill country*]" had caused to bring forth "Loth [*Covering*]",

**11:28**

וַיָּמָת הָרָן עַל פְּנֵי תֶּרַח אָבִיו בְּאֶרֶץ מוֹלַדְתּוֹ בְּאוּר כַּשְׂדִּים

and~he~will~Die "Haran [*Hill country*]" Upon Face~s "Terahh [*Station*]" Father~him in~Land Kindred~him in~"Ur [*Light*]" "Kesad [*Clod breaker*]"~s

and "Haran [*Hill country*]" died upon the face of "Terahh [*Station*]" his father in the land of his kindred in "Ur [*Light*]" of the ones of "Kesad [*Clod breaker*]",

**11:29***

וַיִּקַּח אַבְרָם וְנָחוֹר לָהֶם נָשִׁים שֵׁם אֵשֶׁת אַבְרָם שָׂרָי וְשֵׁם אֵשֶׁת נָחוֹר מִלְכָּה בַּת הָרָן אֲבִי מִלְכָּה וַאֲבִי יִסְכָּה

and~he~will~Take "Avram [*Father raised*]" and~"Nahhor [*Snorting*]" to~them(m) Woman~s Title Woman "Avram [*Father raised*]" "Sarai [*Princess*]" and~Title Woman "Nahhor

and "Avram [*Father raised*]" and "Nahhor [*Snorting*]" took women for them, the title of the woman of "Avram [*Father raised*]" was "Sarai [*Princess*]" and the title of

[*Snorting*]" "Milkah [*Queen*]"
Daughter "Haran [*Hill country*]"
Father~of "Milkah [*Queen*]" and~
Father~of "Yiskah [*He covers*]"

the woman of "Nahhor [*Snorting*]"
was "Milkah [*Queen*]" the daughter
of "Haran [*Hill country*]" the father
of "Milkah [*Queen*]" and the father
of "Yiskah [*He covers*]",

**11:30**

וַתְּהִי שָׂרַי עֲקָרָה אֵין לָהּ וָלָד

and~she~will~Exist "Sarai [*Princess*]"
Sterile Without to~her Child

and "Sarai [*Princess*]" existed
sterile, she was without a child,

**11:31** וַיִּקַּח תֶּרַח אֶת אַבְרָם בְּנוֹ וְאֶת לוֹט בֶּן הָרָן בֶּן בְּנוֹ וְאֶת שָׂרַי
כַּלָּתוֹ אֵשֶׁת אַבְרָם בְּנוֹ וַיֵּצְאוּ אִתָּם מֵאוּר כַּשְׂדִּים לָלֶכֶת אַרְצָה
כְּנַעַן וַיָּבֹאוּ עַד חָרָן וַיֵּשְׁבוּ שָׁם

and~he~will~Take "Terahh [*Station*]"
At "Avram [*Father raised*]" Son~
him and~At "Loth [*Covering*]" Son
"Haran [*Hill country*]" Son Son~him
and~At "Sarai [*Princess*]" Daughter-
in-law~him Woman "Avram [*Father
raised*]" Son~him and~they(m)~will~
Go.out At~them(m) from~"Ur [*Light*]"
"Kesad [*Clod breaker*]"~s to~>~Walk
Land~unto "Kena'an [*Lowered*]" and~
they(m)~will~Come Until "Hharan
[*Burning*]" and~they(m)~will~Settle
There

and "Terahh [*Station*]" took
"Avram [*Father raised*]" his son,
and "Loth [*Covering*]", the son of
"Haran [*Hill country*]", the son of
his son, and "Sarai [*Princess*]", his
daughter-in-law, the woman of
"Avram [*Father raised*]" his son
and they went out from "Ur
[*Light*]" of the ones of "Kesad
[*Clod breaker*]" to walk unto the
land of "Kena'an [*Lowered*]" and
they came as far as "Hharan
[*Burning*]" and they settled there,

**11:32** וַיִּהְיוּ יְמֵי תֶרַח חָמֵשׁ שָׁנִים וּמָאתַיִם שָׁנָה וַיָּמָת תֶּרַח בְּחָרָן

and~they(m)~will~Exist Day~s "Terahh
[*Station*]" Five Year~s and~Hundred~
s2 Year and~he~will~Die "Terahh
[*Station*]" in~"Hharan [*Burning*]"

and the days of "Terahh [*Station*]"
existed two hundred and five years
and "Terahh [*Station*]" died in
"Hharan [*Burning*]",

# Chapter 12

**12:1** וַיֹּאמֶר יְהוָה אֶל אַבְרָם לֶךְ לְךָ מֵאַרְצְךָ וּמִמּוֹלַדְתְּךָ וּמִבֵּית
אָבִיךָ אֶל הָאָרֶץ אֲשֶׁר אַרְאֶךָּ

and~he~will~Say "YHWH [*He
exists*]" To "Avram [*Father raised*]"
!(ms)~Walk to~you(ms) from~Land~
you(ms) and~from~Kindred~you(ms)
and~from~House Father~you(ms) To
the~Land Which i~will~make~See~
you(ms)

and "YHWH [*He exists*]" said to
"Avram [*Father raised*]", walk
yourself from your land and from
your kindred and from the house of
your father to the land which I will
show you,

**12:2** וְאֶעֶשְׂךָ לְגוֹי גָּדוֹל וַאֲבָרֶכְךָ וַאֲגַדְּלָה שְׁמֶךָ וֶהְיֵה בְּרָכָה

and~i~will~Do~you(ms)   to~Nation
Magnificent   and~i~will~much~Kneel~
you(ms)   and~i~will~Magnify   Title~
you(ms)   and~!(ms)~Exist   Present

and I will make you a magnificent nation and I will respect you and I will magnify your title and exist as a present,

**12:3** וַאֲבָרְכָה מְבָרְכֶיךָ וּמְקַלֶּלְךָ אָאֹר וְנִבְרְכוּ בְךָ כֹּל מִשְׁפְּחֹת הָאֲדָמָה

and~i~will~much~Kneel~^   much~Kneel~
ing(mp)~you(ms)   and~much~
Be.insubstantial~ing(mp)~you(ms)   i~
will~Spit.upon   and~they(m)~will~be~
Kneel   in~you(ms)   All   Family~s   the~
Ground

and I will respect ones respecting you and ones making you insubstantial I will spit upon and all of the families of the ground will be respected with you,

**12:4** וַיֵּלֶךְ אַבְרָם כַּאֲשֶׁר דִּבֶּר אֵלָיו יְהֹוָה וַיֵּלֶךְ אִתּוֹ לוֹט וְאַבְרָם בֶּן חָמֵשׁ שָׁנִים וְשִׁבְעִים שָׁנָה בְּצֵאתוֹ מֵחָרָן

and~he~will~Walk "Avram [*Father raised*]" like~Which he~did~much~ Speak To~him "YHWH [*He exists*]" and~he~will~Walk At~him "Loth [*Covering*]" and~"Avram [*Father raised*]" Son Five Year~s and~ Seven~s Year in~>~Go.out~him from~"Hharan [*Burning*]"

and "Avram [*Father raised*]" walked just as "YHWH [*He exists*]" spoke to him and "Loth [*Covering*]" walked with him and "Avram [*Father raised*]" was a son of seventy-five years in his going out from "Hharan [*Burning*]",

**12:5** וַיִּקַּח אַבְרָם אֶת שָׂרַי אִשְׁתּוֹ וְאֶת לוֹט בֶּן אָחִיו וְאֶת כָּל רְכוּשָׁם אֲשֶׁר רָכָשׁוּ וְאֶת הַנֶּפֶשׁ אֲשֶׁר עָשׂוּ בְחָרָן וַיֵּצְאוּ לָלֶכֶת אַרְצָה כְּנַעַן וַיָּבֹאוּ אַרְצָה כְּנָעַן

and~he~will~Take "Avram [*Father raised*]" At "Sarai [*Princess*]" Woman~him and~At "Loth [*Covering*]" Son Brother~him and~At All Goods~them(m) Which they~did~ Accumulate and~At the~Being Which they~did~Do in~"Hharan [*Burning*]" and~they(m)~will~Go.out to~>~Walk Land~unto "Kena'an [*Lowered*]" and~ they(m)~will~Come Land~unto "Kena'an [*Lowered*]"

and "Avram [*Father raised*]" took "Sarai [*Princess*]" his woman and "Loth [*Covering*]" the son of his brother and all of their goods which they accumulated and the beings which they did in "Hharan [*Burning*]" and they went out to walk unto the land of "Kena'an [*Lowered*]" and they came unto the land of "Kena'an [*Lowered*]",

**12:6** וַיַּעֲבֹר אַבְרָם בָּאָרֶץ עַד מְקוֹם שְׁכֶם עַד אֵלוֹן מוֹרֶה וְהַכְּנַעֲנִי אָז בָּאָרֶץ

and~he~will~Cross.over "Avram [*Father raised*]" in~the~Land Until

and "Avram [*Father raised*]" crossed over in the land, as far as

Place "Shekhem [*Shoulder*]" Until Great.tree "Moreh [*Teacher*]" and~ the~"Kena'an [*Lowered*]"~of At.that.time in~the~Land

the place of "Shekhem [*Shoulder*]", as far as the great tree of "Moreh [*Teacher*]" and the one of "Kena'an [*Lowered*]" was at that time in the land,

**12:7** וַיֵּרָא יְהוָה אֶל אַבְרָם וַיֹּאמֶר לְזַרְעֲךָ אֶתֵּן אֶת הָאָרֶץ הַזֹּאת וַיִּבֶן שָׁם מִזְבֵּחַ לַיהוָה הַנִּרְאֶה אֵלָיו

and~he~will~be~See "YHWH [*He exists*]" To "Avram [*Father raised*]" and~he~will~Say to~Seed~you(ms) i~ will~Give At the~Land the~This and~he~will~Build There Altar to~ "YHWH [*He exists*]" the~be~See~ ing(ms) To~him

and "YHWH [*He exists*]" appeared to "Avram [*Father raised*]" and said, to your seed I will give this land, and he built there an altar to "YHWH [*He exists*]" the one appearing to him,

**12:8\*** וַיַּעְתֵּק מִשָּׁם הָהָרָה מִקֶּדֶם לְבֵית אֵל וַיֵּט אָהֳלֹה בֵּית אֵל מִיָּם וְהָעַי מִקֶּדֶם וַיִּבֶן שָׁם מִזְבֵּחַ לַיהוָה וַיִּקְרָא בְּשֵׁם יְהוָה

and~he~will~Advance from~There the~ Hill~unto from~East to~"Beyt-El [*House of El*]" and~he~will~Stretch Tent~her "Beyt-El [*House of El*]" from~Sea and~the~"Ay [*Heap of ruins*]" from~East and~he~will~Build There Altar to~"YHWH [*He exists*]" and~he~will~Call.out in~Title "YHWH [*He exists*]"

and he advanced from there unto the hill, from the east to "Beyt-El [*House of El*]" and he stretched her tent, "Beyt-El [*House of El*]" was from the sea and "Ay [*Heap of ruins*]" was from the east and he built there an altar to "YHWH [*He exists*]" and he called out in the title of "YHWH [*He exists*]",

**12:9** וַיִּסַּע אַבְרָם הָלוֹךְ וְנָסוֹעַ הַנֶּגְבָּה

and~he~will~Journey "Avram [*Father raised*]" >~Walk and~>~Journey the~ South.country~unto

and "Avram [*Father raised*]" journeyed, walking and journeying unto the south country,

**12:10** וַיְהִי רָעָב בָּאָרֶץ וַיֵּרֶד אַבְרָם מִצְרַיְמָה לָגוּר שָׁם כִּי כָבֵד הָרָעָב בָּאָרֶץ

and~he~will~Exist Hunger in~the~Land and~he~will~Go.down "Avram [*Father raised*]" "Mitsrayim [*Troubles*]"~unto to~>~Sojourn There Given.that Heavy the~Hunger in~the~Land

and a hunger existed in the land and "Avram [*Father raised*]" went down unto "Mitsrayim [*Troubles*]" to sojourn there given that the hunger was heavy in the land,

**12:11** וַיְהִי כַּאֲשֶׁר הִקְרִיב לָבוֹא מִצְרָיְמָה וַיֹּאמֶר אֶל שָׂרַי אִשְׁתּוֹ הִנֵּה נָא יָדַעְתִּי כִּי אִשָּׁה יְפַת מַרְאֶה אָתְּ

and~he~will~Exist like~Which he~did~ make~Come.near to~>~Come "Mitsrayim [*Troubles*]"~unto and~he~

and it came to pass just as he come near to come unto "Mitsrayim [*Troubles*]" and he said to "Sarai

will~Say To "Sarai [*Princess*]"
Woman~him Look Please i~did~Know
Given.that Woman Beautiful
Appearance You(fs)

[*Princess*]" his woman, please look,
I know that you are a woman of
beautiful appearance,

**12:12** וְהָיָה כִּי יִרְאוּ אֹתָךְ הַמִּצְרִים וְאָמְרוּ אִשְׁתּוֹ זֹאת וְהָרְגוּ אֹתִי וְאֹתָךְ יְחַיּוּ

and~he~did~Exist Given.that they(m)~
will~See At~you(fs) the~"Mitsrayim
[*Troubles*]"~s and~they~did~Say
Woman~him This and~they~did~Kill
At~me and~At~you(fs) they(m)~will~
much~Live

and it will come to pass that the
ones of "Mitsrayim [*Troubles*]"
will see you and they will say this
is his woman and they will kill me
and they will keep you alive,

**12:13** אִמְרִי נָא אֲחֹתִי אָתְּ לְמַעַן יִיטַב לִי בַעֲבוּרֵךְ וְחָיְתָה נַפְשִׁי בִּגְלָלֵךְ

!(fs)~Say Please Sister~me You(fs)
to~That he~will~Do.well to~me in~
On.account.of~you(fs) and~she~did~Live
Being~me in~Account.of~you(fs)

please say you are my sister so that
it will go well for me so that you
and my being will live on account
of you,

**12:14** וַיְהִי כְּבוֹא אַבְרָם מִצְרָיְמָה וַיִּרְאוּ הַמִּצְרִים אֶת הָאִשָּׁה כִּי יָפָה הִוא מְאֹד

and~he~will~Exist like~>~Come
"Avram [*Father raised*]" "Mitsrayim
[*Troubles*]"~unto and~they(m)~will~See
the~"Mitsrayim [*Troubles*]"~s At the~
Woman Given.that Beautiful She
Many

and it came to pass as "Avram
[*Father raised*]" was coming unto
"Mitsrayim [*Troubles*]" and the
ones of "Mitsrayim [*Troubles*]"
saw the woman given that she was
much beautiful,

**12:15*** וַיִּרְאוּ אֹתָהּ שָׂרֵי פַרְעֹה וַיְהַלְלוּ אֹתָהּ אֶל פַּרְעֹה וַתֻּקַּח הָאִשָּׁה בֵּית פַּרְעֹה

and~they(m)~will~See At~her Noble~s
"Paroh [*Great house*]" and~they(m)~
will~much~Shine At~her To "Paroh
[*Great house*]" and~Take~ed(fs) the~
Woman House "Paroh [*Great house*]"

and the nobles of "Paroh [*Great
house*]" saw her and they
commended her to "Paroh [*Great
house*]" and took the woman to the
house of "Paroh [*Great house*]",

**12:16** וּלְאַבְרָם הֵיטִיב בַּעֲבוּרָהּ וַיְהִי לוֹ צֹאן וּבָקָר וַחֲמֹרִים וַעֲבָדִים וּשְׁפָחֹת וַאֲתֹנֹת וּגְמַלִּים

and~to~"Avram [*Father raised*]" he~
did~make~Do.well in~On.account.of~her
and~he~will~Exist to~him Flocks
and~Cattle and~Donkey~s and~
Servant~s and~Maid~s and~She-
donkey~s and~Camel~s

and to "Avram [*Father raised*]" it
was made well on account of her
and flocks existed for him and
cattle and donkeys and servants and
maids and she donkeys and camels,

**12:17** וַיְנַגַּע יְהֹוָה אֶת פַּרְעֹה נְגָעִים גְּדֹלִים וְאֶת בֵּיתוֹ עַל דְּבַר שָׂרַי אֵשֶׁת אַבְרָם

and~he~will~Touch "YHWH [*He exists*]" At "Paroh [*Great house*]" Plague~s Magnificent~s and~At House~him Upon Word "Sarai [*Princess*]" Woman "Avram [*Father raised*]"

and "YHWH [*He exists*]" touched "Paroh [*Great house*]" and his house with great plagues because of "Sarai [*Princess*]" the woman of "Avram [*Father raised*]",

**12:18** וַיִּקְרָא פַרְעֹה לְאַבְרָם וַיֹּאמֶר מַה זֹּאת עָשִׂיתָ לִּי לָמָּה לֹא הִגַּדְתָּ לִּי כִּי אִשְׁתְּךָ הִוא

and~he~will~Call.out "Paroh [*Great house*]" to~"Avram [*Father raised*]" and~he~will~Say What This you(ms)~did~Do to~me to~What Not you(ms)~did~make~Be.face.to.face to~me Given.that Woman~you(ms) She

and "Paroh [*Great house*]" called out to "Avram [*Father raised*]" and he said, what is this you did to me, why did you not tell to me that she is your woman,

**12:19** לָמָה אָמַרְתָּ אֲחֹתִי הִוא וָאֶקַּח אֹתָהּ לִי לְאִשָּׁה וְעַתָּה הִנֵּה אִשְׁתְּךָ קַח וָלֵךְ

to~What you(ms)~did~Say Sister~me She and~i~will~Take At~her to~me to~Woman and~Now Look Woman~you(ms) !(ms)~Take and~Walk

why did you say she is my sister and I took her for me for a woman and now look, take your woman and walk,

**12:20** וַיְצַו עָלָיו פַּרְעֹה אֲנָשִׁים וַיְשַׁלְּחוּ אֹתוֹ וְאֶת אִשְׁתּוֹ וְאֶת כָּל אֲשֶׁר לוֹ

and~he~will~much~Direct Upon~him "Paroh [*Great house*]" Man~s and~they(m)~will~much~Send At~him and~At Woman~him and~At All Which to~him

and "Paroh [*Great house*]" directed men upon him and they much sent him and his woman and all of the ones which are to him,

# Chapter 13

**13:1** וַיַּעַל אַבְרָם מִמִּצְרַיִם הוּא וְאִשְׁתּוֹ וְכָל אֲשֶׁר לוֹ וְלוֹט עִמּוֹ הַנֶּגְבָּה

and~he~will~Go.up "Avram [*Father raised*]" from~"Mitsrayim [*Troubles*]" He and~Woman~him and~All Which to~him and~"Loth [*Covering*]" With~him the~South.country~unto

and "Avram [*Father raised*]" went up from "Mitsrayim [*Troubles*]", he and his woman and all of the ones which belonged to him and "Loth [*Covering*]" with him unto the south country,

**13:2** וְאַבְרָם כָּבֵד מְאֹד בַּמִּקְנֶה בַּכֶּסֶף וּבַזָּהָב

and~"Avram [*Father raised*]" Heavy Many in~Livestock in~Silver and~in~Gold

and "Avram [*Father raised*]" was much heavy in livestock, in silver and in gold,

**13:3\*** וַיֵּלֶךְ לְמַסָּעָיו מִנֶּגֶב וְעַד בֵּית אֵל עַד הַמָּקוֹם אֲשֶׁר הָיָה שָׁם אָהֳלֹה בַּתְּחִלָּה בֵּין בֵּית אֵל וּבֵין הָעָי

and~he~will~Walk to~Breaking.camp~s~him from~South.country and~Until "Beyt-El [*House of El*]" Until the~Place Which he~did~Exist There Tent~her in~the~First.time Between "Beyt-El [*House of El*]" and~Between the~"Ay [*Heap of ruins*]"

and he walked to the breaking of his camps from the south country and as far as "Beyt-El [*House of El*]", as far as the place where her tent existed, there in the first time between "Beyt-El [*House of El*]" and the "Ay [*Heap of ruins*]",

**13:4\*** אֶל מְקוֹם הַמִּזְבֵּחַ אֲשֶׁר עָשָׂה שָׁם בָּרִאשֹׁנָה וַיִּקְרָא שָׁם אַבְרָם בְּשֵׁם יְהוָה

To Place the~Altar Which he~did~Do There in~the~First and~he~will~Call.out There "Avram [*Father raised*]" in~Title "YHWH [*He exists*]"

to the place of the altar which he made there in the first and there "Avram [*Father raised*]" called out in the title of "YHWH [*He exists*]",

**13:5** וְגַם לְלוֹט הַהֹלֵךְ אֶת אַבְרָם הָיָה צֹאן וּבָקָר וְאֹהָלִים

and~Also to~"Loth [*Covering*]" the~Walk~ing(ms) At "Avram [*Father raised*]" he~did~Exist Flocks and~Cattle and~Tent~s

and also to "Loth [*Covering*]", the one walking with "Avram [*Father raised*]", existed flocks and cattle and tents,

**13:6** וְלֹא נָשָׂא אֹתָם הָאָרֶץ לָשֶׁבֶת יַחְדָּו כִּי הָיָה רְכוּשָׁם רָב וְלֹא יָכְלוּ לָשֶׁבֶת יַחְדָּו

and~Not he~did~Lift.up At~them(m) the~Land to~>~Settle Together Given.that he~did~Exist Goods~them(m) Abundant and~Not they~did~Be.able to~>~Settle Together

and the land did not lift them up to settle together given that their goods existed abundantly and they were not able to settle together,

**13:7** וַיְהִי רִיב בֵּין רֹעֵי מִקְנֵה אַבְרָם וּבֵין רֹעֵי מִקְנֵה לוֹט וְהַכְּנַעֲנִי וְהַפְּרִזִּי אָז יֹשֵׁב בָּאָרֶץ

and~he~will~Exist Strife Between Feed~ing(mp) Livestock "Avram [*Father raised*]" and~Between Feed~ing(mp) Livestock "Loth [*Covering*]" and~the~"Kena'an [*Lowered*]"~of and~the~"Perez [*Peasant*]"~of At.that.time Settle~ing(ms) in~the~Land

and strife existed between the feeders of the livestock of "Avram [*Father raised*]" and the feeders of the livestock of "Loth [*Covering*]" and the one of "Kena'an [*Lowered*]" and the one of "Perez [*Peasant*]" were at that time settling in the land,

**13:8** וַיֹּאמֶר אַבְרָם אֶל לוֹט אַל נָא תְהִי מְרִיבָה בֵּינִי וּבֵינֶךָ וּבֵין רֹעַי
וּבֵין רֹעֶיךָ כִּי אֲנָשִׁים אַחִים אֲנָחְנוּ

| | |
|---|---|
| and~he~will~Say "Avram [*Father raised*]" To "Loth [*Covering*]" No Please she~will~Exist Contention Between~me and~Between~you(ms) and~Between Feed~ing(mp)~me and~ Between Feed~ing(mp)~you(ms) Given.that Man~s Brother~s We | and "Avram [*Father raised*]" said to "Loth [*Covering*]", please, let not contention exist between me and you and between my feeders and your feeders given that we are men of brothers, |

**13:9** הֲלֹא כָל הָאָרֶץ לְפָנֶיךָ הִפָּרֶד נָא מֵעָלָי אִם הַשְּׂמֹאל וְאֵימִנָה
וְאִם הַיָּמִין וְאַשְׂמְאִילָה

| | |
|---|---|
| ?~Not All the~Land to~Face~s~ you(ms) !(ms)~be~Divide.apart Please from~Upon~me If the~Left.hand and~ i~did~make~Go.Right and~If the~ Right.hand and~i~did~make~Go.left | is not all of the land to your face, please be divided apart from upon me, if the left hand, I will go right and if the right hand, I will go left, |

**13:10** וַיִּשָּׂא לוֹט אֶת עֵינָיו וַיַּרְא אֶת כָּל כִּכַּר הַיַּרְדֵּן כִּי כֻלָּהּ מַשְׁקֶה
לִפְנֵי שַׁחֵת יְהֹוָה אֶת סְדֹם וְאֶת עֲמֹרָה כְּגַן יְהֹוָה כְּאֶרֶץ מִצְרַיִם
בֹּאֲכָה צֹעַר

| | |
|---|---|
| and~he~will~Lift.up "Loth [*Covering*]" At Eye~s2~him and~he~will~See At All Roundness the~"Yarden [*Descender*]" Given.that All~her Drinking to~Face~s >~much~Damage "YHWH [*He exists*]" At "Sedom [*Secret*]" and~At "Ghamorah [*Rebellion*]" like~Garden "YHWH [*He exists*]" like~Land "Mitsrayim [*Troubles*]" >~Come~you(ms)~^ "Tso'ar [*Tiny*]" | and "Loth [*Covering*]" lifted up his eyes and he saw all of the roundness of the "Yarden [*Descender*]" given that all of her was drinking, before much damaging of "YHWH [*He exists*]" at "Sedom [*Secret*]" and at "Ghamorah [*Rebellion*]", like the garden of "YHWH [*He exists*]" and like the land of "Mitsrayim [*Troubles*]" as you come to "Tso'ar [*Tiny*]", |

**13:11** וַיִּבְחַר לוֹ לוֹט אֶת כָּל כִּכַּר הַיַּרְדֵּן וַיִּסַּע לוֹט מִקֶּדֶם וַיִּפָּרְדוּ
אִישׁ מֵעַל אָחִיו

| | |
|---|---|
| and~he~will~Choose to~him "Loth [*Covering*]" At All Roundness the~ "Yarden [*Descender*]" and~he~will~ Lift.up "Loth [*Covering*]" from~East and~they(m)~will~Divide.apart Man from~Upon Brother~him | and "Loth [*Covering*]" chose for him all of the roundness of the "Yarden [*Descender*]" and "Loth [*Covering*]" lifted up from the east and they divided apart, each from upon his brother, |

**13:12** אַבְרָם יָשַׁב בְּאֶרֶץ כְּנָעַן וְלוֹט יָשַׁב בְּעָרֵי הַכִּכָּר וַיֶּאֱהַל עַד סְדֹם

"Avram [*Father raised*]" he~had~
Settle in~Land "Kena'an [*Lowered*]"
and~"Loth [*Covering*]" he~had~Settle
in~City~s the~Roundness and~he~will~
Pitch.tent Until "Sedom [*Secret*]"

"Avram [*Father raised*]" had
settled in the land of "Kena'an
[*Lowered*]" and "Loth [*Covering*]"
had settled in the cities of the
roundness and he pitched the tent as
far as "Sedom [*Secret*]",

**13:13** וְאַנְשֵׁי סְדֹם רָעִים וְחַטָּאִים לַיהֹוָה מְאֹד

and~Man~s "Sedom [*Secret*]"
Dysfunctional~s and~Error~s to~
"YHWH [*He exists*]" Many

and the men of "Sedom [*Secret*]"
were ones of dysfunction and ones
of many errors to "YHWH [*He
exists*]",

**13:14** וַיהֹוָה אָמַר אֶל אַבְרָם אַחֲרֵי הִפָּרֶד לוֹט מֵעִמּוֹ שָׂא נָא עֵינֶיךָ
וּרְאֵה מִן הַמָּקוֹם אֲשֶׁר אַתָּה שָׁם צָפֹנָה וָנֶגְבָּה וָקֵדְמָה וָיָמָּה

and~"YHWH [*He exists*]" he~had~Say
To "Avram [*Father raised*]" After
>~be~Divide.apart "Loth [*Covering*]"
from~With~him !(ms)~Lift.up Please
Eye~s2~you(ms) and~!(ms)~See From
the~Place Which You(ms) There
North~unto and~South.country~unto
and~East~unto and~Sea~unto

and "YHWH [*He exists*]" had said
to "Avram [*Father raised*]" after
"Loth [*Covering*]" was divided
apart from him, please lift up your
eyes and see there from the place
which you are unto the north and
unto the south country and unto the
east and unto the sea,

**13:15** כִּי אֶת כָּל הָאָרֶץ אֲשֶׁר אַתָּה רֹאֶה לְךָ אֶתְּנֶנָּה וּלְזַרְעֲךָ עַד עוֹלָם

Given.that At All the~Land Which
You(ms) See~ing(ms) to~you(ms) i~
will~Give~her and~to~Seed~you(ms)
Until Distant.time

given that all of the land which you
are seeing, to you I will give her
and to your seed as far as a distant
time,

**13:16** וְשַׂמְתִּי אֶת זַרְעֲךָ כַּעֲפַר הָאָרֶץ אֲשֶׁר אִם יוּכַל אִישׁ לִמְנוֹת אֶת
עֲפַר הָאָרֶץ גַּם זַרְעֲךָ יִמָּנֶה

and~i~did~Set.in.place At Seed~
you(ms) like~Powder the~Land Which
If he~will~Be.able Man to~>~Reckon
At Powder the~Land Also Seed~
you(ms) he~will~be~Reckon

and I will set your seed in place like
the powder of the land which if a
man will be able to reckon the
powder of the land also your seed
will be reckoned,

**13:17** קוּם הִתְהַלֵּךְ בָּאָרֶץ לְאָרְכָּהּ וּלְרָחְבָּהּ כִּי לְךָ אֶתְּנֶנָּה

!(ms)~Rise !(ms)~self~Walk in~the~
Land to~Length~her and~to~Width~her
Given.that to~you(ms) i~will~Give~her

rise and walk yourself in the land to
her length and to her width given
that I will give her to you,

**13:18** וַיֶּאֱהַל אַבְרָם וַיָּבֹא וַיֵּשֶׁב בְּאֵלֹנֵי מַמְרֵא אֲשֶׁר בְּחֶבְרוֹן וַיִּבֶן שָׁם
מִזְבֵּחַ לַיהֹוָה

and~he~will~Pitch.tent "Avram [*Father
raised*]" and~he~will~Come and~he~

and "Avram [*Father raised*]"
pitched the tent and he came and he

will~Settle in~Great.tree~s "Mamre [*Bitter place*]" Which in~"Hhevron [*Company*]" and~he~will~Build There Altar to~"YHWH [*He exists*]"

settled in the great trees of "Mamre [*Bitter place*]" which is in "Hhevron [*Company*]" and he built there an altar to "YHWH [*He exists*]",

# Chapter 14

**14:1**

וַיְהִי בִּימֵי אַמְרָפֶל מֶלֶךְ שִׁנְעָר אַרְיוֹךְ מֶלֶךְ אֶלָּסָר כְּדָרְלָעֹמֶר מֶלֶךְ עֵילָם וְתִדְעָל מֶלֶךְ גּוֹיִם

and~he~will~Exist in~Day~s "Amraphel [*Speaker of judgement*]" King "Shinar [*Country of two rivers*]" "Aryokh [*Tall*]" King "Elasar [*El is noble*]" "Kedarla'omer [*Attack for sheaves*]" King "Elam [*Ancient*]" and~"Tidal [*Breaker of the yoke*]" King "Goyim [*Nations*]"

and it came to pass in the days of "Amraphel [*Speaker of judgement*]" king of "Shinar [*Country of two rivers*]", "Aryokh [*Tall*]" king of "Elasar [*El is noble*]", "Kedarla'omer [*Attack for sheaves*]" king of "Elam [*Ancient*]" and "Tidal [*Breaker of the yoke*]" king of "Goyim [*Nations*]",

**14:2**

עָשׂוּ מִלְחָמָה אֶת בֶּרַע מֶלֶךְ סְדֹם וְאֶת בִּרְשַׁע מֶלֶךְ עֲמֹרָה שִׁנְאָב מֶלֶךְ אַדְמָה וְשֶׁמְאֵבֶר מֶלֶךְ צְבֹיִים וּמֶלֶךְ בֶּלַע הִיא צֹעַר

they~did~Do Battle At "Bera [*With dysfunction*]" King "Sedom [*Secret*]" and~At "Birsha [*With wickedness*]" King "Ghamorah [*Rebellion*]" "Shinav [*Teeth of father*]" King "Admah [*Red ground*]" and~"Shemever [*Character of wing*]" King "Tseviim [*Gazzells*]" and~King "Bela [*Swallow*]" She "Tso'ar [*Tiny*]"

they did battle with "Bera [*With dysfunction*]" king of "Sedom [*Secret*]" and with "Birsha [*With wickedness*]" king of "Ghamorah [*Rebellion*]", "Shinav [*Teeth of father*]" king of "Admah [*Red ground*]" and "Shemever [*Character of wing*]" king of "Tseviim [*Gazzells*]" and the king of "Bela [*Swallow*]", she is "Tso'ar [*Tiny*]",

**14:3**

כָּל אֵלֶּה חָבְרוּ אֶל עֵמֶק הַשִּׂדִּים הוּא יָם הַמֶּלַח

All These they~did~Couple To Valley the~"Sidim [*Fields*]" He Sea the~Salt

All of these coupled to the valley of the "Sidim [*Fields*]", he is the sea of the salt,

**14:4**

שְׁתֵּים עֶשְׂרֵה שָׁנָה עָבְדוּ אֶת כְּדָרְלָעֹמֶר וּשְׁלֹשׁ עֶשְׂרֵה שָׁנָה מָרָדוּ

Two Ten Year they~did~Serve At "Kedarla'omer [*Attack for sheaves*]" and~Three Ten Year they~did~Rebel

twelve years they served "Kedarla'omer [*Attack for sheaves*]" and the thirteenth year they rebelled,

**14:5** וּבְאַרְבַּע עֶשְׂרֵה שָׁנָה בָּא כְדָרְלָעֹמֶר וְהַמְּלָכִים אֲשֶׁר אִתּוֹ וַיַּכּוּ אֶת רְפָאִים בְּעַשְׁתְּרֹת קַרְנַיִם וְאֶת הַזּוּזִים בְּהָם וְאֵת הָאֵימִים בְּשָׁוֵה קִרְיָתָיִם

and~in~Four Ten Year he~did~Come "Kedarla'omer [Attack for sheaves]" and~the~King~s Which At~him and~they(m)~will~Hit At "Rapha [Heal]"~s in~"Ashterot-Qaraniym [Growths of two horns]" and~At the~"Zuz [Creature]"~s in~"Ham [Roar]" and~At the~"Eym [Terror]"~s in~"Shaweh-Qiryatayim [Plain of cities]"

and in the fourteenth year "Kedarla'omer [Attack for sheaves]" came and the kings which were with him and they hit the ones of "Rapha [Heal]" in "Ashterot-Qaraniym [Growths of two horns]" and the ones of "Zuz [Creature]" in "Ham [Roar]" and the ones of "Eym [Terror]" in "Shaweh-Qiryatayim [Plain of cities]",

**14:6** וְאֶת הַחֹרִי בְּהַרְרָם שֵׂעִיר עַד אֵיל פָּארָן אֲשֶׁר עַל הַמִּדְבָּר

and~At the~"Hhor [Cave Dweller]"~of in~Mount~them(m) "Se'iyr [Hairy]" Until "Eyl-Paran [Post of decoration]" Which Upon the~Wilderness

and the one of "Hhor [Cave dweller]" in their mount of "Se'iyr [Hairy]" as far as "Eyl-Paran [Post of decoration]" which is upon the wilderness,

**14:7** וַיָּשֻׁבוּ וַיָּבֹאוּ אֶל עֵין מִשְׁפָּט הִוא קָדֵשׁ וַיַּכּוּ אֶת כָּל שְׂדֵה הָעֲמָלֵקִי וְגַם אֶת הָאֱמֹרִי הַיֹּשֵׁב בְּחַצְצֹן תָּמָר

and~they(m)~will~Turn.back and~they(m)~will~Come To "Eyn-Mishpat [Eye of judgement]" He "Kadesh [Set apart]" and~they(m)~will~make~Hit At All Field the~"Amaleq [People gathered]"~of and~Also At "Emor [Sayer]"~of the~Settle~ing(ms) in~"Hhats'tson-Tamar [Dividing the palm tree]"

and they turned back and they came to "Eyn-Mishpat [Eye of judgement]", he is "Kadesh [Set apart]", and they hit all of the field of the one of "Amaleq [People gathered]" and also the one of "Emor [Sayer]" settling in "Hhats'tson-Tamar [Dividing the palm tree]",

**14:8** וַיֵּצֵא מֶלֶךְ סְדֹם וּמֶלֶךְ עֲמֹרָה וּמֶלֶךְ אַדְמָה וּמֶלֶךְ צְבֹיִים וּמֶלֶךְ בֶּלַע הִוא צֹעַר וַיַּעַרְכוּ אִתָּם מִלְחָמָה בְּעֵמֶק הַשִּׂדִּים

and~he~will~Go.out King "Sedom [Secret]" and~King "Ghamorah [Rebellion]" and~King "Admah [Red ground]" and~King "Tseviim [Gazzells]" and~King "Bela [Swallow]" She "Tso'ar [Tiny]" and~they(m)~will~Arrange At~them(m) Battle in~Valley the~"Sidim [Fields]"

and the king of "Sedom [Secret]" went out and the king of "Ghamorah [Rebellion]" and the king of "Admah [Red ground]" and the king of "Tseviim [Gazzells]" and the king of "Bela [Swallow]", she is "Tso'ar [Tiny]", and they arranged with them a battle in the valley of "Sidim [*Fields*]",

**14:9** אֵת כְּדָרְלָעֹמֶר מֶלֶךְ עֵילָם וְתִדְעָל מֶלֶךְ גּוֹיִם וְאַמְרָפֶל מֶלֶךְ שִׁנְעָר וְאַרְיוֹךְ מֶלֶךְ אֶלָּסָר אַרְבָּעָה מְלָכִים אֶת הַחֲמִשָּׁה

At "Kedarla'omer [*Attack for sheaves*]" King "Elam [*Ancient*]" and~"Tidal [*Breaker of the yoke*]" King "Goyim [*Nations*]" and~ "Amraphel [*Speaker of judgement*]" King "Shinar [*Country of two rivers*]" and~"Aryokh [*Tall*]" King "Elasar [*El is noble*]" Four King~s At the~Five

with "Kedarla'omer [*Attack for sheaves*]" the king of "Elam [*Ancient*]" and "Tidal [*Breaker of the yoke*]" the king of "Goyim [*Nations*]" and "Amraphel [*Speaker of judgement*]" the king of "Shinar [*Country of two rivers*]" and "Aryokh [*Tall*]" the king of "Elasar [*El is noble*]", four kings with the five,

**14:10** וְעֵמֶק הַשִּׂדִּים בֶּאֱרֹת בֶּאֱרֹת חֵמָר וַיָּנֻסוּ מֶלֶךְ סְדֹם וַעֲמֹרָה וַיִּפְּלוּ שָׁמָּה וְהַנִּשְׁאָרִים הֶרָה נָּסוּ

and~Valley the~"Sidim [*Fields*]" Well~s Well~s Tar and~they(m)~will~ Flee King "Sedom [*Secret*]" and~ "Ghamorah [*Rebellion*]" and~they(m)~ will~Fall There~unto and~the~be~ Remain~ing(mp) Hill~unto they~did~ Flee

and the valley of "Sidim [*Fields*]" was wells of tar and the king of "Sedom [*Secret*]" and "Ghamorah [*Rebellion*]" fled and they fell unto there and the remaining ones fled unto the hill,

**14:11** וַיִּקְחוּ אֶת כָּל רְכֻשׁ סְדֹם וַעֲמֹרָה וְאֶת כָּל אָכְלָם וַיֵּלֵכוּ

and~they(m)~will~Take At All Goods "Sedom [*Secret*]" and~"Ghamorah [*Rebellion*]" and~At All Foodstuff~ them(m) and~they(m)~will~Walk

and they took all of the goods of "Sedom [*Secret*]" and "Ghamorah [*Rebellion*]" and all of their foodstuff and they walked,

**14:12** וַיִּקְחוּ אֶת לוֹט וְאֶת רְכֻשׁוֹ בֶּן אֲחִי אַבְרָם וַיֵּלֵכוּ וְהוּא יֹשֵׁב בִּסְדֹם

and~they(m)~will~Take At "Loth [*Covering*]" and~At Goods~him Son Brother~of "Avram [*Father raised*]" and~they(m)~will~Walk and~He Settle~ing(ms) in~"Sedom [*Secret*]"

and they took "Loth [*Covering*]", the son of the brother of "Avram [*Father raised*]", and his goods and they walked and he settled in "Sedom [*Secret*]",

**14:13** וַיָּבֹא הַפָּלִיט וַיַּגֵּד לְאַבְרָם הָעִבְרִי וְהוּא שֹׁכֵן בְּאֵלֹנֵי מַמְרֵא הָאֱמֹרִי אֲחִי אֶשְׁכֹּל וַאֲחִי עָנֵר וְהֵם בַּעֲלֵי בְרִית אַבְרָם

and~he~will~Come the~Escaped.one and~he~will~make~Be.face.to.face to~ "Avram [*Father raised*]" the~"Ever [*Cross over*]"~of and~He Dwell~ ing(ms) in~Great.tree~s "Mamre

and the escaped one came and he told to "Avram [*Father raised*]", the one of "Ever [*Cross over*]" and he was dwelling in the great trees of "Mamre [*Bitter place*]" and the one

[*Bitter place*]" the~"Emor [*Sayer*]"~of Brother~of "Eshkol [*Cluster*]" and~ Brother~of "Aner [*Answer*]" and~ They(m) Master~s Covenant "Avram [*Father raised*]"

of "Emor [*Sayer*]", the brother of "Eshkol [*Cluster*]" and the brother of "Aner [*Answer*]" who were the masters of the covenant of "Avram [*Father raised*]",

**14:14** וַיִּשְׁמַע אַבְרָם כִּי נִשְׁבָּה אָחִיו וַיָּרֶק אֶת חֲנִיכָיו יְלִידֵי בֵיתוֹ שְׁמֹנָה עָשָׂר וּשְׁלֹשׁ מֵאוֹת וַיִּרְדֹּף עַד דָּן

and~he~will~Hear "Avram [*Father raised*]" Given.that he~did~be~Capture Brother~him and~he~will~Empty At Experienced~s~him Born~s House~him Eight Ten and~Three Hundred~s and~he~will~Pursue Until "Dan [*Moderator*]"

and "Avram [*Father raised*]" heard that his brother was captured and he emptied his three hundred and eighteen experienced ones born of his house and he pursued as far as "Dan [*Moderator*]",

**14:15** וַיֵּחָלֵק עֲלֵיהֶם לַיְלָה הוּא וַעֲבָדָיו וַיַּכֵּם וַיִּרְדְּפֵם עַד חוֹבָה אֲשֶׁר מִשְּׂמֹאל לְדַמָּשֶׂק

and~he~will~be~Apportion Upon~ them(m) Night He and~Servant~s~him and~he~will~Hit~them(m) and~he~will~ Pursue~them(m) Until "Hhovah [*Hiding place*]" Which from~Left.hand to~"Dameseq [*Blood sack*]"

and he and his servants were apportioned upon them at night and he hit them and he pursued them as far as "Hhovah [*Hiding place*]" which is from the left hand to "Dameseq [*Blood sack*]",

**14:16** וַיָּשֶׁב אֵת כָּל הָרְכֻשׁ וְגַם אֶת לוֹט אָחִיו וּרְכֻשׁוֹ הֵשִׁיב וְגַם אֶת הַנָּשִׁים וְאֶת הָעָם

and~he~will~make~Turn.back At All the~Goods and~Also At "Loth [*Covering*]" Brother~him and~Goods~ him he~had~make~Turn.back and~Also At the~Woman~s and~At the~People

and he returned all of the goods and also "Loth [*Covering*]" his brother and his goods he returned and also the women and the people,

**14:17** וַיֵּצֵא מֶלֶךְ סְדֹם לִקְרָאתוֹ אַחֲרֵי שׁוּבוֹ מֵהַכּוֹת אֶת כְּדָרְלָעֹמֶר וְאֶת הַמְּלָכִים אֲשֶׁר אִתּוֹ אֶל עֵמֶק שָׁוֵה הוּא עֵמֶק הַמֶּלֶךְ

and~he~will~Go.out King "Sedom [*Secret*]" to~>~Meet~him After >~ Turn.back~him from~>~make~Hit At "Kedarla'omer [*Attack for sheaves*]" and~At the~King~s Which At~him To Valley "Shaweh [*Plain*]" He Valley the~King

and the king of "Sedom [*Secret*]" came out to meet him after his turning back from hitting "Kedarla'omer [*Attack for sheaves*]" and the kings which were with him, to the valley of "Shaweh [*Plain*]", he is the valley of the king,

**14:18** וּמַלְכִּי צֶדֶק מֶלֶךְ שָׁלֵם הוֹצִיא לֶחֶם וָיָיִן וְהוּא כֹהֵן לְאֵל עֶלְיוֹן

and~"Malkiy-Tsedeq [*King of*

and "Malkiy-Tsedeq [*King of*

77

righteousness]" King "Shalem [Complete]" he~did~make~Go.out Bread and~Wine and~He Priest To Mighty.one Upper

*righteousness*]" was king of "Shalem [*Complete*]" and he brought out bread and wine and he was priest to the upper mighty one,

**14:19** וַיְבָרְכֵהוּ וַיֹּאמַר בָּרוּךְ אַבְרָם לְאֵל עֶלְיוֹן קֹנֵה שָׁמַיִם וָאָרֶץ

and~he~will~much~Kneel~him and~he~will~Say Kneel~ed(ms) "Avram [*Father raised*]" to~Mighty.one Upper Purchase~ing(ms) Sky~s2 and~Land

and he respected him and he said, respected is "Avram [*Father raised*]" to the upper mighty one, the purchaser of the sky and land,

**14:20** וּבָרוּךְ אֵל עֶלְיוֹן אֲשֶׁר מִגֵּן צָרֶיךָ בְּיָדֶךָ וַיִּתֶּן לוֹ מַעֲשֵׂר מִכֹּל

and~Kneel~ed(ms) Mighty.one Upper Which he~did~much~Deliver.up Narrow~s~you(ms) in~Hand~you(ms) and~he~will~Give to~him Tenth.part from~All

and respected is the upper mighty one who delivered up your narrows in your hand and he gave to him a tenth part from all,

**14:21** וַיֹּאמֶר מֶלֶךְ סְדֹם אֶל אַבְרָם תֶּן לִי הַנֶּפֶשׁ וְהָרְכֻשׁ קַח לָךְ

and~he~will~Say King "Sedom [*Secret*]" To "Avram [*Father raised*]" !(ms)~Give to~me the~Being and~the~Goods !(ms)~Take to~you(fs)

and the king of "Sedom [*Secret*]" said to "Avram [*Father raised*]", give to me the being and the goods take for you,

**14:22** וַיֹּאמֶר אַבְרָם אֶל מֶלֶךְ סְדֹם הֲרִמֹתִי יָדִי אֶל יְהֹוָה אֵל עֶלְיוֹן קֹנֵה שָׁמַיִם וָאָרֶץ

and~he~will~Say "Avram [*Father raised*]" To King "Sedom [*Secret*]" i~did~make~Raise Hand~me To "YHWH [*He exists*]" Mighty.one Upper Purchase~ing(ms) Sky~s2 and~Land

and "Avram [*Father raised*]" said to the king of "Sedom [*Secret*]", I made my hand rise to "YHWH [*He exists*]" the upper mighty one, purchaser of the sky and land,

**14:23\*** אִם מִחוּט וְעַד שְׂרוֹךְ נַעַל וְאִם אֶקַּח מִכָּל אֲשֶׁר לָךְ וְלֹא תֹאמַר אֲנִי הֶעֱשַׁרְתִּי אֶת אַבְרָם

If from~Thread and~Until Lace Sandal and~If i~will~Take from~All Which to~you(fs) and~Not you(ms)~will~Say I i~did~make~Be.rich At "Avram [*Father raised*]"

if not from a thread and also not a lace of a sandal and if I do not take from all of the ones which are yours then you will not say, I made "Avram [*Father raised*]" be rich,

**14:24** בִּלְעָדַי רַק אֲשֶׁר אָכְלוּ הַנְּעָרִים וְחֵלֶק הָאֲנָשִׁים אֲשֶׁר הָלְכוּ אִתִּי עָנֵר אֶשְׁכֹּל וּמַמְרֵא הֵם יִקְחוּ חֶלְקָם

Apart.from~me Only Which they~did~Eat the~Young.man~s and~Portion the~Man~s Which they~did~Walk At~me "Aner [*Answer*]" "Eshkol

apart from me only which the young men ate and the portion of the men which walked with me, "Aner [*Answer*]", "Eshkol

[*Cluster*]" and~"Mamre [*Bitter place*]"
They(m) they(m)~will~Take Portion~
them(m)

[*Cluster*]" and "Mamre [*Bitter place*]", they will take their portion,

# Chapter 15

**15:1** אַחַר הַדְּבָרִים הָאֵלֶּה הָיָה דְבַר יְהֹוָה אֶל אַבְרָם בַּמַּחֲזֶה לֵאמֹר אַל תִּירָא אַבְרָם אָנֹכִי מָגֵן לָךְ שְׂכָרְךָ הַרְבֵּה מְאֹד

After the~Word~s the~These he~did~
Exist Word "YHWH [*He exists*]"
To "Avram [*Father raised*]" in~the~
Vision to~>~Say No you(ms)~will~
Fear "Avram [*Father raised*]" I
Shield to~you(fs) Wage~you(ms) >~
make~Increase Many

after these words, the word of "YHWH [*He exists*]", existed for "Avram [*Father raised*]" in the vision saying, "Avram [*Father raised*]" you will not fear, I am your shield, your wages will be made to increase greatly,

**15:2\*** וַיֹּאמֶר אַבְרָם אֲדֹנָי יְהוִה מַה תִּתֶּן לִי וְאָנֹכִי הוֹלֵךְ עֲרִירִי וּבֶן מֶשֶׁק בֵּיתִי הוּא דַּמֶּשֶׂק אֱלִיעֶזֶר

and~he~will~Say "Avram [*Father raised*]" "Adonai [*My lords*]"
"YHWH [*He exists*]" What you(ms)~
will~Give to~me and~I Walk~ing(ms)
Barren and~Son Acquisition House~
me He "Dameseq [*Blood sack*]"
"Eliezer [*My El is a helper*]"

and "Avram [*Father raised*]" said, "Adonai [*My lords*]" of "YHWH [*He exists*]" what will you give to me that I am walking barren and the son of acquisition of my house is "Eliezer [*My El is a helper*]" of "Dameseq [*Blood sack*]",

**15:3** וַיֹּאמֶר אַבְרָם הֵן לִי לֹא נָתַתָּה זָרַע וְהִנֵּה בֶן בֵּיתִי יוֹרֵשׁ אֹתִי

and~he~will~Say "Avram [*Father raised*]" Though to~me Not
you(ms)~did~Give Seed and~Look
Son House~me Inherit~ing(ms) At~me

and "Avram [*Father raised*]" said, though you did not give me seed and look, a son of my house is inheriting me,

**15:4** וְהִנֵּה דְבַר יְהֹוָה אֵלָיו לֵאמֹר לֹא יִירָשְׁךָ זֶה כִּי אִם אֲשֶׁר יֵצֵא מִמֵּעֶיךָ הוּא יִירָשֶׁךָ

and~Look Word "YHWH [*He exists*]" To~him to~>~Say Not he~
will~Inherit~you(ms) This Given.that
If Which he~will~Go.out from~
Abdomen~s~you(ms) He he~will~
Inherit~you(ms)

and look, the word of "YHWH [*He exists*]" was to him saying, this will not inherit you except he which will go out from your abdomens, he will inherit you,

**15:5** וַיּוֹצֵא אֹתוֹ הַחוּצָה וַיֹּאמֶר הַבֶּט נָא הַשָּׁמַיְמָה וּסְפֹר הַכּוֹכָבִים אִם תּוּכַל לִסְפֹּר אֹתָם וַיֹּאמֶר לוֹ כֹּה יִהְיֶה זַרְעֶךָ

and~he~will~make~Go.out At~him the~

and he brought him out unto the

Outside~unto and~he~will~Say !(mp)~make~Stare Please the~Sky~s2~unto and~!(ms)~Count the~Star~s If you(ms)~will~Be.able to~>~Count At~them(m) and~he~will~Say to~him In.this.way he~will~Exist Seed~you(ms)

outside and he said, please stare unto the sky and count the stars if you are able to count them and he said to him, in this way your seed will exist,

**15:6**

וְהֶאֱמִן בַּיהוָה וַיַּחְשְׁבֶהָ לּוֹ צְדָקָה

and~he~will~make~Firm in~"YHWH [*He exists*]" and~he~will~Think~her to~him Correctness

and he was made firm in "YHWH [*He exists*]" and he thought correctness for him,

**15:7** וַיֹּאמֶר אֵלָיו אֲנִי יְהוָה אֲשֶׁר הוֹצֵאתִיךָ מֵאוּר כַּשְׂדִּים לָתֶת לְךָ אֶת הָאָרֶץ הַזֹּאת לְרִשְׁתָּהּ

and~he~will~Say To~him I "YHWH [*He exists*]" Which i~did~make~Go.out~you(ms) from~"Ur [*Light*]" "Kesad [*Clod breaker*]"~s to~>~Give to~you(ms) At the~Land the~This to~>~Inherit~her

and he said to him, I am "YHWH [*He exists*]" who brought you out from "Ur [*Light*]" of the ones of "Kesad [*Clod breaker*]" to give to you this land to inherit her,

**15:8** וַיֹּאמַר אֲדֹנָי יְהוִה בַּמָּה אֵדַע כִּי אִירָשֶׁנָּה

and~he~will~Say "Adonai [*My lords*]" "YHWH [*He exists*]" in~What i~will~Know Given.that i~will~Inherit~her

and he said, "Adonai [*My lords*]" of "YHWH [*He exists*]" how will I know that I will inherit her,

**15:9** וַיֹּאמֶר אֵלָיו קְחָה לִי עֶגְלָה מְשֻׁלֶּשֶׁת וְעֵז מְשֻׁלֶּשֶׁת וְאַיִל מְשֻׁלָּשׁ וְתֹר וְגוֹזָל

and~he~will~Say To~him !(ms)~Take to~me Heifer much~Be.threefold~ing(fs) and~She-goat much~Be.threefold~ing(fs) and~Strong.One much~Be.threefold~ing(ms) and~Turtledove and~Young.pigeon

and he said to him, take for me a heifer being threefold and a she-goat being a threefold and a strong one being a threefold and a turtledove and a young pigeon,

**15:10** וַיִּקַּח לוֹ אֶת כָּל אֵלֶּה וַיְבַתֵּר אֹתָם בַּתָּוֶךְ וַיִּתֵּן אִישׁ בִּתְרוֹ לִקְרַאת רֵעֵהוּ וְאֶת הַצִּפֹּר לֹא בָתָר

and~he~will~Take to~him At All These and~he~will~Cut.in.two At~them(m) in~the~Midst and~he~will~Give Man Cut.piece~him to~>~Meet Companion~him and~At the~Bird Not he~did~Cut.in.two

and he took to him all these and he cut them in two in the middle and he gave each cut piece to meet his companion and the bird he did not cut in two,

**15:11** וַיֵּרֶד הָעַיִט עַל הַפְּגָרִים וַיַּשֵּׁב אֹתָם אַבְרָם

and~he~will~Go.down the~Bird.of.prey

and the bird of prey went down

Upon the~Carcass~s and~he~will~make~Gust At~them(m) "Avram [*Father raised*]"

upon the carcasses and "Avram [*Father raised*]" made a gust at them,

**15:12** וַיְהִי הַשֶּׁמֶשׁ לָבוֹא וְתַרְדֵּמָה נָפְלָה עַל אַבְרָם וְהִנֵּה אֵימָה חֲשֵׁכָה גְדֹלָה נֹפֶלֶת עָלָיו

and~he~will~Exist the~Sun to~>~Come Trance she~had~Fall Upon "Avram [*Father raised*]" and~Look Terror Dark Magnificent Fall~ing(fs) Upon~him

and the sun existed to come, a trance had fallen upon "Avram [*Father raised*]" and look, a terror of a magnificent darkness was falling upon him,

**15:13** וַיֹּאמֶר לְאַבְרָם יָדֹעַ תֵּדַע כִּי גֵר יִהְיֶה זַרְעֲךָ בְּאֶרֶץ לֹא לָהֶם וַעֲבָדוּם וְעִנּוּ אֹתָם אַרְבַּע מֵאוֹת שָׁנָה

and~he~will~Say to~"Avram [*Father raised*]" >~Know you(ms)~will~Know Given.that Stranger he~will~Exist Seed~you(ms) in~Land Not to~them(m) and~they~did~Serve~them(m) and~they~did~much~Afflict At~them(m) Four Hundred~s Year

and he said to "Avram [*Father raised*]", you will surely know that your seed will exist as a stranger in a land not for them and they will serve them and they will much afflict them four hundred years,

**15:14** וְגַם אֶת הַגּוֹי אֲשֶׁר יַעֲבֹדוּ דָּן אָנֹכִי וְאַחֲרֵי כֵן יֵצְאוּ בִּרְכֻשׁ גָּדוֹל

and~Also At the~Nation Which they(m)~will~Serve Moderate~ing(ms) I and~After So they(m)~will~Go.out in~Goods Magnificent

and also the nation which they will serve, I am moderating, and afterward they will go out with magnificent goods,

**15:15** וְאַתָּה תָּבוֹא אֶל אֲבֹתֶיךָ בְּשָׁלוֹם תִּקָּבֵר בְּשֵׂיבָה טוֹבָה

and~You(ms) you(ms)~will~Come To Father~s~you(ms) in~Completeness you(ms)~will~be~Bury in~Gray.headed Functional

and you will come to your fathers in completeness, you will be buried with a functional gray head,

**15:16** וְדוֹר רְבִיעִי יָשׁוּבוּ הֵנָּה כִּי לֹא שָׁלֵם עֲוֹן הָאֱמֹרִי עַד הֵנָּה

and~Generation Fourth they(m)~will~Turn.back Thus.far Given.that Not Complete Iniquity the~"Emor [*Sayer*]"~of Until Thus.far

and the fourth generation will turn back thus far given that the iniquity of the one of "Emor [*Sayer*]" is not yet complete,

**15:17** וַיְהִי הַשֶּׁמֶשׁ בָּאָה וַעֲלָטָה הָיָה וְהִנֵּה תַנּוּר עָשָׁן וְלַפִּיד אֵשׁ אֲשֶׁר עָבַר בֵּין הַגְּזָרִים הָאֵלֶּה

and~he~will~Exist the~Sun she~did~Come and~Twilight he~did~Exist and~Look Oven Smoke and~Torch Fire Which he~did~Cross.over Between the~Divided.part~s the~These

and it came to pass, the sun came and he was twilight and look, an oven of smoke and a torch of fire which crossed over between these divided parts,

**81**

**15:18**  בַּיּוֹם הַהוּא כָּרַת יְהוָה אֶת אַבְרָם בְּרִית לֵאמֹר לְזַרְעֲךָ נָתַתִּי אֶת הָאָרֶץ הַזֹּאת מִנְּהַר מִצְרַיִם עַד הַנָּהָר הַגָּדֹל נְהַר פְּרָת

in~the~Day the~He he~did~Cut "YHWH [*He exists*]" At "Avram [*Father raised*]" Covenant to~>~Say to~Seed~you(ms) i~will~Give At the~Land the~This from~River from~ "Mitsrayim [*Troubles*]" Until the~River the~Magnificent River "Perat [*Break*]"

in that day "YHWH [*He exists*]" cut with "Avram [*Father raised*]" a covenant saying, to your seed I will give this land from the river of "Mitsrayim [*Troubles*]" as far as the magnificent river, the river "Perat [*Break*]",

**15:19**  אֶת הַקֵּינִי וְאֶת הַקְּנִזִּי וְאֵת הַקַּדְמֹנִי

At the~"Qayin [*Acquired*]"~of and~At "Qeniz [*Hunter*]"~of and~At the~ "Qadmon [*Ancient one*]"~of

the one of "Qayin [*Acquired*]" and the one of "Qeniz [*Hunter*]" and the one of "Qadmon [*Ancient one*]",

**15:20**  וְאֶת הַחִתִּי וְאֶת הַפְּרִזִּי וְאֶת הָרְפָאִים

and~At the~"Hhet [*Shattered*]"~of and~At the~"Perez [*Peasant*]"~of and~At the~"Rapha [*Heal*]"~s

and the one of "Hhet [*Shattered*]" and the one of "Perez [*Peasant*]" and the one of "Rapha [*Heal*]",

**15:21**  וְאֶת הָאֱמֹרִי וְאֶת הַכְּנַעֲנִי וְאֶת הַגִּרְגָּשִׁי וְאֶת הַיְבוּסִי

and~At the~"Emor [*Sayer*]"~of and~At the~"Kena'an [*Lowered*]"~of and~At the~"Girgash [*Stranger on clods*]"~of and~At the~"Yevus [*He threshes*]"~of

and the one of "Emor [*Sayer*]" and the one of "Kena'an [*Lowered*]" and the one of "Girgash [*Stranger on clods*]" and the one of "Yevus [*He threshes*]",

# Chapter 16

**16:1**  וְשָׂרַי אֵשֶׁת אַבְרָם לֹא יָלְדָה לוֹ וְלָהּ שִׁפְחָה מִצְרִית וּשְׁמָהּ הָגָר

and~"Sarai [*Princess*]" Woman "Avram [*Father raised*]" Not she~did~Bring.forth to~him and~to~her Maid "Mitsrayim [*Troubles*]"~s and~Title~her "Hagar [*Stranger*]"

and "Sarai [*Princess*]", the woman of "Avram [*Father raised*]", did not bring forth for him and to her was a maid of "Mitsrayim [*Troubles*]" and her title was "Hagar [*Stranger*]",

**16:2**  וַתֹּאמֶר שָׂרַי אֶל אַבְרָם הִנֵּה נָא עֲצָרַנִי יְהוָה מִלֶּדֶת בֹּא נָא אֶל שִׁפְחָתִי אוּלַי אִבָּנֶה מִמֶּנָּה וַיִּשְׁמַע אַבְרָם לְקוֹל שָׂרָי

and~she~will~Say "Sarai [*Princess*]" To "Avram [*Father raised*]" Look Please he~did~Stop~me "YHWH [*He exists*]" from~>~Bring.forth !(ms)~

and "Sarai [*Princess*]" said to "Avram [*Father raised*]", please look, "YHWH [*He exists*]" stopped me from bringing forth, please

Come Please To Maid~me Possibly i~will~Build From~her and~he~will~Hear "Avram [*Father raised*]" to~Voice "Sarai [*Princess*]"

come to my maid possibly I will build from her and "Avram [*Father raised*]" heard the voice of "Sarai [*Princess*]",

**16:3** וַתִּקַּח שָׂרַי אֵשֶׁת אַבְרָם אֶת הָגָר הַמִּצְרִית שִׁפְחָתָהּ מִקֵּץ עֶשֶׂר שָׁנִים לְשֶׁבֶת אַבְרָם בְּאֶרֶץ כְּנָעַן וַתִּתֵּן אֹתָהּ לְאַבְרָם אִישָׁהּ לוֹ לְאִשָּׁה

and~she~will~Take "Sarai [*Princess*]" Woman "Avram [*Father raised*]" At "Hagar [*Stranger*]" the~"Mitsrayim [*Troubles*]"~of Maid~her from~Conclusion Ten Year~s to~>~Settle "Avram [*Father raised*]" in~Land "Kena'an [*Lowered*]" and~she~will~Give At~her to~"Avram [*Father raised*]" Man~her to~him to~Woman

and "Sarai [*Princess*]", the woman of "Avram [*Father raised*]", took "Hagar [*Stranger*]", the of "Mitsrayim [*Troubles*]", her maid, from the conclusion of ten years for the settling of "Avram [*Father raised*]" in the land of "Kena'an [*Lowered*]" and she gave her to "Avram [*Father raised*]", her man, for him for a woman,

**16:4** וַיָּבֹא אֶל הָגָר וַתַּהַר וַתֵּרֶא כִּי הָרָתָה וַתֵּקַל גְּבִרְתָּהּ בְּעֵינֶיהָ

and~he~will~Come To "Hagar [*Stranger*]" and~she~will~Conceive and~she~will~See Given.that she~did~Conceive and~she~will~Be.insubstantial Female.owner~her in~Eye~s2~her

and he came to "Hagar [*Stranger*]" and she conceived and she saw that she conceived and her female owner was insubstantial in her eyes,

**16:5** וַתֹּאמֶר שָׂרַי אֶל אַבְרָם חֲמָסִי עָלֶיךָ אָנֹכִי נָתַתִּי שִׁפְחָתִי בְּחֵיקֶךָ וַתֵּרֶא כִּי הָרָתָה וָאֵקַל בְּעֵינֶיהָ יִשְׁפֹּט יְהוָה בֵּינִי וּבֵינֶיךָ

and~she~will~Say "Sarai [*Princess*]" To "Avram [*Father raised*]" Violence~me Upon~you(ms) I i~did~Give Maid~me in~Bosom~you(ms) and~she~will~See Given.that she~did~Conceive and~i~will~Be.insubstantial in~Eye~s2~her he~will~Judge "YHWH [*He exists*]" Between~me and~Between~you(ms)

and "Sarai [*Princess*]" said to "Avram [*Father raised*]", my violence is upon you, I gave my maid in your bosom and she saw that she conceived and I am insubstantial in her eyes, "YHWH [*He exists*]" will judge between me and you,

**16:6** וַיֹּאמֶר אַבְרָם אֶל שָׂרַי הִנֵּה שִׁפְחָתֵךְ בְּיָדֵךְ עֲשִׂי לָהּ הַטּוֹב בְּעֵינָיִךְ וַתְּעַנֶּהָ שָׂרַי וַתִּבְרַח מִפָּנֶיהָ

and~he~will~Say "Avram [*Father raised*]" To "Sarai [*Princess*]" Look Maid~you(fs) in~Hand~you(fs) !(ms)~Do to~her the~Functional in~Eye~s2~you(fs) and~she~will~Afflict~her "Sarai [*Princess*]" and~she~will~Flee.away

and "Avram [*Father raised*]" said to "Sarai [*Princess*]", look, your maid is in your hand do to her the functional thing in your eyes and "Sarai [*Princess*]" afflicted her and she fled from her face, from~Face~s~her

**16:7** וַיִּמְצָאָהּ מַלְאַךְ יְהוָה עַל עֵין הַמַּיִם בַּמִּדְבָּר עַל הָעַיִן בְּדֶרֶךְ שׁוּר

and~he~will~Find~her Messenger "YHWH [*He exists*]" Upon Eye the~Water~s2 in~Wilderness Upon the~Eye in~Road "Shur [*Caravan*]"

and the messenger of "YHWH [*He exists*]" found her upon the eye of the water in the wilderness upon the eye in the road of "Shur [*Caravan*]",

**16:8** וַיֹּאמַר הָגָר שִׁפְחַת שָׂרַי אֵי מִזֶּה בָאת וְאָנָה תֵלֵכִי וַתֹּאמֶר מִפְּנֵי שָׂרַי גְּבִרְתִּי אָנֹכִי בֹּרַחַת

and~he~will~Say "Hagar [*Stranger*]" Maid "Sarai [*Princess*]" Where from~This you(fs)~did~Come and~ Wherever you(fs)~will~Walk and~she~ will~Say from~Face~s "Sarai [*Princess*]" Female.owner~me I Flee.away~ing(fs)

and he said, "Hagar [*Stranger*]", the maid of "Sarai [*Princess*]", from where did you come and wherever are you walking and she said, from the face of "Sarai [*Princess*]" my female owner I am fleeing away,

**16:9** וַיֹּאמֶר לָהּ מַלְאַךְ יְהוָה שׁוּבִי אֶל גְּבִרְתֵּךְ וְהִתְעַנִּי תַּחַת יָדֶיהָ

and~he~will~Say to~her Messenger "YHWH [*He exists*]" !(fs)~Turn.back To Female.owner~you(fs) and~!(fs)~ self~Afflict Under Hand~s2~her

and the messenger of "YHWH [*He exists*]" said to her, turn back to your female owner and afflict yourself under her hands,

**16:10** וַיֹּאמֶר לָהּ מַלְאַךְ יְהוָה הַרְבָּה אַרְבֶּה אֶת זַרְעֵךְ וְלֹא יִסָּפֵר מֵרֹב

and~he~will~Say to~her Messenger "YHWH [*He exists*]" >~make~ Increase i~will~make~Increase At Seed~you(fs) and~Not he~will~be~ Count from~Abundance

and the messenger of "YHWH [*He exists*]" said to her, I will make your seed an increase of an increase and he will not be counted from an abundance,

**16:11** וַיֹּאמֶר לָהּ מַלְאַךְ יְהוָה הִנָּךְ הָרָה וְיֹלַדְתְּ בֵּן וְקָרָאת שְׁמוֹ יִשְׁמָעֵאל כִּי שָׁמַע יְהוָה אֶל עָנְיֵךְ

and~he~will~Say to~her Messenger "YHWH [*He exists*]" Look~you(fs) Pregnant and~you(fs)~did~Bring.forth Son and~you(fs)~did~Call.out Title~ him "Yishma'el [*El will listen*]" Given.that he~will~Hear "YHWH [*He exists*]" To Affliction~you(fs)

and the messenger of "YHWH [*He exists*]" said to her, look, you are pregnant and you will bring forth a son and you will call out his title "Yishma'el [*El will listen*]" given that "YHWH [*He exists*]" will hear your affliction,

**16:12** וְהוּא יִהְיֶה פֶּרֶא אָדָם יָדוֹ בַכֹּל וְיַד כֹּל בּוֹ וְעַל פְּנֵי כָל אֶחָיו יִשְׁכֹּן

and~He he~will~Exist Wild.ass Human Hand~him in~the~All and~

and he will exist as a wild ass of a human, his hand with all and a hand

Hand All in~him and~Upon Face~s All Brother~s~him he~will~Dwell

of all of the ones with him and upon the face of all of his brothers he will dwell,

**16:13** וַתִּקְרָא שֵׁם יְהוָה הַדֹּבֵר אֵלֶיהָ אַתָּה אֵל רֳאִי כִּי אָמְרָה הֲגַם הֲלֹם רָאִיתִי אַחֲרֵי רֹאִי

and~she~will~Call.out Title "YHWH [He exists]" the~Speak~ing(ms) To~ her You(ms) "El-Ra'iy [El seeing me]" Given.that she~did~Say ?~Also At.this.point i~will~See After See~ ing(ms)~me

and she called out the title of "YHWH [He exists]", the one speaking to her, you are "El-Ra'iy [El seeing me]" given that she said also, at this point will I see after seeing me,

**16:14** עַל כֵּן קָרָא לַבְּאֵר בְּאֵר לַחַי רֹאִי הִנֵּה בֵין קָדֵשׁ וּבֵין בָּרֶד

Upon So he~did~Call.out to~the~Well "Be'er-Lahhiy-Ro'iy [Well for the living seeing me]" Look Between "Kadesh [Set apart]" and~Between "Bered [Hail]"

therefore he called out to the well "Be'er-Lahhiy-Ro'iy [Well for the living seeing me]", look, it is between "Kadesh [Set apart]" and "Bered [Hail]",

**16:15** וַתֵּלֶד הָגָר לְאַבְרָם בֵּן וַיִּקְרָא אַבְרָם שֵׁם בְּנוֹ אֲשֶׁר יָלְדָה הָגָר יִשְׁמָעֵאל

and~she~will~Bring.forth "Hagar [Stranger]" to~"Avram [Father raised]" Son and~he~will~Call.out "Avram [Father raised]" Title Son~ him Which she~did~Bring.forth "Hagar [Stranger]" "Yishma'el [El will listen]"

and "Hagar [Stranger]" brought forth for "Avram [Father raised]" a son and "Avram [Father raised]" called out the title of his son which "Hagar [Stranger]" brought forth "Yishma'el [El will listen]",

**16:16** וְאַבְרָם בֶּן שְׁמֹנִים שָׁנָה וְשֵׁשׁ שָׁנִים בְּלֶדֶת הָגָר אֶת יִשְׁמָעֵאל לְאַבְרָם

and~"Avram [Father raised]" Son Eight~s Year and~Six Year~s in~>~ Bring.forth "Hagar [Stranger]" At "Yishma'el [El will listen]" to~ "Avram [Father raised]"

and "Avram [Father raised]" was a son of eighty six years in the giving birth of "Hagar [Stranger]" to "Yishma'el [El will listen]" for "Avram [Father raised]",

# Chapter 17

**17:1** וַיְהִי אַבְרָם בֶּן תִּשְׁעִים שָׁנָה וְתֵשַׁע שָׁנִים וַיֵּרָא יְהוָה אֶל אַבְרָם וַיֹּאמֶר אֵלָיו אֲנִי אֵל שַׁדַּי הִתְהַלֵּךְ לְפָנַי וֶהְיֵה תָמִים

and~he~will~Exist "Avram [Father raised]" Son Nine~s Year and~Nine

and "Avram [Father raised]" existed a son of ninety nine years

Year~s and~he~will~be~See "YHWH [*He exists*]" To "Avram [*Father raised*]" and~he~will~Say To~him I Mighty.one "Shaddai [*My breasts*]" >~self~Walk to~Face~s~me and~!(ms)~Exist Whole

and "YHWH [*He exists*]" appeared to "Avram [*Father raised*]" and he said to him, I am a mighty one of "Shaddai [*My breasts*]" walk yourself to my face and exist whole,

**17:2** וְאֶתְּנָה בְרִיתִי בֵּינִי וּבֵינֶךָ וְאַרְבֶּה אוֹתְךָ בִּמְאֹד מְאֹד

and~i~will~Give~her Covenant~me Between~me and~Between~you(ms) and~i~will~make~Increase At~you(ms) in~Many Many

and I will give my covenant between me and you and I will make you a very great increase,

**17:3** וַיִּפֹּל אַבְרָם עַל פָּנָיו וַיְדַבֵּר אִתּוֹ אֱלֹהִים לֵאמֹר

and~he~will~Fall "Avram [*Father raised*]" Upon Face~s~him and~he~will~much~Speak At~him "Elohiym [*Powers*]" to~>~Say

and "Avram [*Father raised*]" fell upon his face and "Elohiym [*Powers*]" spoke with him saying,

**17:4** אֲנִי הִנֵּה בְרִיתִי אִתָּךְ וְהָיִיתָ לְאַב הֲמוֹן גּוֹיִם

I Look Covenant~me At~you(ms) and~you(ms)~will~Exist to~Father Multitude Nation~s

look, I am here, my covenant is with you and you will exist for a father of a multitude of nations,

**17:5** וְלֹא יִקָּרֵא עוֹד אֶת שִׁמְךָ אַבְרָם וְהָיָה שִׁמְךָ אַבְרָהָם כִּי אַב הֲמוֹן גּוֹיִם נְתַתִּיךָ

and~Not he~will~be~Call.out Yet.again At Title~you(ms) "Avram [*Father raised*]" and~he~did~Exist Title~you(ms) "Avraham [*Father lifted*]" Given.that Father Multitude Nation~s i~did~Give~you(ms)

and your title will not again be called "Avram [*Father raised*]" and your title will exist as "Avraham [*Father lifted*]" given that a father of a multitude of nations I give you,

**17:6** וְהִפְרֵתִי אֹתְךָ בִּמְאֹד מְאֹד וּנְתַתִּיךָ לְגוֹיִם וּמְלָכִים מִמְּךָ יֵצֵאוּ

and~i~did~make~Reproduce At~you(ms) in~Many Many and~i~did~Give~you(ms) to~Nation~s and~King~s From~you(ms) they(m)~will~Go.out

and I will make you reproduce very greatly and I will give you for nations and kings will go out from you,

**17:7** וַהֲקִמֹתִי אֶת בְּרִיתִי בֵּינִי וּבֵינֶךָ וּבֵין זַרְעֲךָ אַחֲרֶיךָ לְדֹרֹתָם לִבְרִית עוֹלָם לִהְיוֹת לְךָ לֵאלֹהִים וּלְזַרְעֲךָ אַחֲרֶיךָ

and~i~did~make~Rise At Covenant~me Between~me and~Between~you(ms) and~Between Seed~you(ms) After~you(ms) to~Generation~s~them(m) to~Covenant Distant.time to~>~Exist to~you(ms) to~"Elohiym [*Powers*]" and~

and I will make my covenant rise between me and you and your seed after you to their generations for a covenant of a distant time, to exist for you for "Elohiym [*Powers*]" and for your seed after you,

to~Seed~you(ms)   After~you(ms)

**17:8**   וְנָתַתִּי לְךָ וּלְזַרְעֲךָ אַחֲרֶיךָ אֵת אֶרֶץ מְגֻרֶיךָ אֵת כָּל אֶרֶץ כְּנַעַן
לַאֲחֻזַּת עוֹלָם וְהָיִיתִי לָהֶם לֵאלֹהִים

and~i~did~Give  to~you(ms)  and~to~ Seed~you(ms)  After~you(ms)  At  Land Pilgrimage  At  All  Land  "Kena'an [Lowered]"  to~Holdings  Distant.time and~i~did~Exist  to~them(m)  to~ "Elohiym  [Powers]"

and I will give to you and to your seed after you a land of pilgrimage, all of the land of "Kena'an [Lowered]" for a holdings of a distant time and I will exist for them for "Elohiym [Powers]",

**17:9**   וַיֹּאמֶר אֱלֹהִים אֶל אַבְרָהָם וְאַתָּה אֶת בְּרִיתִי תִשְׁמֹר אַתָּה
וְזַרְעֲךָ אַחֲרֶיךָ לְדֹרֹתָם

and~he~will~Say  "Elohiym  [Powers]" To  "Avraham  [Father lifted]"  and~ You(ms)  At  Covenant~me  you(ms)~ will~Guard  You(ms)  and~Seed~ you(ms)  After~you(ms)  to~Generation~ s~them(m)

and "Elohiym [Powers]" said to "Avraham [Father lifted]", and you, you will guard my covenant, you and your seed after you for their generations,

**17:10**   זֹאת בְּרִיתִי אֲשֶׁר תִּשְׁמְרוּ בֵּינִי וּבֵינֵיכֶם וּבֵין זַרְעֲךָ אַחֲרֶיךָ
הִמּוֹל לָכֶם כָּל זָכָר

This  Covenant~me  Which  you(mp)~ will~Guard  Between~me  and~Between~ you(mp)  and~Between  Seed~you(ms) After~you(ms)  >~be~Circumcise  to~ you(mp)  All  Male

this is my covenant which you will guard between me and you and your seed after you, all of your males be circumcised,

**17:11**   וּנְמַלְתֶּם אֵת בְּשַׂר עָרְלַתְכֶם וְהָיָה לְאוֹת בְּרִית בֵּינִי וּבֵינֵיכֶם

and~you(mp)~did~Cut.off  At  Flesh Foreskin~you(mp)  and~he~did~Exist to~Sign  Covenant  Between~me  and~ Between~you(mp)

and you will cut off the flesh of your foreskin and he will exist for a sign of the covenant between me and you,

**17:12**   וּבֶן שְׁמֹנַת יָמִים יִמּוֹל לָכֶם כָּל זָכָר לְדֹרֹתֵיכֶם יְלִיד בָּיִת
וּמִקְנַת כֶּסֶף מִכֹּל בֶּן נֵכָר אֲשֶׁר לֹא מִזַּרְעֲךָ הוּא

and~Son  Eight  Day~s  he~will~be~ Circumcise  to~you(mp)  All  Male  to~ Generation~s~you(mp)  Born  House and~Acquired  Silver  from~All  Son Foreign  Which  Not  from~Seed~ you(ms)  He

and he that is a son of eight days will be circumcised for you, all of the males to your generations born of the house and acquired of silver from all of the sons of a foreign one which is not from your seed,

**17:13**   הִמּוֹל יִמּוֹל יְלִיד בֵּיתְךָ וּמִקְנַת כַּסְפֶּךָ וְהָיְתָה בְרִיתִי בִּבְשַׂרְכֶם
לִבְרִית עוֹלָם

>~be~Circumcise  he~will~be~Circumcise

be circumcised, one born of your

Born House~you(ms) and~Acquired Silver~you(ms) and~she~did~Exist Covenant~me in~Flesh to~Covenant Distant.time

house and acquired of your silver, he will be circumcised and my covenant will exist in the flesh for a covenant of a distant time,

**17:14** וְעָרֵל זָכָר אֲשֶׁר לֹא יִמּוֹל אֶת בְּשַׂר עָרְלָתוֹ וְנִכְרְתָה הַנֶּפֶשׁ הַהוּא מֵעַמֶּיהָ אֶת בְּרִיתִי הֵפַר

and~Uncircumcised Male Which Not he~will~be~Circumcise At Flesh Foreskin~him and~she~did~be~Cut the~Being the~She from~People~s~her At Covenant~me he~had~make~Break

and an uncircumcised male whose flesh of his foreskin is not being circumcised then that being will be cut from her people, he has made my covenant broken,

**17:15** וַיֹּאמֶר אֱלֹהִים אֶל אַבְרָהָם שָׂרַי אִשְׁתְּךָ לֹא תִקְרָא אֶת שְׁמָהּ שָׂרָי כִּי שָׂרָה שְׁמָהּ

and~he~will~Say "Elohiym [Powers]" To "Avraham [Father lifted]" "Sarai [Princess]" Woman~you(ms) Not you(ms)~will~Call.out At Title~her "Sarai [Princess]" Given.that "Sarah [Noblewoman]" Title~her

and "Elohiym [Powers]" said to "Avraham [Father lifted]", you will not call out the title of "Sarai [Princess]" your woman "Sarai [Princess]" given that "Sarah [Noblewoman]" is her title,

**17:16\*** וּבֵרַכְתִּי אֹתָהּ וְגַם נָתַתִּי מִמֶּנָּה לְךָ בֵּן וּבֵרַכְתִּיהָ וְהָיְתָה לְגוֹיִם מַלְכֵי עַמִּים מִמֶּנָּה יִהְיוּ

and~i~did~much~Kneel At~her and~Also i~did~Give From~her to~you(ms) Son and~i~did~much~Kneel~her and~she~did~Exist to~Nation~s King~s People~s From~her they(m)~will~Exist

and I will respect her and also from her I will give to you a son and I will respect her and she will exist for nations, kings of peoples will exist from her,

**17:17** וַיִּפֹּל אַבְרָהָם עַל פָּנָיו וַיִּצְחָק וַיֹּאמֶר בְּלִבּוֹ הַלְּבֶן מֵאָה שָׁנָה יִוָּלֵד וְאִם שָׂרָה הֲבַת תִּשְׁעִים שָׁנָה תֵּלֵד

and~he~will~Fall "Avraham [Father lifted]" Upon Face~s~him and~he~will~Laugh and~he~will~Say in~Heart~him ?~to~Son Hundred Year he~will~be~Bring.forth and~If "Sarah [Noblewoman]" the~Daughter Nine~s Year she~will~Bring.forth□

and "Avraham [Father lifted]" fell upon his face and he laughed and he said in his heart, will he be given in birth to one who is a son of a hundred years and if "Sarah [Noblewoman]" is the daughter of ninety years will she bring forth,

**17:18** וַיֹּאמֶר אַבְרָהָם אֶל הָאֱלֹהִים לוּ יִשְׁמָעֵאל יִחְיֶה לְפָנֶיךָ

and~he~will~Say "Avraham [Father lifted]" To the~"Elohiym [Powers]" Would.that "Yishma'el [El will listen]" he~will~Live to~Face~s~

and "Avraham [Father lifted]" said to the "Elohiym [Powers]", would that "Yishma'el [El will listen]" will live to your face,

you(ms)

**17:19** וַיֹּאמֶר אֱלֹהִים אֲבָל שָׂרָה אִשְׁתְּךָ יֹלֶדֶת לְךָ בֵּן וְקָרָאתָ אֶת שְׁמוֹ יִצְחָק וַהֲקִמֹתִי אֶת בְּרִיתִי אִתּוֹ לִבְרִית עוֹלָם לְזַרְעוֹ אַחֲרָיו

and~he~will~Say "Elohiym [*Powers*]" Nevertheless "Sarah [*Noblewoman*]" Woman~you(ms) Bring.forth~ing(fs) to~you(ms) Son and~you(ms)~did~ Call.out At Title~him "Yits'hhaq [*He laughs*]" and~i~did~make~Rise At Covenant~me At~him to~Covenant Distant.time to~Seed~him After~him

and "Elohiym [*Powers*]" said, nevertheless, "Sarah [*Noblewoman*]" your woman is giving birth for you a son and you will call out his title "Yits'hhaq [*He laughs*]" and I will make my covenant rise with him for a covenant of a distant time for his seed after him,

**17:20** וּלְיִשְׁמָעֵאל שְׁמַעְתִּיךָ הִנֵּה בֵּרַכְתִּי אֹתוֹ וְהִפְרֵיתִי אֹתוֹ וְהִרְבֵּיתִי אֹתוֹ בִּמְאֹד מְאֹד שְׁנֵים עָשָׂר נְשִׂיאִם יוֹלִיד וּנְתַתִּיו לְגוֹי גָּדוֹל

and~to~"Yishma'el [*El will listen*]" i~did~Hear~you(ms) Look i~did~ much~Kneel At~him and~i~did~make~ Reproduce At~him and~i~did~make~ Increase At~him in~Many Many Two Ten Captain~s he~will~make~ Bring.forth and~i~did~Give~him to~ Nation Magnificent

and to "Yishma'el [*El will listen*]", I heard you, look, I respected him and I will make him reproduce and I will make him increase with a great many, he will cause to bring forth twelve captains and I will give him for a magnificent nation,

**17:21** וְאֶת בְּרִיתִי אָקִים אֶת יִצְחָק אֲשֶׁר תֵּלֵד לְךָ שָׂרָה לַמּוֹעֵד הַזֶּה בַּשָּׁנָה הָאַחֶרֶת

and~At Covenant~me i~will~make~ Rise At "Yits'hhaq [*He laughs*]" Which she~will~Bring.forth to~you(ms) "Sarah [*Noblewoman*]" to~the~ Appointed the~This in~the~Year the~ Other

and I will make my covenant rise with "Yits'hhaq [*He laughs*]" which "Sarah [*Noblewoman*]" will bring forth for you to this appointed time in another year,

**17:22** וַיְכַל לְדַבֵּר אִתּוֹ וַיַּעַל אֱלֹהִים מֵעַל אַבְרָהָם

and~he~will~much~Finish to~>~Speak At~him and~he~will~Go.up "Elohiym [*Powers*]" from~Upon "Avraham [*Father lifted*]"

and he finished speaking with him and "Elohiym [*Powers*]" went up from upon "Avraham [*Father lifted*]",

**17:23** וַיִּקַּח אַבְרָהָם אֶת יִשְׁמָעֵאל בְּנוֹ וְאֵת כָּל יְלִידֵי בֵיתוֹ וְאֵת כָּל מִקְנַת כַּסְפּוֹ כָּל זָכָר בְּאַנְשֵׁי בֵּית אַבְרָהָם וַיָּמָל אֶת בְּשַׂר עָרְלָתָם בְּעֶצֶם הַיּוֹם הַזֶּה כַּאֲשֶׁר דִּבֶּר אִתּוֹ אֱלֹהִים

and~he~will~Take "Avraham [*Father lifted*]" At "Yishma'el [*El will

and "Avraham [*Father lifted*]" took "Yishma'el [*El will listen*]" his son

listen]" Son~him and~At All Born~s
House~him and~At All Acquired
Silver~him All Male in~Man~s
House "Avraham [*Father lifted*]"
and~he~will~Circumcise At Flesh
Foreskin~them(m) in~Bone the~Day
the~This like~Which he~did~much~
Speak At~him "Elohiym [*Powers*]"

and all of the ones born of his
house and all of the ones acquired
of his silver, all of the males with
the men of the house of "Avraham
[*Father lifted*]" and he circumcised
the flesh of their foreskin in the
bone of this day just as "Elohiym
[*Powers*]" spoke with him,

**17:24** וְאַבְרָהָם בֶּן תִּשְׁעִים וָתֵשַׁע שָׁנָה בְּהִמֹּלוֹ בְּשַׂר עָרְלָתוֹ

and~"Avraham [*Father lifted*]" Son
Nine~s and~Nine Year in~>~
make.be~Circumcise~him Flesh
Foreskin~him

and "Avraham [*Father lifted*]" was
a son of ninety nine years in his
being made circumcised of the flesh
of his foreskin,

**17:25** וְיִשְׁמָעֵאל בְּנוֹ בֶּן שְׁלֹשׁ עֶשְׂרֵה שָׁנָה בְּהִמֹּלוֹ אֵת בְּשַׂר עָרְלָתוֹ

and~"Yishma'el [*El will listen*]"
Son~him Son Three Ten Year in~
>~make.be~Circumcise~him At Flesh
Foreskin~him

and "Yishma'el [*El will listen*]" his
son was a son of thirteen years in
his being made circumcised with
the flesh of his foreskin,

**17:26** בְּעֶצֶם הַיּוֹם הַזֶּה נִמּוֹל אַבְרָהָם וְיִשְׁמָעֵאל בְּנוֹ

in~Bone the~Day the~This he~did~
be~Circumcise "Avraham [*Father
lifted*]" and~"Yishma'el [*El will
listen*]" Son~him

in the bone of this day "Avraham
[*Father lifted*]" was circumcised
and "Yishma'el [*El will listen*]" his
son,

**17:27** וְכָל אַנְשֵׁי בֵיתוֹ יְלִיד בָּיִת וּמִקְנַת כֶּסֶף מֵאֵת בֶּן נֵכָר נִמֹּלוּ אִתּוֹ

and~All Man~s House~him Born
House and~Acquired Silver from~At
Son Foreign they~did~be~Circumcise
At~him

and all of the men of his house born
of the house and acquired of silver
from a son of a foreign one were
circumcised with him,

# Chapter 18

**18:1\*** וַיֵּרָא אֵלָיו יְהוָה בְּאֵלֹנֵי מַמְרֵא וְהוּא יֹשֵׁב פֶּתַח הָאֹהֶל כְּחֹם הַיּוֹם

and~he~will~be~See To~him "YHWH
[*He exists*]" in~Great.tree~s "Mamre
[*Bitter place*]" and~He Settle~ing(ms)
Opening the~Tent like~Hot the~Day

and "YHWH [*He exists*]" appeared
to him in the great trees of "Mamre
[*Bitter place*]" and he was settling
in the opening of the tent in the heat
of the day,

**18:2** וַיִּשָּׂא עֵינָיו וַיַּרְא וְהִנֵּה שְׁלֹשָׁה אֲנָשִׁים נִצָּבִים עָלָיו וַיַּרְא וַיָּרָץ לִקְרָאתָם מִפֶּתַח הָאֹהֶל וַיִּשְׁתַּחוּ אָרְצָה

and~he~will~Lift.up Eye~s2~him and~
he~will~See and~Look Three Man~s
be~Stand.erect~ing(mp) Upon~him
and~he~will~See and~he~will~Run to~
>~Meet~them(m) from~Opening the~
Tent and~he~will~self~Bend.down
Land~unto

and he lifted up his eyes and he saw
and look, three men were standing
erect upon him and he saw and he
ran from the opening of the tent to
meet them, he bent himself down
unto the land,

**18:3\*** וַיֹּאמַר אֲדֹנָי אִם נָא מָצָאתִי חֵן בְּעֵינֶיךָ אַל נָא תַעֲבֹר מֵעַל
עַבְדֶּךָ

and~he~will~Say "Adonai [*My lords*]"
If Please i~did~Find Beauty in~Eye~
s2~you(ms) No Please you(ms)~will~
Cross.over from~Upon Servant~you(ms)

and he said, "Adonai [*My lords*]",
please, if I find beauty in your eyes
please do not cross over from upon
your servant,

**18:4** יֻקַּח נָא מְעַט מַיִם וְרַחֲצוּ רַגְלֵיכֶם וְהִשָּׁעֲנוּ תַּחַת הָעֵץ

he~will~much.be~Take Please
Small.amount Water~s2 and~!(mp)~
Wash Foot~s~you(mp) and~!(ms)~be~
Lean Under the~Tree

Please, a small amount of water
will be taken and wash your feet
and lean under the tree,

**18:5** וְאֶקְחָה פַת לֶחֶם וְסַעֲדוּ לִבְּכֶם אַחַר תַּעֲבֹרוּ כִּי עַל כֵּן עֲבַרְתֶּם
עַל עַבְדְּכֶם וַיֹּאמְרוּ כֵּן תַּעֲשֶׂה כַּאֲשֶׁר דִּבַּרְתָּ

and~i~did~Take~her Fragment Bread
and~!(mp)~Hold.up Heart~you(mp)
After you(mp)~will~Cross.over
Given.that Upon So you(mp)~did~
Cross.over Upon Servant~you(mp)
and~they(m)~will~Say So you(ms)~
will~Do like~Which you(ms)~did~
much~Say

and I will take a fragment of bread
and hold up your heart after you
cross over since you crossed over
upon your servant and they said,
you will do so just as you said,

**18:6** וַיְמַהֵר אַבְרָהָם הָאֹהֱלָה אֶל שָׂרָה וַיֹּאמֶר מַהֲרִי שְׁלֹשׁ סְאִים
קֶמַח סֹלֶת לוּשִׁי וַעֲשִׂי עֻגוֹת

and~he~will~much~Hurry "Avraham
[*Father lifted*]" the~Tent~unto To
"Sarah [*Noblewoman*]" and~he~will~
Say !(fs)~Hurry Three Se'ah~s
Grain.flour Flour !(fs)~Knead and~
!(fs)~Do Bread.cake~s

and "Avraham [*Father lifted*]"
much hurried unto the tent to
"Sarah [*Noblewoman*]" and he said
hurry, knead three se'ahs of grain
flour and make bread cakes,

**18:7** וְאֶל הַבָּקָר רָץ אַבְרָהָם וַיִּקַּח בֶּן בָּקָר רַךְ וָטוֹב וַיִּתֵּן אֶל הַנַּעַר
וַיְמַהֵר לַעֲשׂוֹת אֹתוֹ

and~To the~Cattle he~did~Run
"Avraham [*Father lifted*]" and~he~
will~Take Son Cattle Tender and~

and "Avraham [*Father lifted*]" ran
to the cattle and he took a son of the
cattle, tender and functional and he

**91**

Functional and~he~will~Give To the~Young.man and~he~will~much~Hurry to~>~Do At~him

gave it to the young man and he much hurried to make him,

**18:8** וַיִּקַּח חֶמְאָה וְחָלָב וּבֶן הַבָּקָר אֲשֶׁר עָשָׂה וַיִּתֵּן לִפְנֵיהֶם וְהוּא עֹמֵד עֲלֵיהֶם תַּחַת הָעֵץ וַיֹּאכֵלוּ

and~he~will~Take Cheese and~Fat and~Son the~Cattle Which he~did~Do and~he~will~Give to~Face~s~them(m) and~He Stand~ing(ms) Upon~them(m) Under the~Tree and~they(m)~will~Eat

and he took cheese and fat and a son of the cattle which he made and he gave it to their face and he was standing upon them under the tree and they ate,

**18:9** וַיֹּאמְרוּ אֵלָיו אַיֵּה שָׂרָה אִשְׁתֶּךָ וַיֹּאמֶר הִנֵּה בָאֹהֶל

and~they(m)~will~Say To~him Where "Sarah [Noblewoman]" Woman~you(ms) and~he~will~Say Look in~the~Tent

and they said to him, where is "Sarah [Noblewoman]" your woman, and he said, look, in the tent,

**18:10*** וַיֹּאמֶר שׁוֹב אָשׁוּב אֵלֶיךָ כָּעֵת חַיָּה וְהִנֵּה בֵן לְשָׂרָה אִשְׁתֶּךָ וְשָׂרָה שֹׁמַעַת פֶּתַח הָאֹהֶל וְהוּא אַחֲרָיו

and~he~will~Say >~Turn.back i~will~Turn.back To~you(ms) like~the~Appointed.time Life and~Look Son to~"Sarah [Noblewoman]" Woman~you(ms) and~"Sarah [Noblewoman]" Hear~ing(fs) Opening the~Tent and~He After~him

and he said, I will surely turn back to you at the appointed time of life and look, a son for "Sarah [Noblewoman]" your woman and "Sarah [Noblewoman]" was hearing in the opening of the tent and he was behind him,

**18:11** וְאַבְרָהָם וְשָׂרָה זְקֵנִים בָּאִים בַּיָּמִים חָדַל לִהְיוֹת לְשָׂרָה אֹרַח כַּנָּשִׁים

and~"Avraham [Father lifted]" and~"Sarah [Noblewoman]" Beard~s Come~ing(mp) in~the~Day~s he~did~Terminate to~>~Exist to~"Sarah [Noblewoman]" Path like~the~Woman~s

and "Avraham [Father lifted]" and "Sarah [Noblewoman]" were bearded ones coming in the days, the path like the women terminated to exist for "Sarah [Noblewoman]",

**18:12** וַתִּצְחַק שָׂרָה בְּקִרְבָּהּ לֵאמֹר אַחֲרֵי בְלֹתִי הָיְתָה לִּי עֶדְנָה וַאדֹנִי זָקֵן

and~she~will~Laugh "Sarah [Noblewoman]" in~Within~her to~>~Say After i~>~Wear.Out she~did~Exist to~me Pleasure and~Lord~me Beard

and "Sarah [Noblewoman]" laughed within her saying, after I am worn out, pleasure exists for me and my lord is a bearded one,

**18:13** וַיֹּאמֶר יְהוָה אֶל אַבְרָהָם לָמָּה זֶּה צָחֲקָה שָׂרָה לֵאמֹר הַאַף

אָמְנָם אֵלֵד וַאֲנִי זָקַנְתִּי

and~he~will~Say "YHWH [*He exists*]" To "Avraham [*Father lifted*] to~What This she~did~Laugh "Sarah [*Noblewoman*]" to~>~Say the~ Moreover Indeed i~will~Bring.forth and~I i~did~Be.old

and "YHWH [*He exists*]" said to "Avraham [*Father lifted*]", why is this, "Sarah [*Noblewoman*]" laughed saying, moreover indeed, will I bring forth and I am old,

**18:14** הֲיִפָּלֵא מֵיהוָה דָּבָר לַמּוֹעֵד אָשׁוּב אֵלֶיךָ כָּעֵת חַיָּה וּלְשָׂרָה בֵן

?~he~did~Perform from~"YHWH [*He exists*]" Word to~the~Appointed i~ will~Turn.back To~you(ms) like~the~ Appointed.time Life and~to~"Sarah [*Noblewoman*]" Son

can the word from "YHWH [*He exists*]" perform at the appointed time, I will turn back to you at the appointed time of life and to "Sarah [*Noblewoman*]" will be a son,

**18:15** וַתְּכַחֵשׁ שָׂרָה לֵאמֹר לֹא צָחַקְתִּי כִּי יָרֵאָה כִּי יָאמֶר לֹא כִּי צָחָקְתְּ

and~she~will~Deny "Sarah [*Noblewoman*]" to~>~Say Not i~did~ Laugh Given.that she~did~Fear and~ he~will~Say Not Given.that you(fs)~ did~Laugh

and "Sarah [*Noblewoman*]" denied saying, I did not laugh, given that she feared and he said, no, given that you laughed,

**18:16** וַיָּקֻמוּ מִשָּׁם הָאֲנָשִׁים וַיַּשְׁקִפוּ עַל פְּנֵי סְדֹם וְאַבְרָהָם הֹלֵךְ עִמָּם לְשַׁלְּחָם

and~they(m)~will~Rise from~There the~Man~s and~they(m)~will~make~ Look.down Upon Face~s "Sedom [*Secret*]" and~"Avraham [*Father lifted*]" Walk~ing(ms) With~them(m) to~>~much~Send~them(m)

and the men rose from there and they looked down upon the face of "Sedom [*Secret*]" and "Avraham [*Father lifted*]" was walking with them to send them off,

**18:17** וַיהוָה אָמָר הַמְכַסֶּה אֲנִי מֵאַבְרָהָם אֲשֶׁר אֲנִי עֹשֶׂה

and~"YHWH [*He exists*]" he~had~Say ?~much~Conceal~ing(ms) I from~ "Avraham [*Father lifted*]" Which I Do~ing(ms)

and "YHWH [*He exists*]" had said, am I concealing from "Avraham [*Father lifted*]" what I am doing,

**18:18** וְאַבְרָהָם הָיוֹ יִהְיֶה לְגוֹי גָּדוֹל וְעָצוּם וְנִבְרְכוּ בוֹ כֹּל גּוֹיֵי הָאָרֶץ

and~"Avraham [*Father lifted*]" >~ Exist he~will~Exist to~Nation Magnificent and~Multiple and~ they(m)~did~be~Kneel in~him All Nation~s the~Land

and "Avraham [*Father lifted*]" will greatly exist for a magnificent and multiple nation and all of the nations of the land will be respected with him,

**18:19** כִּי יְדַעְתִּיו לְמַעַן אֲשֶׁר יְצַוֶּה אֶת בָּנָיו וְאֶת בֵּיתוֹ אַחֲרָיו וְשָׁמְרוּ דֶּרֶךְ יְהוָה לַעֲשׂוֹת צְדָקָה וּמִשְׁפָּט לְמַעַן הָבִיא יְהוָה עַל אַבְרָהָם

אֶת אֲשֶׁר דִּבֶּר עָלָיו

Given.that i~did~Know~him to~That Which he~will~much~Direct At Son~s~him and~At House~him After~him and~they~did~Guard Road "YHWH [*He exists*]" to~>~Do Correctness and~Judgement to~That >~make~Come "YHWH [*He exists*]" Upon "Avraham [*Father lifted*]" At Which he~did~much~Speak Upon~him

given that I knew him that what he will direct his sons and his house after him and they will guard the road of "YHWH [*He exists*]" to do correctness and judgement so that "YHWH [*He exists*]" is bringing upon "Avraham [*Father lifted*]" with what he spoke upon him,

**18:20** וַיֹּאמֶר יְהֹוָה זַעֲקַת סְדֹם וַעֲמֹרָה כִּי רָבָּה כִּי וְחַטָּאתָם כִּי כָבְדָה מְאֹד

and~he~will~Say "YHWH [*He exists*]" Outcry "Sedom [*Secret*]" and~"Ghamorah [*Rebellion*]" Given.that she~had~Increase.in.number and~Error~them(m) Given.that she~had~Be.heavy Many

and "YHWH [*He exists*]" said, given that the outcry of "Sedom [*Secret*]" and "Ghamorah [*Rebellion*]" had increased in number and given that their error had become very heavy,

**18:21** אֵרֲדָה נָּא וְאֶרְאֶה הַכְּצַעֲקָתָהּ הַבָּאָה אֵלַי עָשׂוּ כָּלָה וְאִם לֹא אֵדָעָה

i~will~Go.down~her Please and~i~did~See the~like~Outcry~her ?~she~did~Come To~me they~did~Do Completion and~If Not i~will~Know

please, I will go down to her and I will see, is her outcry that is coming to me completed, if not I will know,

**18:22** וַיִּפְנוּ מִשָּׁם הָאֲנָשִׁים וַיֵּלְכוּ סְדֹמָה וְאַבְרָהָם עוֹדֶנּוּ עֹמֵד לִפְנֵי יְהֹוָה

and~they(m)~will~Turn from~There the~Man~s and~they(m)~will~Walk "Sedom [*Secret*]"~unto and~"Avraham [*Father lifted*]" Yet.again~him Stand~ing(ms) to~Face~s "YHWH [*He exists*]"

and the men turned from there and they walked unto "Sedom [*Secret*]" and yet again "Avraham [*Father lifted*]" was standing to the face of "YHWH [*He exists*]",

**18:23** וַיִּגַּשׁ אַבְרָהָם וַיֹּאמַר הַאַף תִּסְפֶּה צַדִּיק עִם רָשָׁע

and~he~will~Draw.near "Avraham [*Father lifted*]" and~he~will~Say ?~Moreover you(ms)~will~Consume Correct With Lost

and "Avraham [*Father lifted*]" drew near and he said, moreover, will you consume the correct with the lost,

**18:24** אוּלַי יֵשׁ חֲמִשִּׁים צַדִּיקִם בְּתוֹךְ הָעִיר הַאַף תִּסְפֶּה וְלֹא תִשָּׂא לַמָּקוֹם לְמַעַן חֲמִשִּׁים הַצַּדִּיקִם אֲשֶׁר בְּקִרְבָּהּ

Possibly There.is Five~s Correct~s in~Midst the~City ?~Nose you(ms)~

possibly there are fifty correct ones in the midst of the city, will your

**94**

will~Consume and~Not you(ms)~will~
Lift.up to~the~Place to~That Five~s
the~Correct~s Which in~Within~her

anger consume and not lift up to
that place of the fifty correct ones
which are within her,

**18:25** חָלִלָה לְּךָ מֵעֲשֹׂת כַּדָּבָר הַזֶּה לְהָמִית צַדִּיק עִם רָשָׁע וְהָיָה
כַּצַּדִּיק כָּרָשָׁע חָלִלָה לָּךְ הֲשֹׁפֵט כָּל הָאָרֶץ לֹא יַעֲשֶׂה מִשְׁפָּט

Far.be.it to~you(ms) from~>~Do like~
the~Word the~This to~>~make~Die
Correct With Lost and~he~did~Exist
like~the~Correct like~the~Lost Far.be.it
to~you(fs) ?~Judge~ing(ms) All the~
Land Not he~will~Do Judgement

far be it to you from doing in this
manner to kill the correct with the
lost and the correct will be like the
lost, far be it to you, will the judge
of all of the land not do judgement,

**18:26** וַיֹּאמֶר יְהֹוָה אִם אֶמְצָא בִסְדֹם חֲמִשִּׁים צַדִּיקִם בְּתוֹךְ הָעִיר
וְנָשָׂאתִי לְכָל הַמָּקוֹם בַּעֲבוּרָם

and~he~will~Say "YHWH [*He
exists*]" If i~will~Find in~"Sedom
[*Secret*]" Five~s Correct~s in~Midst
the~City and~i~did~Lift.up to~All
the~Place in~On.account.of~them(m)

and "YHWH [*He exists*]" said, if I
will find in "Sedom [*Secret*]" fifty
correct ones in the midst of the city
I will lift up to all of the place on
account of them,

**18:27** וַיַּעַן אַבְרָהָם וַיֹּאמַר הִנֵּה נָא הוֹאַלְתִּי לְדַבֵּר אֶל אֲדֹנָי וְאָנֹכִי
עָפָר וָאֵפֶר

and~he~will~Answer "Avraham [*Father
lifted*]" and~he~will~Say Look Please
i~will~make~Take.upon to~>~much~
Speak To "Adonai [*My lords*]"
and~I Powder and~Ash

and "Avraham [*Father lifted*]"
answered and he said, please look, I
take upon to speak to "Adonai [*My
lords*]" and I am powder and dust,

**18:28** אוּלַי יַחְסְרוּן חֲמִשִּׁים הַצַּדִּיקִם חֲמִשָּׁה הֲתַשְׁחִית בַּחֲמִשָּׁה אֶת
כָּל הָעִיר וַיֹּאמֶר לֹא אַשְׁחִית אִם אֶמְצָא שָׁם אַרְבָּעִים וַחֲמִשָּׁה

Possibly they(m)~will~Diminish Five~s
Correct~s Five ?~you(ms)~will~make~
Damage in~the~Five At All the~City
and~he~will~Say Not i~will~make~
Damage If i~will~Find There Four~s
and~Five

possibly the fifty correct ones
diminish by five, will you destroy
all of the city with the five, and he
said, I will not cause damage if I
will find there forty-five,

**18:29** וַיֹּסֶף עוֹד לְדַבֵּר אֵלָיו וַיֹּאמַר אוּלַי יִמָּצְאוּן שָׁם אַרְבָּעִים
וַיֹּאמֶר לֹא אֶעֱשֶׂה בַּעֲבוּר הָאַרְבָּעִים

and~he~will~make~Add Yet.again to~
>~much~Speak To~him and~he~will~
Say Possibly they(m)~will~be~Find
There Four~s and~he~will~Say Not
i~will~Do in~On.account.of the~Four~s

and he continued to speak to him
and he said, possibly forty will be
found there, and he said, I will not
do on account of the forty,

**18:30** וַיֹּאמֶר אַל נָא יִחַר לַאדֹנָי וַאֲדַבֵּרָה אוּלַי יִמָּצְאוּן שָׁם שְׁלֹשִׁים וַיֹּאמֶר לֹא אֶעֱשֶׂה אִם אֶמְצָא שָׁם שְׁלֹשִׁים

and~he~will~Say No Please he~will~Flare.up to~"Adonai [*My lords*]" and~i~did~much~Speak~^ Possibly they(m)~will~be~Find There Three~s and~he~will~Say Not i~will~Do If i~will~Find There Three~s

and he said to "Adonai [*My lords*]", please do not flare up and I will speak, possibly thirty will be found there, and he said, I will not do if I will find there thirty,

**18:31** וַיֹּאמֶר הִנֵּה נָא הוֹאַלְתִּי לְדַבֵּר אֶל אֲדֹנָי אוּלַי יִמָּצְאוּן שָׁם עֶשְׂרִים וַיֹּאמֶר לֹא אַשְׁחִית בַּעֲבוּר הָעֶשְׂרִים

and~he~will~Say Look Please i~will~make~Take.upon to~>~much~Speak To "Adonai [*My lords*]" Possibly they(m)~will~be~Find There Ten~s and~he~will~Say Not i~will~Do in~On.account.of the~Ten~s

and he said, please look, I will take upon to speak to "Adonai [*My lords*]", possibly twenty will be found there, and he said, I will not do on account of the twenty,

**18:32** וַיֹּאמֶר אַל נָא יִחַר לַאדֹנָי וַאֲדַבְּרָה אַךְ הַפַּעַם אוּלַי יִמָּצְאוּן שָׁם עֲשָׂרָה וַיֹּאמֶר לֹא אַשְׁחִית בַּעֲבוּר הָעֲשָׂרָה

and~he~will~Say No Please he~will~Flare.up to~"Adonai [*My lords*]" and~i~did~much~Speak Surely the~Stroke.of.time Possibly they(m)~will~be~Find There Ten and~he~will~Say Not i~will~Do in~On.account.of the~Ten

and he said to "Adonai [*My lords*]", please do no flare up and I will speak, surely this time, possibly ten will be found there, and he said I will not do on account of the ten,

**18:33** וַיֵּלֶךְ יְהֹוָה כַּאֲשֶׁר כִּלָּה לְדַבֵּר אֶל אַבְרָהָם וְאַבְרָהָם שָׁב לִמְקֹמוֹ

and~he~will~Walk "YHWH [*He exists*]" like~Which he~did~much~Finish to~>~much~Speak To "Avraham [*Father lifted*]" and~"Avraham [*Father lifted*]" he~did~Turn.back to~Place~him

and "YHWH [*He exists*]" walked just as he finished to speak to "Avraham [*Father lifted*]" and "Avraham [*Father lifted*]" turned back to his place,

# Chapter 19

**19:1** וַיָּבֹאוּ שְׁנֵי הַמַּלְאָכִים סְדֹמָה בָּעֶרֶב וְלוֹט יֹשֵׁב בְּשַׁעַר סְדֹם וַיַּרְא לוֹט וַיָּקָם לִקְרָאתָם וַיִּשְׁתַּחוּ אַפַּיִם אָרְצָה

and~they(m)~will~Come Two the~Messenger~s "Sedom [*Secret*]"~unto in~the~Evening and~"Loth [*Covering*]"

and two of the messengers came unto "Sedom [*Secret*]" in the evening and "Loth [*Covering*]" was

Settle~ing(ms) in~Gate "Sedom [*Secret*]" and~he~will~See "Loth [*Covering*]" and~he~will~Rise to~>~ Meet~them(m) and~he~will~self~ Bend.down Nose~s2 Land~unto

settling in the gate of "Sedom [*Secret*]" and "Loth [*Covering*]" saw and he rose to meet them and he bent himself down, nostrils unto the land,

**19:2**

וַיֹּאמֶר הִנֶּה נָּא אֲדֹנַי סוּרוּ נָא אֶל בֵּית עַבְדְּכֶם וְלִינוּ וְרַחֲצוּ רַגְלֵיכֶם וְהִשְׁכַּמְתֶּם וַהֲלַכְתֶּם לְדַרְכְּכֶם וַיֹּאמְרוּ לֹא כִּי בָרְחוֹב נָלִין

and~he~will~Say Look Please Lord~ s~me !(mp)~Turn.aside Please To House Servant~you(mp) and~!(mp)~ Stay.the.night and~!(mp)~Wash Foot~s~ you(mp) and~you(mp)~did~make~ Depart.early and~you(mp)~did~Walk to~Road~you(mp) and~they(m)~will~Say Not Given.that in~the~Street we~will~ Stay.the.night

and he said, please look my lords, please turn aside to the house of your servant and stay the night and wash your feet and you will depart early and you will walk to your road and they said, no, given that in the street we will stay the night,

**19:3**

וַיִּפְצַר בָּם מְאֹד וַיָּסֻרוּ אֵלָיו וַיָּבֹאוּ אֶל בֵּיתוֹ וַיַּעַשׂ לָהֶם מִשְׁתֶּה וּמַצּוֹת אָפָה וַיֹּאכֵלוּ

and~he~will~Press.hard in~them(m) Many and~they(m)~will~Turn.aside To~him and~they(m)~will~Come To House~him and~he~will~Do to~ them(m) Feast and~Unleavened.bread he~did~Bake and~they(m)~will~Eat

and he pressed very hard with them and they turned aside to him and they came to his house and he made for them a feast and he baked unleavened bread and they ate,

**19:4***

טֶרֶם יִשְׁכָּבוּ וְאַנְשֵׁי הָעִיר אַנְשֵׁי סְדֹם נָסַבּוּ עַל הַבַּיִת מִנַּעַר וְעַד זָקֵן כָּל הָעָם מִקָּצֶה

Before they(m)~will~Lay.down and~ Man~s the~City Man~s "Sedom [*Secret*]" they~did~be~Go.around Upon the~House from~Young.man and~Until Beard All the~People from~Far.end

before they laid down, the men of the city, men of "Sedom [*Secret*]", from the young men and also the bearded ones, all of the people from the far end, went around upon the house,

**19:5**

וַיִּקְרְאוּ אֶל לוֹט וַיֹּאמְרוּ לוֹ אַיֵּה הָאֲנָשִׁים אֲשֶׁר בָּאוּ אֵלֶיךָ הַלַּיְלָה הוֹצִיאֵם אֵלֵינוּ וְנֵדְעָה אֹתָם

and~they(m)~will~Call.out To "Loth [*Covering*]" and~they(m)~will~Say to~ him Where the~Man~s Which they(m)~did~Come To~you(ms) the~ Night !(mp)~make~Go.out~them(m) To~us and~we~did~Know At~them(m)

and they called out to "Loth [*Covering*]" and they said to him, where are the men which came to you tonight, bring them out to us and we will know them,

**19:6**

וַיֵּצֵא אֲלֵהֶם לוֹט הַפֶּתְחָה וְהַדֶּלֶת סָגַר אַחֲרָיו

and~he~will~Go.out To~them(m) "Loth [*Covering*]" the~Opening~unto and~the~Door he~did~Shut After~him

and "Loth [*Covering*]" went out to them, unto the opening and he shut the door after him,

**19:7**

וַיּאמַר אַל נָא אַחַי תָּרֵעוּ

and~he~will~Say No Please Brother~s~me you(mp)~will~make~Be.dysfunctional

and he said, please no my brothers, you will be made dysfunctional,

**19:8**

הִנֵּה נָא לִי שְׁתֵּי בָנוֹת אֲשֶׁר לֹא יָדְעוּ אִישׁ אוֹצִיאָה נָּא אֶתְהֶן אֲלֵיכֶם וַעֲשׂוּ לָהֶן כַּטּוֹב בְּעֵינֵיכֶם רַק לָאֲנָשִׁים הָאֵל אַל תַּעֲשׂוּ דָבָר כִּי עַל כֵּן בָּאוּ בְּצֵל קֹרָתִי

Look Please to~me Two Daughter~s Which Not they~did~Know Man i~will~make~Go.out Please At~them(f) To~you(mp) and~!(mp)~Do to~them(f) like~the~Functional in~Eye~s2~you(mp) Only to~the~Man~s the~These No you(mp)~will~Do Word Given.that Upon So they~did~Come in~Shadow Rafter~me

please look, I have two daughters which do not know a man, please, I will bring them out to you and do to them as is functional in your eyes only to these men you will not do a thing because they came in the shadow of my rafter,

**19:9**

וַיּאמְרוּ גֶּשׁ הָלְאָה וַיּאמְרוּ הָאֶחָד בָּא לָגוּר וַיִּשְׁפֹּט שָׁפוֹט עַתָּה נָרַע לְךָ מֵהֶם וַיִּפְצְרוּ בָאִישׁ בְּלוֹט מְאֹד וַיִּגְּשׁוּ לִשְׁבֹּר הַדָּלֶת

and~they(m)~will~Say !(ms)~Draw.near Distant and~they(m)~will~Say the~Unit he~did~Come to~>~Sojourn and~he~will~Judge >~Judge Now we~will~make~Be.dysfunctional to~you(ms) from~them(m) and~they(m)~will~Press.hard in~the~Man in~"Loth [*Covering*]" Many and~they(m)~will~Draw.near to~Burst the~Door

and they said, draw near to a distance, and they said, the one had come to sojourn and he will judge a judgement, now we will cause you to be dysfunctional rather than them and they pressed very hard with the man, with "Loth [*Covering*]", and they drew near to burst the door,

**19:10**

וַיִּשְׁלְחוּ הָאֲנָשִׁים אֶת יָדָם וַיָּבִיאוּ אֶת לוֹט אֲלֵיהֶם הַבָּיְתָה וְאֶת הַדֶּלֶת סָגָרוּ

and~they(m)~will~Send the~Man~s At Hand~them(m) and~they(m)~will~make~Come At "Loth [*Covering*]" To~them(m) the~House~unto and~At the~Door they~did~Shut

and the men sent their hand and they made "Loth [*Covering*]" come to them unto the house and they shut the door,

**19:11**

וְאֶת הָאֲנָשִׁים אֲשֶׁר פֶּתַח הַבַּיִת הִכּוּ בַּסַּנְוֵרִים מִקָּטֹן וְעַד גָּדוֹל וַיִּלְאוּ לִמְצֹא הַפָּתַח

and~At the~Man~s Which Opening the~House they~did~make~Hit in~the~ Blindness from~Small and~Until Magnificent and~they(m)~will~Weary to~>~Find the~Opening

they hit the men which were at the opening of the house with the blindness from the small and also the magnificent and they were weary for finding the opening,

**19:12** וַיֹּאמְרוּ הָאֲנָשִׁים אֶל לוֹט עֹד מִי לְךָ פֹה חָתָן וּבָנֶיךָ וּבְנֹתֶיךָ וְכֹל אֲשֶׁר לְךָ בָּעִיר הוֹצֵא מִן הַמָּקוֹם

and~they(m)~will~Say the~Man~s To "Loth [*Covering*]" Yet.again Who to~you(ms) Here In-law and~Son~s~ you(ms) and~Daughter~s~you(ms) and~ All Which to~you(ms) in~the~City !(ms)~Go.out From the~Place

and the men said to "Loth [*Covering*]" yet again, who also belongs to you here, in-laws and your sons and your daughters and all of the ones which belong to you in the city, go out from the place,

**19:13** כִּי מַשְׁחִתִים אֲנַחְנוּ אֶת הַמָּקוֹם הַזֶּה כִּי גָדְלָה צַעֲקָתָם אֶת פְּנֵי יְהוָה וַיְשַׁלְּחֵנוּ יְהוָה לְשַׁחֲתָהּ

Given.that make~Damage~ing(mp) We At the~Place the~This Given.that she~will~Magnify Cry~them(m) At Face~s "YHWH [*He exists*]" and~ he~will~Send~us "YHWH [*He exists*]" to~>~Damage~her

given that we will destroy this place, given that their cry will magnify at the face of "YHWH [*He exists*]" and "YHWH [*He exists*]" sent us to damage her,

**19:14** וַיֵּצֵא לוֹט וַיְדַבֵּר אֶל חֲתָנָיו לֹקְחֵי בְנֹתָיו וַיֹּאמֶר קוּמוּ צְּאוּ מִן הַמָּקוֹם הַזֶּה כִּי מַשְׁחִית יְהוָה אֶת הָעִיר וַיְהִי כִמְצַחֵק בְּעֵינֵי חֲתָנָיו

and~he~will~Go.out "Loth [*Covering*]" and~he~will~Speak To In-law~s~him Take~ing(mp) Daughter~s~him and~ he~will~Say !(mp)~Rise !(mp)~Go.out From the~Place the~This Given.that make~Damage~ing(ms) "YHWH [*He exists*]" At the~City and~he~will~ Exist like~much~Laugh~ing(ms) in~ Eye~s2 In-law~s~him

and "Loth [*Covering*]" went out and he spoke to his in-laws, ones taking his daughters, and he said rise, go out from this place given that "YHWH [*He exists*]" will destroy the city and he was like one greatly laughing in the eyes of his in-laws,

**19:15** וּכְמוֹ הַשַּׁחַר עָלָה וַיָּאִיצוּ הַמַּלְאָכִים בְּלוֹט לֵאמֹר קוּם קַח אֶת אִשְׁתְּךָ וְאֶת שְׁתֵּי בְנֹתֶיךָ הַנִּמְצָאֹת פֶּן תִּסָּפֶה בַּעֲוֹן הָעִיר

and~like~That.one the~Dawn he~had~ Go.up and~they(m)~will~make~Compel the~Messenger~s in~"Loth [*Covering*]" to~>~Say !(ms)~Rise !(ms)~Take At Woman~you(ms) and~At Two Daughter~s~you(ms) the~be~Find~ ing(fp) Otherwise you(ms)~will~be~

and as the dawn had come up, then the messengers compelled "Loth [*Covering*]" saying, rise, take your woman and your two daughters, the ones being found, otherwise you will be consumed in the iniquity of the city,

Consume in~Iniquity the~City

**19:16** וַיִּתְמַהְמָהּ וַיַּחֲזִיקוּ הָאֲנָשִׁים בְּיָדוֹ וּבְיַד אִשְׁתּוֹ וּבְיַד שְׁתֵּי בְנֹתָיו בְּחֶמְלַת יְהוָה עָלָיו וַיֹּצִאֻהוּ וַיַּנִּחֻהוּ מִחוּץ לָעִיר

and~he~will~self-Linger and~they(m)~will~make-Seize the~Man~s in~Hand~him and~in~Hand Woman~him and~in~Hand Two Daughter~s~him in~Compassionate "YHWH [*He exists*]" Upon~him and~they(m)~will~make-Go.out~him and~they(m)~will~make-Rest~him from~Outside to~the~City

and he lingered himself and the men seized his hand and the hand of his woman and with the hand of his two daughters, "YHWH [*He exists*]" with compassion upon him and they brought him out and they left him outside the city,

**19:17** וַיְהִי כְהוֹצִיאָם אֹתָם הַחוּצָה וַיֹּאמֶר הִמָּלֵט עַל נַפְשֶׁךָ אַל תַּבִּיט אַחֲרֶיךָ וְאַל תַּעֲמֹד בְּכָל הַכִּכָּר הָהָרָה הִמָּלֵט פֶּן תִּסָּפֶה

and~he~will~Exist like~>~make-Go.out~them(m) At~them(m) the~Outside~unto and~he~will~Say !(ms)~be-Slip.away Upon Being~you(ms) No you(ms)~will~make-Stare After~you(ms) and~No you(ms)~will~Stand in~All the~Roundness the~Hill~unto !(ms)~be-Slip.away Otherwise you(ms)~will~be-Consume

and it came to pass as they brought them out unto the outside and he said, slip away upon your being, you will not stare behind you and you will not stand in all of the roundness, slip away unto the hill, otherwise you will be consumed,

**19:18** וַיֹּאמֶר לוֹט אֲלֵהֶם אַל נָא אֲדֹנָי

and~he~will~Say "Loth [*Covering*]" To~them(m) No Please Lord~s~me

and "Loth [*Covering*]" said to them, please no my lord,

**19:19** הִנֵּה נָא מָצָא עַבְדְּךָ חֵן בְּעֵינֶיךָ וַתַּגְדֵּל חַסְדְּךָ אֲשֶׁר עָשִׂיתָ עִמָּדִי לְהַחֲיוֹת אֶת נַפְשִׁי וְאָנֹכִי לֹא אוּכַל לְהִמָּלֵט הָהָרָה פֶּן תִּדְבָּקַנִי הָרָעָה וָמַתִּי

Look Please he~did-Find Servant~you(ms) Beauty in~Eye~s2~you(ms) and~you(ms)~will~make-Magnify Kindness~you(ms) Which you(ms)~did-Do By~me to~>~make-Live At Being~me and~I Not i~will-Be.able to~>~make-Slip.away the~Hill~unto Otherwise she~will~Adhere~me the~Dysfunctional and~i~did~Die

please look, your servant found beauty in your eyes and you magnified your kindness which you did by me, making my being live and I will not be able to slip away unto the hill otherwise dysfunction will adhere to me and I will die,

**19:20** הִנֵּה נָא הָעִיר הַזֹּאת קְרֹבָה לָנוּס שָׁמָּה וְהִוא מִצְעָר אִמָּלְטָה נָּא שָׁמָּה הֲלֹא מִצְעָר הִוא וּתְחִי נַפְשִׁי

Look Please the~City the~This Near to~>~Flee There~unto and~She Few

please look, this city is near, to flee unto there and she is few, please, I

i~will~be~Slip.away Please There~unto ?~Not Few She and~she~will~Live Being~me

will slip away unto there, is she not few, and my being will live,

**19:21** וַיֹּאמֶר אֵלָיו הִנֵּה נָשָׂאתִי פָנֶיךָ גַּם לַדָּבָר הַזֶּה לְבִלְתִּי הָפְכִּי אֶת הָעִיר אֲשֶׁר דִּבַּרְתָּ

and~he~will~Say To~him Look i~did~Lift.up Face~s~you(ms) Also to~the~Word the~This to~Except >~Overturn~me At the~City Which you(ms)~did~much~Speak

and he said to him, look, I lifted up your face also to this word for I will not overturn the city which you spoke,

**19:22** מַהֵר הִמָּלֵט שָׁמָּה כִּי לֹא אוּכַל לַעֲשׂוֹת דָּבָר עַד בֹּאֲךָ שָׁמָּה עַל כֵּן קָרָא שֵׁם הָעִיר צוֹעַר

!(ms)~Hurry !(ms)~be~Slip.away There~unto Given.that Not i~will~Be.able to~>~Do Word Until >~Come~you(ms) There~unto Upon So he~did~Call.out Title the~City "Tso'ar [Tiny]"

hurry, slip away unto there given that I will not be able to do a word until you come unto there, therefore he called out the title of the city "Tso'ar [Tiny]",

**19:23** הַשֶּׁמֶשׁ יָצָא עַל הָאָרֶץ וְלוֹט בָּא צֹעֲרָה

the~Sun he~did~Go.out Upon the~Land and~"Loth [Covering]" he~did~Come "Tso'ar [Tiny]"~unto

the sun went out upon the land and "Loth [Covering]" came unto "Tso'ar [Tiny]",

**19:24** וַיהוָה הִמְטִיר עַל סְדֹם וְעַל עֲמֹרָה גָּפְרִית וָאֵשׁ מֵאֵת יְהוָה מִן הַשָּׁמָיִם

and~"YHWH [He exists]" he~did~make~Precipitate Upon "Sedom [Secret]" and~Upon "Ghamorah [Rebellion]" Brimstone and~Fire from~At "YHWH [He exists]" From the~Sky~s2

and "YHWH [He exists]" caused to precipitate upon "Sedom [Secret]" and upon "Ghamorah [Rebellion]" brimstone and fire from "YHWH [He exists]" from the sky,

**19:25** וַיַּהֲפֹךְ אֶת הֶעָרִים הָאֵל וְאֵת כָּל הַכִּכָּר וְאֵת כָּל יֹשְׁבֵי הֶעָרִים וְצֶמַח הָאֲדָמָה

and~he~will~Overturn At the~City~s the~These and~At All the~Roundness and~At All Settle~ing(mp) the~City~s and~Spring.up the~Ground

and he overturned these cities and all of the roundness and all of the settlers of the cities and the spring up things of the ground,

**19:26** וַתַּבֵּט אִשְׁתּוֹ מֵאַחֲרָיו וַתְּהִי נְצִיב מֶלַח

and~she~will~make~Stare Woman~him from~After~him and~she~will~Exist Post Salt

and his woman stared from behind him and she existed as a post of salt,

**19:27** וַיַּשְׁכֵּם אַבְרָהָם בַּבֹּקֶר אֶל הַמָּקוֹם אֲשֶׁר עָמַד שָׁם אֶת פְּנֵי יְהוָה

and~he~will~Depart.early "Avraham [*Father lifted*]" in~the~Morning To the~Place Which he~did~Stand There At Face~s "YHWH [*He exists*]"

and "Avraham [*Father lifted*]" departed early in the morning to the place where he stood there with the face of "YHWH [*He exists*]",

**19:28** וַיַּשְׁקֵף עַל פְּנֵי סְדֹם וַעֲמֹרָה וְעַל כָּל פְּנֵי אֶרֶץ הַכִּכָּר וַיַּרְא וְהִנֵּה עָלָה קִיטֹר הָאָרֶץ כְּקִיטֹר הַכִּבְשָׁן

and~he~will~make~Look.down Upon Face~s "Sedom [*Secret*]" and~ "Ghamorah [*Rebellion*]" and~Upon All Face~s Land the~Roundness and~he~will~See and~Look he~did~Go.up Smoldering the~Land like~Smoldering the~Furnace

and he looked down upon the face of "Sedom [*Secret*]" and "Ghamorah [*Rebellion*]" and upon all of the face of the land of the roundness and he saw and look, a smoldering of the land went up like a smoldering furnace,

**19:29** וַיְהִי בְּשַׁחֵת אֱלֹהִים אֶת עָרֵי הַכִּכָּר וַיִּזְכֹּר אֱלֹהִים אֶת אַבְרָהָם וַיְשַׁלַּח אֶת לוֹט מִתּוֹךְ הַהֲפֵכָה בַּהֲפֹךְ אֶת הֶעָרִים אֲשֶׁר יָשַׁב בָּהֵן לוֹט

and~he~will~Exist in~>~much~Damage "Elohiym [*Powers*]" At City~s the~ Roundness and~he~will~Remember "Elohiym [*Powers*]" At "Avraham [*Father lifted*]" and~he~will~much~ Send At "Loth [*Covering*]" from~ Midst the~Overturning in~>~Overturn At the~City~s Which he~did~Settle in~them(f) "Loth [*Covering*]"

and it came to pass "Elohiym [*Powers*]" greatly damaged the cities of the roundness and "Elohiym [*Powers*]" remembered "Avraham [*Father lifted*]" and he sent "Loth [*Covering*]" from the midst of the overturning, in overturning the cities which "Loth [*Covering*]" settled in,

**19:30** וַיַּעַל לוֹט מִצּוֹעַר וַיֵּשֶׁב בָּהָר וּשְׁתֵּי בְנֹתָיו עִמּוֹ כִּי יָרֵא לָשֶׁבֶת בְּצוֹעַר וַיֵּשֶׁב בַּמְּעָרָה הוּא וּשְׁתֵּי בְנֹתָיו

and~he~will~Go.up "Loth [*Covering*]" from~"Tso'ar [*Tiny*]" and~he~will~ Settle in~the~Hill and~Two Daughter~ s~him With~him Given.that he~did~ Fear to~>~Settle in~"Tso'ar [*Tiny*]" and~he~will~Settle in~Cave He and~ Two Daughter~s~him

and "Loth [*Covering*]" and his two daughters with him, went up from "Tso'ar [*Tiny*]" and settled in the hill given that he feared to settle in "Tso'ar [*Tiny*]" and he and his two daughters settled in the cave,

**19:31** וַתֹּאמֶר הַבְּכִירָה אֶל הַצְּעִירָה אָבִינוּ זָקֵן וְאִישׁ אֵין בָּאָרֶץ לָבוֹא עָלֵינוּ כְּדֶרֶךְ כָּל הָאָרֶץ

and~she~will~Say the~Firstborn.female To the~Little.one Father~us he~did~ Be.old and~Man Without in~the~Land

and the firstborn woman said to the little one, our father is old and not a man in the land to come upon us

to~>~Come Upon~us like~Road All the~Land

like the road of all of the land,

**19:32** לְכָה נַשְׁקֶה אֶת אָבִינוּ יַיִן וְנִשְׁכְּבָה עִמּוֹ וּנְחַיֶּה מֵאָבִינוּ זָרַע

Walk we~will~make~Drink At Father~us Wine and~we~will~Lay.down With~him and~we~will~Live from~Father~us Seed

walk, we will make our father drink wine and we will lay down with him and we will live from our father a seed,

**19:33** וַתַּשְׁקֶיןָ אֶת אֲבִיהֶן יַיִן בַּלַּיְלָה הוּא וַתָּבֹא הַבְּכִירָה וַתִּשְׁכַּב אֶת אָבִיהָ וְלֹא יָדַע בְּשִׁכְבָהּ וּבְקוּמָהּ

and~they(f)~will~make~Drink At Father~them(f) Wine in~the~Night He and~she~will~Come the~Firstborn.female and~she~will~Lay.down At Father~her and~Not he~did~Know in~>~ Lay.down~her and~in~>~Rise~her

and they made their father drink wine in that night and the firstborn woman came and she laid down with her father and he did not know in her laying down and in her rising,

**19:34** וַיְהִי מִמָּחֳרָת וַתֹּאמֶר הַבְּכִירָה אֶל הַצְּעִירָה הֵן שָׁכַבְתִּי אֶמֶשׁ אֶת אָבִי נַשְׁקֶנּוּ יַיִן גַּם הַלַּיְלָה וּבֹאִי שִׁכְבִי עִמּוֹ וּנְחַיֶּה מֵאָבִינוּ זָרַע

and~he~will~Exist from~Tomorrow and~she~will~Say the~Firstborn.female To the~Little.one Though i~did~ Lay.down Last.night At Father~me we~will~make~Drink~him Wine Also the~Night and~!(fs)~Come !(fs)~ Lay.down With~him and~we~will~Live from~Father~us Seed

and it came to pass the next day and the firstborn woman said to the little one, though I laid down last night with my father we will make him drink wine also tonight and come and lay down with him and we will live from our father a seed,

**19:35** וַתַּשְׁקֶיןָ גַּם בַּלַּיְלָה הַהוּא אֶת אֲבִיהֶן יַיִן וַתָּקָם הַצְּעִירָה וַתִּשְׁכַּב עִמּוֹ וְלֹא יָדַע בְּשִׁכְבָהּ וּבְקֻמָהּ

and~they(f)~will~make~Drink Also in~ the~Night the~He At Father~them(m) Wine and~she~will~Rise the~Little.one and~she~will~Lay.down With~him and~Not he~did~Know in~>~ Lay.down~her and~in~>~Rise~her

and they made their father drink wine also in that night and the little one rose and she laid down with him and he did not know in her laying down and in her rising,

**19:36** וַתַּהֲרֶיןָ שְׁתֵּי בְנוֹת לוֹט מֵאֲבִיהֶן

and~they(f)~will~Conceive Two Daughter~s "Loth [*Covering*]" from~ Father~them(f)

and the two daughters of "Loth [*Covering*]" conceived from their father,

**19:37** וַתֵּלֶד הַבְּכִירָה בֵּן וַתִּקְרָא שְׁמוֹ מוֹאָב הוּא אֲבִי מוֹאָב עַד הַיּוֹם

and~she~will~Bring.forth the~ Firstborn.female Son and~she~will~

and the firstborn woman brought forth a son and she called out his

**103**

Call.out Title~him "Mo'av [*From father*]" He Father~of "Mo'av [*From father*]" Until the~Day

title "Mo'av [*From father*]", he is the father of the "Mo'av [*From father*]" until today,

**19:38**

וְהַצְּעִירָה גַם הִוא יָלְדָה בֵּן וַתִּקְרָא שְׁמוֹ בֶּן עַמִּי הוּא אֲבִי בְנֵי עַמּוֹן עַד הַיּוֹם

and~the~Little.one Also She she~did~Bring.forth Son and~she~will~Call.out Title~him "Ben-Amiy [*Son of my people*]" He Father~of Son~s "Amon [*Tribe*]" Until the~Day

and the little one, she also brought forth a son and she called out his title "Ben-Amiy [*Son of my people*]", he is the father of the sons of "Amon [*Tribe*]" until today,

# Chapter 20

**20:1**

וַיִּסַּע מִשָּׁם אַבְרָהָם אַרְצָה הַנֶּגֶב וַיֵּשֶׁב בֵּין קָדֵשׁ וּבֵין שׁוּר וַיָּגָר בִּגְרָר

and~he~will~Lift.up from~There "Avraham [*Father lifted*]" Land~unto the~South.country and~he~will~Settle Between "Kadesh [*Set apart*]" and~Between "Shur [*Caravan*]" and~he~will~Sojourn in~"Gerar [*Chew*]"

and "Avraham [*Father lifted*]" lifted up from there unto the land of the south country and he settled between "Kadesh [*Set apart*]" and "Shur [*Caravan*]" and he sojourned in "Gerar [*Chew*]",

**20:2\***

וַיֹּאמֶר אַבְרָהָם אֶל שָׂרָה אִשְׁתּוֹ אֲחֹתִי הִוא וַיִּשְׁלַח אֲבִימֶלֶךְ מֶלֶךְ גְּרָר וַיִּקַּח אֶת שָׂרָה

and~he~will~Say "Avraham [*Father lifted*]" To "Sarah [*Noblewoman*]" Woman~him Sister~me She and~he~will~Send "Aviymelekh [*My father is king*]" King "Gerar [*Chew*]" and~he~will~Take At "Sarah [*Noblewoman*]"

and "Avraham [*Father lifted*]" said to "Sarah [*Noblewoman*]" his woman, she is my sister and "Aviymelekh [*My father is king*]" the king of "Gerar [*Chew*]" sent and he took "Sarah [*Noblewoman*]",

**20:3**

וַיָּבֹא אֱלֹהִים אֶל אֲבִימֶלֶךְ בַּחֲלוֹם הַלָּיְלָה וַיֹּאמֶר לוֹ הִנְּךָ מֵת עַל הָאִשָּׁה אֲשֶׁר לָקַחְתָּ וְהִוא בְּעֻלַת בָּעַל

and~he~will~Come "Elohiym [*Powers*]" To "Aviymelekh [*My father is king*]" in~the~Dream in~Night and~he~will~Say to~him Look~you(ms) Die~ing(ms) Upon the~Woman Which you(ms)~did~Take and~She Marry~ed(fs) Master

and "Elohiym [*Powers*]" came to "Aviymelekh [*My father is king*]" in the dream in the night and he said to him, look at you, dying because of the woman which you took and she is the married of a master,

**20:4**

וַאֲבִימֶלֶךְ לֹא קָרַב אֵלֶיהָ וַיֹּאמַר אֲדֹנָי הֲגוֹי גַּם צַדִּיק תַּהֲרֹג

and~"Aviymelekh [*My father is king*]" Not he~had~Come.near To~her and~he~will~Say "Adonai [*My lords*]" ?~Nation Also Correct you(ms)~will~Kill

and "Aviymelekh [*My father is king*]" had not come near to her and he said, "Adonai [*My lords*]" will you kill also a correct nation,

**20:5** הֲלֹא הוּא אָמַר לִי אֲחֹתִי הִוא וְהִיא גַם הִוא אָמְרָה אָחִי הוּא בְּתָם לְבָבִי וּבְנִקְיֹן כַּפַּי עָשִׂיתִי זֹאת

?~Not He he~did~Say to~me Sister~me She and~She Also She she~did~Say Brother~me He in~Mature Mind~me and~in~Innocence Palm~s2~me i~did~Do This

did he not say to me she is my sister and she also said he is my brother, in the maturity of my mind and in the innocence of my palms I did this,

**20:6\*** וַיֹּאמֶר אֵלָיו הָאֱלֹהִים בַּחֲלֹם גַּם אָנֹכִי יָדַעְתִּי כִּי בְתָם לְבָבְךָ עָשִׂיתָ זֹּאת וָאֶחְשֹׂךְ גַּם אָנֹכִי אוֹתְךָ מֵחֲטוֹ לִי עַל כֵּן לֹא נְתַתִּיךָ לִנְגֹּעַ אֵלֶיהָ

and~he~will~Say To~him the~"Elohiym [*Powers*]" in~the~Dream Also I i~did~Know Given.that in~Mature Mind~you(ms) you(ms)~did~Do This and~i~will~Keep.back Also I At~you(ms) from~Fault~him to~me Upon So Not i~did~Give~you(ms) to~>~Touch To~her

and the "Elohiym [*Powers*]" said to him in the dream, I also knew given that in the maturity of your mind you did this and I also kept you back from his fault to me therefore, I did not give you to touch her,

**20:7** וְעַתָּה הָשֵׁב אֵשֶׁת הָאִישׁ כִּי נָבִיא הוּא וְיִתְפַּלֵּל בַּעַדְךָ וֶחְיֵה וְאִם אֵינְךָ מֵשִׁיב דַּע כִּי מוֹת תָּמוּת אַתָּה וְכָל אֲשֶׁר לָךְ

and~Now !(mp)~make~Turn.back Woman the~Man Given.that Prophet He and~he~will~self~Plead Round.about~you(ms) and~!(ms)~Live and~If Without~you(ms) make~Turn.back~ing(ms) !(ms)~Know Given.that >~Die you(ms)~will~Die You(ms) and~All Which to~you(fs)

and now make the woman of the man return given that he is a prophet and he will plead round about you and live and if you do not make a returning know that you will surely die,

**20:8** וַיַּשְׁכֵּם אֲבִימֶלֶךְ בַּבֹּקֶר וַיִּקְרָא לְכָל עֲבָדָיו וַיְדַבֵּר אֵת כָּל הַדְּבָרִים הָאֵלֶּה בְּאָזְנֵיהֶם וַיִּירְאוּ הָאֲנָשִׁים מְאֹד

and~he~will~make~Depart.early "Aviymelekh [*My father is king*]" in~the~Morning and~he~will~Call.out to~All Servant~s~him and~he~will~Speak At All the~Word~s the~These in~Ear~s2~them(m) and~they(m)~will~Fear the~Man~s Many

and "Aviymelekh [*My father is king*]" departed early in the morning and he called out to all of his servants and he spoke all of these words in their ears and the men greatly feared,

**20:9** וַיִּקְרָא אֲבִימֶלֶךְ לְאַבְרָהָם וַיֹּאמֶר לוֹ מֶה עָשִׂיתָ לָּנוּ וּמֶה חָטָאתִי לָךְ כִּי הֵבֵאתָ עָלַי וְעַל מַמְלַכְתִּי חֲטָאָה גְדֹלָה מַעֲשִׂים אֲשֶׁר לֹא יֵעָשׂוּ עָשִׂיתָ עִמָּדִי

and~he~will~Call.out "Aviymelekh [*My father is king*]" to~"Avraham [*Father lifted*]" and~he~will~Say to~him What you(ms)~did~Do to~us and~What i~did~Err to~you(fs) Given.that you(ms)~did~make~Come Upon~me and~Upon Kingdom.place~me Error Magnificent Work~s Which Not they~did~be~Do you(ms)~did~Do By~me

and "Aviymelekh [*My father is king*]" called out to "Avraham [*Father lifted*]" and said, to him what did you do to us and how did I err to you given that you brought upon me and upon my kingdom place a magnificent error, works which were not done, you did by me,

**20:10** וַיֹּאמֶר אֲבִימֶלֶךְ אֶל אַבְרָהָם מָה רָאִיתָ כִּי עָשִׂיתָ אֶת הַדָּבָר הַזֶּה

and~he~will~Say "Aviymelekh [*My father is king*]" To "Avraham [*Father lifted*]" What you(ms)~did~See Given.that you(ms)~did~Do At the~Word the~This

and "Aviymelekh [*My father is king*]" said to "Avraham [*Father lifted*]", what did you see given that you did this word,

**20:11** וַיֹּאמֶר אַבְרָהָם כִּי אָמַרְתִּי רַק אֵין יִרְאַת אֱלֹהִים בַּמָּקוֹם הַזֶּה וַהֲרָגוּנִי עַל דְּבַר אִשְׁתִּי

and~he~will~Say "Avraham [*Father lifted*]" Given.that i~did~Say Only Without Fearfulness "Elohiym [*Powers*]" in~the~Place the~This and~they~did~Kill~me Upon Word Woman~me

and "Avraham [*Father lifted*]" said, given that I said, fearfulness of "Elohiym [*Powers*]" is not at all in this place and they will kill me because of my woman,

**20:12** וְגַם אָמְנָה אֲחֹתִי בַת אָבִי הוּא אַךְ לֹא בַת אִמִּי וַתְּהִי לִי לְאִשָּׁה

and~Also Sure Sister~me Daughter Father~me She Surely Not Daughter Mother~me and~she~will~Exist to~me to~Woman

and indeed she is my sister, daughter of my father, surely not the daughter of my mother and she exists to me for a woman,

**20:13** וַיְהִי כַּאֲשֶׁר הִתְעוּ אֹתִי אֱלֹהִים מִבֵּית אָבִי וָאֹמַר לָהּ זֶה חַסְדֵּךְ אֲשֶׁר תַּעֲשִׂי עִמָּדִי אֶל כָּל הַמָּקוֹם אֲשֶׁר נָבוֹא שָׁמָּה אִמְרִי לִי אָחִי הוּא

and~he~will~Exist like~Which they~did~make~Wander At~me "Elohiym [*Powers*]" from~House Father~me and~i~will~Say to~her This

and it came to pass just as "Elohiym [*Powers*]" caused me to wander from the house of my father and I said to her, this is your

Kindness~you(fs) Which you(fs)~will~ Do By~me To All the~Place Which we~will~Come There~unto !(ms)~Say to~me Brother~me He

kindness which you will do by me to all of the places which we will come unto, say for me he is my brother,

**20:14** וַיִּקַּח אֲבִימֶלֶךְ צֹאן וּבָקָר וַעֲבָדִים וּשְׁפָחֹת וַיִּתֵּן לְאַבְרָהָם וַיָּשֶׁב לוֹ אֵת שָׂרָה אִשְׁתּוֹ

and~he~will~Take "Aviymelekh [*My father is king*]" Flocks and~Cattle and~Servant~s and~Maid~s and~he~ will~Give to~"Avraham [*Father lifted*]" and~he~will~Turn.back to~him At "Sarah [*Noblewoman*]" Woman~ him

and "Aviymelekh [*My father is king*]" took flocks and cattle and servants and maids and he gave to "Avraham [*Father lifted*]" and turned "Sarah [*Noblewoman*]" his woman back to him,

**20:15** וַיֹּאמֶר אֲבִימֶלֶךְ הִנֵּה אַרְצִי לְפָנֶיךָ בַּטּוֹב בְּעֵינֶיךָ שֵׁב

and~he~will~Say "Aviymelekh [*My father is king*]" Look Land~me to~ Face~s~you(ms) in~the~Functional in~ Eye~s2~you(ms) !(ms)~Settle

and "Aviymelekh [*My father is king*]" said, look, my land is to your face, functional in your eyes, settle,

**20:16** וּלְשָׂרָה אָמַר הִנֵּה נָתַתִּי אֶלֶף כֶּסֶף לְאָחִיךְ הִנֵּה הוּא לָךְ כְּסוּת עֵינַיִם לְכֹל אֲשֶׁר אִתָּךְ וְאֵת כֹּל וְנֹכָחַת

and~to~"Sarah [*Noblewoman*]" he~did~ Say Look i~did~Give Thousand Silver to~Brother~you(fs) Look He to~you(fs) Raiment Eye~s2 to~All Which At~you(fs) and~At All and~ be~Convict~ing(fs)

and to "Sarah [*Noblewoman*]" he said, look, I gave a thousand silver to your brother look, he is to you a raiment of the eyes to all who are with you and with all and being convicted,

**20:17** וַיִּתְפַּלֵּל אַבְרָהָם אֶל הָאֱלֹהִים וַיִּרְפָּא אֱלֹהִים אֶת אֲבִימֶלֶךְ וְאֶת אִשְׁתּוֹ וְאַמְהֹתָיו וַיֵּלֵדוּ

and~he~will~self~Plead "Avraham [*Father lifted*]" To the~"Elohiym [*Powers*]" and~he~will~Heal "Elohiym [*Powers*]" At "Aviymelekh [*My father is king*]" and~At Woman~him and~Bondwoman~s~him and~they(m)~ will~Bring.forth

and "Avraham [*Father lifted*]" pleaded to the "Elohiym [*Powers*]" and "Elohiym [*Powers*]" healed "Aviymelekh [*My father is king*]" and his woman and his bondwomen and they brought forth,

**20:18** כִּי עָצֹר עָצַר יְהוָה בְּעַד כָּל רֶחֶם לְבֵית אֲבִימֶלֶךְ עַל דְּבַר שָׂרָה אֵשֶׁת אַבְרָהָם

Given.that >~Stop he~did~Stop "YHWH [*He exists*]" Round.about All Bowels to~House "Aviymelekh [*My father is king*]" Upon Word

given that "YHWH [*He exists*]" stopped round about all the bowels to the house of "Aviymelekh [*My father is king*]" because of "Sarah

"Sarah [*Noblewoman*]" Woman "Avraham [*Father lifted*]"

[*Noblewoman*]" the woman of "Avraham [*Father lifted*]",

# Chapter 21

**21:1** וַיהוָה פָּקַד אֶת שָׂרָה כַּאֲשֶׁר אָמָר וַיַּעַשׂ יְהוָה לְשָׂרָה כַּאֲשֶׁר דִּבֵּר

and~"YHWH [*He exists*]" he~had~Visit At "Sarah [*Noblewoman*]" like~Which he~did~Say and~he~will~Do "YHWH [*He exists*]" to~"Sarah [*Noblewoman*]" like~Which he~did~much~Speak

and "YHWH [*He exists*]" had visited "Sarah [*Noblewoman*]" just as he said and "YHWH [*He exists*]" did to "Sarah [*Noblewoman*]" just as he spoke,

**21:2** וַתַּהַר וַתֵּלֶד שָׂרָה לְאַבְרָהָם בֵּן לִזְקֻנָיו לַמּוֹעֵד אֲשֶׁר דִּבֶּר אֹתוֹ אֱלֹהִים

and~she~will~Conceive and~she~will~Bring.forth "Sarah [*Noblewoman*]" to~"Avraham [*Father lifted*]" Son to~Extreme.old.age~s~him to~the~Appointed Which he~did~much~Speak At~him "Elohiym [*Powers*]"

and "Sarah [*Noblewoman*]" conceived and she brought forth for "Avraham [*Father lifted*]" a son to his extreme old age to the appointed time which "Elohiym [*Powers*]" spoke to him,

**21:3** וַיִּקְרָא אַבְרָהָם אֶת שֵׁם בְּנוֹ הַנּוֹלַד לוֹ אֲשֶׁר יָלְדָה לוֹ שָׂרָה יִצְחָק

and~he~will~Call.out "Avraham [*Father lifted*]" At Title Son~him the~be~Bring.forth~ing(ms) to~him Which she~did~Bring.forth to~him "Sarah [*Noblewoman*]" "Yits'hhaq [*He laughs*]"

and "Avraham [*Father lifted*]" called out the title of his son, being brought forth for him which "Sarah [*Noblewoman*]" brought forth for him, "Yits'hhaq [*He laughs*]",

**21:4** וַיָּמָל אַבְרָהָם אֶת יִצְחָק בְּנוֹ בֶּן שְׁמֹנַת יָמִים כַּאֲשֶׁר צִוָּה אֹתוֹ אֱלֹהִים

and~he~will~Circumcise "Avraham [*Father lifted*]" At "Yits'hhaq [*He laughs*]" Son~him Son Eight Day~s like~Which he~did~much~Direct At~him "Elohiym [*Powers*]"

and "Avraham [*Father lifted*]" circumcised "Yits'hhaq [*He laughs*]" his son, a son of eight days just as "Elohiym [*Powers*]" directed him,

**21:5** וְאַבְרָהָם בֶּן מְאַת שָׁנָה בְּהִוָּלֶד לוֹ אֵת יִצְחָק בְּנוֹ

and~"Avraham [*Father lifted*]" Son Hundred Year in~>~be~Bring.forth to~him At "Yits'hhaq [*He laughs*]"

and "Avraham [*Father lifted*]" was a son of a hundred years with "Yits'hhaq [*He laughs*]" his son,

Son~him

being brought forth for him,

**21:6** וַתֹּאמֶר שָׂרָה צְחֹק עָשָׂה לִי אֱלֹהִים כָּל הַשֹּׁמֵעַ יִצְחַק לִי

and~she~will~Say "Sarah [*Noblewoman*]" Laughter he~did~Do to~me "Elohiym [*Powers*]" All the~Hear~ing(ms) he~will~Laugh to~me

and "Sarah [*Noblewoman*]" said, "Elohiym [*Powers*] did laughter to me, all the ones hearing will laugh for me,

**21:7** וַתֹּאמֶר מִי מִלֵּל לְאַבְרָהָם הֵינִיקָה בָנִים שָׂרָה כִּי יָלַדְתִּי בֵן לִזְקֻנָיו

and~she~will~Say Who he~did~much~Talk to~"Avraham [*Father lifted*]" she~did~make~Suckle Son~s "Sarah [*Noblewoman*]" Given.that i~did~Bring.forth Son to~Extreme.old.age~s~him

and she said, who talked to "Avraham [*Father lifted*]", "Sarah [*Noblewoman*]" made sons suckle given that I brought forth a son to his extreme old age,

**21:8** וַיִּגְדַּל הַיֶּלֶד וַיִּגָּמַל וַיַּעַשׂ אַבְרָהָם מִשְׁתֶּה גָדוֹל בְּיוֹם הִגָּמֵל אֶת יִצְחָק

and~he~will~Magnify the~Boy and~he~will~be~Yield and~he~will~Do "Avraham [*Father lifted*]" Feast Magnificent in~Day >~be~Yield At "Yits'hhaq [*He laughs*]"

and the boy will magnify and he will be yielded and "Avraham [*Father lifted*]" will do a magnificent feast in the day "Yits'hhaq [*He laughs*]" is being yielded,

**21:9** וַתֵּרֶא שָׂרָה אֶת בֶּן הָגָר הַמִּצְרִית אֲשֶׁר יָלְדָה לְאַבְרָהָם מְצַחֵק

and~she~will~See "Sarah [*Noblewoman*]" At Son "Hagar [*Stranger*]" the~"Mitsrayim [*Troubles*]"~of Which she~did~Bring.forth to~"Avraham [*Father lifted*]" much~Laugh~ing(ms)

and "Sarah [*Noblewoman*]" saw the son of "Hagar [*Stranger*]", the one of "Mitsrayim [*Troubles*]" which brought forth for "Avraham [*Father lifted*]", much mocking,

**21:10** וַתֹּאמֶר לְאַבְרָהָם גָּרֵשׁ הָאָמָה הַזֹּאת וְאֶת בְּנָהּ כִּי לֹא יִירַשׁ בֶּן הָאָמָה הַזֹּאת עִם בְּנִי עִם יִצְחָק

and~she~will~Say to~"Avraham [*Father lifted*]" >~much~Cast.out the~Bondwoman the~This and~At Son~her Given.that Not he~will~Inherit Son the~Bondwoman the~This With Son~me With "Yits'hhaq [*He laughs*]"

and she said to "Avraham [*Father lifted*]", cast out this bondwoman and her son given that the son of this bondwoman will not inherit with my son "Yits'hhaq [*He laughs*]",

**21:11** וַיֵּרַע הַדָּבָר מְאֹד בְּעֵינֵי אַבְרָהָם עַל אוֹדֹת בְּנוֹ

and~he~will~Be.dysfunctional the~Word Many in~Eye~s2 "Avraham [*Father lifted*]" Upon Concerning Son~him

and the word was very dysfunctional in the eyes of "Avraham [*Father lifted*]" concerning his son,

**21:12** וַיֹּאמֶר אֱלֹהִים אֶל אַבְרָהָם אַל יֵרַע בְּעֵינֶיךָ עַל הַנַּעַר וְעַל אֲמָתֶךָ כֹּל אֲשֶׁר תֹּאמַר אֵלֶיךָ שָׂרָה שְׁמַע בְּקֹלָהּ כִּי בְיִצְחָק יִקָּרֵא לְךָ זָרַע

and~he~will~Say "Elohiym [*Powers*]" To "Avraham [*Father lifted*]" No he~will~Be.dysfunctional in~Eye~s2~ you(ms) Upon the~Young.man and~ Upon Bondwoman~you(ms) All Which she~will~Say To~you(ms) "Sarah [*Noblewoman*]" !(ms)~Hear in~ Voice~her Given.that in~"Yits'hhaq [*He laughs*]" he~will~be~Call.out to~ you(ms) Seed

and "Elohiym [*Powers*]" said to "Avraham [*Father lifted*]", it is not dysfunctional in your eyes upon the young man and upon your bondwoman, all which "Sarah [*Noblewoman*]" says to you, hear in her voice given that in "Yits'hhaq [*He laughs*]", seed will be called out to you,

**21:13** וְגַם אֶת בֶּן הָאָמָה לְגוֹי אֲשִׂימֶנּוּ כִּי זַרְעֲךָ הוּא

and~Also At Son the~Bondwoman to~Nation i~will~Set.in.place~him Given.that Seed~you(ms) He

and also I will set in place the son of the bondwoman for a nation given that he is your seed,

**21:14** וַיַּשְׁכֵּם אַבְרָהָם בַּבֹּקֶר וַיִּקַּח לֶחֶם וְחֵמַת מַיִם וַיִּתֵּן אֶל הָגָר שָׂם עַל שִׁכְמָהּ וְאֶת הַיֶּלֶד וַיְשַׁלְּחֶהָ וַתֵּלֶךְ וַתֵּתַע בְּמִדְבַּר בְּאֵר שָׁבַע

and~he~will~Depart.early "Avraham [*Father lifted*]" in~the~Morning and~ he~will~Take Bread and~Skin.bag Water~s2 and~he~will~Give To "Hagar [*Stranger*]" Set.in.place~ing(ms) Upon Shoulder~her and~At the~Boy and~he~will~Send~her and~she~will~ Walk and~she~will~Wander in~ Wilderness "B'er-Sheva [*Well of oath*]"

and "Avraham [*Father lifted*]" departed early in the morning and he took bread and a skin bag of water and he gave to "Hagar [*Stranger*]" setting the boy in place upon her shoulder and he sent her and she walked and she wandered in the wilderness of "B'er-Sheva [*Well of oath*]",

**21:15** וַיִּכְלוּ הַמַּיִם מִן הַחֵמֶת וַתַּשְׁלֵךְ אֶת הַיֶּלֶד תַּחַת אַחַד הַשִּׂיחִם

and~they(m)~will~Finish the~Water~s2 From the~Skin.bag and~she~will~ Throw.out At the~Boy Under Unit the~Shrub

and they finished the water from the skin bag and she threw out the boy under one of the shrubs,

**21:16** וַתֵּלֶךְ וַתֵּשֶׁב לָהּ מִנֶּגֶד הַרְחֵק כִּמְטַחֲוֵי קֶשֶׁת כִּי אָמְרָה אַל אֶרְאֶה בְּמוֹת הַיָּלֶד וַתֵּשֶׁב מִנֶּגֶד וַתִּשָּׂא אֶת קֹלָהּ וַתֵּבְךְּ

and~she~will~Walk and~she~will~Settle to~her from~Opposite >~make~Be.far like~much~Hurl~ing(mp) Bow

and she walked and she settled herself opposite a far, like the hurling of a bow, given that she

Given.that she~did~Say No i~will~See in~Death the~Boy and~she~will~Settle from~Opposite and~she~will~Lift.up At Voice~her and~she~will~Weep

said I will not see in the death of the boy and she settled opposite and she lifted up her voice and she wept,

**21:17** וַיִּשְׁמַע אֱלֹהִים אֶת קוֹל הַנַּעַר וַיִּקְרָא מַלְאַךְ אֱלֹהִים אֶל הָגָר מִן הַשָּׁמַיִם וַיֹּאמֶר לָהּ מַה לָּךְ הָגָר אַל תִּירְאִי כִּי שָׁמַע אֱלֹהִים אֶל קוֹל הַנַּעַר בַּאֲשֶׁר הוּא שָׁם

and~he~will~Hear "Elohiym [*Powers*]" At Voice the~Young.man and~he~will~Call.out Messenger "Elohiym [*Powers*]" To "Hagar [*Stranger*]" From the~Sky~s2 and~he~will~Say to~her What to~you(fs) "Hagar [*Stranger*]" No you(fs)~will~Fear Given.that he~did~Hear "Elohiym [*Powers*]" At Voice the~Young.man in~Which He There

and "Elohiym [*Powers*]" heard the voice of the young man and the messenger of "Elohiym [*Powers*]" called out to "Hagar [*Stranger*]" from the sky and he said to her, what is to you "Hagar [*Stranger*]", you will not fear given that "Elohiym [*Powers*]" heard the voice of the young man whereas he is there,

**21:18** קוּמִי שְׂאִי אֶת הַנַּעַר וְהַחֲזִיקִי אֶת יָדֵךְ בּוֹ כִּי לְגוֹי גָּדוֹל אֲשִׂימֶנּוּ

!(ms)~Rise !(ms)~Lift.up At the~Young.man and~!(ms)~make~Seize At Hand~you(fs) in~him Given.that to~Nation Magnificent i~will~Set.in.place~him

rise, lift up the young man and make your hand seize with him given that I will set him in place for a magnificent nation,

**21:19** וַיִּפְקַח אֱלֹהִים אֶת עֵינֶיהָ וַתֵּרֶא בְּאֵר מָיִם וַתֵּלֶךְ וַתְּמַלֵּא אֶת הַחֵמֶת מַיִם וַתַּשְׁקְ אֶת הַנָּעַר

and~he~will~Open.up "Elohiym [*Powers*]" At Eye~s2~her and~she~will~See Well Water~s2 and~she~will~Walk and~she~will~Fill At the~Skin.bag Water~s2 and~she~will~make~Drink At the~Young.man

and "Elohiym [*Powers*]" opened up her eyes and she saw a well of water and she walked and she filled the skin bag of water and she made the young man drink,

**21:20** וַיְהִי אֱלֹהִים אֶת הַנַּעַר וַיִּגְדָּל וַיֵּשֶׁב בַּמִּדְבָּר וַיְהִי רֹבֶה קַשָּׁת

and~he~will~Exist "Elohiym [*Powers*]" At the~Young.man and~he~will~Magnify and~he~will~Settle in~the~Wilderness and~he~will~Exist Increase~ing(ms) Bow

and "Elohiym [*Powers*]" existed with the young man and he magnified and he settled in the wilderness and he existed increasing of a bow,

**21:21** וַיֵּשֶׁב בְּמִדְבַּר פָּארָן וַתִּקַּח לוֹ אִמּוֹ אִשָּׁה מֵאֶרֶץ מִצְרָיִם

and~he~will~Settle in~Wilderness "Paran [*Decoration*]" and~she~will~

and he settled in the wilderness of "Paran [*Decoration*]" and his

Take to~him Mother Woman from~
Land "Mitsrayim [*Troubles*]"

mother took for him a woman from
the land of "Mitsrayim [*Troubles*]",

**21:22** וַיְהִי בָּעֵת הַהִוא וַיֹּאמֶר אֲבִימֶלֶךְ וּפִיכֹל שַׂר צְבָאוֹ אֶל אַבְרָהָם
לֵאמֹר אֱלֹהִים עִמְּךָ בְּכֹל אֲשֶׁר אַתָּה עֹשֶׂה

and~he~will~Exist in~the~
Appointed.time the~He and~he~will~
Say "Aviymelekh [*My father is
king*]" and~"Pikhol [Face of all]"
Noble Army~him To "Avraham
[*Father lifted*]" to~>~Say "Elohiym
[*Powers*]" With~you(ms) in~All
Which You(ms) Do~ing(ms)

and it came to pass in that
appointed time "Aviymelekh [*My
father is king*]" and "Pikhol [Face
of all]", the noble of his army, said
to "Avraham [*Father lifted*]"
saying, "Elohiym [*Powers*]" is with
you in all which you are doing,

**21:23** וְעַתָּה הִשָּׁבְעָה לִּי בֵאלֹהִים הֵנָּה אִם תִּשְׁקֹר לִי וּלְנִינִי וּלְנֶכְדִּי
כַּחֶסֶד אֲשֶׁר עָשִׂיתִי עִמְּךָ תַּעֲשֶׂה עִמָּדִי וְעִם הָאָרֶץ אֲשֶׁר גַּרְתָּה
בָּהּ

and~Now !(ms)~be~Swear to~me in~
"Elohiym [*Powers*]" Thus.far If
you(ms)~will~Lie to~me and~to~Heir~
me and~to~Posterity~me like~the~
Kindness Which i~did~Do With~
you(ms) you(ms)~will~Do By~me
and~With the~Land Which you(ms)~
did~Sojourn in~her

and now swear to me in "Elohiym
[*Powers*]" thus far, if you will lie to
me and to my heir and to my
prosperity like the kindness which I
did with you, you will do by me
and with the land which you
sojourned in,

**21:24** וַיֹּאמֶר אַבְרָהָם אָנֹכִי אִשָּׁבֵעַ

and~he~will~Say "Avraham [*Father
lifted*]" I i~will~be~Swear

and "Avraham [*Father lifted*]" said,
I will be sworn,

**21:25** וְהוֹכִחַ אַבְרָהָם אֶת אֲבִימֶלֶךְ עַל אֹדוֹת בְּאֵר הַמַּיִם אֲשֶׁר גָּזְלוּ
עַבְדֵי אֲבִימֶלֶךְ

and~he~will~make~Convict "Avraham
[*Father lifted*]" At "Aviymelekh [*My
father is king*]" Upon Concerning
Well the~Water~s2 Which they~did~
Pluck.away Servant~s "Aviymelekh
[*My father is king*]"

and "Avraham [*Father lifted*]"
convicted "Aviymelekh [*My father
is king*]" concerning the well of
water which the servants of
"Aviymelekh [*My father is king*]"
plucked away,

**21:26** וַיֹּאמֶר אֲבִימֶלֶךְ לֹא יָדַעְתִּי מִי עָשָׂה אֶת הַדָּבָר הַזֶּה וְגַם אַתָּה
לֹא הִגַּדְתָּ לִּי וְגַם אָנֹכִי לֹא שָׁמַעְתִּי בִּלְתִּי הַיּוֹם

and~he~will~Say "Aviymelekh [*My
father is king*]" Not i~did~Know
Who he~did~Do At the~Word the~
This and~Also You(ms) Not
you(ms)~did~make~Be.face.to.face to~

and "Aviymelekh [*My father is
king*]" said, I do not know who did
this thing and also you did not tell
me and also I did not hear except
today,

me   and~Also   I   Not   i~did~Hear
Except   the~Day

**21:27**   וַיִּקַּח אַבְרָהָם צֹאן וּבָקָר וַיִּתֵּן לַאֲבִימֶלֶךְ וַיִּכְרְתוּ שְׁנֵיהֶם בְּרִית

and~he~will~Take   "Avraham [*Father lifted*]"   Flocks   and~Cattle   and~he~will~Give   to~"Aviymelekh [*My father is king*]"   and~they(m)~will~Cut   Two~them(m)   Covenant

and "Avraham [*Father lifted*]" took flocks and cattle and he gave to "Aviymelekh [*My father is king*]" and the two of them cut a covenant,

**21:28**   וַיַּצֵּב אַבְרָהָם אֶת שֶׁבַע כִּבְשֹׂת הַצֹּאן לְבַדְּהֶן

and~he~will~make~Stand.erect   "Avraham [*Father lifted*]"   At   Seven   Ewe.lamb   the~Flocks   to~Separated.thing~them(f)

and "Avraham [*Father lifted*]" made seven ewe lambs of the flock stand erect by themselves,

**21:29**   וַיֹּאמֶר אֲבִימֶלֶךְ אֶל אַבְרָהָם מָה הֵנָּה שֶׁבַע כְּבָשֹׂת הָאֵלֶּה אֲשֶׁר הִצַּבְתָּ לְבַדָּנָה

and~he~will~Say   "Aviymelekh [*My father is king*]"   To   "Avraham [*Father lifted*]"   What   Thus.far   Seven   Ewe.lamb   the~These   Which   you(ms)~did~make~Stand.erect   to~Separated.thing~them(f)

and "Aviymelekh [*My father is king*]" said to "Avraham [*Father lifted*]", what is this these seven ewe lamb which you made stand erect by themselves,

**21:30**   וַיֹּאמֶר כִּי אֶת שֶׁבַע כְּבָשֹׂת תִּקַּח מִיָּדִי בַּעֲבוּר תִּהְיֶה לִּי לְעֵדָה כִּי חָפַרְתִּי אֶת הַבְּאֵר הַזֹּאת

and~he~will~Say   Given.that   At   Seven   Ewe.lamb   you(ms)~will~Take   from~Hand~me   in~On.account.of   she~will~Exist   to~me   to~Company   Given.that   i~did~Dig.out   At   the~Well   the~This

and he said, given that you will take the seven ewe lambs from my hand so that she will exist for me for a witness given that I dug out this well,

**21:31**   עַל כֵּן קָרָא לַמָּקוֹם הַהוּא בְּאֵר שָׁבַע כִּי שָׁם נִשְׁבְּעוּ שְׁנֵיהֶם

Upon   So   he~did~Call.out   to~the~Place   the~He   "B'er-Sheva [*Well of oath*]"   Given.that   There   they~did~be~Swear   Two~them(m)

therefore he called out to that place "B'er-Sheva [*Well of oath*]" given that there the two of them were sworn,

**21:32**   וַיִּכְרְתוּ בְרִית בִּבְאֵר שָׁבַע וַיָּקָם אֲבִימֶלֶךְ וּפִיכֹל שַׂר צְבָאוֹ וַיָּשֻׁבוּ אֶל אֶרֶץ פְּלִשְׁתִּים

and~they(m)~will~Cut   Covenant   in~"B'er-Sheva [*Well of oath*]"   and~he~will~Rise   "Aviymelekh [*My father is king*]"   and~"Pikhol [*Face of all*]"   Noble   Army~him   and~they(m)~will~Turn.back   To   Land   "Peleshet

and they cut a covenant in "B'er-Sheva [*Well of oath*]" and "Aviymelekh [*My father is king*]" rose and "Pikhol [Face of all]" the noble of his army and they turned back to the land of the ones of

[*Immigrant*]"~s

"Peleshet [*Immigrant*]",

**21:33**

וַיִּטַּע אֶשֶׁל בִּבְאֵר שָׁבַע וַיִּקְרָא שָׁם בְּשֵׁם יְהוָה אֵל עוֹלָם

and~he~will~Plant Tamarisk in~"B'er-Sheva [*Well of oath*]" and~he~will~Meet There in~Title "YHWH [*He exists*]" Mighty.one Distant.time

and he planted a tamarisk in "B'er-Sheva [*Well of oath*]" and he met there with the title of "YHWH [*He exists*]", a mighty one of a distant time,

**21:34**

וַיָּגָר אַבְרָהָם בְּאֶרֶץ פְּלִשְׁתִּים יָמִים רַבִּים

and~he~will~Sojourn "Avraham [*Father lifted*]" in~Land "Peleshet [*Immigrant*]"~s Day~s Abundant~s

and "Avraham [*Father lifted*]" sojourned in the land of the ones of "Peleshet [*Immigrant*]" an abundant days,

# Chapter 22

**22:1**

וַיְהִי אַחַר הַדְּבָרִים הָאֵלֶּה וְהָאֱלֹהִים נִסָּה אֶת אַבְרָהָם וַיֹּאמֶר אֵלָיו אַבְרָהָם וַיֹּאמֶר הִנֵּנִי

and~he~will~Exist After the~Word~s the~These and~the~"Elohiym [*Powers*]" he~did~much~Test At "Avraham [*Father lifted*]" and~he~will~Say To~him "Avraham [*Father lifted*]" and~he~will~Say Look~me

and it came to pass after these words and the "Elohiym [*Powers*]" greatly tested "Avraham [*Father lifted*]" and he said to him, "Avraham [*Father lifted*]", and he said here am I,

**22:2**

וַיֹּאמֶר קַח נָא אֶת בִּנְךָ אֶת יְחִידְךָ אֲשֶׁר אָהַבְתָּ אֶת יִצְחָק וְלֶךְ לְךָ אֶל אֶרֶץ הַמֹּרִיָּה וְהַעֲלֵהוּ שָׁם לְעֹלָה עַל אַחַד הֶהָרִים אֲשֶׁר אֹמַר אֵלֶיךָ

and~he~will~Say !(ms)~Take Please At Son~you(ms) At Solitary~you(ms) Which you(ms)~did~Love At "Yits'hhaq [*He laughs*]" and~!(ms)~Walk to~you(ms) To Land the~"Moriyah [*Appearance of Yah*]" and~!(ms)~make~Go.up~him There to~Rising Upon Unit the~Hill~s Which i~will~Say To~you(ms)

and he said, please take your son, your solitary one which you love, "Yits'hhaq [*He laughs*]" and you will walk to the land of "Moriyah [*Appearance of Yah*]" and make him go up there for a rising upon one of the hills which I will say to you,

**22:3**

וַיַּשְׁכֵּם אַבְרָהָם בַּבֹּקֶר וַיַּחֲבֹשׁ אֶת חֲמֹרוֹ וַיִּקַּח אֶת שְׁנֵי נְעָרָיו אִתּוֹ וְאֵת יִצְחָק בְּנוֹ וַיְבַקַּע עֲצֵי עֹלָה וַיָּקָם וַיֵּלֶךְ אֶל הַמָּקוֹם אֲשֶׁר אָמַר לוֹ הָאֱלֹהִים

and~he~will~Depart.early "Avraham [*Father lifted*]" in~the~Morning and~

and "Avraham [*Father lifted*]" departed early in the morning and

he~will~Saddle At Donkey~him and~
he~will~Take At Two Young.man~s~
him At~him and~At "Yits'hhaq [*He
laughs*]" Son~him and~he~will~Cleave
Tree~s Rising and~he~will~Rise and~
he~will~Walk To the~Place Which
he~did~Say to~him the~"Elohiym
[*Powers*]"

he saddled his donkey and took two of his young men with him and with "Yits'hhaq [*He laughs*]" his son and he cleaved trees of the rising and he rose and he walked to the place which the "Elohiym [*Powers*]" said to him,

**22:4** בַּיּוֹם הַשְּׁלִישִׁי וַיִּשָּׂא אַבְרָהָם אֶת עֵינָיו וַיַּרְא אֶת הַמָּקוֹם מֵרָחֹק

in~the~Day the~Third and~he~will~Lift.up "Avraham [*Father lifted*]" At Eye~s2~him and~he~will~See At the~Place from~Distance

in the third day "Avraham [*Father lifted*]" lifted up his eyes and saw the place from a distance,

**22:5** וַיֹּאמֶר אַבְרָהָם אֶל נְעָרָיו שְׁבוּ לָכֶם פֹּה עִם הַחֲמוֹר וַאֲנִי וְהַנַּעַר נֵלְכָה עַד כֹּה וְנִשְׁתַּחֲוֶה וְנָשׁוּבָה אֲלֵיכֶם

and~he~will~Say "Avraham [*Father lifted*]" To Young.man~s~him !(mp)~Settle to~you(mp) Here With the~Donkey and~I and~the~Young.man we~will~Walk Until In.this.way and~we~did~self~Bend.down and~we~did~Turn.back To~you(mp)

and "Avraham [*Father lifted*]" said to his young men, you will settle here with the donkey and I and the young man will walk as far as this way and we will bow ourselves down and we will turn back to you,

**22:6** וַיִּקַּח אַבְרָהָם אֶת עֲצֵי הָעֹלָה וַיָּשֶׂם עַל יִצְחָק בְּנוֹ וַיִּקַּח בְּיָדוֹ אֶת הָאֵשׁ וְאֶת הַמַּאֲכֶלֶת וַיֵּלְכוּ שְׁנֵיהֶם יַחְדָּו

and~he~will~Take "Avraham [*Father lifted*]" At Tree~s the~Rising and~he~will~Set.in.place Upon "Yits'hhaq [*He laughs*]" Son~him and~he~will~Take in~Hand~him At the~Fire and~At the~Knife and~they(m)~will~Walk Two~them(m) Together

and "Avraham [*Father lifted*]" took trees of the rising and set in place upon "Yits'hhaq [*He laughs*]" his son and he took in his hand the fire and the knife and the two of them walked together,

**22:7** וַיֹּאמֶר יִצְחָק אֶל אַבְרָהָם אָבִיו וַיֹּאמֶר אָבִי וַיֹּאמֶר הִנֶּנִּי בְנִי וַיֹּאמֶר הִנֵּה הָאֵשׁ וְהָעֵצִים וְאַיֵּה הַשֶּׂה לְעֹלָה

and~he~will~Say "Yits'hhaq [*He laughs*]" To "Avraham [*Father lifted*]" Father~him and~he~will~Say Father~me and~he~will~Say Look~me Son~me and~he~will~Say Look the~Fire and~the~Tree~s and~Where the~One.of.the.flock to~Rising

and "Yits'hhaq [*He laughs*]" said to "Avraham [*Father lifted*]" his father and he said, my father, and he said, here am I my son, and he said, look, the fire and the trees and where is the one of the flock for the rising,

**22:8** וַיֹּאמֶר אַבְרָהָם אֱלֹהִים יִרְאֶה לּוֹ הַשֶּׂה לְעֹלָה בְּנִי וַיֵּלְכוּ שְׁנֵיהֶם יַחְדָּו

and~he~will~Say "Avraham [*Father lifted*]" "Elohiym [*Powers*]" he~will~See to~him the~One.of.the.flock to~Rising Son~me and~they(m)~will~Walk Two~them(m) Together

and "Avraham [*Father lifted*]" said, "Elohiym [*Powers*]" will see to him the one of the flock for a rising my son and the two of them walked together,

**22:9** וַיָּבֹאוּ אֶל הַמָּקוֹם אֲשֶׁר אָמַר לוֹ הָאֱלֹהִים וַיִּבֶן שָׁם אַבְרָהָם אֶת הַמִּזְבֵּחַ וַיַּעֲרֹךְ אֶת הָעֵצִים וַיַּעֲקֹד אֶת יִצְחָק בְּנוֹ וַיָּשֶׂם אֹתוֹ עַל הַמִּזְבֵּחַ מִמַּעַל לָעֵצִים

and~they(m)~will~Come To Place Which he~did~Say to~him the~"Elohiym [*Powers*]" and~he~will~Build There "Avraham [*Father lifted*]" At the~Altar and~he~will~Arrange At the~Tree~s and~he~will~Bind At "Yits'hhaq [*He laughs*]" Son~him and~he~will~Set.in.place At~him Upon the~Altar from~Upward to~the~Tree~s

and they came to the place which the "Elohiym [*Powers*]" said to him and "Avraham [*Father lifted*]" built there the altar and arranged the trees and he bound "Yits'hhaq [*He laughs*]" his son and he set him in place upon the altar, upon the trees,

**22:10** וַיִּשְׁלַח אַבְרָהָם אֶת יָדוֹ וַיִּקַּח אֶת הַמַּאֲכֶלֶת לִשְׁחֹט אֶת בְּנוֹ

and~he~will~Send "Avraham [*Father lifted*]" At Hand~him and~he~will~Take At the~Knife to~>~Slay At Son~him

and "Avraham [*Father lifted*]" sent his hand and he took the knife to slay his son,

**22:11** וַיִּקְרָא אֵלָיו מַלְאַךְ יְהֹוָה מִן הַשָּׁמַיִם וַיֹּאמֶר אַבְרָהָם אַבְרָהָם וַיֹּאמֶר הִנֵּנִי

and~he~will~Call.out To~him Messenger "YHWH [*He exists*]" From the~Sky~s2 and~he~will~Say "Avraham [*Father lifted*]" "Avraham [*Father lifted*]" and~he~will~Say Look~me

and the messenger of "YHWH [*He exists*]" called out to him from the sky and he said, "Avraham [*Father lifted*]", "Avraham [*Father lifted*]", and he said, here am I,

**22:12** וַיֹּאמֶר אַל תִּשְׁלַח יָדְךָ אֶל הַנַּעַר וְאַל תַּעַשׂ לוֹ מְאוּמָה כִּי עַתָּה יָדַעְתִּי כִּי יְרֵא אֱלֹהִים אַתָּה וְלֹא חָשַׂכְתָּ אֶת בִּנְךָ אֶת יְחִידְךָ מִמֶּנִּי

and~he~will~Say No you(ms)~will~Send Hand~you(ms) To the~Young.man and~No you(ms)~will~Do to~him Nothing Given.that Now i~did~Know Given.that Fearful "Elohiym [*Powers*]" You(ms) and~Not

and he said, you will not send your hand to the young man and you will not do to him anything given that now I know that you are fearful of "Elohiym [*Powers*]" and you did not keep back your solitary son

you(ms)~did~Keep.back At Son~ you(ms) At Solitary~you(ms) From~me

from me,

**22:13**

וַיִּשָּׂא אַבְרָהָם אֶת עֵינָיו וַיַּרְא וְהִנֵּה אַיִל אַחַר נֶאֱחַז בַּסְּבַךְ בְּקַרְנָיו וַיֵּלֶךְ אַבְרָהָם וַיִּקַּח אֶת הָאַיִל וַיַּעֲלֵהוּ לְעֹלָה תַּחַת בְּנוֹ

and~he~will~Lift.up "Avraham [*Father lifted*]" At Eye~s2~him and~he~will~See and~Look Strong.One After he~did~be~Hold in~Net in~Horn~s~him and~he~will~Walk "Avraham [*Father lifted*]" and~he~will~Take At the~Strong.One and~he~will~make~Go.up~him to~Rising Under Son~him

and "Avraham [*Father lifted*]" lifted up his eyes and he saw and look, a strong one was behind and he was held in a net with his horns and "Avraham [*Father lifted*]" walked and he took the strong one and he made him go up for a rising in place of his son,

**22:14**

וַיִּקְרָא אַבְרָהָם שֵׁם הַמָּקוֹם הַהוּא יְהוָה יִרְאֶה אֲשֶׁר יֵאָמֵר הַיּוֹם בְּהַר יְהוָה יֵרָאֶה

and~he~will~Call.out "Avraham [*Father lifted*]" Title the~Place the~He "YHWH-Yireh [*YHWH will see*]" Which he~will~be~Say the~Day in~Hill "YHWH [*He exists*]" he~will~be~See

and "Avraham [*Father lifted*]" called out the title of that place "YHWH-Yireh [*YHWH will see*]" which today will be said, in a hill "YHWH [*He exists*]" appeared,

**22:15**

וַיִּקְרָא מַלְאַךְ יְהוָה אֶל אַבְרָהָם שֵׁנִית מִן הַשָּׁמָיִם

and~he~will~Call.out Messenger "YHWH [*He exists*]" To "Avraham [*Father lifted*]" Second From the~Sky~s2

and the messenger of "YHWH [*He exists*]" called out to "Avraham [*Father lifted*]" a second time from the sky,

**22:16**

וַיֹּאמֶר בִּי נִשְׁבַּעְתִּי נְאֻם יְהוָה כִּי יַעַן אֲשֶׁר עָשִׂיתָ אֶת הַדָּבָר הַזֶּה וְלֹא חָשַׂכְתָּ אֶת בִּנְךָ אֶת יְחִידֶךָ

and~he~will~Say in~me i~did~be~Swear Utterance "YHWH [*He exists*]" Given.that Seeing.as Which you(ms)~did~Do At the~Word the~This and~Not you(ms)~did~Keep.back At Son~you(ms) At Solitary~you(ms)

and he said, in me I was sworn an utterance of "YHWH [*He exists*]" seeing that you did this thing and you did not keep back your solitary son,

**22:17**

כִּי בָרֵךְ אֲבָרֶכְךָ וְהַרְבָּה אַרְבֶּה אֶת זַרְעֲךָ כְּכוֹכְבֵי הַשָּׁמַיִם וְכַחוֹל אֲשֶׁר עַל שְׂפַת הַיָּם וְיִרַשׁ זַרְעֲךָ אֵת שַׁעַר אֹיְבָיו

Given.that >~much~Kneel i~will~much~Kneel~you(ms) and~>~make~Increase i~will~make~Increase At Seed~you(ms) like~Star~s the~Sky~s2 and~like~the~Sand Which Upon Lip

given that I will greatly respect and I will greatly make an increase of your seed like the stars of the sky and like the sand which is upon the lip of the sea and your seed will

the~Sea and~he~will~Inherit Seed~ you(ms) At Gate Hostile~ing(ms)~s~ him

inherit the gate of his hostile ones,

**22:18** וְהִתְבָּרְכוּ בְזַרְעֲךָ כֹּל גּוֹיֵי הָאָרֶץ עֵקֶב אֲשֶׁר שָׁמַעְתָּ בְּקֹלִי

and~they~did~self~Kneel in~Seed~ you(ms) All Nation~s the~Land Since Which you(ms)~did~Hear in~ Voice~me

and all nations of the land will respect themselves with your seed because you heard in my voice,

**22:19** וַיָּשָׁב אַבְרָהָם אֶל נְעָרָיו וַיָּקֻמוּ וַיֵּלְכוּ יַחְדָּו אֶל בְּאֵר שָׁבַע וַיֵּשֶׁב אַבְרָהָם בִּבְאֵר שָׁבַע

and~he~will~Turn.back "Avraham [*Father lifted*]" To Young.man~s~him and~they~will~Rise and~they~will~Walk Together To "B'er-Sheva [*Well of oath*]" and~he~will~Settle "Avraham [*Father lifted*]" in~"B'er-Sheva [*Well of oath*]"

and "Avraham [*Father lifted*]" turned back to his young men and they rose and they walked together to "B'er-Sheva [*Well of oath*]" and "Avraham [*Father lifted*]" settled in "B'er-Sheva [*Well of oath*]",

**22:20** וַיְהִי אַחֲרֵי הַדְּבָרִים הָאֵלֶּה וַיֻּגַּד לְאַבְרָהָם לֵאמֹר הִנֵּה יָלְדָה מִלְכָּה גַם הִוא בָּנִים לְנָחוֹר אָחִיךָ

and~he~will~Exist After the~Word~s the~These and~he~will~make.be~ Be.face.to.face to~"Avraham [*Father lifted*]" to~>~Say Look she~did~ Bring.forth "Milkah [*Queen*]" Also She Son~s to~"Nahhor [*Snorting*]" Brother~you(ms)

and it came to pass after these words and he told to "Avraham [*Father lifted*]" saying, look, "Milkah [*Queen*]" also brought forth sons for "Nahhor [*Snorting*]" your brother,

**22:21** אֶת עוּץ בְּכֹרוֹ וְאֶת בּוּז אָחִיו וְאֶת קְמוּאֵל אֲבִי אֲרָם

At "Uts [*Counsel*]" Firstborn~him and~At "Buz [*Despise*]" Brother~him and~At "Qemu'el [*Raised of El*]" Father~of "Aram [*Palace*]"

"Uts [*Counsel*]" his firstborn and "Buz [*Despise*]" his brother and "Qemu'el [*Raised of El*]" the father of "Aram [*Palace*]",

**22:22** וְאֶת כֶּשֶׂד וְאֶת חֲזוֹ וְאֶת פִּלְדָּשׁ וְאֶת יִדְלָף וְאֶת בְּתוּאֵל

and~At "Kesad [*Clod breaker*]" and~ At "Hhazo [*Vision*]" and~At "Pildash [*Bean thresher*]" and~At "Yidlap [*He will drip*]" and~At "Betu'el [*Destruction of El*]"

and "Kesad [*Clod breaker*]" and "Hhazo [*Vision*]" and "Pildash [*Bean thresher*]" and "Yidlap [*He will drip*]" and "Betu'el [*Destruction of El*]",

**22:23** וּבְתוּאֵל יָלַד אֶת רִבְקָה שְׁמֹנָה אֵלֶּה יָלְדָה מִלְכָּה לְנָחוֹר אֲחִי אַבְרָהָם

and~"Betu'el [*Destruction of El*]" he~did~Bring.forth At "Rivqah

and "Betu'el [*Destruction of El*]" brought forth "Rivqah [*Ensnarer*]",

[*Ensnarer*]" Eight These she~did~ Bring.forth "Milkah [*Queen*]" to~ "Nahhor [*Snorting*]" Brother~of "Avraham [*Father lifted*]"

these eight "Milkah [*Queen*]" brought forth for "Nahhor [*Snorting*]" the brother of "Avraham [*Father lifted*]",

**22:24** וּפִילַגְשׁוֹ וּשְׁמָהּ רְאוּמָה וַתֵּלֶד גַּם הִוא אֶת טֶבַח וְאֶת גַּחַם וְאֶת תַּחַשׁ וְאֶת מַעֲכָה

and~Concubine~him and~Title~her "Re'umah [*Lifted up*]" and~she~will~ Bring.forth Also She At "Thevahh [*Slaughtering*]" and~At "Gahham [*Burning*]" and~At "Tahhash [*Badger*]" and~At "Ma'akhah [*Cursing*]"

and his concubine and her title was "Re'umah [*Lifted up*]" and she also brought "Thevahh [*Slaughtering*]" and "Gahham [*Burning*]" and "Tahhash [*Badger*]" and "Ma'akhah [*Cursing*]",

# Chapter 23

**23:1** וַיִּהְיוּ חַיֵּי שָׂרָה מֵאָה שָׁנָה וְעֶשְׂרִים שָׁנָה וְשֶׁבַע שָׁנִים שְׁנֵי חַיֵּי שָׂרָה

and~they(m)~will~Exist Life~s "Sarah [*Noblewoman*]" Hundred Year and~ Ten~s Year and~Seven Year~s Year~s Life~s "Sarah [*Noblewoman*]"

and the life of "Sarah [*Noblewoman*]" existed a hundred and twenty and seven years, the years of the life of "Sarah [*Noblewoman*]",

**23:2** וַתָּמָת שָׂרָה בְּקִרְיַת אַרְבַּע הִוא חֶבְרוֹן בְּאֶרֶץ כְּנָעַן וַיָּבֹא אַבְרָהָם לִסְפֹּד לְשָׂרָה וְלִבְכֹּתָהּ

and~she~will~Die "Sarah [*Noblewoman*]" in~"Qiryat-Arba [*City of four*]" She "Hhevron [*Company*]" in~Land "Kena'an [*Lowered*]" and~ he~will~Come "Avraham [*Father lifted*]" to~>~Lament to~"Sarah [*Noblewoman*]" and~to~>~Weep~her

and "Sarah [*Noblewoman*]" died in "Qiryat-Arba [*City of four*]", she is "Hhevron [*Company*]" in the land of "Kena'an [*Lowered*]" and "Avraham [*Father lifted*]" came to lament for "Sarah [*Noblewoman*]" and to weep for her,

**23:3** וַיָּקָם אַבְרָהָם מֵעַל פְּנֵי מֵתוֹ וַיְדַבֵּר אֶל בְּנֵי חֵת לֵאמֹר

and~he~will~Rise "Avraham [*Father lifted*]" from~Upon Face~s Die~ ing(ms)~him and~he~will~Speak To Son~s "Hhet [*Shattered*]" to~>~Say

and "Avraham [*Father lifted*]" rose from upon the face of his dead and he spoke to the sons of "Hhet [*Shattered*]" saying,

**23:4** גֵּר וְתוֹשָׁב אָנֹכִי עִמָּכֶם תְּנוּ לִי אֲחֻזַּת קֶבֶר עִמָּכֶם וְאֶקְבְּרָה מֵתִי מִלְּפָנָי

Stranger and~Sojourner I With~

I am a stranger and sojourner with

**119**

you(mp) !(mp)~Give to~me Holdings
Grave With~you(mp) and~i~will~Bury~
^ Die~ing(ms)~me from~to~Face~s

you, give to me a holdings of a
grave with you and I will bury my
dead from before me,

**23:5** וַיַּעֲנוּ בְנֵי חֵת אֶת אַבְרָהָם לֵאמֹר לוֹ

and~they(m)~will~Answer Son~s "Hhet
[*Shattered*]" At "Avraham [*Father
lifted*]" to~>~Say to~him

and the sons of "Hhet [*Shattered*]"
answered "Avraham [*Father
lifted*]" saying to him,

**23:6** שְׁמָעֵנוּ אֲדֹנִי נְשִׂיא אֱלֹהִים אַתָּה בְּתוֹכֵנוּ בְּמִבְחַר קְבָרֵינוּ קְבֹר
אֶת מֵתֶךָ אִישׁ מִמֶּנּוּ אֶת קִבְרוֹ לֹא יִכְלֶה מִמְּךָ מִקְּבֹר מֵתֶךָ

!(ms)~Hear~us Lord~me Captain
"Elohiym [*Powers*]" You(ms) in~
Midst~us in~Chosen Grave~s~us
!(ms)~Bury At Die~ing(ms)~you(ms)
Man From~us At Grave~him Not
he~will~Restrict From~you(ms) from~
>~Bury Die~ing(ms)~you(ms)

hear us my lord you are a captain
of "Elohiym [*Powers*]" in the midst
of us, with the chosen of our graves
bury your dead, not a man from us
will restrict his grave from you
from burying your dead,

**23:7** וַיָּקָם אַבְרָהָם וַיִּשְׁתַּחוּ לְעַם הָאָרֶץ לִבְנֵי חֵת

and~he~will~Rise "Avraham [*Father
lifted*]" and~he~will~self~Bend.down
to~People the~Land to~Son~s "Hhet
[*Shattered*]"

and "Avraham [*Father lifted*]" rose
and bent himself down to the
people of the land, to the sons of
"Hhet [*Shattered*]",

**23:8** וַיְדַבֵּר אִתָּם לֵאמֹר אִם יֵשׁ אֶת נַפְשְׁכֶם לִקְבֹּר אֶת מֵתִי מִלְּפָנַי
שְׁמָעוּנִי וּפִגְעוּ לִי בְּעֶפְרוֹן בֶּן צֹחַר

and~he~will~Speak At~them(m) to~>~
Say If There.is At Being~you(ms)
to~>~Bury At Die~ing(ms)~me from~
to~Face~s~me !(mp)~Hear~me and~
!(mp)~Reach to~me in~"Ephron
[*Powdery*]" Son "Tsohhar [*White*]"

and he spoke to them saying, if it is
your being to bury my dead from
before me, hear me and reach for
me with "Ephron [*Powdery*]" the
son of "Tsohhar [*White*]",

**23:9** וְיִתֶּן לִי אֶת מְעָרַת הַמַּכְפֵּלָה אֲשֶׁר לוֹ אֲשֶׁר בִּקְצֵה שָׂדֵהוּ בְּכֶסֶף
מָלֵא יִתְּנֶנָּה לִי בְּתוֹכְכֶם לַאֲחֻזַּת קָבֶר

and~he~will~Give to~me At Cave
the~"Makhpelah [*Double*]" Which to~
him Which in~Far.end Field~him in~
Silver Full he~will~Give~her to~me
in~Midst~you(mp) to~Holdings Grave

and he will give to me the cave
"Makhpelah [*Double*]" which
belongs to him which is in the far
end of his field, with full silver he
will give to me in your midst for a
holdings of a grave,

**23:10*** וְעֶפְרוֹן יֹשֵׁב בְּתוֹךְ בְּנֵי חֵת וַיַּעַן עֶפְרוֹן הַחִתִּי אֶת אַבְרָהָם
בְּאָזְנֵי בְנֵי חֵת לְכֹל בָּאֵי שַׁעַר עִירוֹ לֵאמֹר

and~"Ephron [*Powdery*]" Settle~ing(ms)
in~Midst Son~s "Hhet [*Shattered*]"

and "Ephron [*Powdery*]" was
settling in the midst of the sons of

and~he~will~Answer "Ephron [*Powdery*]" the~"Hhet [*Shattered*]"~of At "Avraham [*Father lifted*]" in~ Ear~s Son~s "Hhet [*Shattered*]" to~ All Come~ing(mp) Gate City~him to~>~Say

"Hhet [*Shattered*]" and "Ephron [*Powdery*]", the one of "Hhet [*Shattered*]", answered in the ears of the sons of "Hhet [*Shattered*]" to all coming to the gate of his city saying,

**23:11** לֹא אֲדֹנִי שְׁמָעֵנִי הַשָּׂדֶה נָתַתִּי לָךְ וְהַמְּעָרָה אֲשֶׁר בּוֹ לְךָ נְתַתִּיהָ לְעֵינֵי בְנֵי עַמִּי נְתַתִּיהָ לָּךְ קְבֹר מֵתֶךָ

Not Lord~me !(ms)~Hear~me the~ Field i~did~Give to~you(fs) and~the~ Cave Which in~him to~you(ms) i~ did~Give~her to~Eye~s2 Son~s People~me i~did~Give~her to~you(fs) !(ms)~Bury Die~ing(ms)~you(ms)

No my lord hear me, the field I give to you and the cave which is in him I give her to you to the eyes of the sons of my people I give her to you, bury your dead,

**23:12** וַיִּשְׁתַּחוּ אַבְרָהָם לִפְנֵי עַם הָאָרֶץ

and~he~will~self~Bend.down "Avraham [*Father lifted*]" to~Face~s People the~Land

and "Avraham [*Father lifted*]" bent himself down to the face of the people of the land,

**23:13** וַיְדַבֵּר אֶל עֶפְרוֹן בְּאָזְנֵי עַם הָאָרֶץ לֵאמֹר אַךְ אִם אַתָּה לוּ שְׁמָעֵנִי נָתַתִּי כֶּסֶף הַשָּׂדֶה קַח מִמֶּנִּי וְאֶקְבְּרָה אֶת מֵתִי שָׁמָּה

and~he~will~Speak To "Ephron [*Powdery*]" in~Ear~s People the~Land to~>~Say Surely If You(ms) Would.that !(ms)~Hear~me i~did~Give Silver the~Field !(ms)~Take From~me and~i~will~Bury At Die~ing(ms)~me There~unto

and he spoke to "Ephron [*Powdery*]" in the ears of the people of the land saying, surely, if you would hear me, I give the silver of the field, take from me and I will bury my dead unto there,

**23:14** וַיַּעַן עֶפְרוֹן אֶת אַבְרָהָם לֵאמֹר לוֹ

and~he~will~Answer "Ephron [*Powdery*]" To "Avraham [*Father lifted*]" to~>~Say to~him

and "Ephron [*Powdery*]" answered "Avraham [*Father lifted*]" saying to him,

**23:15** אֲדֹנִי שְׁמָעֵנִי אֶרֶץ אַרְבַּע מֵאֹת שֶׁקֶל כֶּסֶף בֵּינִי וּבֵינְךָ מַה הִוא וְאֶת מֵתְךָ קְבֹר

Lord~me !(ms)~Hear~me Land Four Hundred Sheqel Silver Between~me and~Between~you(ms) What She and~ At Die~ing(ms)~you(ms) !(ms)~Bury

my lord, hear me, what is a land of four hundred sheqels of silver between me and you, bury your dead,

**23:16** וַיִּשְׁמַע אַבְרָהָם אֶל עֶפְרוֹן וַיִּשְׁקֹל אַבְרָהָם לְעֶפְרֹן אֶת הַכֶּסֶף אֲשֶׁר דִּבֶּר בְּאָזְנֵי בְנֵי חֵת אַרְבַּע מֵאוֹת שֶׁקֶל כֶּסֶף עֹבֵר לַסֹּחֵר

and~he~will~Hear "Avraham [*Father lifted*]" To "Ephron [*Powdery*]" and~

and "Avraham [*Father lifted*]" heard "Ephron [*Powdery*]" and he~will~Weigh "Avraham [*Father lifted*]" to~"Ephron [*Powdery*]" At the~Silver Which he~did~much~Speak in~Ear~s Son~s "Hhet [*Shattered*]" Four Hundred~s Sheqel Silver Cross.over~ing(ms) to~the~Trade~ing(ms)

"Avraham [*Father lifted*]" weighed to "Ephron [*Powdery*]" the silver which he spoke in the ears of the sons of "Hhet [*Shattered*]", four hundred sheqels of silver, a crossing over for the trading,

**23:17** וַיָּקָם שְׂדֵה עֶפְרוֹן אֲשֶׁר בַּמַּכְפֵּלָה אֲשֶׁר לִפְנֵי מַמְרֵא הַשָּׂדֶה וְהַמְּעָרָה אֲשֶׁר בּוֹ וְכָל הָעֵץ אֲשֶׁר בַּשָּׂדֶה אֲשֶׁר בְּכָל גְּבֻלוֹ סָבִיב

and~he~will~Rise Field "Ephron [*Powdery*]" Which in~"Makhpelah [*Double*]" Which to~Face~s "Mamre [*Bitter place*]" the~Field and~the~Cave Which in~him and~All the~Tree Which in~the~Field Which in~All Border~him Around

and the field of "Ephron [*Powdery*]" rose, which is in "Makhpelah [*Double*]" which is to the face of "Mamre [*Bitter place*]", the field and the cave which is in him and all the trees which are in the field which are in all his borders around,

**23:18** לְאַבְרָהָם לְמִקְנָה לְעֵינֵי בְנֵי חֵת בְּכֹל בָּאֵי שַׁעַר עִירוֹ

to~"Avraham [*Father lifted*]" to~Livestock to~Eye~s2 Son~s "Hhet [*Shattered*]" in~All Come Gate City~him

to "Avraham [*Father lifted*]" for livestock to the eyes of the sons of "Hhet [*Shattered*]" with all coming at the gate of his city,

**23:19** וְאַחֲרֵי כֵן קָבַר אַבְרָהָם אֶת שָׂרָה אִשְׁתּוֹ אֶל מְעָרַת שְׂדֵה הַמַּכְפֵּלָה עַל פְּנֵי מַמְרֵא הוא חֶבְרוֹן בְּאֶרֶץ כְּנָעַן

and~After So he~did~Bury "Avraham [*Father lifted*]" At "Sarah [*Noblewoman*]" Woman~him To Cave Field the~"Makhpelah [*Double*]" Upon Face~s "Mamre [*Bitter place*]" She "Hhevron [*Company*]" in~Land "Kena'an [*Lowered*]"

and afterward, "Avraham [*Father lifted*]" buried "Sarah [*Noblewoman*]" his woman to the cave of the field of "Makhpelah [*Double*]" upon the face of "Mamre [*Bitter place*]", she is "Hhevron [*Company*]", in the land of "Kena'an [*Lowered*]",

**23:20** וַיָּקָם הַשָּׂדֶה וְהַמְּעָרָה אֲשֶׁר בּוֹ לְאַבְרָהָם לַאֲחֻזַּת קָבֶר מֵאֵת בְּנֵי חֵת

and~he~will~Rise the~Field and~the~Cave Which in~him to~"Avraham [*Father lifted*]" to~Holdings Grave from~At Son~s "Hhet [*Shattered*]"

and the field rose, and the cave which is in him, belonging to "Avraham [*Father lifted*]" for a holdings of a grave from the sons of "Hhet [*Shattered*]",

# Chapter 24

**24:1** וְאַבְרָהָם זָקֵן בָּא בַּיָּמִים וַיהוָה בֵּרַךְ אֶת אַבְרָהָם בַּכֹּל

and~"Avraham [*Father lifted*]" he~did~Be.old he~did~Come in~the~Day~s and~"YHWH [*He exists*]" he~had~much~Kneel At "Avraham [*Father lifted*]" in~the~All

and "Avraham [*Father lifted*]" was old, he came in the days and "YHWH [*He exists*]" had respected "Avraham [*Father lifted*]" in all,

**24:2** וַיֹּאמֶר אַבְרָהָם אֶל עַבְדּוֹ זְקַן בֵּיתוֹ הַמֹּשֵׁל בְּכָל אֲשֶׁר לוֹ שִׂים נָא יָדְךָ תַּחַת יְרֵכִי

and~he~will~Say "Avraham [*Father lifted*]" To Servant~him Beard House~him the~Regulate~ing(ms) in~All Which to~him !(ms)~Set.in.place Please Hand~you(ms) Under Midsection~me

and "Avraham [*Father lifted*]" said to his servant, the bearded one of his house the one regulating in all which belonged to him, please set your hand in place under my midsection,

**24:3** וְאַשְׁבִּיעֲךָ בַּיהוָה אֱלֹהֵי הַשָּׁמַיִם וֵאלֹהֵי הָאָרֶץ אֲשֶׁר לֹא תִקַּח אִשָּׁה לִבְנִי מִבְּנוֹת הַכְּנַעֲנִי אֲשֶׁר אָנֹכִי יוֹשֵׁב בְּקִרְבּוֹ

and~i~will~make~Swear~you(ms) in~"YHWH [*He exists*]" Power~s the~Sky~s2 and~Power~s the~Land Which Not you(ms)~will~Take Woman to~Son~me from~Daughter~s the~"Kena'an [*Lowered*]"~of Which I Settle~ing(ms) in~Within~him

and I will make you swear with "YHWH [*He exists*]" of the powers of the sky and the powers of the land that you will not take a woman for my son from the daughters of the ones of "Kena'an [*Lowered*]" which I am settling within,

**24:4** כִּי אֶל אַרְצִי וְאֶל מוֹלַדְתִּי תֵּלֵךְ וְלָקַחְתָּ אִשָּׁה לִבְנִי לְיִצְחָק

Given.that To Land~me and~To Kindred~me you(ms)~will~Walk and~you(ms)~did~Take Woman to~Son~me to~"Yits'hhaq [*He laughs*]"

given that to my land and to my kindred you will walk and you will take a woman for my son "Yits'hhaq [*He laughs*]",

**24:5** וַיֹּאמֶר אֵלָיו הָעֶבֶד אוּלַי לֹא תֹאבֶה הָאִשָּׁה לָלֶכֶת אַחֲרַי אֶל הָאָרֶץ הַזֹּאת הֶהָשֵׁב אָשִׁיב אֶת בִּנְךָ אֶל הָאָרֶץ אֲשֶׁר יָצָאתָ מִשָּׁם

and~he~will~Say To~him the~Servant Possibly Not she~will~Consent the~Woman to~>~Walk After To the~Land the~This ?~>~make~Turn.back i~will~make~Turn.back At Son~you(ms) To the~Land Which you(ms)~did~Go.out from~There

and the servant said to him, possibly the woman will not consent to walk after to this land, will I return your son to the land which you went out from,

**24:6** וַיֹּאמֶר אֵלָיו אַבְרָהָם הִשָּׁמֶר לְךָ פֶּן תָּשִׁיב אֶת בְּנִי שָׁמָּה

and~he~will~Say To~him "Avraham [*Father lifted*]" !(ms)~be~Guard to~you(ms) Otherwise you(ms)~will~Turn.back At Son~me There~unto

and "Avraham [*Father lifted*]" said to him, you be guarded otherwise you will turn my son back unto there,

**24:7** יְהֹוָה אֱלֹהֵי הַשָּׁמַיִם אֲשֶׁר לְקָחַנִי מִבֵּית אָבִי וּמֵאֶרֶץ מוֹלַדְתִּי וַאֲשֶׁר דִּבֶּר לִי וַאֲשֶׁר נִשְׁבַּע לִי לֵאמֹר לְזַרְעֲךָ אֶתֵּן אֶת הָאָרֶץ הַזֹּאת הוּא יִשְׁלַח מַלְאָכוֹ לְפָנֶיךָ וְלָקַחְתָּ אִשָּׁה לִבְנִי מִשָּׁם

"YHWH [*He exists*]" Power~s the~Sky~s2 Which he~did~Take~me from~House Father~me and~from~Land Kindred~me and~Which he~did~much~Speak to~me and~Which he~did~be~Swear to~me to~>~Say to~Seed~you(ms) i~will~Give At the~Land the~This He he~will~Send Messenger~him to~Face~s~you(ms) and~you(ms)~did~Take Woman to~Son~me from~There

"YHWH [*He exists*]" of the powers of the sky who took me from the house of my father and from the land of my kindred and who spoke to me and who was sworn to me saying, I will give to your seed this land, he will send his messenger to your face and you will take a woman for my son from there,

**24:8** וְאִם לֹא תֹאבֶה הָאִשָּׁה לָלֶכֶת אַחֲרֶיךָ וְנִקִּיתָ מִשְּׁבֻעָתִי זֹאת רַק אֶת בְּנִי לֹא תָשֵׁב שָׁמָּה

and~If Not she~will~Consent the~Woman to~>~Walk After~you(ms) and~you(ms)~will~be~Acquit from~Swearing~me This Only At Son~me Not you(ms)~will~Turn.back There~unto

and if the woman will not consent to walk after you then you will be acquitted from my swearing of this, only you will not turn back my son unto there,

**24:9** וַיָּשֶׂם הָעֶבֶד אֶת יָדוֹ תַּחַת יֶרֶךְ אַבְרָהָם אֲדֹנָיו וַיִּשָּׁבַע לוֹ עַל הַדָּבָר הַזֶּה

and~he~will~Set.in.place the~Servant At Hand~him Under Midsection "Avraham [*Father lifted*]" Lord~him and~he~will~be~Swear to~him Upon the~Word the~This

and the servant sat his hand in place under the midsection of "Avraham [*Father lifted*]" his lord and he was sworn to him upon this word,

**24:10** וַיִּקַּח הָעֶבֶד עֲשָׂרָה גְמַלִּים מִגְּמַלֵּי אֲדֹנָיו וַיֵּלֶךְ וְכָל טוּב אֲדֹנָיו בְּיָדוֹ וַיָּקָם וַיֵּלֶךְ אֶל אֲרַם נַהֲרַיִם אֶל עִיר נָחוֹר

and~he~will~Take the~Servant Ten Camel~s from~Camel~s Lord~him and~he~will~Walk and~All Functional Lord~him in~Hand~him and~he~will~Rise and~he~will~Walk To "Aram-

and the servant took ten camels from the camels of his lord and he walked and all the functional ones of his lord were in his hand and he rose and he walked to "Aram-

Nahhara'im [*Palace of two rivers*]"
To City "Nahhor [*Snorting*]"

Nahhara'im [*Palace of two rivers*]",
to the city of "Nahhor [*Snorting*]",

**24:11** וַיַּבְרֵךְ הַגְּמַלִּים מִחוּץ לָעִיר אֶל בְּאֵר הַמָּיִם לְעֵת עֶרֶב לְעֵת צֵאת הַשֹּׁאֲבֹת

and~he~will~make~Kneel the~Camel~s
from~Outside to~the~City To Well
the~Water~s2 to~Appointed.time
Evening to~Appointed.time >~Go.out
the~Draw.water~ing(fp)

and he made the camels kneel
outside the city to the well of the
water to the appointed time of the
evening, to the appointed time the
water drawers go out,

**24:12** וַיֹּאמַר יְהוָה אֱלֹהֵי אֲדֹנִי אַבְרָהָם הַקְרֵה נָא לְפָנַי הַיּוֹם וַעֲשֵׂה חֶסֶד עִם אֲדֹנִי אַבְרָהָם

and~he~will~Say "YHWH [*He
exists*]" Power~s Lord~me "Avraham
[*Father lifted*]" !(ms)~make~Meet
Please to~Face~s the~Day and~!(ms)~
Do Kindness With Lord~me
"Avraham [*Father lifted*]"

and he said, "YHWH [*He exists*]"
of the powers of my lord "Avraham
[*Father lifted*]" please make a
meeting before today and do
kindness with my lord "Avraham
[*Father lifted*]",

**24:13** הִנֵּה אָנֹכִי נִצָּב עַל עֵין הַמָּיִם וּבְנוֹת אַנְשֵׁי הָעִיר יֹצְאֹת לִשְׁאֹב מָיִם

Look I be~Stand.erect~ing(ms) Upon
Eye the~Water~s2 and~Daughter~s
Man~s the~City Go.out~ing(fp) to~>~
Draw.water Water~s2

look, I am standing erect upon the
eye of the water and the daughters
of the men of the city are going out
to draw water,

**24:14** וְהָיָה הַנַּעֲרָ אֲשֶׁר אֹמַר אֵלֶיהָ הַטִּי נָא כַדֵּךְ וְאֶשְׁתֶּה וְאָמְרָה שְׁתֵה וְגַם גְּמַלֶּיךָ אַשְׁקֶה אֹתָהּ הֹכַחְתָּ לְעַבְדְּךָ לְיִצְחָק וּבָהּ אֵדַע כִּי עָשִׂיתָ חֶסֶד עִם אֲדֹנִי

and~he~did~Exist the~Young.woman
Which i~will~Say To~her !(fs)~make~
Stretch Please Jar~you(fs) and~i~will~
Gulp and~she~did~Say !(ms)~Gulp~^
and~Also Camel~s~you(ms) i~will~
make~Drink At~her you(ms)~did~
make~Convict to~Servant~you(ms) to~
"Yits'hhaq [*He laughs*]" and~in~her
i~will~Know Given.that you(ms)~did~
Do Kindness With Lord~me

and it will come to pass the young
woman which I will say to her,
please make your jar stretch and I
will gulp and she will say, gulp and
I will also make your camels drink,
you made her convicted to your
servant "Yits'hhaq [*He laughs*]"
and in her I will know that you did
kindness with my lord,

**24:15** וַיְהִי הוּא טֶרֶם כִּלָּה לְדַבֵּר וְהִנֵּה רִבְקָה יֹצֵאת אֲשֶׁר יֻלְּדָה לִבְתוּאֵל בֶּן מִלְכָּה אֵשֶׁת נָחוֹר אֲחִי אַבְרָהָם וְכַדָּהּ עַל שִׁכְמָהּ

and~he~will~Exist He Before he~did~
much~Finish to~>~Speak and~Look
"Rivqah [*Ensnarer*]" Go.out~ing(fs)

and it came to pass before he
finished speaking and look,
"Rivqah [*Ensnarer*]" was going

**125**

Which she~did~be~Bring.forth to~ "Betu'el [*Destruction of El*]" Son "Milkah [*Queen*]" Woman "Nahhor [*Snorting*]" Brother~of "Avraham [*Father lifted*]" and~Jar~her Upon Shoulder~her

out, who was brought forth to "Betu'el [*Destruction of El*]", the son of "Milkah [*Queen*]", the woman of "Nahhor [*Snorting*]", the brother of "Avraham [*Father lifted*]" and her jar was upon her shoulder,

**24:16** וְהַנַּעֲרָ טֹבַת מַרְאֶה מְאֹד בְּתוּלָה וְאִישׁ לֹא יְדָעָהּ וַתֵּרֶד הָעַיְנָה וַתְּמַלֵּא כַדָּהּ וַתָּעַל

and~the~Young.woman Functional Appearance Many Virgin and~Man Not he~had~Know~her and~she~will~ Go.down the~Eye~unto and~she~will~ Fill Jar~her and~she~will~Go.up

and the young woman was very functional of appearance, a virgin and a man had not known her and she went down unto the eye and she filled her jar and she got up,

**24:17** וַיָּרָץ הָעֶבֶד לִקְרָאתָהּ וַיֹּאמֶר הַגְמִיאִינִי נָא מְעַט מַיִם מִכַּדֵּךְ

and~he~will~Run the~Servant to~>~ Meet~her and~he~will~Say !(ms)~ make~Guzzle~me Please Small.amount Water~s2 from~Jar~you(fs)

and the servant ran to meet her and he said, please make me guzzle a small amount of water from your jar,

**24:18** וַתֹּאמֶר שְׁתֵה אֲדֹנִי וַתְּמַהֵר וַתֹּרֶד כַּדָּהּ עַל יָדָהּ וַתַּשְׁקֵהוּ

and~she~will~Say !(ms)~Gulp Lord~me and~she~will~much~Hurry and~she~ will~make~Go.down Jar~her Upon Hand~her and~she~will~make~Drink~ him

and she said, gulp my lord and she much hurried and she made her jar go down upon her hand and she made him drink,

**24:19** וַתְּכַל לְהַשְׁקֹתוֹ וַתֹּאמֶר גַּם לִגְמַלֶּיךָ אֶשְׁאָב עַד אִם כִּלּוּ לִשְׁתֹּת

and~she~will~much~Finish to~>~make~ Drink~him and~she~will~Say Also to~Camel~s~you(ms) i~will~Draw.water Until If they~did~much~Finish to~>~ Gulp

and she finished making him drink and she said, I will also draw water for your camels until they finish gulping,

**24:20** וַתְּמַהֵר וַתְּעַר כַּדָּהּ אֶל הַשֹּׁקֶת וַתָּרָץ עוֹד אֶל הַבְּאֵר לִשְׁאֹב וַתִּשְׁאַב לְכָל גְּמַלָּיו

and~she~will~much~Hurry and~she~ will~much~Uncover Jar~her To the~ Watering.trough and~she~will~Run Yet.again To the~Well to~>~ Draw.water and~she~will~Draw.water to~All Camel~s~him

and she much hurried and she uncovered her jar to the watering trough and she ran yet again to the well to draw water and she drew water for all his camels,

**24:21** וְהָאִישׁ מִשְׁתָּאֵה לָהּ מַחֲרִישׁ לָדַעַת הַהִצְלִיחַ יְהוָה דַּרְכּוֹ אִם לֹא

and~the~Man self~Crash~ing(ms) to~ her make~Keep.silent~ing(ms) to~>~ Know ?~he~did~make~Prosper "YHWH [*He exists*]" Road~him If Not

and the man was crashing himself to her, keeping silent, to know, did "YHWH [*He exists*]" make his road prosper or not,

**24:22** וַיְהִי כַּאֲשֶׁר כִּלּוּ הַגְּמַלִּים לִשְׁתּוֹת וַיִּקַּח הָאִישׁ נֶזֶם זָהָב בֶּקַע מִשְׁקָלוֹ וּשְׁנֵי צְמִידִים עַל יָדֶיהָ עֲשָׂרָה זָהָב מִשְׁקָלָם

and~he~will~Exist like~Which they~ did~much~Finish the~Camel~s to~>~ Gulp and~he~will~Take the~Man Ring Gold Beqa Weight~him and~ Two Bracelet~s Upon Hand~s2~her Ten Gold Weight~them(m)

and it came to pass just as the camels finished gulping and the man took a ring of gold of a beqa weight and two bracelets upon her hands, ten weights of gold,

**24:23** וַיֹּאמֶר בַּת מִי אַתְּ הַגִּידִי נָא לִי הֲיֵשׁ בֵּית אָבִיךְ מָקוֹם לָנוּ לָלִין

and~he~will~Say Daughter Who You(fs) !(fs)~make~Be.face.to.face Please to~me ?~There.is House Father~you(fs) Place to~us to~>~ Stay.the.night

and he said whose daughter are you, please tell me, is there a house of your father, a place for us to stay the night,

**24:24** וַתֹּאמֶר אֵלָיו בַּת בְּתוּאֵל אָנֹכִי בֶּן מִלְכָּה אֲשֶׁר יָלְדָה לְנָחוֹר

and~she~will~Say To~him Daughter "Betu'el [*Destruction of El*]" I Son "Milkah [*Queen*]" Which she~did~ Bring.forth to~"Nahhor [*Snorting*]"

and she said to him, I am the daughter of "Betu'el [*Destruction of El*]" the son of "Milkah [*Queen*]" who was brought forth to "Nahhor [*Snorting*]",

**24:25** וַתֹּאמֶר אֵלָיו גַּם תֶּבֶן גַּם מִסְפּוֹא רַב עִמָּנוּ גַּם מָקוֹם לָלוּן

and~she~will~Say To~him Also Straw Also Provender Abundant With~us Also Place to~>~Stay.the.night

and she said to him, also straw, also abundant provender with us, also a place to stay the night,

**24:26** וַיִּקֹּד הָאִישׁ וַיִּשְׁתַּחוּ לַיהוָה

and~he~will~Bow.the.head the~Man and~he~will~self~Bend.down to~ "YHWH [*He exists*]"

and the man bowed the head and he bent himself down to "YHWH [*He exists*]",

**24:27** וַיֹּאמֶר בָּרוּךְ יְהוָה אֱלֹהֵי אֲדֹנִי אַבְרָהָם אֲשֶׁר לֹא עָזַב חַסְדּוֹ וַאֲמִתּוֹ מֵעִם אֲדֹנִי אָנֹכִי בַּדֶּרֶךְ נָחַנִי יְהוָה בֵּית אֲחֵי אֲדֹנִי

and~he~will~Say be~Kneel~ed(ms) "YHWH [*He exists*]" Power~s Lord~ me "Avraham [*Father lifted*]" Which Not he~did~Leave Kindness~him and~Truth~him from~With Lord~me I in~the~Road he~did~Guide~me

and he said, respected is "YHWH [*He exists*]" of the powers of my lord "Avraham [*Father lifted*]" who did not leave his kindness and his truth from my lord, I am in the road of the house of the brothers of my

"YHWH [*He exists*]" House Brother~s Lord~me

lord, "YHWH [*He exists*]" guided me,

**24:28**

וַתָּרָץ הַנַּעֲרָ וַתַּגֵּד לְבֵית אִמָּהּ כַּדְּבָרִים הָאֵלֶּה

and~she~will~Run the~Young.woman and~she~will~make~Be.face.to.face to~House Mother~her like~the~Word~s the~These

and the young woman ran and she told to the house of her mother these words,

**24:29**

וּלְרִבְקָה אָח וּשְׁמוֹ לָבָן וַיָּרָץ לָבָן אֶל הָאִישׁ הַחוּצָה אֶל הָעָיִן

and~to~"Rivqah [*Ensnarer*]" Brother and~Title~him "Lavan [*White*]" and~he~will~Run "Lavan [*White*]" To the~Man the~Outside~unto To the~Eye

and to "Rivqah [*Ensnarer*]" was a brother and his title was "Lavan [*White*]" and "Lavan [*White*]" ran unto the man outside, to the eye,

**24:30**

וַיְהִי כִּרְאֹת אֶת הַנֶּזֶם וְאֶת הַצְּמִדִים עַל יְדֵי אֲחֹתוֹ וּכְשָׁמְעוֹ אֶת דִּבְרֵי רִבְקָה אֲחֹתוֹ לֵאמֹר כֹּה דִבֶּר אֵלַי הָאִישׁ וַיָּבֹא אֶל הָאִישׁ וְהִנֵּה עֹמֵד עַל הַגְּמַלִּים עַל הָעָיִן

and~he~will~Exist like~>~See At the~Ring and~At the~Bracelet~s Upon Hand~s2 Sister~him and~like~>~Hear~him At Word~s "Rivqah [*Ensnarer*]" Sister~him to~>~Say In.this.way he~did~much~Speak To~me the~Man and~he~will~Come To the~Man and~Look Stand~ing(ms) Upon the~Camel~s Upon the~Eye

and it came to pass at seeing the ring and the bracelets upon the hands of his sister and at the hearing of the words of "Rivqah [*Ensnarer*]" his sister saying, in this way the man spoke to me and he came to the man and look, standing upon the camels, upon the eye,

**24:31**

וַיֹּאמֶר בּוֹא בְּרוּךְ יְהוָה לָמָּה תַעֲמֹד בַּחוּץ וְאָנֹכִי פִּנִּיתִי הַבַּיִת וּמָקוֹם לַגְּמַלִּים

and~he~will~Say !(ms)~Come be~Kneel~ed(ms) "YHWH [*He exists*]" to~What you(ms)~will~Stand in~the~Outside and~I i~did~Turn the~House and~Place to~the~Camel~s

and he said, come, respected is "YHWH [*He exists*]", why will you stand in the outside and I turned the house and the place for the camels,

**24:32**

וַיָּבֹא הָאִישׁ הַבַּיְתָה וַיְפַתַּח הַגְּמַלִּים וַיִּתֵּן תֶּבֶן וּמִסְפּוֹא לַגְּמַלִּים וּמַיִם לִרְחֹץ רַגְלָיו וְרַגְלֵי הָאֲנָשִׁים אֲשֶׁר אִתּוֹ

and~he~will~Come the~Man the~House~unto and~he~will~Open the~Camel~s and~he~will~Give Straw and~Provender to~the~Camel~s and~Water~s2 to~>~Wash Foot~s~him and~Foot~s the~Man~s Which At~him

and the man came unto the house and he opened the camels and he gave straw and provender to the camels and water to wash his feet and the feet of the men who were with him,

**24:33** וַיּיּשֶׂם (וַיּוּשַׂם) לְפָנָיו לֶאֱכֹל וַיֹּאמֶר לֹא אֹכַל עַד אִם דִּבַּרְתִּי דְּבָרָי וַיֹּאמֶר דַּבֵּר

and~he~will~Put  to~Face~s~him  to~>~
Eat  and~he~will~Say  Not  i~will~Eat
Until  If  i~did~Speak  Word~s~me
and~he~will~Say  >~much~Speak

and he put to his face to eat and he said, I will not eat until I speak my words, and he said, speak,

**24:34** וַיֹּאמַר עֶבֶד אַבְרָהָם אָנֹכִי

and~he~will~Say  Servant  "Avraham
[*Father lifted*]"  I

and he said, I am a servant of "Avraham [*Father lifted*]",

**24:35** וַיהוָה בֵּרַךְ אֶת אֲדֹנִי מְאֹד וַיִּגְדָּל וַיִּתֶּן לוֹ צֹאן וּבָקָר וְכֶסֶף וְזָהָב וַעֲבָדִם וּשְׁפָחֹת וּגְמַלִּים וַחֲמֹרִים

and~"YHWH  [*He exists*]"  he~had~
much~Kneel  At  Lord~me  Many
and~he~will~Magnify  and~he~will~Give
to~him  Flocks  and~Cattle  and~Silver
and~Gold  and~Servant~s  and~Maid~s
and~Camel~s  and~Donkey~s

and "YHWH [*He exists*]" had respected my lord and he magnified and he gave to him flocks and cattle and silver and gold and servants and maids and camels and donkeys,

**24:36** וַתֵּלֶד שָׂרָה אֵשֶׁת אֲדֹנִי בֵן לַאדֹנִי אַחֲרֵי זִקְנָתָהּ וַיִּתֶּן לוֹ אֶת כָּל אֲשֶׁר לוֹ

and~she~will~Bring.forth  "Sarah
[*Noblewoman*]"  Woman  Lord~me  Son
to~Lord~me  After  Old.age~her  and~
he~will~Give  to~him  At  All  Which
to~him

and "Sarah [*Noblewoman*]", the woman of my lord, brought forth a son for my lord after her old age and he gave to him all which belongs to him,

**24:37** וַיַּשְׁבִּעֵנִי אֲדֹנִי לֵאמֹר לֹא תִקַּח אִשָּׁה לִבְנִי מִבְּנוֹת הַכְּנַעֲנִי אֲשֶׁר אָנֹכִי יֹשֵׁב בְּאַרְצוֹ

and~he~will~make~Swear~me  Lord~me
to~>~Say  Not  you(ms)~will~Take
Woman  to~Son~me  from~Daughter~s
the~"Kena'an [*Lowered*]"~of  Which  I
Settle~ing(ms)  in~Land~him

and my lord made me swear saying, you will not take a woman for my son from the daughters of the one of "Kena'an [*Lowered*]" where I am settling in his land,

**24:38** אִם לֹא אֶל בֵּית אָבִי תֵּלֵךְ וְאֶל מִשְׁפַּחְתִּי וְלָקַחְתָּ אִשָּׁה לִבְנִי

If  Not  To  House  Father~me
you(ms)~will~Walk  and~To  Family~me
and~you(ms)~did~Take  Woman  to~
Son~me

but to the house of my father you will walk and to my family and you will take a woman for my son,

**24:39** וָאֹמַר אֶל אֲדֹנִי אֻלַי לֹא תֵלֵךְ הָאִשָּׁה אַחֲרָי

and~i~will~Say  To  Lord~me  Possibly
Not  she~will~Walk  the~Woman
After~me

and I said to my lord, possibly the woman will not walk after me,

**24:40** וַיֹּאמֶר אֵלָי יְהוָה אֲשֶׁר הִתְהַלַּכְתִּי לְפָנָיו יִשְׁלַח מַלְאָכוֹ אִתָּךְ וְהִצְלִיחַ דַּרְכֶּךָ וְלָקַחְתָּ אִשָּׁה לִבְנִי מִמִּשְׁפַּחְתִּי וּמִבֵּית אָבִי

and~he~will~Say To~me "YHWH [*He exists*]" Which i~did~self~Walk to~ Face~s~him he~will~Send Messenger~ him At~you(fs) and~he~did~make~ Prosper Road~you(ms) and~you(ms)~ did~Take Woman to~Son~me from~ Family~me and~from~House Father~ me

and he said to me, I walked myself to the face of "YHWH [*He exists*]", he will send his messenger to you and he will make your road prosper and you will take a woman for my son from my family and from the house of my father,

**24:41** אָז תִּנָּקֶה מֵאָלָתִי כִּי תָבוֹא אֶל מִשְׁפַּחְתִּי וְאִם לֹא יִתְּנוּ לָךְ וְהָיִיתָ נָקִי מֵאָלָתִי

At.that.time you(ms)~will~be~Innocent from~Oath~me Given.that you(ms)~ will~Come To Family~me and~If Not they(m)~will~Give to~you(fs) and~you(ms)~did~Exist Acquit from~ Oath~me

at that time you will be innocent from my oath given that you will come to my family and if they will not give to you and you will exist acquitted from my oath,

**24:42** וָאָבֹא הַיּוֹם אֶל הָעָיִן וָאֹמַר יְהוָה אֱלֹהֵי אֲדֹנִי אַבְרָהָם אִם יֶשְׁךָ נָּא מַצְלִיחַ דַּרְכִּי אֲשֶׁר אָנֹכִי הֹלֵךְ עָלֶיהָ

and~i~will~Come the~Day To the~ Eye and~i~will~Say "YHWH [*He exists*]" Power~s Lord~me "Avraham [*Father lifted*]" If There.is~you(ms) Please make~Prosper~ing(ms) Road~me Which I Walk~ing(ms) Upon~her

and I came today to the eye and I said, "YHWH [*He exists*]" of the powers of my lord "Avraham [*Father lifted*]", if you are there please make my road which I am walking upon prosper,

**24:43** הִנֵּה אָנֹכִי נִצָּב עַל עֵין הַמָּיִם וְהָיָה הָעַלְמָה הַיֹּצֵאת לִשְׁאֹב וְאָמַרְתִּי אֵלֶיהָ הַשְׁקִינִי נָא מְעַט מַיִם מִכַּדֵּךְ

Look I be~Stand.erect~ing(ms) Upon Eye the~Water~s2 and~he~did~Exist the~Young.maiden the~Go.out~ing(fs) to~>~Draw.water and~i~did~Say To~ her !(fs)~make~Drink Please Small.amount Water~s2 from~Jar~ you(fs)

look, I am standing erect upon the eye of the water and it came to pass the young maiden was going out to draw water and I said to her please make drink a small amount of water from your jar,

**24:44** וְאָמְרָה אֵלַי גַּם אַתָּה שְׁתֵה וְגַם לִגְמַלֶּיךָ אֶשְׁאָב הִוא הָאִשָּׁה אֲשֶׁר הֹכִיחַ יְהוָה לְבֶן אֲדֹנִי

and~she~did~Say To~me Also You(ms) !(ms)~Gulp and~Also to~ Camel~s~you(ms) i~will~Draw.water She the~Woman Which he~did~

and she said to me, you also gulp and also for your camels, I will draw water, she is the woman which "YHWH [*He exists*]" made

make~Convict "YHWH [*He exists*]" to~Son Lord~me

convict for the son of my lord,

**24:45** אֲנִי טֶרֶם אֲכַלֶּה לְדַבֵּר אֶל לִבִּי וְהִנֵּה רִבְקָה יֹצֵאת וְכַדָּהּ עַל שִׁכְמָהּ וַתֵּרֶד הָעַיְנָה וַתִּשְׁאָב וָאֹמַר אֵלֶיהָ הַשְׁקִינִי נָא

I Before i~will~much~Finish to~>~ much~Speak To Heart~me and~Look "Rivqah [*Ensnarer*]" Go.out~ing(fs) and~Jar~her Upon Shoulder~her and~ she~will~Go.down the~Eye~unto and~ she~will~Draw.water and~i~will~Say To~her !(fs)~make~Drink~me Please

before I finished speaking to my heart and behold "Rivqah [*Ensnarer*]" was going out and her jar was upon her shoulder and she went down unto the eye and she drew water and I said to her, please make me drink,

**24:46** וַתְּמַהֵר וַתּוֹרֶד כַּדָּהּ מֵעָלֶיהָ וַתֹּאמֶר שְׁתֵה וְגַם גְּמַלֶּיךָ אַשְׁקֶה וָאֵשְׁתְּ וְגַם הַגְּמַלִּים הִשְׁקָתָה

and~she~will~Hurry and~she~will~ make~Go.down Jar~her from~Upon~her and~she~will~Say !(ms)~Gulp and~ Also Camel~s~you(ms) i~will~make~ Drink and~i~will~Gulp and~Also the~ Camel~s she~did~make~Drink

and she hurried and she made her jar go down from upon her and she said, gulp and also your camels I will make drink and I gulped and also the camels she made drink,

**24:47** וָאֶשְׁאַל אֹתָהּ וָאֹמַר בַּת מִי אַתְּ וַתֹּאמֶר בַּת בְּתוּאֵל בֶּן נָחוֹר אֲשֶׁר יָלְדָה לּוֹ מִלְכָּה וָאָשִׂם הַנֶּזֶם עַל אַפָּהּ וְהַצְּמִידִים עַל יָדֶיהָ

and~i~will~Inquire At~her and~i~will~ Say Daughter Who You(fs) and~she~ will~Say Daughter "Betu'el [*Destruction of El*]" Son "Nahhor [*Snorting*]" Which she~did~Bring.forth to~him "Milkah [*Queen*]" and~i~will~ Set.in.place the~Ring Upon Nose~her and~the~Bracelet~s Upon Hand~s2~her

and I inquired of her and I said whose daughter are you and she said the daughter of "Betu'el [*Destruction of El*]", the son of "Nahhor [*Snorting*]" who "Milkah [*Queen*]" brought forth to him and I set in place the ring upon her nose and the bracelets upon her hands,

**24:48** וָאֶקֹּד וָאֶשְׁתַּחֲוֶה לַיהוָה וָאֲבָרֵךְ אֶת יְהוָה אֱלֹהֵי אֲדֹנִי אַבְרָהָם אֲשֶׁר הִנְחַנִי בְּדֶרֶךְ אֱמֶת לָקַחַת אֶת בַּת אֲחִי אֲדֹנִי לִבְנוֹ

and~i~will~Bow.the.head and~i~will~ self~Bend.down to~"YHWH [*He exists*]" and~i~will~much~Kneel At "YHWH [*He exists*]" Power~s Lord~ me "Avraham [*Father lifted*]" Which he~did~make~Guide~me in~Road Truth to~>~Take At Daughter Brother~of Lord~me to~Son~him

and I bowed the head and I bent myself down to "YHWH [*He exists*]" and I respected "YHWH [*He exists*]" of the powers of my lord "Avraham [*Father lifted*]" which he guided me in the road of truth to take a daughter of the brother of my lord for his son,

**24:49** וְעַתָּה אִם יֶשְׁכֶם עֹשִׂים חֶסֶד וֶאֱמֶת אֶת אֲדֹנִי הַגִּידוּ לִי וְאִם לֹא הַגִּידוּ לִי וְאֶפְנֶה עַל יָמִין אוֹ עַל שְׂמֹאל

and~Now If There.is~you(mp) Do~ing(mp) Kindness and~Truth At Lord~me !(mp)~make~Be.face.to.face to~me and~If Not !(mp)~make~Be.face.to.face to~me and~i~did~Turn Upon Right.hand Or Upon Left.hand

and now if you will do kindness and truth to my lord tell to me and if not tell to me and I will turn upon the right hand or upon the left hand,

**24:50** וַיַּעַן לָבָן וּבְתוּאֵל וַיֹּאמְרוּ מֵיְהֹוָה יָצָא הַדָּבָר לֹא נוּכַל דַּבֵּר אֵלֶיךָ רַע אוֹ טוֹב

and~he~will~Answer "Lavan [*White*]" and~"Betu'el [*Destruction of El*]" and~they(m)~will~Say from~"YHWH [*He exists*]" he~did~Go.out the~Word Not we~will~Be.able >~much~Speak To~you(ms) Dysfunctional Or Functional

and "Lavan [*White*]" answered and "Betu'el [*Destruction of El*]", and they said, the word went out from "YHWH [*He exists*]", we will not be able to speak to you dysfunction or function,

**24:51** הִנֵּה רִבְקָה לְפָנֶיךָ קַח וָלֵךְ וּתְהִי אִשָּׁה לְבֶן אֲדֹנֶיךָ כַּאֲשֶׁר דִּבֶּר יְהֹוָה

Look "Rivqah [*Ensnarer*]" to~Face~s~you(ms) !(ms)~Take and~!(ms)~Walk and~she~will~Exist Woman to~Son Lord~s~you(ms) like~Which he~did~much~Speak "YHWH [*He exists*]"

look, "Rivqah [*Ensnarer*]" is to your face, take and walk and she will exist a woman for the son of your lord just as "YHWH [*He exists*]" spoke,

**24:52** וַיְהִי כַּאֲשֶׁר שָׁמַע עֶבֶד אַבְרָהָם אֶת דִּבְרֵיהֶם וַיִּשְׁתַּחוּ אַרְצָה לַיהֹוָה

and~he~will~Exist like~Which he~did~Hear Servant "Avraham [*Father lifted*]" At Word~s~them(m) and~he~will~self~Bend.down Land~unto to~"YHWH [*He exists*]"

and it came to pass just as the servant of "Avraham [*Father lifted*]" heard their words and bent himself down unto the land to "YHWH [*He exists*]",

**24:53** וַיּוֹצֵא הָעֶבֶד כְּלֵי כֶסֶף וּכְלֵי זָהָב וּבְגָדִים וַיִּתֵּן לְרִבְקָה וּמִגְדָּנֹת נָתַן לְאָחִיהָ וּלְאִמָּהּ

and~he~will~make~Go.out the~Servant Instrument~s Silver and~Instrument~s Gold and~Garment~s and~he~will~Give to~"Rivqah [*Ensnarer*]" and~Ornament~s he~did~Give to~Brother~her and~to~Mother~her

and the servant brought out instruments of silver and instruments of gold and garments and he gave to "Rivqah [*Ensnarer*]" and he gave ornaments to her brother and to her mother,

**24:54** וַיֹּאכְלוּ וַיִּשְׁתּוּ הוּא וְהָאֲנָשִׁים אֲשֶׁר עִמּוֹ וַיָּלִינוּ וַיָּקוּמוּ בַבֹּקֶר וַיֹּאמֶר שַׁלְּחֻנִי לַאדֹנִי

and~they(m)~will~Eat and~they(m)~will~Gulp He and~the~Man~s Which

and they ate and they gulped, he and the men which were with him

With~him and~they(m)~will~
Stay.the.night and~they(m)~will~Rise
in~the~Morning and~he~will~Say
!(mp)~Send~me to~Lord~me

and they stayed the night and they
rose in the morning and he said,
send me to my lord,

**24:55** וַיֹּאמֶר אָחִיהָ וְאִמָּהּ תֵּשֵׁב הַנַּעַר אִתָּנוּ יָמִים אוֹ עָשׂוֹר אַחַר
תֵּלֵךְ

and~he~will~Say Brother~her and~
Mother~her she~will~Settle the~
Young.woman At~us Day~s Or
Tenth.one After !(ms)~will~Walk

and her brother said, and her
mother, the young woman will
settle days or the tenth one,
afterward, walk,

**24:56** וַיֹּאמֶר אֲלֵהֶם אַל תְּאַחֲרוּ אֹתִי וַיהוָה הִצְלִיחַ דַּרְכִּי שַׁלְּחוּנִי
וְאֵלְכָה לַאדֹנִי

and~he~will~Say To~them(m) No
you(mp)~will~Delay At~me and~
"YHWH [*He exists*]" he~had~make~
Prosper Road~me !(mp)~Send~me
and~i~will~Walk to~Lord~me

and he said to them, you will not
delay me and "YHWH [*He exists*]"
has made my road prosper, send me
and I will walk to my lord,

**24:57** וַיֹּאמְרוּ נִקְרָא לַנַּעַר וְנִשְׁאֲלָה אֶת פִּיהָ

and~they(m)~will~Say we~will~Call.out
to~Young.woman and~we~will~Inquire
At Mouth~her

and they said we will call out to the
young woman and inquire at her
mouth,

**24:58** וַיִּקְרְאוּ לְרִבְקָה וַיֹּאמְרוּ אֵלֶיהָ הֲתֵלְכִי עִם הָאִישׁ הַזֶּה וַתֹּאמֶר
אֵלֵךְ

and~they(m)~will~Call.out to~"Rivqah
[*Ensnarer*]" and~they(m)~will~Say To~
her ?~you(fs)~will~Walk With the~
Man the~This and~she~will~Say i~
will~Walk

and they called out to "Rivqah
[*Ensnarer*]" and they said to her,
will you walk with this man and she
said, I will walk,

**24:59** וַיְשַׁלְּחוּ אֶת רִבְקָה אֲחֹתָם וְאֶת מֵנִקְתָּהּ וְאֶת עֶבֶד אַבְרָהָם
וְאֶת אֲנָשָׁיו

and~they(m)~will~Send At "Rivqah
[*Ensnarer*]" Sister~them(m) and~At
make~Suckle~ing(fs)~her and~At
Servant "Avraham [*Father lifted*]"
and~At Man~s~him

and they sent "Rivqah [*Ensnarer*]"
their sister and her nurse and the
servant of "Avraham [*Father
lifted*]" and his men,

**24:60** וַיְבָרְכוּ אֶת רִבְקָה וַיֹּאמְרוּ לָהּ אֲחֹתֵנוּ אַתְּ הֲיִי לְאַלְפֵי רְבָבָה
וְיִירַשׁ זַרְעֵךְ אֵת שַׁעַר שֹׂנְאָיו

and~they(m)~will~much~Kneel At
"Rivqah [*Ensnarer*]" and~they(m)~will~
Say to~her Sister~us You(fs) !(fs)~

and they respected "Rivqah
[*Ensnarer*]" and they said to her,
you are our sister, exist for a

Exist to~Thousand~s Myriad and~he~will~Inherit Seed~you(fs) At Gate Hate~ing(mp)~him

myriad thousands and your seed will inherit the gate of the ones hating him,

**24:61** וַתָּקָם רִבְקָה וְנַעֲרֹתֶיהָ וַתִּרְכַּבְנָה עַל הַגְּמַלִּים וַתֵּלַכְנָה אַחֲרֵי הָאִישׁ וַיִּקַּח הָעֶבֶד אֶת רִבְקָה וַיֵּלַךְ

and~she~will~Rise "Rivqah [*Ensnarer*]" and~Young.woman~s~her and~they(f)~will~Ride Upon the~Camel~s and~they(f)~will~Walk After the~Man and~he~will~Take the~Servant At "Rivqah [*Ensnarer*]" and~he~will~Walk

and "Rivqah [*Ensnarer*]" rose and her young women and they rode upon the camels and they walked after the man and the servant took "Rivqah [*Ensnarer*]" and he walked,

**24:62** וְיִצְחָק בָּא מִבּוֹא בְּאֵר לַחַי רֹאִי וְהוּא יוֹשֵׁב בְּאֶרֶץ הַנֶּגֶב

and~"Yits'hhaq [*He laughs*]" he~had~Come from~>~Come "Be'er-Lahhiy-Ro'iy [*Well for the living seeing me*]" and~He Settle~ing(ms) in~Land the~South.country

and "Yits'hhaq [*He laughs*]" had come from coming of "Be'er-Lahhiy-Ro'iy [*Well for the living seeing me*]" and he settled in the land of the south country,

**24:63** וַיֵּצֵא יִצְחָק לָשׂוּחַ בַּשָּׂדֶה לִפְנוֹת עָרֶב וַיִּשָּׂא עֵינָיו וַיַּרְא וְהִנֵּה גְמַלִּים בָּאִים

and~he~will~Go.out "Yits'hhaq [*He laughs*]" to~Meditate in~the~Field to~>~Turn Evening and~he~will~Lift.up Eye~s2~him and~he~will~See and~Look Camel~s Come~ing(mp)

and "Yits'hhaq [*He laughs*]" went out to meditate in the field to the turning of the evening and he lifted up his eyes and he saw and look, camels were coming,

**24:64** וַתִּשָּׂא רִבְקָה אֶת עֵינֶיהָ וַתֵּרֶא אֶת יִצְחָק וַתִּפֹּל מֵעַל הַגָּמָל

and~she~will~Lift.up "Rivqah [*Ensnarer*]" At Eye~s2~her and~she~will~See At "Yits'hhaq [*He laughs*]" and~she~will~Fall from~Upon the~Camel

and "Rivqah [*Ensnarer*]" lifted up her eyes and she saw "Yits'hhaq [*He laughs*]" and she fell from upon the camel,

**24:65** וַתֹּאמֶר אֶל הָעֶבֶד מִי הָאִישׁ הַלָּזֶה הַהֹלֵךְ בַּשָּׂדֶה לִקְרָאתֵנוּ וַיֹּאמֶר הָעֶבֶד הוּא אֲדֹנִי וַתִּקַּח הַצָּעִיף וַתִּתְכָּס

and~she~will~Say To the~Servant Who the~Man This.one the~Walk~ing(ms) in~the~Field to~>~Meet~us and~he~will~Say the~Servant He Lord~me and~she~will~Take the~Veil and~she~will~self~Conceal

and she said to the servant, who is this man, the one walking in the field to meet us and the servant said, he is my lord and she took the veil and concealed herself,

**24:66** וַיְסַפֵּר הָעֶבֶד לְיִצְחָק אֵת כָּל הַדְּבָרִים אֲשֶׁר עָשָׂה

and~he~will~much~Count the~Servant to~"Yits'hhaq [*He laughs*]" At All

and the servant recounted to "Yits'hhaq [*He laughs*]" all the

the~Word~s   Which   he~did~Do

words which he did,

**24:67**   וַיְבִאֶהָ יִצְחָק הָאֹהֱלָה שָׂרָה אִמּוֹ וַיִּקַּח אֶת רִבְקָה וַתְּהִי לוֹ
לְאִשָּׁה וַיֶּאֱהָבֶהָ וַיִּנָּחֵם יִצְחָק אַחֲרֵי אִמּוֹ

and~he~will~make~Come~her
"Yits'hhaq [*He laughs*]" the~Tent~unto "Sarah [*Noblewoman*]" Mother~him and~he~will~Take At "Rivqah [*Ensnarer*]" and~she~will~Exist to~him to~Woman and~he~will~Love~her and~he~will~be~Comfort "Yits'hhaq [*He laughs*]" After Mother~him

and "Yits'hhaq [*He laughs*]" brought her unto the tent of "Sarah [*Noblewoman*]" his mother and he took "Rivqah [*Ensnarer*]" and she existed to him for a woman and loved her and "Yits'hhaq [*He laughs*]" was comforted after his mother,

# Chapter 25

**25:1**   וַיֹּסֶף אַבְרָהָם וַיִּקַּח אִשָּׁה וּשְׁמָהּ קְטוּרָה

and~he~will~make~Add "Avraham [*Father lifted*]" and~he~will~Take Woman and~Title~her "Qethurah [*Incense*]"

and "Avraham [*Father lifted*]" again took a woman and her title was "Qethurah [*Incense*]",

**25:2**   וַתֵּלֶד לוֹ אֶת זִמְרָן וְאֶת יָקְשָׁן וְאֶת מְדָן וְאֶת מִדְיָן וְאֶת יִשְׁבָּק
וְאֶת שׁוּחַ

and~she~will~Bring.forth to~him At "Zimran [*Musician*]" and~At "Yaq'shan [*Snarer*]" and~At "Medan [*Quarrel*]" and~At "Midian [*Strife*]" and~At "Yish'baq [*He will leave alone*]" and~At "Shu'ahh [*Sinking*]"

and she brought forth to him "Zimran [*Musician*]" and "Yaq'shan [*Snarer*]" and "Medan [*Quarrel*]" and "Midian [*Strife*]" and "Yish'baq [*He will leave alone*]" and "Shu'ahh [*Sinking*]",

**25:3**   וְיָקְשָׁן יָלַד אֶת שְׁבָא וְאֶת דְּדָן וּבְנֵי דְדָן הָיוּ אַשּׁוּרִם וּלְטוּשִׁם
וּלְאֻמִּים

and~"Yaq'shan [*Snarer*]" he~had~Bring.forth At "Sheva [*Seven*]" and~At "Dedan [*Friendship*]" and~Son~s "Dedan [*Friendship*]" they~did~Exist "Ashur [*Step*]"~s and~"Lethush [*Sharpened*]"~s and~"Le'um [*Peoples*]"~s

and "Yaq'shan [*Snarer*]" had brought forth "Sheva [*Seven*]" and "Dedan [*Friendship*]" and the sons of "Dedan [*Friendship*]" existed, the ones of "Ashur [*Step*]" and the ones of "Lethush [*Sharpened*]" and the ones of "Le'um [*Peoples*]",

**25:4**   וּבְנֵי מִדְיָן עֵיפָה וָעֵפֶר וַחֲנֹךְ וַאֲבִידָע וְאֶלְדָּעָה כָּל אֵלֶּה בְּנֵי
קְטוּרָה

and~Son~s "Midian [*Strife*]" "Eyphah [*Darkness*]" and~"Epher [*Calf*]" and~

are "Eyphah [*Darkness*]" and

"Hhanokh [*Dedicated*]" and~"Avida [*My father knows*]" and~"Elda'ah [*El knows*]" All These Son~s "Qethurah [*Incense*]"

"Epher [*Calf*]" and "Hhanokh [*Dedicated*]" and "Avida [*My father knows*]" and "Elda'ah [*El knows*]", all these are the sons of "Qethurah [*Incense*]",

**25:5**

וַיִּתֵּן אַבְרָהָם אֶת כָּל אֲשֶׁר לוֹ לְיִצְחָק

and~he~will~Give "Avraham [*Father lifted*]" At All Which to~him to~ "Yits'hhaq [*He laughs*]"

and "Avraham [*Father lifted*]" gave all which belonged to him to "Yits'hhaq [*He laughs*]",

**25:6**

וְלִבְנֵי הַפִּילַגְשִׁים אֲשֶׁר לְאַבְרָהָם נָתַן אַבְרָהָם מַתָּנֹת וַיְשַׁלְּחֵם מֵעַל יִצְחָק בְּנוֹ בְּעוֹדֶנּוּ חַי קֵדְמָה אֶל אֶרֶץ קֶדֶם

and~to~Son~s the~Concubine~s Which to~"Avraham [*Father lifted*]" he~did~ Give "Avraham [*Father lifted*]" Contribution~s and~he~will~much~ Send~them(m) from~Upon "Yits'hhaq [*He laughs*]" Son~him in~Yet.again~ him Life East~unto To Land East

and to the sons of the concubines which were to "Avraham [*Father lifted*]", "Avraham [*Father lifted*]" gave contributions and he sent them from upon "Yits'hhaq [*He laughs*]" his son, while he was alive unto the east, to the land of the east,

**25:7**

וְאֵלֶּה יְמֵי שְׁנֵי חַיֵּי אַבְרָהָם אֲשֶׁר חָי מְאַת שָׁנָה וְשִׁבְעִים שָׁנָה וְחָמֵשׁ שָׁנִים

and~These Day~s Year~s Life~s "Avraham [*Father lifted*]" Which Life Hundred Year and~Seven~s Year and~Five Year~s

and these were the days of the years of the life of "Avraham [*Father lifted*]" which was a life of a hundred and seventy five years,

**25:8**

וַיִּגְוַע וַיָּמָת אַבְרָהָם בְּשֵׂיבָה טוֹבָה זָקֵן וְשָׂבֵעַ וַיֵּאָסֶף אֶל עַמָּיו

and~he~will~Expire and~he~will~Die "Avraham [*Father lifted*]" in~ Gray.headed Functional Beard and~ Plenty and~he~will~be~Gather To People~s~him

and "Avraham [*Father lifted*]" expired and he died with a gray head, functional beard and plenty and he was gathered to his people,

**25:9**

וַיִּקְבְּרוּ אֹתוֹ יִצְחָק וְיִשְׁמָעֵאל בָּנָיו אֶל מְעָרַת הַמַּכְפֵּלָה אֶל שְׂדֵה עֶפְרֹן בֶּן צֹחַר הַחִתִּי אֲשֶׁר עַל פְּנֵי מַמְרֵא

and~they(m)~will~Bury At~him "Yits'hhaq [*He laughs*]" and~ "Yishma'el [*El will listen*]" Son~s~ him To Cave the~"Makhpelah [*Double*]" To Field "Ephron [*Powdery*]" Son "Tsohhar [*White*]" the~"Hhet [*Shattered*]"~s Which Upon Face~s "Mamre [*Bitter place*]"

and "Yits'hhaq [*He laughs*]" and "Yishma'el [*El will listen*]" his sons buried him at the cave of "Makhpelah [*Double*]", at the field of "Ephron [*Powdery*]", the son of "Tsohhar [*White*]" of the ones of "Hhet [*Shattered*]" which is upon the face of "Mamre [*Bitter place*]",

**25:10**

הַשָּׂדֶה אֲשֶׁר קָנָה אַבְרָהָם מֵאֵת בְּנֵי חֵת שָׁמָּה קֻבַּר אַבְרָהָם

וְשָׂרָה אִשְׁתּוֹ

the~Field Which he~did~Purchase "Avraham [*Father lifted*]" from~At Son~s "Hhet [*Shattered*]" There~unto he~did~much.be~Bury "Avraham [*Father lifted*]" and~"Sarah [*Noblewoman*]" Woman~him

the field which "Avraham [*Father lifted*]" purchased from the sons of "Hhet [*Shattered*]", unto there "Avraham [*Father lifted*]" was buried and "Sarah [*Noblewoman*]" his woman,

**25:11** וַיְהִי אַחֲרֵי מוֹת אַבְרָהָם וַיְבָרֶךְ אֱלֹהִים אֶת יִצְחָק בְּנוֹ וַיֵּשֶׁב יִצְחָק עִם בְּאֵר לַחַי רֹאִי

and~he~will~Exist After Death "Avraham [*Father lifted*]" and~he~will~much~Kneel "Elohiym [*Powers*]" At "Yits'hhaq [*He laughs*]" Son~him and~he~will~Settle "Yits'hhaq [*He laughs*]" With "Be'er-Lahhiy-Ro'iy [*Well for the living seeing me*]"

and it came to pass after the death of "Avraham [*Father lifted*]" and "Elohiym [*Powers*]" respected "Yits'hhaq [*He laughs*]" his son and "Yits'hhaq [*He laughs*]" settled by "Be'er-Lahhiy-Ro'iy [*Well for the living seeing me*]",

**25:12** וְאֵלֶּה תֹּלְדֹת יִשְׁמָעֵאל בֶּן אַבְרָהָם אֲשֶׁר יָלְדָה הָגָר הַמִּצְרִית שִׁפְחַת שָׂרָה לְאַבְרָהָם

and~These Birthing~s "Yishma'el [*El will listen*]" Son "Avraham [*Father lifted*]" Which she~did~Bring.forth "Hagar [*Stranger*]" the~"Mitsrayim [*Troubles*]"~of Maid "Sarah [*Noblewoman*]" to~"Avraham [*Father lifted*]"

and these are the birthings of "Yishma'el [*El will listen*]" the son of "Avraham [*Father lifted*]" who "Hagar [*Stranger*]", the one of the "Mitsrayim [*Troubles*]", the maid of "Sarah [*Noblewoman*]", brought forth to "Avraham [*Father lifted*]",

**25:13** וְאֵלֶּה שְׁמוֹת בְּנֵי יִשְׁמָעֵאל בִּשְׁמֹתָם לְתוֹלְדֹתָם בְּכֹר יִשְׁמָעֵאל נְבָיֹת וְקֵדָר וְאַדְבְּאֵל וּמִבְשָׂם

and~These Title~s Son~s "Yishma'el [*El will listen*]" in~Title~s~them(m) to~Birthing~s~them(m) Firstborn "Yishma'el [*El will listen*]" "Nevayot [*Flourishings*]" and~"Qedar [*Dark*]" and~"Adbe'el [*Grief of El*]" and~ "Mivsam [*Sweet odor*]"

and these are the titles of the sons of "Yishma'el [*El will listen*]" in their titles to their birthings, the firstborn of "Yishma'el [*El will listen*]" was "Nevayot [*Flourishings*]" and "Qedar [*Dark*]" and "Adbe'el [*Grief of El*]" and "Mivsam [*Sweet odor*]",

**25:14** וּמִשְׁמָע וְדוּמָה וּמַשָּׂא

and~"Mishma [*Hearing*]" and~"Dumah [*Silence*]" and~"Masa [*Burden*]"

and "Mishma [*Hearing*]" and "Dumah [*Silence*]" and "Masa [*Burden*]",

**25:15** חֲדַד וְתֵימָא יְטוּר נָפִישׁ וָקֵדְמָה

"Hhadar [*Chamber*]" and~"Teyma

"Hhadar [*Chamber*]" and "Teyma

[*Wonder*]" "Yethur [*He rows*]" "Naphish [*Refreshed*]" and~"Qedmah [*Original*]"

[*Wonder*]", "Yethur [*He rows*]", "Naphish [*Refreshed*]" and "Qedmah [*Original*]",

**25:16**

אֵלֶּה הֵם בְּנֵי יִשְׁמָעֵאל וְאֵלֶּה שְׁמֹתָם בְּחַצְרֵיהֶם וּבְטִירֹתָם שְׁנֵים עָשָׂר נְשִׂיאִם לְאֻמֹתָם

These They(m) Son~s "Yishma'el [*El will listen*]" and~These Title~s~them(m) in~Yard~s~them(m) and~in~Village~s~them(m) Two Ten Captain~s to~Tribe~s~them(m)

these are the sons of "Yishma'el [*El will listen*]" and these are their titles in their yards and in their villages, twelve captains to their tribes,

**25:17**

וְאֵלֶּה שְׁנֵי חַיֵּי יִשְׁמָעֵאל מְאַת שָׁנָה וּשְׁלֹשִׁים שָׁנָה וְשֶׁבַע שָׁנִים וַיִּגְוַע וַיָּמָת וַיֵּאָסֶף אֶל עַמָּיו

and~These Year~s Live~s "Yishma'el [*El will listen*]" Hundred Year and~Three~s Year and~Seven Year~s and~he~will~Expire and~he~will~Die and~he~will~be~Gather To People~him

and these are the years of the life of "Yishma'el [*El will listen*]", a hundred and thirty seven years and he expired and he died and he was gathered to his people,

**25:18**

וַיִּשְׁכְּנוּ מֵחֲוִילָה עַד שׁוּר אֲשֶׁר עַל פְּנֵי מִצְרַיִם בֹּאֲכָה אַשּׁוּרָה עַל פְּנֵי כָל אֶחָיו נָפָל

and~they(m)~will~Dwell from~"Hhawilah [*Twisting*]" Until "Shur [*Caravan*]" Which Upon Face~s "Mitsrayim [*Troubles*]" >~Come~you(ms) "Ashur [*Step*]"~unto Upon Face~s All Brother~s~him he~did~Fall

and they dwelt from "Hhawilah [*Twisting*]" as far as "Shur [*Caravan*]" which is upon the face of "Mitsrayim [*Troubles*]" as you come unto "Ashur [*Step*]", upon the face of all his brothers he fell,

**25:19**

וְאֵלֶּה תּוֹלְדֹת יִצְחָק בֶּן אַבְרָהָם אַבְרָהָם הוֹלִיד אֶת יִצְחָק

and~These Birthing~s "Yits'hhaq [*He laughs*]" Son "Avraham [*Father lifted*]" "Avraham [*Father lifted*]" he~had~make~Bring.forth At "Yits'hhaq [*He laughs*]"

and these are the birthings of "Yits'hhaq [*He laughs*]", the son of "Avraham [*Father lifted*]", "Avraham [*Father lifted*]" had caused to bring forth "Yits'hhaq [*He laughs*]",

**25:20**

וַיְהִי יִצְחָק בֶּן אַרְבָּעִים שָׁנָה בְּקַחְתּוֹ אֶת רִבְקָה בַּת בְּתוּאֵל הָאֲרַמִּי מִפַּדַּן אֲרָם אֲחוֹת לָבָן הָאֲרַמִּי לוֹ לְאִשָּׁה

and~he~will~Exist "Yits'hhaq [*He laughs*]" Son Four~s Year in~>~Take~him At "Rivqah [*Ensnarer*]" Daughter "Betu'el [*Destruction of El*]" the~"Aram [*Palace*]"~of from~"Padan-Aram [*Field palace*]" Sister

and "Yits'hhaq [*He laughs*]" existed a son of forty years in his taking of "Rivqah [*Ensnarer*]", the daughter of "Betu'el [*Destruction of El*]" the one of "Aram [*Palace*]", from "Padan-Aram [*Field palace*]", the

"Lavan [*White*]" the~"Aram [*Palace*]"~of to~him to~Woman

sister of "Lavan [*White*]", the one of "Aram [*Palace*]", to him for a woman,

**25:21** וַיֶּעְתַּר יִצְחָק לַיהוָה לְנֹכַח אִשְׁתּוֹ כִּי עֲקָרָה הִוא וַיֵּעָתֶר לוֹ יְהוָה וַתַּהַר רִבְקָה אִשְׁתּוֹ

and~he~will~Intercede "Yits'hhaq [*He laughs*]" to~"YHWH [*He exists*]" to~In.front Woman~him Given.that Sterile She and~he~will~be~Intercede to~him "YHWH [*He exists*]" and~she~will~Conceive "Rivqah [*Ensnarer*]" Woman~him

and "Yits'hhaq [*He laughs*]" interceded to "YHWH [*He exists*]" in front of his woman given that she was sterile and "YHWH [*He exists*]" was interceded to him and "Rivqah [*Ensnarer*]", his woman, conceived,

**25:22** וַיִּתְרֹצֲצוּ הַבָּנִים בְּקִרְבָּהּ וַתֹּאמֶר אִם כֵּן לָמָּה זֶּה אָנֹכִי וַתֵּלֶךְ לִדְרֹשׁ אֶת יְהוָה

and~they(m)~will~self~Crush the~Son~s in~Within~her and~she~will~Say If So to~What This I and~she~will~Walk to~>~Seek At "YHWH [*He exists*]"

and the sons crushed themselves within her and she said, if it is so, why am I this and she walked to seek "YHWH [*He exists*]",

**25:23** וַיֹּאמֶר יְהוָה לָהּ שְׁנֵי גִיִּים בְּבִטְנֵךְ וּשְׁנֵי לְאֻמִּים מִמֵּעַיִךְ יִפָּרֵדוּ וּלְאֹם מִלְאֹם יֶאֱמָץ וְרַב יַעֲבֹד צָעִיר

and~he~will~Say "YHWH [*He exists*]" to~her Two Nation~s in~Womb~you(fs) and~Two Community~s from~Abdomen~s~you(fs) they~will~be~Divide.apart and~Community from~Community he~will~Be.strong and~Abundant he~will~Serve Little.one□

and "YHWH [*He exists*]" said to her, two nations are in your womb and two communities from your abdomens will be divided apart and the community from the community will be strong and abundant, he will serve the little one,

**25:24** וַיִּמְלְאוּ יָמֶיהָ לָלֶדֶת וְהִנֵּה תוֹמִם בְּבִטְנָהּ

and~they(m)~will~Fill Day~s~her to~>~Bring.forth and~Look Twin~s in~Womb~her

and her days were filled to bring forth and look, twins are in her womb,

**25:25** וַיֵּצֵא הָרִאשׁוֹן אַדְמוֹנִי כֻּלּוֹ כְּאַדֶּרֶת שֵׂעָר וַיִּקְרְאוּ שְׁמוֹ עֵשָׂו

and~he~will~Go.out the~First Ruddy All~him like~Robe Hair and~they(m)~will~Call.out Title~him "Esav [*Doing*]"

and the first went out ruddy, all of him was like a robe of hair and they called out his title "Esav [*Doing*]",

**25:26** וְאַחֲרֵי כֵן יָצָא אָחִיו וְיָדוֹ אֹחֶזֶת בַּעֲקֵב עֵשָׂו וַיִּקְרָא שְׁמוֹ יַעֲקֹב וְיִצְחָק בֶּן שִׁשִּׁים שָׁנָה בְּלֶדֶת אֹתָם

and~After So he~did~Go.out Brother~

and afterward, his brother went out

him and~Hand~him Hold~ing(fs) in~ Heel "Esav [*Doing*]" and~he~will~ Call.out Title~him "Ya'aqov [*He restrains*]" and~"Yits'hhaq [*He laughs*]" Son Six~s Year in~>~ Bring.forth At~them(m)

and his hand was holding in the heel of "Esav [*Doing*]" and he called out his title "Ya'aqov [*He restrains*]" and "Yits'hhaq [*He laughs*]" was a son of sixty years in bringing them forth,

**25:27** וַיִּגְדְּלוּ הַנְּעָרִים וַיְהִי עֵשָׂו אִישׁ יֹדֵעַ צַיִד אִישׁ שָׂדֶה וְיַעֲקֹב אִישׁ תָּם יֹשֵׁב אֹהָלִים

and~they(m)~will~Magnify the~ Young.man~s and~he~will~Exist "Esav [*Doing*]" Man Know~ing(ms) Game Man Field and~"Ya'aqov [*He restrains*]" Man Mature Settle~ing(ms) Tent~s

and the young men magnified and "Esav [*Doing*]" existed a man knowing game and a man of the field and "Ya'aqov [*He restrains*]" was a man of maturity a settler of tents,

**25:28** וַיֶּאֱהַב יִצְחָק אֶת עֵשָׂו כִּי צַיִד בְּפִיו וְרִבְקָה אֹהֶבֶת אֶת יַעֲקֹב

and~he~will~Love "Yits'hhaq [*He laughs*]" At "Esav [*Doing*]" Given.that Game in~Mouth~him and~ "Rivqah [*Ensnarer*]" Love~ing(fs) At "Ya'aqov [*He restrains*]"

and "Yits'hhaq [*He laughs*]" loved "Esav [*Doing*]" given that game was in his mouth and "Rivqah [*Ensnarer*]" was loving "Ya'aqov [*He restrains*]",

**25:29** וַיָּזֶד יַעֲקֹב נָזִיד וַיָּבֹא עֵשָׂו מִן הַשָּׂדֶה וְהוּא עָיֵף

and~he~will~make~Seethe "Ya'aqov [*He restrains*]" Stew and~he~will~ Come "Esav [*Doing*]" From the~ Field and~He Tired

and "Ya'aqov [*He restrains*]" seethed a stew and "Esav [*Doing*]" came from the field and he was tired,

**25:30** * וַיֹּאמֶר עֵשָׂו אֶל יַעֲקֹב הַלְעִיטֵנִי נָא מִן הָאָדֹם הָאָדֹם הַזֶּה כִּי עָיֵף אָנֹכִי עַל כֵּן קָרָא שְׁמוֹ אֱדוֹם

and~he~will~Say "Esav [*Doing*]" To "Ya'aqov [*He restrains*]" !(ms)~make~ Provide.food~me Please From the~Red the~Red the~This Given.that Tired I Upon So he~did~Call.out Title~him "Edom [*Red*]"

and "Esav [*Doing*]" said to "Ya'aqov [*He restrains*]" please provide food to me from the red thing given that I am tired, therefore, he called out his title "Edom [*Red*]",

**25:31** וַיֹּאמֶר יַעֲקֹב מִכְרָה כַיּוֹם אֶת בְּכֹרָתְךָ לִי

and~he~will~Say "Ya'aqov [*He restrains*]" !(ms)~Sell like~the~Day At Birthright~you(ms) to~me

and "Ya'aqov [*He restrains*]" said, as of today, sell your birthright to me,

**25:32** וַיֹּאמֶר עֵשָׂו הִנֵּה אָנֹכִי הוֹלֵךְ לָמוּת וְלָמָּה זֶּה לִי בְּכֹרָה

and~he~will~Say "Esav [*Doing*]" Look I Walk~ing(ms) to~>~Die and~ to~What This to~me Birthright

and "Esav [*Doing*]" said, look, I am walking to die and what is this birthright to me,

**25:33** וַיֹּאמֶר יַעֲקֹב הִשָּׁבְעָה לִּי כַּיּוֹם וַיִּשָּׁבַע לוֹ וַיִּמְכֹּר אֶת בְּכֹרָתוֹ לְיַעֲקֹב

and~he~will~Say "Ya'aqov [*He restrains*]" !(ms)~be~Swear to~me like~the~Day and~he~will~be~Swear to~him and~he~will~Sell At Birthright~him to~"Ya'aqov [*He restrains*]"

and "Ya'aqov [*He restrains*]" said be sworn to me as of today and he was sworn to him and he sold his birthright to "Ya'aqov [*He restrains*]",

**25:34** וְיַעֲקֹב נָתַן לְעֵשָׂו לֶחֶם וּנְזִיד עֲדָשִׁים וַיֹּאכַל וַיֵּשְׁתְּ וַיָּקָם וַיֵּלַךְ וַיִּבֶז עֵשָׂו אֶת הַבְּכֹרָה

and~"Ya'aqov [*He restrains*]" he~had~Give to~"Esav [*Doing*]" Bread and~Stew Lentil~s and~he~will~Eat and~he~will~Gulp and~he~will~Rise and~he~will~Walk and~he~will~Disdain "Esav [*Doing*]" At the~Birthright

and "Ya'aqov [*He restrains*]" had given to "Esav [*Doing*]" bread and stew of lintels and he ate and he gulped and he rose and he walked and "Esav [*Doing*]" disdained the birthright,

# Chapter 26

**26:1** וַיְהִי רָעָב בָּאָרֶץ מִלְּבַד הָרָעָב הָרִאשׁוֹן אֲשֶׁר הָיָה בִּימֵי אַבְרָהָם וַיֵּלֶךְ יִצְחָק אֶל אֲבִימֶלֶךְ מֶלֶךְ פְּלִשְׁתִּים גְּרָרָה

and~he~will~Exist Hunger in~Land from~to~Separated.thing the~Hunger the~First Which he~did~Exist in~Day~s "Avraham [*Father lifted*]" and~he~will~Walk "Yits'hhaq [*He laughs*]" To "Aviymelekh [*My father is king*]" King "Peleshet [*Immigrant*]"~s "Gerar [*Chew*]"~unto

and hunger existed in the land besides the first hunger which existed in the days of "Avraham [*Father lifted*]" and "Yits'hhaq [*He laughs*]" walked to "Aviymelekh [*My father is king*]" king of the ones of "Peleshet [*Immigrant*]" unto "Gerar [*Chew*]",

**26:2** וַיֵּרָא אֵלָיו יְהוָה וַיֹּאמֶר אַל תֵּרֵד מִצְרָיְמָה שְׁכֹן בָּאָרֶץ אֲשֶׁר אֹמַר אֵלֶיךָ

and~he~will~be~See To~him "YHWH [*He exists*]" and~he~will~Say No you(ms)~will~Go.down "Mitsrayim [*Troubles*]"~unto !(ms)~Dwell in~the~Land Which i~will~Say To~you(ms)

and "YHWH [*He exists*]" appeared to him and he said, you will not go down unto "Mitsrayim [*Troubles*]", dwell in the land which I will say to you,

**26:3** גּוּר בָּאָרֶץ הַזֹּאת וְאֶהְיֶה עִמְּךָ וַאֲבָרְכֶךָּ כִּי לְךָ וּלְזַרְעֲךָ אֶתֵּן אֶת כָּל הָאֲרָצֹת הָאֵל וַהֲקִמֹתִי אֶת הַשְּׁבֻעָה אֲשֶׁר נִשְׁבַּעְתִּי לְאַבְרָהָם אָבִיךָ

!(ms)~Sojourn in~the~Land the~This

sojourn in this land and I will exist

141

and~i~did~Exist With~you(ms) and~i~
did~much~Kneel~you(ms) Given.that
to~you(ms) and~to~Seed~you(ms) i~
will~Give At All the~Land~s the~
These and~i~did~make~Rise At the~
Swearing Which i~did~be~Swear to~
"Avraham [*Father lifted*]" Father~
you(ms)

with you and I will respect you
given that to you and to your seed I
will give all these lands and I will
make rise the swearing which I was
sworn to "Avraham [*Father lifted*]"
your father,

**26:4** וְהִרְבֵּיתִי אֶת זַרְעֲךָ כְּכוֹכְבֵי הַשָּׁמַיִם וְנָתַתִּי לְזַרְעֲךָ אֵת כָּל הָאֲרָצֹת הָאֵל וְהִתְבָּרְכוּ בְזַרְעֲךָ כֹּל גּוֹיֵי הָאָרֶץ

and~i~did~make~Increase At Seed~
you(ms) like~Star~s the~Sky~s2 and~
i~will~Give to~Seed~you(ms) At All
the~Land~s the~These and~they~did~
self~Kneel in~Seed~you(ms) All
Nation~s the~Land

and I will make your seed increase
like the stars of the sky and I will
give to your seed all these lands and
all the nations of the land will
respect themselves with your seed,

**26:5** עֵקֶב אֲשֶׁר שָׁמַע אַבְרָהָם בְּקֹלִי וַיִּשְׁמֹר מִשְׁמַרְתִּי מִצְוֹתַי חֻקּוֹתַי וְתוֹרֹתַי

Since Which he~did~much~Hear
"Avraham [*Father lifted*]" in~Voice~
me and~he~will~Guard Charge~me
Directive~s~me Custom~s~me and~
Teaching~s~me

because "Avraham [*Father lifted*]"
heard in my voice and he guarded
my charge, my directives, my
customs and my teachings,

**26:6** וַיֵּשֶׁב יִצְחָק בִּגְרָר

and~he~will~Settle "Yits'hhaq [*He
laughs*]" in~"Gerar [*Chew*]"

and "Yits'hhaq [*He laughs*]" settled
in "Gerar [*Chew*]",

**26:7** וַיִּשְׁאֲלוּ אַנְשֵׁי הַמָּקוֹם לְאִשְׁתּוֹ וַיֹּאמֶר אֲחֹתִי הִוא כִּי יָרֵא לֵאמֹר אִשְׁתִּי פֶּן יַהַרְגֻנִי אַנְשֵׁי הַמָּקוֹם עַל רִבְקָה כִּי טוֹבַת מַרְאֶה הִוא

and~they(m)~will~Inquire Man~s the~
Place to~Woman~him and~he~will~Say
Sister~me She Given.that he~did~Fear
to~>~Say Woman~me Otherwise
they(m)~will~Kill~me Man~s the~Place
Upon "Rivqah [*Ensnarer*]" Given.that
Functional Appearance She

and the men inquired to his woman
and he said, she is my sister, given
that he feared saying, my woman,
otherwise the men of the place will
kill me because of "Rivqah
[*Ensnarer*]" given that she is
functional in appearance,

**26:8** וַיְהִי כִּי אָרְכוּ לוֹ שָׁם הַיָּמִים וַיַּשְׁקֵף אֲבִימֶלֶךְ מֶלֶךְ פְּלִשְׁתִּים בְּעַד הַחַלּוֹן וַיַּרְא וְהִנֵּה יִצְחָק מְצַחֵק אֵת רִבְקָה אִשְׁתּוֹ

and~he~will~Exist Given.that they~did~
Prolong to~him There the~Day~s
and~he~will~make~Look.down

and it came to pass that the days
were prolonged to him there and
"Aviymelekh [*My father is king*]"

"Aviymelekh [*My father is king*]" King "Peleshet [*Immigrant*]"~s Round.about the~Window and~he~will~ See and~Look "Yits'hhaq [*He laughs*]" much~Laugh~ing(ms) At "Rivqah [*Ensnarer*]" Woman~him

the king of the ones of "Peleshet [*Immigrant*]" looked down round about the window and he saw and look, "Yits'hhaq [*He laughs*]" was laughing with "Rivqah [*Ensnarer*]" his woman,

**26:9**

וַיִּקְרָא אֲבִימֶלֶךְ לְיִצְחָק וַיֹּאמֶר אַךְ הִנֵּה אִשְׁתְּךָ הִוא וְאֵיךְ אָמַרְתָּ אֲחֹתִי הִוא וַיֹּאמֶר אֵלָיו יִצְחָק כִּי אָמַרְתִּי פֶּן אָמוּת עָלֶיהָ

and~he~will~Call.out "Aviymelekh [*My father is king*]" to~"Yits'hhaq [*He laughs*]" and~he~will~Say Surely Look Woman~you(ms) She and~ Where you(ms)~did~Say Sister~me She and~he~will~Say To~him "Yits'hhaq [*He laughs*]" Given.that i~ did~Say Otherwise i~will~Die Upon~ her

and "Aviymelekh [*My father is king*]" called out to "Yits'hhaq [*He laughs*]" and he said, surely look, she is your woman and why did you say, she is my sister and "Yits'hhaq [*He laughs*]" said to him given that I said otherwise I will die because of her,

**26:10**

וַיֹּאמֶר אֲבִימֶלֶךְ מַה זֹּאת עָשִׂיתָ לָּנוּ כִּמְעַט שָׁכַב אַחַד הָעָם אֶת אִשְׁתֶּךָ וְהֵבֵאתָ עָלֵינוּ אָשָׁם

and~he~will~Say "Aviymelekh [*My father is king*]" What This you(ms)~did~Do to~us like~ Small.amount he~did~Lay.down Unit the~People At Woman~you(ms) and~ you(ms)~did~make~Come Upon~us Guilt

and "Aviymelekh [*My father is king*]" said what is this you did to us, one of the people might have laid down with your woman and you will make guilt come upon us,

**26:11**

וַיְצַו אֲבִימֶלֶךְ אֶת כָּל הָעָם לֵאמֹר הַנֹּגֵעַ בָּאִישׁ הַזֶּה וּבְאִשְׁתּוֹ מוֹת יוּמָת

and~he~will~much~Direct "Aviymelekh [*My father is king*]" At All the~ People to~>~Say the~Touch~ing(ms) in~the~Man the~This and~in~Woman~ him >~Die he~will~make.be~Die

and "Aviymelekh [*My father is king*]" directed all the people saying, the touching with this man and with his woman, he will be made very dead,

**26:12**

וַיִּזְרַע יִצְחָק בָּאָרֶץ הַהִוא וַיִּמְצָא בַּשָּׁנָה הַהִוא מֵאָה שְׁעָרִים וַיְבָרֲכֵהוּ יְהוָה

and~he~will~Sow "Yits'hhaq [*He laughs*]" in~the~Land the~She and~ he~will~Find in~the~Year the~He Hundred Sha'ar~s and~he~will~much~ Kneel~him "YHWH [*He exists*]"

and "Yits'hhaq [*He laughs*]" sowed in that land and he found in that year a hundred sha'ars and "YHWH [*He exists*]" respected him,

**26:13** וַיִּגְדַּל הָאִישׁ וַיֵּלֶךְ הָלוֹךְ וְגָדֵל עַד כִּי גָדַל מְאֹד

and~he~will~Magnify the~Man and~he~will~Walk >~Walk and~Magnified Until Given.that he~did~Magnify Many

and the man magnified and he walked a walking and magnified until he much magnified,

**26:14** וַיְהִי לוֹ מִקְנֵה צֹאן וּמִקְנֵה בָקָר וַעֲבֻדָּה רַבָּה וַיְקַנְאוּ אֹתוֹ פְּלִשְׁתִּים

and~he~will~Exist to~him Livestock Flocks and~Livestock Cattle and~Service Abundant and~they(m)~will~much~Be.zealous At~him "Peleshet [*Immigrant*]"~s

and livestock of flocks and livestock of cattle and an abundant household existed to him and the ones of "Peleshet [*Immigrant*]" were envious of him,

**26:15*** וְכָל הַבְּאֵרֹת אֲשֶׁר חָפְרוּ עַבְדֵי אָבִיו בִּימֵי אַבְרָהָם אָבִיו סִתְּמוּם פְּלִשְׁתִּים וַיְמַלְאוּם עָפָר

and~All the~Well~s Which they~did~Dig.out Servant~s Father~him in~Day~s "Avraham [*Father lifted*]" Father~him they~did~much~Shut.up~them(m) "Peleshet [*Immigrant*]"~s and~they(m)~will~much~Fill~them(m) Powder

and all the wells which the servants of his father dug out in the days of "Avraham [*Father lifted*]" his father, the ones of "Peleshet [*Immigrant*]" shut them up and they filled them with powder,

**26:16** וַיֹּאמֶר אֲבִימֶלֶךְ אֶל יִצְחָק לֵךְ מֵעִמָּנוּ כִּי עָצַמְתָּ מִמֶּנּוּ מְאֹד

and~he~will~Say "Aviymelekh [*My father is king*]" To "Yits'hhaq [*He laughs*]" !(ms)~Walk from~With~us Given.that you(ms)~did~Be.abundant From~us Many

and "Aviymelekh [*My father is king*]" said to "Yits'hhaq [*He laughs*]", walk from us given that you are much more abundant from us,

**26:17** וַיֵּלֶךְ מִשָּׁם יִצְחָק וַיִּחַן בְּנַחַל גְּרָר וַיֵּשֶׁב שָׁם

and~he~will~Walk from~There "Yits'hhaq [*He laughs*]" and~he~will~Camp in~Wadi "Gerar [*Chew*]" and~he~will~Settle There

and "Yits'hhaq [*He laughs*]" walked from there and he camped in the wadi of "Gerar [*Chew*]" and settled there,

**26:18** וַיָּשָׁב יִצְחָק וַיַּחְפֹּר אֶת בְּאֵרֹת הַמַּיִם אֲשֶׁר חָפְרוּ בִּימֵי אַבְרָהָם אָבִיו וַיְסַתְּמוּם פְּלִשְׁתִּים אַחֲרֵי מוֹת אַבְרָהָם וַיִּקְרָא לָהֶן שֵׁמוֹת כַּשֵּׁמֹת אֲשֶׁר קָרָא לָהֶן אָבִיו

and~he~will~Turn.back "Yits'hhaq [*He laughs*]" and~he~will~Dig.out At Well~s the~Water~s2 Which they~did~Dig.out in~Day~s "Avraham [*Father lifted*]" Father~him they~did~much~Shut.up~them(m) "Peleshet

and "Yits'hhaq [*He laughs*]" turned back and dug out the wells of water which they dug out in the days of "Avraham [*Father lifted*]" his father and the ones of "Peleshet [*Immigrant*]" shut them up after the

[*Immigrant*]"~s After Death "Avraham [*Father lifted*]" and~he~will~Call.out to~them(f) Title~s like~Title~s Which he~did~Call.out to~them(f) Father~him

death of "Avraham [*Father lifted*]" and he called out to them titles like the titles which his father called out to them,

**26:19** וַיַּחְפְּרוּ עַבְדֵי יִצְחָק בַּנָּחַל וַיִּמְצְאוּ שָׁם בְּאֵר מַיִם חַיִּים

and~they(m)~will~Dig.out Servant~s "Yits'hhaq [*He laughs*]" in~the~Wadi and~they(m)~will~Find There Well Water~s2 Life~s

and the servants of "Yits'hhaq [*He laughs*]" dug out in the wadi and they found there a well of water of life,

**26:20** וַיָּרִיבוּ רֹעֵי גְרָר עִם רֹעֵי יִצְחָק לֵאמֹר לָנוּ הַמָּיִם וַיִּקְרָא שֵׁם הַבְּאֵר עֵשֶׂק כִּי הִתְעַשְּׂקוּ עִמּוֹ

and~they(m)~will~Dispute Feed~ing(mp) "Gerar [*Chew*]" With Feed~ing(mp) "Yits'hhaq [*He laughs*]" to~>~Say to~us the~Water~s2 and~he~will~ Call.out There the~Well "Eseq [*Quarrel*]" Given.that they~did~self~ Quarrel With~him

and the feeders of "Gerar [*Chew*]" disputed with the feeders of "Yits'hhaq [*He laughs*]" saying, the water is to us, and he called out there the well "Eseq [*Quarrel*]" given that they quarreled with themselves with him,

**26:21** וַיַּחְפְּרוּ בְּאֵר אַחֶרֶת וַיָּרִיבוּ גַּם עָלֶיהָ וַיִּקְרָא שְׁמָהּ שִׂטְנָה

and~they(m)~will~Dig.out Well Other and~they(m)~will~Dispute Also Upon~ her and~he~will~Call.out Title~her "Sithnah [*Accusation*]"

and they dug out another well and they also disputed upon her and he called out her title "Sithnah [*Accusation*]",

**26:22** וַיַּעְתֵּק מִשָּׁם וַיַּחְפֹּר בְּאֵר אַחֶרֶת וְלֹא רָבוּ עָלֶיהָ וַיִּקְרָא שְׁמָהּ רְחֹבוֹת וַיֹּאמֶר כִּי עַתָּה הִרְחִיב יְהוָה לָנוּ וּפָרִינוּ בָאָרֶץ

and~he~will~make~Advance from~There and~he~will~Dig.out Well Other and~ Not they~did~Dispute Upon~her and~ he~will~Call.out Title~her "Rehhovot [*Wide streets*]" and~he~will~Say Given.that Now he~did~make~Widen "YHWH [*He exists*]" to~us and~we~ will~Reproduce in~the~Land

and he made an advance from there and he dug out another well and they did not dispute upon her and he called out her title "Rehhovot [*Wide streets*]" and he said given that now "YHWH [*He exists*]" made a widening for us and we will reproduce in the land,

**26:23\*** וַיַּעַל מִשָּׁם בְּאֵר שָׁבַע

and~he~will~Go.up from~There "B'er-Sheva [*Well of oath*]"

and he went up from there to "B'er-Sheva [*Well of oath*]",

**26:24** וַיֵּרָא אֵלָיו יְהוָה בַּלַּיְלָה הַהוּא וַיֹּאמֶר אָנֹכִי אֱלֹהֵי אַבְרָהָם אָבִיךָ אַל תִּירָא כִּי אִתְּךָ אָנֹכִי וּבֵרַכְתִּיךָ וְהִרְבֵּיתִי אֶת זַרְעֲךָ בַּעֲבוּר אַבְרָהָם עַבְדִּי

and~he~will~be~See To~him "YHWH [*He exists*]" in~the~Night the~He

and "YHWH [*He exists*]" appeared to him in that night and he said, I

and~he~will~Say I Power~s
"Avraham [*Father lifted*]" Father~
you(ms) No you(ms)~will~Fear
Given.that At~you(ms) I and~i~did~
much~Kneel~you(ms) and~i~did~make~
Increase At Seed~you(ms) in~
On.account.of "Avraham [*Father
lifted*]" Servant~me

am the powers of "Avraham
[*Father lifted*]" your father, you
will not fear given that I am with
you, I will respect you and I will
make an increase to your seed on
account of "Avraham [*Father
lifted*]" my servant,

**\* 26:25**   וַיִּבֶן שָׁם מִזְבֵּחַ וַיִּקְרָא בְּשֵׁם יְהוָה וַיֵּט שָׁם אָהֳלוֹ וַיִּכְרוּ שָׁם עַבְדֵי יִצְחָק בְּאֵר

and~he~will~Build There Altar and~
he~will~Call.out in~Title "YHWH [*He
exists*]" and~he~will~Stretch There
Tent~him and~they(m)~will~Dig There
Servant~s "Yits'hhaq [*He laughs*]"
Well

and he built an altar there and
called out in the title of "YHWH
[*He exists*]" and he will stretch his
tent there and the servants of
"Yits'hhaq [*He laughs*]" dug a well
there,

**26:26**   וַאֲבִימֶלֶךְ הָלַךְ אֵלָיו מִגְּרָר וַאֲחֻזַּת מֵרֵעֵהוּ וּפִיכֹל שַׂר צְבָאוֹ

and~"Aviymelekh [*My father is
king*]" he~had~Walk To~him from~
"Gerar [*Chew*]" and~"Ahhuzat
[*Holdings*]" Partner~him and~"Pikhol
[*Face of all*]" Noble Army~him

and "Aviymelekh [*My father is
king*]" had walked to him from
"Gerar [*Chew*]" and "Ahhuzat
[*Holdings*]" his partner and "Pikhol
[*Face of all*]" the noble of his army,

**26:27**   וַיֹּאמֶר אֲלֵהֶם יִצְחָק מַדּוּעַ בָּאתֶם אֵלָי וְאַתֶּם שְׂנֵאתֶם אֹתִי וַתְּשַׁלְּחוּנִי מֵאִתְּכֶם

and~he~will~Say To~them(m)
"Yits'hhaq [*He laughs*]" Why
you(mp)~did~Come To~me and~
You(ms) you(mp)~did~Hate At~me
and~you(mp)~will~Send~me from~At~
you(mp)

and "Yits'hhaq [*He laughs*]" said to
them, why did you come to me and
you hated me and you sent me from
you,

**\* 26:28**   וַיֹּאמְרוּ רָאוֹ רָאִינוּ כִּי הָיָה יְהוָה עִמָּךְ וַנֹּאמֶר תְּהִי נָא אָלָה בֵּינוֹתֵינוּ בֵּינֵינוּ וּבֵינֶךָ וְנִכְרְתָה בְרִית עִמָּךְ

and~they(m)~will~Say >~See we~did~
See Given.that he~did~Exist "YHWH
[*He exists*]" With~you(fs) and~we~
will~Say she~will~Exist Please Oath
Between~s~us Between~s~us and~
Between~you(ms) and~we~will~Cut
Covenant With~you(fs)

and they said, we surely see that
"YHWH [*He exists*]" existed with
you and we said, please, an oath
will exist between us and you and
we will cut a covenant with you,

**\* 26:29**   אִם תַּעֲשֵׂה עִמָּנוּ רָעָה כַּאֲשֶׁר לֹא נְגַעֲנוּךָ וְכַאֲשֶׁר עָשִׂינוּ עִמְּךָ רַק טוֹב וַנְּשַׁלֵּחֲךָ בְּשָׁלוֹם אַתָּה עַתָּה בְּרוּךְ יְהוָה

If you(ms)~will~Do With~us
Dysfunctional like~Which Not we~
did~Touch and~like~Which we~did~Do
With~you(ms) Only Functional and~
we~will~much~Send~you(ms) in~
Complete You(ms) Now Kneel~ed(ms)
"YHWH [*He exists*]"

if you will not do dysfunction with
us just as we did not touch and just
as we did with you only function
and we sent you in completeness,
you are now respected of "YHWH
[*He exists*]",

## 26:30

וַיַּעַשׂ לָהֶם מִשְׁתֶּה וַיֹּאכְלוּ וַיִּשְׁתּוּ

and~he~will~Do to~them(m) Feast
and~they(m)~will~Eat and~they(m)~
will~Gulp

and he made for them a feast and
they ate and they gulped,

## 26:31

וַיַּשְׁכִּימוּ בַבֹּקֶר וַיִּשָּׁבְעוּ אִישׁ לְאָחִיו וַיְשַׁלְּחֵם יִצְחָק וַיֵּלְכוּ
מֵאִתּוֹ בְּשָׁלוֹם

and~they(m)~will~make~Depart.early in~
the~Morning and~they(m)~will~be~
Swear Man to~Brother~him and~he~
will~much~Send~them(m) "Yits'hhaq
[*He laughs*]" and~they(m)~will~Walk
from~At~him in~Complete

and they departed early in the
morning and each were sworn to
his brother and "Yits'hhaq [*He
laughs*]" sent them and they walked
from him in completeness,

## 26:32

וַיְהִי בַּיּוֹם הַהוּא וַיָּבֹאוּ עַבְדֵי יִצְחָק וַיַּגִּדוּ לוֹ עַל אֹדוֹת הַבְּאֵר
אֲשֶׁר חָפָרוּ וַיֹּאמְרוּ לוֹ מָצָאנוּ מָיִם

and~he~will~Exist in~the~Day the~He
and~they(m)~will~Come Servant~s
"Yits'hhaq [*He laughs*]" and~they(m)~
will~make~Be.face.to.face to~him Upon
Concerning the~Well Which they~
did~Dig.out and~they(m)~will~Say to~
him we~did~Find Water~s2

and it came to pass in that day and
the servants of "Yits'hhaq [*He
laughs*]" came and they told to him
concerning the well which they dug
out and they said to him we found
water,

## 26:33

וַיִּקְרָא אֹתָהּ שִׁבְעָה עַל כֵּן שֵׁם הָעִיר בְּאֵר שֶׁבַע עַד הַיּוֹם הַזֶּה

and~he~will~Call.out At~her "Shivah
[*Oath*]" Upon So Title the~City
"B'er-Sheva [*Well of oath*]" Until
the~Day the~This

and he called her "Shivah [*Oath*]"
therefore the title of the city is
"B'er-Sheva [*Well of oath*]" until
this day,

## 26:34

וַיְהִי עֵשָׂו בֶּן אַרְבָּעִים שָׁנָה וַיִּקַּח אִשָּׁה אֶת יְהוּדִית בַּת בְּאֵרִי
הַחִתִּי וְאֶת בָּשְׂמַת בַּת אֵילֹן הַחִתִּי

and~he~will~Exist "Esav [*Doing*]"
Son Four~s Year and~he~will~Take
Woman At "Yehudit [*Praised*]"
Daughter "Be'eri [*My well*]" the~
"Hhet [*Shattered*]"~of and~At
"Basmat [*Spice*]" Daughter "Eylon

and "Esav [*Doing*]" existed a son of
forty years and he took a woman,
"Yehudit [*Praised*]", the daughter
of "Be'eri [*My well*]", the one of
"Hhet [*Shattered*]" and "Basmat
[*Spice*]" the daughter of "Eylon

[*Strength*]" the~"Hhet [*Shattered*]"~of

[*Strength*]", the one of "Hhet [*Shattered*]",

**26:35**

וַתִּהְיֶיןָ מֹרַת רוּחַ לְיִצְחָק וּלְרִבְקָה

and~they(f)~will~Exist Grief Wind to~"Yits'hhaq [*He laughs*]" and~to~ "Rivqah [*Ensnarer*]"

and they existed a grief of wind to "Yits'hhaq [*He laughs*]" and to "Rivqah [*Ensnarer*]",

# Chapter 27

**27:1**

וַיְהִי כִּי זָקֵן יִצְחָק וַתִּכְהֶיןָ עֵינָיו מֵרְאֹת וַיִּקְרָא אֶת עֵשָׂו בְּנוֹ הַגָּדֹל וַיֹּאמֶר אֵלָיו בְּנִי וַיֹּאמֶר אֵלָיו הִנֵּנִי

and~he~will~Exist Given.that he~did~ Be.old "Yits'hhaq [*He laughs*]" and~ they(f)~will~Dim Eye~s2~him from~>~ See and~he~will~Call.out At "Esav [*Doing*]" Son~him the~Magnificent and~he~will~Say To~him Son~me and~he~will~Say To~him Look~me

and it came to pass that "Yits'hhaq [*He laughs*]" was old and his eyes dimmed from seeing and he called out "Esav [*Doing*]" his magnificent son and he said to him, my son, and he said to him, here am I,

**27:2**

וַיֹּאמֶר הִנֵּה נָא זָקַנְתִּי לֹא יָדַעְתִּי יוֹם מוֹתִי

and~he~will~Say Look Please i~did~ Be.old Not i~did~Know Day Death~ me

and he said, please look, I am old, I do not know the day of my death,

**27:3**

וְעַתָּה שָׂא נָא כֵלֶיךָ תֶּלְיְךָ וְקַשְׁתֶּךָ וְצֵא הַשָּׂדֶה וְצוּדָה לִי צידה (צָיִד)

and~Now !(ms)~Lift.up Please Instrument~you(ms) Quiver~you(ms) and~Bow~you(ms) and~!(ms)~Go.out the~Field and~!(ms)~Hunt to~me Provisions

and now please lift up your instrument, your quiver and your bow and go out to the field and hunt for me provisions,

**27:4**

וַעֲשֵׂה לִי מַטְעַמִּים כַּאֲשֶׁר אָהַבְתִּי וְהָבִיאָה לִּי וְאֹכֵלָה בַּעֲבוּר תְּבָרֶכְךָ נַפְשִׁי בְּטֶרֶם אָמוּת

and~!(ms)~Do to~me Delicacy~s like~ Which i~did~Love and~!(ms)~make~ Come to~me and~i~did~Eat in~ On.account.of she~will~much~Kneel~ you(ms) Being~me in~Before i~will~ Die

and do for me delicacies just as I love and bring to me and I will eat so that my being will respect you before I die,

**27:5**

וְרִבְקָה שֹׁמַעַת בְּדַבֵּר יִצְחָק אֶל עֵשָׂו בְּנוֹ וַיֵּלֶךְ עֵשָׂו הַשָּׂדֶה לָצוּד צַיִד לְהָבִיא

and~"Rivqah [*Ensnarer*]" Hear~ing(fs)

and "Rivqah [*Ensnarer*]" was

in~>~much~Speak "Yits'hhaq [*He laughs*]" To "Esav [*Doing*]" Son~him and~he~will~Walk "Esav [*Doing*]" the~Field to~>~Hunt Game to~>~make~Come

hearing in the speaking of "Yits'hhaq [*He laughs*]" to "Esav [*Doing*]" his son and "Esav [*Doing*]" walked to the field to hunt game to bring,

**27:6** וְרִבְקָה אָמְרָה אֶל יַעֲקֹב בְּנָהּ לֵאמֹר הִנֵּה שָׁמַעְתִּי אֶת אָבִיךָ מְדַבֵּר אֶל עֵשָׂו אָחִיךָ לֵאמֹר

and~"Rivqah [*Ensnarer*]" she~had~Say To "Ya'aqov [*He restrains*]" Son~her to~>~Say Look i~did~Hear At Father~you(ms) >~much~Speak~ing(ms) To "Esav [*Doing*]" Brother~you(ms) to~>~Say

and "Rivqah [*Ensnarer*]" had said to "Ya'aqov [*He restrains*]" her son saying, look, I heard your father speaking to "Esav [*Doing*]" your brother saying,

**27:7** הָבִיאָה לִּי צַיִד וַעֲשֵׂה לִי מַטְעַמִּים וְאֹכֵלָה וַאֲבָרֶכְכָה לִפְנֵי יְהוָה לִפְנֵי מוֹתִי

!(ms)~make~Come to~me Game and~!(ms)~Do to~me Delicacy~s and~i~will~Eat and~i~will~much~Kneel~you(ms) to~Face~s "YHWH [*He exists*]" to~Face~s Death~me

bring to me game and make for me delicacies and I will eat and I will respect you before "YHWH [*He exists*]", before my death,

**27:8** וְעַתָּה בְנִי שְׁמַע בְּקֹלִי לַאֲשֶׁר אֲנִי מְצַוָּה אֹתָךְ

and~Now Son~me !(ms)~Hear in~Voice~me to~Which I much~Direct~ing(fs) At~you(ms)

and now my son, hear in my voice which I am directing you,

**27:9** לֶךְ נָא אֶל הַצֹּאן וְקַח לִי מִשָּׁם שְׁנֵי גְּדָיֵי עִזִּים טֹבִים וְאֶעֱשֶׂה אֹתָם מַטְעַמִּים לְאָבִיךָ כַּאֲשֶׁר אָהֵב

!(ms)~Walk Please To the~Flocks and~!(ms)~Take to~me from~There Two Male.kid~s She-goat~s Functional~s and~i~will~Do At~them(m) Delicacy~s to~Father~you(ms) like~Which he~did~Love

please walk to the flocks and take for me from there two functional male kids of the she-goats and I will make them, delicacies for your father just as he loves,

**27:10** וְהֵבֵאתָ לְאָבִיךָ וְאָכָל בַּעֲבֻר אֲשֶׁר יְבָרֶכְךָ לִפְנֵי מוֹתוֹ

and~you(ms)~did~make~Come to~Father~you(ms) and~he~did~Eat in~On.account.of Which he~will~much~Kneel~you(ms) to~Face~s Death~him

and you will bring to your father and he will eat so that he will respect you before his death,

**27:11** וַיֹּאמֶר יַעֲקֹב אֶל רִבְקָה אִמּוֹ הֵן עֵשָׂו אָחִי אִישׁ שָׂעִר וְאָנֹכִי אִישׁ חָלָק

and~he~will~Say "Ya'aqov [*He restrains*]" To "Rivqah [*Ensnarer*]"

and "Ya'aqov [*He restrains*]" said to "Rivqah [*Ensnarer*]" his mother,

Mother~him  Though  "Esav [*Doing*]"
Brother~me  Man  Hair  and~I  Man
Slick

though "Esav [*Doing*]" my brother
is a man of hair and I am a slick
man,

**27:12** אוּלַי יְמֻשֵּׁנִי אָבִי וְהָיִיתִי בְעֵינָיו כִּמְתַעְתֵּעַ וְהֵבֵאתִי עָלַי קְלָלָה וְלֹא בְרָכָה

Possibly  he~will~Feel~me  Father~me
and~i~did~Exist  in~Eye~s2~him  like~
much~Imitate~ing(ms)  and~i~will~
make~Come  Upon~me  Annoyance
and~Not  Present

possibly my father will feel me and
I will exist in his eyes as imitating
and I will bring upon me an
annoyance and not a present,

**27:13** וַתֹּאמֶר לוֹ אִמּוֹ עָלַי קִלְלָתְךָ בְּנִי אַךְ שְׁמַע בְּקֹלִי וְלֵךְ קַח לִי

and~she~will~Say  to~him  Mother~him
Upon~me  Annoyance~you(ms)  Son~me
Surely  !(ms)~Hear  in~Voice~me  and~
!(ms)~Walk  !(ms)~Take  to~me

and his mother said to him, your
annoyance is upon me my son,
surely, hear in my voice and walk,
take for me,

**27:14** וַיֵּלֶךְ וַיִּקַּח וַיָּבֵא לְאִמּוֹ וַתַּעַשׂ אִמּוֹ מַטְעַמִּים כַּאֲשֶׁר אָהֵב אָבִיו

and~he~will~Walk  and~he~will~Take
and~he~will~make~Come  to~Mother~
him  and~she~will~Do  Mother~him
Delicacy~s  like~Which  he~did~Love
Father~him

and he walked and he took and he
brought to his mother and his
mother made delicacies just as his
father loved,

**27:15** וַתִּקַּח רִבְקָה אֶת בִּגְדֵי עֵשָׂו בְּנָהּ הַגָּדֹל הַחֲמֻדֹת אֲשֶׁר אִתָּהּ בַּבָּיִת וַתַּלְבֵּשׁ אֶת יַעֲקֹב בְּנָהּ הַקָּטָן

and~she~will~Take  "Rivqah
[*Ensnarer*]"  At  Garment~s  "Esav
[*Doing*]"  Son~her  the~Magnificent
the~Pleasant~s  Which  At~her  in~the~
House  and~she~will~make~Clothe  At
"Ya'aqov [*He restrains*]"  Son~her
the~Small

and "Rivqah [*Ensnarer*]" took
garments of "Esav [*Doing*]" her
magnificent son which were with
her in the house and she clothed
"Ya'aqov [*He restrains*]" her small
son,

**27:16** וְאֵת עֹרֹת גְּדָיֵי הָעִזִּים הִלְבִּישָׁה עַל יָדָיו וְעַל חֶלְקַת צַוָּארָיו

and~At  Skin~s  Male.kid~s  the~She-
goat~s  she~did~make~Clothe  Upon
Hand~s2~him  and~Upon  Smooth
Back.of.the.neck~s~him

and with the skins of the male kids
of the she-goats she clothed his
hands and the smooth of the back of
his neck,

**27:17** וַתִּתֵּן אֶת הַמַּטְעַמִּים וְאֶת הַלֶּחֶם אֲשֶׁר עָשָׂתָה בְּיַד יַעֲקֹב בְּנָהּ

and~she~will~Give  At  Delicacy~s
and~At  the~Bread  Which  she~did~Do
in~Hand  "Ya'aqov [*He restrains*]"
Son~her

and she gave delicacies and bread
which she made in the hand of
"Ya'aqov [*He restrains*]" her son,

**27:18**

וַיָּבֹא אֶל אָבִיו וַיֹּאמֶר אָבִי וַיֹּאמֶר הִנֶּנִּי מִי אַתָּה בְּנִי

and~he~will~Come To Father~him and~he~will~Say Father~me and~he~will~Say Look~me Who You(ms) Son~me

and he came to his father and he said, my father, and he said, here am I, who are you my son,

**27:19**

וַיֹּאמֶר יַעֲקֹב אֶל אָבִיו אָנֹכִי עֵשָׂו בְּכֹרֶךָ עָשִׂיתִי כַּאֲשֶׁר דִּבַּרְתָּ אֵלָי קוּם נָא שְׁבָה וְאָכְלָה מִצֵּידִי בַּעֲבוּר תְּבָרֲכַנִּי נַפְשֶׁךָ

and~he~will~Say "Ya'aqov [*He restrains*]" To Father~him I "Esav [*Doing*]" Firstborn~you(ms) i~did~Do like~Which you(ms)~did~Speak To~me !(ms)~Rise Please !(ms)~Settle~^ and~!(ms)~Eat from~Game~me in~On.account.of she~will~much~Kneel~me Being~you(ms)

and "Ya'aqov [*He restrains*]" said to his father, I am "Esav [*Doing*]" your firstborn I did just as you spoke to me, please rise, settle and eat from my game so that your being will respect me,

**27:20**

וַיֹּאמֶר יִצְחָק אֶל בְּנוֹ מַה זֶּה מִהַרְתָּ לִמְצֹא בְּנִי וַיֹּאמֶר כִּי הִקְרָה יְהֹוָה אֱלֹהֶיךָ לְפָנָי

and~he~will~Say "Yits'hhaq [*He laughs*]" To Son~him What This you(ms)~did~much~Hurry to~>>Find Son~me and~he~will~Say Given.that he~did~make~Meet "YHWH [*He exists*]" Power~s~you(ms) to~Face~s~me

and "Yits'hhaq [*He laughs*]" said to his son, what is this you quickly hurried to find my son, and he said, given that "YHWH [*He exists*]" of your powers caused to meet before me,

**27:21**

וַיֹּאמֶר יִצְחָק אֶל יַעֲקֹב גְּשָׁה נָּא וַאֲמֻשְׁךָ בְּנִי הַאַתָּה זֶה בְּנִי עֵשָׂו אִם לֹא

and~he~will~Say "Yits'hhaq [*He laughs*]" To "Ya'aqov [*He restrains*]" !(ms)~Draw.near Please and~i~will~Grope Son~me the~You(ms) This Son~me "Esav [*Doing*]" If Not

and "Yits'hhaq [*He laughs*]" said to "Ya'aqov [*He restrains*]", please draw near and I will grope my son, is this you my son "Esav [*Doing*]" or not,

**27:22**

וַיִּגַּשׁ יַעֲקֹב אֶל יִצְחָק אָבִיו וַיְמֻשֵּׁהוּ וַיֹּאמֶר הַקֹּל קוֹל יַעֲקֹב וְהַיָּדַיִם יְדֵי עֵשָׂו

and~he~will~Draw.near "Ya'aqov [*He restrains*]" To "Yits'hhaq [*He laughs*]" Father~him and~he~will~Grope~him and~he~will~Say the~Voice Voice "Ya'aqov [*He restrains*]" and~the~Hand~s2 Hand~s2 "Esav [*Doing*]"

and "Ya'aqov [*He restrains*]" drew near to "Yits'hhaq [*He laughs*]" his father and he groped him and he said, the voice is the voice of "Ya'aqov [*He restrains*]" and the hands are the hands of "Esav [*Doing*]",

**27:23**

וְלֹא הִכִּירוֹ כִּי הָיוּ יָדָיו כִּידֵי עֵשָׂו אָחִיו שְׂעִרֹת וַיְבָרֲכֵהוּ

and~Not   he~did~make~Recognize~him
Given.that   they~did~Exist   Hand~s2~
him   like~Hand~s2 "Esav [*Doing*]"
Brother~him   Hair~s   and~he~will~
much~Kneel~him

and he did not recognize him given
that his hands existed like the hands
of "Esav [*Doing*]" his brother was
hairy, and he respected him,

**27:24**   וַיֹּאמֶר אַתָּה זֶה בְּנִי עֵשָׂו וַיֹּאמֶר אָנִי

and~he~will~Say   You(ms)   This   Son~
me "Esav [*Doing*]"   and~he~will~Say
I

and he said, this is you my son
"Esav [*Doing*]", and he said, I am,

**27:25**   וַיֹּאמֶר הַגִּשָׁה לִּי וְאֹכְלָה מִצֵּיד בְּנִי לְמַעַן תְּבָרֶכְךָ נַפְשִׁי וַיַּגֶּשׁ לוֹ
וַיֹּאכַל וַיָּבֵא לוֹ יַיִן וַיֵּשְׁתְּ

and~he~will~Say   !(ms)~make~Draw.near
to~me   and~i~will~Eat   from~Game
Son~me   to~That   she~will~much~
Kneel~you(ms)   Being~me   and~he~
will~make~Draw.near   to~him   and~he~
will~Eat   and~he~will~make~Come   to~
him   Wine   and~he~will~Gulp

and he said, draw near to me and I
will eat from the game of my son
that my being will respect you, and
he drew near to him and he ate and
he brought wine to him and he
gulped,

**27:26**   וַיֹּאמֶר אֵלָיו יִצְחָק אָבִיו גְּשָׁה נָּא וּשְׁקָה לִּי בְּנִי

and~he~will~Say   To~him   "Yits'hhaq
[*He laughs*]"   Father~him   !(ms)~
Draw.near   Please   and~!(ms)~Kiss   to~
me   Son~me

and "Yits'hhaq [*He laughs*]" his
father said to him, please draw near
and kiss me my son,

**27:27**   וַיִּגַּשׁ וַיִּשַּׁק לוֹ וַיָּרַח אֶת רֵיחַ בְּגָדָיו וַיְבָרְכֵהוּ וַיֹּאמֶר רְאֵה רֵיחַ
בְּנִי כְּרֵיחַ שָׂדֶה אֲשֶׁר בֵּרְכוֹ יְהֹוָה

and~he~will~Draw.near   and~he~will~
Kiss   to~him   and~he~will~make~Smell
At   Aroma   Garment~s~him   and~he~
will~much~Kneel~him   and~he~will~Say
!(ms)~See   Aroma   Son~me   like~
Aroma   Field   Which   he~did~much~
Kneel~him   "YHWH [*He   exists*]"

and he drew near and he kissed him
and he smelled the aroma of his
garments and he respected him and
he said, see the aroma of my son is
like the aroma of the field which
"YHWH [*He exists*]" presented him
many gifts,

**27:28 ***   וְיִתֶּן לְךָ הָאֱלֹהִים מִטַּל הַשָּׁמַיִם וּמִשְׁמַנֵּי הָאָרֶץ וְרֹב דָּגָן
וְתִירֹשׁ

and~he~will~Give   to~you(ms)   the~
"Elohiym [*Powers*]"   from~Dew   the~
Sky~s2   and~from~Oil~s   the~Land
and~Abundance   Cereal   and~Fresh.Wine

and the "Elohiym [*Powers*]" gave
to you from the dew of the sky and
from the oil of the land and the
abundance of cereal and fresh wine,

**27:29**   יַעַבְדוּךָ עַמִּים וְיִשְׁתַּחוּ (וְיִשְׁתַּחֲווּ) לְךָ לְאֻמִּים הֱוֵה גְבִיר לְאַחֶיךָ
וְיִשְׁתַּחֲווּ לְךָ בְּנֵי אִמֶּךָ אֹרְרֶיךָ אָרוּר וּמְבָרְכֶיךָ בָּרוּךְ

they(m)~will~Serve~you(ms)   People~s

peoples will serve you and the

and~they(m)~will~Bend.down to~ you(ms) Community~s !(ms)~Be Owner to~Brother~s~you(ms) and~ they(m)~will~Bend.down to~you(ms) Son~s Mother~you(ms) Spit.upon~ ing(mp)~you(ms) Spit.upon~ed(ms) much~Kneel~ing(mp)~you(ms) Kneel~ ed(ms)

communities will bend down to you, be an owner to your brothers and the sons of your mother will bend down to you, one spitting upon you is spitted upon, one respecting you is respected,

**27:30** וַיְהִי כַּאֲשֶׁר כִּלָּה יִצְחָק לְבָרֵךְ אֶת יַעֲקֹב וַיְהִי אַךְ יָצֹא יָצָא יַעֲקֹב מֵאֵת פְּנֵי יִצְחָק אָבִיו וְעֵשָׂו אָחִיו בָּא מִצֵּידוֹ

and~he~will~Exist like~Which he~did~ much~Finish "Yits'hhaq [He laughs]" to~>~much~Kneel At "Ya'aqov [He restrains]" and~he~will~Exist Surely >~Go.out he~did~Go.out "Ya'aqov [He restrains]" from~At Face~s "Yits'hhaq [He laughs]" Father~him and~"Esav [Doing]" Brother~him he~ did~Come from~Game~him

and it came to pass just as "Yits'hhaq [He laughs]" finished respecting "Ya'aqov [He restrains]" and he was surely going out, "Ya'aqov [He restrains]" went out from the face of "Yits'hhaq [He laughs]" his father and "Esav [Doing]" his brother came from his game,

**27:31** וַיַּעַשׂ גַּם הוּא מַטְעַמִּים וַיָּבֵא לְאָבִיו וַיֹּאמֶר לְאָבִיו יָקֻם אָבִי וְיֹאכַל מִצֵּיד בְּנוֹ בַּעֲבֻר תְּבָרֲכַנִּי נַפְשֶׁךָ

and~he~will~Do Also He Delicacy~s and~he~will~make~Come to~Father~him and~he~will~Say to~Father~him he~ will~Rise Father~me and~he~will~Eat from~Game Son~him in~On.account.of she~will~much~Kneel~me Being~ you(ms)

and he also made delicacies and brought to his father and he said to his father, my father will rise and he will eat from the game of his son so that your being will respect me,

**27:32** וַיֹּאמֶר לוֹ יִצְחָק אָבִיו מִי אָתָּה וַיֹּאמֶר אֲנִי בִּנְךָ בְכֹרְךָ עֵשָׂו

and~he~will~Say to~him "Yits'hhaq [He laughs]" Father~him Who You(ms) and~he~will~Say I Son~ you(ms) Firstborn~you(ms) "Esav [Doing]"

and "Yits'hhaq [He laughs]" his father said to him, who are you, and he said, I am your son, your firstborn "Esav [Doing]",

**27:33** וַיֶּחֱרַד יִצְחָק חֲרָדָה גְּדֹלָה עַד מְאֹד וַיֹּאמֶר מִי אֵפוֹא הוּא הַצָּד צַיִד וַיָּבֵא לִי וָאֹכַל מִכֹּל בְּטֶרֶם תָּבוֹא וָאֲבָרֲכֵהוּ גַּם בָּרוּךְ יִהְיֶה

and~he~will~Tremble "Yits'hhaq [He laughs]" Trembling Magnificent Until Many and~he~will~Say Who Then He the~Hunt Game and~he~will~ make~Come to~me and~i~will~Eat from~All in~Before you(ms)~will~

and "Yits'hhaq [He laughs]" trembled a magnificent trembling and many more and he said who then is he of the hunt of the game and he brought to me and I ate from all before you came and I respected

Come and~i~will~much~Kneel~him Also Kneel~ed(ms) he~will~Exist

him, also, the one respected will exist,

**27:34** כִּשְׁמֹעַ עֵשָׂו אֶת דִּבְרֵי אָבִיו וַיִּצְעַק צְעָקָה גְּדֹלָה וּמָרָה עַד מְאֹד וַיֹּאמֶר לְאָבִיו בָּרֲכֵנִי גַם אָנִי אָבִי

like~>~Hear "Esav [*Doing*]" At Word~s Father~him and~he~will~Cry.out Cry Magnificent and~Bitter Until Many and~he~will~Say to~Father~him >~much~Kneel~me Also I Father~me

as "Esav [*Doing*]" heard the words of his father and he cried out a magnificent and bitter cry and many more and he said to his father, respect me, also me my father,

**27:35** וַיֹּאמֶר בָּא אָחִיךָ בְּמִרְמָה וַיִּקַּח בִּרְכָתֶךָ

and~he~will~Say he~did~Come Brother~you(ms) in~Deceit and~he~will~Take Present~you(ms)

and he said, your brother came in deceit and he took your present,

**27:36** וַיֹּאמֶר הֲכִי קָרָא שְׁמוֹ יַעֲקֹב וַיַּעְקְבֵנִי זֶה פַעֲמַיִם אֶת בְּכֹרָתִי לָקָח וְהִנֵּה עַתָּה לָקַח בִּרְכָתִי וַיֹּאמַר הֲלֹא אָצַלְתָּ לִי בְּרָכָה

and~he~will~Say ?~Given.that he~did~Call.out Title~him "Ya'aqov [*He restrains*]" and~he~will~Restrain~me This Stroke.of.time~s2 At Birthright~me he~did~Take and~Look Now he~did~Take Present~me and~he~will~Say ?~Not you(ms)~did~Set-aside to~me Present

and he said, is it that he called out his title "Ya'aqov [*He restrains*]" and he restrained me these two times, he took my birthright and look, now he took my present, and he said, did you not set aside for me a present,

**27:37** וַיַּעַן יִצְחָק וַיֹּאמֶר לְעֵשָׂו הֵן גְּבִיר שַׂמְתִּיו לָךְ וְאֶת כָּל אֶחָיו נָתַתִּי לוֹ לַעֲבָדִים וְדָגָן וְתִירֹשׁ סְמַכְתִּיו וּלְכָה אֵפוֹא מָה אֶעֱשֶׂה בְּנִי

and~he~will~Answer "Yits'hhaq [*He laughs*]" and~he~will~Say to~"Esav [*Doing*]" Though Owner i~did~Set.in.place~him to~you(fs) and~At All Brother~s~him i~did~Give to~him to~the~Servant~s and~Cereal and~Fresh.Wine i~did~Support~him and~to~you(ms) Then What i~will~Do Son~me

and "Yits'hhaq [*He laughs*]" answered and he said to "Esav [*Doing*]", though I set him in place as owner to you and all his brothers I gave to him for servants and cereal and fresh wine and I supported him and to you then, what will I do my son,

**27:38** וַיֹּאמֶר עֵשָׂו אֶל אָבִיו הַבְרָכָה אַחַת הִוא לְךָ אָבִי בָּרֲכֵנִי גַם אָנִי אָבִי וַיִּשָּׂא עֵשָׂו קֹלוֹ וַיֵּבְךְּ

and~he~will~Say "Esav [*Doing*]" To Father~him ?~Present Unit She to~you(ms) Father~me !(ms)~much~

and "Esav [*Doing*]" said to his father, is there to you one present my father, respect me, also me my

Kneel~me Also I Father~me and~
he~will~Lift.up "Esav [*Doing*]"
Voice~him and~he~will~Weep

father and "Esav [*Doing*]" lifted up
his voice and he wept,

**27:39**  וַיַּעַן יִצְחָק אָבִיו וַיֹּאמֶר אֵלָיו הִנֵּה מִשְׁמַנֵּי הָאָרֶץ יִהְיֶה מוֹשָׁבֶךָ
וּמִטַּל הַשָּׁמַיִם מֵעָל

and~he~will~Answer "Yits'hhaq [*He
laughs*]" Father~him and~he~will~Say
To~him Look from~Oil~s the~Land
he~will~Exist Settling and~from~Dew
the~Sky~s2 from~Upon

and "Yits'hhaq [*He laughs*]" his
father answered and he said to him,
look, from the oils of the land a
settling will exist and from the dew
of the sky from above,

**27:40**  וְעַל חַרְבְּךָ תִחְיֶה וְאֶת אָחִיךָ תַּעֲבֹד וְהָיָה כַּאֲשֶׁר תָּרִיד וּפָרַקְתָּ
עֻלּוֹ מֵעַל צַוָּארֶךָ

and~Upon Sword~you(ms) you(ms)~
will~Live and~At Brother~you(ms)
you(ms)~will~Serve and~he~did~Exist
like~Which you(ms)~will~make~Roam
and~you(ms)~did~Tear.away Yoke~him
from~Upon Back.of.the.neck~you(ms)

and upon your sword you will live
and you will serve your brother and
it will come to pass, you will roam
and you will tear away his yoke
from upon the back of your neck,

**27:41**  וַיִּשְׂטֹם עֵשָׂו אֶת יַעֲקֹב עַל הַבְּרָכָה אֲשֶׁר בֵּרְכוֹ אָבִיו וַיֹּאמֶר
עֵשָׂו בְּלִבּוֹ יִקְרְבוּ יְמֵי אֵבֶל אָבִי וְאַהַרְגָה אֶת יַעֲקֹב אָחִי

and~he~will~Hold.a.grudge "Esav
[*Doing*]" At "Ya'aqov [*He restrains*]"
Upon the~Present Which he~did~
much~Kneel Father~him and~he~will~
Say "Esav [*Doing*]" in~Heart~him
they(m)~will~Come.near Day~s
Mourning Father~me and~i~will~Kill
At "Ya'aqov [*He restrains*]" Brother~
me

and "Esav [*Doing*]" held a grudge
at "Ya'aqov [*He restrains*]" because
of the present which his father
respected and "Esav [*Doing*]" said
in his heart, the days of mourning
of my father will come near and I
will kill "Ya'aqov [*He restrains*]"
my brother,

**27:42**  וַיֻּגַּד לְרִבְקָה אֶת דִּבְרֵי עֵשָׂו בְּנָהּ הַגָּדֹל וַתִּשְׁלַח וַתִּקְרָא לְיַעֲקֹב
בְּנָהּ הַקָּטָן וַתֹּאמֶר אֵלָיו הִנֵּה עֵשָׂו אָחִיךָ מִתְנַחֵם לְךָ לְהָרְגֶךָ

and~he~make.be~Be.face.to.face to~
"Rivqah [*Ensnarer*]" At Word~s
"Esav [*Doing*]" Son~her the~
Magnificent and~she~will~Send and~
she~will~Call.out to~"Ya'aqov [*He
restrains*]" Son~her the~Small and~
she~will~Say To~him Look "Esav
[*Doing*]" Brother~you(ms) self~
Comfort~ing(ms) to~you(ms) to~>~
Kill~you(ms)

and he told to "Rivqah [*Ensnarer*]"
the words of "Esav [*Doing*]" her
magnificent son and she sent and
she called out to "Ya'aqov [*He
restrains*]" her small son and she
said to him, look, "Esav [*Doing*]"
your brother is comforting himself
for you to kill you,

**155**

**27:43**

וְעַתָּה בְנִי שְׁמַע בְּקֹלִי וְקוּם בְּרַח לְךָ אֶל לָבָן אָחִי חָרָנָה

and~Now Son~me !(ms)~Hear in~Voice~me and~!(ms)~Rise !(ms)~Flee.away to~you(ms) To "Lavan [*White*]" Brother~me "Hharan [*Burning*]"~unto

and now my son, hear in my voice and rise, flee away for you to "Lavan [*White*]" my brother unto "Hharan [*Burning*]",

**27:44**

וְיָשַׁבְתָּ עִמּוֹ יָמִים אֲחָדִים עַד אֲשֶׁר תָּשׁוּב חֲמַת אָחִיךָ

and~you(ms)~did~Settle With~him Day~s Unit~s Until Which she~will~Turn.back Fury Brother~you(ms)

and you will settle with him a few days until the fury of your brother turns back,

**27:45**

עַד שׁוּב אַף אָחִיךָ מִמְּךָ וְשָׁכַח אֵת אֲשֶׁר עָשִׂיתָ לּוֹ וְשָׁלַחְתִּי וּלְקַחְתִּיךָ מִשָּׁם לָמָה אֶשְׁכַּל גַּם שְׁנֵיכֶם יוֹם אֶחָד

Until >~Turn.back Nose Brother~you(ms) From~you(ms) and~he~did~Forget At Which you(ms)~did~Do to~him and~i~did~Send and~i~did~Take~you(ms) from~There to~What i~will~Be.childless Also Two~you(mp) Day Unit

until the nose of your brother turns back from you and he forgets what you did to him and I will send and I will take you from there, why should I be childless of the two of you of one day,

**27:46**

וַתֹּאמֶר רִבְקָה אֶל יִצְחָק קַצְתִּי בְחַיַּי מִפְּנֵי בְּנוֹת חֵת אִם לֹקֵחַ יַעֲקֹב אִשָּׁה מִבְּנוֹת חֵת כָּאֵלֶּה מִבְּנוֹת הָאָרֶץ לָמָה לִי חַיִּים

and~she~will~Say "Rivqah [*Ensnarer*]" To "Yits'hhaq [*He laughs*]" i~will~Loathe in~Life~me from~Face~s Daughter~s "Hhet [*Shattered*]" If Take~ing(ms) "Ya'aqov [*He restrains*]" Woman from~Daughter~s "Hhet [*Shattered*]" like~These from~Daughter~s the~Land to~What to~me Life~s

and "Rivqah [*Ensnarer*]" said to "Yits'hhaq [*He laughs*]", I will loathe in my life from the faces of the daughters of "Hhet [*Shattered*]", if "Ya'aqov [*He restrains*]" is taking a woman from the daughters of "Hhet [*Shattered*]" such as these from the daughters of the land what is to me a life,

# Chapter 28

**28:1**

וַיִּקְרָא יִצְחָק אֶל יַעֲקֹב וַיְבָרֶךְ אֹתוֹ וַיְצַוֵּהוּ וַיֹּאמֶר לוֹ לֹא תִקַּח אִשָּׁה מִבְּנוֹת כְּנָעַן

and~he~will~Call.out "Yits'hhaq [*He laughs*]" To "Ya'aqov [*He restrains*]" and~he~will~much~Kneel At~him and~he~will~much~Direct~him and~he~will~Say to~him Not you(ms)~will~Take Woman from~Daughter~s "Kena'an

and "Yits'hhaq [*He laughs*]" called out to "Ya'aqov [*He restrains*]" and he respected him and he directed him and he said to him, you will not take a woman from the daughters of "Kena'an [*Lowered*]",

[*Lowered*]"

**28:2**

קוּם לֵךְ פַּדֶּנָה אֲרָם בֵּיתָה בְתוּאֵל אֲבִי אִמֶּךָ וְקַח לְךָ מִשָּׁם אִשָּׁה מִבְּנוֹת לָבָן אֲחִי אִמֶּךָ

!(ms)~Rise !(ms)~Walk "Padan-Aram [*Field palace*]"~unto House~unto "Betu'el [*Destruction of El*]" Father~ of Mother~you(ms) and~!(ms)~Take to~you(ms) from~There Woman from~Daughter~s "Lavan [*White*]" Brother~of Mother~you(ms)

rise, walk unto "Padan-Aram [*Field palace*]", unto the house of "Betu'el [*Destruction of El*]" the father of your mother and take for you from there a woman, from the daughters of "Lavan [*White*]", the brother of your mother,

**28:3**

וְאֵל שַׁדַּי יְבָרֵךְ אֹתְךָ וְיַפְרְךָ וְיַרְבֶּךָ וְהָיִיתָ לִקְהַל עַמִּים

and~Mighty.one "Shaddai [*My breasts*]" he~will~much~Kneel At~ you(ms) and~he~will~make~Reproduce~ you(ms) and~he~will~make~Increase~ you(ms) and~you(ms)~did~Exist to~ Assembled.flock People~s

and the mighty one of "Shaddai [*My breasts*]" will respect you and he will make you reproduce and he will make you increase and you will exist for an assembled flock of peoples,

**28:4**

וְיִתֶּן לְךָ אֶת בִּרְכַּת אַבְרָהָם לְךָ וּלְזַרְעֲךָ אִתָּךְ לְרִשְׁתְּךָ אֶת אֶרֶץ מְגֻרֶיךָ אֲשֶׁר נָתַן אֱלֹהִים לְאַבְרָהָם

and~he~will~Give to~you(ms) At Present "Avraham [*Father lifted*]" to~you(ms) and~to~Seed~you(ms) At~ you(ms) to~>~Inherit~you(ms) At Land Pilgrimage~s~you(ms) Which he~did~Give "Elohiym [*Powers*]" to~ "Avraham [*Father lifted*]"

and he gave to you the present of "Avraham [*Father lifted*]" for you and for your seed with you for you to inherit the land of your pilgrimages which "Elohiym [*Powers*]" gave to "Avraham [*Father lifted*]",

**28:5**

וַיִּשְׁלַח יִצְחָק אֶת יַעֲקֹב וַיֵּלֶךְ פַּדֶּנָה אֲרָם אֶל לָבָן בֶּן בְּתוּאֵל הָאֲרַמִּי אֲחִי רִבְקָה אֵם יַעֲקֹב וְעֵשָׂו

and~he~will~Send "Yits'hhaq [*He laughs*]" At "Ya'aqov [*He restrains*]" and~he~will~Walk "Padan-Aram [*Field palace*]"~unto To "Lavan [*White*]" Son "Betu'el [*Destruction of El*]" the~"Aram [*Palace*]"~of Brother~of "Rivqah [*Ensnarer*]" Mother "Ya'aqov [*He restrains*]" and~"Esav [*Doing*]"

and "Yits'hhaq [*He laughs*]" sent "Ya'aqov [*He restrains*]" and he walked unto "Padan-Aram [*Field palace*]" to "Lavan [*White*]" the son of "Betu'el [*Destruction of El*]" the one of "Aram [*Palace*]" the brother of "Rivqah [*Ensnarer*]" the mother of "Ya'aqov [*He restrains*]" and "Esav [*Doing*]",

**28:6**

וַיַּרְא עֵשָׂו כִּי בֵרַךְ יִצְחָק אֶת יַעֲקֹב וְשִׁלַּח אֹתוֹ פַּדֶּנָה אֲרָם לָקַחַת לוֹ מִשָּׁם אִשָּׁה בְּבָרֲכוֹ אֹתוֹ וַיְצַו עָלָיו לֵאמֹר לֹא תִקַּח אִשָּׁה מִבְּנוֹת כְּנָעַן

and~he~will~See "Esav [*Doing*]"

and "Esav [*Doing*]" saw that

Given.that and~he~will~much~Kneel "Yits'hhaq [*He laughs*]" At "Ya'aqov [*He restrains*]" and~he~did~much~Send At~him "Padan-Aram [*Field palace*]"~ unto to~>~Take to~him from~There Woman in~>~much~Kneel~him At~ him and~he~will~much~Direct Upon~ him to~>~Say Not you(ms)~will~Take Woman from~Daughter~s "Kena'an [*Lowered*]"

"Yits'hhaq [*He laughs*]" respected "Ya'aqov [*He restrains*]" and he sent him unto "Padan-Aram [*Field palace*]" to take for him from there a woman, in respecting him and he directed upon him saying, you will not take a woman from the daughters of "Kena'an [*Lowered*]",

**28:7**

וַיִּשְׁמַע יַעֲקֹב אֶל אָבִיו וְאֶל אִמּוֹ וַיֵּלֶךְ פַּדֶּנָה אֲרָם

and~he~will~Hear "Ya'aqov [*He restrains*]" To Father~him and~To Mother~him and~he~will~Walk "Padan-Aram [*Field palace*]"~unto

and "Ya'aqov [*He restrains*]" heard his father and his mother and he walked unto "Padan-Aram [*Field palace*]",

**28:8**

וַיַּרְא עֵשָׂו כִּי רָעוֹת בְּנוֹת כְּנָעַן בְּעֵינֵי יִצְחָק אָבִיו

and~he~will~See "Esav [*Doing*]" Given.that Dysfunctional~s Daughter~s "Kena'an [*Lowered*]" in~Eye~s2 "Yits'hhaq [*He laughs*]" Father~him

and "Esav [*Doing*]" saw that the daughters of "Kena'an [*Lowered*]" were dysfunctional in the eyes of "Yits'hhaq [*He laughs*]" his father,

**28:9**

וַיֵּלֶךְ עֵשָׂו אֶל יִשְׁמָעֵאל וַיִּקַּח אֶת מָחֲלַת בַּת יִשְׁמָעֵאל בֶּן אַבְרָהָם אֲחוֹת נְבָיוֹת עַל נָשָׁיו לוֹ לְאִשָּׁה

and~he~will~Walk "Esav [*Doing*]" To "Yishma'el [*El will listen*]" and~he~ will~Take At "Mahhalat [*Stringed instrument*]" Daughter "Yishma'el [*El will listen*]" Son "Avraham [*Father lifted*]" Sister "Nevayot [*Flourishings*]" Upon Woman~s~him to~him to~Woman

and "Esav [*Doing*]" walked to "Yishma'el [*El will listen*]" and he took "Mahhalat [*Stringed instrument*]" the daughter of "Yishma'el [*El will listen*]" the son of "Avraham [*Father lifted*]", the sister of "Nevayot [*Flourishings*]", for him for a woman in addition to his women,

**28:10**

וַיֵּצֵא יַעֲקֹב מִבְּאֵר שָׁבַע וַיֵּלֶךְ חָרָנָה

and~he~will~Go.out "Ya'aqov [*He restrains*]" from~"B'er-Sheva [*Well of oath*]" and~he~will~Walk "Hharan [*Burning*]"~unto

and "Ya'aqov [*He restrains*]" went out from "B'er-Sheva [*Well of oath*]" and he walked unto "Hharan [*Burning*]",

**28:11**

וַיִּפְגַּע בַּמָּקוֹם וַיָּלֶן שָׁם כִּי בָא הַשֶּׁמֶשׁ וַיִּקַּח מֵאַבְנֵי הַמָּקוֹם וַיָּשֶׂם מְרַאֲשֹׁתָיו וַיִּשְׁכַּב בַּמָּקוֹם הַהוּא

and~he~will~Reach in~the~Place and~ he~will~Stay.the.night There Given.that he~did~Come the~Sun and~he~will~ Take from~Stone~s Place and~he~

and he reached the place and he stayed the night there given that the sun came and he took from the stones of the place and he set his

will~Set.in.place  Headrest~s~him  and~
he~will~Lay.down  in~the~Place  the~He

headrest in place and he laid down in that place,

**28:12**  וַיַּחֲלֹם וְהִנֵּה סֻלָּם מֻצָּב אַרְצָה וְרֹאשׁוֹ מַגִּיעַ הַשָּׁמָיְמָה וְהִנֵּה מַלְאֲכֵי אֱלֹהִים עֹלִים וְיֹרְדִים בּוֹ

and~he~will~Visualize  and~Look
Ladder  make.be~Stand.erect~ing(ms)
Land~unto  and~Head~him  make~
Touch~ing(ms)  the~Sky~s2~unto  and~
Look  Messenger~s  "Elohiym
[*Powers*]"  Go.up~ing(mp)  and~
Go.down~ing(mp)  in~him

and he visualized and look, a ladder is standing erect unto the land and his head was touching unto the sky and look, messengers of "Elohiym [*Powers*]" were going up and going down him,

**28:13**  וְהִנֵּה יְהוָה נִצָּב עָלָיו וַיֹּאמַר אֲנִי יְהוָה אֱלֹהֵי אַבְרָהָם אָבִיךָ וֵאלֹהֵי יִצְחָק הָאָרֶץ אֲשֶׁר אַתָּה שֹׁכֵב עָלֶיהָ לְךָ אֶתְּנֶנָּה וּלְזַרְעֶךָ

and~Look  "YHWH [*He exists*]"  be~
Stand.erect~ing(ms)  Upon~him  and~he~
will~Say  I  "YHWH [*He exists*]"
Power~s  "Avraham [*Father lifted*]"
Father~you(ms)  and~Power~s
"Yits'hhaq [*He laughs*]"  the~Land
Which  You(ms)  Lay.down~ing(ms)
Upon~her  to~you(ms)  i~will~Give~her
and~to~Seed~you(ms)

and look, "YHWH [*He exists*]" is standing erect upon him and he said, I am "YHWH [*He exists*]" of the powers of "Avraham [*Father lifted*]" your father and the powers of "Yits'hhaq [*He laughs*]", the land which you are laying down upon I will give her to you and to your seed,

**28:14**  וְהָיָה זַרְעֲךָ כַּעֲפַר הָאָרֶץ וּפָרַצְתָּ יָמָּה וָקֵדְמָה וְצָפֹנָה וָנֶגְבָּה וְנִבְרְכוּ בְךָ כָּל מִשְׁפְּחֹת הָאֲדָמָה וּבְזַרְעֶךָ

and~he~did~Exist  Seed~you(ms)  like~
Powder  the~Land  and~you(ms)~did~
Break.out  Sea~unto  and~East~unto
and~North~unto  and~South.country~unto
and~they~did~be~Kneel  in~you(ms)  All
Family~s  the~Ground  and~in~Seed~
you(ms)

and your seed will exist like the powder of the land and you will break out unto the sea and unto the east and unto the north and unto the south country and all the families of the ground will be respected with you and with your seed,

**28:15**  וְהִנֵּה אָנֹכִי עִמָּךְ וּשְׁמַרְתִּיךָ בְּכֹל אֲשֶׁר תֵּלֵךְ וַהֲשִׁבֹתִיךָ אֶל הָאֲדָמָה הַזֹּאת כִּי לֹא אֶעֱזָבְךָ עַד אֲשֶׁר אִם עָשִׂיתִי אֵת אֲשֶׁר דִּבַּרְתִּי לָךְ

and~Look  I  With~you(ms)  and~i~did~
Guard~you(ms)  in~All  Which
you(ms)~will~Walk  and~i~did~make~
Turn.back~you(ms)  To  the~Ground
the~This  Given.that  Not  i~will~
Leave~you(ms)  Until  Which  If  i~
did~Do  At  Which  i~did~Speak  to~
you(fs)

and look, I am with you and will guard you in all where you will walk and I will return you to this ground given that I will not leave you until I do which I spoke to you,

# Jeff A. Benner

**28:16** וַיִּיקַץ יַעֲקֹב מִשְּׁנָתוֹ וַיֹּאמֶר אָכֵן יֵשׁ יְהוָה בַּמָּקוֹם הַזֶּה וְאָנֹכִי לֹא יָדָעְתִּי

and~he~will~Awake "Ya'aqov [*He restrains*]" from~Snooze~him and~he~will~Say Surely There.is "YHWH [*He exists*]" in~the~Place the~This and~I Not i~did~Know

and "Ya'aqov [*He restrains*]" awoke from his snooze and he said, surely "YHWH [*He exists*]" is in this place and I did not know,

**28:17** וַיִּירָא וַיֹּאמַר מַה נּוֹרָא הַמָּקוֹם הַזֶּה אֵין זֶה כִּי אִם בֵּית אֱלֹהִים וְזֶה שַׁעַר הַשָּׁמָיִם

and~he~will~Fear and~he~will~Say What be~Fear~ing(ms) the~Place the~This Without This Given.that If House "Elohiym [*Powers*]" and~This Gate the~Sky~s2

and he feared and he said, what is being feared of this place this is nothing except the house of "Elohiym [*Powers*]" and this is the gate of the sky,

**28:18** וַיַּשְׁכֵּם יַעֲקֹב בַּבֹּקֶר וַיִּקַּח אֶת הָאֶבֶן אֲשֶׁר שָׂם מְרַאֲשֹׁתָיו וַיָּשֶׂם אֹתָהּ מַצֵּבָה וַיִּצֹק שֶׁמֶן עַל רֹאשָׁהּ

and~he~will~make~Depart.early "Ya'aqov [*He restrains*]" in~the~Morning and~he~will~Take At the~Stone Which he~did~Set.in.place Headrest~s~him and~he~will~Set.in.place At~her Monument and~he~will~Pour.down Oil Upon Head~her

and "Ya'aqov [*He restrains*]" departed early in the morning and he took the stone which he set in place as his headrest, and he set her in place as a monument and poured down oil upon her head,

**28:19** וַיִּקְרָא אֶת שֵׁם הַמָּקוֹם הַהוּא בֵּית אֵל וְאוּלָם לוּז שֵׁם הָעִיר לָרִאשֹׁנָה

and~he~will~Call.out At Title the~Place the~He "Beyt-El [*House of El*]" and~But "Luz [*Almond*]" Title the~City to~the~First

and he called out the title of that place "Beyt-El [*House of El*]" but "Luz [*Almond*]" was the title of the city at first,

**28:20** וַיִּדַּר יַעֲקֹב נֶדֶר לֵאמֹר אִם יִהְיֶה אֱלֹהִים עִמָּדִי וּשְׁמָרַנִי בַּדֶּרֶךְ הַזֶּה אֲשֶׁר אָנֹכִי הוֹלֵךְ וְנָתַן לִי לֶחֶם לֶאֱכֹל וּבֶגֶד לִלְבֹּשׁ

and~he~will~Make.a.vow "Ya'aqov [*He restrains*]" Vow to~>~Say If "YHWH [*He exists*]" "Elohiym [*Powers*]" By~me and~he~did~Guard~me in~the~Road the~This Which I Walk~ing(ms) and~he~did~Give to~me Bread to~>~Eat and~Garment to~>~Clothe

and "Ya'aqov [*He restrains*]" vowed a vow saying, if "YHWH [*He exists*]" of "Elohiym [*Powers*]" is by me and he will guard me in this road which I am walking and he will give to me bread to eat and garments to clothe,

**28:21**

וְשַׁבְתִּי בְשָׁלוֹם אֶל בֵּית אָבִי וְהָיָה יְהוָה לִי לֵאלֹהִים

and~i~did~Turn.back in~Completeness To House Father~me and~he~did~Exist "YHWH [*He exists*]" to~me to~"Elohiym [*Powers*]"

and I will turn back in completeness to the house of my father then "YHWH [*He exists*]" will exist for me for "Elohiym [*Powers*]",

**28:22**

וְהָאֶבֶן הַזֹּאת אֲשֶׁר שַׂמְתִּי מַצֵּבָה יִהְיֶה בֵּית אֱלֹהִים וְכֹל אֲשֶׁר תִּתֶּן לִי עַשֵּׂר אֲעַשְּׂרֶנּוּ לָךְ

and~the~Stone the~This Which i~did~Set.in.place Monument he~will~Exist House "Elohiym [*Powers*]" and~All Which you(ms)~will~Give to~me >~ much~Give.a.tenth i~will~much~Give.a.tenth~him to~you(fs)

and this stone which I set in place as a monument will exist as the house of "Elohiym [*Powers*]" and all which you will give to me I will surely give a tenth of him to you,

# Chapter 29

**29:1**

וַיִּשָּׂא יַעֲקֹב רַגְלָיו וַיֵּלֶךְ אַרְצָה בְנֵי קֶדֶם

and~he~will~Lift.up "Ya'aqov [*He restrains*]" Foot~s~him and~he~will~Walk Land~unto Son~s East

and "Ya'aqov [*He restrains*]" lifted up his feet and he walked unto the land of the sons the east,

**29:2**

וַיַּרְא וְהִנֵּה בְאֵר בַּשָּׂדֶה וְהִנֵּה שָׁם שְׁלֹשָׁה עֶדְרֵי צֹאן רֹבְצִים עָלֶיהָ כִּי מִן הַבְּאֵר הַהִוא יַשְׁקוּ הָעֲדָרִים וְהָאֶבֶן גְּדֹלָה עַל פִּי הַבְּאֵר

and~he~will~See and~Look Well in~the~Field and~Look There Three Drove~s Flocks Stretch.out~ing(mp) Upon~her Given.that From the~Well the~She they(m)~will~Drink the~Drove~s and~the~Stone Magnificent Upon Mouth the~Well

and he saw and look, a well in the field and look, there were three droves of flocks stretching out upon her given that from that well the droves will drink and the stone upon the mouth of the well was magnificent,

**29:3**

וְנֶאֶסְפוּ שָׁמָּה כָל הָעֲדָרִים וְגָלְלוּ אֶת הָאֶבֶן מֵעַל פִּי הַבְּאֵר וְהִשְׁקוּ אֶת הַצֹּאן וְהֵשִׁיבוּ אֶת הָאֶבֶן עַל פִּי הַבְּאֵר לִמְקֹמָהּ

and~they~will~be~Gather There~unto All the~Drove~s and~they~will~Roll At the~Stone from~Upon Mouth the~Well and~they~will~make~Drink At the~Flocks and~they~will~make~Turn.back At the~Stone Upon Mouth the~Well to~Place~her

and all the droves gathered unto there and they rolled the stone from upon the mouth of the well and the flocks drank and they returned the stone back upon the mouth of the well to her place,

**29:4**

וַיֹּאמֶר לָהֶם יַעֲקֹב אַחַי מֵאַיִן אַתֶּם וַיֹּאמְרוּ מֵחָרָן אֲנָחְנוּ

and~he~will~Say to~them(m) "Ya'aqov [*He restrains*]" Brother~s~me from~Without You(mp) and~they(m)~will~Say from~"Hharan [*Burning*]" We

and "Ya'aqov [*He restrains*]" said to them, my brothers, from where are you and they said, we are from "Hharan [*Burning*]",

**29:5**

וַיֹּאמֶר לָהֶם הַיְדַעְתֶּם אֶת לָבָן בֶּן נָחוֹר וַיֹּאמְרוּ יָדָעְנוּ

and~he~will~Say to~them(m) ?~you(mp)~did~Know At "Lavan [*White*]" Son "Nahhor [*Snorting*]" and~they(m)~will~Say we~did~Know

and he said to them, do you know "Lavan [*White*]" the son of "Nahhor [*Snorting*]" and they said we know,

**29:6**

וַיֹּאמֶר לָהֶם הַשָּׁלוֹם לוֹ וַיֹּאמְרוּ שָׁלוֹם וְהִנֵּה רָחֵל בִּתּוֹ בָּאָה עִם הַצֹּאן

and~he~will~Say to~them(m) ?~Completeness to~him and~they(m)~will~Say Completeness and~Look "Rahhel [*Ewe*]" Daughter~him Come~ing(fs) With the~Flocks

and he said to them, is completeness to him and they said completeness and look, "Rahhel [*Ewe*]" his daughter was coming with the flocks,

**29:7**

וַיֹּאמֶר הֵן עוֹד הַיּוֹם גָּדוֹל לֹא עֵת הֵאָסֵף הַמִּקְנֶה הַשְׁקוּ הַצֹּאן וּלְכוּ רְעוּ

and~he~will~Say Though Yet.again the~Day Magnificent Not Appointed.time >~be~Gather the~Livestock !(mp)~make~Drink the~Flocks and~!(mp)~Walk !(mp)~Feed

and he said, while it is yet a magnificent day it is not the appointed time for the gathering of the livestock, make the flocks drink, walk and feed,

**29:8**

וַיֹּאמְרוּ לֹא נוּכַל עַד אֲשֶׁר יֵאָסְפוּ כָּל הָעֲדָרִים וְגָלְלוּ אֶת הָאֶבֶן מֵעַל פִּי הַבְּאֵר וְהִשְׁקִינוּ הַצֹּאן

and~they(m)~will~Say Not we~will~Be.able Until Which they(m)~will~be~Gather All the~Drove~s and~they~will~Roll At the~Stone from~Upon Mouth the~Well and~they~will~make~Drink the~Flocks

and they said, we will not be able until all the droves be gathered and they will roll the stone from upon the mouth of the well and they will make the flocks drink,

**29:9**

עוֹדֶנּוּ מְדַבֵּר עִמָּם וְרָחֵל בָּאָה עִם הַצֹּאן אֲשֶׁר לְאָבִיהָ כִּי רֹעָה הִוא

Yet.again~him much~Speak~ing(ms) With~them(m) and~"Rahhel [*Ewe*]" Come~ing(fs) With the~Flocks Which to~Father~her Given.that Feed~ing(fs) She

while he was speaking with them then "Rahhel [*Ewe*]" was coming with the flocks which belonged to her father given that she was feeding,

**29:10**

וַיְהִי כַּאֲשֶׁר רָאָה יַעֲקֹב אֶת רָחֵל בַּת לָבָן אֲחִי אִמּוֹ וְאֶת צֹאן

לָבָן אֲחִי אִמּוֹ וַיִּגַּשׁ יַעֲקֹב וַיָּגֶל אֶת הָאֶבֶן מֵעַל פִּי הַבְּאֵר וַיַּשְׁקְ
אֶת צֹאן לָבָן אֲחִי אִמּוֹ

| | |
|---|---|
| and~he~will~Exist like~Which he~did~See "Ya'aqov [*He restrains*]" At "Rahhel [*Ewe*]" Daughter "Lavan [*White*]" Brother~of Mother~him and~At Flocks "Lavan [*White*]" Brother~of Mother~him and~he~will~Draw.near "Ya'aqov [*He restrains*]" and~he~will~Roll At the~Stone from~Upon Mouth the~Well and~he~will~make~Drink At Flocks "Lavan [*White*]" Brother~of Mother~him | and it came to pass just as "Ya'aqov [*He restrains*]" saw "Rahhel [*Ewe*]" the daughter of "Lavan [*White*]" the brother of his mother and the flocks of "Lavan [*White*]" the brother of his mother and "Ya'aqov [*He restrains*]" drew near and he rolled the stone from upon the mouth of the well and he made the flocks of "Lavan [*White*]", the brother of his mother, drink, |

**29:11**

וַיִּשַּׁק יַעֲקֹב לְרָחֵל וַיִּשָּׂא אֶת קֹלוֹ וַיֵּבְךְּ

| | |
|---|---|
| and~he~will~Kiss "Ya'aqov [*He restrains*]" to~"Rahhel [*Ewe*]" and~he~will~Lift.up At Voice~him and~he~will~Weep | and "Ya'aqov [*He restrains*]" kissed "Rahhel [*Ewe*]" and he lifted up his voice and he wept, |

**29:12**

וַיַּגֵּד יַעֲקֹב לְרָחֵל כִּי אֲחִי אָבִיהָ הוּא וְכִי בֶן רִבְקָה הוּא וַתָּרָץ
וַתַּגֵּד לְאָבִיהָ

| | |
|---|---|
| and~he~will~make~Be.face.to.face "Ya'aqov [*He restrains*]" to~"Rahhel [*Ewe*]" Given.that Brother~of Father~her He and~Given.that Son "Rivqah [*Ensnarer*]" He and~she~will~Run and~she~will~make~Be.face.to.face to~Father~her | and "Ya'aqov [*He restrains*]" told "Rahhel [*Ewe*]" that he was the brother of her father and that he was the son of "Rivqah [*Ensnarer*]" and she ran and she told her father, |

**29:13**

וַיְהִי כִשְׁמֹעַ לָבָן אֶת שֵׁמַע יַעֲקֹב בֶּן אֲחֹתוֹ וַיָּרָץ לִקְרָאתוֹ
וַיְחַבֶּק לוֹ וַיְנַשֶּׁק לוֹ וַיְבִיאֵהוּ אֶל בֵּיתוֹ וַיְסַפֵּר לְלָבָן אֶת כָּל
הַדְּבָרִים הָאֵלֶּה

| | |
|---|---|
| and~he~will~Exist like~>~Hear "Lavan [*White*]" At Report "Ya'aqov [*He restrains*]" Son Sister~him and~he~will~Run to~>~Meet~him and~he~will~much~Embrace to~him and~he~will~much~Kiss to~him and~he~will~make~Come~him To House~him and~he~will~much~Count to~"Lavan [*White*]" At All the~Word~s the~These | and it came to pass as "Lavan [*White*]" heard the report of "Ya'aqov [*He restrains*]" the son of his sister and he ran to meet him and he embraced him and he kissed him and he brought him to his house and he recounted to "Lavan [*White*]" all these words, |

**29:14**

וַיֹּאמֶר לוֹ לָבָן אַךְ עַצְמִי וּבְשָׂרִי אָתָּה וַיֵּשֶׁב עִמּוֹ חֹדֶשׁ יָמִים

| | |
|---|---|
| and~he~will~Say to~him "Lavan | and "Lavan [*White*]" said to him |

| | |
|---|---|
| [White]" Surely Bone~me and~Flesh~ me You(ms) and~he~will~Settle With~him New.moon Day~s | surely you are my bone and my flesh and he settled with him a new moon of days, |

**29:15** וַיֹּאמֶר לָבָן לְיַעֲקֹב הֲכִי אָחִי אַתָּה וַעֲבַדְתַּנִי חִנָּם הַגִּידָה לִּי מַה מַּשְׂכֻּרְתֶּךָ

| | |
|---|---|
| and~he~will~Say "Lavan [White]" to~ "Ya'aqov [He restrains]" ?~Given.that Brother~me You(ms) and~you(ms)~ did~Serve~me Freely !(ms)~make~ Be.face.to.face to~me What Payment~ you(ms) | and "Lavan [White]" said to "Ya'aqov [He restrains]", given that you are my brother, will you serve me freely, tell me what is your payment, |

**29:16** וּלְלָבָן שְׁתֵּי בָנוֹת שֵׁם הַגְּדֹלָה לֵאָה וְשֵׁם הַקְּטַנָּה רָחֵל

| | |
|---|---|
| and~to~"Lavan [White]" Two Daughter~s Title the~Magnificent "Le'ah [Weary]" and~Title the~Small "Rahhel [Ewe]" | and to "Lavan [White]" were two daughters, the title of the magnicent one was "Le'ah [Weary]" and the title of the small one was "Rahhel [Ewe]", |

**29:17** וְעֵינֵי לֵאָה רַכּוֹת וְרָחֵל הָיְתָה יְפַת תֹּאַר וִיפַת מַרְאֶה

| | |
|---|---|
| and~Eye~s2 "Le'ah [Weary]" Tender~ s and~"Rahhel [Ewe]" she~had~Exist Beautiful Shape and~Beautiful Appearance | and the eyes of "Le'ah [Weary]" were tender and "Rahhel [Ewe]" had existed beautiful of shape and beautiful of appearance, |

**29:18** וַיֶּאֱהַב יַעֲקֹב אֶת רָחֵל וַיֹּאמֶר אֶעֱבָדְךָ שֶׁבַע שָׁנִים בְּרָחֵל בִּתְּךָ הַקְּטַנָּה

| | |
|---|---|
| and~he~will~Love "Ya'aqov [He restrains]" At "Rahhel [Ewe]" and~ he~will~Say i~will~Serve~you(ms) Seven Year~s in~"Rahhel [Ewe]" Daughter~you(ms) the~Small | and "Ya'aqov [He restrains]" loved "Rahhel [Ewe]" and he said, I will serve you seven years in "Rahhel [Ewe]" your small daughter, |

**29:19** וַיֹּאמֶר לָבָן טוֹב תִּתִּי אֹתָהּ לָךְ מִתִּתִּי אֹתָהּ לְאִישׁ אַחֵר שְׁבָה עִמָּדִי

| | |
|---|---|
| and~he~will~Say "Lavan [White]" Functional >~Give~me At~her to~ you(fs) from~>~Give~me At~her to~ Man Other !(ms)~Settle~^ By~me | and "Lavan [White]" said, it is functional that I give her to you rather than give her to another man, settle by me, |

**29:20** וַיַּעֲבֹד יַעֲקֹב בְּרָחֵל שֶׁבַע שָׁנִים וַיִּהְיוּ בְעֵינָיו כְּיָמִים אֲחָדִים בְּאַהֲבָתוֹ אֹתָהּ

| | |
|---|---|
| and~he~will~Serve "Ya'aqov [He restrains]" in~"Rahhel [Ewe]" Seven Year~s and~they(m)~will~Exist in~ Eye~s2~him like~Day~s Unit~s in~ | and "Ya'aqov [He restrains]" served in "Rahhel [Ewe]" seven years and they existed in his eyes like a few days with the affection to |

Affection   At~her

her,

---

**29:21**

נִיֹּאמֶר יַעֲקֹב אֶל לָבָן הָבָה אֶת אִשְׁתִּי כִּי מָלְאוּ יָמָי וְאָבוֹאָה אֵלֶיהָ

and~he~will~Say "Ya'aqov [He restrains]" To "Lavan [White]" !(fs)~ Provide At Woman~me Given.that they~did~Fill Day~s~me and~i~will~ Come~^ To~her

and "Ya'aqov [He restrains]" said to "Lavan [White]", provide my woman given that my days are filled and I will come to her,

---

**29:22**

וַיֶּאֱסֹף לָבָן אֶת כָּל אַנְשֵׁי הַמָּקוֹם וַיַּעַשׂ מִשְׁתֶּה

and~he~will~Gather "Lavan [White]" At All Man~s the~Place and~he~ will~Do Feast

and "Lavan [White]" gathered all the men of the place and he made a feast,

---

**29:23**

וַיְהִי בָעֶרֶב וַיִּקַּח אֶת לֵאָה בִתּוֹ וַיָּבֵא אֹתָהּ אֵלָיו וַיָּבֹא אֵלֶיהָ

and~he~will~Exist in~the~Evening and~he~will~Take At "Le'ah [Weary]" Daughter~him and~he~will~make~Come At~her To~him and~he~will~Come To~her

and it came to pass in the evening and he took "Le'ah [Weary]" his daughter and he brought her to him and he came to her,

---

**29:24\***

וַיִּתֵּן לָבָן לָהּ אֶת זִלְפָּה שִׁפְחָתוֹ לְלֵאָה בִתּוֹ שִׁפְחָה

and~he~will~Give "Lavan [White]" to~her At "Zilpah [Trickling]" Maid~ him to~"Le'ah [Weary]" Daughter~him Maid

and "Lavan [White]" gave her "Zilpah [Trickling]", his maid, to "Le'ah [Weary]", his daughter, for a maid,

---

**29:25**

וַיְהִי בַבֹּקֶר וְהִנֵּה הִוא לֵאָה וַיֹּאמֶר אֶל לָבָן מַה זֹּאת עָשִׂיתָ לִּי הֲלֹא בְרָחֵל עָבַדְתִּי עִמָּךְ וְלָמָּה רִמִּיתָנִי

and~he~will~Exist in~the~Morning and~Look She "Le'ah [Weary]" and~ he~will~Say To "Lavan [White]" What This you(ms)~did~Do to~me ?~Not in~"Rahhel [Ewe]" i~did~Serve With~you(fs) and~to~What you(ms)~ did~much~Betray~me

and it came to pass in the morning and look, she is "Le'ah [Weary]", and he said to "Lavan [White]" what is this you did to me, did I not serve in "Rahhel [Ewe]" with you and why did you betray me,

---

**29:26**

וַיֹּאמֶר לָבָן לֹא יֵעָשֶׂה כֵן בִּמְקוֹמֵנוּ לָתֵת הַצְּעִירָה לִפְנֵי הַבְּכִירָה

and~he~will~Say "Lavan [White]" Not he~will~be~Do So in~Place~us to~>~ Give the~Little.one to~Face~s the~ Firstborn.female

and "Lavan [White]" said, he will not be done so in our place, to give the little one before the firstborn woman,

---

**29:27**

מַלֵּא שְׁבֻעַ זֹאת וְנִתְּנָה לְךָ גַּם אֶת זֹאת בַּעֲבֹדָה אֲשֶׁר תַּעֲבֹד עִמָּדִי עוֹד שֶׁבַע שָׁנִים אֲחֵרוֹת

!(ms)~much~Fill Week This and~we~will~Give to~you(ms) Also At This in~the~Service Which~you(ms) will~Serve By~me Yet.again Seven Year~s Other~s

fulfill this week and we will also give to you this one with the service which you will serve by me yet again another seven years,

**29:28**    וַיַּעַשׂ יַעֲקֹב כֵּן וַיְמַלֵּא שְׁבֻעַ זֹאת וַיִּתֶּן לוֹ אֶת רָחֵל בִּתּוֹ לוֹ לְאִשָּׁה

and~he~will~Do "Ya'aqov [*He restrains*]" So and~he~will~much~Fill Week This and~he~will~Give to~him At "Rahhel [*Ewe*]" Daughter~him to~him to~Woman

and "Ya'aqov [*He restrains*]" did so and he fulfilled this week and he gave to him "Rahhel [*Ewe*]", his daughter, for him for a woman,

**29:29**    וַיִּתֶּן לָבָן לְרָחֵל בִּתּוֹ אֶת בִּלְהָה שִׁפְחָתוֹ לָהּ לְשִׁפְחָה

and~he~will~Give "Lavan [*White*]" to~"Rahhel [*Ewe*]" Daughter~him At "Bilhah [*Wear out*]" Maid~him to~her to~Maid

and "Lavan [*White*]" gave "Rahhel [*Ewe*]", his daughter, "Bilhah [*Wear out*]" his maid to her for a maid,

**29:30**    וַיָּבֹא גַּם אֶל רָחֵל וַיֶּאֱהַב גַּם אֶת רָחֵל מִלֵּאָה וַיַּעֲבֹד עִמּוֹ עוֹד שֶׁבַע שָׁנִים אֲחֵרוֹת

and~he~will~Come Also To "Rahhel [*Ewe*]" and~he~will~Love Also At "Rahhel [*Ewe*]" from~"Le'ah [*Weary*]" and~he~will~Serve With~him Yet.again Seven Year~s Other~s

and he also came to "Rahhel [*Ewe*]" and he also loved "Rahhel [*Ewe*]" rather than "Le'ah [*Weary*]" and he served with him yet again another seven years,

**29:31**    וַיַּרְא יְהֹוָה כִּי שְׂנוּאָה לֵאָה וַיִּפְתַּח אֶת רַחְמָהּ וְרָחֵל עֲקָרָה

and~he~will~See "YHWH [*He exists*]" Given.that Hate~ed(fs) "Le'ah [*Weary*]" and~he~will~Open At Bowels~her and~"Rahhel [*Ewe*]" Sterile

and "YHWH [*He exists*]" saw that "Le'ah [*Weary*]" was hated and he opened her bowels and "Rahhel [*Ewe*]" was sterile,

**29:32**    וַתַּהַר לֵאָה וַתֵּלֶד בֵּן וַתִּקְרָא שְׁמוֹ רְאוּבֵן כִּי אָמְרָה כִּי רָאָה יְהֹוָה בְּעָנְיִי כִּי עַתָּה יֶאֱהָבַנִי אִישִׁי

and~she~will~Conceive "Le'ah [*Weary*]" and~she~will~Bring.forth Son and~she~will~Call.out Title~him "Re'uven [*See a son*]" Given.that she~did~Say Given.that he~did~See "YHWH [*He exists*]" in~Affliction~me Given.that Now he~will~Love~me Man~me

and "Le'ah [*Weary*]" conceived and she brought forth a son and she called out his title "Re'uven [*See a son*]" given that she said, given that "YHWH [*He exists*]" saw in my affliction, given that now my man will love me,

**29:33**    וַתַּהַר עוֹד וַתֵּלֶד בֵּן וַתֹּאמֶר כִּי שָׁמַע יְהֹוָה כִּי שְׂנוּאָה אָנֹכִי

וַיִּתֶּן לִי גַּם אֶת זֶה וַתִּקְרָא שְׁמוֹ שִׁמְעוֹן

and~she~will~Conceive Yet.again and~she~will~Bring.forth Son and~she~will~Say Given.that he~did~Hear "YHWH [*He exists*]" Given.that Hate~ed(fs) I and~he~will~Give to~me Also At This and~she~will~Call.out Title~him "Shimon [*Heard*]"

and she conceived yet again and she brought forth a son and she said, given that "YHWH [*He exists*]" heard, given that I am hated and he also gave to me this and she called out his title "Shimon [*Heard*]",

**29:34 ***
וַתַּהַר עוֹד וַתֵּלֶד בֵּן וַתֹּאמֶר עַתָּה הַפַּעַם יִלָּוֶה אִישִׁי אֵלַי כִּי יָלַדְתִּי לוֹ שְׁלֹשָׁה בָנִים עַל כֵּן קָרָא שְׁמוֹ לֵוִי

and~she~will~Conceive Yet.again and~she~will~Bring.forth Son and~she~will~Say Now the~Stroke.of.time he~will~be~Join Man~me To~me Given.that i~did~Bring.forth to~him Three Son~s Upon So he~did~Call.out Title~him "Lewi [*Joined*]"

and she conceived yet again and she brought forth a son and she said, now this time my man will be joined to me given that I brought forth to him three sons therefore, she called out his title "Lewi [*Joined*]",

**29:35**
וַתַּהַר עוֹד וַתֵּלֶד בֵּן וַתֹּאמֶר הַפַּעַם אוֹדֶה אֶת יְהֹוָה עַל כֵּן קָרְאָה שְׁמוֹ יְהוּדָה וַתַּעֲמֹד מִלֶּדֶת

and~she~will~Conceive Yet.again and~she~will~Bring.forth Son and~she~will~Say the~Stroke.of.time i~will~make~Throw.the.hand At "YHWH [*He exists*]" Upon So she~did~Call.out Title~him "Yehudah [*Praised*]" and~she~will~Stand from~>~Bring.forth

and she conceived yet again and she brought forth a son and she said, this time I will thank "YHWH [*He exists*]" therefore she called out his title "Yehudah [*Praised*]" and she stood from bringing forth,

# Chapter 30

**30:1**
וַתֵּרֶא רָחֵל כִּי לֹא יָלְדָה לְיַעֲקֹב וַתְּקַנֵּא רָחֵל בַּאֲחֹתָהּ וַתֹּאמֶר אֶל יַעֲקֹב הָבָה לִּי בָנִים וְאִם אַיִן מֵתָה אָנֹכִי

and~she~will~See "Rahhel [*Ewe*]" Given.that Not she~did~Bring.forth to~"Ya'aqov [*He restrains*]" and~she~will~Be.zealous "Rahhel [*Ewe*]" in~Sister~her and~she~will~Say To "Ya'aqov [*He restrains*]" !(ms)~Provide to~me Son~s and~If Without Die~ing(fs) I

and "Rahhel [*Ewe*]" saw that she did not bring forth for "Ya'aqov [*He restrains*]" and "Rahhel [*Ewe*]" was envious with her sister and she said to "Ya'aqov [*He restrains*]", provide me sons and if not I am dead,

**30:2**
וַיִּחַר אַף יַעֲקֹב בְּרָחֵל וַיֹּאמֶר הֲתַחַת אֱלֹהִים אָנֹכִי אֲשֶׁר מָנַע מִמֵּךְ פְּרִי בָטֶן

# Jeff A. Benner

and~he~will~Flare.up Nose "Ya'aqov [*He restrains*]" in~"Rahhel [*Ewe*]" and~he~will~Say ?~Under "Elohiym [*Powers*]" I Which he~did~Withhold From~you(fs) Produce Womb

and the nose of "Ya'aqov [*He restrains*]" flared up with "Rahhel [*Ewe*]" and he said, am I in the place of "Elohiym [*Powers*]" who withheld from you the produce of the womb,

**30:3** נַתֹּאמֶר הִנֵּה אֲמָתִי בִלְהָה בֹּא אֵלֶיהָ וְתֵלֵד עַל בִּרְכַּי וְאִבָּנֶה גַם אָנֹכִי מִמֶּנָּה

and~she~will~Say Look Bondwoman~me "Bilhah [*Wear out*]" !(ms)~Come To~her and~she~will~Bring.forth Upon Knee~me and~i~will~be~Build Also I From~her

and she said, look, my bondwoman "Bilhah [*Wear out*]", come to her and she will bring forth upon my knee and I will also be built from her,

**30:4** וַתִּתֶּן לוֹ אֶת בִּלְהָה שִׁפְחָתָהּ לְאִשָּׁה וַיָּבֹא אֵלֶיהָ יַעֲקֹב

and~she~will~Give to~him At "Bilhah [*Wear out*]" Maid~her to~Woman and~he~will~Come To~her "Ya'aqov [*He restrains*]"

and she gave to him "Bilhah [*Wear out*]" her maid for a woman and "Ya'aqov [*He restrains*]" came to her,

**30:5** וַתַּהַר בִּלְהָה וַתֵּלֶד לְיַעֲקֹב בֵּן

and~she~will~Conceive "Bilhah [*Wear out*]" and~she~will~Bring.forth to~"Ya'aqov [*He restrains*]" Son

and "Bilhah [*Wear out*]" conceived and she brought forth for "Ya'aqov [*He restrains*]" a son,

**30:6** וַתֹּאמֶר רָחֵל דָּנַנִּי אֱלֹהִים וְגַם שָׁמַע בְּקֹלִי וַיִּתֶּן לִי בֵּן עַל כֵּן קָרְאָה שְׁמוֹ דָּן

and~she~will~Say "Rahhel [*Ewe*]" he~did~Moderate~me "Elohiym [*Powers*]" and~Also he~did~Hear in~Voice~you(ms) and~he~will~Give to~me Son Upon So she~did~Call.out Title~him "Dan [*Moderator*]"

and "Rahhel [*Ewe*]" said, "Elohiym [*Powers*]" will moderate me and he also heard in your voice and he gave to me a son therefore she called out his title "Dan [*Moderator*]",

**30:7** וַתַּהַר עוֹד וַתֵּלֶד בִּלְהָה שִׁפְחַת רָחֵל בֵּן שֵׁנִי לְיַעֲקֹב

and~she~will~Conceive Yet.again and~she~will~Bring.forth "Bilhah [*Wear out*]" Maid "Rahhel [*Ewe*]" Son Second to~"Ya'aqov [*He restrains*]"

and she conceived yet again and "Bilhah [*Wear out*]", the maid of "Rahhel [*Ewe*]", brought forth a second son for "Ya'aqov [*He restrains*]",

**30:8** וַתֹּאמֶר רָחֵל נַפְתּוּלֵי אֱלֹהִים נִפְתַּלְתִּי עִם אֲחֹתִי גַם יָכֹלְתִּי וַתִּקְרָא שְׁמוֹ נַפְתָּלִי

and~she~will~Say "Rahhel [*Ewe*]" Wrestle~s Power~s i~did~be~Entwine With Sister~me Also i~did~Be.able

and "Rahhel [*Ewe*]" said, wrestlings of powers I was entwined with my sister also, I was

**168**

and~she~will~Call.out   Title~him
"Naphtali [*Wrestling*]"

able and she called out his title
"Naphtali [*Wrestling*]",

**30:9**

וַתֵּרֶא לֵאָה כִּי עָמְדָה מִלֶּדֶת וַתִּקַּח אֶת זִלְפָּה שִׁפְחָתָהּ וַתִּתֵּן
אֹתָהּ לְיַעֲקֹב לְאִשָּׁה

and~she~will~See   "Le'ah [*Weary*]"
Given.that   she~did~Stand   from~>~
Bring.forth   and~she~will~Take   At
"Zilpah [*Trickling*]"   Maid~her   and~
she~will~Give   At~her   to~"Ya'aqov
[*He restrains*]"   to~Woman

and "Le'ah [*Weary*]" saw that she
stood from bringing forth and she
took "Zilpah [*Trickling*]" her maid
and she gave her to "Ya'aqov [*He
restrains*]" for a woman,

**30:10**

וַתֵּלֶד זִלְפָּה שִׁפְחַת לֵאָה לְיַעֲקֹב בֵּן

and~she~will~Bring.forth   "Zilpah
[*Trickling*]"   Maid   "Le'ah [*Weary*]"
to~"Ya'aqov [*He restrains*]"   Son

and "Zilpah [*Trickling*]" the maid
of "Le'ah [*Weary*]" brought forth
for "Ya'aqov [*He restrains*]" a son,

**30:11***

וַתֹּאמֶר לֵאָה בגד (בָּא גָד) וַתִּקְרָא אֶת שְׁמוֹ גָּד

and~she~will~Say   "Le'ah [*Weary*]"
in~Fortune   and~she~will~Call.out   At
Title~him   "Gad [*Fortune*]"

and "Le'ah [*Weary*]" said, fortune
came, and she called out his title
"Gad [*Fortune*]",

**30:12**

וַתֵּלֶד זִלְפָּה שִׁפְחַת לֵאָה בֵּן שֵׁנִי לְיַעֲקֹב

and~she~will~Bring.forth   "Zilpah
[*Trickling*]"   Maid   "Le'ah [*Weary*]"
Son   Second   to~"Ya'aqov [*He
restrains*]"

and "Zilpah [*Trickling*]", the maid
of "Le'ah [*Weary*]", brought forth a
second son for "Ya'aqov [*He
restrains*]",

**30:13**

וַתֹּאמֶר לֵאָה בְּאָשְׁרִי כִּי אִשְּׁרוּנִי בָּנוֹת וַתִּקְרָא אֶת שְׁמוֹ אָשֵׁר

and~she~will~Say   "Le'ah [*Weary*]"
in~Happiness~me   Given.that   they~did~
much~Happy~me   Daughter~s   and~she~
will~Call.out   At   Title~him   "Asher
[*Happy*]"

and "Le'ah [*Weary*]" said, I am in
happiness given that the daughters
are very happy for me and she
called out his title "Asher
[*Happy*]",

**30:14**

וַיֵּלֶךְ רְאוּבֵן בִּימֵי קְצִיר חִטִּים וַיִּמְצָא דוּדָאִים בַּשָּׂדֶה וַיָּבֵא
אֹתָם אֶל לֵאָה אִמּוֹ וַתֹּאמֶר רָחֵל אֶל לֵאָה תְּנִי נָא לִי מִדּוּדָאֵי
בְּנֵךְ

and~he~will~Walk   "Re'uven [*See a
son*]"   in~Day~s   Harvest   Wheat~s
and~he~will~Find   Mandrakes~s   in~the~
Field   and~he~will~make~Come   At~
them(m)   To   "Le'ah [*Weary*]"
Mother~him   and~she~will~Say   "Rahhel
[*Ewe*]"   To   "Le'ah [*Weary*]"   !(fs)~
Give   Please   to~me   from~Mandrakes~s
Son~you(fs)

and "Re'uven [*See a son*]" walked
in the days of the wheat harvest and
he found mandrakes in the field and
he brought them to "Le'ah [*Weary*]"
his mother and "Rahhel [*Ewe*]" said
to "Le'ah [*Weary*]", please give me
from the mandrakes of your son,

**30:15**

וַתֹּאמֶר לָהּ הַמְעַט קַחְתֵּךְ אֶת אִישִׁי וְלָקַחַת גַּם אֶת דּוּדָאֵי בְּנִי וַתֹּאמֶר רָחֵל לָכֵן יִשְׁכַּב עִמָּךְ הַלַּיְלָה תַּחַת דּוּדָאֵי בְנֵךְ

and~she~will~Say to~her ?~ Small.amount >~Take~you(fs) At Man~me and~to~>~Take Also At Mandrakes~s Son~me and~she~will~ Say "Rahhel [Ewe]" to~So he~will~ Lay.down With~you(fs) the~Night Under Mandrakes~s Son~you(fs)

and she said to her, is it a small thing for you to take my man and also to take the mandrakes of my son and "Rahhel [Ewe]" said, because of this he will lay down with you tonight under the mandrakes of your son,

**30:16**

וַיָּבֹא יַעֲקֹב מִן הַשָּׂדֶה בָּעֶרֶב וַתֵּצֵא לֵאָה לִקְרָאתוֹ וַתֹּאמֶר אֵלַי תָּבוֹא כִּי שָׂכֹר שְׂכַרְתִּיךָ בְּדוּדָאֵי בְּנִי וַיִּשְׁכַּב עִמָּהּ בַּלַּיְלָה הוּא

and~he~will~Come "Ya'aqov [He restrains]" From the~Field in~the~ Evening and~she~will~Go.out "Le'ah [Weary]" to~>~Meet~him and~she~ will~Say To~me you(ms)~will~Come Given.that >~Hire i~did~Hire~you(ms) in~Mandrakes~s Son~me and~he~will~ Lay.down With~her in~the~Night He

and "Ya'aqov [He restrains]" came from the field in the evening and "Le'ah [Weary]" went out to meet him and she said, you will come to me given that I surely hired you with the mandrakes of my son and he laid down with her in that night,

**30:17**

וַיִּשְׁמַע אֱלֹהִים אֶל לֵאָה וַתַּהַר וַתֵּלֶד לְיַעֲקֹב בֵּן חֲמִישִׁי

and~he~will~Hear "Elohiym [Powers]" To "Le'ah [Weary]" and~she~will~ Conceive and~she~will~Bring.forth to~ "Ya'aqov [He restrains]" Son Fifth

and "Elohiym [Powers]" heard "Le'ah [Weary]" and she conceived and she brought forth for "Ya'aqov [He restrains]" a fifth son,

**30:18**

וַתֹּאמֶר לֵאָה נָתַן אֱלֹהִים שְׂכָרִי אֲשֶׁר נָתַתִּי שִׁפְחָתִי לְאִישִׁי וַתִּקְרָא שְׁמוֹ יִשָּׂשכָר

and~she~will~Say "Le'ah [Weary]" he~did~Give "Elohiym [Powers]" Wage~me Which i~did~Give Maid~ me to~Man~me and~she~will~Call.out Title~him "Yis'sas'kar [He will lift up the wage]"

and "Le'ah [Weary]" said, "Elohiym [Powers]" gave my wage because I gave my maid to my man and she called out his title "Yis'sas'kar [He will lift up the wage]",

**30:19**

וַתַּהַר עוֹד לֵאָה וַתֵּלֶד בֵּן שִׁשִּׁי לְיַעֲקֹב

and~she~will~Conceive Yet.again "Le'ah [Weary]" and~she~will~ Bring.forth Son Sixth to~"Ya'aqov [He restrains]"

and "Le'ah [Weary]" conceived yet again and she brought forth a sixth son for "Ya'aqov [He restrains]",

**30:20**

וַתֹּאמֶר לֵאָה זְבָדַנִי אֱלֹהִים אֹתִי זֵבֶד טוֹב הַפַּעַם יִזְבְּלֵנִי אִישִׁי כִּי יָלַדְתִּי לוֹ שִׁשָּׁה בָנִים וַתִּקְרָא אֶת שְׁמוֹ זְבֻלוּן

and~she~will~Say "Le'ah [Weary]" he~did~Endow~me "Elohiym [Powers]"

and "Le'ah [Weary]" said, "Elohiym [Powers]" endowed me a

At~me Dowry Functional the~
Stroke.of.time he~will~Reside~me
Man~me Given.that i~did~Bring.forth
to~him Six Son~s and~she~will~
Call.out At Title~him "Zevulun
[*Residence*]"

functional dowry, will my man reside with me this time given that I brought forth for him six sons and she called out his title "Zevulun [*Residence*]",

**30:21**

וְאַחַר יָלְדָה בַת וַתִּקְרָא אֶת שְׁמָהּ דִּינָה

and~After she~did~Bring.forth
Daughter and~she~will~Call.out At
Title~her "Dinah [*Judgement*]"

and afterward she brought forth a daughter and she called out her title "Dinah [*Judgement*]",

**30:22**

וַיִּזְכֹּר אֱלֹהִים אֶת רָחֵל וַיִּשְׁמַע אֵלֶיהָ אֱלֹהִים וַיִּפְתַּח אֶת רַחְמָהּ

and~he~will~Remember "Elohiym
[*Powers*]" At "Rahhel [*Ewe*]" and~
he~will~Hear To~her "Elohiym
[*Powers*]" and~he~will~Open At
Bowels~her

and "Elohiym [*Powers*]" remembered "Rahhel [*Ewe*]" and "Elohiym [*Powers*]" heard her and he opened her bowels,

**30:23**

וַתַּהַר וַתֵּלֶד בֵּן וַתֹּאמֶר אָסַף אֱלֹהִים אֶת חֶרְפָּתִי

and~she~will~Conceive and~she~will~
Bring.forth Son and~she~will~Say he~
did~Gather "Elohiym [*Powers*]" At
Disgrace~me

and she conceived and she brought forth a son and she said "Elohiym [*Powers*]" gathered my disgrace,

**30:24**

וַתִּקְרָא אֶת שְׁמוֹ יוֹסֵף לֵאמֹר יְהֹוָה לִי בֵּן אַחֵר

and~she~will~Call.out At Title~him
"Yoseph [*Adding*]" to~>~Say he~will~
make~Add "YHWH [*He exists*]" to~
me Son Other

and she called out his title "Yoseph [*Adding*]" saying, "YHWH [*He exists*]" will add to me another son,

**30:25**

וַיְהִי כַּאֲשֶׁר יָלְדָה רָחֵל אֶת יוֹסֵף וַיֹּאמֶר יַעֲקֹב אֶל לָבָן שַׁלְּחֵנִי וְאֵלְכָה אֶל מְקוֹמִי וּלְאַרְצִי

and~he~will~Exist like~Which she~
will~Bring.forth "Rahhel [*Ewe*]" At
"Yoseph [*Adding*]" and~he~will~Say
"Ya'aqov [*He restrains*]" To "Lavan
[*White*]" !(ms)~much~Send~me and~i~
will~Walk To Place~me and~to~
Land~me

and it came to pass, just as "Rahhel [*Ewe*]" brought forth "Yoseph [*Adding*]", "Ya'aqov [*He restrains*]" said to "Lavan [*White*]", send me and I will walk to my place and to my land,

**30:26**

תְּנָה אֶת נָשַׁי וְאֶת יְלָדַי אֲשֶׁר עָבַדְתִּי אֹתְךָ בָּהֵן וְאֵלֵכָה כִּי אַתָּה יָדַעְתָּ אֶת עֲבֹדָתִי אֲשֶׁר עֲבַדְתִּיךָ

!(ms)~Give~^ At Woman~s~me and~
At Boy~s~me Which i~did~Serve
At~you(ms) in~them(f) and~i~will~

give my women and my boys which I served with you in them and I will walk given that you knew

**171**

Walk~^ Given.that You(ms) you(ms)~ did~Know At Service~me Which i~ did~Serve~you(ms)

my service which I served you,

**30:27** וַיֹּאמֶר אֵלָיו לָבָן אִם נָא מָצָאתִי חֵן בְּעֵינֶיךָ נִחַשְׁתִּי וַיְבָרְכֵנִי יְהוָה בִּגְלָלֶךָ

and~he~will~Say To~him "Lavan [*White*]" If Please i~did~Find Beauty in~Eye~s2~you(ms) i~did~much~Divine and~he~will~much~Kneel~me "YHWH [*He exists*]" in~Account.of~you(ms)

and "Lavan [*White*]" said to him please, if I found beauty in your eyes, I will divine and "YHWH [*He exists*]" respected me on account of you,

**30:28** וַיֹּאמַר נָקְבָה שְׂכָרְךָ עָלַי וְאֶתֵּנָה

and~he~will~Say !(ms)~Pierce.through~^ Wage~you(ms) Upon~me and~i~will~ Give~^

and he said, pierce through your wage upon me and I will give,

**30:29** וַיֹּאמֶר אֵלָיו אַתָּה יָדַעְתָּ אֵת אֲשֶׁר עֲבַדְתִּיךָ וְאֵת אֲשֶׁר הָיָה מִקְנְךָ אִתִּי

and~he~will~Say To~him You(ms) you(ms)~did~Know At Which i~did~ Serve~you(ms) and~At Which he~ did~Exist Livestock~you(ms) At~me

and he said to him, you know that I served you, that your livestock existed with me,

**30:30** כִּי מְעַט אֲשֶׁר הָיָה לְךָ לְפָנַי וַיִּפְרֹץ לָרֹב וַיְבָרֶךְ יְהוָה אֹתְךָ לְרַגְלִי וְעַתָּה מָתַי אֶעֱשֶׂה גַם אָנֹכִי לְבֵיתִי

Given.that Small.amount Which he~ did~Exist to~you(ms) to~Face~s~me and~he~will~Break.out to~the~ Abundance and~he~will~much~Kneel "YHWH [*He exists*]" At~you(ms) to~Foot~me and~Now How.long i~ will~Do Also I to~House~me

given that the small amount which existed to you before me and he will break out to the abundance and "YHWH [*He exists*]" will respect you to my foot and now, how long will I make also for my house,

**30:31** וַיֹּאמֶר מָה אֶתֶּן לָךְ וַיֹּאמֶר יַעֲקֹב לֹא תִתֶּן לִי מְאוּמָה אִם תַּעֲשֶׂה לִּי הַדָּבָר הַזֶּה אָשׁוּבָה אֶרְעֶה צֹאנְךָ אֶשְׁמֹר

and~he~will~Say What i~will~Give to~you(fs) and~he~will~Say "Ya'aqov [*He restrains*]" Not you(ms)~will~ Give to~me Nothing If you(ms)~ will~Do to~me the~Word the~This i~will~Turn.back~^ i~will~Feed Flocks~you(ms) i~will~Guard

and he said, what will I give to you, and "Ya'aqov [*He restrains*]" said, you will not give to me anything if you will do to me this word, I will turn back, I will feed your flock, I will guard,

**30:32** אֶעֱבֹר בְּכָל צֹאנְךָ הַיּוֹם הָסֵר מִשָּׁם כָּל שֶׂה נָקֹד וְטָלוּא וְכָל שֶׂה חוּם בַּכְּשָׂבִים וְטָלוּא וְנָקֹד בָּעִזִּים וְהָיָה שְׂכָרִי

i~will~Cross.over in~All Flocks~
you(ms) the~Day >~make~Turn.aside
from~There All One.of.the.flock
Speckled and~Spot~ed(ms) and~All
One.of.the.flock Black in~the~Sheep~s
and~Spot~ed(ms) and~Speckled in~the~
She-goat~s and~he~did~Exist Wage~
me

I will cross over in all your flocks today, removing from there all the speckled and spotted ones of the flock and all of the black ones of the flock with the sheep and the spotted and speckled with the she-goats and he will exist as my wage,

**30:33** וְעָנְתָה בִּי צִדְקָתִי בְּיוֹם מָחָר כִּי תָבוֹא עַל שְׂכָרִי לְפָנֶיךָ כֹּל אֲשֶׁר אֵינֶנּוּ נָקֹד וְטָלוּא בָּעִזִּים וְחוּם בַּכְּשָׂבִים גָּנוּב הוּא אִתִּי

and~she~did~Answer in~me
Correctness~me in~Day Later
Given.that you(ms)~will~Come Upon
Wage~me to~Face~s~you(ms) All
Which Without~him Speckled and~
Spot~ed(ms) in~the~She-goat~s and~
Black in~the~Sheep~s Steal~ed(ms)
He At~me

and my correctness will answer in me in a later day given that you will come because of my wage before you, all which are without the speckled and the spotted in the she-goats and the black in the sheep, he is stolen with me,

**30:34** וַיֹּאמֶר לָבָן הֵן לוּ יְהִי כִדְבָרֶךָ

and~he~will~Say "Lavan [*White*]"
Though Would.that he~will~Exist
like~Word~you(ms)

and "Lavan [*White*]" said, though that would exist like your word,

**30:35** וַיָּסַר בַּיּוֹם הַהוּא אֶת הַתְּיָשִׁים הָעֲקֻדִּים וְהַטְּלֻאִים וְאֵת כָּל הָעִזִּים הַנְּקֻדּוֹת וְהַטְּלֻאֹת כֹּל אֲשֶׁר לָבָן בּוֹ וְכָל חוּם בַּכְּשָׂבִים וַיִּתֵּן בְּיַד בָּנָיו

and~he~will~make~Turn.aside in~the~
Day the~He At the~He-goat~s the~
Striped~s and~the~Spot~ed(ms)~s and~
At All the~She-goat~s the~Speckled~s
and~the~Spot~ed(ms)~s All Which
White in~him and~All Black in~the~
Sheep~s and~he~will~Give in~Hand
Son~s~him

and he removed in that day the stripped and spotted he-goats and all the speckled and spotted she-goats, all which was white in him and all the black in the sheep and he gave in the hand of his sons,

**30:36** וַיָּשֶׂם דֶּרֶךְ שְׁלֹשֶׁת יָמִים בֵּינוֹ וּבֵין יַעֲקֹב וְיַעֲקֹב רֹעֶה אֶת צֹאן לָבָן הַנּוֹתָרֹת

and~he~will~Set.in.place Road Three
Day~s Between~him and~Between
"Ya'aqov [*He restrains*]" and~
"Ya'aqov [*He restrains*]" Feed~
ing(ms) At Flocks "Lavan [*White*]"
the~be~Reserve~ing(fp)

and he sat in place a road of three days between him and "Ya'aqov [*He restrains*]" and "Ya'aqov [*He restrains*]" was feeding the flocks of "Lavan [*White*]", the ones being reserved,

**30:37** וַיִּקַּח לוֹ יַעֲקֹב מַקַּל לִבְנֶה לַח וְלוּז וְעַרְמוֹן וַיְפַצֵּל בָּהֵן פְּצָלוֹת לְבָנוֹת מַחְשֹׂף הַלָּבָן אֲשֶׁר עַל הַמַּקְלוֹת

and~he~will~Take to~him "Ya'aqov [*He restrains*]" Rod Poplar Moist and~Hazel and~Chestnut and~he~will~much~Peel in~them(f) Strip White~s Expose the~White Which Upon the~Rod~s

and "Ya'aqov [*He restrains*]" took to him a rod of a moist poplar and hazel and chestnut and he peeled white strips in them exposing the white which was upon the rods,

**30:38** וַיַּצֵּג אֶת הַמַּקְלוֹת אֲשֶׁר פִּצֵּל בָּרְהָטִים בְּשִׁקֲתוֹת הַמָּיִם אֲשֶׁר תָּבֹאןָ הַצֹּאן לִשְׁתּוֹת לְנֹכַח הַצֹּאן וַיֵּחַמְנָה בְּבֹאָן לִשְׁתּוֹת

and~he~will~make~Set At the~Rod~s Which he~did~much~Peel in~Trough~s in~Watering.trough~s the~Water~s2 Which they(f)~will~Come the~Flocks to~>~Gulp to~In.front the~Flocks and~they(m)~will~Heat in~>~Come~them(f) to~>~Gulp

and he set the rods which he peeled in troughs, in the watering troughs of water where the flocks come to gulp, to the front of the flocks, and they will heat in their coming to gulp,

**30:39** וַיֶּחֱמוּ הַצֹּאן אֶל הַמַּקְלוֹת וַתֵּלַדְןָ הַצֹּאן עֲקֻדִּים נְקֻדִּים וּטְלֻאִים

and~they(m)~will~Heat the~Flocks To the~Rod~s and~they(f)~will~Bring.forth the~Flocks Striped~s Speckled~s and~the~Spot~ed(ms)

and the flocks will heat to the rods and the flocks brought forth striped ones, speckled ones and spotted ones,

**30:40** וְהַכְּשָׂבִים הִפְרִיד יַעֲקֹב וַיִּתֵּן פְּנֵי הַצֹּאן אֶל עָקֹד וְכָל חוּם בְּצֹאן לָבָן וַיָּשֶׁת לוֹ עֲדָרִים לְבַדּוֹ וְלֹא שָׁתָם עַל צֹאן לָבָן

and~the~Sheep~s he~did~make~Divide.apart "Ya'aqov [*He restrains*]" and~he~will~Give Face~s the~Flocks To Striped and~All Black in~Flocks "Lavan [*White*]" and~he~will~Set.down to~him Drove~s to~Separated.thing~him and~Not he~did~Set.down~them(m) Upon Flocks "Lavan [*White*]"

and "Ya'aqov [*He restrains*]" divided apart the sheep and he gave the faces of the flocks to the striped and all the black in the flocks of "Lavan [*White*]" and he set down to him droves by himself and he did not set them down upon the flocks of "Lavan [*White*]",

**30:41** וְהָיָה בְּכָל יַחֵם הַצֹּאן הַמְקֻשָּׁרוֹת וְשָׂם יַעֲקֹב אֶת הַמַּקְלוֹת לְעֵינֵי הַצֹּאן בָּרְהָטִים לְיַחְמֵנָּה בַּמַּקְלוֹת

and~he~did~Exist in~All >~much~Heat the~Flocks the~much.be~Tie~ing(fp) and~he~did~Set.in.place "Ya'aqov [*He restrains*]" At the~Rod~s to~Eye~s2 the~Flocks in~Trough~s to~>~much~

and it came to pass in all the heating of the robust flocks and "Ya'aqov [*He restrains*]" set in place the rods to the eyes of the flocks in the troughs, for her

Heat~her in~the~Rod~s

heating in the rods,

**30:42** וּבְהַעֲטִיף הַצֹּאן לֹא יָשִׂים וְהָיָה הָעֲטֻפִים לְלָבָן וְהַקְּשֻׁרִים לְיַעֲקֹב

and~in~>~make~Turn.over the~Flocks Not he~will~Set.in.place and~he~did~ Exist the~Turn.over~ed(mp) to~"Lavan [*White*]" and~the~Tie~ed(mp) to~ "Ya'aqov [*He restrains*]"

and with the feeble of the flocks he will not set in place and the feeble ones existed to "Lavan [*White*]" and the robust ones to "Ya'aqov [*He restrains*]",

**30:43** וַיִּפְרֹץ הָאִישׁ מְאֹד מְאֹד וַיְהִי לוֹ צֹאן רַבּוֹת וּשְׁפָחוֹת וַעֲבָדִים וּגְמַלִּים וַחֲמֹרִים

and~he~will~Break.out the~Man Many Many and~he~will~Exist to~him Flocks Abundant~s and~Maid~s and~ Servant~s and~Camel~s and~Donkey~s

and the man broke out very greatly and he existed to him abundant flocks and maids and servants and camels and donkeys,

# Chapter 31

**31:1** וַיִּשְׁמַע אֶת דִּבְרֵי בְנֵי לָבָן לֵאמֹר לָקַח יַעֲקֹב אֵת כָּל אֲשֶׁר לְאָבִינוּ וּמֵאֲשֶׁר לְאָבִינוּ עָשָׂה אֵת כָּל הַכָּבֹד הַזֶּה

and~he~will~Hear At Word~s Son~s "Lavan [*White*]" to~>~Say he~did~ Take "Ya'aqov [*He restrains*]" At All Which to~Father~us and~from~ Which to~Father~us he~will~Do At All the~Honor the~This

and he heard the words of the sons of "Lavan [*White*]" saying, "Ya'aqov [*He restrains*]" took all which belongs to our father and from which belongs to our father he will do all this honor,

**31:2** וַיַּרְא יַעֲקֹב אֶת פְּנֵי לָבָן וְהִנֵּה אֵינֶנּוּ עִמּוֹ כִּתְמוֹל שִׁלְשׁוֹם

and~he~will~See "Ya'aqov [*He restrains*]" At Face~s "Lavan [*White*]" and~Look Without~him With~him like~Yesterday Three.days.ago

and "Ya'aqov [*He restrains*]" saw the face of "Lavan [*White*]" and look, it was not with him previously,

**31:3** וַיֹּאמֶר יְהֹוָה אֶל יַעֲקֹב שׁוּב אֶל אֶרֶץ אֲבוֹתֶיךָ וּלְמוֹלַדְתֶּךָ וְאֶהְיֶה עִמָּךְ

and~he~will~Say "YHWH [*He exists*]" To "Ya'aqov [*He restrains*]" !(ms)~Turn.back To Land Father~s~ you(ms) and~to~Kindred~you(ms) and~ i~will~Exist With~you(fs)

and "YHWH [*He exists*]" said to "Ya'aqov [*He restrains*]", turn back to the land of your father and to your kindred and I will exist with you,

**31:4\*** וַיִּשְׁלַח יַעֲקֹב וַיִּקְרָא לְרָחֵל וּלְלֵאָה הַשָּׂדֶה אֶל צֹאנוֹ

and~he~will~Send "Ya'aqov [*He*

and "Ya'aqov [*He restrains*]" sent

restrains]" and~he~will~Call.out to~ "Rahhel [*Ewe*]" and~to~"Le'ah [*Weary*]" the~Field To Flocks~him

and he called out to "Rahhel [*Ewe*]" and to "Le'ah [*Weary*]" to the field of his flock,

### 31:5

וַיֹּאמֶר לָהֶן רֹאֶה אָנֹכִי אֶת פְּנֵי אֲבִיכֶן כִּי אֵינֶנּוּ אֵלַי כִּתְמֹל שִׁלְשֹׁם וֵאלֹהֵי אָבִי הָיָה עִמָּדִי

and~he~will~Say to~them(f) Seeing(ms) I At Face~s Father~you(fp) Given.that Without~him To~me like~ Yesterday Three.days.ago and~Power~s Father~me he~did~Exist By~me

and he said to them, I am seeing the face of your father given that it was not to me as previously and the powers of my father existed by me,

### 31:6

וְאַתֵּנָה יְדַעְתֶּן כִּי בְּכָל כֹּחִי עָבַדְתִּי אֶת אֲבִיכֶן

and~You(fs) you(fp)~did~Know Given.that in~All Strength~me i~did~ Serve At Father~you(fp)

and you know that in all my strength I served your father,

### 31:7

וַאֲבִיכֶן הֵתֶל בִּי וְהֶחֱלִף אֶת מַשְׂכֻּרְתִּי עֲשֶׂרֶת מֹנִים וְלֹא נְתָנוֹ אֱלֹהִים לְהָרַע עִמָּדִי

and~Father~you(fp) he~had~make~ Deal.deceitfully in~me and~he~did~ make~Pass.over At Payment~me Ten Time~s and~Not he~did~Give~him "Elohiym [*Powers*]" to~>~make~ Be.dysfunctional By~me

and your father had dealt deceitfully in me and he changed my payment ten times and "Elohiym [*Powers*]" did not give him to be made dysfunctional by me,

### 31:8

אִם כֹּה יֹאמַר נְקֻדִּים יִהְיֶה שְׂכָרֶךָ וְיָלְדוּ כָל הַצֹּאן נְקֻדִּים וְאִם כֹּה יֹאמַר עֲקֻדִּים יִהְיֶה שְׂכָרֶךָ וְיָלְדוּ כָל הַצֹּאן עֲקֻדִּים

If In.this.way he~will~Say Speckled~s he~will~Exist Wage~you(ms) and~ they~will~Bring.forth All the~Flocks Speckled~s and~If In.this.way he~ will~Say Striped~s he~will~Exist Wage~you(ms) and~they~will~ Bring.forth All the~Flocks Striped~s

if in this way he will say, the speckled ones will exist as your wage then all of the flocks will bring forth speckled ones and if in this way he will say, striped ones will exist as your wage then all of the flocks will bring forth striped ones,

### 31:9

וַיַּצֵּל אֱלֹהִים אֶת מִקְנֵה אֲבִיכֶם וַיִּתֶּן לִי

and~he~will~make~Deliver "Elohiym [*Powers*]" At Livestock Father~ you(mp) and~he~will~Give to~me

and "Elohiym [*Powers*]" delivered the livestock of your father and he gave to me,

### 31:10

וַיְהִי בְּעֵת יַחֵם הַצֹּאן וָאֶשָּׂא עֵינַי וָאֵרֶא בַּחֲלוֹם וְהִנֵּה הָעַתֻּדִים הָעֹלִים עַל הַצֹּאן עֲקֻדִּים נְקֻדִּים וּבְרֻדִּים

and~he~will~Exist in~Appointed.time >~much~Heat the~Flocks and~i~will~ Lift.up Eye~s2~me and~i~will~See

and it came to pass in the appointed time of the heat of the flocks and I lifted up my eyes and I saw in the

in~the~Dream and~Look the~Male.goat~s the~Go.up~ing(mp) Upon the~Flocks Striped~s Speckled~s and~Spotted~s

dream and look, the male goats going up upon the flocks were striped ones, speckled ones and spotted ones,

**31:11** וַיֹּאמֶר אֵלַי מַלְאַךְ הָאֱלֹהִים בַּחֲלוֹם יַעֲקֹב וָאֹמַר הִנֵּנִי

and~he~will~Say To~me Messenger the~"Elohiym [Powers]" in~the~Dream "Ya'aqov [He restrains]" and~i~will~Say Look~me

and the messenger of the "Elohiym [Powers]" said to me in the dream, "Ya'aqov [He restrains]", and I said, here am I,

**31:12** וַיֹּאמֶר שָׂא נָא עֵינֶיךָ וּרְאֵה כָּל הָעַתֻּדִים הָעֹלִים עַל הַצֹּאן עֲקֻדִּים נְקֻדִּים וּבְרֻדִּים כִּי רָאִיתִי אֵת כָּל אֲשֶׁר לָבָן עֹשֶׂה לָּךְ

and~he~will~Say !(ms)~Lift.up Please Eye~s2~you(ms) and~!(ms)~See All the~Male.goat~s the~Go.up~ing(mp) Upon the~Flocks Striped~s Speckled~s and~Spotted~s Given.that i~did~See At All Which "Lavan [White]" Do~ing(ms) to~you(fs)

and he said, please lift up your eyes and see all the male goats going up upon the flocks were striped ones, speckled ones and spotted ones given that I saw all which "Lavan [White]" is doing to you,

**31:13** אָנֹכִי הָאֵל בֵּית אֵל אֲשֶׁר מָשַׁחְתָּ שָּׁם מַצֵּבָה אֲשֶׁר נָדַרְתָּ לִּי שָׁם נֶדֶר עַתָּה קוּם צֵא מִן הָאָרֶץ הַזֹּאת וְשׁוּב אֶל אֶרֶץ מוֹלַדְתֶּךָ

I the~Mighty.one "Beyt-El [House of El]" Which you(ms)~did~Smear There Monument Which you(ms)~did~Make.a.vow to~me There Vow Now !(ms)~Rise !(ms)~Go.out From the~Land the~This and~!(ms)~Turn.back To Land Kindred~you(ms)

I am the mighty one of "Beyt-El [House of El]" where you smeared there a monument where you made a vow to me there a vow, now rise, go out from this land and turn back to the land of your kindred,

**31:14** וַתַּעַן רָחֵל וְלֵאָה וַתֹּאמַרְנָה לוֹ הַעוֹד לָנוּ חֵלֶק וְנַחֲלָה בְּבֵית אָבִינוּ

and~she~will~Answer "Rahhel [Ewe]" and~"Le'ah [Weary]" and~they(f)~will~Say to~him ?~Yet.again to~us Portion and~Inheritance in~House Father~us

and "Rahhel [Ewe]" answered, and "Le'ah [Weary]", and they said to him, is there also for us a portion and inheritance in the house of our father,

**31:15** הֲלוֹא נָכְרִיּוֹת נֶחְשַׁבְנוּ לוֹ כִּי מְכָרָנוּ וַיֹּאכַל גַּם אָכוֹל אֶת כַּסְפֵּנוּ

?~Not Foreigner~s we~did~be~Think to~him Given.that he~did~Sell~us and~he~will~Eat Also >~Eat At Silver~us

were we not thought of as foreigners to him given that he sold us and he also greatly ate our silver,

**31:16** כִּי כָל הָעֹשֶׁר אֲשֶׁר הִצִּיל אֱלֹהִים מֵאָבִינוּ לָנוּ הוּא וּלְבָנֵינוּ וְעַתָּה כֹּל אֲשֶׁר אָמַר אֱלֹהִים אֵלֶיךָ עֲשֵׂה

**177**

Given.that All the~Riches Which he~ did~make~Deliver "Elohiym [*Powers*]" from~Father~us to~us He and~to~ Son~s~us and~Now All Which he~ did~Say "Elohiym [*Powers*]" To~ you(ms) !(ms)~Do

given that all the riches which "Elohiym [*Powers*]" delivered from our father, to us is he and to our sons and now all which "Elohiym [*Powers*]" said to you, do,

**31:17**  וַיָּקָם יַעֲקֹב וַיִּשָּׂא אֶת בָּנָיו וְאֶת נָשָׁיו עַל הַגְּמַלִּים

and~he~will~Rise "Ya'aqov [*He restrains*]" and~he~will~Lift.up At Son~s~him and~At Woman~s~him Upon the~Camel~s

and "Ya'aqov [*He restrains*]" rose and he lifted up his sons and his women upon the camels,

**31:18**  וַיִּנְהַג אֶת כָּל מִקְנֵהוּ וְאֶת כָּל רְכֻשׁוֹ אֲשֶׁר רָכָשׁ מִקְנֵה קִנְיָנוֹ אֲשֶׁר רָכַשׁ בְּפַדַּן אֲרָם לָבוֹא אֶל יִצְחָק אָבִיו אַרְצָה כְּנָעַן

and~he~will~Drive At All Livestock~ him and~At All Goods~him Which he~did~Accumulate Livestock Possession~him Which he~did~ Accumulate in~"Padan-Aram [*Field palace*]" to~>~Come To "Yits'hhaq [*He laughs*]" Father~him Land~unto "Kena'an [*Lowered*]"

and he drove all his livestock and all his goods which he accumulated, the livestock of his possession which he accumulated in "Padan-Aram [*Field palace*]", to come to "Yits'hhaq [*He laughs*]" his father, unto the land of "Kena'an [*Lowered*]",

**31:19**  וְלָבָן הָלַךְ לִגְזֹז אֶת צֹאנוֹ וַתִּגְנֹב רָחֵל אֶת הַתְּרָפִים אֲשֶׁר לְאָבִיהָ

and~"Lavan [*White*]" he~had~Walk to~>~Shear At Flocks~him and~she~ will~Steal "Rahhel [*Ewe*]" At the~ Family.idol~s Which to~Father~her

and "Lavan [*White*]" had walked to shear his flocks and "Rahhel [*Ewe*]" stole the family idols which belonged to her father,

**31:20**  וַיִּגְנֹב יַעֲקֹב אֶת לֵב לָבָן הָאֲרַמִּי עַל בְּלִי הִגִּיד לוֹ כִּי בֹרֵחַ הוּא

and~he~will~Steal "Ya'aqov [*He restrains*]" At Heart "Lavan [*White*]" the~"Aram [*Palace*]"~of Upon Unaware he~will~make~Be.face.to.face to~him Given.that Flee.away~ing(ms) He

and "Ya'aqov [*He restrains*]" stole the heart of "Lavan [*White*]", the one of "Aram [*Palace*]", because it was not told to him that he was fleeing away,

**31:21 \***  וַיִּבְרַח הוּא וְכָל אֲשֶׁר לוֹ וַיָּקָם וַיַּעֲבֹר אֶת הַנָּהָר וַיָּשֶׂם אֶת פָּנָיו הַר הַגִּלְעָד

and~he~will~Flee.away He and~All Which to~him and~he~will~Rise and~ he~will~Cross.over At the~River and~ he~will~Set.in.place At Face~s~him Hill the~"Gil'ad [*Mound of witness*]"

and he fled away and all which belonged to him and he rose and he crossed over the river and he set his face in place toward the hill of "Gil'ad [*Mound of witness*]",

**31:22**

וַיֻּגַּד לְלָבָן בַּיּוֹם הַשְּׁלִישִׁי כִּי בָרַח יַעֲקֹב

and~he~will~make.be~Be.face.to.face to~ "Lavan [*White*]" in~the~Day the~ Third Given.that he~did~Flee.away "Ya'aqov [*He restrains*]"

and he told to "Lavan [*White*]" in the third day that "Ya'aqov [*He restrains*]" fled away,

**31:23**

וַיִּקַּח אֶת אֶחָיו עִמּוֹ וַיִּרְדֹּף אַחֲרָיו דֶּרֶךְ שִׁבְעַת יָמִים וַיַּדְבֵּק אֹתוֹ בְּהַר הַגִּלְעָד

and~he~will~Take At Brother~s~him With~him and~he~will~Pursue After~ him Road Seven Day~s and~he~ will~make~Adhere At~him in~Hill the~"Gil'ad [*Mound of witness*]"

and he took his brothers with him and he pursued after him a road of seven of the days and he adhered to him in the hill of "Gil'ad [*Mound of witness*]",

**31:24**

וַיָּבֹא אֱלֹהִים אֶל לָבָן הָאֲרַמִּי בַּחֲלֹם הַלָּיְלָה וַיֹּאמֶר לוֹ הִשָּׁמֶר לְךָ פֶּן תְּדַבֵּר עִם יַעֲקֹב מִטּוֹב עַד רָע

and~he~will~Come "Elohiym [*Powers*]" To "Lavan [*White*]" the~ "Aram [*Palace*]"~of in~Dream the~ Night and~he~will~Say To~him !(ms)~be~Guard to~you(ms) Otherwise you(ms)~will~much~Speak With "Ya'aqov [*He restrains*]" from~ Functional Until Dysfunctional

and "Elohiym [*Powers*]" came to "Lavan [*White*]", the one of "Aram [*Palace*]", in a dream of the night and he said to him, be guarded to yourself, otherwise you will speak with "Ya'aqov [*He restrains*]" out of function as well as dysfunction,

**31:25**

וַיַּשֵּׂג לָבָן אֶת יַעֲקֹב וְיַעֲקֹב תָּקַע אֶת אָהֳלוֹ בָּהָר וְלָבָן תָּקַע אֶת אֶחָיו בְּהַר הַגִּלְעָד

and~he~will~make~Overtake "Lavan [*White*]" At "Ya'aqov [*He restrains*]" and~"Ya'aqov [*He restrains*]" he~had~ Thrust At Tent~him in~the~Hill and~"Lavan [*White*]" he~had~Thrust At Brother~s~him in~the~Hill "Gil'ad [*Mound of witness*]"

and "Lavan [*White*]" overtook "Ya'aqov [*He restrains*]" and "Ya'aqov [*He restrains*]" had thrust his tent in the hill and "Lavan [*White*]" had thrust his brothers in the hill of "Gil'ad [*Mound of witness*]",

**31:26**

וַיֹּאמֶר לָבָן לְיַעֲקֹב מֶה עָשִׂיתָ וַתִּגְנֹב אֶת לְבָבִי וַתְּנַהֵג אֶת בְּנֹתַי כִּשְׁבֻיוֹת חָרֶב

and~he~will~Say "Lavan [*White*]" to~ "Ya'aqov [*He restrains*]" What you(ms)~did~Do and~you(ms)~will~ Steal At Mind~me and~you(ms)~will~ much~Drive At Daughter~s~me like~ Capture~ed(fp) Sword

and "Lavan [*White*]" said to "Ya'aqov [*He restrains*]", what did you do and you stole my heart and you drove my daughters like captured ones of the sword,

**31:27**

לָמָּה נַחְבֵּאתָ לִבְרֹחַ וַתִּגְנֹב אֹתִי וְלֹא הִגַּדְתָּ לִּי וָאֲשַׁלֵּחֲךָ

בְּשִׂמְחָה וּבְשִׁרִים בְּתֹף וּבְכִנּוֹר

| | |
|---|---|
| to~What you(ms)~did~be~Withdraw to~>~Flee.away and~you(ms)~will~Steal At~me and~Not you(ms)~did~make~ Be.face.to.face to~me and~i~will~ much~Send~you(ms) in~Joy and~in~ Song~s in~Tambourine and~in~Harp | why did you withdraw to flee away and you stole me and you did not tell me and I sent you in joy and in songs, in tambourine and in harp, |

**31:28**   וְלֹא נְטַשְׁתַּנִי לְנַשֵּׁק לְבָנַי וְלִבְנֹתָי עַתָּה הִסְכַּלְתָּ עֲשׂוֹ

| | |
|---|---|
| and~Not you(ms)~did~Let.alone~me to~>~much~Kiss to~Son~s~me and~to~ Daughter~s~me Now you(ms)~did~ make~Foolish >~Do~him | and you did not let me alone to kiss my sons and my daughters, now you did foolishly, |

**31:29**   יֶשׁ לְאֵל יָדִי לַעֲשׂוֹת עִמָּכֶם רָע וֵאלֹהֵי אֲבִיכֶם אֶמֶשׁ אָמַר אֵלַי לֵאמֹר הִשָּׁמֶר לְךָ מִדַּבֵּר עִם יַעֲקֹב מִטּוֹב עַד רָע

| | |
|---|---|
| There.is to~Mighty.one Hand~me to~ >~Do With~you(mp) Dysfunctional and~Power~s Father~you(mp) Last.night he~had~Say To~me to~>~ Say !(ms)~be~Guard to~you(ms) from~>~much~Speak With "Ya'aqov [*He restrains*]" from~Functional Until Dysfunctional | there is belonging to the might of my hand to do dysfunction with you and the powers of your father had said to me last night saying, be guarded to yourself from speaking with "Ya'aqov [*He restrains*]" out of function as well as dysfunction, |

**31:30**   וְעַתָּה הָלֹךְ הָלַכְתָּ כִּי נִכְסֹף נִכְסַפְתָּה לְבֵית אָבִיךָ לָמָּה גָנַבְתָּ אֶת אֱלֹהָי

| | |
|---|---|
| and~Now >~Walk you(ms)~did~Walk Given.that >~be~Craving you(ms)~did~ be~Craving to~House Father~you(ms) to~What you(ms)~did~Steal At Power~s~me | and now, you quickly walked given that you were greatly craving for the house of your father, why did you steal my powers, |

**31:31**   וַיַּעַן יַעֲקֹב וַיֹּאמֶר לְלָבָן כִּי יָרֵאתִי כִּי אָמַרְתִּי פֶּן תִּגְזֹל אֶת בְּנוֹתֶיךָ מֵעִמִּי

| | |
|---|---|
| and~he~will~Answer "Ya'aqov [*He restrains*]" and~he~will~Say to~"Lavan [*White*]" Given.that i~did~Fear Given.that i~did~Say Otherwise you(ms)~will~Pluck.away At Daughter~ s~you(ms) from~With~me | and "Ya'aqov [*He restrains*]" answered and he said to "Lavan [*White*]", given that I feared, given that I said, otherwise you will pluck away your daughters from me, |

**31:32**   עִם אֲשֶׁר תִּמְצָא אֶת אֱלֹהֶיךָ לֹא יִחְיֶה נֶגֶד אַחֵינוּ הַכֶּר לְךָ מָה עִמָּדִי וְקַח לָךְ וְלֹא יָדַע יַעֲקֹב כִּי רָחֵל גְּנָבָתַם

| | |
|---|---|
| With Which you(ms)~will~Find At Power~s~you(ms) Not he~will~Live | whoever you find with your powers, he will not live, in the face |

Opposite Brother~s~us !(ms)~make~ Recognize to~you(ms) What By~me and~!(ms)~Take to~you(fs) and~Not he~did~Know "Ya'aqov [*He restrains*]" Given.that "Rahhel [*Ewe*]" she~did~Steal~them(m)

of our brothers recognize what belongs to you by me and take to you and "Ya'aqov [*He restrains*]" did not know that "Rahhel [*Ewe*]" stole them,

**31:33**   וַיָּבֹא לָבָן בְּאֹהֶל יַעֲקֹב וּבְאֹהֶל לֵאָה וּבְאֹהֶל שְׁתֵּי הָאֲמָהֹת וְלֹא מָצָא וַיֵּצֵא מֵאֹהֶל לֵאָה וַיָּבֹא בְּאֹהֶל רָחֵל

and~he~will~Come "Lavan [*White*]" in~Tent "Ya'aqov [*He restrains*]" and~in~Tent "Le'ah [*Weary*]" and~in~ Tent Two the~Bondwoman~s and~Not he~did~Find and~he~will~Go.out from~Tent "Le'ah [*Weary*]" and~he~ will~Come in~Tent "Rahhel [*Ewe*]"

and "Lavan [*White*]" came in the tent of "Ya'aqov [*He restrains*]" and in the tent of "Le'ah [*Weary*]" and in the tent of the two bondwomen and he did not find and he went out from the tent of "Le'ah [*Weary*]" and he came in the tent of "Rahhel [*Ewe*]",

**31:34**   וְרָחֵל לָקְחָה אֶת הַתְּרָפִים וַתְּשִׂמֵם בְּכַר הַגָּמָל וַתֵּשֶׁב עֲלֵיהֶם וַיְמַשֵּׁשׁ לָבָן אֶת כָּל הָאֹהֶל וְלֹא מָצָא

and~"Rahhel [*Ewe*]" she~had~Take At the~Family.idol~s and~she~will~ Set.in.place~them(m) in~Hollow the~ Camel and~she~will~Settle Upon~ them(m) and~he~will~much~Grope "Lavan [*White*]" At All the~Tent and~Not he~did~Find

and "Rahhel [*Ewe*]" had taken the family idols and she set them in place in the hollow of the camel and she settled upon them and "Lavan [*White*]" quickly groped all the tent and he did not find,

**31:35**   וַתֹּאמֶר אֶל אָבִיהָ אַל יִחַר בְּעֵינֵי אֲדֹנִי כִּי לוֹא אוּכַל לָקוּם מִפָּנֶיךָ כִּי דֶרֶךְ נָשִׁים לִי וַיְחַפֵּשׂ וְלֹא מָצָא אֶת הַתְּרָפִים

and~she~will~Say To Father~her No he~will~Flare.up in~Eye~s2 Lord~me Given.that Not i~will~Be.able to~>~ Rise from~Face~s~you(ms) Given.that Road Woman~s to~me and~he~will~ much~Search and~Not he~did~Find At the~Family.idol~s

and she said to her father, he will not flare up in the eyes of my lord given that I will not be able to rise from your face given that the road of women is to me and he quickly searched and he did not find the family idols,

**31:36**   וַיִּחַר לְיַעֲקֹב וַיָּרֶב בְּלָבָן וַיַּעַן יַעֲקֹב וַיֹּאמֶר לְלָבָן מַה פִּשְׁעִי מַה חַטָּאתִי כִּי דָלַקְתָּ אַחֲרָי

and~he~will~Flare.up to~"Ya'aqov [*He restrains*]" and~he~will~Dispute in~ "Lavan [*White*]" and~he~will~Answer "Ya'aqov [*He restrains*]" and~he~ will~Say to~"Lavan [*White*]" What Revolution~me What Error~me

and "Ya'aqov [*He restrains*]" flared up and he disputed with "Lavan [*White*]" and "Ya'aqov [*He restrains*]" answered and he said to "Lavan [*White*]", what is my revolution, what is my error that

Given.that you(ms)~did~Inflame After~me

you inflamed after me,

**31:37** כִּי מִשַּׁשְׁתָּ אֶת כָּל כֵּלַי מַה מָּצָאתָ מִכֹּל כְּלֵי בֵיתֶךָ שִׂים כֹּה נֶגֶד אַחַי וְאַחֶיךָ וְיוֹכִיחוּ בֵּין שְׁנֵינוּ

Given.that you(ms)~did~much~Grope At All Instrument~me What you(ms)~did~Find from~All Instrument~s House~you(ms) !(ms)~Set.in.place In.this.way Opposite Brother~s~me and~Brother~s~you(ms) and~they(m)~will~make~Convict Between Two~us

given that you quickly groped all my instruments what did you find from all the instruments of your house, set in place in this way opposite my brothers and your brothers and they will make a conviction between the two us,

**31:38** זֶה עֶשְׂרִים שָׁנָה אָנֹכִי עִמָּךְ רְחֵלֶיךָ וְעִזֶּיךָ לֹא שִׁכֵּלוּ וְאֵילֵי צֹאנְךָ לֹא אָכָלְתִּי

This Ten~s Year I With~you(fs) Ewe~s~you(ms) and~She-goat~s~you(ms) Not they~had~much~Be.childless and~Strong.One~s Flocks~you(ms) Not i~did~Eat

this twenty years I was with you, your ewes and your she-goats had not been childless and the strong ones of your flocks I did not eat,

**31:39** טְרֵפָה לֹא הֵבֵאתִי אֵלֶיךָ אָנֹכִי אֲחַטֶּנָּה מִיָּדִי תְּבַקְשֶׁנָּה גְּנֻבְתִי יוֹם וּגְנֻבְתִי לָיְלָה

Torn Not i~did~make~Come To~you(ms) I i~will~much~Err~her from~Hand~me you(ms)~will~Search.out~her Steal~ed(fs) Day and~Steal~ed(fs) Night

a torn thing I did not bring to you, I will reconcile her, from my hand you will search her out, stolen of the day and stolen of the night,

**31:40** הָיִיתִי בַיּוֹם אֲכָלַנִי חֹרֶב וְקֶרַח בַּלָּיְלָה וַתִּדַּד שְׁנָתִי מֵעֵינָי

i~did~Exist in~the~Day he~did~Eat~me Parching.heat and~Ice in~the~Night and~she~will~Toss Snooze~me from~Eye~s2~me

I existed in the day, the parching heat ate me and ice in the night and my snooze tossed from my eyes,

**31:41** זֶה לִּי עֶשְׂרִים שָׁנָה בְּבֵיתֶךָ עֲבַדְתִּיךָ אַרְבַּע עֶשְׂרֵה שָׁנָה בִּשְׁתֵּי בְנֹתֶיךָ וְשֵׁשׁ שָׁנִים בְּצֹאנֶךָ וַתַּחֲלֵף אֶת מַשְׂכֻּרְתִּי עֲשֶׂרֶת מֹנִים

This to~me Ten~s Year in~House~you(ms) i~did~Serve~you(ms) Four Ten Year in~Two Daughter~s~you(ms) and~Six Year~s in~Flocks~you(ms) and~you(ms)~will~make~Pass.over At Payment~me Ten Time~s

this is to me twenty years in your house, I served you fourteen years with two of your daughters and six years with your flocks and you changed my payment ten times,

**31:42** לוּלֵי אֱלֹהֵי אָבִי אֱלֹהֵי אַבְרָהָם וּפַחַד יִצְחָק הָיָה לִי כִּי עַתָּה

רֵיקָם שַׁלַּחְתַּנִי אֶת עָנְיִי וְאֶת יְגִיעַ כַּפַּי רָאָה אֱלֹהִים וַיּוֹכַח
אָמֶשׁ

Unless Power~s Father~me Power~s "Avraham [*Father lifted*]" and~Awe "Yits'hhaq [*He laughs*]" he~did~Exist to~me Given.that Now Emptiness you(ms)~did~much~Send~me At Affliction~me and~At Toil Palm~s2~ me he~did~See "Elohiym [*Powers*]" and~he~will~make~Convict Last.night

unless the powers of my father, the powers of "Avraham [*Father lifted*]" and the awe of "Yits'hhaq [*He laughs*]" existed for me given that now is an emptiness, you sent me my affliction and the toil of my palms, "Elohiym [*Powers*]" saw and he convicted last night,

**31:43** וַיַּעַן לָבָן וַיֹּאמֶר אֶל יַעֲקֹב הַבָּנוֹת בְּנֹתַי וְהַבָּנִים בָּנַי וְהַצֹּאן
צֹאנִי וְכֹל אֲשֶׁר אַתָּה רֹאֶה לִי הוּא וְלִבְנֹתַי מָה אֶעֱשֶׂה לָאֵלֶּה
הַיּוֹם אוֹ לִבְנֵיהֶן אֲשֶׁר יָלָדוּ

and~he~will~Answer "Lavan [*White*]" and~he~will~Say To "Ya'aqov [*He restrains*]" the~Daughter~s Daughter~s~ me and~the~Son~s Son~s~me and~ the~Flocks Flocks~me and~All Which You(ms) See~ing(ms) to~me He and~to~Daughter~s~me What i~will~ Do to~These the~Day Or to~Son~s~ them(f) Which they~did~Bring.forth

and "Lavan [*White*]" answered and he said to "Ya'aqov [*He restrains*]", the daughters are my daughters and the sons are my sons and the flocks are my flocks and all which you are seeing, he belongs to me and what will I do this day to my daughters or to their sons which they brought forth,

**31:44** וְעַתָּה לְכָה נִכְרְתָה בְרִית אֲנִי וָאָתָּה וְהָיָה לְעֵד בֵּינִי וּבֵינֶךָ

and~Now !(ms)~Walk~^ we~will~Cut~ ^ Covenant I and~You(ms) and~he~ did~Exist to~Witness Between~me and~Between~you(ms)

and now walk, we will cut a covenant, I and you and he will exist for a witness between me and you,

**31:45** וַיִּקַּח יַעֲקֹב אָבֶן וַיְרִימֶהָ מַצֵּבָה

and~he~will~Take "Ya'aqov [*He restrains*]" Stone and~he~will~Raise~ her Monument

and "Ya'aqov [*He restrains*]" took a stone and he raised her a monument,

**31:46** וַיֹּאמֶר יַעֲקֹב לְאֶחָיו לִקְטוּ אֲבָנִים וַיִּקְחוּ אֲבָנִים וַיַּעֲשׂוּ גָל
וַיֹּאכְלוּ שָׁם עַל הַגָּל

and~he~will~Say "Ya'aqov [*He restrains*]" to~Brother~s~him !(mp)~ Pick.up Stone~s and~they(m)~will~ Take Stone~s and~they(m)~will~Do Mound and~they(m)~will~Eat There Upon the~Mound

and "Ya'aqov [*He restrains*]" said to his brothers, pick up the stones, and they took the stones and they made a mound and they ate there upon the mound,

**31:47** וַיִּקְרָא לוֹ לָבָן יְגַר שָׂהֲדוּתָא וְיַעֲקֹב קָרָא לוֹ גַּלְעֵד

and~he~will~Call.out to~him "Lavan

and "Lavan [*White*]" called out to

[*White*]" "Yegar-Sa'haduta [*Fear of a witness*]" and~"Ya'aqov [*He restrains*]" he~had~Call.out to~him "Galeyd [*Mound of witness*]"

him, "Yegar-Sa'haduta [*Fear of a witness*]", and "Ya'aqov [*He restrains*]" had called out to him, "Galeyd [*Mound of witness*]",

**31:48** וַיֹּאמֶר לָבָן הַגַּל הַזֶּה עֵד בֵּינִי וּבֵינְךָ הַיּוֹם עַל כֵּן קָרָא שְׁמוֹ גַּלְעֵד

and~he~will~Say "Lavan [*White*]" the~Mound the~This Witness Between~me and~Between~you(ms) the~Day Upon So he~did~Call.out Title~him "Galeyd [*Mound of witness*]"

and "Lavan [*White*]" said, this mound is a witness between me and you today therefore, he called out his title "Galeyd [*Mound of witness*]",

**31:49** וְהַמִּצְפָּה אֲשֶׁר אָמַר יִצֶף יְהוָה בֵּינִי וּבֵינֶךָ כִּי נִסָּתֵר אִישׁ מֵרֵעֵהוּ

and~the~"Hamitspah [*Watchtower*]" Which he~did~Say he~will~Keep.watch "YHWH [*He exists*]" Between~me and~Between~you(ms) Given.that we~will~be~Hide Man from~Dysfunctional~him

and "Hamitspah [*Watchtower*]" because he said, "YHWH [*He exists*]" will keep watch between me and you given that we will be hidden, a man from his dysfunction,

**31:50** אִם תְּעַנֶּה אֶת בְּנֹתַי וְאִם תִּקַּח נָשִׁים עַל בְּנֹתַי אֵין אִישׁ עִמָּנוּ רְאֵה אֱלֹהִים עֵד בֵּינִי וּבֵינֶךָ

If you(ms)~will~Afflict At Daughter~s~me and~If you(ms)~will~Take Woman~s Upon Daughter~s~me Without Man With~us !(ms)~See "Elohiym [*Powers*]" Witness Between~me and~Between~you(ms)

if you will afflict my daughters and if you will take women in addition to my daughters, not a man with us, see, "Elohiym [*Powers*]" is a witness between me and you,

**31:51** וַיֹּאמֶר לָבָן לְיַעֲקֹב הִנֵּה הַגַּל הַזֶּה וְהִנֵּה הַמַּצֵּבָה אֲשֶׁר יָרִיתִי בֵּינִי וּבֵינֶךָ

and~he~will~Say "Lavan [*White*]" to~"Ya'aqov [*He restrains*]" Look the~Mound the~This and~Look the~Monument Which i~did~Throw Between~me and~Between~you(ms)

and "Lavan [*White*]" said to "Ya'aqov [*He restrains*]", look, this mound, and look, the monument which I threw between me and you,

**31:52** עֵד הַגַּל הַזֶּה וְעֵדָה הַמַּצֵּבָה אִם אָנִי לֹא אֶעֱבֹר אֵלֶיךָ אֶת הַגַּל הַזֶּה וְאִם אַתָּה לֹא תַעֲבֹר אֵלַי אֶת הַגַּל הַזֶּה וְאֶת הַמַּצֵּבָה הַזֹּאת לְרָעָה

Witness the~Mound the~This and~Witness the~Monument If I Not i~will~Cross.over To~you(ms) At the~

a witness is this mound and a witness is the monument, if I do not cross over this mound to you and if

Mound the~This and~If You(ms) Not you(ms)~will~Cross.over To~me At the~Mound the~This and~At the~Monument the~This to~Dysfunctional

you do not cross over this mound and this monument, to me, it is for dysfunction,

**31:53** אֱלֹהֵי אַבְרָהָם וֵאלֹהֵי נָחוֹר יִשְׁפְּטוּ בֵינֵינוּ אֱלֹהֵי אֲבִיהֶם וַיִּשָּׁבַע יַעֲקֹב בְּפַחַד אָבִיו יִצְחָק

Power~s "Avraham [*Father lifted*]" and~Power~s "Nahhor [*Snorting*]" they(m)~will~Judge Between~us Power~s Father~s~them(m) and~he~will~be~Swear "Ya'aqov [*He restrains*]" in~Awe Father~him "Yits'hhaq [*He laughs*]"

the powers of "Avraham [*Father lifted*]" and the powers of "Nahhor [*Snorting*]" will judge between us, the powers of their fathers and "Ya'aqov [*He restrains*]" was sworn in the awe of his father "Yits'hhaq [*He laughs*]",

**31:54** וַיִּזְבַּח יַעֲקֹב זֶבַח בָּהָר וַיִּקְרָא לְאֶחָיו לֶאֱכָל לָחֶם וַיֹּאכְלוּ לֶחֶם וַיָּלִינוּ בָּהָר

and~he~will~Sacrifice "Ya'aqov [*He restrains*]" Thing.of.sacrifice in~the~Hill and~he~will~Call.out to~Brother~s~him to~>~Eat Bread and~they(m)~will~Eat Bread and~they(m)~will~Stay.the.night in~the~Hill

and "Ya'aqov [*He restrains*]" sacrificed a thing of sacrifice in the hill and he called out to his brothers to eat bread and they ate bread and they stayed the night in the hill,

# Chapter 32

**32:1\*** וַיַּשְׁכֵּם לָבָן בַּבֹּקֶר וַיְנַשֵּׁק לְבָנָיו וְלִבְנוֹתָיו וַיְבָרֶךְ אֶתְהֶם וַיֵּלֶךְ וַיָּשָׁב לָבָן לִמְקֹמוֹ

and~he~will~make~Depart.early "Lavan [*White*]" in~the~Morning and~he~will~much~Kiss to~Son~s~him and~to~Daughter~s~him and~he~will~much~Kneel At~them(m) and~he~will~Walk and~he~will~Turn.back "Lavan [*White*]" to~Place~him

and "Lavan [*White*]" departed early in the morning and he kissed his sons and his daughters and he respected them and he walked and "Lavan [*White*]" turned to his place,

**32:2** וְיַעֲקֹב הָלַךְ לְדַרְכּוֹ וַיִּפְגְּעוּ בוֹ מַלְאֲכֵי אֱלֹהִים

and~"Ya'aqov [*He restrains*]" he~had~Walk to~Road~him and~they~did~Reach in~him Messenger~s "Elohiym [*Powers*]"

and "Ya'aqov [*He restrains*]" had walked to his road and messengers of "Elohiym [*Powers*]" reached him,

**32:3** וַיֹּאמֶר יַעֲקֹב כַּאֲשֶׁר רָאָם מַחֲנֵה אֱלֹהִים זֶה וַיִּקְרָא שֵׁם הַמָּקוֹם הַהוּא מַחֲנָיִם

and~he~will~Say "Ya'aqov [*He restrains*]" like~Which he~did~See~them(m) Campsite "Elohiym [*Powers*]" This and~he~will~Call.out Title the~Place the~He "Mahhanayim [*Two camps*]"

and "Ya'aqov [*He restrains*]" said just as he saw them, this is the campsite of "Elohiym [*Powers*]" and he called out the title of that place "Mahhanayim [*Two camps*]",

### 32:4 וַיִּשְׁלַח יַעֲקֹב מַלְאָכִים לְפָנָיו אֶל עֵשָׂו אָחִיו אַרְצָה שֵׂעִיר שְׂדֵה אֱדוֹם

and~he~will~Send "Ya'aqov [*He restrains*]" Messenger~s to~Face~s~him To "Esav [*Doing*]" Brother~him Land~unto "Se'iyr [*Hairy*]" Field "Edom [*Red*]"

and "Ya'aqov [*He restrains*]" sent messengers before him to "Esav [*Doing*]" his brother, unto the land of "Se'iyr [*Hairy*]", the field of "Edom [*Red*]",

### 32:5 וַיְצַו אֹתָם לֵאמֹר כֹּה תֹאמְרוּן לַאדֹנִי לְעֵשָׂו כֹּה אָמַר עַבְדְּךָ יַעֲקֹב עִם לָבָן גַּרְתִּי וָאֵחַר עַד עָתָּה

and~he~will~much~Direct At~them(m) to~>~Say In.this.way you(ms)~will~Say to~Lord~me to~"Esav [*Doing*]" In.this.way he~did~Say Servant~you(ms) "Ya'aqov [*He restrains*]" With "Lavan [*White*]" i~had~Sojourn and~i~will~Delay Until Now

and he directed them saying, in this way you will say to my lord, to "Esav [*Doing*]", in this way your servant "Ya'aqov [*He restrains*]" said, I had sojourned with "Lavan [*White*]" and I delayed until now,

### 32:6 וַיְהִי לִי שׁוֹר וַחֲמוֹר צֹאן וְעֶבֶד וְשִׁפְחָה וָאֶשְׁלְחָה לְהַגִּיד לַאדֹנִי לִמְצֹא חֵן בְּעֵינֶיךָ

and~he~will~Exist to~me Ox and~Donkey Flocks and~Servant and~Maid and~i~will~Send~^ to~>~make~Be.face.to.face to~Lord~me to~>~Find Beauty in~Eye~s2~you(ms)

and it came to pass, I have ox and donkey, flocks and servant and maid and I sent to tell to my lord to find beauty in your eyes,

### 32:7 וַיָּשֻׁבוּ הַמַּלְאָכִים אֶל יַעֲקֹב לֵאמֹר בָּאנוּ אֶל אָחִיךָ אֶל עֵשָׂו וְגַם הֹלֵךְ לִקְרָאתְךָ וְאַרְבַּע מֵאוֹת אִישׁ עִמּוֹ

and~they(m)~will~Turn.back the~Messenger~s To "Ya'aqov [*He restrains*]" to~>~Say we~did~Come To Brother~you(ms) To "Esav [*Doing*]" and~Also Walk~ing(ms) to~>~Meet~you(ms) and~Four Hundred~s Man With~him

and the messengers turned back to "Ya'aqov [*He restrains*]" saying, we came to your brother, to "Esav [*Doing*]" and also walking to meet you and four hundred men with him,

### 32:8 וַיִּירָא יַעֲקֹב מְאֹד וַיֵּצֶר לוֹ וַיַּחַץ אֶת הָעָם אֲשֶׁר אִתּוֹ וְאֶת הַצֹּאן וְאֶת הַבָּקָר וְהַגְּמַלִּים לִשְׁנֵי מַחֲנוֹת

and~he~will~Fear "Ya'aqov [*He restrains*]"

and "Ya'aqov [*He restrains*]"

restrains]" Many and~he~will~Mold
to~him and~he~will~Divide At the~
People Which At~him and~At the~
Flocks and~At the~Cattle and~the~
Camel~s to~Two Campsite~s

greatly feared and he distressed for
him and he divided the people
which were with him and the flocks
and the cattle and the camels to two
campsites,

**32:9** וַיֹּאמֶר אִם יָבוֹא עֵשָׂו אֶל הַמַּחֲנֶה הָאַחַת וְהִכָּהוּ וְהָיָה הַמַּחֲנֶה הַנִּשְׁאָר לִפְלֵיטָה

and~he~will~Say If he~will~Come
"Esav [*Doing*]" To the~Campsite
the~Unit and~he~did~make~Hit~him
and~he~did~Exist the~Campsite the~
be~Remain~ing(ms) to~Escape

and he said, if "Esav [*Doing*]" will
come to the one campsite and he hit
him then the campsite remaining
will exist for an escape,

**32:10** וַיֹּאמֶר יַעֲקֹב אֱלֹהֵי אָבִי אַבְרָהָם וֵאלֹהֵי אָבִי יִצְחָק יְהוָה הָאֹמֵר אֵלַי שׁוּב לְאַרְצְךָ וּלְמוֹלַדְתְּךָ וְאֵיטִיבָה עִמָּךְ

and~he~will~Say "Ya'aqov [*He
restrains*]" Power~s Father~me
"Avraham [*Father lifted*]" and~
Power~s Father~me "Yits'hhaq [*He
laughs*]" "YHWH [*He exists*]" the~
Say~ing(ms) To~me !(ms)~Turn.back
to~Land~you(ms) and~to~Kindred~
you(ms) and~i~will~make~Do.well~^
With~you(fs)

and "Ya'aqov [*He restrains*]" said,
the powers of my father "Avraham
[*Father lifted*]", the powers of my
father "Yits'hhaq [*He laughs*]",
"YHWH [*He exists*]" is the one
saying to me, turn back to your land
and to your kindred and I will make
it do well with you,

**32:11** קָטֹנְתִּי מִכֹּל הַחֲסָדִים וּמִכָּל הָאֱמֶת אֲשֶׁר עָשִׂיתָ אֶת עַבְדֶּךָ כִּי בְמַקְלִי עָבַרְתִּי אֶת הַיַּרְדֵּן הַזֶּה וְעַתָּה הָיִיתִי לִשְׁנֵי מַחֲנוֹת

i~did~Be.small from~All the~
Kindness~s and~from~All the~Truth
Which you(ms)~did~Do At Servant~
you(ms) Given.that in~Rod~me i~did~
Cross.over At the~"Yarden
[*Descender*]" the~This and~Now i~
did~Exist to~Two Campsite~s

I am small from all the kindnesses
and from all the truth which you did
to your servant given that with my
rod I crossed over this "Yarden
[*Descender*]" and now I exist as
two campsites,

**32:12** הַצִּילֵנִי נָא מִיַּד אָחִי מִיַּד עֵשָׂו כִּי יָרֵא אָנֹכִי אֹתוֹ פֶּן יָבוֹא וְהִכַּנִי אֵם עַל בָּנִים

!(ms)~make~Deliver~me Please from~
Hand Brother~me from~Hand "Esav
[*Doing*]" Given.that Fear~ing(ms) I
At~him Otherwise he~will~Come
and~he~did~make~Hit~me Mother
Upon Son~s

please deliver me from the hand of
my brother, from the hand of "Esav
[*Doing*]" given that I am fearing
him otherwise he will come and he
will hit me, mother upon sons,

**32:13** וְאַתָּה אָמַרְתָּ הֵיטֵב אֵיטִיב עִמָּךְ וְשַׂמְתִּי אֶת זַרְעֲךָ כְּחוֹל הַיָּם

אֲשֶׁר לֹא יִסָּפֵר מֵרֹב

and~You(ms) you(ms)~did~Say >~ make~Do.well i~will~make~Do.well With~you(fs) and~i~did~Set.in.place At Seed~you(ms) like~Sand the~Sea Which Not he~will~be~Count from~ Abundance

and you said, I will surely make it do well with you and I set your seed in place like the sand of the sea which cannot be counted out of the abundance,

**32:14** וַיָּלֶן שָׁם בַּלַּיְלָה הַהוּא וַיִּקַּח מִן הַבָּא בְיָדוֹ מִנְחָה לְעֵשָׂו אָחִיו

and~he~will~Stay.the.night There in~ the~Night the~He and~he~will~Take From the~Come~ing(ms) in~Hand~him Donation to~"Esav [*Doing*]" Brother~ him

and he stayed the night there in that night and he took from the one coming in his hand a donation for "Esav [*Doing*]" his brother,

**32:15** עִזִּים מָאתַיִם וּתְיָשִׁים עֶשְׂרִים רְחֵלִים מָאתַיִם וְאֵילִים עֶשְׂרִים

She-goat~s Hundred~s2 and~He-goat~s Ten~s Ewe~s Hundred~s2 and~ Strong.One~s Ten~s

two hundred she-goats and twenty he-goats, two hundred ewes and twenty strong ones,

**32:16** גְּמַלִּים מֵינִיקוֹת וּבְנֵיהֶם שְׁלֹשִׁים פָּרוֹת אַרְבָּעִים וּפָרִים עֲשָׂרָה אֲתֹנֹת עֶשְׂרִים וַעְיָרִם עֲשָׂרָה

Camel~s make~Suckle~ing(fs) and~ Son~s~them(m) Three~s Cow~s Four~ s and~Bull~s Ten She-donkey~s Ten~s Colt~s Ten

thirty nurse camels and their sons, forty cows and ten bulls, twenty she-donkeys, ten colts,

**32:17** וַיִּתֵּן בְּיַד עֲבָדָיו עֵדֶר עֵדֶר לְבַדּוֹ וַיֹּאמֶר אֶל עֲבָדָיו עִבְרוּ לְפָנַי וְרֶוַח תָּשִׂימוּ בֵּין עֵדֶר וּבֵין עֵדֶר

and~he~will~Give in~Hand Servant~s~ him Drove Drove to~Separated.thing~ him and~he~will~Say To Servant~s !(mp)~Cross.over to~Face~s~me and~ Wind you(mp)~will~Set.in.place Between Drove and~Between Drove

and he gave a drove in the hand of his servants, a drove by himself and he said to the servants, cross over to my face and you will set a wind in place between a drove and a drove,

**32:18** וַיְצַו אֶת הָרִאשׁוֹן לֵאמֹר כִּי יִפְגָּשְׁךָ עֵשָׂו אָחִי וּשְׁאֵלְךָ לֵאמֹר לְמִי אַתָּה וְאָנָה תֵלֵךְ וּלְמִי אֵלֶּה לְפָנֶיךָ

and~he~will~much~Direct At the~First to~>~Say Given.that he~will~ Encounter~you(ms) "Esav [*Doing*]" Brother~me and~he~did~Inquire~ you(ms) to~>~Say to~Who You(ms) and~Wherever you(ms)~will~Walk and~to~Who These to~Face~s~you(ms)

and he directed to the first saying, given that "Esav [*Doing*]" my brother will encounter you and he will inquire of you saying, to who are you, and wherever are you walking, and to who are these to your face,

**32:19** וְאָמַרְתָּ לְעַבְדְּךָ לְיַעֲקֹב מִנְחָה הִוא שְׁלוּחָה לַאדֹנִי לְעֵשָׂו וְהִנֵּה

גַם הוּא אַחֲרֵינוּ

and~you(ms)~did~Say   to~Servant~
you(ms)   to~"Ya'aqov [*He restrains*]"
Donation   She   Send~ing(fs)   to~Lord~
me   to~"Esav [*Doing*]"   and~Look
Also   He   After~us

and you will say, to your servant, to
"Ya'aqov [*He restrains*]", she is a
donation being sent to my lord, to
"Esav [*Doing*]" and look, he is also
behind us,

**32:20**   וַיְצַו גַּם אֶת הַשֵּׁנִי גַּם אֶת הַשְּׁלִישִׁי גַּם אֶת כָּל הַהֹלְכִים אַחֲרֵי
הָעֲדָרִים לֵאמֹר כַּדָּבָר הַזֶּה תְּדַבְּרוּן אֶל עֵשָׂו בְּמֹצַאֲכֶם אֹתוֹ

and~he~will~much~Direct   Also   At
the~Second   Also   At   the~Third   Also
At   All   the~Walk~ing(mp)   After   the~
Drove~s   to~>~Say   like~the~Word
the~This   you(ms)~will~Speak   To
"Esav [*Doing*]"   in~>~Find~you(mp)
At~him

and he also directed the second,
also the third, also all the ones
walking after the droves saying, in
this manner you will speak to "Esav
[*Doing*]" with your finding him,

**32:21**   וַאֲמַרְתֶּם גַּם הִנֵּה עַבְדְּךָ יַעֲקֹב אַחֲרֵינוּ כִּי אָמַר אֲכַפְּרָה פָנָיו
בַּמִּנְחָה הַהֹלֶכֶת לְפָנָי וְאַחֲרֵי כֵן אֶרְאֶה פָנָיו אוּלַי יִשָּׂא פָנָי

and~you(mp)~did~Say   Also   Look
Servant~you(ms)   "Ya'aqov [*He
restrains*]"   After~us   Given.that   he~
did~Say   i~will~much~Cover~^   Face~s~
him   in~the~Donation   the~Walk~ing(fs)
to~Face~s~me   and~After   So   i~will~
See   Face~s~him   Possibly   he~will~
Lift.up   Face~s~me

and you will also say, look, your
servant "Ya'aqov [*He restrains*]" is
behind us given that he said, I will
cover his face with the donation
walking to my face and afterward I
will see his face, possibly he will
lift up my face,

**32:22**   וַתַּעֲבֹר הַמִּנְחָה עַל פָּנָיו וְהוּא לָן בַּלַּיְלָה הַהוּא בַּמַּחֲנֶה

and~she~will~Cross.over   the~Donation
Upon   Face~s~him   and~He   he~did~
Stay.the.night   in~the~Night   the~He
in~the~Campsite

and the donation crossed over upon
his face and he stayed the night, in
that night, in the campsite,

**32:23**   וַיָּקָם בַּלַּיְלָה הוּא וַיִּקַּח אֶת שְׁתֵּי נָשָׁיו וְאֶת שְׁתֵּי שִׁפְחֹתָיו וְאֶת
אַחַד עָשָׂר יְלָדָיו וַיַּעֲבֹר אֵת מַעֲבַר יַבֹּק

and~he~will~Rise   in~the~Night   He
and~he~will~Take   At   Two   Woman~
s~him   and~At   Two   Maid~s~him
and~At   Unit   Ten   Boy~s~him   and~
he~will~Cross.over   At   Crossing
"Yaboq [*Emptying*]"

and he rose in that night and he
took two of his women and two of
his maids and eleven of his boys
and he crossed over the crossing of
the "Yaboq [*Emptying*]",

**32:24**   וַיִּקָּחֵם וַיַּעֲבִרֵם אֶת הַנָּחַל וַיַּעֲבֵר אֶת אֲשֶׁר לוֹ

and~he~will~Take~them(m)   and~he~
will~make~Cross.over~them(m)   At   the~

and took them and he made them
cross over the wadi and he made

Wadi and~he~will~make~Cross.over At Which to~him

which belongs to him cross over,

**32:25**

וַיִּוָּתֵר יַעֲקֹב לְבַדּוֹ וַיֵּאָבֵק אִישׁ עִמּוֹ עַד עֲלוֹת הַשָּׁחַר

and~he~will~be~Reserve "Ya'aqov [*He restrains*]" to~Separated.thing~him and~he~will~be~Grapple Man With~him Until >~Go.up the~Dawn

and "Ya'aqov [*He restrains*]" was reserved by himself and he was grappling a man with him until the going up of the dawn,

**32:26**

וַיַּרְא כִּי לֹא יָכֹל לוֹ וַיִּגַּע בְּכַף יְרֵכוֹ וַתֵּקַע כַּף יֶרֶךְ יַעֲקֹב בְּהֵאָבְקוֹ עִמּוֹ

and~he~will~See Given.that Not he~did~Be.able to~him and~he~will~Touch in~Palm Midsection~him and~she~will~Dislocate Palm Midsection "Ya'aqov [*He restrains*]" in~>~be~Grapple~him With~him

and he saw that he was not able and he touched with the palm of his midsection and the palm of the midsection of "Ya'aqov [*He restrains*]" was dislocated in his grappling with him,

**32:27**

וַיֹּאמֶר שַׁלְּחֵנִי כִּי עָלָה הַשָּׁחַר וַיֹּאמֶר לֹא אֲשַׁלֵּחֲךָ כִּי אִם בֵּרַכְתָּנִי

and~he~will~Say !(ms)~much~Send~me Given.that he~did~Go.up the~Dawn and~he~will~Say Not i~will~much~Send~you(ms) Given.that If you(ms)~did~much~Kneel~me

and he said, send me given that the dawn went up and he said, I will not send you unless you respect me,

**32:28**

וַיֹּאמֶר אֵלָיו מַה שְּׁמֶךָ וַיֹּאמֶר יַעֲקֹב

and~he~will~Say To~him What Title~you(ms) and~he~will~Say "Ya'aqov [*He restrains*]"

and he said to him, what is your title, and he said, "Ya'aqov [*He restrains*]",

**32:29**

וַיֹּאמֶר לֹא יַעֲקֹב יֵאָמֵר עוֹד שִׁמְךָ כִּי אִם יִשְׂרָאֵל כִּי שָׂרִיתָ עִם אֱלֹהִים וְעִם אֲנָשִׁים וַתּוּכָל

and~he~will~Say Not "Ya'aqov [*He restrains*]" he~will~be~Say Yet.again Title~you(ms) Given.that If "Yisra'el [*He turns El*]" Given.that you(ms)~did~Turn.away With "Elohiym [*Powers*]" and~With Man~s and~you(ms)~Be.able ☐

and he said, "Ya'aqov [*He restrains*]" will not be said again as your title, instead "Yisra'el [*He turns El*]" given that you turned away with "Elohiym [*Powers*]" and with men and you were able,

**32:30**

וַיִּשְׁאַל יַעֲקֹב וַיֹּאמֶר הַגִּידָה נָּא שְׁמֶךָ וַיֹּאמֶר לָמָּה זֶּה תִּשְׁאַל לִשְׁמִי וַיְבָרֶךְ אֹתוֹ שָׁם

and~he~will~Inquire "Ya'aqov [*He restrains*]" and~he~will~Say !(ms)~make~Be.face.to.face~^ Please Title~you(ms) and~he~will~Say to~What

and "Ya'aqov [*He restrains*]" inquired and he said, please tell your title, and he said, why is this you inquire for my title, and he

This you(ms)~will~Inquire to~Title~me and~he~will~much~Kneel At~him There

respected him there,

**32:31** \* וַיִּקְרָא יַעֲקֹב שֵׁם הַמָּקוֹם פְּנִיאֵל כִּי רָאִיתִי אֱלֹהִים פָּנִים אֶל פָּנִים וַתִּנָּצֵל נַפְשִׁי

and~he~will~Call.out "Ya'aqov [*He restrains*]" Title the~Place "Peni'el [*Face of El*]" Given.that i~did~See "Elohiym [*Powers*]" Face~s To Face~s and~she~will~be~Deliver Being~me

and "Ya'aqov [*He restrains*]" called out the title of the place "Peni'el [*Face of El*]" given that he said, I saw "Elohiym [*Powers*]" face to face and my being was delivered,

**32:32** וַיִּזְרַח לוֹ הַשֶּׁמֶשׁ כַּאֲשֶׁר עָבַר אֶת פְּנוּאֵל וְהוּא צֹלֵעַ עַל יְרֵכוֹ

and~he~will~Come.up to~him the~Sun like~Which he~did~Cross.over At "Peni'el [*Face of El*]" and~He Limp~ing(ms) Upon Midsection~him

and the sun came up to him just as he crossed over "Peni'el [*Face of El*]" and he was limping upon his midsection,

**32:33** עַל כֵּן לֹא יֹאכְלוּ בְנֵי יִשְׂרָאֵל אֶת גִּיד הַנָּשֶׁה אֲשֶׁר עַל כַּף הַיָּרֵךְ עַד הַיּוֹם הַזֶּה כִּי נָגַע בְּכַף יֶרֶךְ יַעֲקֹב בְּגִיד הַנָּשֶׁה

Upon So Not they(m)~will~Eat Son~s "Yisra'el [*He turns El*]" At Sinew the~Hip Which Upon Palm the~Midsection Until the~Day the~This Given.that he~did~Touch in~Palm Midsection "Ya'aqov [*He restrains*]" in~Sinew the~Hip

therefore the sons of "Yisra'el [*He turns El*]" will not eat the sinew of the hip which is upon the palm of the midsection until this day given that he touched in the palm of the midsection of "Ya'aqov [*He restrains*]" in the sinew of the hip,

# Chapter 33

**33:1** וַיִּשָּׂא יַעֲקֹב עֵינָיו וַיַּרְא וְהִנֵּה עֵשָׂו בָּא וְעִמּוֹ אַרְבַּע מֵאוֹת אִישׁ וַיַּחַץ אֶת הַיְלָדִים עַל לֵאָה וְעַל רָחֵל וְעַל שְׁתֵּי הַשְּׁפָחוֹת

and~he~will~Lift.up "Ya'aqov [*He restrains*]" Eye~s2~him and~he~will~See and~Look "Esav [*Doing*]" Come~ing(ms) and~With~him Four Hundred~s Man and~he~will~Divide At the~Boy~s Upon "Le'ah [*Weary*]" and~Upon "Rahhel [*Ewe*]" and~Upon Two the~Maid~s

and "Ya'aqov [*He restrains*]" lifted up his eyes and he saw and look, "Esav [*Doing*]" was coming and with him were four hundred men and he divided the boys upon "Le'ah [*Weary*]" and upon "Rahhel [*Ewe*]" and upon the two maids,

**33:2** וַיָּשֶׂם אֶת הַשְּׁפָחוֹת וְאֶת יַלְדֵיהֶן רִאשֹׁנָה וְאֶת לֵאָה וִילָדֶיהָ אַחֲרֹנִים וְאֶת רָחֵל וְאֶת יוֹסֵף אַחֲרֹנִים

and~he~will~Set.in.place  At  the~Maid~s  and~At  Boy~s~them(f)  First  and~At  "Le'ah [*Weary*]"  and~Boy~s~her  Behind~s  and~At  "Rahhel [*Ewe*]"  and~At  "Yoseph [*Adding*]"  Behind~s

and he set in place the maids and their boys first and "Le'ah [*Weary*]" and her boys behind and "Rahhel [*Ewe*]" and "Yoseph [*Adding*]" behind,

**33:3** וְהוּא עָבַר לִפְנֵיהֶם וַיִּשְׁתַּחוּ אַרְצָה שֶׁבַע פְּעָמִים עַד גִּשְׁתּוֹ עַד אָחִיו

and~He  he~did~Cross.over  to~Face~s~them(m)  and~he~will~self~Bend.down  Land~unto  Seven  Stroke.of.time~s  Until  >~Draw.near~him  Until  Brother~him

and he crossed over to their face and bent himself down unto the land seven times until drawing near him, until his brother,

**33:4** וַיָּרָץ עֵשָׂו לִקְרָאתוֹ וַיְחַבְּקֵהוּ וַיִּפֹּל עַל צַוָּארָו וַיִּשָּׁקֵהוּ וַיִּבְכּוּ

and~he~will~Run  "Esav [*Doing*]"  to~>~Meet~him  and~he~will~much~Embrace~him  and~he~will~Fall  Upon  Back.of.the.neck~him  and~he~will~Kiss~him  and~they(m)~will~Weep

and "Esav [*Doing*]" ran to meet him and he embraced him and he fell upon the back of his neck and he kissed him and they wept,

**33:5** וַיִּשָּׂא אֶת עֵינָיו וַיַּרְא אֶת הַנָּשִׁים וְאֶת הַיְלָדִים וַיֹּאמֶר מִי אֵלֶּה לָּךְ וַיֹּאמַר הַיְלָדִים אֲשֶׁר חָנַן אֱלֹהִים אֶת עַבְדֶּךָ

and~he~will~Lift.up  At  Eye~s2~him  and~he~will~See  At  the~Woman~s  and~At  the~Boy~s  and~he~will~Say  Who  These  to~you(fs)  and~he~will~Say  the~Boy~s  Which  he~did~Show.beauty  "Elohiym [*Powers*]"  At  Servant~you(ms)

and he lifted up his eyes and he saw the women and the boys and he said, who are these belonging to you and he said, the boys which "Elohiym [*Powers*]" showed beauty to your servant,

**33:6** וַתִּגַּשְׁןָ הַשְּׁפָחוֹת הֵנָּה וְיַלְדֵיהֶן וַתִּשְׁתַּחֲוֶיןָ

and~they(f)~will~Draw.near  the~Maid~s  They(f)  and~the~Boy~s~them(f)  and~they(f)~will~self~Bend.down

and the maids drew near, they and their boys and they bent themselves down,

**33:7** וַתִּגַּשׁ גַּם לֵאָה וִילָדֶיהָ וַיִּשְׁתַּחֲווּ וְאַחַר נִגַּשׁ יוֹסֵף וְרָחֵל וַיִּשְׁתַּחֲווּ

and~she~will~Draw.near  Also  "Le'ah [*Weary*]"  and~Boy~s~her  and~they(m)~will~self~Bend.down  and~After  he~did~be~Draw.near  "Yoseph [*Adding*]"  and~"Rahhel [*Ewe*]"  and~they(m)~will~self~Bend.down

and "Le'ah [*Weary*]" also drew near and her boys and they bent themselves down and after, "Yoseph [*Adding*]" was drawn near and "Rahhel [*Ewe*]" and they bent themselves down,

**33:8** וַיֹּאמֶר מִי לְךָ כָּל הַמַּחֲנֶה הַזֶּה אֲשֶׁר פָּגָשְׁתִּי וַיֹּאמֶר לִמְצֹא חֵן בְּעֵינֵי אֲדֹנִי

and~he~will~Say Who to~you(ms) All the~Campsite the~This Which i~did~Encounter and~he~will~Say to~>~Find Beauty in~Eye~s2 Lord~me

and he said, who belongs to you of all this campsite which I encountered, and he said, to find beauty in the eyes of my lord,

**33:9** וַיֹּאמֶר עֵשָׂו יֶשׁ לִי רָב אָחִי יְהִי לְךָ אֲשֶׁר לָךְ

and~he~will~Say "Esav [*Doing*]" There.is to~me Abundant Brother~me he~will~Exist to~you(ms) Which to~you(fs)

and "Esav [*Doing*]" said, there is an abundance belonging to me my brother, he will exist for you which is to you,

**33:10** וַיֹּאמֶר יַעֲקֹב אַל נָא אִם נָא מָצָאתִי חֵן בְּעֵינֶיךָ וְלָקַחְתָּ מִנְחָתִי מִיָּדִי כִּי עַל כֵּן רָאִיתִי פָנֶיךָ כִּרְאֹת פְּנֵי אֱלֹהִים וַתִּרְצֵנִי

and~he~will~Say "Ya'aqov [*He restrains*]" No Please If Please i~did~Find Beauty in~Eye~s2~you(ms) and~you(ms)~did~Take Donation~me from~Hand~me Given.that Upon So i~did~See Face~s~you(ms) like~>~See Face~s "Elohiym [*Powers*]" and~you(ms)~will~Accept~me

and "Ya'aqov [*He restrains*]" said, please no, please, if I found beauty in your eyes then you will take my donation from my hand since I saw your face it is like seeing the face of "Elohiym [*Powers*]" and you accepted me,

**33:11** קַח נָא אֶת בִּרְכָתִי אֲשֶׁר הֻבָאת לָךְ כִּי חַנַּנִי אֱלֹהִים וְכִי יֶשׁ לִי כֹל וַיִּפְצַר בּוֹ וַיִּקָּח

!(ms)~Take Please At Present~me Which she~did~make.be~Come to~you(fs) Given.that he~did~Show.beauty~me "Elohiym [*Powers*]" and~Given.that There.is to~me All and~he~will~Press.hard in~him and~he~will~Take

please take my present which was brought to you given that "Elohiym [*Powers*]" showed me beauty and given that there is belonging to me all and he pressed hard with him and he took,

**33:12** וַיֹּאמֶר נִסְעָה וְנֵלֵכָה וְאֵלְכָה לְנֶגְדֶּךָ

and~he~will~Say we~will~Journey and~we~will~Walk~^ and~i~will~Walk~^ to~Be.face.to.face~you(ms)

and he said, we will journey and we will walk and I will walk to be face to face with you,

**33:13** וַיֹּאמֶר אֵלָיו אֲדֹנִי יֹדֵעַ כִּי הַיְלָדִים רַכִּים וְהַצֹּאן וְהַבָּקָר עָלוֹת עָלָי וּדְפָקוּם יוֹם אֶחָד וָמֵתוּ כָּל הַצֹּאן

and~he~will~Say To~him Lord~me Know~ing(ms) Given.that the~Boy~s Tender and~the~Flocks and~the~Cattle Give.milk~ing(fp) Upon~me and~we~did~Knock~them(m) Day Unit and~they~did~Die All the~Flocks

and he said to him, my lord is knowing that the boys are tender and the flocks and the cattle giving milk are upon me and we will knock them one day and all the flocks will die,

**33:14** יַעֲבָר נָא אֲדֹנִי לִפְנֵי עַבְדּוֹ וַאֲנִי אֶתְנָהֲלָה לְאִטִּי לְרֶגֶל הַמְּלָאכָה

אֲשֶׁר לְפָנַי וּלְרֶגֶל הַיְלָדִים עַד אֲשֶׁר אָבֹא אֶל אֲדֹנִי שֵׂעִירָה

he~will~Cross.over Please Lord~me to~Face~s Servant~him and~I i~will~self~Lead~^ to~Gentle~me to~Foot the~Occupation Which to~Face~s~me and~to~Foot the~Boy~s Until Which i~will~Come To Lord~me "Se'iyr [*Hairy*]"~unto

please, my lord will cross over to the face of his servant and I will lead myself for my gentleness, for the foot of the occupation which is to my face and to the foot of the boys, until I come to my lord, unto "Se'iyr [*Hairy*]",

**33:15** וַיֹּאמֶר עֵשָׂו אַצִּיגָה נָּא עִמְּךָ מִן הָעָם אֲשֶׁר אִתִּי וַיֹּאמֶר לָמָּה זֶּה אֶמְצָא חֵן בְּעֵינֵי אֲדֹנִי

and~he~will~Say "Esav [*Doing*]" i~will~make~Set~^ Please With~you(ms) From the~People Which At~me and~he~will~Say to~What This i~will~Find Beauty in~Eye~s2 Lord~me

and "Esav [*Doing*]" said, please, I will make set with you from the people which are with me, and he said, why is this, I will find beauty in the eyes of my lord,

**33:16** וַיָּשָׁב בַּיּוֹם הַהוּא עֵשָׂו לְדַרְכּוֹ שֵׂעִירָה

and~he~will~Turn.back in~the~Day the~He "Esav [*Doing*]" to~Road~him "Se'iyr [*Hairy*]"~unto

and "Esav [*Doing*]" turned back in that day to his road unto "Se'iyr [*Hairy*]",

**33:17** וְיַעֲקֹב נָסַע סֻכֹּתָה וַיִּבֶן לוֹ בָּיִת וּלְמִקְנֵהוּ עָשָׂה סֻכֹּת עַל כֵּן קָרָא שֵׁם הַמָּקוֹם סֻכּוֹת

and~"Ya'aqov [*He restrains*]" he~had~Journey "Sukot [*Booths*]"~unto and~he~will~Build to~him House and~to~Livestock~him he~did~Do Booth~s Upon So he~did~Call.out Title the~Place "Sukot [*Booths*]"

and "Ya'aqov [*He restrains*]" had journeyed unto "Sukot [*Booths*]" and built for himself a house and for his livestock he made booths therefore, he called out the title of the place "Sukot [*Booths*]",

**33:18*** וַיָּבֹא יַעֲקֹב שָׁלֵם עִיר שְׁכֶם אֲשֶׁר בְּאֶרֶץ כְּנַעַן בְּבֹאוֹ מִפַּדַּן אֲרָם וַיִּחַן אֶת פְּנֵי הָעִיר

and~he~will~Come "Ya'aqov [*He restrains*]" "Shalem [*Complete*]" City "Shekhem [*Shoulder*]" Which in~Land "Kena'an [*Lowered*]" in~>~Come~him from~"Padan-Aram [*Field palace*]" and~he~will~Camp At Face~s the~City

and "Ya'aqov [*He restrains*]" came to "Shalem [*Complete*]", a city of "Shekhem [*Shoulder*]" which is in the land of "Kena'an [*Lowered*]", in his coming from "Padan-Aram [*Field palace*]" and he camped at the face of the city,

**33:19** וַיִּקֶן אֶת חֶלְקַת הַשָּׂדֶה אֲשֶׁר נָטָה שָׁם אָהֳלוֹ מִיַּד בְּנֵי חֲמוֹר אֲבִי שְׁכֶם בְּמֵאָה קְשִׂיטָה

and~he~will~Purchase At Parcel the~Field Which he~did~Stretch There Tent~him from~Hand Son~s "Hhamor

and he purchased a parcel of the field, where he stretched there his tent, from the hand of the sons of

[*Donkey*]" Father~of "Shekhem [*Shoulder*]" in~Hundred Qeshiytah

"Hhamor [*Donkey*]", the father of "Shekhem [*Shoulder*]", with a hundred qeshiytah,

**33:20** וַיַּצֶּב שָׁם מִזְבֵּחַ וַיִּקְרָא לוֹ אֵל אֱלֹהֵי יִשְׂרָאֵל

and~he~will~make~Stand.erect There Altar and~he~will~Call.out to~him "El-Elohey-Yisra'el [*El of the powers of Yisra'el*]"

and he caused to stand erect an altar there and he called out to him, "El-Elohey-Yisra'el [*El of the powers of Yisra'el*]",

# Chapter 34

**34:1** וַתֵּצֵא דִינָה בַּת לֵאָה אֲשֶׁר יָלְדָה לְיַעֲקֹב לִרְאוֹת בִּבְנוֹת הָאָרֶץ

and~she~will~Go.out "Dinah [*Judgement*]" Daughter "Le'ah [*Weary*]" Which she~did~Bring.forth to~"Ya'aqov [*He restrains*]" to~>~See in~Daughter~s the~Land

and "Dinah [*Judgement*]", the daughter of "Le'ah [*Weary*]" which she brought forth to "Ya'aqov [*He restrains*]", went out to see in the daughters of the land,

**34:2** וַיַּרְא אֹתָהּ שְׁכֶם בֶּן חֲמוֹר הַחִוִּי נְשִׂיא הָאָרֶץ וַיִּקַּח אֹתָהּ וַיִּשְׁכַּב אֹתָהּ וַיְעַנֶּהָ

and~he~will~See At~her "Shekhem [*Shoulder*]" Son "Hhamor [*Donkey*]" the~"Hhiw [*Village*]"~of Captain the~Land and~he~will~Take At~her and~he~will~Lay.down At~her and~he~will~much~Afflict~her

and "Shekhem [*Shoulder*]", the son of "Hhamor [*Donkey*]" the one of "Hhiw [*Village*]", the captain of the land, saw her and he took her and he laid her down and he afflicted her,

**34:3** וַתִּדְבַּק נַפְשׁוֹ בְּדִינָה בַּת יַעֲקֹב וַיֶּאֱהַב אֶת הַנַּעֲרָ וַיְדַבֵּר עַל לֵב הַנַּעֲרָ

and~she~will~Adhere Being~him in~"Dinah [*Judgement*]" Daughter "Ya'aqov [*He restrains*]" and~he~will~Love At the~Young.woman and~he~will~much~Speak Upon Heart the~Young.woman

and his being adhered with "Dinah [*Judgement*]", the daughter of "Ya'aqov [*He restrains*]", and he loved the young woman and spoke upon the heart of the young woman,

**34:4** וַיֹּאמֶר שְׁכֶם אֶל חֲמוֹר אָבִיו לֵאמֹר קַח לִי אֶת הַיַּלְדָּה הַזֹּאת לְאִשָּׁה

and~he~will~Say "Shekhem [*Shoulder*]" To "Hhamor [*Donkey*]" Father~him to~>~Say !(ms)~Take to~me At the~Girl the~This to~Woman

and "Shekhem [*Shoulder*]" said to "Hhamor [*Donkey*]" his father saying, take for me this girl for a woman,

**34:5** וְיַעֲקֹב שָׁמַע כִּי טִמֵּא אֶת דִּינָה בִתּוֹ וּבָנָיו הָיוּ אֶת מִקְנֵהוּ

**195**

בַּשָּׂדֶה וְהֶחֱרִשׁ יַעֲקֹב עַד בֹּאָם

and~"Ya'aqov [*He restrains*]" he~had~ Hear Given.that he~did~much~ Be.unclean At "Dinah [*Judgement*]" Daughter~him and~Son~s~him they~ did~Exist At Livestock~him in~the~ Field and~he~did~make~Keep.silent "Ya'aqov [*He restrains*]" Until >~ Come~them(m)

and "Ya'aqov [*He restrains*]" had heard that he defiled "Dinah [*Judgement*]" his daughter and his sons existed with his livestock in the field and "Ya'aqov [*He restrains*]" kept silent until they came,

**34:6** וַיֵּצֵא חֲמוֹר אֲבִי שְׁכֶם אֶל יַעֲקֹב לְדַבֵּר אִתּוֹ

and~he~will~Go.out "Hhamor [*Donkey*]" Father~of "Shekhem [*Shoulder*]" To "Ya'aqov [*He restrains*]" to~>~Speak At~him

and "Hhamor [*Donkey*]", the father of "Shekhem [*Shoulder*]", went out to "Ya'aqov [*He restrains*]" to speak with him,

**34:7** וּבְנֵי יַעֲקֹב בָּאוּ מִן הַשָּׂדֶה כְּשָׁמְעָם וַיִּתְעַצְּבוּ הָאֲנָשִׁים וַיִּחַר לָהֶם מְאֹד כִּי נְבָלָה עָשָׂה בְיִשְׂרָאֵל לִשְׁכַּב אֶת בַּת יַעֲקֹב וְכֵן לֹא יֵעָשֶׂה

and~Son~s "Ya'aqov [*He restrains*]" they~had~Come From the~Field like~ >~Hear~them(m) and~they(m)~will~ self~Distress the~Man~s and~he~will~ Flare.up to~them(m) Many Given.that Folly he~did~Do in~"Yisra'el [*He turns El*]" to~>~Lay.down At Daughter "Ya'aqov [*He restrains*]" and~So Not he~will~be~Do

and the sons of "Ya'aqov [*He restrains*]" had come from the field and the men were distressed and they greatly flared up given the folly he did in "Yisra'el [*He turns El*]", to lay down with the daughter of "Ya'aqov [*He restrains*]" and so he will not be done,

**34:8** וַיְדַבֵּר חֲמוֹר אִתָּם לֵאמֹר שְׁכֶם בְּנִי חָשְׁקָה נַפְשׁוֹ בְּבִתְּכֶם תְּנוּ נָא אֹתָהּ לוֹ לְאִשָּׁה

and~he~will~much~Speak "Hhamor [*Donkey*]" At~them(m) to~>~Say "Shekhem [*Shoulder*]" Son~me she~ did~Attach Being~him in~Daughter~ them(m) !(mp)~Give Please At~her to~him to~Woman

and "Hhamor [*Donkey*]" spoke with them saying, the being of "Shekhem [*Shoulder*]" my son is attached with their daughter, please give her to him for a woman,

**34:9** וְהִתְחַתְּנוּ אֹתָנוּ בְּנֹתֵיכֶם תִּתְּנוּ לָנוּ וְאֶת בְּנֹתֵינוּ תִּקְחוּ לָכֶם

and~!(mp)~self~Relate At~us Daughter~s~you(mp) you(mp)~will~Give to~us and~At Daughter~s~us you(mp)~will~Take to~you(mp)

and relate yourselves with us, you will give your daughters to us and you will take our daughters to you,

**34:10** וְאִתָּנוּ תֵּשֵׁבוּ וְהָאָרֶץ תִּהְיֶה לִפְנֵיכֶם שְׁבוּ וּסְחָרוּהָ וְהֵאָחֲזוּ בָּהּ

and~At~us you(mp)~will~Turn.back

and you will turn back with us and

and~the~Land she~will~Exist to~Face~
s~you(mp) !(mp)~Settle and~!(mp)~
Trade~her and~!(mp)~be~Hold in~her

the land will exist to your face,
settle and trade her and be held in
her,

**34:11** וַיֹּאמֶר שְׁכֶם אֶל אָבִיהָ וְאֶל אַחֶיהָ אֶמְצָא חֵן בְּעֵינֵיכֶם וַאֲשֶׁר
תֹּאמְרוּ אֵלַי אֶתֵּן

and~he~will~Say "Shekhem
[*Shoulder*]" To Father~her and~To
Brother~s~her i~will~Find Beauty in~
Eye~s2~you(mp) and~Which you(mp)~
will~Say To~me i~will~Give

and "Shekhem [*Shoulder*]" said to
her father and to her brothers, I will
find beauty in your eyes and what
you will say to me I will give,

**34:12** הַרְבּוּ עָלַי מְאֹד מֹהַר וּמַתָּן וְאֶתְּנָה כַּאֲשֶׁר תֹּאמְרוּ אֵלָי וּתְנוּ לִי
אֶת הַנַּעֲרָ לְאִשָּׁה

!(mp)~make~Increase Upon~me Many
Bride.price and~Gift and~i~will~Give~
^ like~Which you(mp)~will~Say To~
me and~!(mp)~Give to~me At the~
Young.woman to~Woman

make increase upon me a great
bride price and gift and I will give
just as you say to me and give to
me the young woman for a woman,

**34:13** וַיַּעֲנוּ בְנֵי יַעֲקֹב אֶת שְׁכֶם וְאֶת חֲמוֹר אָבִיו בְּמִרְמָה וַיְדַבֵּרוּ
אֲשֶׁר טִמֵּא אֵת דִּינָה אֲחֹתָם

and~they(m)~will~Answer Son~s
"Ya'aqov [*He restrains*]" At
"Shekhem [*Shoulder*]" and~At
"Hhamor [*Donkey*]" Father~him in~
Deceit and~they(m)~will~Speak Which
he~did~much~Be.unclean At "Dinah
[*Judgement*]" Sister~them(m)

and the sons of "Ya'aqov [*He
restrains*]" answered "Shekhem
[*Shoulder*]" and "Hhamor
[*Donkey*]" his father in deceit and
they spoke because he defiled
"Dinah [*Judgement*]" their sister,

**34:14** וַיֹּאמְרוּ אֲלֵיהֶם לֹא נוּכַל לַעֲשׂוֹת הַדָּבָר הַזֶּה לָתֵת אֶת אֲחֹתֵנוּ
לְאִישׁ אֲשֶׁר לוֹ עָרְלָה כִּי חֶרְפָּה הוּא לָנוּ

and~they(m)~will~Say To~them(m) Not
we~will~Be.able to~>~Do the~Word
the~This to~>~Give At Sister~us to~
Man Which to~him Foreskin
Given.that Disgrace She to~us

and they said to them, we will not
be able to do this word, to give our
sister to a man who has a foreskin
given that she is a disgrace to us,

**34:15** אַךְ בְּזֹאת נֵאוֹת לָכֶם אִם תִּהְיוּ כָמֹנוּ לְהִמֹּל לָכֶם כָּל זָכָר
Surely in~This we~will~be~Agree to~
you(mp) If you(mp)~will~Exist like~
That.one~us to~>~be~Circumcise to~
you(mp) All Male

surely in this we will be agreed to
you if you will exist like one of us,
all males belonging to you to be
circumcised,

**34:16** וְנָתַנּוּ אֶת בְּנֹתֵינוּ לָכֶם וְאֶת בְּנֹתֵיכֶם נִקַּח לָנוּ וְיָשַׁבְנוּ אִתְּכֶם
וְהָיִינוּ לְעַם אֶחָד

and~we~did~Give At Daughter~s~us
to~you(mp) and~At Daughter~s~
you(mp) we~will~Take to~us and~
we~did~Settle At~you(mp) and~we~
did~Exist to~People Unit

and we will give our daughters to
you and your daughters we will
take for us and we will settle with
you and we will exist for a people
unit,

**34:17** וְאִם לֹא תִשְׁמְעוּ אֵלֵינוּ לְהִמּוֹל וְלָקַחְנוּ אֶת בִּתֵּנוּ וְהָלָכְנוּ

and~If Not you(mp)~will~Hear To~us
to~>~be~Circumcise and~we~did~Take
At Daughter~us and~we~did~Walk

and if you will not hear to us, to be
circumcised, then we will take our
daughter and we will walk,

**34:18** וַיִּיטְבוּ דִבְרֵיהֶם בְּעֵינֵי חֲמוֹר וּבְעֵינֵי שְׁכֶם בֶּן חֲמוֹר

and~they(m)~will~Do.well Word~s~
them(m) in~Eye~s2 "Hhamor
[*Donkey*]" and~in~Eye~s2 "Shekhem
[*Shoulder*]" Son "Hhamor [*Donkey*]"

and their words did well in the eyes
of "Hhamor [*Donkey*]" and in the
eyes of "Shekhem [*Shoulder*]", the
son of "Hhamor [*Donkey*]",

**34:19** וְלֹא אֵחַר הַנַּעַר לַעֲשׂוֹת הַדָּבָר כִּי חָפֵץ בְּבַת יַעֲקֹב וְהוּא נִכְבָּד
מִכֹּל בֵּית אָבִיו

and~Not he~did~much~Delay the~
Young.man to~>~Do the~Word~s
Given.that he~did~Delight in~Daughter
"Ya'aqov [*He restrains*]" and~He
be~Be.heavy~ing(ms) from~All House
Father~him

and the young man did not delay to
do the words, given that he
delighted in the daughter of
"Ya'aqov [*He restrains*]" and he
was a heavy one out of all the
house of his father,

**34:20** וַיָּבֹא חֲמוֹר וּשְׁכֶם בְּנוֹ אֶל שַׁעַר עִירָם וַיְדַבְּרוּ אֶל אַנְשֵׁי עִירָם
לֵאמֹר

and~he~will~Come "Hhamor [*Donkey*]"
and~"Shekhem [*Shoulder*]" Son~him
To Gate City~them(m) and~they(m)~
will~Speak To Man~s City~them(m)
to~>~Say

and "Hhamor [*Donkey*]" came, and
"Shekhem [*Shoulder*]" his son, to
the gate of their city and they spoke
to the men of the city saying,

**34:21** הָאֲנָשִׁים הָאֵלֶּה שְׁלֵמִים הֵם אִתָּנוּ וְיֵשְׁבוּ בָאָרֶץ וְיִסְחֲרוּ אֹתָהּ
וְהָאָרֶץ הִנֵּה רַחֲבַת יָדַיִם לִפְנֵיהֶם אֶת בְּנֹתָם נִקַּח לָנוּ לְנָשִׁים
וְאֶת בְּנֹתֵינוּ נִתֵּן לָהֶם

the~Man~s the~These Complete~s
They(m) At~us and~they(m)~will~
Settle in~the~Land and~they(m)~will~
Trade At~her and~the~Land Look
Wide Hand~s2 to~Face~s~them(m) At
Daughter~s~them(m) we~will~Take to~
us to~Woman~s and~At Daughter~s~
us we~will~Give to~them(m)

these men are complete with us and
they settled in the land and they
traded with her and look, the land is
wide of hands to their face, we will
take their daughters for us for
women and we will give our
daughters to them,

**34:22** אַךְ בְּזֹאת יֵאֹתוּ לָנוּ הָאֲנָשִׁים לָשֶׁבֶת אִתָּנוּ לִהְיוֹת לְעַם אֶחָד

בְּהִמּוֹל לָנוּ כָּל זָכָר כַּאֲשֶׁר הֵם נִמֹּלִים

Surely in~This they(m)~will~Agree
to~us the~Man~s to~>~Settle At~us
to~>~Exist to~People Unit in~>~be~
Circumcise to~us All Male like~
Which They(m) be~Circumcise~ing(mp)

surely in this, the men will agree
with us to settle with us, to exist for
a people unit, with all males
belonging to us being circumcised
just as they are being circumcised,

**34:23** מִקְנֵהֶם וְקִנְיָנָם וְכָל בְּהֶמְתָּם הֲלוֹא לָנוּ הֵם אַךְ נֵאוֹתָה לָהֶם וְיֵשְׁבוּ אִתָּנוּ

Livestock~them(m) and~Possession~
them(m) and~All Beast~them(m) ?~
Not to~us They(m) Surely we~will~
be~Agree to~them(m) and~they(m)~
will~Settle At~us

their livestock and their possessions
and all their beasts, do they not
belong to us, surely we will be
agreed to them and they will settle
with us,

**34:24** וַיִּשְׁמְעוּ אֶל חֲמוֹר וְאֶל שְׁכֶם בְּנוֹ כָּל יֹצְאֵי שַׁעַר עִירוֹ וַיִּמֹּלוּ כָּל זָכָר כָּל יֹצְאֵי שַׁעַר עִירוֹ

and~they(m)~will~Hear To "Hhamor
[*Donkey*]" and~To "Shekhem
[*Shoulder*]" Son~him All Go.out~
ing(mp) Gate City~him and~they(m)~
will~be~Circumcise All Male All
Go.out~ing(mp) Gate City~him

and all going out of the gate of his
city heard "Hhamor [*Donkey*]" and
to "Shekhem [*Shoulder*]" his son
and all the males, all going out of
the gate of his city, were
circumcised,

**34:25** וַיְהִי בַיּוֹם הַשְּׁלִישִׁי בִּהְיוֹתָם כֹּאֲבִים וַיִּקְחוּ שְׁנֵי בְנֵי יַעֲקֹב שִׁמְעוֹן וְלֵוִי אֲחֵי דִינָה אִישׁ חַרְבּוֹ וַיָּבֹאוּ עַל הָעִיר בֶּטַח וַיַּהַרְגוּ כָּל זָכָר

and~he~did~Exist in~the~Day the~
Third in~>~Exist~them(m)
Be.in.misery~ing(mp) and~they(m)~will~
Take Two Son~s "Ya'aqov [*He
restrains*]" "Shimon [*Heard*]" and~
"Lewi [*Joined*]" Brother~s "Dinah
[*Judgement*]" Man Sword~him and~
they(m)~will~Come Upon the~City
Safely and~they(m)~will~Kill All
Male

and it came to pass, in the third day,
with them being in misery, then the
two sons of "Ya'aqov [*He
restrains*]", "Shimon [*Heard*]" and
"Lewi [*Joined*]", brothers of
"Dinah [*Judgement*]", took each his
sword and they came upon the city
safely and they killed all the males,

**34:26** וְאֶת חֲמוֹר וְאֶת שְׁכֶם בְּנוֹ הָרְגוּ לְפִי חָרֶב וַיִּקְחוּ אֶת דִּינָה מִבֵּית שְׁכֶם וַיֵּצֵאוּ

and~At "Hhamor [*Donkey*]" and~At
"Shekhem [*Shoulder*]" Son~him they~
did~Kill to~Mouth Sword and~
they(m)~will~Take At "Dinah
[*Judgement*]" from~House "Shekhem
[*Shoulder*]" and~they(m)~will~Go.out

and "Hhamor [*Donkey*]" and
"Shekhem [*Shoulder*]", his son,
they killed at the mouth of the
sword and they took "Dinah
[*Judgement*]" from the house of
"Shekhem [*Shoulder*]" and they

went out,

**34:27** בְּנֵי יַעֲקֹב בָּאוּ עַל הַחֲלָלִים וַיָּבֹזּוּ הָעִיר אֲשֶׁר טִמְּאוּ אֲחוֹתָם

Son~s "Ya'aqov [*He restrains*]" they~had~Come Upon the~Pierced~s and~they(m)~will~Plunder the~City Which they~did~much~Be.unclean Sister~them(m)

the sons of "Ya'aqov [*He restrains*]" had come upon the pierced ones and they plundered the city because they defiled their sister,

**34:28** אֶת צֹאנָם וְאֶת בְּקָרָם וְאֶת חֲמֹרֵיהֶם וְאֵת אֲשֶׁר בָּעִיר וְאֶת אֲשֶׁר בַּשָּׂדֶה לָקָחוּ

At Flocks~them(m) and~At Cattle~them(m) and~At Donkey~s~them(m) and~At Which in~the~City and~At Which in~the~Field they~did~Take

their flocks and their cattle and their donkeys and what was in the city and what was in the field, they took,

**34:29** וְאֶת כָּל חֵילָם וְאֶת כָּל טַפָּם וְאֶת נְשֵׁיהֶם שָׁבוּ וַיָּבֹזּוּ וְאֵת כָּל אֲשֶׁר בַּבָּיִת

and~At All Force~them(m) and~At All Children~them(m) and~At Woman~s~them(m) they~did~Capture and~they(m)~will~Plunder and~At All Which in~the~House

and all their force and all their children and their women they captured and they plundered all which was in the house,

**34:30** וַיֹּאמֶר יַעֲקֹב אֶל שִׁמְעוֹן וְאֶל לֵוִי עֲכַרְתֶּם אֹתִי לְהַבְאִישֵׁנִי בְּיֹשֵׁב הָאָרֶץ בַּכְּנַעֲנִי וּבַפְּרִזִּי וַאֲנִי מְתֵי מִסְפָּר וְנֶאֶסְפוּ עָלַי וְהִכּוּנִי וְנִשְׁמַדְתִּי אֲנִי וּבֵיתִי

and~he~will~Say "Ya'aqov [*He restrains*]" To "Shimon [*Heard*]" and~To "Lewi [*Joined*]" you(mp)~did~Disturb At~me to~>~make~Stink~me in~Settle~ing(ms) the~Land in~"Kena'an [*Lowered*]"~of and~in~"Perez [*Peasant*]"~of and~I Mortal.man~s Number and~they~did~Gather Upon~me and~they~did~make~Hit~me and~i~did~be~Destroy I and~House~me

and "Ya'aqov [*He restrains*]" said to "Shimon [*Heard*]" and to "Lewi [*Joined*]", you disturbed me, to make me stink with the ones settling the land, with the one of "Kena'an [*Lowered*]" and with the one of "Perez [*Peasant*]" and I of mortal men of a number and they will gather upon me and they will hit me and I will be destroyed, I and my house,

**34:31** וַיֹּאמְרוּ הַכְזוֹנָה יַעֲשֶׂה אֶת אֲחוֹתֵנוּ

and~they(m)~will~Say ?~like~Be.a.whore~ing(fs) he~will~Do At Sister~us

and they said, will he make our sister be like a whore,

**200**

# Chapter 35

**35:1\***

וַיֹּאמֶר אֱלֹהִים אֶל יַעֲקֹב קוּם עֲלֵה בֵית אֵל וְשֶׁב שָׁם וַעֲשֵׂה
שָׁם מִזְבֵּחַ לָאֵל הַנִּרְאֶה אֵלֶיךָ בְּבָרְחֲךָ מִפְּנֵי עֵשָׂו אָחִיךָ

and~he~will~Say "Elohiym [*Powers*]" To "Ya'aqov [*He restrains*]" !(ms)~Rise !(ms)~Go.up "Beyt-El [*House of El*]" and~!(ms)~Settle There and~!(ms)~Do There Altar to~Mighty.one the~be~See~ing(ms) To~you(ms) in~>~Flee.away~you(ms) from~Face~s "Esav [*Doing*]" Brother~you(ms)

and "Elohiym [*Powers*]" said to "Ya'aqov [*He restrains*]", rise, go up to "Beyt-El [*House of El*]" and settle there and make an altar there to the mighty one, the one appearing to you in your fleeing away from the face of "Esav [*Doing*]" your brother,

**35:2**

וַיֹּאמֶר יַעֲקֹב אֶל בֵּיתוֹ וְאֶל כָּל אֲשֶׁר עִמּוֹ הָסִרוּ אֶת אֱלֹהֵי
הַנֵּכָר אֲשֶׁר בְּתֹכְכֶם וְהִטַּהֲרוּ וְהַחֲלִיפוּ שִׂמְלֹתֵיכֶם

and~he~will~Say "Ya'aqov [*He restrains*]" To House~him and~To All Which With~him !(ms)~make~Turn.aside At Power~s the~Foreign Which in~Midst~you(mp) and~!(mp)~make~Be.clean and~!(mp)~make~Pass.over Apparel~s~you(mp)

and "Ya'aqov [*He restrains*]" said to his house and to all which were with him, remove the powers of the foreign one which is in the midst of you and be clean and change your apparels,

**35:3\***

וְנָקוּמָה וְנַעֲלֶה בֵּית אֵל וְאֶעֱשֶׂה שָּׁם מִזְבֵּחַ לָאֵל הָעֹנֶה אֹתִי
בְּיוֹם צָרָתִי וַיְהִי עִמָּדִי בַּדֶּרֶךְ אֲשֶׁר הָלָכְתִּי

and~we~will~Rise~^ and~we~will~Go.up~^ "Beyt-El [*House of El*]" and~i~will~Do There Altar to~Mighty.one the~Answer~ing(ms) At~me in~Day Trouble~me and~he~will~Exist By~me in~the~Road Which i~did~Walk

and we will rise and we will go up to "Beyt-El [*House of El*]" and I will make an altar there to the mighty one, the one answering me in the day of my trouble and he existed by me in the road which I walked,

**35:4**

וַיִּתְּנוּ אֶל יַעֲקֹב אֵת כָּל אֱלֹהֵי הַנֵּכָר אֲשֶׁר בְּיָדָם וְאֶת הַנְּזָמִים
אֲשֶׁר בְּאָזְנֵיהֶם וַיִּטְמֹן אֹתָם יַעֲקֹב תַּחַת הָאֵלָה אֲשֶׁר עִם שְׁכֶם

and~they(m)~will~Give To "Ya'aqov [*He restrains*]" At All Power~s the~Foreign Which in~Hand~them(m) and~At the~Ring~s Which in~Ear~s~them(m) and~he~will~Submerge At~them(m) "Ya'aqov [*He restrains*]" Under the~Oak Which With "Shekhem [*Shoulder*]"

and they gave to "Ya'aqov [*He restrains*]" all the powers of the foreign one which was in their hand and the rings which were in their ears and "Ya'aqov [*He restrains*]" submerged them under the oak which was with "Shekhem [*Shoulder*]",

**35:5** וַיִּסָּעוּ וַיְהִי חִתַּת אֱלֹהִים עַל הֶעָרִים אֲשֶׁר סְבִיבוֹתֵיהֶם וְלֹא רָדְפוּ אַחֲרֵי בְּנֵי יַעֲקֹב

and~they(m)~will~Journey and~he~will~Exist Dread "Elohiym [*Powers*]" Upon the~City~s Which Around~s~them(m) and~Not they~did~Pursue After Son~s "Ya'aqov [*He restrains*]"

and they journeyed and the dread of "Elohiym [*Powers*]" existed upon the cities which were around them and they did not pursue after the sons of "Ya'aqov [*He restrains*]",

**35:6** וַיָּבֹא יַעֲקֹב לוּזָה אֲשֶׁר בְּאֶרֶץ כְּנַעַן הִוא בֵּית אֵל הוּא וְכָל הָעָם אֲשֶׁר עִמּוֹ

and~he~will~Come "Ya'aqov [*He restrains*]" "Luz [*Almond*]"~unto Which in~Land "Kena'an [*Lowered*]" She "Beyt-El [*House of El*]" He and~All the~People Which With~him

and "Ya'aqov [*He restrains*]" came unto "Luz [*Almond*]" which was in the land of "Kena'an [*Lowered*]", she is "Beyt-El [*House of El*]", he and all the people which were with him,

**35:7** וַיִּבֶן שָׁם מִזְבֵּחַ וַיִּקְרָא לַמָּקוֹם אֵל בֵּית אֵל כִּי שָׁם נִגְלוּ אֵלָיו הָאֱלֹהִים בְּבָרְחוֹ מִפְּנֵי אָחִיו

and~he~will~Build There Altar and~he~will~Call.out to~the~Place "El-Beyt-El [*El of Beyt El*]" Given.that There they~did~be~Remove.the.cover To~him the~"Elohiym [*Powers*]" in~>~Flee.away~him from~Face~s Brother~him

and he built an altar there and called out to the place "El-Beyt-El [*El of Beyt El*]" given that their powers were uncovered to him in his fleeing away from the face of his brother,

**35:8** וַתָּמָת דְּבֹרָה מֵינֶקֶת רִבְקָה וַתִּקָּבֵר מִתַּחַת לְבֵית אֵל תַּחַת הָאַלּוֹן וַיִּקְרָא שְׁמוֹ אַלּוֹן בָּכוּת

and~she~will~Die "Devorah [*Bee*]" make~Suckle~ing(fs) "Rivqah [*Ensnarer*]" and~she~will~be~Bury from~Under to~"Beyt-El [*House of El*]" Under the~Great.tree and~he~will~Call.out Title~him "Alon-Bakhut [*Oak of weeping*]"

and "Devorah [*Bee*]", the nurse of "Rivqah [*Ensnarer*]", died and she was buried under "Beyt-El [*House of El*]", under the great tree and he called out his title "Alon-Bakhut [*Oak of weeping*]",

**35:9** וַיֵּרָא אֱלֹהִים אֶל יַעֲקֹב עוֹד בְּבֹאוֹ מִפַּדַּן אֲרָם וַיְבָרֶךְ אֹתוֹ

and~he~will~be~See "Elohiym [*Powers*]" To "Ya'aqov [*He restrains*]" Yet.again in~>~Come~him from~"Padan-Aram [*Field palace*]" and~he~will~much~Kneel At~him

and "Elohiym [*Powers*]" appeared to "Ya'aqov [*He restrains*]" yet again in his coming from "Padan-Aram [*Field palace*]" and he respected him,

**35:10** וַיֹּאמֶר לוֹ אֱלֹהִים שִׁמְךָ יַעֲקֹב לֹא יִקָּרֵא שִׁמְךָ עוֹד יַעֲקֹב כִּי

אִם יִשְׂרָאֵל יִהְיֶה שְׁמֶךָ וַיִּקְרָא אֶת שְׁמוֹ יִשְׂרָאֵל

and~he~will~Say to~him "Elohiym [*Powers*]" Title~you(ms) "Ya'aqov [*He restrains*]" Not he~will~be~ Call.out Title~you(ms) Yet.again "Ya'aqov [*He restrains*]" Given.that If "Yisra'el [*He turns El*]" he~will~ Exist Title~you(ms) and~he~will~ Call.out At Title~him "Yisra'el [*He turns El*]"

and "Elohiym [*Powers*]" said to him, your title is "Ya'aqov [*He restrains*]", your title will not be called yet again "Ya'aqov [*He restrains*]" instead your title will exist as "Yisra'el [*He turns El*]" and he called out his title "Yisra'el [*He turns El*]",

**35:11** וַיֹּאמֶר לוֹ אֱלֹהִים אֲנִי אֵל שַׁדַּי פְּרֵה וּרְבֵה גּוֹי וּקְהַל גּוֹיִם יִהְיֶה מִמֶּךָּ וּמְלָכִים מֵחֲלָצֶיךָ יֵצֵאוּ

and~he~will~Say to~him "Elohiym [*Powers*]" I Mighty.one "Shaddai [*My breasts*]" !(ms)~Reproduce and~ !(ms)~Increase Nation and~ Assembled.flock Nation~s he~will~ Exist From~you(ms) and~King~s from~Loins~you(ms) they(m)~will~ Go.out

and "Elohiym [*Powers*]" said to him, I am the mighty one of "Shaddai [*My breasts*]", reproduce and increase, a nation and assembled flock of nations will exist from you and kings will go out from your loins,

**35:12** וְאֶת הָאָרֶץ אֲשֶׁר נָתַתִּי לְאַבְרָהָם וּלְיִצְחָק לְךָ אֶתְּנֶנָּה וּלְזַרְעֲךָ אַחֲרֶיךָ אֶתֵּן אֶת הָאָרֶץ

and~At the~Land Which i~did~Give to~"Avraham [*Father lifted*]" and~to~ "Yits'hhaq [*He laughs*]" to~you(ms) i~will~Give~her and~to~Seed~you(ms) After~you(ms) i~will~Give At the~ Land

and the land which I gave to "Avraham [*Father lifted*]" and to "Yits'hhaq [*He laughs*]" I will give her to you, and to your seed after you I will give the land,

**35:13** וַיַּעַל מֵעָלָיו אֱלֹהִים בַּמָּקוֹם אֲשֶׁר דִּבֶּר אִתּוֹ

and~he~will~Go.up from~Upon~him "Elohiym [*Powers*]" in~the~Place Which he~did~much~Speak At~him

and "Elohiym [*Powers*]" went up from upon him in the place which he spoke to him,

**35:14** וַיַּצֵּב יַעֲקֹב מַצֵּבָה בַּמָּקוֹם אֲשֶׁר דִּבֶּר אִתּוֹ מַצֶּבֶת אָבֶן וַיַּסֵּךְ עָלֶיהָ נֶסֶךְ וַיִּצֹק עָלֶיהָ שָׁמֶן

and~he~will~make~Stand.erect "Ya'aqov [*He restrains*]" Monument in~the~ Place Which he~did~much~Speak At~ him Monument Stone and~he~will~ make~Pour Upon~her Pouring and~ he~will~Pour.down Upon~her Oil

and "Ya'aqov [*He restrains*]" made a monument stand erect in the place which he spoke to him, a monument of stone, and he poured upon her a pouring, and he poured down oil upon her,

**35:15** וַיִּקְרָא יַעֲקֹב אֶת שֵׁם הַמָּקוֹם אֲשֶׁר דִּבֶּר אִתּוֹ שָׁם אֱלֹהִים בֵּית

**203**

אֶל

and~he~will~Call.out "Ya'aqov [*He restrains*]" At Title the~Place Which he~did~much~Speak At~him There "Elohiym [*Powers*]" "Beyt-El [*House of El*]"

and "Ya'aqov [*He restrains*]" called out the title of the place which "Elohiym [*Powers*]" spoke to him there, "Beyt-El [*House of El*]",

**35:16**

וַיִּסְעוּ מִבֵּית אֵל וַיְהִי עוֹד כִּבְרַת הָאָרֶץ לָבוֹא אֶפְרָתָה וַתֵּלֶד רָחֵל וַתְּקַשׁ בְּלִדְתָּהּ

and~they(m)~will~Journey from~"Beyt-El [*House of El*]" and~he~will~Exist Yet.again Short the~Land to~>~Come "Ephrat [*Fruitful*]"~unto and~she~will~Bring.forth "Rahhel [*Ewe*]" and~she~will~much~Be.hard in~>~Bring.forth~her

and they journeyed from "Beyt-El [*House of El*]" and a short distance yet existed to come unto "Ephrat [*Fruitful*]" and "Rahhel [*Ewe*]" brought forth and she was very hard in her bringing forth,

**35:17**

וַיְהִי בְהַקְשֹׁתָהּ בְּלִדְתָּהּ וַתֹּאמֶר לָהּ הַמְיַלֶּדֶת אַל תִּירְאִי כִּי גַם זֶה לָךְ בֵּן

and~he~will~Exist in~>~make~Be.hard~her in~>~Bring.forth~her and~she~will~Say to~her the~much~Bring.forth~ing(fs) No you(fs)~will~Fear Given.that Also This to~you(fs) Son

and it came to pass with her bringing forth being hard, the midwife said to her, you will not fear given that this also is to you a son,

**35:18**

וַיְהִי בְּצֵאת נַפְשָׁהּ כִּי מֵתָה וַתִּקְרָא שְׁמוֹ בֶּן אוֹנִי וְאָבִיו קָרָא לוֹ בִנְיָמִין

and~he~will~Exist in~>~Go.out Being~her Given.that she~did~Die and~she~will~Call.out Title~him "Ben-Oni [*Son of my sorrow*]" and~Father~him he~did~Call.out to~him "Binyamin [*Son of the right hand*]"

and it came to pass with the going out of her being that she died and she called out his title "Ben-Oni [*Son of my sorrow*]" and his father called out to him "Binyamin [*Son of the right hand*]",

**35:19**

וַתָּמָת רָחֵל וַתִּקָּבֵר בְּדֶרֶךְ אֶפְרָתָה הִוא בֵּית לָחֶם

and~she~will~Die "Rahhel [*Ewe*]" and~she~will~be~Bury in~Road "Ephrat [*Fruitful*]"~unto She "Beyt-Lehhem [*House of bread*]"

and "Rahhel [*Ewe*]" died and she was buried in the road unto "Ephrat [*Fruitful*]", she is "Beyt-Lehhem [*House of bread*]",

**35:20**

וַיַּצֵּב יַעֲקֹב מַצֵּבָה עַל קְבֻרָתָהּ הִוא מַצֶּבֶת קְבֻרַת רָחֵל עַד הַיּוֹם

and~he~will~make~Stand.erect "Ya'aqov [*He restrains*]" Monument Upon Burial.place~her She Monument Burial.place "Rahhel [*Ewe*]" Yet.again

and "Ya'aqov [*He restrains*]" made a monument stand erect upon her burial place, she is the monument of the burial place of "Rahhel the~Day

[*Ewe*]" also today,

**35:21\*** וַיִּסַּע יִשְׂרָאֵל וַיֵּט אָהֳלֹה מֵהָלְאָה לְמִגְדַּל־עֵדֶר

and~he~will~Journey "Yisra'el [*He turns El*]" and~he~will~Stretch Tent~ her from~Distant to~"Migdal-Eyder [*Tower of the flock*]"

and "Yisra'el [*He turns El*]" journeyed and he stretched her tent beyond "Migdal-Eyder [*Tower of the flock*]",

**35:22** וַיְהִי בִּשְׁכֹּן יִשְׂרָאֵל בָּאָרֶץ הַהִוא וַיֵּלֶךְ רְאוּבֵן וַיִּשְׁכַּב אֶת בִּלְהָה פִּילֶגֶשׁ אָבִיו וַיִּשְׁמַע יִשְׂרָאֵל וַיִּהְיוּ בְנֵי יַעֲקֹב שְׁנֵים עָשָׂר

and~he~will~Exist in~>~Dwell "Yisra'el [*He turns El*]" in~the~Land the~She and~he~will~Walk "Re'uven [*See a son*]" and~he~will~Lay.down At "Bilhah [*Wear out*]" Concubine Father~him and~he~will~Hear "Yisra'el [*He turns El*]" and~they(m)~will~ Exist Son~s "Ya'aqov [*He restrains*]" Two Ten

and it came to pass with "Yisra'el [*He turns El*]" dwelling in that land and "Re'uven [*See a son*]" walked and he laid down with "Bilhah [*Wear out*]", the concubine of his father and "Yisra'el [*He turns El*]" heard, and the sons of "Ya'aqov [*He restrains*]" existed as twelve,

**35:23** בְּנֵי לֵאָה בְּכוֹר יַעֲקֹב רְאוּבֵן וְשִׁמְעוֹן וְלֵוִי וִיהוּדָה וְיִשָּׂשכָר וּזְבֻלוּן

Son~s "Le'ah [*Weary*]" Firstborn "Ya'aqov [*He restrains*]" "Re'uven [*See a son*]" and~"Shimon [*Heard*]" and~"Lewi [*Joined*]" and~"Yehudah [*Praised*]" and~"Yis'sas'kar [*He will lift up the wage*]" and~"Zevulun [*Residence*]"

the sons of "Le'ah [*Weary*]" were "Re'uven [*See a son*]", the firstborn of "Ya'aqov [*He restrains*]", and "Shimon [*Heard*]" and "Lewi [*Joined*]" and "Yehudah [*Praised*]" and "Yis'sas'kar [*He will lift up the wage*]" and "Zevulun [*Residence*]",

**35:24** בְּנֵי רָחֵל יוֹסֵף וּבִנְיָמִן

Son~s "Rahhel [*Ewe*]" "Yoseph [*Adding*]" and~"Binyamin [*Son of the right hand*]"

the sons of "Rahhel [*Ewe*]" were "Yoseph [*Adding*]" and "Binyamin [*Son of the right hand*]",

**35:25** וּבְנֵי בִלְהָה שִׁפְחַת רָחֵל דָּן וְנַפְתָּלִי

and~Son~s "Bilhah [*Wear out*]" Maid "Rahhel [*Ewe*]" "Dan [*Moderator*]" and~"Naphtali [*Wrestling*]"

and the sons of "Bilhah [*Wear out*]", the maid of "Rahhel [*Ewe*]" were "Dan [*Moderator*]" and "Naphtali [*Wrestling*]",

**35:26** וּבְנֵי זִלְפָּה שִׁפְחַת לֵאָה גָּד וְאָשֵׁר אֵלֶּה בְּנֵי יַעֲקֹב אֲשֶׁר יֻלַּד לוֹ בְּפַדַּן אֲרָם

and~Son~s "Zilpah [*Trickling*]" Maid "Le'ah [*Weary*]" "Gad [*Fortune*]" and~"Asher [*Happy*]" These Son~s "Ya'aqov [*He restrains*]" Which he~

and the sons of "Zilpah [*Trickling*]", the maid of "Le'ah [*Weary*]" were "Gad [*Fortune*]" and "Asher [*Happy*]", these are the

did~much.be~Bring.forth to~him in~
"Padan-Aram [*Field palace*]"

sons of "Ya'aqov [*He restrains*]"
which was brought forth to him in
"Padan-Aram [*Field palace*]",

**35:27\***    וַיָּבֹא יַעֲקֹב אֶל יִצְחָק אָבִיו מַמְרֵא קִרְיַת הָאַרְבַּע הִוא חֶבְרוֹן
אֲשֶׁר גָּר שָׁם אַבְרָהָם וְיִצְחָק

and~he~will~Come "Ya'aqov [*He
restrains*]" To "Yits'hhaq [*He
laughs*]" Father~him "Mamre [*Bitter
place*]" "Qiryat-Arba [*City of four*]"
She "Hhevron [*Company*]" Which
he~did~Sojourn There "Avraham
[*Father lifted*]" and~"Yits'hhaq [*He
laughs*]"

and "Ya'aqov [*He restrains*]" came
to "Yits'hhaq [*He laughs*]" his
father, to "Mamre [*Bitter place*]",
to "Qiryat-Arba [*City of four*]", she
is "Hhevron [*Company*]", where
"Avraham [*Father lifted*]"
sojourned there and "Yits'hhaq [*He
laughs*]",

**35:28**    וַיִּהְיוּ יְמֵי יִצְחָק מְאַת שָׁנָה וּשְׁמֹנִים שָׁנָה

and~they(m)~will~Exist Day~s
"Yits'hhaq [*He laughs*]" Hundred
Year and~Eight~s Year

and the days of "Yits'hhaq [*He
laughs*]" existed a hundred and
eighty years,

**35:29**    וַיִּגְוַע יִצְחָק וַיָּמָת וַיֵּאָסֶף אֶל עַמָּיו זָקֵן וּשְׂבַע יָמִים וַיִּקְבְּרוּ
אֹתוֹ עֵשָׂו וְיַעֲקֹב בָּנָיו

and~he~will~Expire "Yits'hhaq [*He
laughs*]" and~he~will~Die and~he~
will~be~Gather To People~him Beard
and~Plenty Day~s and~they(m)~will~
Bury At~him "Esav [*Doing*]" and~
"Ya'aqov [*He restrains*]" Son~s~him

and "Yits'hhaq [*He laughs*]"
expired and he died and he was
gathered to his people, bearded and
plenty of days, and "Esav [*Doing*]"
and "Ya'aqov [*He restrains*]", his
sons, buried him,

# Chapter 36

**36:1**    וְאֵלֶּה תֹּלְדוֹת עֵשָׂו הוּא אֱדוֹם

and~These Birthing "Esav [*Doing*]"
He "Edom [*Red*]"

and these are the birthings of "Esav
[*Doing*]", he is "Edom [*Red*]",

**36:2**    עֵשָׂו לָקַח אֶת נָשָׁיו מִבְּנוֹת כְּנָעַן אֶת עָדָה בַּת אֵילוֹן הַחִתִּי וְאֶת
אָהֳלִיבָמָה בַּת עֲנָה בַּת צִבְעוֹן הַחִוִּי

"Esav [*Doing*]" he~had~Take At
Woman~s~him from~Daughter~s
"Kena'an [*Lowered*]" At "Adah
[*Ornament*]" Daughter "Eylon
[*Strength*]" the~"Hhet [*Shattered*]"~of
and~At "Ahalivamah [*Tent of the
high place*]" Daughter "Anah
[*Answer*]" Daughter "Tsiv'ghon

Esav had taken his women from the
daughters of "Kena'an [*Lowered*]",
"Adah [*Ornament*]", the daughter
of "Eylon [*Strength*]" the one of
"Hhet [*Shattered*]" and
"Ahalivamah [*Tent of the high
place*]", the daughter of "Anah
[*Answer*]", the daughter of

[Colored]" the~"Hhiw [Village]"~of

"Tsiv'ghon [Colored]" the one of "Hhiw [Village]",

## 36:3

וְאֶת בָּשְׂמַת בַּת יִשְׁמָעֵאל אֲחוֹת נְבָיוֹת

and~At "Basmat [Spice]" Daughter "Yishma'el [El will listen]" Sister "Nevayot [Flourishings]"

and "Basmat [Spice]" the daughter of "Yishma'el [El will listen]", the sister of "Nevayot [Flourishings]",

## 36:4

וַתֵּלֶד עָדָה לְעֵשָׂו אֶת אֱלִיפָז וּבָשְׂמַת יָלְדָה אֶת רְעוּאֵל

and~she~will~Bring.forth "Adah [Ornament]" to~"Esav [Doing]" At "Eliphaz [My El is pure gold]" and~"Basmat [Spice]" she~did~ Bring.forth At "Re'uel [Companion of El]"

and "Adah [Ornament]" brought forth for "Esav [Doing]" "Eliphaz [My El is pure gold]" and "Basmat [Spice]", she brought forth "Re'u'el [Companion of El]",

## 36:5

וְאָהֳלִיבָמָה יָלְדָה אֶת יעיש (יְעוּשׁ) וְאֶת יַעְלָם וְאֶת קֹרַח אֵלֶּה בְּנֵי עֵשָׂו אֲשֶׁר יֻלְּדוּ לוֹ בְּאֶרֶץ כְּנָעַן

and~"Ahalivamah [Tent of the high place]" she~did~Bring.forth At "Ye'ush [He will assemble]" and~At "Yalam [He is concealed]" and~At "Qorahh [Bald]" These Son~s "Esav [Doing]" Which he~did~much.be~ Bring.forth to~him in~Land "Kena'an [Lowered]"

and "Ahalivamah [Tent of the high place]" brought forth "Ye'ush [He will assemble]" and "Yalam [He is concealed]" and "Qorahh [Bald]", these are the sons of "Esav [Doing]" which were brought forth to him in the land of "Kena'an [Lowered]",

## 36:6

וַיִּקַּח עֵשָׂו אֶת נָשָׁיו וְאֶת בָּנָיו וְאֶת בְּנֹתָיו וְאֶת כָּל נַפְשׁוֹת בֵּיתוֹ וְאֶת מִקְנֵהוּ וְאֶת כָּל בְּהֶמְתּוֹ וְאֶת כָּל קִנְיָנוֹ אֲשֶׁר רָכַשׁ בְּאֶרֶץ כְּנָעַן וַיֵּלֶךְ אֶל אֶרֶץ מִפְּנֵי יַעֲקֹב אָחִיו

and~he~will~Take "Esav [Doing]" At Woman~s~him and~At Son~s~him and~At Daughter~s~him and~At All Being~s House~him and~At Livestock~him and~At All Beast~him and~At All Possession~him Which he~did~Accumulate in~Land "Kena'an [Lowered]" and~he~did~Walk To Land from~Face~s "Ya'aqov [He restrains]" Brother~him

and "Esav [Doing]" took his women and his sons and his daughters and all the beings of his house and his livestock and all his beasts and all his possessions which he accumulated in the land of "Kena'an [Lowered]" and he walked to the land from the face of "Ya'aqov [He restrains]" his brother,

## 36:7

כִּי הָיָה רְכוּשָׁם רָב מִשֶּׁבֶת יַחְדָּו וְלֹא יָכְלָה אֶרֶץ מְגוּרֵיהֶם לָשֵׂאת אֹתָם מִפְּנֵי מִקְנֵיהֶם

Given.that he~did~Exist Goods~ them(m) Abundant from~>~Settle Together and~Not she~did~Be.able

given that their goods existed abundantly from their settling together and the land of their

Land Pilgrimage~s~them(m) to~>~ Lift.up At~them(m) from~Face~s Livestock~them(m)

pilgrimages was not able to lift them up from the face of their livestock,

**36:8**

וַיֵּשֶׁב עֵשָׂו בְּהַר שֵׂעִיר עֵשָׂו הוּא אֱדוֹם

and~he~will~Settle "Esav [*Doing*]" in~Hill "Se'iyr [*Hairy*]" "Esav [*Doing*]" He "Edom [*Red*]"

and "Esav [*Doing*]" settled in the hill of "Se'iyr [*Hairy*]", "Esav [*Doing*]", he is "Edom [*Red*]",

**36:9**

וְאֵלֶּה תֹּלְדוֹת עֵשָׂו אֲבִי אֱדוֹם בְּהַר שֵׂעִיר

and~These Birthing~s "Esav [*Doing*]" Father~of "Edom [*Red*]" in~Hill "Se'iyr [*Hairy*]"

and these are the birthings of "Esav [*Doing*]", the father of "Edom [*Red*]" in the hill of "Se'iyr [*Hairy*]",

**36:10**

אֵלֶּה שְׁמוֹת בְּנֵי עֵשָׂו אֱלִיפַז בֶּן עָדָה אֵשֶׁת עֵשָׂו רְעוּאֵל בֶּן בָּשְׂמַת אֵשֶׁת עֵשָׂו

These Title~s Son~s "Esav [*Doing*]" "Eliphaz [*My El is pure gold*]" Son "Adah [*Ornament*]" Woman "Esav [*Doing*]" "Re'u'el [*Companion of El*]" Son "Basmat [*Spice*]" Woman "Esav [*Doing*]"

these are the titles of the sons of "Esav [*Doing*]", "Eliphaz [*My El is pure gold*]", the son of "Adah [*Ornament*]", the woman of "Esav [*Doing*]", "Re'u'el [*Companion of El*]", the son of "Basmat [*Spice*]", the woman of "Esav [*Doing*]",

**36:11**

וַיִּהְיוּ בְּנֵי אֱלִיפַז תֵּימָן אוֹמָר צְפוֹ וְגַעְתָּם וּקְנַז

and~they(m)~will~Exist Son~s "Eliphaz [*My El is pure gold*]" "Teyman [*South*]" "Omar [*Speaker*]" "Tsepho [*Watcher*]" and~"Gatam [*Burnt valley*]" and~"Qeniz [*Hunter*]"

and the sons of "Eliphaz [*My El is pure gold*]" existed, "Teyman [*South*]", "Omar [*Speaker*]", "Tsepho [*Watcher*]" and "Gatam [*Burnt valley*]" and "Qeniz [*Hunter*]",

**36:12**

וְתִמְנַע הָיְתָה פִילֶגֶשׁ לֶאֱלִיפַז בֶּן עֵשָׂו וַתֵּלֶד לֶאֱלִיפַז אֶת עֲמָלֵק אֵלֶּה בְּנֵי עָדָה אֵשֶׁת עֵשָׂו

and~"Timna [*Withhold*]" she~had~Exist Concubine to~"Eliphaz [*My El is pure gold*]" Son "Esav [*Doing*]" and~she~will~Bring.forth to~"Eliphaz [*My El is pure gold*]" At "Amaleq [*People gathered*]" These Son~s "Adah [*Ornament*]" Woman "Esav [*Doing*]"

and "Timna [*Withhold*]" had existed as the concubine to "Eliphaz [*My El is pure gold*]", the son of "Esav [*Doing*]", and she brought forth to "Eliphaz [*My El is pure gold*]", "Amaleq [*People gathered*]", these are the sons of "Adah [*Ornament*]", the woman of "Esav [*Doing*]",

**36:13**

וְאֵלֶּה בְּנֵי רְעוּאֵל נַחַת וָזֶרַח שַׁמָּה וּמִזָּה אֵלֶּה הָיוּ בְּנֵי בָשְׂמַת אֵשֶׁת עֵשָׂו

and~These Son~s "Re'u'el [*Companion of El*]" "Nahhat [*Rest*]" and~"Zerahh [*Dawn*]" "Sham'mah [*Desolate*]" and~ "Miz'zah [*Faint*]" These they~did~ Exist Son~s "Basmat [*Spice*]" Woman "Esav [*Doing*]"

and these are the sons of "Re'u'el [*Companion of El*]", "Nahhat [*Rest*]" and "Zerahh [*Dawn*]", "Sham'mah [*Desolate*]" and "Miz'zah [*Faint*]", these sons existed of "Basmat [*Spice*]", the woman of "Esav [*Doing*]",

**36:14** וְאֵלֶּה הָיוּ בְּנֵי אָהֳלִיבָמָה בַת עֲנָה בַּת צִבְעוֹן אֵשֶׁת עֵשָׂו וַתֵּלֶד לְעֵשָׂו אֶת יְעִישׁ (יְעוּשׁ) וְאֶת יַעְלָם וְאֶת קֹרַח

and~These they~did~Exist Son~s "Ahalivamah [*Tent of the high place*]" Daughter "Anah [*Answer*]" Daughter "Tsiv'ghon [*Colored*]" Woman "Esav [*Doing*]" and~she~ will~Bring.forth to~"Esav [*Doing*]" At "Ye'ush [*He will assemble*]" and~At "Yalam [*He is concealed*]" and~At "Qorahh [*Bald*]"

and these sons existed of "Ahalivamah [*Tent of the high place*]", the daughter of "Anah [*Answer*]", the daughter of "Tsiv'ghon [*Colored*]", woman of "Esav [*Doing*]", and she brought forth to "Esav [*Doing*]" "Ye'ush [*He will assemble*]" and "Yalam [*He is concealed*]" and "Qorahh [*Bald*]",

**36:15** אֵלֶּה אַלּוּפֵי בְנֵי עֵשָׂו בְּנֵי אֱלִיפַז בְּכוֹר עֵשָׂו אַלּוּף תֵּימָן אַלּוּף אוֹמָר אַלּוּף צְפוֹ אַלּוּף קְנַז

These Chief~s Son~s "Esav [*Doing*]" Son~s "Eliphaz [*My El is pure gold*]" Firstborn "Esav [*Doing*]" Chief "Teyman [*South*]" Chief "Omar [*Speaker*]" Chief "Tsepho [*Watcher*]" Chief "Qeniz [*Hunter*]"

these are the chiefs of the sons of "Esav [*Doing*]", sons of "Eliphaz [*My El is pure gold*]", the firstborn of "Esav [*Doing*]", chief "Teyman [*South*]", chief "Omar [*Speaker*]", chief "Tsepho [*Watcher*]", chief "Qeniz [*Hunter*]",

**36:16** אַלּוּף קֹרַח אַלּוּף גַּעְתָּם אַלּוּף עֲמָלֵק אֵלֶּה אַלּוּפֵי אֱלִיפַז בְּאֶרֶץ אֱדוֹם אֵלֶּה בְּנֵי עָדָה

Chief "Qorahh [*Bald*]" Chief "Gatam [*Burnt valley*]" Chief "Amaleq [*People gathered*]" These Chief~s "Eliphaz [*My El is pure gold*]" in~ Land "Edom [*Red*]" These Son~s "Adah [*Ornament*]"

chief "Qorahh [*Bald*]", chief "Gatam [*Burnt valley*]", chief "Amaleq [*People gathered*]", these are the chiefs of "Eliphaz [*My El is pure gold*]" in the land of "Edom [*Red*]", these are the sons of "Adah [*Ornament*]",

**36:17** וְאֵלֶּה בְּנֵי רְעוּאֵל בֶּן עֵשָׂו אַלּוּף נַחַת אַלּוּף זֶרַח אַלּוּף שַׁמָּה אַלּוּף מִזָּה אֵלֶּה אַלּוּפֵי רְעוּאֵל בְּאֶרֶץ אֱדוֹם אֵלֶּה בְּנֵי בָשְׂמַת אֵשֶׁת עֵשָׂו

and~These Son~s "Re'u'el [*Companion of El*]" Son "Esav [*Doing*]" Chief

and these are the sons of "Re'u'el [*Companion of El*]", the son of

"Nahhat [*Rest*]" Chief "Zerahh [*Dawn*]" Chief "Sham'mah [*Desolate*]" Chief "Miz'zah [*Faint*]" These Chief~s "Re'u'el [*Companion of El*]" in~Land "Edom [*Red*]" These Son~s "Basmat [*Spice*]" Woman "Esav [*Doing*]"

"Esav [*Doing*]", chief "Nahhat [*Rest*]", chief "Zerahh [*Dawn*]", chief "Sham'mah [*Desolate*]", chief "Miz'zah [*Faint*]", these are the chiefs of "Re'u'el [*Companion of El*]" in the land of "Edom [*Red*]", these are the sons of "Basmat [*Spice*]", the woman of "Esav [*Doing*]",

**36:18**   וְאֵלֶּה בְּנֵי אָהֳלִיבָמָה אֵשֶׁת עֵשָׂו אַלּוּף יְעוּשׁ אַלּוּף יַעְלָם אַלּוּף קֹרַח אֵלֶּה אַלּוּפֵי אָהֳלִיבָמָה בַּת עֲנָה אֵשֶׁת עֵשָׂו

and~These Son~s "Ahalivamah [*Tent of the high place*]" Woman "Esav [*Doing*]" Chief "Ye'ush [*He will assemble*]" Chief "Yalam [*He is concealed*]" Chief "Qorahh [*Bald*]" These Chief~s "Ahalivamah [*Tent of the high place*]" Daughter "Anah [*Answer*]" Woman "Esav [*Doing*]"

and these are the sons of "Ahalivamah [*Tent of the high place*]", the woman of "Esav [*Doing*]", chief "Ye'ush [*He will assemble*]", chief "Yalam [*He is concealed*]", chief "Qorahh [*Bald*]", these are the chiefs of "Ahalivamah [*Tent of the high place*]", the daughter of "Anah [*Answer*]", the woman of "Esav [*Doing*]",

**36:19**   אֵלֶּה בְנֵי עֵשָׂו וְאֵלֶּה אַלּוּפֵיהֶם הוּא אֱדוֹם

These Son~s "Esav [*Doing*]" and~These Chief~s~them(m) He "Edom [*Red*]"

these are the sons of "Esav [*Doing*]" and these are their chiefs, he is "Edom [*Red*]",

**36:20**   אֵלֶּה בְנֵי שֵׂעִיר הַחֹרִי יֹשְׁבֵי הָאָרֶץ לוֹטָן וְשׁוֹבָל וְצִבְעוֹן וַעֲנָה

These Son~s "Se'iyr [*Hairy*]" the~"Hhor [*Cave Dweller*]"~of Settle~ing(mp) the~Land "Lothan [*Covering*]" and~"Shoval [*Leg*]" and~"Tsiv'ghon [*Colored*]" and~"Anah [*Answer*]"

these are the sons of "Se'iyr [*Hairy*]", the one of "Hhor [*Cave Dweller*]", the ones settling in the land, "Lothan [*Covering*]" and "Shoval [*Leg*]" and "Tsiv'ghon [*Colored*]" and "Anah [*Answer*]",

**36:21**   וְדִשׁוֹן וְאֵצֶר וְדִישָׁן אֵלֶּה אַלּוּפֵי הַחֹרִי בְּנֵי שֵׂעִיר בְּאֶרֶץ אֱדוֹם

and~"Dishon [*Threshing*]" and~"Eytser [*Restraint*]" and~"Dishan [*Thresher*]" These Chief~s the~"Hhor [*Cave Dweller*]"~of Son~s "Se'iyr [*Hairy*]" in~Land "Edom [*Red*]"

and "Dishon [*Threshing*]" and "Eytser [*Restraint*]" and "Dishan [*Thresher*]", these are the chiefs of the one of "Hhor [*Cave Dweller*]", the sons of "Se'iyr [*Hairy*]" in the land of "Edom [*Red*]",

**36:22**   וַיִּהְיוּ בְנֵי לוֹטָן חֹרִי וְהֵימָם וַאֲחוֹת לוֹטָן תִּמְנָע

and~they(m)~will~Exist Son~s "Lothan

and the sons of "Lothan

[Covering]" "Hhoriy [Cave dweller]"
and~"Heymam [Exterminating]" and~
Sister "Lothan [Covering]" "Timna
[Withhold]"

[Covering]" existed, "Hhoriy [Cave
dweller]" and "Heymam
[Exterminating]" and the sister of
"Lothan [Covering]" was "Timna
[Withhold]",

**36:23**

וְאֵלֶּה בְּנֵי שׁוֹבָל עַלְוָן וּמָנַחַת וְעֵיבָל שְׁפוֹ וְאוֹנָם

and~These Son~s "Shoval [Leg]"
"Alwan [Tall]" and~"Manahhat [Rest]"
and~"Eyval [Stone]" "Shepho [Bare
place]" and~"Onam [Vigorous]"

and these are the sons of "Shoval
[Leg]", "Alwan [Tall]" and
"Manahhat [Rest]" and "Eyval
[Stone]", "Shepho [Bare place]"
and "Onam [Vigorous]",

**36:24***

וְאֵלֶּה בְנֵי צִבְעוֹן וְאַיָּה וַעֲנָה הוּא עֲנָה אֲשֶׁר מָצָא אֶת הַיֵּמִם
בַּמִּדְבָּר בִּרְעֹתוֹ אֶת הַחֲמֹרִים לְצִבְעוֹן אָבִיו

and~These Son~s "Tsiv'ghon
[Colored]" and~"Ayah [Falcon]" and~
"Anah [Answer]" He "Anah
[Answer]" Which he~did~Find At
the~Hot.spring in~the~Wilderness in~
>~Feed~him At the~Donkey~s to~
"Tsiv'ghon [Colored]" Father~him

and these are the sons of "Tsiv'ghon
[Colored]", and "Ayah [Falcon]"
and "Anah [Answer]", he is the
"Anah [Answer]" who found the
hot spring in the wilderness in his
feeding of the donkeys belonging to
"Tsiv'ghon [Colored]" his father,

**36:25**

וְאֵלֶּה בְנֵי עֲנָה דִּשֹׁן וְאָהֳלִיבָמָה בַּת עֲנָה

and~These Son~s "Anah [Answer]"
"Dishon [Threshing]" and~"Ahalivamah
[Tent of the high place]" Daughter
"Anah [Answer]"

and these are the sons of "Anah
[Answer]", "Dishon [Threshing]"
and "Ahalivamah [Tent of the high
place]", the daughter of "Anah
[Answer]",

**36:26***

וְאֵלֶּה בְּנֵי דִישָׁן חֶמְדָּן וְאֶשְׁבָּן וְיִתְרָן וּכְרָן

and~These Son~s "Dishan [Thresher]"
"Hhemdan [Desireable]" and~"Eshban
[Fire of understanding]" and~"Yitran
[Remainder]" and~"Keran [Lyre]"

and these are the sons of "Dishan
[Thresher]" "Hhemdan
[Desireable]" and "Eshban [Fire of
understanding]" and "Yitran
[Remainder]" and "Keran [Lyre]",

**36:27**

אֵלֶּה בְּנֵי אֵצֶר בִּלְהָן וְזַעֲוָן וַעֲקָן

and~These Son~s "Eytser [Restraint]"
"Bilhan [Worn out]" and~"Za'awan
[Trembling]" and~"Aqan [Sharp
sighted]"

and these are the sons of "Eytser
[Restraint]", "Bilhan [Worn out]"
and "Za'awan [Trembling]" and
"Aqan [Sharp sighted]",

**36:28**

אֵלֶּה בְנֵי דִישָׁן עוּץ וַאֲרָן

and~These Son~s "Dishan [Thresher]"
"Uts [Counsel]" and~"Aran [Joyous]"

and these are the sons of "Dishan
[Thresher]", "Uts [Counsel]" and
"Aran [Joyous]",

**36:29** אֵלֶּה אַלּוּפֵי הַחֹרִי אַלּוּף לוֹטָן אַלּוּף שׁוֹבָל אַלּוּף צִבְעוֹן אַלּוּף עֲנָה

These Chief~s the~"Hhor [*Cave Dweller*]"~of Chief "Lothan [*Covering*]" Chief "Shoval [*Leg*]" Chief "Tsiv'ghon [*Colored*]" and~ Chief "Anah [*Answer*]"

these are the chiefs of the one of "Hhor [*Cave Dweller*]", chief "Lothan [*Covering*]", chief "Shoval [*Leg*]", chief "Tsiv'ghon [*Colored*]" and chief "Anah [*Answer*]",

**36:30** אַלּוּף דִּשֹׁן אַלּוּף אֵצֶר אַלּוּף דִּישָׁן אֵלֶּה אַלּוּפֵי הַחֹרִי לְאַלֻּפֵיהֶם בְּאֶרֶץ שֵׂעִיר

Chief "Dishon [*Threshing*]" Chief "Eytser [*Restraint*]" Chief "Dishan [*Thresher*]" These Chief~s the~"Hhor [*Cave Dweller*]"~of to~Chief~s~ them(m) in~Land "Se'iyr [*Hairy*]"

chief "Dishon [*Threshing*]", chief "Eytser [*Restraint*]", chief "Dishan [*Thresher*]", these are the chiefs of the one of "Hhor [*Cave Dweller*]", to their chiefs in the land of "Se'iyr [*Hairy*]",

**36:31** וְאֵלֶּה הַמְּלָכִים אֲשֶׁר מָלְכוּ בְּאֶרֶץ אֱדוֹם לִפְנֵי מְלָךְ מֶלֶךְ לִבְנֵי יִשְׂרָאֵל

and~These the~King~s Which they~ did~Reign in~Land "Edom [*Red*]" to~Face~s >~Reign King to~Son~s "Yisra'el [*He turns El*]"

and these are the kings which reigned in the land of "Edom [*Red*]" before the reigning of a king to the sons of "Yisra'el [*He turns El*]",

**36:32** וַיִּמְלֹךְ בֶּאֱדוֹם בֶּלַע בֶּן בְּעוֹר וְשֵׁם עִירוֹ דִּנְהָבָה

and~he~will~Reign in~"Edom [*Red*]" "Bela [*Swallow*]" Son "Be'or [*Burning*]" and~Title City~him "Dinhavah [*Give judgement*]"

and "Bela [*Swallow*]", the son of "Be'or [*Burning*]", reigned in "Edom [*Red*]", and the title of his city was "Dinhavah [*Give judgement*]",

**36:33** וַיָּמָת בָּלַע וַיִּמְלֹךְ תַּחְתָּיו יוֹבָב בֶּן זֶרַח מִבָּצְרָה

and~he~will~Die "Bela [*Swallow*]" and~he~will~Reign Under~him "Yovav [*Howler*]" Son "Zerahh [*Dawn*]" from~"Batsrah [*Sheepfold*]"

and "Bela [*Swallow*]" died and "Yovav [*Howler*]", the son of "Zerahh [*Dawn*]" from "Batsrah [*Sheepfold*]", reigned in place of him,

**36:34** וַיָּמָת יוֹבָב וַיִּמְלֹךְ תַּחְתָּיו חֻשָׁם מֵאֶרֶץ הַתֵּימָנִי

and~he~will~Die "Yovav [*Howler*]" and~he~will~Reign Under~him "Hhusham [*Haste*]" from~Land the~ "Teyman [*South*]"~of

and "Yovav [*Howler*]" died and "Hhusham [*Haste*]", from the land of the one of "Teyman [*South*]", reigned in place of him,

**36:35** וַיָּמָת חֻשָׁם וַיִּמְלֹךְ תַּחְתָּיו הֲדַד בֶּן בְּדַד הַמַּכֶּה אֶת מִדְיָן בִּשְׂדֵה

מוֹאָב וְשֵׁם עִירוֹ עֲוִית

and~he~will~Die "Hhusham [*Haste*]" and~he~will~Reign Under~him "Hadad [*The beloved*]" Son "Bedad [*Solitary*]" make~Hit~ing(ms) At "Midian [*Strife*]" in~Field "Mo'av [*From father*]" and~Title City~him "Awit [*Crooked*]"

and "Hhusham [*Haste*]" died and "Hadad [*The beloved*]", the son of "Bedad [*Solitary*]", the one hitting "Midian [*Strife*]" in the field of "Mo'av [*From father*]", reigned in place of him, and the title of his city was "Awit [*Crooked*]",

**36:36**

וַיָּמָת הֲדָד וַיִּמְלֹךְ תַּחְתָּיו שַׂמְלָה מִמַּשְׂרֵקָה

and~he~will~Die "Hadad [*The beloved*]" and~he~will~Reign Under~him "Samlah [*Garment*]" from~ "Masreyqah [*Choice vine*]"

and "Hadad [*The beloved*]" died and "Samlah [*Garment*]", from "Masreyqah [*Choice vine*]", reigned in place of him,

**36:37**

וַיָּמָת שַׂמְלָה וַיִּמְלֹךְ תַּחְתָּיו שָׁאוּל מֵרְחֹבוֹת הַנָּהָר

and~he~will~Die "Samlah [*Garment*]" and~he~will~Reign Under~him "Sha'ul [*Unknown*]" from~"Rehhovot [*Wide streets*]" the~River

and "Samlah [*Garment*]" died and "Sha'ul [*Unknown*]", from "Rehhovot [*Wide streets*]" of the river, reigned in place of him,

**36:38**

וַיָּמָת שָׁאוּל וַיִּמְלֹךְ תַּחְתָּיו בַּעַל חָנָן בֶּן עַכְבּוֹר

and~he~will~Die "Sha'ul [*Unknown*]" and~he~will~Reign Under~him "Ba'al-Hhanan [*Master of beauty*]" Son "Akhbor [*Mouse*]"

and "Sha'ul [*Unknown*]" died and "Ba'al-Hhanan [*Master of beauty*]", the son of "Akhbor [*Mouse*]", reigned in place of him,

**36:39**

וַיָּמָת בַּעַל חָנָן בֶּן עַכְבּוֹר וַיִּמְלֹךְ תַּחְתָּיו הֲדַר וְשֵׁם עִירוֹ פָּעוּ וְשֵׁם אִשְׁתּוֹ מְהֵיטַבְאֵל בַּת מַטְרֵד בַּת מֵי זָהָב

and~he~will~Die "Ba'al-Hhanan [*Master of beauty*]" Son "Akhbor [*Mouse*]" and~he~will~Reign Under~him "Hadar [*Honor*]" and~Title City~him "Pa'u [*Screaming*]" and~Title Woman~him "Meheythaveyl [*Favoured of El*]" Daughter "Mathreyd [*Driven*]" Daughter "Mey-Zahav [*Water of gold*]"

and "Ba'al-Hhanan [*Master of beauty*]", the son of "Akhbor [*Mouse*]", died and "Hadar [*Honor*]" reigned in place of him and the title of his city was "Pa'u [*Screaming*]" and the title of his woman was "Meheythaveyl [*Favoured of El*]", the daughter of "Mathreyd [*Driven*]", the daughter of "Mey-Zahav [*Water of gold*]",

**36:40**

וְאֵלֶּה שְׁמוֹת אַלּוּפֵי עֵשָׂו לְמִשְׁפְּחֹתָם לִמְקֹמֹתָם בִּשְׁמֹתָם אַלּוּף תִּמְנָע אַלּוּף עַלְוָה אַלּוּף יְתֵת

and~These Title~s Chief~s "Esav [*Doing*]" to~Family~s~them(m) to~Place~s~them(m) in~Title~s~them(m) Chief "Timna [*Withhold*]" Chief

and these are the titles of the chiefs of "Esav [*Doing*]", to their families, to their places, in their titles, chief "Timna [*Withhold*]", chief "Alwah

"Alwah [*Wicked*]" Chief "Yetet [*Nail*]"

[*Wicked*]", chief "Yetet [*Nail*]",

**36:41**

אַלּוּף אׇהֳלִיבׇמָה אַלּוּף אֵלָה אַלּוּף פִּינֹן

Chief "Ahalivamah [*Tent of the high place*]" Chief "Eylah [*Oak*]" Chief "Pinon [*Darkness*]"

chief "Ahalivamah [*Tent of the high place*]", chief "Eylah [*Oak*]", chief "Pinon [*Darkness*]",

**36:42**

אַלּוּף קְנַז אַלּוּף תֵּימָן אַלּוּף מִבְצָר

Chief "Qeniz [*Hunter*]" Chief "Teyman [*South*]" Chief "Mivtsar [*Fortress*]"

chief "Qeniz [*Hunter*]", chief "Teyman [*South*]", chief "Mivtsar [*Fortress*]",

**36:43**

אַלּוּף מַגְדִּיאֵל אַלּוּף עִירָם אֵלֶּה אַלּוּפֵי אֱדוֹם לְמֹשְׁבֹתָם בְּאֶרֶץ אֲחֻזָּתָם הוּא עֵשָׂו אֲבִי אֱדוֹם

Chief "Magdi'eyl [*Prince of El*]" Chief "Iyram [*Their city*]" These Chief~s "Edom [*Red*]" to~Settling~s~ them(m) in~Land Holdings~them(m) He "Esav [*Doing*]" Father~of "Edom [*Red*]"

chief "Magdi'eyl [*Prince of El*]", chief "Iyram [*Their city*]", these are the chiefs of "Edom [*Red*]" to their settlings in the land of their holdings, he is "Esav [*Doing*]", the father of "Edom [*Red*]",

# Chapter 37

**37:1**

וַיֵּשֶׁב יַעֲקֹב בְּאֶרֶץ מְגוּרֵי אָבִיו בְּאֶרֶץ כְּנָעַן

and~he~will~Settle "Ya'aqov [*He restrains*]" in~Land Pilgrimage~s Father~him in~Land "Kena'an [*Lowered*]"

and "Ya'aqov [*He restrains*]" settled in the land of the pilgrimages of his father, in the land of "Kena'an [*Lowered*]",

**37:2**

אֵלֶּה תֹּלְדוֹת יַעֲקֹב יוֹסֵף בֶּן שְׁבַע עֶשְׂרֵה שָׁנָה הָיָה רֹעֶה אֶת אֶחָיו בַּצֹּאן וְהוּא נַעַר אֶת בְּנֵי בִלְהָה וְאֶת בְּנֵי זִלְפָּה נְשֵׁי אָבִיו וַיָּבֵא יוֹסֵף אֶת דִּבָּתָם רָעָה אֶל אֲבִיהֶם

These Birthing~s "Ya'aqov [*He restrains*]" "Yoseph [*Adding*]" Son Seven Ten Year he~did~Exist Feed~ ing(ms) At Brother~s~him in~the~ Flocks and~He Young.man At Son~s "Bilhah [*Wear out*]" and~At Son~s "Zilpah [*Trickling*]" Woman~s Father~ him and~he~will~make~Come "Yoseph [*Adding*]" At Slander~them(m) Dysfunctional To Father~them(m)

these are the birthings of "Ya'aqov [*He restrains*]", "Yoseph [*Adding*]", the son of seventeen years, he existed the feeder with his brothers in the flocks and he was a young man with the sons of "Bilhah [*Wear out*]" and with the sons of "Zilpah [*Trickling*]", the women of his father, and "Yoseph [*Adding*]" brought their dysfunctional slander to their father,

**37:3** וַיִּשְׂרָאֵל אָהַב אֶת יוֹסֵף מִכָּל בָּנָיו כִּי בֶן זְקֻנִים הוּא לוֹ וְעָשָׂה לוֹ כְּתֹנֶת פַּסִּים

and~"Yisra'el [*He turns El*]" he~had~Love At "Yoseph [*Adding*]" from~All Son~s~him Given.that Son Extreme.old.age~s He to~him and~he~did~Do to~him Tunic Wrist~s

and "Yisra'el [*He turns El*]" had loved "Yoseph [*Adding*]" out of all his sons given that he was the son of his extreme old age and he made for him a tunic of wrists,

**37:4** וַיִּרְאוּ אֶחָיו כִּי אֹתוֹ אָהַב אֲבִיהֶם מִכָּל אֶחָיו וַיִּשְׂנְאוּ אֹתוֹ וְלֹא יָכְלוּ דַּבְּרוֹ לְשָׁלֹם

and~they(m)~will~See Brother~s~him Given.that At~him he~did~Love Father~them(m) from~All Brother~s~him and~they(m)~will~Hate At~him and~Not they~will~Be.able >~much~Speak~him to~Completeness

and his brothers saw that their father loved him out of all his brothers and they hated him and they were not able to speak to him for completeness,

**37:5** וַיַּחֲלֹם יוֹסֵף חֲלוֹם וַיַּגֵּד לְאֶחָיו וַיּוֹסִפוּ עוֹד שְׂנֹא אֹתוֹ

and~he~will~Visualize "Yoseph [*Adding*]" Dream and~he~will~make~Be.face.to.face to~Brother~s~him and~they(m)~will~make~Add Yet.again >~Hate At~him

and "Yoseph [*Adding*]" visualized a dream and he told it to his brothers and they continued to hate him,

**37:6** וַיֹּאמֶר אֲלֵיהֶם שִׁמְעוּ נָא הַחֲלוֹם הַזֶּה אֲשֶׁר חָלָמְתִּי

and~he~will~Say To~them(m) !(mp)~Hear Please the~Dream the~This Which i~did~Visualize

and he said to them, please hear this dream which I visualized,

**37:7** וְהִנֵּה אֲנַחְנוּ מְאַלְּמִים אֲלֻמִּים בְּתוֹךְ הַשָּׂדֶה וְהִנֵּה קָמָה אֲלֻמָּתִי וְגַם נִצָּבָה וְהִנֵּה תְסֻבֶּינָה אֲלֻמֹּתֵיכֶם וַתִּשְׁתַּחֲוֶיןָ לַאֲלֻמָּתִי

and~Look We much~Bind.up~ing(mp) Sheaf~s in~Midst the~Field and~Look she~did~Rise Sheaf~me and~Also she~did~be~Stand.erect and~Look they(f)~did~Go.around Sheaf~s~you(mp) and~they(f)~will~self~Bend.down to~Sheaf~me

and look, we were binding sheaves in the midst of the field and look, my sheaf rose and she was also standing erect and look, your sheaves went around and they bent themselves down to my sheaf,

**37:8** וַיֹּאמְרוּ לוֹ אֶחָיו הֲמָלֹךְ תִּמְלֹךְ עָלֵינוּ אִם מָשׁוֹל תִּמְשֹׁל בָּנוּ וַיּוֹסִפוּ עוֹד שְׂנֹא אֹתוֹ עַל חֲלֹמֹתָיו וְעַל דְּבָרָיו

and~they(m)~will~Say to~him Brother~s~him ?~>~Reign you(ms)~will~Reign Upon~us If >~Regulate you(ms)~will~Regulate in~us and~they(m)~will~make~Add Yet.again >~Hate At~him

and his brothers said to him, will you reign upon us or will you regulate in us and they continued to hate him because of his dreams and because of his words,

Upon Dream~s~him and~Upon and~
Word~s~him

37:9

וַיַּחֲלֹם עוֹד חֲלוֹם אַחֵר וַיְסַפֵּר אֹתוֹ לְאֶחָיו וַיֹּאמֶר הִנֵּה חָלַמְתִּי
חֲלוֹם עוֹד וְהִנֵּה הַשֶּׁמֶשׁ וְהַיָּרֵחַ וְאַחַד עָשָׂר כּוֹכָבִים מִשְׁתַּחֲוִים
לִי

and~he~will~Visualize Yet.again Dream Other and~he~will~much~Count At~ him to~Brother~s~him and~he~will~ Say Look i~did~Visualize Dream Yet.again and~Look the~Sun and~the~ Moon and~Unit Ten Star~s self~ Bend.down~ing(mp) to~me

and he visualized yet again another dream and he recounted him to his brothers and he said, look, I visualized a dream yet again and look, the sun and the moon and eleven stars were bending themselves down to me,

37:10

וַיְסַפֵּר אֶל אָבִיו וְאֶל אֶחָיו וַיִּגְעַר בּוֹ אָבִיו וַיֹּאמֶר לוֹ מָה
הַחֲלוֹם הַזֶּה אֲשֶׁר חָלָמְתָּ הֲבוֹא נָבוֹא אֲנִי וְאִמְּךָ וְאַחֶיךָ
לְהִשְׁתַּחֲוֹת לְךָ אָרְצָה

and~he~will~much~Count To Father~ him and~To Brother~s~him and~he~ will~Rebuke in~him Father~him and~ he~will~Say to~him What the~Dream the~This Which you(ms)~did~Visualize ?~>~Come we~will~Come I and~ Mother~you(ms) and~Brother~s~you(ms) to~>~self~Bend.down to~you(ms) Land~unto

and he recounted it to his father and to his brothers and his father rebuked him and he said to him, what is this dream which you visualized, will I and your mother and your brothers come to bend ourselves down to you unto the land,

37:11

וַיְקַנְאוּ בוֹ אֶחָיו וְאָבִיו שָׁמַר אֶת הַדָּבָר

and~they(m)~will~much~Be.zealous in~ him Brother~s~him and~Father~him he~had~Guard At the~Word

and his brothers were envious with him and his father had guarded the word,

37:12

וַיֵּלְכוּ אֶחָיו לִרְעוֹת אֶת צֹאן אֲבִיהֶם בִּשְׁכֶם

and~they(m)~will~Walk Brother~s~him to~>~Feed At Flocks Father~them(m) in~"Shekhem [Shoulder]"

and his brothers walked to feed the flocks of their father in "Shekhem [Shoulder]",

37:13

וַיֹּאמֶר יִשְׂרָאֵל אֶל יוֹסֵף הֲלוֹא אַחֶיךָ רֹעִים בִּשְׁכֶם לְכָה
וְאֶשְׁלָחֲךָ אֲלֵיהֶם וַיֹּאמֶר לוֹ הִנֵּנִי

and~he~will~Say "Yisra'el [He turns El]" To "Yoseph [Adding]" ?~Not Brother~s~you(ms) Feed~ing(mp) in~ "Shekhem [Shoulder]" !(ms)~Walk~^ and~i~will~Send~you(ms) To~them(m) and~he~will~Say to~him Look~me

and "Yisra'el [He turns El]" said to "Yoseph [Adding]", are your brothers not feeding in "Shekhem [Shoulder]", walk and I will send you to them, and he said to him, here am I,

**37:14** וַיֹּאמֶר לוֹ לֶךְ נָא רְאֵה אֶת שְׁלוֹם אַחֶיךָ וְאֶת שְׁלוֹם הַצֹּאן וַהֲשִׁבֵנִי דָּבָר וַיִּשְׁלָחֵהוּ מֵעֵמֶק חֶבְרוֹן וַיָּבֹא שְׁכֶמָה

and~he~will~Say to~him !(ms)~Walk Please !(ms)~See At Completeness Brother~s~you(ms) and~At Completeness the~Flocks and~!(ms)~make~Turn.back~me Word and~he~will~Send~him from~Valley "Hhevron [*Company*]" and~he~will~Come "Shekhem [*Shoulder*]"~unto

and he said to him, please walk, see the completeness of your brothers and the completeness of the flocks and return to me a word, and he sent him from the valley of "Hhevron [*Company*]" and he came unto "Shekhem [*Shoulder*]",

**37:15** וַיִּמְצָאֵהוּ אִישׁ וְהִנֵּה תֹעֶה בַּשָּׂדֶה וַיִּשְׁאָלֵהוּ הָאִישׁ לֵאמֹר מַה תְּבַקֵּשׁ

and~he~will~Find~him Man and~Look Wander~ing(ms) in~Field and~he~will~Inquire~him the~Man to~>~Say What you(ms)~will~much~Search.out

and a man found him and look, he was wandering in the field and the man inquired of him saying, what are you searching out,

**37:16** וַיֹּאמֶר אֶת אַחַי אָנֹכִי מְבַקֵּשׁ הַגִּידָה נָּא לִי אֵיפֹה הֵם רֹעִים

and~he~will~Say At Brother~s~me I much~Search.out~ing(ms) !(ms)~make~Be.face.to.face~^ Please to~me Where They(m) Feed~ing(mp)

and he said, I am searching out my brothers, please tell me where are they feeding,

**37:17** וַיֹּאמֶר הָאִישׁ נָסְעוּ מִזֶּה כִּי שָׁמַעְתִּי אֹמְרִים נֵלְכָה דֹּתָיְנָה וַיֵּלֶךְ יוֹסֵף אַחַר אֶחָיו וַיִּמְצָאֵם בְּדֹתָן

and~he~will~Say the~Man they~did~Journey from~This Given.that i~did~Hear Say~ing(mp) we~will~Walk~^ "Dotan [*Well*]"~unto and~he~will~Walk "Yoseph [*Adding*]" After Brother~s~him and~he~will~Find~them(m) in~"Dotan [*Well*]"

and the man said, they journeyed from this one given that I heard them saying, we will walk unto "Dotan [*Well*]", and "Yoseph [*Adding*]" walked after his brothers and he found them in "Dotan [*Well*]",

**37:18** וַיִּרְאוּ אֹתוֹ מֵרָחֹק וּבְטֶרֶם יִקְרַב אֲלֵיהֶם וַיִּתְנַכְּלוּ אֹתוֹ לַהֲמִיתוֹ

and~they(m)~will~See At~him from~Distance and~in~Before he~will~Come.near To~them(m) and~they(m)~will~self~Be.crafty At~him to~>~make~Die~him

and they saw him from a distance and before he came near to them, and they acted craftily with him to kill him,

**37:19** וַיֹּאמְרוּ אִישׁ אֶל אָחִיו הִנֵּה בַּעַל הַחֲלֹמוֹת הַלָּזֶה בָּא

and~they(m)~will~Say Man To Brother~him Look Master the~Dream~s This.one Come~ing(ms)

and they said, each to his brother, look, this master of the dreams is coming,

**37:20** וְעַתָּה לְכוּ וְנַהַרְגֵהוּ וְנַשְׁלִכֵהוּ בְּאַחַד הַבֹּרוֹת וְאָמַרְנוּ חַיָּה רָעָה
אֲכָלָתְהוּ וְנִרְאֶה מַה יִּהְיוּ חֲלֹמֹתָיו

and~Now !(mp)~Walk and~we~will~
Kill~him and~we~will~make~
Throw.out~him in~Unit the~Cistern~s
and~we~did~Say Life Dysfunctional
she~had~Eat~him and~we~will~See~^
What they(m)~will~Exist Dream~s~him

and now walk and we will kill him
and we will cause him to be thrown
out in one of the cisterns and we
will say a dysfunctional living one
had eaten him and we will see how
his dreams will exist,

**37:21*** וַיִּשְׁמַע רְאוּבֵן וַיַּצִּלֵהוּ מִיָּדָם וַיֹּאמֶר לֹא נַכֶּנּוּ נָפֶשׁ

and~he~will~Hear "Re'uven [*See a
son*]" and~he~will~make~Deliver~him
from~Hand~them(m) and~he~will~Say
Not we~will~make~Hit~him Being

and "Re'uven [*See a son*]" heard
and he delivered him from their
hand and he said, we will not hit his
being,

**37:22** וַיֹּאמֶר אֲלֵהֶם רְאוּבֵן אַל תִּשְׁפְּכוּ דָם הַשְׁלִיכוּ אֹתוֹ אֶל הַבּוֹר
הַזֶּה אֲשֶׁר בַּמִּדְבָּר וְיָד אַל תִּשְׁלְחוּ בוֹ לְמַעַן הַצִּיל אֹתוֹ מִיָּדָם
לַהֲשִׁיבוֹ אֶל אָבִיו

and~he~will~Say To~them(m) "Re'uven
[*See a son*]" No you(mp)~will~
Pour.out Blood !(mp)~make~Throw.out
At~him To the~Cistern the~This
Which in~the~Wilderness and~Hand
No you(mp)~will~Send in~him to~
That >~make~Deliver At~him from~
Hand~them(m) to~>~make~Turn.back~
him To Father~him

and "Re'uven [*See a son*]" said to
them, you will not pour out the
blood, throw him out to this cistern
which is in the wilderness and you
will not send a hand in him, to
deliver him from their hand to
return him to his father,

**37:23** וַיְהִי כַּאֲשֶׁר בָּא יוֹסֵף אֶל אֶחָיו וַיַּפְשִׁיטוּ אֶת יוֹסֵף אֶת כֻּתָּנְתּוֹ
אֶת כְּתֹנֶת הַפַּסִּים אֲשֶׁר עָלָיו

and~he~will~Exist like~Which he~did~
Come "Yoseph [*Adding*]" To
Brother~s~him and~they(m)~will~make~
Peel.off At "Yoseph [*Adding*]" At
Tunic~him At Tunic the~Wrist~s
Which Upon~him

and it came to pass just as "Yoseph
[*Adding*]" came to his brothers that
they peeled off "Yoseph [*Adding*]",
his tunic, the tunic of the wrists
which was upon him,

**37:24** וַיִּקָּחֻהוּ וַיַּשְׁלִכוּ אֹתוֹ הַבֹּרָה וְהַבּוֹר רֵק אֵין בּוֹ מָיִם

and~they(m)~will~Take~him and~
they(m)~will~make~Throw.out At~him
the~Cistern~unto and~the~Cistern
Empty Without in~him Water~s2

and they took him and they threw
him out unto the cistern and the
cistern was empty, without water in
him,

**37:25** וַיֵּשְׁבוּ לֶאֱכָל לֶחֶם וַיִּשְׂאוּ עֵינֵיהֶם וַיִּרְאוּ וְהִנֵּה אֹרְחַת
יִשְׁמְעֵאלִים בָּאָה מִגִּלְעָד וּגְמַלֵּיהֶם נֹשְׂאִים נְכֹאת וּצְרִי וָלֹט

הוֹלְכִים לְהוֹרִיד מִצְרָיְמָה

and~they(m)~will~Settle to~>~Eat Bread and~they(m)~will~Lift.up Eye~s2~them(m) and~they(m)~will~See and~Look Caravan "Yishma'el [*El will listen*]"~s Come~ing(fs) from~ "Gil'ad [*Mound of witness*]" and~ Camel~s~them(m) Lift.up~ing(mp) Spice and~Balm and~Myrrh Walk~ing(mp) to~>~make~Go.down "Mitsrayim [*Troubles*]"~unto

and they settled to eat bread and they lifted up their eyes and they saw and look, a caravan of the ones of "Yishma'el [*El will listen*]" was coming from "Gil'ad [*Mound of witness*]" and their camels were lifting up spice and balm and myrrh, walking to go down unto "Mitsrayim [*Troubles*]",

**37:26** וַיֹּאמֶר יְהוּדָה אֶל אֶחָיו מַה בֶּצַע כִּי נַהֲרֹג אֶת אָחִינוּ וְכִסִּינוּ אֶת דָּמוֹ

and~he~will~Say "Yehudah [*Praised*]" To Brother~s~him What Profit Given.that we~will~Kill At Brother~us and~we~did~Conceal At Blood~him

and "Yehudah [*Praised*]" said to his brothers, what is the profit given that we kill our brother and we conceal his blood,

**37:27** לְכוּ וְנִמְכְּרֶנּוּ לַיִּשְׁמְעֵאלִים וְיָדֵנוּ אַל תְּהִי בוֹ כִּי אָחִינוּ בְשָׂרֵנוּ הוּא וַיִּשְׁמְעוּ אֶחָיו

!(mp)~Walk and~we~will~Sell~him to~ "Yishma'el [*El will listen*]"~s and~ Hand~us No she~will~Exist in~him Given.that Brother~us Flesh~us He and~they(m)~will~Hear Brother~s~him

walk and we will sell him to the ones of "Yishma'el [*El will listen*]" and our hand will not exist in him given that he is our brother, our flesh and his brothers heard,

**37:28** וַיַּעַבְרוּ אֲנָשִׁים מִדְיָנִים סֹחֲרִים וַיִּמְשְׁכוּ וַיַּעֲלוּ אֶת יוֹסֵף מִן הַבּוֹר וַיִּמְכְּרוּ אֶת יוֹסֵף לַיִּשְׁמְעֵאלִים בְּעֶשְׂרִים כָּסֶף וַיָּבִיאוּ אֶת יוֹסֵף מִצְרָיְמָה

and~they(m)~will~Cross.over Man~s "Midian [*Strife*]"~s Trade~ing(mp) and~they(m)~will~Draw and~they(m)~ will~make~Go.up At "Yoseph [*Adding*]" From the~Cistern and~ they(m)~will~Sell At "Yoseph [*Adding*]" to~"Yishma'el [*El will listen*]"~s in~Ten~s Silver and~ they(m)~will~make~Come At "Yoseph [*Adding*]" "Mitsrayim [*Troubles*]"~unto

and the men, traders of "Midian [*Strife*]", crossed over and they drew and they brought up "Yoseph [*Adding*]" from the cistern and they sold "Yoseph [*Adding*]" to the ones of "Yishma'el [*El will listen*]" with twenty silver and they brought "Yoseph [*Adding*]" unto "Mitsrayim [*Troubles*]",

**37:29** וַיָּשָׁב רְאוּבֵן אֶל הַבּוֹר וְהִנֵּה אֵין יוֹסֵף בַּבּוֹר וַיִּקְרַע אֶת בְּגָדָיו

and~he~will~Turn.back "Re'uven [*See a son*]" To the~Cistern and~Look Without "Yoseph [*Adding*]" in~the~ Cistern and~he~will~Tear At

and "Re'uven [*See a son*]" turned back to the cistern and look, "Yoseph [*Adding*]" was not in the cistern and he tore his garment,

Garment~s~him

**37:30** וַיָּשָׁב אֶל אֶחָיו וַיֹּאמַר הַיֶּלֶד אֵינֶנּוּ וַאֲנִי אָנָה אֲנִי בָא

and~he~will~Turn.back  To  Brother~s~him  and~he~will~Say  the~Boy  Without~us  and~I  Wherever  I  Come~ing(ms)

and he turned back to his brothers and he said, the boy is not with us and I, wherever am I coming,

**37:31** וַיִּקְחוּ אֶת כְּתֹנֶת יוֹסֵף וַיִּשְׁחֲטוּ שְׂעִיר עִזִּים וַיִּטְבְּלוּ אֶת הַכֻּתֹּנֶת בַּדָּם

and~they(m)~will~Take  At  Tunic  "Yoseph  [Adding]"  and~they(m)~will~Slay  Goat  She-goat~s  and~they(m)~will~Dip  At  the~Tunic  in~the~Blood

and they took the tunic of "Yoseph [Adding]" and they slew a she-goat and they dipped the tunic in the blood,

**37:32** וַיְשַׁלְּחוּ אֶת כְּתֹנֶת הַפַּסִּים וַיָּבִיאוּ אֶל אֲבִיהֶם וַיֹּאמְרוּ זֹאת מָצָאנוּ הַכֶּר נָא הַכְּתֹנֶת בִּנְךָ הִוא אִם לֹא

and~they(m)~will~much~Send  At  Tunic  the~Wrist  and~they(m)~will~make~Come  To  Father~them(m)  and~they(m)~will~Say  This  we~did~Find  !(ms)~make~Recognize  Please  the~Tunic  Son~you(ms)  She  If  Not

and they sent the tunic of the wrist and they brought to their father and they said, we found this, please recognize the tunic of your son, is she or not,

**37:33** וַיַּכִּירָהּ וַיֹּאמֶר כְּתֹנֶת בְּנִי חַיָּה רָעָה אֲכָלָתְהוּ טָרֹף טֹרַף יוֹסֵף

and~he~will~make~Recognize~her  and~he~will~Say  Tunic  Son~me  Life  Dysfunctional  she~did~Eat~him  >~Tear.into.pieces  Tear.into.pieces~ed(ms)  "Yoseph  [Adding]"

and he recognized her and he said, the tunic of my son, a dysfunctional living one ate him, "Yoseph [Adding]" is completely torn into pieces,

**37:34** וַיִּקְרַע יַעֲקֹב שִׂמְלֹתָיו וַיָּשֶׂם שַׂק בְּמָתְנָיו וַיִּתְאַבֵּל עַל בְּנוֹ יָמִים רַבִּים

and~he~will~Tear  "Ya'aqov  [He restrains]"  Apparel~s~him  and~he~will~Set.in.place  Sack  in~Waist~him  and~he~will~self~Mourn  Upon  Son~him  Day~s  Abundant~s

and "Ya'aqov [He restrains]" tore his apparels and he set in place a sack in his waist and he mourned upon his son an abundant days,

**37:35** וַיָּקֻמוּ כָל בָּנָיו וְכָל בְּנֹתָיו לְנַחֲמוֹ וַיְמָאֵן לְהִתְנַחֵם וַיֹּאמֶר כִּי אֵרֵד אֶל בְּנִי אָבֵל שְׁאֹלָה וַיֵּבְךְ אֹתוֹ אָבִיו

and~they(m)~will~Rise  All  Son~s~him  and~All  Daughter~s~him  to~>~much~Comfort~him  and~he~will~much~Refuse  to~>~self~Comfort  and~he~will~Say  Given.that  i~will~Go.down  To  Son~me  Mourning  Underworld~unto  and~

and all his sons and all his daughters rose to comfort him and he refused to comfort himself and said, given that I will go down to my son mourning, unto the underworld and his father wept for

he~will~Weep   At~him   Father~him       him,

**37:36**   וְהַמְּדָנִים מָכְרוּ אֹתוֹ אֶל מִצְרָיִם לְפוֹטִיפַר סְרִיס פַּרְעֹה שַׂר הַטַּבָּחִים

and~the~"Midian [*Strife*]"~s   they~had~Sell   At~him   To   "Mitsrayim [*Troubles*]"   to~"Potiphar [*Belonging to the sun*]"   Eunuch   "Paroh [*Great house*]"   Noble   the~Slaughtering~s

and the ones of "Midian [*Strife*]" had sold him to "Mitsrayim [*Troubles*]", to "Potiphar [*Belonging to the sun*]", the eunuch of "Paroh [*Great house*]", the noble of the slaughtering ones,

# Chapter 38

**38:1**   וַיְהִי בָּעֵת הַהִוא וַיֵּרֶד יְהוּדָה מֵאֵת אֶחָיו וַיֵּט עַד אִישׁ עֲדֻלָּמִי וּשְׁמוֹ חִירָה

and~he~will~Exist   in~the~Appointed.time   the~She   and~he~will~Go.down   "Yehudah [*Praised*]"   from~At   Brother~him   and~he~will~Stretch   Until   Man   "Adulam [*Witness of the people*]"~of   and~Title~him   "Hhiyrah [*Bleached white*]"

and it came to pass in that appointed time, "Yehudah [*Praised*]" went down from his brothers and he stretched unto a man, one of "Adulam [*Witness of the people*]", and his title was "Hhiyrah [*Bleached white*],

**38:2**   וַיַּרְא שָׁם יְהוּדָה בַּת אִישׁ כְּנַעֲנִי וּשְׁמוֹ שׁוּעַ וַיִּקָּחֶהָ וַיָּבֹא אֵלֶיהָ

and~he~will~See   There   "Yehudah [*Praised*]"   Daughter   Man   "Kena'an [*Lowered*]"~of   and~Title~him   "Shu'a [*Wealthy*]"   and~he~will~Take~her   and~he~will~Come   To~her

and "Yehudah [*Praised*]" saw there a daughter of a man, one of "Kena'an [*Lowered*]" and his title was "Shu'a [*Wealthy*]" and he took her and he came to her,

**38:3**   וַתַּהַר וַתֵּלֶד בֵּן וַיִּקְרָא אֶת שְׁמוֹ עֵר

and~she~will~Conceive   and~she~will~Bring.forth   Son   and~he~will~Call.out   At   Title~him   "Eyr [*Awake*]"

and she conceived and she brought forth a son and he called out his title "Eyr [*Awake*]",

**38:4**   וַתַּהַר עוֹד וַתֵּלֶד בֵּן וַתִּקְרָא אֶת שְׁמוֹ אוֹנָן

and~she~will~Conceive   Yet.again   and~she~will~Bring.forth   Son   and~she~will~Call.out   At   Title~him   "Onan [*Strong*]"

and she conceived again and she brought forth a son and she called out his title "Onan [*Strong*]",

**38:5**   וַתֹּסֶף עוֹד וַתֵּלֶד בֵּן וַתִּקְרָא אֶת שְׁמוֹ שֵׁלָה וְהָיָה בִכְזִיב בְּלִדְתָּהּ אֹתוֹ

and~she~will~Add   Yet.again   and~she~will~Bring.forth   Son   and~she~will~

and she continued and she brought forth a son and she called out his

# Jeff A. Benner

Call.out At Title~him "Sheylah [*Petition*]" and~he~did~Exist in~"Keziv [*False*]" in~>~Bring.forth~her At~him

title "Sheylah [*Petition*]" and he existed in "Keziv [*False*]" with her bringing him forth,

**38:6** וַיִּקַּח יְהוּדָה אִשָּׁה לְעֵר בְּכוֹרוֹ וּשְׁמָהּ תָּמָר

and~he~will~Take "Yehudah [*Praised*]" Woman to~"Eyr [*Awake*]" Firstborn~him and~Title~her "Tamar [*Palm tree*]"

and "Yehudah [*Praised*]" took a woman for "Eyr [*Awake*]" his firstborn and her title was "Tamar [*Palm tree*]",

**38:7** וַיְהִי עֵר בְּכוֹר יְהוּדָה רַע בְּעֵינֵי יְהֹוָה וַיְמִתֵהוּ יְהֹוָה

and~he~will~Exist "Eyr [*Awake*]" Firstborn "Yehudah [*Praised*]" Dysfunctional in~Eye~s2 "YHWH [*He exists*]" and~he~will~make~Die~him "YHWH [*He exists*]"

and "Eyr [*Awake*]", the firstborn of "Yehudah [*Praised*]", existed dysfunctional in the eyes of "YHWH [*He exists*]" and "YHWH [*He exists*]" killed him,

**38:8** וַיֹּאמֶר יְהוּדָה לְאוֹנָן בֹּא אֶל אֵשֶׁת אָחִיךָ וְיַבֵּם אֹתָהּ וְהָקֵם זֶרַע לְאָחִיךָ

and~he~will~Say "Yehudah [*Praised*]" to~"Onan [*Strong*]" !(ms)~Come To Woman Brother~you(ms) and~!(ms)~Do.the.marriage.duty At~her and~!(ms)~make~Rise Seed to~Brother~you(ms)

and "Yehudah [*Praised*]" said to "Onan [*Strong*]", come to the woman of your brother and do the marriage duty to her and make a seed rise for your brother,

**38:9** וַיֵּדַע אוֹנָן כִּי לֹא לוֹ יִהְיֶה הַזָּרַע וְהָיָה אִם בָּא אֶל אֵשֶׁת אָחִיו וְשִׁחֵת אַרְצָה לְבִלְתִּי נְתָן זֶרַע לְאָחִיו

and~he~will~Know "Onan [*Strong*]" Given.that Not to~him he~will~Exist the~Seed and~he~did~Exist If he~did~Come To Woman Brother~him and~he~did~much~Damage Land~unto to~Except >~Give Seed to~Brother~him

and "Onan [*Strong*]" knew that the seed did not exist for him and it came to pass that he came to the woman of his brother and he did damage unto the land to not give seed to his brother,

**38:10** וַיֵּרַע בְּעֵינֵי יְהֹוָה אֲשֶׁר עָשָׂה וַיָּמֶת גַּם אֹתוֹ

and~he~will~Be.dysfunctional in~Eye~s2 "YHWH [*He exists*]" Which he~did~Do and~he~will~make~Die Also At~him

and he was dysfunctional in the eyes of "YHWH [*He exists*]" because of what he did and he killed him also,

**38:11** וַיֹּאמֶר יְהוּדָה לְתָמָר כַּלָּתוֹ שְׁבִי אַלְמָנָה בֵית אָבִיךְ עַד יִגְדַּל שֵׁלָה בְנִי כִּי אָמַר פֶּן יָמוּת גַּם הוּא כְּאֶחָיו וַתֵּלֶךְ תָּמָר וַתֵּשֶׁב בֵּית אָבִיהָ

and~he~will~Say "Yehudah [*Praised*]" to~"Tamar [*Palm tree*]" Daughter-in-

and "Yehudah [*Praised*]" said to "Tamar [*Palm tree*]" his daughter-

222

law~him !(fs)~Settle Widow House Father~you(fs) Until he~will~Magnify "Sheylah [*Petition*]" Son~me Given.that he~did~Say Otherwise he~will~Die Also He like~Brother~him and~she~will~Walk "Tamar [*Palm tree*]" and~she~will~Settle House Father~her

in-law, settle, a widow of the house of your father until "Sheylah [*Petition*]", my son, will magnify given that he said otherwise he will also die like his brother and "Tamar [*Palm tree*]" walked and she settled the house of her father,

**38:12** וַיִּרְבּוּ הַיָּמִים וַתָּמָת בַּת שׁוּעַ אֵשֶׁת יְהוּדָה וַיִּנָּחֶם יְהוּדָה וַיַּעַל עַל גֹּזֲזֵי צֹאנוֹ הוּא וְחִירָה רֵעֵהוּ הָעֲדֻלָּמִי תִּמְנָתָה

and~they(m)~will~Increase the~Day~s and~she~will~Die Daughter "Shu'a [*Wealthy*]" Woman "Yehudah [*Praised*]" and~he~will~be~Comfort "Yehudah [*Praised*]" and~he~will~Go.up Upon Shear~ing(mp) Flocks~him He and~"Hhiyrah [*Bleached white*]" Companion~him the~"Adulam [*Witness of the people*]"~of "Timnat [*Portion*]"~unto

and the days increased and the daughter of "Shu'a [*Wealthy*]", the woman of "Yehudah [*Praised*]", died and "Yehudah [*Praised*]" was comforted and he went up upon the shearing of his flocks, he and "Hhiyrah [*Bleached white*]" his companion, the one of "Adulam [*Witness of the people*]", unto "Timnat [*Portion*]",

**38:13** וַיֻּגַּד לְתָמָר לֵאמֹר הִנֵּה חָמִיךְ עֹלֶה תִמְנָתָה לָגֹז צֹאנוֹ

and~he~will~make.be~Be.face.to.face to~"Tamar [*Palm tree*]" to~>>~Say Look Father-in-law~you(fs) Go.up~ing(ms) "Timnat [*Portion*]"~unto to~>>~Shear Flocks~him

and he was told to "Tamar [*Palm tree*]" saying, look, your father-in-law is going up unto "Timnat [*Portion*]" to shear his flocks,

**38:14** וַתָּסַר בִּגְדֵי אַלְמְנוּתָהּ מֵעָלֶיהָ וַתְּכַס בַּצָּעִיף וַתִּתְעַלָּף וַתֵּשֶׁב בְּפֶתַח עֵינַיִם אֲשֶׁר עַל דֶּרֶךְ תִּמְנָתָה כִּי רָאֲתָה כִּי גָדַל שֵׁלָה וְהִוא לֹא נִתְּנָה לוֹ לְאִשָּׁה

and~she~will~make~Turn.aside Garment~s Widowhood~her from~Upon~her and~she~will~much~Conceal in~the~Veil and~she~will~self~Wrap and~she~will~Settle in~Opening "Eynayim [*Double spring*]" Which Upon Road "Timnat [*Portion*]"~unto Given.that she~did~See Given.that he~did~Magnify "Sheylah [*Petition*]" and~She Not she~did~be~Give to~him to~Woman

and she removed the garments of her widowhood, from upon her and she concealed with the veil and wrapped herself and she settled in the opening of "Eynayim [*Double spring*]" which is upon the road unto "Timnat [*Portion*]", given that she saw that "Sheylah [*Petition*]" magnified and she was not given to him for a woman,

**38:15** וַיִּרְאֶהָ יְהוּדָה וַיַּחְשְׁבֶהָ לְזוֹנָה כִּי כִסְּתָה פָּנֶיהָ

and~he~will~See~her "Yehudah

and "Yehudah [*Praised*]" saw her

[*Praised*]" and~he~will~Think~her to~Be.a.whore~ing(fs) Given.that she~did~much~Conceal Face~s~her

and he thought her to be a whore given that she concealed her face,

**38:16** וַיֵּט אֵלֶיהָ אֶל הַדֶּרֶךְ וַיֹּאמֶר הָבָה נָּא אָבוֹא אֵלַיִךְ כִּי לֹא יָדַע כִּי כַלָּתוֹ הִוא וַתֹּאמֶר מַה תִּתֶּן לִי כִּי תָבוֹא אֵלָי

and~he~will~Stretch To~her To the~Road and~he~will~Say !(ms)~Provide~ ^ Please i~will~Come To~you(fs) Given.that Not he~did~Know Given.that Daughter-in-law~him She and~she~will~Say What you(ms)~will~Give to~me Given.that you(ms)~will~Come To~me

and he stretched to her by the road and he said, please provide, given that he did not know that she was his daughter-in-law, and she said, what will you give to me given that you will come to me,

**38:17** וַיֹּאמֶר אָנֹכִי אֲשַׁלַּח גְּדִי עִזִּים מִן הַצֹּאן וַתֹּאמֶר אִם תִּתֵּן עֵרָבוֹן עַד שָׁלְחֶךָ

and~he~will~Say I i~will~much~Send Male.kid She-goat~s From the~Flocks and~she~will~Say If you(ms)~will~Give Token Until >~Send~you(ms)

and he said, I will send a male-kid from the she-goats from the flocks, and she said, if you will give a token until you send,

**38:18** וַיֹּאמֶר מָה הָעֵרָבוֹן אֲשֶׁר אֶתֶּן לָךְ וַתֹּאמֶר חֹתָמְךָ וּפְתִילֶךָ וּמַטְּךָ אֲשֶׁר בְּיָדֶךָ וַיִּתֶּן לָהּ וַיָּבֹא אֵלֶיהָ וַתַּהַר לוֹ

and~he~will~Say What the~Token Which i~will~Give to~you(fs) and~she~will~Say Signet~you(ms) and~Cord~you(ms) and~Stave~you(ms) Which in~Hand~you(ms) and~he~will~Give to~her and~he~will~Come To~her and~she~will~Conceive to~him

and he said, what is the token which I will give to you, and she said, your signet and your cord and your stave which is in your hand, and he gave to her and he came to her and she conceived to him,

**38:19** וַתָּקָם וַתֵּלֶךְ וַתָּסַר צְעִיפָהּ מֵעָלֶיהָ וַתִּלְבַּשׁ בִּגְדֵי אַלְמְנוּתָהּ

and~she~will~Rise and~she~will~Walk and~she~will~make~Turn.aside Veil from~Upon~her and~she~will~Clothe Garment~s Widowhood~her

and she rose and she walked and she removed the veil from upon her and she clothed garments of her widowhood,

**38:20** וַיִּשְׁלַח יְהוּדָה אֶת גְּדִי הָעִזִּים בְּיַד רֵעֵהוּ הָעֲדֻלָּמִי לָקַחַת הָעֵרָבוֹן מִיַּד הָאִשָּׁה וְלֹא מְצָאָהּ

and~he~will~Send "Yehudah [*Praised*]" At Male.kid She-goat~s in~Hand Companion~him "Adulam [*Witness of the people*]"~of to~Take the~Token from~Hand the~Woman and~Not he~did~Find~her

and "Yehudah [*Praised*]" sent the male-kid of the she-goats in the hand of his companion, the one of "Adulam [*Witness of the people*]", to take the token from the hand of the woman and he did not find her,

**38:21** וַיִּשְׁאַל אֶת אַנְשֵׁי מְקֹמָהּ לֵאמֹר אַיֵּה הַקְּדֵשָׁה הִוא בָעֵינַיִם עַל הַדָּרֶךְ וַיֹּאמְרוּ לֹא הָיְתָה בָזֶה קְדֵשָׁה

and~he~will~Inquire At Man~s Place~ her to~>~Say Where the~Prostitute She in~"Eynayim [*Double spring*]" Upon the~Road and~they(m)~will~Say Not she~did~Exist in~This Prostitute

and he inquired the men of her place saying, where is the prostitute, she was in "Eynayim [*Double spring*]", upon the road, and they said, a prostitute does not exist here,

**38:22** וַיָּשָׁב אֶל יְהוּדָה וַיֹּאמֶר לֹא מְצָאתִיהָ וְגַם אַנְשֵׁי הַמָּקוֹם אָמְרוּ לֹא הָיְתָה בָזֶה קְדֵשָׁה

and~he~will~Turn.back To "Yehudah [*Praised*]" and~he~will~Say Not i~ did~Find~her and~Also Man~s the~ Place they~had~Say Not she~did~ Exist in~This Prostitute

and he turned back to "Yehudah [*Praised*]" and he said, I did not find her and also the men of the place had said, a prostitute does not exist here,

**38:23** וַיֹּאמֶר יְהוּדָה תִּקַּח לָהּ פֶּן נִהְיֶה לָבוּז הִנֵּה שָׁלַחְתִּי הַגְּדִי הַזֶּה וְאַתָּה לֹא מְצָאתָהּ

and~he~will~Say "Yehudah [*Praised*]" she~will~Take to~her Otherwise we~ will~Exist to~Despise Look i~did~ Send the~Male.kid the~This and~ You(ms) Not you(ms)~did~Find~her

and "Yehudah [*Praised*]" said, she will take for her otherwise, we will exist to be despised, look, I sent this male-kid and you did not find her,

**38:24** וַיְהִי כְּמִשְׁלֹשׁ חֳדָשִׁים וַיֻּגַּד לִיהוּדָה לֵאמֹר זָנְתָה תָּמָר כַּלָּתֶךָ וְגַם הִנֵּה הָרָה לִזְנוּנִים וַיֹּאמֶר יְהוּדָה הוֹצִיאוּהָ וְתִשָּׂרֵף

and~he~will~Exist like~from~Three New.moon~s and~he~will~make.be~ Be.face.to.face to~"Yehudah [*Praised*]" to~>~Say she~did~Be.a.whore "Tamar [*Palm tree*]" Daughter-in-law~you(ms) and~Also Look Pregnant to~ Prostitution~s and~he~will~Say "Yehudah [*Praised*]" !(ms)~make~ Go.out~her and~she~will~be~Cremate

and it came to pass about three new moons and "Yehudah [*Praised*]" was told saying, "Tamar [*Palm tree*]", your daughter-in-law, was a whore and also look, pregnant for prostitutions and "Yehudah [*Praised*]" said, bring her out and she will be cremated,

**38:25** הִוא מוּצֵאת וְהִיא שָׁלְחָה אֶל חָמִיהָ לֵאמֹר לְאִישׁ אֲשֶׁר אֵלֶּה לּוֹ אָנֹכִי הָרָה וַתֹּאמֶר הַכֶּר נָא לְמִי הַחֹתֶמֶת וְהַפְּתִילִים וְהַמַּטֶּה הָאֵלֶּה

She make.be~Go.out~ing(fs) and~She she~did~Send To Father-in-law~her to~>~Say to~Man Which These to~ him I Pregnant and~she~will~Say !(ms)~make~Recognize Please to~Who

she was being brought out and she sent to her father-in-law saying, to the man who these belong, to him I am pregnant, and she said, please recognize to who this signet and

**225**

the~Signet and~the~Cord~s and~the~
Stave the~These

this cord and this stave,

**38:26** נַיַּכֵּר יְהוּדָה וַיֹּאמֶר צָדְקָה מִמֶּנִּי כִּי עַל כֵּן לֹא נְתַתִּיהָ לְשֵׁלָה
בְּנִי וְלֹא יָסַף עוֹד לְדַעְתָּהּ

and~he~will~make~Recognize "Yehudah
[Praised]" and~he~will~Say she~did~
Be.correct From~me Given.that Upon
So Not i~did~Give~her to~"Sheylah
[Petition]" Son~me and~Not he~did~
Add Yet.again to~>~Know~her

and "Yehudah [Praised]"
recognized and he said, she is more
correct than I since I did not give
her to "Sheylah [Petition]" my son
and he did not continue to know
her,

**38:27** וַיְהִי בְּעֵת לִדְתָּהּ וְהִנֵּה תְאוֹמִים בְּבִטְנָהּ

and~he~will~Exist in~the~
Appointed.time >~Know~her and~Look
Twin~s in~Womb~her

and it came to pass in the appointed
time of her knowing and look,
twins were in her womb,

**38:28** וַיְהִי בְלִדְתָּהּ וַיִּתֶּן יָד וַתִּקַּח הַמְיַלֶּדֶת וַתִּקְשֹׁר עַל יָדוֹ שָׁנִי
לֵאמֹר זֶה יָצָא רִאשֹׁנָה

and~he~will~Exist in~>~Bring.forth~her
and~he~will~Give Hand and~she~will~
Take the~much~Bring.forth~ing(fs)
and~she~will~Tie Upon Hand~him
Scarlet to~>~Say This he~did~Go.out
First

and it came to pass in her bringing
forth and he gave a hand and the
midwife took and she tied upon his
hand a scarlet saying, this went out
first,

**38:29** וַיְהִי כְּמֵשִׁיב יָדוֹ וְהִנֵּה יָצָא אָחִיו וַתֹּאמֶר מַה פָּרַצְתָּ עָלֶיךָ פָּרֶץ
וַיִּקְרָא שְׁמוֹ פָּרֶץ

and~he~will~Exist like~make~
Turn.back~ing(ms) Hand~him and~
Look he~did~Go.out Brother~him
and~she~will~Say What you(ms)~did~
Break.out Upon~you(ms) Breach and~
he~will~Call.out Title~him "Perets
[Breach]"

and it came to pass as his hand was
returning and look, his brother went
out and she said, how did you break
out upon you a breach and he called
out his title "Perets [Breach]",

**38:30** וְאַחַר יָצָא אָחִיו אֲשֶׁר עַל יָדוֹ הַשָּׁנִי וַיִּקְרָא שְׁמוֹ זָרַח

and~After he~did~Go.out Brother~him
Which Upon Hand~him the~Scarlet
and~he~will~Call.out Title~him
"Zerahh [Dawn]"

and after, his brother went out
which had the scarlet upon his
hand, and he called out his title
"Zerahh [Dawn]",

# Chapter 39

**39:1** וְיוֹסֵף הוּרַד מִצְרָיְמָה וַיִּקְנֵהוּ פּוֹטִיפַר סְרִיס פַּרְעֹה שַׂר הַטַּבָּחִים אִישׁ מִצְרִי מִיַּד הַיִּשְׁמְעֵאלִים אֲשֶׁר הוֹרִדֻהוּ שָׁמָּה

and~"Yoseph [*Adding*]" he~had~ make.be~Go.down "Mitsrayim [*Troubles*]"~unto and~he~will~Purchase~ him "Potiphar [*Belonging to the sun*]" Eunuch "Paroh [*Great house*]" Noble the~Slaughtering~s Man "Mitsrayim [*Troubles*]"~of from~Hand the~"Yishma'el [*El will listen*]"~s Which they~had~make~Go.down~him There~unto

and "Yoseph [*Adding*]" had been brought down unto "Mitsrayim [*Troubles*]" and "Potiphar [*Belonging to the sun*]", the eunuch of "Paroh [*Great house*]", the noble of the slaughtering ones, man of "Mitsrayim [*Troubles*]", purchased him from the hand of the ones of "Yishma'el [*El will listen*]" who had brought him down unto there,

**39:2*** וַיְהִי יְהוָה אֶת יוֹסֵף וַיְהִי אִישׁ מַצְלִיחַ וַיְהִי בְּבֵית אֲדֹנָיו הַמִּצְרִי

and~he~will~Exist "YHWH [*He exists*]" At "Yoseph [*Adding*]" and~ he~will~Exist Man make~Prosper~ ing(ms) and~he~will~Exist in~House Lord~s~him the~"Mitsrayim [*Troubles*]"~of

and "YHWH [*He exists*]" existed with "Yoseph [*Adding*]" and he existed as a man making prosper and he existed in the house of his lord, the one of "Mitsrayim [*Troubles*]",

**39:3** וַיַּרְא אֲדֹנָיו כִּי יְהוָה אִתּוֹ וְכֹל אֲשֶׁר הוּא עֹשֶׂה יְהוָה מַצְלִיחַ בְּיָדוֹ

and~he~will~See Lord~s~him Given.that "YHWH [*He exists*]" At~ him and~All Which He Do~ing(ms) "YHWH [*He exists*]" make~Prosper~ ing(ms) in~Hand~him

and his lord saw that "YHWH [*He exists*]" was with him and all which he was doing, "YHWH [*He exists*]" was making prosper in his hand,

**39:4** וַיִּמְצָא יוֹסֵף חֵן בְּעֵינָיו וַיְשָׁרֶת אֹתוֹ וַיַּפְקִדֵהוּ עַל בֵּיתוֹ וְכָל יֶשׁ לוֹ נָתַן בְּיָדוֹ

and~he~will~Find "Yoseph [*Adding*]" Beauty in~Eye~s2~him and~he~will~ much~Minister At~him and~he~will~ make~Visit~him Upon House~him and~All There.is to~him he~did~Give in~Hand~him

and "Yoseph [*Adding*]" found beauty in his eyes and he ministered him and he set him over his house and all there is belonging to him he gave in his hand,

**39:5** וַיְהִי מֵאָז הִפְקִיד אֹתוֹ בְּבֵיתוֹ וְעַל כָּל אֲשֶׁר יֶשׁ לוֹ וַיְבָרֶךְ יְהוָה אֶת בֵּית הַמִּצְרִי בִּגְלַל יוֹסֵף וַיְהִי בִּרְכַּת יְהוָה בְּכָל אֲשֶׁר יֶשׁ לוֹ בַּבַּיִת וּבַשָּׂדֶה

and~he~will~Exist   from~At.that.time
he~did~make~Visit   At~him   in~House~
him   and~Upon   All   Which   There.is
to~him   and~he~will~much~Kneel
"YHWH   [*He   exists*]"   At   House
the~"Mitsrayim   [*Troubles*]"~s   in~
Account.of   "Yoseph   [*Adding*]"   and~
he~will~Exist   Present   "YHWH   [*He
exists*]"   in~All   Which   There.is   to~
him   in~the~House   and~in~the~Field

and it came to pass from the time
that he set him over in his house
and upon all which there is
belonging to him, that "YHWH [*He
exists*]" respected the house of the
one of "Mitsrayim [*Troubles*]" on
account of "Yoseph [*Adding*]" and
a present of "YHWH [*He exists*]"
existed in all which there is
belonging to him, in the house and
in the field,

**39:6**   וַיַּעֲזֹב כָּל אֲשֶׁר לוֹ בְּיַד יוֹסֵף וְלֹא יָדַע אִתּוֹ מְאוּמָה כִּי אִם
הַלֶּחֶם אֲשֶׁר הוּא אוֹכֵל וַיְהִי יוֹסֵף יְפֵה תֹאַר וִיפֵה מַרְאֶה

and~he~will~Leave   All   Which   to~him
in~Hand   "Yoseph   [*Adding*]"   and~Not
he~did~Know   At~him   Nothing
Given.that   If   the~Bread   Which   He
Eat~ing(ms)   and~he~will~Exist
"Yoseph   [*Adding*]"   Beautiful   Shape
and~Beautiful   Appearance

and he left all which belonged to
him in the hand of "Yoseph
[*Adding*]" and he did not know
anything of him except the bread
which he was eating and "Yoseph
[*Adding*]" existed beautiful of
shape and beautiful of appearance,

**39:7**   וַיְהִי אַחַר הַדְּבָרִים הָאֵלֶּה וַתִּשָּׂא אֵשֶׁת אֲדֹנָיו אֶת עֵינֶיהָ אֶל
יוֹסֵף וַתֹּאמֶר שִׁכְבָה עִמִּי

and~he~will~Exist   After   the~Word~s
the~These   and~she~will~Lift.up
Woman   Lord~s~him   At   Eye~s2~her
To   "Yoseph   [*Adding*]"   and~she~will~
Say   !(ms)~Lay.down~^   With~me

and it came to pass after these
words and the woman of his lord
lifted up her eyes to "Yoseph
[*Adding*]" and she said, lay down
with me,

**39:8**   וַיְמָאֵן וַיֹּאמֶר אֶל אֵשֶׁת אֲדֹנָיו הֵן אֲדֹנִי לֹא יָדַע אִתִּי מַה בַּבָּיִת
וְכֹל אֲשֶׁר יֶשׁ לוֹ נָתַן בְּיָדִי

and~he~will~Refuse   and~he~will~Say
To   Woman   Lord~s~him   Though
Lord~me   Not   he~did~Know   At~me
What   in~the~House   and~All   Which
There.is   to~him   he~did~Give   in~
Hand~me

and he refused and he said to the
woman of his lord, though my lord
does not know what is with me in
the house and all which there is
belonging to him he gave in my
hand,

**39:9**   אֵינֶנּוּ גָדוֹל בַּבַּיִת הַזֶּה מִמֶּנִּי וְלֹא חָשַׂךְ מִמֶּנִּי מְאוּמָה כִּי אִם
אוֹתָךְ בַּאֲשֶׁר אַתְּ אִשְׁתּוֹ וְאֵיךְ אֶעֱשֶׂה הָרָעָה הַגְּדֹלָה הַזֹּאת
וְחָטָאתִי לֵאלֹהִים

Without~him   Magnificent   in~the~House
the~This   From~me   and~Not   he~did~
Keep.back   From~me   Nothing
Given.that   If   At~you(fs)   in~Which

not one is magnificent in this house
more than me, nothing except you,
whereas you are his woman, and
how will I do this magnificent

You(fs) Woman~him and~Where i~will~Do the~Dysfunctional the~Magnificent the~This and~i~did~Err to~"Elohiym [*Powers*]"

dysfunction and err to "Elohiym [*Powers*]",

**39:10** נַיְהִי כְּדַבְּרָהּ אֶל יוֹסֵף יוֹם יוֹם וְלֹא שָׁמַע אֵלֶיהָ לִשְׁכַּב אֶצְלָהּ לִהְיוֹת עִמָּהּ

and~he~will~Exist like~>~much~Speak~her To "Yoseph [*Adding*]" Day Day and~Not he~did~Hear To~her to~>~Lay.down Beside~her to~>~Exist With~her

and it came to pass at her speaking to "Yoseph [*Adding*]" day by day, that he did not hear her to lay down beside her, to exist with her,

**39:11** נַיְהִי כְּהַיּוֹם הַזֶּה וַיָּבֹא הַבַּיְתָה לַעֲשׂוֹת מְלַאכְתּוֹ וְאֵין אִישׁ מֵאַנְשֵׁי הַבַּיִת שָׁם בַּבָּיִת

and~he~will~Exist like~the~Day the~This and~he~will~Come the~House~unto to~>~Do Occupation~him and~Without Man from~Man~s the~House There in~the~House

and it came to pass at this day and he came unto the house to do his occupation and not a man out of the men of the house was there in the house,

**39:12** וַתִּתְפְּשֵׂהוּ בְּבִגְדוֹ לֵאמֹר שִׁכְבָה עִמִּי וַיַּעֲזֹב בִּגְדוֹ בְּיָדָהּ וַיָּנָס וַיֵּצֵא הַחוּצָה

and~she~will~Seize.hold~him in~Garment~him to~>~Say !(ms)~Lay.down~^ With~me and~he~will~Leave Garment~him in~Hand~her and~he~will~Flee and~he~will~Go.out the~Outside~unto

and she seized hold of him with his garment saying, lay down with me, and he left his garment in her hand and he fled and he went out unto the outside,

**39:13** וַיְהִי כִּרְאוֹתָהּ כִּי עָזַב בִּגְדוֹ בְּיָדָהּ וַיָּנָס הַחוּצָה

and~he~will~Exist like~>~See~her Given.that he~did~Leave Garment~him in~Hand~her and~he~will~Flee the~Outside~unto

and it came to pass at her seeing that he left his garment in her hand and he fled unto the outside,

**39:14** וַתִּקְרָא לְאַנְשֵׁי בֵיתָהּ וַתֹּאמֶר לָהֶם לֵאמֹר רְאוּ הֵבִיא לָנוּ אִישׁ עִבְרִי לְצַחֶק בָּנוּ בָּא אֵלַי לִשְׁכַּב עִמִּי וָאֶקְרָא בְּקוֹל גָּדוֹל

and~she~will~Call.out to~Man~s House~her and~she~will~Say to~them(m) to~>~Say !(mp)~See he~did~make~Come to~us Man "Ever [*Cross over*]"~of to~>~much~Laugh in~us he~did~Come To~me to~>~Lay.down With~me and~i~will~Call.out in~Voice Magnificent

and she called out to the men of her house and she said to them saying, see, he brought to us a man of "Ever [*Cross over*]" to mock in us, he came to me to lay down with me and I called out with a magnificent voice,

**39:15** וַיְהִי כְשָׁמְעוֹ כִּי הֲרִימֹתִי קוֹלִי וָאֶקְרָא וַיַּעֲזֹב בִּגְדוֹ אֶצְלִי וַיָּנָס וַיֵּצֵא הַחוּצָה

and~he~will~Exist like~>~Hear~him Given.that i~did~make~Rise Voice~me and~i~will~Call.out and~he~will~Leave Garment~him Beside~me and~he~will~Flee and~he~will~Go.out the~Outside~unto

and it came to pass at his hearing, that I rose my voice and I called out and he left his garment beside me and he fled and he went out unto the outside,

**39:16** וַתַּנַּח בִּגְדוֹ אֶצְלָהּ עַד בּוֹא אֲדֹנָיו אֶל בֵּיתוֹ

and~she~will~make~Rest Garment~him Beside~her Until >~Come Lord~s~him To House~him

and she left his garment beside her until his lord comes to his house,

**39:17** וַתְּדַבֵּר אֵלָיו כַּדְּבָרִים הָאֵלֶּה לֵאמֹר בָּא אֵלַי הָעֶבֶד הָעִבְרִי אֲשֶׁר הֵבֵאתָ לָּנוּ לְצַחֶק בִּי

and~she~will~much~Speak To~him like~the~Word~s the~These to~>~Say he~did~Come To~me the~Servant the~"Ever [*Cross over*]"~of Which you(ms)~did~make~Come to~us to~>~much~Laugh in~me

and she spoke to him like these words saying, the servant, the one of "Ever [*Cross over*]", who you brought to us, came to me to mock in me,

**39:18** וַיְהִי כַּהֲרִימִי קוֹלִי וָאֶקְרָא וַיַּעֲזֹב בִּגְדוֹ אֶצְלִי וַיָּנָס הַחוּצָה

and~he~will~Exist like~>~make~Raise~me Voice~me and~i~will~Call.out and~he~will~Leave Garment~him Beside~me and~he~will~Flee the~Outside~unto

and it came to pass at my raising of my voice and I called out and he left his garment beside me and he fled unto the outside,

**39:19** וַיְהִי כִשְׁמֹעַ אֲדֹנָיו אֶת דִּבְרֵי אִשְׁתּוֹ אֲשֶׁר דִּבְּרָה אֵלָיו לֵאמֹר כַּדְּבָרִים הָאֵלֶּה עָשָׂה לִי עַבְדֶּךָ וַיִּחַר אַפּוֹ

and~he~will~Exist like~>~Hear Lord~s~him At Word Woman~him Which she~did~much~Speak To~him to~>~Say like~the~Word~s the~These he~did~Do to~me Servant~you(ms) and~he~will~Flare.up Nose~him

and it came to pass at the hearing of his lord of the word of his woman which she spoke to him saying, like these words your servant did to me and he flared up his nose,

**39:20** וַיִּקַּח אֲדֹנֵי יוֹסֵף אֹתוֹ וַיִּתְּנֵהוּ אֶל בֵּית הַסֹּהַר מְקוֹם אֲשֶׁר אסורי (אֲסִירֵי) הַמֶּלֶךְ אֲסוּרִים וַיְהִי שָׁם בְּבֵית הַסֹּהַר

and~he~will~Take Lord~s "Yoseph [*Adding*]" At~him and~he~will~Give~him To House the~Prison Place Which Tie.up~ed(mp) the~King Tie.up~ed(mp) and~he~will~Exist

and the lord of "Yoseph [*Adding*]" took him and he gave him to the house of the prison, the place where the tied up ones of the king are tied up,

There in~House the~Prison

**39:21** וַיְהִי יְהוָה אֶת יוֹסֵף וַיֵּט אֵלָיו חָסֶד וַיִּתֵּן חִנּוֹ בְּעֵינֵי שַׂר בֵּית הַסֹּהַר

and~he~will~Exist "YHWH [He exists]" At "Yoseph [Adding]" and~he~will~Stretch To~him Kindness and~he~will~Give Beauty~him in~Eye~s2 Noble House the~Prison

and "YHWH [He exists]" existed with "Yoseph [Adding]" and stretched kindness to him and he gave his beauty in the eyes of the noble of the house of the prison,

**39:22** וַיִּתֵּן שַׂר בֵּית הַסֹּהַר בְּיַד יוֹסֵף אֵת כָּל הָאֲסִירִם אֲשֶׁר בְּבֵית הַסֹּהַר וְאֵת כָּל אֲשֶׁר עֹשִׂים שָׁם הוּא הָיָה עֹשֶׂה

and~he~will~Give Noble House the~Prison in~Hand "Yoseph [Adding]" At All the~Prisoner~s Which in~House the~Prison and~At All Which Do~ing(mp) There He he~did~Exist Do~ing(ms)

and the noble of the house of the prison gave in the hand of "Yoseph [Adding]" all the prisoners which were in the house of the prison and all which was doing there, he was doing,

**39:23** אֵין שַׂר בֵּית הַסֹּהַר רֹאֶה אֶת כָּל מְאוּמָה בְּיָדוֹ בַּאֲשֶׁר יְהוָה אִתּוֹ וַאֲשֶׁר הוּא עֹשֶׂה יְהוָה מַצְלִיחַ

Without Noble House the~Prison See~ing(ms) At All Nothing in~Hand~him in~Which "YHWH [He exists]" At~him and~Which He Do~ing(ms) "YHWH [He exists]" make~Prosper~ing(ms)

the noble of the house of the prison was seeing nothing at all, nothing was in his hand, whereas "YHWH [He exists]" was with him and what he was doing, "YHWH [He exists]" made prosper,

# Chapter 40

**40:1\*** וַיְהִי אַחַר הַדְּבָרִים הָאֵלֶּה חָטְאוּ מַשְׁקֵה מֶלֶךְ מִצְרַיִם וְהָאֹפֶה לַאֲדֹנֵיהֶם לְמֶלֶךְ מִצְרַיִם

and~he~will~Exist After the~Word~s the~These they~did~Err make~Drink~ing(ms) King "Mitsrayim [Troubles]" and~the~Bake~ing(ms) to~Lord~s~them(m) to~King "Mitsrayim [Troubles]"

and it came to pass after these words, the drinker of the king of "Mitsrayim [Troubles]" and the baker erred to their lord, to the king of "Mitsrayim [Troubles]",

**40:2** וַיִּקְצֹף פַּרְעֹה עַל שְׁנֵי סָרִיסָיו עַל שַׂר הַמַּשְׁקִים וְעַל שַׂר הָאוֹפִים

and~he~will~Snap "Paroh [Great house]" Upon Two Eunuch~s~him Upon Noble the~make~Drink~ing(mp)

and "Paroh [Great house]" snapped upon his two eunuchs, upon the noble of the drinkers and upon the

| and~Upon Noble the~Bake~ing(mp) | noble of the bakers, |

**40:3** נַיִּתֵּן אֹתָם בְּמִשְׁמַר בֵּית שַׂר הַטַּבָּחִים אֶל בֵּית הַסֹּהַר מְקוֹם אֲשֶׁר יוֹסֵף אָסוּר שָׁם

| and~he~will~Give At~them(m) in~Custody House Noble the~Slaughtering~s To House the~Prison Place Which "Yoseph [Adding]" Tie.up~ed(ms) There | and he gave them in the custody of the house of the noble of the slaughtering ones, to the house of the prison, the place where "Yoseph [Adding]" was tied up there, |

**40:4\*** נַיִּפְקֹד שַׂר הַטַּבָּחִים אֶת יוֹסֵף אִתָּם וַיְשָׁרֶת אֹתָם וַיִּהְיוּ יָמִים בְּמִשְׁמָר

| and~he~will~Visit Noble the~Slaughtering~s At "Yoseph [Adding]" At~them(m) and~he~will~much~Minister At~them(m) and~they(m)~will~Exist Day~s in~Custody | and the noble of the slaughtering ones set "Yoseph [Adding]" over them and he ministered them and they existed days in custody, |

**40:5** וַיַּחַלְמוּ חֲלוֹם שְׁנֵיהֶם אִישׁ חֲלֹמוֹ בְּלַיְלָה אֶחָד אִישׁ כְּפִתְרוֹן חֲלֹמוֹ הַמַּשְׁקֶה וְהָאֹפֶה אֲשֶׁר לְמֶלֶךְ מִצְרַיִם אֲשֶׁר אֲסוּרִים בְּבֵית הַסֹּהַר

| and~they(m)~will~Visualize Dream Two~them(m) Man Dream~him in~Night Unit Man like~Interpretation Dream~him the~Drinking and~the~Bake~ing(ms) Which to~King "Mitsrayim [Troubles]" Which Tie.up~ed(mp) in~House the~Prison | and the two of them visualized a dream, each had his dream in one night, each according to the interpretation of his dream, the drinker and the baker which belonged to the king of "Mitsrayim [Troubles]", which was tied up in the house of the prison, |

**40:6** וַיָּבֹא אֲלֵיהֶם יוֹסֵף בַּבֹּקֶר וַיַּרְא אֹתָם וְהִנָּם זֹעֲפִים

| and~he~will~Come To~them(m) "Yoseph [Adding]" in~the~Morning and~he~will~See At~them(m) and~Look~them(m) Be.sad~ing(mp) | and "Yoseph [Adding]" came to them in the morning and he saw them and look, they were being sad, |

**40:7** וַיִּשְׁאַל אֶת סְרִיסֵי פַרְעֹה אֲשֶׁר אִתּוֹ בְמִשְׁמַר בֵּית אֲדֹנָיו לֵאמֹר מַדּוּעַ פְּנֵיכֶם רָעִים הַיּוֹם

| and~he~will~Inquire At Eunuch~s "Paroh [Great house]" Which At~him in~Custody House Lord~s~him to~>~ Say Why Face~s~you(ms) Dysfunctional~s the~Day | and he inquired of the eunuchs of "Paroh [Great house]" which were with him in the custody of the house of his lord, saying, why are your faces dysfunctional today, |

**40:8** וַיֹּאמְרוּ אֵלָיו חֲלוֹם חָלַמְנוּ וּפֹתֵר אֵין אֹתוֹ וַיֹּאמֶר אֲלֵהֶם

יוֹסֵף הֲלוֹא לֵאלֹהִים פִּתְרֹנִים סַפְּרוּ נָא לִי

| | |
|---|---|
| and~they(m)~will~Say To~him Dream we~had~Visualize and~Interpret~ing(ms) Without At~him and~he~will~Say To~them(m) "Yoseph [*Adding*]" ?~ Not to~"Elohiym [*Powers*]" Interpretation~s !(mp)~>~much~Count Please to~me | and they said to him, we had visualized a dream and no interpreter for him, and "Yoseph [*Adding*]" said to them, is not interpretations to "Elohiym [*Powers*]", please recount to me, |

**40:9** וַיְסַפֵּר שַׂר הַמַּשְׁקִים אֶת חֲלֹמוֹ לְיוֹסֵף וַיֹּאמֶר לוֹ בַּחֲלוֹמִי וְהִנֵּה גֶפֶן לְפָנָי

| | |
|---|---|
| and~he~will~much~Count Noble the~make~Drink~ing(mp) At Dream~him to~"Yoseph [*Adding*]" and~he~will~Say to~him in~Dream~me and~Look Grapevine to~Face~s~me | and the noble of the drinkers recounted his dream to "Yoseph [*Adding*]" saying to him, in my dream, look, a grapevine to my face, |

**40:10** וּבַגֶּפֶן שְׁלֹשָׁה שָׂרִיגִם וְהִוא כְפֹרַחַת עָלְתָה נִצָּהּ הִבְשִׁילוּ אַשְׁכְּלֹתֶיהָ עֲנָבִים

| | |
|---|---|
| and~in~the~Grapevine Three Branch~s and~She like~Burst.out~ing(fs) she~did~Go.up Blossom~her they~did~make~Boil Cluster~s~her Grape~s | and in the grapevine were three branches and she was as bursting out, her blossom went up, her clusters of grapes were ripened, |

**40:11** וְכוֹס פַּרְעֹה בְּיָדִי וָאֶקַּח אֶת הָעֲנָבִים וָאֶשְׂחַט אֹתָם אֶל כּוֹס פַּרְעֹה וָאֶתֵּן אֶת הַכּוֹס עַל כַּף פַּרְעֹה

| | |
|---|---|
| and~Cup "Paroh [*Great house*]" in~Hand~me and~i~will~Take At the~Grape~s and~i~will~Press At~them(m) To Cup "Paroh [*Great house*]" and~i~will~Give At the~Cup Upon Palm "Paroh [*Great house*]" | and the cup of "Paroh [*Great house*]" was in my hand and I took the grapes and I pressed them to the cup of "Paroh [*Great house*]" and I gave the cup upon the palm of "Paroh [*Great house*]", |

**40:12** וַיֹּאמֶר לוֹ יוֹסֵף זֶה פִּתְרֹנוֹ שְׁלֹשֶׁת הַשָּׂרִגִים שְׁלֹשֶׁת יָמִים הֵם

| | |
|---|---|
| and~he~will~Say to~him "Yoseph [*Adding*]" This Interpretation~him Three the~Branch~s Three Day~s They(m) | and "Yoseph [*Adding*]" said to him, this is his interpretation, the three branches, they are three days, |

**40:13** בְּעוֹד שְׁלֹשֶׁת יָמִים יִשָּׂא פַרְעֹה אֶת רֹאשֶׁךָ וַהֲשִׁיבְךָ עַל כַּנֶּךָ וְנָתַתָּ כוֹס פַּרְעֹה בְּיָדוֹ כַּמִּשְׁפָּט הָרִאשׁוֹן אֲשֶׁר הָיִיתָ מַשְׁקֵהוּ

| | |
|---|---|
| in~Yet.again Three Day~s he~will~Lift.up "Paroh [*Great house*]" At Head~you(ms) and~he~did~make~Turn.back~you(ms) Upon Base~you(ms) and~you(ms)~did~Give Cup | within three days "Paroh [*Great house*]" will lift up your head and he will return you upon your base and you will give the cup of "Paroh [*Great house*]" in his hand, like the |

"Paroh [*Great house*]" in~Hand~him like~the~Judgement the~First Which you(ms)~did~Exist make~Drink~ing(ms)~him

first judgement when you existed as his drinker,

**40:14** כִּי אִם זְכַרְתַּנִי אִתְּךָ כַּאֲשֶׁר יִיטַב לָךְ וְעָשִׂיתָ נָּא עִמָּדִי חָסֶד וְהִזְכַּרְתַּנִי אֶל פַּרְעֹה וְהוֹצֵאתַנִי מִן הַבַּיִת הַזֶּה

Given.that If you(ms)~did~Remember~me At~you(ms) like~Which he~will~Do.well to~you(fs) and~you(ms)~did~Do Please By~me Kindness and~you(ms)~did~make~Remember~me To "Paroh [*Great house*]" and~you(ms)~did~make~Go.out~me From the~House the~This

but if you can remember me with you, just as he will do well to you, and please, you will do kindness by me, and you will mention me to "Paroh [*Great house*]" and you will bring me from this house,

**40:15** כִּי גֻנֹּב גֻּנַּבְתִּי מֵאֶרֶץ הָעִבְרִים וְגַם פֹּה לֹא עָשִׂיתִי מְאוּמָה כִּי שָׂמוּ אֹתִי בַּבּוֹר

Given.that >~much.be~Steal i~did~much.be~Steal from~Land the~"Ever [*Cross over*]"~s and~Also Here Not i~did~Do Nothing Given.that they~did~Set.in.place At~me in~the~Cistern

given that I was surely stolen away from the land of the ones of "Ever [*Cross over*]" and also here I did not do anything that they set me in place in the cistern,

**40:16** וַיַּרְא שַׂר הָאֹפִים כִּי טוֹב פָּתָר וַיֹּאמֶר אֶל יוֹסֵף אַף אֲנִי בַּחֲלוֹמִי וְהִנֵּה שְׁלֹשָׁה סַלֵּי חֹרִי עַל רֹאשִׁי

and~he~will~See Noble the~Bake~ing(mp) Given.that Functional he~did~Interpret and~he~will~Say To "Yoseph [*Adding*]" Moreover I in~Dream~me and~Look Three Basket~s White.bread Upon Head~me

and the noble of the bakers saw that he interpreted functionally and he said to "Yoseph [*Adding*]", I was also in my dream and look, three baskets of white bread were upon my head,

**40:17** וּבַסַּל הָעֶלְיוֹן מִכֹּל מַאֲכַל פַּרְעֹה מַעֲשֵׂה אֹפֶה וְהָעוֹף אֹכֵל אֹתָם מִן הַסַּל מֵעַל רֹאשִׁי

and~in~the~Basket the~Upper from~All Nourishment "Paroh [*Great house*]" Work Bake~ing(ms) and~the~Flyer Eat~ing(ms) At~them(m) From the~Basket from~Upon Head~me

and in the upper basket were all kinds of nourishment of "Paroh [*Great house*]", work of the bakers, and the flyer was eating them from the basket upon my head,

**40:18** וַיַּעַן יוֹסֵף וַיֹּאמֶר זֶה פִּתְרֹנוֹ שְׁלֹשֶׁת הַסַּלִּים שְׁלֹשֶׁת יָמִים הֵם

and~he~will~Answer "Yoseph [*Adding*]" and~he~will~Say This Interpretation~him Three the~Basket~s Three Day~s They(m)

and "Yoseph [*Adding*]" answered and he said, this is his interpretation, the three baskets, they are three days,

**40:19** בְּעוֹד שְׁלֹשֶׁת יָמִים יִשָּׂא פַרְעֹה אֶת רֹאשְׁךָ מֵעָלֶיךָ וְתָלָה אוֹתְךָ עַל עֵץ וְאָכַל הָעוֹף אֶת בְּשָׂרְךָ מֵעָלֶיךָ

in~Yet.again Three Day~s he~will~ Lift.up "Paroh [*Great house*]" At Head~you(ms) from~Upon~you(ms) and~he~did~Hang At~you(ms) Upon Tree and~he~did~Eat the~Flyer At Flesh~you(ms) from~Upon~you(ms)

within three days "Paroh [*Great house*]" will lift up your head from upon you and will hang you upon a tree and the flyer will eat your flesh from upon you,

**40:20** וַיְהִי בַּיּוֹם הַשְּׁלִישִׁי יוֹם הֻלֶּדֶת אֶת פַּרְעֹה וַיַּעַשׂ מִשְׁתֶּה לְכָל עֲבָדָיו וַיִּשָּׂא אֶת רֹאשׁ שַׂר הַמַּשְׁקִים וְאֶת רֹאשׁ שַׂר הָאֹפִים בְּתוֹךְ עֲבָדָיו

and~he~will~Exist in~the~Day the~ Third Day >~make.be~Bring.forth At "Paroh [*Great house*]" and~he~will~Do Feast to~All Servant~s~him and~he~ will~Lift.up At Head Noble make~ Drink~ing(mp) and~At Head Noble the~Bake~ing(mp) in~Midst Servant~s~ him

and it came to pass in the third day, the day "Paroh [*Great house*]" was brought forth, and he did a feast for all his servants and he lifted up the head of the noble of the drinkers and the head of the noble of the bakers in the midst of his servants,

**40:21** וַיָּשֶׁב אֶת שַׂר הַמַּשְׁקִים עַל מַשְׁקֵהוּ וַיִּתֵּן הַכּוֹס עַל כַּף פַּרְעֹה

and~he~will~make~Turn.back At Noble the~make~Drink~ing(mp) Upon Drinking~him and~he~will~Give the~ Cup Upon Palm "Paroh [*Great house*]"

and the noble of the drinkers was restored upon his drinking and he gave the cup upon the palm of "Paroh [*Great house*]",

**40:22** וְאֶת שַׂר הָאֹפִים תָּלָה כַּאֲשֶׁר פָּתַר לָהֶם יוֹסֵף

and~At Noble the~Bake~ing(mp) he~ did~Hang like~Which he~did~Interpret to~them(m) "Yoseph [*Adding*]"

and he hung the noble of the bakers just as "Yoseph [*Adding*]" interpreted to them,

**40:23** וְלֹא זָכַר שַׂר הַמַּשְׁקִים אֶת יוֹסֵף וַיִּשְׁכָּחֵהוּ

and~Not he~did~Remember Noble the~make~Drink~ing(mp) At "Yoseph [*Adding*]" and~he~will~Forget~him

and the noble of the drinkers did not remember "Yoseph [*Adding*]" and he forgot him,

# Chapter 41

**41:1** וַיְהִי מִקֵּץ שְׁנָתַיִם יָמִים וּפַרְעֹה חֹלֵם וְהִנֵּה עֹמֵד עַל הַיְאֹר

and~he~will~Exist from~Conclusion Year~s2 Day~s and~"Paroh [*Great house*]" Visualize~ing(ms) and~Look

and it came to pass at the conclusion of two years of days and "Paroh [*Great house*]" was

Stand~ing(ms)  Upon  the~Stream

visualizing and look, he was standing upon the stream,

**41:2** וְהִנֵּה מִן הַיְאֹר עֹלת שֶׁבַע פָּרוֹת יְפוֹת מַרְאֶה וּבְרִיאֹת בָּשָׂר וַתִּרְעֶינָה בָּאָחוּ

and~Look  From  the~Stream  Go.up~ing(fp)  Seven  Cow~s  Beautiful~s  Appearance  and~Fed.fat~s  Flesh  and~they(f)~will~Feed  in~the~Marsh.Grass

and look, from the stream are going up seven cows, beautiful of appearance and fed fat of flesh, and they fed in the marsh grass,

**41:3** וְהִנֵּה שֶׁבַע פָּרוֹת אֲחֵרוֹת עֹלוֹת אַחֲרֵיהֶן מִן הַיְאֹר רָעוֹת מַרְאֶה וְדַקּוֹת בָּשָׂר וַתַּעֲמֹדְנָה אֵצֶל הַפָּרוֹת עַל שְׂפַת הַיְאֹר

and~Look  Seven  Cow~s  Other~s  Go.up~ing(fp)  After~them(f)  From  the~Stream  Dysfunctional~s  Appearance  and~Emaciated~s  Flesh  and~they(f)~will~Stand  Beside  the~Cow~s  Upon  Lip  the~Stream

and look, seven other cows are going up after them from the stream, dysfunctional of appearance and emaciated of flesh, and they stood beside the cows upon the lip of the stream,

**41:4** וַתֹּאכַלְנָה הַפָּרוֹת רָעוֹת הַמַּרְאֶה וְדַקֹּת הַבָּשָׂר אֵת שֶׁבַע הַפָּרוֹת יְפֹת הַמַּרְאֶה וְהַבְּרִיאֹת וַיִּיקַץ פַּרְעֹה

and~they(f)~will~Eat  the~Cow~s  Dysfunctional~s  the~Appearance  and~Emaciated~s  the~Flesh  At  Seven  the~Cow~s  Beautiful~s  the~Appearance  and~the~Fed.fat~s  and~he~will~Awake  "Paroh [*Great   house*]"

and the cows, dysfunctional of appearance and emaciated of flesh, ate the seven cows, beautiful of appearance and fed fat, and "Paroh [*Great house*]" awoke,

**41:5** וַיִּישָׁן וַיַּחֲלֹם שֵׁנִית וְהִנֵּה שֶׁבַע שִׁבֳּלִים עֹלוֹת בְּקָנֶה אֶחָד בְּרִיאוֹת וְטֹבוֹת

and~he~will~Sleep  and~he~will~Visualize  Second  and~Look  Seven  Head.of.grain~s  Go.up~ing(fp)  in~Stalk  Unit  Fed.fat~s  and~Functional~s

and he slept and he visualized a second one and look, seven heads of grain were going up in one stalk, fed fat and functional,

**41:6** וְהִנֵּה שֶׁבַע שִׁבֳּלִים דַּקּוֹת וּשְׁדוּפֹת קָדִים צֹמְחוֹת אַחֲרֵיהֶן

and~Look  Seven  Head.of.grain~s  Emaciated~s  and~Blast~ed(fp)  East.wind  Spring.up~ing(fp)  After~them(f)

and look, seven heads of grain, emaciated and blasted of the east wind, springing up after them,

**41:7** וַתִּבְלַעְנָה הַשִּׁבֳּלִים הַדַּקּוֹת אֵת שֶׁבַע הַשִּׁבֳּלִים הַבְּרִיאוֹת וְהַמְּלֵאוֹת וַיִּיקַץ פַּרְעֹה וְהִנֵּה חֲלוֹם

and~they(f)~will~Swallow  the~Head.of.grain~s  the~Emaciated~s  At  Seven  the~Head.of.grain~s  the~Fed.fat~

and the emaciated heads of grain swallowed the seven fed fat and full heads of grain and "Paroh [*Great*

s and~the~Full~s and~he~will~Awake "Paroh [*Great house*]" and~Look Dream

house]" awoke and look, it was a dream,

**41:8**

וַיְהִי בַבֹּקֶר וַתִּפָּעֶם רוּחוֹ וַיִּשְׁלַח וַיִּקְרָא אֶת כָּל חַרְטֻמֵּי מִצְרַיִם וְאֶת כָּל חֲכָמֶיהָ וַיְסַפֵּר פַּרְעֹה לָהֶם אֶת חֲלֹמוֹ וְאֵין פּוֹתֵר אוֹתָם לְפַרְעֹה

and~he~will~Exist in~the~Morning and~she~will~be~Beat Wind~him and~he~will~Send and~he~will~Call.out At All Magician~s "Mitsrayim [*Troubles*]" and~At All Wise~her and~he~will~much~Count "Paroh [*Great house*]" to~them(m) At Dream~him and~Without Interpret~ing(ms) At~them(m) to~"Paroh [*Great house*]"

and it came to pass in the morning and his wind was beat and he sent and he called out all his magicians of "Mitsrayim [*Troubles*]" and all her wise ones and "Paroh [*Great house*]" recounted to them his dream and they were without an interpretation for "Paroh [*Great house*]",

**41:9**

וַיְדַבֵּר שַׂר הַמַּשְׁקִים אֶת פַּרְעֹה לֵאמֹר אֶת חֲטָאַי אֲנִי מַזְכִּיר הַיּוֹם

and~he~will~much~Speak Noble the~make~Drink~ing(mp) At "Paroh [*Great house*]" to~>>~Say At Fault~s~me I make~Remember~ing(ms) the~Day

and the noble of the drinkers spoke to "Paroh [*Great house*]" saying, I am remembering my faults today,

**41:10**

פַּרְעֹה קָצַף עַל עֲבָדָיו וַיִּתֵּן אֹתִי בְּמִשְׁמַר בֵּית שַׂר הַטַּבָּחִים אֹתִי וְאֵת שַׂר הָאֹפִים

"Paroh [*Great house*]" he~had~Snap Upon Servant~s~him and~he~will~Give At~me in~Custody House Noble the~Slaughtering~s At~me and~At Noble the~Bake~ing(mp)

"Paroh [*Great house*]" had snapped upon his servants and he gave me in the custody of the house of the noble of the slaughtering ones, me and the noble of the bakers,

**41:11**

וַנַּחַלְמָה חֲלוֹם בְּלַיְלָה אֶחָד אֲנִי וָהוּא אִישׁ כְּפִתְרוֹן חֲלֹמוֹ חָלָמְנוּ

and~we~will~Visualize~^ Dream in~Night Unit I and~He Man like~Interpretation Dream~him we~did~Visualize

and we visualized a dream in one night, I and he, each according to his dream we visualized,

**41:12**

וְשָׁם אִתָּנוּ נַעַר עִבְרִי עֶבֶד לְשַׂר הַטַּבָּחִים וַנְּסַפֶּר לוֹ וַיִּפְתָּר לָנוּ אֶת חֲלֹמֹתֵינוּ אִישׁ כַּחֲלֹמוֹ פָּתָר

and~There At~us Young.man "Ever [*Cross over*]"~of Servant to~Noble the~Slaughtering~s and~we~will~much~Count to~him and~he~will~Interpret

and there was with us a young man, one of "Ever [*Cross over*]", a servant to the noble of the slaughtering ones, and we

to~us   At   Dream~s~us   Man   like~
Dream~him   he~did~Interpret

recounted to him and he interpreted to us our dreams, each according to his dream and he interpreted,

**41:13**   וַיְהִי כַּאֲשֶׁר פָּתַר לָנוּ כֵּן הָיָה אֹתִי הֵשִׁיב עַל כַּנִּי וְאֹתוֹ תָלָה

and~he~will~Exist   like~Which   he~did~
Interpret   to~us   So   he~did~Exist   At~
me   he~did~make~Turn.back   Upon
Base~me   and~At~him   he~did~Hang

and it came to pass just as he interpreted to us, so it existed, he returned me upon my base and he hanged him,

**41:14**   וַיִּשְׁלַח פַּרְעֹה וַיִּקְרָא אֶת יוֹסֵף וַיְרִיצֻהוּ מִן הַבּוֹר וַיְגַלַּח וַיְחַלֵּף שִׂמְלֹתָיו וַיָּבֹא אֶל פַּרְעֹה

and~he~will~Send   "Paroh [*Great house*]"   and~he~will~Call.out   At
"Yoseph [*Adding*]"   and~they~will~
make~Run~him   From   the~Cistern
and~he~will~much~Shave   and~he~will~
much~Pass.over   Apparel~s~him   and~
he~will~Come   To   "Paroh [*Great house*]"

and "Paroh [*Great house*]" sent and he called out to "Yoseph [*Adding*]" and they quickly brought him from the cistern and he shaved and he changed his apparels and he came to "Paroh [*Great house*]",

**41:15**   וַיֹּאמֶר פַּרְעֹה אֶל יוֹסֵף חֲלוֹם חָלַמְתִּי וּפֹתֵר אֵין אֹתוֹ וַאֲנִי שָׁמַעְתִּי עָלֶיךָ לֵאמֹר תִּשְׁמַע חֲלוֹם לִפְתֹּר אֹתוֹ

and~we~will~Say   "Paroh [*Great house*]"   To   "Yoseph [*Adding*]"
Dream   i~did~Visualize   and~Interpret~
ing(ms)   Without   At~him   and~I   i~
did~Hear   Upon~you(ms)   to~>~Say
you(ms)~will~Hear   Dream   to~>~
Interpret   At~him

and "Paroh [*Great house*]" said to "Yoseph [*Adding*]", a dream I visualized and he is without an interpreter, and I heard about you saying you will hear a dream to interpret him,

**41:16**   וַיַּעַן יוֹסֵף אֶת פַּרְעֹה לֵאמֹר בִּלְעָדָי אֱלֹהִים יַעֲנֶה אֶת שְׁלוֹם פַּרְעֹה

and~he~will~Answer   "Yoseph [*Adding*]"   At   "Paroh [*Great house*]"
to~>~Say   Apart.from~me   "Elohiym [*Powers*]"   he~will~Answer   At
Completeness   "Paroh [*Great house*]"

and "Yoseph [*Adding*]" answered "Paroh [*Great house*]" saying, apart from me, "Elohiym [*Powers*]" will answer "Paroh [*Great house*]" with completeness,

**41:17**   וַיְדַבֵּר פַּרְעֹה אֶל יוֹסֵף בַּחֲלֹמִי הִנְנִי עֹמֵד עַל שְׂפַת הַיְאֹר

and~he~will~much~Speak   "Paroh [*Great house*]"   To   "Yoseph [*Adding*]"   in~
Dream~me   Look~me   Stand~ing(ms)
Upon   Lip   the~Stream

and "Paroh [*Great house*]" spoke to "Yoseph [*Adding*]", in my dream, look, here am I standing upon the lip of the stream,

**41:18**   וְהִנֵּה מִן הַיְאֹר עֹלֹת שֶׁבַע פָּרוֹת בְּרִיאוֹת בָּשָׂר וִיפֹת תֹּאַר וַתִּרְעֶינָה בָּאָחוּ

and~Look From the~Stream Go.up~ing(fp) Seven Cow~s Fed.fat~s Flesh and~Beautiful~s Shape and~they(f)~will~Feed in~the~Marsh.Grass

and look, from the stream is going up seven cows, fed fat of flesh and beautiful of shape and they fed in the marsh grass,

**41:19** וְהִנֵּה שֶׁבַע פָּרוֹת אֲחֵרוֹת עֹלוֹת אַחֲרֵיהֶן דַּלּוֹת וְרָעוֹת תֹּאַר מְאֹד וְרַקּוֹת בָּשָׂר לֹא רָאִיתִי כָהֵנָּה בְּכָל אֶרֶץ מִצְרַיִם לָרֹעַ

and~Look Seven Cow~s Other~s Go.up~ing(fp) After~them(f) Weak~s and~Dysfunctional~s Shape Many and~Thin~s Flesh Not i~did~See like~They(f) in~All Land "Mitsrayim [*Troubles*]" to~the~Dysfunctional

and look, seven other cows were going up after them, weak and very dysfunctional of shape and thin of flesh, I did not see such as them in all the land of "Mitsrayim [*Troubles*]" for the dysfunction,

**41:20** וַתֹּאכַלְנָה הַפָּרוֹת הָרַקּוֹת וְהָרָעוֹת אֵת שֶׁבַע הַפָּרוֹת הָרִאשֹׁנוֹת הַבְּרִיאֹת

and~they(f)~will~Eat the~Cow~s the~Thin~s and~the~Dysfunctional~s At Seven the~Cow~s the~First~s the~Fed.fat~s

and the thin and dysfuctional cows ate the seven first fed fat cows,

**41:21** וַתָּבֹאנָה אֶל קִרְבֶּנָה וְלֹא נוֹדַע כִּי בָאוּ אֶל קִרְבֶּנָה וּמַרְאֵיהֶן רַע כַּאֲשֶׁר בַּתְּחִלָּה וָאִיקָץ

and~they(f)~will~Come To Within~them(f) and~Not he~did~be~Know Given.that they~did~Come To Within~them(f) and~Appearance~s~them(f) Dysfunctional like~Which in~the~First.time and~i~will~Awake

and they came to within them and it is not known that they came to within them because their appearance was dysfunctional just as in the first time and I awoke,

**41:22** וָאֵרֶא בַּחֲלֹמִי וְהִנֵּה שֶׁבַע שִׁבֳּלִים עֹלֹת בְּקָנֶה אֶחָד מְלֵאֹת וְטֹבוֹת

and~i~will~See in~Dream~me and~Look Seven Head.of.grain~s Go.up~ing(fp) in~Stalk Unit Full~s and~Functional~s

and I saw in my dream, and look, seven heads of grain were going up in one stalk, full and functional,

**41:23** וְהִנֵּה שֶׁבַע שִׁבֳּלִים צְנֻמוֹת דַּקּוֹת שְׁדֻפוֹת קָדִים צֹמְחוֹת אַחֲרֵיהֶם

and~Look Seven Head.of.grain~s Wither~ed(fp) Thin~s Blast~ed(fp) East.wind Spring.up~ing(fp) After~them(m)

and look, seven heads of grain, withered, thin, blasted of the west wind were springing up after them,

**41:24** וַתִּבְלַעְןָ הַשִּׁבֳּלִים הַדַּקֹּת אֵת שֶׁבַע הַשִּׁבֳּלִים הַטֹּבוֹת וָאֹמַר אֶל הַחַרְטֻמִּים וְאֵין מַגִּיד לִי

and~they(f)~will~Swallow the~ Head.of.grain~s the~Thin~s At Seven the~Head.of.grain~s the~Functional~s and~i~will~Say To the~Magician~s and~Without make~Be.face.to.face~ ing(ms) to~me

and the thin heads of grain swallowed the seven functional heads of grain and I said to the magicians and without telling to me,

**41:25** וַיֹּאמֶר יוֹסֵף אֶל פַּרְעֹה חֲלוֹם פַּרְעֹה אֶחָד הוּא אֵת אֲשֶׁר הָאֱלֹהִים עֹשֶׂה הִגִּיד לְפַרְעֹה

and~he~will~Say "Yoseph [*Adding*]" To "Paroh [*Great house*]" Dream "Paroh [*Great house*]" Unit He At Which the~"Elohiym [*Powers*]" Do~ ing(ms) he~did~make~Be.face.to.face to~"Paroh [*Great house*]"

and "Yoseph [*Adding*]" said to "Paroh [*Great house*]", the dream of "Paroh [*Great house*]" is a unit, what the "Elohiym [*Powers*]" is doing, he told to "Paroh [*Great house*]",

**41:26** שֶׁבַע פָּרֹת הַטֹּבֹת שֶׁבַע שָׁנִים הֵנָּה וְשֶׁבַע הַשִּׁבֳּלִים הַטֹּבֹת שֶׁבַע שָׁנִים הֵנָּה חֲלוֹם אֶחָד הוּא

Seven Cow~s the~Functional~s Seven Year~s They(f) and~Seven Head.of.grain~s the~Functional~s Seven Year~s They(f) Dream Unit He

the seven functional cows, they are seven years, and the seven functional heads of grain, they are seven years, the dream is a unit,

**41:27** וְשֶׁבַע הַפָּרוֹת הָרַקּוֹת וְהָרָעֹת הָעֹלֹת אַחֲרֵיהֶן שֶׁבַע שָׁנִים הֵנָּה וְשֶׁבַע הַשִּׁבֳּלִים הָרֵקוֹת שְׁדֻפוֹת הַקָּדִים יִהְיוּ שֶׁבַע שְׁנֵי רָעָב

and~Seven the~Cow~s the~Thin~s and~the~Dysfunctional~s the~Go.up~ ing(fp) After~them(f) Seven Year~s They(f) and~Seven the~Head.of.grain~s the~Empty~s Blast~ed(fp) the~ East.wind they(m)~will~Exist Seven Year~s Hunger

and seven thin and dysfunctional cows going up after them, they are seven years, and seven empty heads of grain, blasted of the east wind, they exist as seven years of hunger,

**41:28** הוּא הַדָּבָר אֲשֶׁר דִּבַּרְתִּי אֶל פַּרְעֹה אֲשֶׁר הָאֱלֹהִים עֹשֶׂה הֶרְאָה אֶת פַּרְעֹה

He the~Word Which i~did~much~ Speak To "Paroh [*Great house*]" Which the~"Elohiym [*Powers*]" Do~ ing(ms) he~did~make~See At "Paroh [*Great house*]"

he is the word which I spoke to "Paroh [*Great house*]" which the "Elohiym [*Powers*]" is doing he made "Paroh [*Great house*]" see,

**41:29** הִנֵּה שֶׁבַע שָׁנִים בָּאוֹת שָׂבָע גָּדוֹל בְּכָל אֶרֶץ מִצְרָיִם

Look Seven Year~s Come~ing(fp) Plenty Magnificent in~All Land "Mitsrayim [*Troubles*]"

look, seven years are coming of magnificent plenty in all the land of "Mitsrayim [*Troubles*]",

**41:30** וְקָמוּ שֶׁבַע שְׁנֵי רָעָב אַחֲרֵיהֶן וְנִשְׁכַּח כָּל הַשָּׂבָע בְּאֶרֶץ מִצְרָיִם

וְכִלָּה הָרָעָב אֶת הָאָרֶץ

| | |
|---|---|
| and~they~did~Rise Seven Year~s Hunger After~them(f) and~he~did~be~ Forget All the~Plenty in~Land "Mitsrayim [*Troubles*]" and~he~did~ much~Finish the~Hunger At the~Land | and seven years of hunger will rise after them and all the plenty in the land of "Mitsrayim [*Troubles*]" will be forgotten and the hunger will finish the land, |

**41:31** וְלֹא יִוָּדַע הַשָּׂבָע בָּאָרֶץ מִפְּנֵי הָרָעָב הַהוּא אַחֲרֵי כֵן כִּי כָבֵד הוּא מְאֹד

| | |
|---|---|
| and~Not he~will~be~Know the~Plenty in~Land from~Face~s the~Hunger the~He After So Given.that Heavy He Many | and the plenty in the land will not be known from the face of that hunger afterward because he was great, |

**41:32** וְעַל הִשָּׁנוֹת הַחֲלוֹם אֶל פַּרְעֹה פַּעֲמָיִם כִּי נָכוֹן הַדָּבָר מֵעִם הָאֱלֹהִים וּמְמַהֵר הָאֱלֹהִים לַעֲשֹׂתוֹ

| | |
|---|---|
| and~Upon >~be~Change the~Dream To "Paroh [*Great house*]" Stroke.of.time~s2 Given.that be~Fixed~ ing(ms) the~Word from~With the~ "Elohiym [*Powers*]" and~much~Hurry~ ing(ms) the~"Elohiym [*Powers*]" to~ >~Do~him | and because the dream repeated to "Paroh [*Great house*]" a second time given that the word from the "Elohiym [*Powers*]" was fixed and the "Elohiym [*Powers*]" is hurrying to do him, |

**41:33** וְעַתָּה יֵרֶא פַרְעֹה אִישׁ נָבוֹן וְחָכָם וִישִׁיתֵהוּ עַל אֶרֶץ מִצְרָיִם

| | |
|---|---|
| and~Now he~will~See "Paroh [*Great house*]" Man be~Understand~ing(ms) and~Wise and~he~will~Set.down~him Upon Land "Mitsrayim [*Troubles*]" | and now, "Paroh [*Great house*]" will see a man being understanding and wise and he will set him down upon the land of "Mitsrayim [*Troubles*]", |

**41:35** וְיִקְבְּצוּ אֶת כָּל אֹכֶל הַשָּׁנִים הַטֹּבוֹת הַבָּאֹת הָאֵלֶּה וְיִצְבְּרוּ בָר תַּחַת יַד פַּרְעֹה אֹכֶל בֶּעָרִים וְשָׁמָרוּ

| | |
|---|---|
| and~they(m)~will~Gather.together At All Foodstuff the~Year~s the~ Functional~s the~Come~ing(fp) the~ These and~they(m)~will~Pile.up Grain Under Hand "Paroh [*Great house*]" Foodstuff in~City~s and~they~did~ Guard | and they will gather together all the foodstuff of these coming functional years and they will pile up grain under the hand of "Paroh [*Great house*]", foodstuff in the cities and they will guard, |

**41:36** וְהָיָה הָאֹכֶל לְפִקָּדוֹן לָאָרֶץ לְשֶׁבַע שְׁנֵי הָרָעָב אֲשֶׁר תִּהְיֶיןָ בְּאֶרֶץ מִצְרָיִם וְלֹא תִכָּרֵת הָאָרֶץ בָּרָעָב

| | |
|---|---|
| and~he~did~Exist the~Foodstuff to~ Deposited to~the~Land to~Seven Year~s the~Hunger Which they(f)~ | and the foodstuff existed for a deposit to the land for the seven years of hunger which will exist in |

will~Exist in~Land "Mitsrayim [*Troubles*]" and~Not she~will~be~Cut the~Land in~the~Hunger

the land of "Mitsrayim [*Troubles*]" and the land will not be cut in the hunger,

**41:37**

וַיִּיטַב הַדָּבָר בְּעֵינֵי פַרְעֹה וּבְעֵינֵי כָּל עֲבָדָיו

and~he~will~Do.well the~Word in~Eye~s2 "Paroh [*Great house*]" and~in~Eye~s2 All Servant~s~him

and the word did well in the eyes of "Paroh [*Great house*]" and in the eyes of all his servants,

**41:38**

וַיֹּאמֶר פַּרְעֹה אֶל עֲבָדָיו הֲנִמְצָא כָזֶה אִישׁ אֲשֶׁר רוּחַ אֱלֹהִים בּוֹ

and~he~will~Say "Paroh [*Great house*]" To Servant~s~him ?~he~did~be~Find like~This Man Which Wind the~"Elohiym [*Powers*]" in~him

and "Paroh [*Great house*]" said to his servants, can one be found like this man which has the wind of the "Elohiym [*Powers*]" in him,

**41:39** *

וַיֹּאמֶר פַּרְעֹה אֶל יוֹסֵף אַחֲרֵי הוֹדִיעַ אֱלֹהִים אוֹתְךָ אֶת כָּל זֹאת אֵין נָבוֹן וְחָכָם כָּמוֹךָ

and~he~will~Say "Paroh [*Great house*]" To "Yoseph [*Adding*]" After >~make~Know "Elohiym [*Powers*]" At~you(ms) At All This Without be~Understand~ing(ms) and~Wise like~That.one~you(ms)

and "Paroh [*Great house*]" said to "Yoseph [*Adding*]" afterward, "Elohiym [*Powers*]" made known to you all this, none is understanding and wise like you,

**41:40** *

אַתָּה תִּהְיֶה עַל בֵּיתִי וְעַל פִּיךָ יִשַּׁק כָּל עַמִּי רַק הַכִּסֵּא אֶגְדַּל מִמֶּךָּ

You(ms) you(ms)~will~Exist Upon House~me and~Upon Mouth~you(ms) he~will~Kiss All People~me Only the~Seat i~will~Magnify From~you(ms)

you will exist upon my house and upon your mouth he will kiss all my people, only the seat I will magnify more than you,

**41:41**

וַיֹּאמֶר פַּרְעֹה אֶל יוֹסֵף רְאֵה נָתַתִּי אֹתְךָ עַל כָּל אֶרֶץ מִצְרָיִם

and~he~will~Say "Paroh [*Great house*]" To "Yoseph [*Adding*]" !(ms)~See i~did~Give At~you(ms) Upon All Land "Mitsrayim [*Troubles*]"

and "Paroh [*Great house*]" said to "Yoseph [*Adding*]", see, I gave you upon all the land of "Mitsrayim [*Troubles*]",

**41:42**

וַיָּסַר פַּרְעֹה אֶת טַבַּעְתּוֹ מֵעַל יָדוֹ וַיִּתֵּן אֹתָהּ עַל יַד יוֹסֵף וַיַּלְבֵּשׁ אֹתוֹ בִּגְדֵי שֵׁשׁ וַיָּשֶׂם רְבִד הַזָּהָב עַל צַוָּארוֹ

and~he~will~Turn.aside "Paroh [*Great house*]" At Signet.ring~him from~Upon Hand~him and~he~will~Give At~her Upon Hand "Yoseph [*Adding*]" and~he~will~make~Clothe At~him Garment~s Linen and~he~will~Set.in.place Chain the~Gold

and "Paroh [*Great house*]" turned aside his signet ring from upon his hand and he gave her upon the hand of "Yoseph [*Adding*]" and he clothed him, garments of linen, and he set in place a chain of gold upon the back of his neck,

Upon    Back.of.the.neck~him

**41:43**    וַיַּרְכֵּב אֹתוֹ בְּמִרְכֶּבֶת הַמִּשְׁנֶה אֲשֶׁר לוֹ וַיִּקְרְאוּ לְפָנָיו אַבְרֵךְ
וְנָתוֹן אֹתוֹ עַל כָּל אֶרֶץ מִצְרָיִם

and~he~will~make~Ride  At~him  in~ Chariot  the~Double  Which  to~him and~they(m)~will~Call.out  to~Face~s~ him  Bend.the.knee  and~>~Give  At~ him  Upon  All  Land  "Mitsrayim [*Troubles*]"

and he will make him ride in the double chariot which belonged to him and they will call out to his face, bend the knee and give him upon all the land of "Mitsrayim [*Troubles*]",

**41:44**    וַיֹּאמֶר פַּרְעֹה אֶל יוֹסֵף אֲנִי פַּרְעֹה וּבִלְעָדֶיךָ לֹא יָרִים אִישׁ אֶת
יָדוֹ וְאֶת רַגְלוֹ בְּכָל אֶרֶץ מִצְרָיִם

and~he~will~Say  "Paroh [*Great house*]"  To  "Yoseph [*Adding*]"  I  "Paroh [*Great house*]"  and~Apart.from~ you(ms)  Not  he~will~make~Raise  Man  At  Hand~him  and~At  Foot~him  in~All  Land  "Mitsrayim [*Troubles*]"

and "Paroh [*Great house*]" said to "Yoseph [*Adding*]", I am "Paroh [*Great house*]" and apart from you no man will raise his hand and his foot in all the land of "Mitsrayim [*Troubles*]",

**41:45**    וַיִּקְרָא פַּרְעֹה שֵׁם יוֹסֵף צָפְנַת פַּעְנֵחַ וַיִּתֶּן לוֹ אֶת אָסְנַת בַּת
פּוֹטִי פֶרַע כֹּהֵן אֹן לְאִשָּׁה וַיֵּצֵא יוֹסֵף עַל אֶרֶץ מִצְרָיִם

and~he~will~Call.out  "Paroh [*Great house*]"  Title  "Yoseph [*Adding*]"  "Tsaphnat-Paneyahh [*Treasury of the rest*]"  and~he~will~Give  to~him  At  "Asnat [*Belonging to Nat*]"  Daughter  "Pothee-Phera [*He whom the Ra gave*]"  Priest  "On [*Vigor*]"  to~ Woman  and~he~will~Go.out  "Yoseph [*Adding*]"  Upon  Land  "Mitsrayim [*Troubles*]"

and "Paroh [*Great house*]" called out the title of "Yoseph [*Adding*]", "Tsaphnat-Paneyahh [*Treasury of the rest*]", and he gave to him "Asnat [*Belonging to Nat*]", the daughter of "Pothee-Phera [*He whom the Ra gave*]", priest of "On [*Vigor*]", for a woman, and "Yoseph [*Adding*]" went out upon the land of "Mitsrayim [*Troubles*]",

**41:46**    וְיוֹסֵף בֶּן שְׁלֹשִׁים שָׁנָה בְּעָמְדוֹ לִפְנֵי פַּרְעֹה מֶלֶךְ מִצְרָיִם וַיֵּצֵא
יוֹסֵף מִלִּפְנֵי פַרְעֹה וַיַּעֲבֹר בְּכָל אֶרֶץ מִצְרָיִם

and~"Yoseph [*Adding*]"  Son  Three~s  Year  in~>~Stand~him  to~Face~s  "Paroh [*Great house*]"  King  "Mitsrayim [*Troubles*]"  and~he~will~ Go.out  "Yoseph [*Adding*]"  from~to~ Face~s  "Paroh [*Great house*]"  and~ he~will~Cross.over  in~All  the~Land  "Mitsrayim [*Troubles*]"

and "Yoseph [*Adding*]" was a son of thirty years in his standing to the face of "Paroh [*Great house*]", king of "Mitsrayim [*Troubles*]", and "Yoseph [*Adding*]" went out from the face of "Paroh [*Great house*]" and crossed over in all the land of "Mitsrayim [*Troubles*]",

**41:47**    וַתַּעַשׂ הָאָרֶץ בְּשֶׁבַע שְׁנֵי הַשָּׂבָע לִקְמָצִים

and~she~will~Do  the~Land  in~Seven

and the land did in the seven years

Year~s  the~Plenty  to~Handful~s          of plenty for handfuls,

**41:48**  וַיִּקְבֹּץ אֶת כָּל אֹכֶל שֶׁבַע שָׁנִים אֲשֶׁר הָיוּ בְּאֶרֶץ מִצְרַיִם וַיִּתֶּן אֹכֶל בֶּעָרִים אֹכֶל שְׂדֵה הָעִיר אֲשֶׁר סְבִיבֹתֶיהָ נָתַן בְּתוֹכָהּ

and~he~will~Gather.together  At  All Foodstuff  Seven  Year~s  Which  they~ did~Exist  in~Land  "Mitsrayim [*Troubles*]"  and~he~will~Give Foodstuff  in~the~City~s  Foodstuff Field  the~City  Which  Around~her he~did~Give  in~Midst~her

and he gathered together all the foodstuffs of the seven years which existed in the land of "Mitsrayim [*Troubles*]"  and  he  gave  the foodstuff in the cities, the foodstuff of the field which was around the city he gave in her midst,

**41:49**  וַיִּצְבֹּר יוֹסֵף בָּר כְּחוֹל הַיָּם הַרְבֵּה מְאֹד עַד כִּי חָדַל לִסְפֹּר כִּי אֵין מִסְפָּר

and~he~will~Pile.up  "Yoseph [*Adding*]" Grain  like~Sand  the~Sea  >~make~ Increase  Many  Until  Given.that  he~ did~Terminate  to~>~Count  Given.that Without  Number

and  "Yoseph [*Adding*]"  piled  up grain like sand of the sea, making an  increase  of  much,  until  he terminated to count, given that it was without number,

**41:50**  וּלְיוֹסֵף יֻלַּד שְׁנֵי בָנִים בְּטֶרֶם תָּבוֹא שְׁנַת הָרָעָב אֲשֶׁר יָלְדָה לּוֹ אָסְנַת בַּת פּוֹטִי פֶרַע כֹּהֵן אוֹן

and~to~"Yoseph  [*Adding*]"  he~ much.be~Bring.forth  Two  Son~s  in~ Before  she~will~Come  Year  the~ Hunger  Which  she~did~Bring.forth to~him  "Asnat [*Belonging  to  Nat*]" Daughter  "Pothee-Phera [*He  whom the  Ra  gave*]"  Priest  "On [*Vigor*]"
☐

and  to  "Yoseph [*Adding*]"  he brought forth two sons before the year of the hunger came which "Asnat [*Belonging to Nat*]", the daughter of "Pothee-Phera [*He whom the Ra gave*]", priest of "On [*Vigor*]", brought forth,

**41:51**  וַיִּקְרָא יוֹסֵף אֶת שֵׁם הַבְּכוֹר מְנַשֶּׁה כִּי נַשַּׁנִי אֱלֹהִים אֶת כָּל עֲמָלִי וְאֵת כָּל בֵּית אָבִי

and~he~will~Call.out  "Yoseph [*Adding*]"  At  Title  the~Firstborn "Menasheh [*Causing  to  overlook*]" Given.that  he~did~much~Overlook "Elohiym [*Powers*]"  At  All  Labor~ me  and~At  All  House  Father~me

and  "Yoseph [*Adding*]"  called  out the title of the firstborn, "Menasheh [*Causing to overlook*]"  given that "Elohiym [*Powers*]"  overlooked all my labor and all the house of my father,

**41:52**  וְאֵת שֵׁם הַשֵּׁנִי קָרָא אֶפְרָיִם כִּי הִפְרַנִי אֱלֹהִים בְּאֶרֶץ עָנְיִי

and~At  Title  the~Second  he~did~ Call.out  "Ephrayim [*Double fruitfulness*]"  Given.that  he~did~make~ Reproduce~me  "Elohiym [*Powers*]" in~Land  Affliction~me

and the title of the second he called out,  "Ephrayim  [*Double fruitfulness*]"  given that "Elohiym [*Powers*]" reproduced me in the land of my affliction,

**41:53** וַתִּכְלֶינָה שֶׁבַע שְׁנֵי הַשָּׂבָע אֲשֶׁר הָיָה בְּאֶרֶץ מִצְרָיִם

and~they(f)~will~Finish Seven Year~s the~Plenty Which he~did~Exist Land "Mitsrayim [*Troubles*]"

and the seven years of the plenty which existed in the land of "Mitsrayim [*Troubles*]" finished,

**41:54** וַתְּחִלֶּינָה שֶׁבַע שְׁנֵי הָרָעָב לָבוֹא כַּאֲשֶׁר אָמַר יוֹסֵף וַיְהִי רָעָב בְּכָל הָאֲרָצוֹת וּבְכָל אֶרֶץ מִצְרַיִם הָיָה לָחֶם

and~they(f)~will~Pierce Seven Year~s the~Hunger to~>~Come like~Which he~did~Say "Yoseph [*Adding*]" and~ he~will~Exist Hunger in~All the~ Land~s and~in~All Land "Mitsrayim [*Troubles*]" he~did~Exist Bread

and the seven years of the hunger pierced to come just as "Yoseph [*Adding*]" said and hunger existed in all the lands and in all the land of "Mitsrayim [*Troubles*]" bread existed,

**41:55** וַתִּרְעַב כָּל אֶרֶץ מִצְרַיִם וַיִּצְעַק הָעָם אֶל פַּרְעֹה לַלָּחֶם וַיֹּאמֶר פַּרְעֹה לְכָל מִצְרַיִם לְכוּ אֶל יוֹסֵף אֲשֶׁר יֹאמַר לָכֶם תַּעֲשׂוּ

and~she~will~Be.hungry All Land "Mitsrayim [*Troubles*]" and~he~will~ Cry.out the~People To "Paroh [*Great house*]" to~Bread and~he~will~Say "Paroh [*Great house*]" to~All "Mitsrayim [*Troubles*]" !(mp)~Walk To "Yoseph [*Adding*]" Which he~ will~Say to~you(mp) you(mp)~will~Do

and all the land of "Mitsrayim [*Troubles*]" was hungry and the people cried out to "Paroh [*Great house*]" for bread and "Paroh [*Great house*]" said to all "Mitsrayim [*Troubles*]", walk to "Yoseph [*Adding*]" what he will say to you, you will do,

**41:56** וְהָרָעָב הָיָה עַל כָּל פְּנֵי הָאָרֶץ וַיִּפְתַּח יוֹסֵף אֶת כָּל אֲשֶׁר בָּהֶם וַיִּשְׁבֹּר לְמִצְרַיִם וַיֶּחֱזַק הָרָעָב בְּאֶרֶץ מִצְרָיִם

and~the~Hunger he~did~Exist Upon All Face~s the~Land and~he~will~ Open "Yoseph [*Adding*]" At All Which in~them(m) and~he~will~ Exchange to~"Mitsrayim [*Troubles*]" and~he~will~Seize the~Hunger in~Land "Mitsrayim [*Troubles*]"

and the hunger existed upon all the face of the land and "Yoseph [*Adding*]" opened all which was in them and he exchanged to "Mitsrayim [*Troubles*]" and the hunger seized in the land of "Mitsrayim [*Troubles*]",

**41:57** וְכָל הָאָרֶץ בָּאוּ מִצְרַיְמָה לִשְׁבֹּר אֶל יוֹסֵף כִּי חָזַק הָרָעָב בְּכָל הָאָרֶץ

and~All the~Land they~had~Come "Mitsrayim [*Troubles*]"~unto to~>~ Exchange To "Yoseph [*Adding*]" Given.that he~did~Seize the~Hunger in~All the~Land

and all the land had come unto "Mitsrayim [*Troubles*]" to exchange to "Yoseph [*Adding*]" given that he seized the hunger in all the land,

# Chapter 42

**42:1** וַיַּרְא יַעֲקֹב כִּי יֶשׁ שֶׁבֶר בְּמִצְרָיִם וַיֹּאמֶר יַעֲקֹב לְבָנָיו לָמָּה תִּתְרָאוּ

and~he~will~See "Ya'aqov [*He restrains*]" Given.that There.is Barley in~"Mitsrayim [*Troubles*]" and~he~will~Say "Ya'aqov [*He restrains*]" to~Son~s~him to~What you(mp)~will~self~See

and "Ya'aqov [*He restrains*]" saw that there was barley in "Mitsrayim [*Troubles*]" and "Ya'aqov [*He restrains*]" said to his sons, why do you look at yourselves,

**42:2** וַיֹּאמֶר הִנֵּה שָׁמַעְתִּי כִּי יֶשׁ שֶׁבֶר בְּמִצְרָיִם רְדוּ שָׁמָּה וְשִׁבְרוּ לָנוּ מִשָּׁם וְנִחְיֶה וְלֹא נָמוּת

and~he~will~Say Look i~did~Hear Given.that There.is Barley in~"Mitsrayim [*Troubles*]" !(mp)~Go.down There~unto and~!(mp)~Exchange to~us from~There and~we~will~Live and~Not we~will~Die

and he said, look, I heard that there is barley in "Mitsrayim [*Troubles*]", go down unto there and exchange for us from there and we will live and we will not die,

**42:3** וַיֵּרְדוּ אֲחֵי יוֹסֵף עֲשָׂרָה לִשְׁבֹּר בָּר מִמִּצְרָיִם

and~they(m)~will~Go.down Brother~s "Yoseph [*Adding*]" Ten to~>~Exchange Grain from~"Mitsrayim [*Troubles*]"

and the ten brothers of "Yoseph [*Adding*]" went down to exchange grain from "Mitsrayim [*Troubles*]",

**42:4** וְאֶת בִּנְיָמִין אֲחִי יוֹסֵף לֹא שָׁלַח יַעֲקֹב אֶת אֶחָיו כִּי אָמַר פֶּן יִקְרָאֶנּוּ אָסוֹן

and~At "Binyamin [*Son of the right hand*]" Brother~of "Yoseph [*Adding*]" Not he~did~Send "Ya'aqov [*He restrains*]" At Brother~s~him Given.that he~did~Say Otherwise he~will~Meet~us Harm

and "Binyamin [*Son of the right hand*]", brother of "Yoseph [*Adding*]", "Ya'aqov [*He restrains*]" did not send with his brothers given that he said, otherwise harm will meet us,

**42:5** וַיָּבֹאוּ בְּנֵי יִשְׂרָאֵל לִשְׁבֹּר בְּתוֹךְ הַבָּאִים כִּי הָיָה הָרָעָב בְּאֶרֶץ כְּנָעַן

and~they(m)~will~Come Son~s "Yisra'el [*He turns El*]" to~>~Exchange in~Midst the~Come~ing(mp) Given.that he~did~Exist the~Hunger in~Land "Kena'an [*Lowered*]"

and the sons of "Yisra'el [*He turns El*]" came to exchange in the midst of the ones coming given that the hunger existed in the land of "Kena'an [*Lowered*]",

**42:6** וְיוֹסֵף הוּא הַשַּׁלִּיט עַל הָאָרֶץ הוּא הַמַּשְׁבִּיר לְכָל עַם הָאָרֶץ

וַיָּבֹאוּ אֲחֵי יוֹסֵף וַיִּשְׁתַּחֲווּ לוֹ אַפַּיִם אָרְצָה

| and~"Yoseph [Adding]" He the~ Governor Upon the~Land He make~ Exchange~ing(ms) to~All People the~ Land and~they(m)~will~Come Brother~ s "Yoseph [Adding]" and~they(m)~ will~self~Bend.down to~him Nose~s2 Land~unto | and "Yoseph [Adding]" was the governor upon the land making exchange to all the people of the land and the brothers of "Yoseph [Adding]" came and they bent themselves down to him, nostrils unto the land, |
|---|---|

**42:7** וַיַּרְא יוֹסֵף אֶת אֶחָיו וַיַּכִּרֵם וַיִּתְנַכֵּר אֲלֵיהֶם וַיְדַבֵּר אִתָּם קָשׁוֹת וַיֹּאמֶר אֲלֵהֶם מֵאַיִן בָּאתֶם וַיֹּאמְרוּ מֵאֶרֶץ כְּנַעַן לִשְׁבָּר אֹכֶל

| and~he~will~See "Yoseph [Adding]" At Brother~s~him and~he~will~make~ Recognize~them(m) and~he~will~self~ Recognize To~them(m) and~he~will~ much~Speak At~them(m) Hard~s and~he~will~Say To~them(m) from~ Without you(mp)~did~Come and~ they(m)~will~Say from~Land "Kena'an [Lowered]" to~>~Exchange Foodstuff | and "Yoseph [Adding]" saw his brothers and he recognized them and he made himself unrecognizable to them and he spoke to them hard, from where did you come, and they said, from the land of "Kena'an [Lowered]" to exchange foodstuff, |
|---|---|

**42:8** וַיַּכֵּר יוֹסֵף אֶת אֶחָיו וְהֵם לֹא הִכִּרֻהוּ

| and~he~will~make~Recognize "Yoseph [Adding]" At Brother~s~him and~ They(m) Not they~will~Recognize~him | and "Yoseph [Adding]" recognized his brothers and they did not recognize him, |
|---|---|

**42:9** וַיִּזְכֹּר יוֹסֵף אֵת הַחֲלֹמוֹת אֲשֶׁר חָלַם לָהֶם וַיֹּאמֶר אֲלֵהֶם מְרַגְּלִים אַתֶּם לִרְאוֹת אֶת עֶרְוַת הָאָרֶץ בָּאתֶם

| and~he~will~Remember "Yoseph [Adding]" At the~Dream~s Which he~did~Visualize to~them(m) and~he~ will~Say To~them(m) much~ Tread.about~ing(mp) You(mp) to~>~ See At Nakedness the~Land you(mp)~did~Come | and "Yoseph [Adding]" remembered the dreams which he visualized to them and he said to them, you are spies, you came to see the nakedness of the land, |
|---|---|

**42:10** וַיֹּאמְרוּ אֵלָיו לֹא אֲדֹנִי וַעֲבָדֶיךָ בָּאוּ לִשְׁבָּר אֹכֶל

| and~they(m)~will~Say To~him Not Lord~me and~Servant~s~you(ms) they~ had~Come to~>~Exchange Foodstuff | and they said to him, no my lord and your servants had come to exchange foodstuff, |
|---|---|

**42:11** כֻּלָּנוּ בְּנֵי אִישׁ אֶחָד נָחְנוּ כֵּנִים אֲנַחְנוּ לֹא הָיוּ עֲבָדֶיךָ מְרַגְּלִים

| All~us Son~s Man Unit We Base~s We Not they~did~Exist Servant~s~ you(ms) much~Tread.about~ing(mp) | all of us are the sons of one man, we are bases, your servants do not exist as spies, |
|---|---|

**42:12** וַיֹּאמֶר אֲלֵהֶם לֹא כִּי עֶרְוַת הָאָרֶץ בָּאתֶם לִרְאוֹת

and~he~will~Say To~them(m) Not Given.that Nakedness the~Land you(mp)~did~Come to~>~See

and he said to them, no, but the nakedness of the land you came to see,

**42:13** וַיֹּאמְרוּ שְׁנֵים עָשָׂר עֲבָדֶיךָ אַחִים אֲנַחְנוּ בְּנֵי אִישׁ אֶחָד בְּאֶרֶץ כְּנָעַן וְהִנֵּה הַקָּטֹן אֶת אָבִינוּ הַיּוֹם וְהָאֶחָד אֵינֶנּוּ

and~they(m)~will~Say Two Ten Servant~s~you(ms) Brother~s We Son~s Man Unit in~Land "Kena'an [Lowered]" and~Look the~Small At Father~us the~Day and~the~Unit Without~us

and they said, we are twelve of your servants, we are brothers, sons of one man in the land of "Kena'an [Lowered]" and look, the small one is with our father today and the one is not with us,

**42:14** וַיֹּאמֶר אֲלֵהֶם יוֹסֵף הוּא אֲשֶׁר דִּבַּרְתִּי אֲלֵכֶם לֵאמֹר מְרַגְּלִים אַתֶּם

and~he~will~Say To~them(m) "Yoseph [Adding]" He Which i~did~Speak To~you(mp) to~>~Say much~Tread.about~ing(mp) You(mp)

and "Yoseph [Adding]" said to them, that is what I spoke to you saying, you are spies,

**42:15** בְּזֹאת תִּבָּחֵנוּ חֵי פַרְעֹה אִם תֵּצְאוּ מִזֶּה כִּי אִם בְּבוֹא אֲחִיכֶם הַקָּטֹן הֵנָּה

in~This you(mp)~will~be~Examine Life "Paroh [Great house]" If you(mp)~will~Go.out from~This Given.that If >~Come Brother~you(mp) the~Small Look

in this, you will be examined, the life of "Paroh [Great house]" if you go out from this unless your small brother comes here,

**42:16** שִׁלְחוּ מִכֶּם אֶחָד וְיִקַּח אֶת אֲחִיכֶם וְאַתֶּם הֵאָסְרוּ וְיִבָּחֲנוּ דִּבְרֵיכֶם הַאֱמֶת אִתְּכֶם וְאִם לֹא חֵי פַרְעֹה כִּי מְרַגְּלִים אַתֶּם

!(mp)~Send from~you(mp) Unit and~he~will~Take At Brother~you(mp) and~You(mp) !(mp)~be~Tie.up and~they(m)~will~be~Examine Word~s~you(mp) ?~Truth At~you(mp) and~If Not Life "Paroh [Great house]" Given.that much~Tread.about~ing(mp) You(mp)

send from you one and he will take your brother and you will be tied up and your words will be examined, is truth with you, and if not, the life of "Paroh [Great house]" that you are spies,

**42:17** וַיֶּאֱסֹף אֹתָם אֶל מִשְׁמָר שְׁלֹשֶׁת יָמִים

and~he~will~Gather At~them(m) To Custody Three Day~s

and he gathered them for a custody of three days,

**42:18** וַיֹּאמֶר אֲלֵהֶם יוֹסֵף בַּיּוֹם הַשְּׁלִישִׁי זֹאת עֲשׂוּ וִחְיוּ אֶת הָאֱלֹהִים אֲנִי יָרֵא

and~he~will~Say To~them(m) "Yoseph [*Adding*]" in~the~Day the~Third This !(mp)~Do and~!(mp)~Live Λt the~"Elohiym [*Powers*]" I Fear~ing(ms)

and "Yoseph [*Adding*]" said to them in the third day, this do and live, I am fearing the "Elohiym [*Powers*]",

**42:19\*** אִם כֵּנִים אַתֶּם אֲחִיכֶם אֶחָד יֵאָסֵר בְּבֵית מִשְׁמַרְכֶם וְאַתֶּם לְכוּ הָבִיאוּ שֶׁבֶר רַעֲבוֹן בָּתֵּיכֶם

If Base~s You(mp) Brother~you(mp) Unit he~will~be~Tie.up in~House Custody~you(mp) and~You(mp) !(mp)~Walk !(mp)~make~Come Barley Famine House~s~you(mp)

If you are bases, your one brother will be tied up in the house of your custody and you will walk, bring barley to the famine of your house,

**42:20** וְאֶת אֲחִיכֶם הַקָּטֹן תָּבִיאוּ אֵלַי וְיֵאָמְנוּ דִבְרֵיכֶם וְלֹא תָמוּתוּ וַיַּעֲשׂוּ כֵן

and~At Brother~you(mp) the~Small you(mp)~will~make~Come To~me and~they(m)~will~be~Firm Word~s~you(mp) and~Not you(mp)~will~Die and~they(m)~will~Do So

and you will bring to me your small brother than your words will be firm and you will not die and they did so,

**42:21** וַיֹּאמְרוּ אִישׁ אֶל אָחִיו אֲבָל אֲשֵׁמִים אֲנַחְנוּ עַל אָחִינוּ אֲשֶׁר רָאִינוּ צָרַת נַפְשׁוֹ בְּהִתְחַנְנוֹ אֵלֵינוּ וְלֹא שָׁמָעְנוּ עַל כֵּן בָּאָה אֵלֵינוּ הַצָּרָה הַזֹּאת

and~they(m)~will~Say Man To~Brother~him Nevertheless Guilt~s We Upon Brother~us Which we~did~See Trouble Being~him in~>~self~Show.beauty~him To~us and~Not we~did~Hear Upon So she~did~Come To~us the~Trouble the~This

and they said each to his brother, nevertheless we are guilty about our brother because we saw the trouble of his being in his beseeching to us and we did not hear, therefore this trouble came to us,

**42:22** וַיַּעַן רְאוּבֵן אֹתָם לֵאמֹר הֲלוֹא אָמַרְתִּי אֲלֵיכֶם לֵאמֹר אַל תֶּחֶטְאוּ בַיֶּלֶד וְלֹא שְׁמַעְתֶּם וְגַם דָּמוֹ הִנֵּה נִדְרָשׁ

and~he~will~Answer "Re'uven [*See a son*]" At~them(m) to~>~Say ?~Not i~did~Say To~you(mp) to~>~Say No you(mp)~will~Err in~the~Boy and~Not you(mp)~did~Hear and~Also Blood~him Look be~Seek~ing(ms)

and "Re'uven [*See a son*]" answered them saying, did I not say to you saying, you will not err in the boy and you did not hear and also look, his blood is required,

**42:23** וְהֵם לֹא יָדְעוּ כִּי שֹׁמֵעַ יוֹסֵף כִּי הַמֵּלִיץ בֵּינֹתָם

and~They(m) Not they~did~Know Given.that Hear~ing(ms) "Yoseph [*Adding*]" Given.that the~make~Mimic~ing(ms) Between~them(m)

and they did not know that "Yoseph [*Adding*]" was listening given that the interpreter was between them,

**42:24**

וַיִּסֹּב מֵעֲלֵיהֶם וַיֵּבְךְּ וַיָּשָׁב אֲלֵהֶם וַיְדַבֵּר אֲלֵהֶם וַיִּקַּח מֵאִתָּם אֶת שִׁמְעוֹן וַיֶּאְסֹר אֹתוֹ לְעֵינֵיהֶם

and~he~will~Go.around from~Upon~them(m) and~he~will~Weep and~he~will~Turn.back To~them(m) and~he~will~Speak To~them(m) and~he~will~Take from~At~them(m) At "Shimon [*Heard*]" and~he~will~Tie.up At~him to~Eye~s2~them(m)

and he went around from upon them and he wept and he turned back to them and he spoke to them and he took from them "Shimon [*Heard*]" and he tied him up to their eyes,

**42:25***

וַיְצַו יוֹסֵף וַיְמַלְאוּ אֶת כְּלֵיהֶם בָּר וּלְהָשִׁיב כַּסְפֵּיהֶם אִישׁ אֶל שַׂקּוֹ וְלָתֵת לָהֶם צֵדָה לַדָּרֶךְ וַיַּעַשׂ לָהֶם כֵּן

and~he~will~much~Direct "Yoseph [*Adding*]" and~they(m)~will~much~Fill At Instrument~them(m) Grain and~to~>~make~Turn.back Silver~s~them(m) Man To Sack~him and~to~>~Give to~them(m) Provisions to~the~Road and~he~will~Do to~them(m) So

and "Yoseph [*Adding*]" directed and they filled their instruments of grain and returned their silver, each to his sack and gave to them provisions for the road and he did to them so,

**42:26**

וַיִּשְׂאוּ אֶת שִׁבְרָם עַל חֲמֹרֵיהֶם וַיֵּלְכוּ מִשָּׁם

and~they(m)~will~Lift.up At Barley~them(m) Upon Donkey~s~them(m) and~they(m)~will~Walk from~There

and they lifted up their barley upon their donkeys and they walked from there,

**42:27**

וַיִּפְתַּח הָאֶחָד אֶת שַׂקּוֹ לָתֵת מִסְפּוֹא לַחֲמֹרוֹ בַּמָּלוֹן וַיַּרְא אֶת כַּסְפּוֹ וְהִנֵּה הוּא בְּפִי אַמְתַּחְתּוֹ

and~he~will~Open the~Unit At Sack~him to~>~Give Provender to~Donkey~him in~the~Place.of.lodging and~he~will~See At Silver~him and~Look He in~Mouth Bag~him

and one opened his sack to give provender to his donkey in the place of lodging and he saw his silver and look, he was in the mouth of his bag,

**42:28**

וַיֹּאמֶר אֶל אֶחָיו הוּשַׁב כַּסְפִּי וְגַם הִנֵּה בְאַמְתַּחְתִּי וַיֵּצֵא לִבָּם וַיֶּחֶרְדוּ אִישׁ אֶל אָחִיו לֵאמֹר מַה זֹּאת עָשָׂה אֱלֹהִים לָנוּ

and~he~will~Say To Brother~s~him he~did~make.be~Turn.back Silver~me and~Also Look in~Bag~me and~he~will~Go.out Heart~them(m) and~they(m)~will~Tremble Man To Brother~him to~>~Say What This he~did~Do "Elohiym [*Powers*]" to~us

and he said to his brothers, my silver was returned and also look in my bag, and their heart went out and they trembled, each to his brother saying, what is this "Elohiym [*Powers*]" did to us,

**42:29**

וַיָּבֹאוּ אֶל יַעֲקֹב אֲבִיהֶם אַרְצָה כְּנָעַן וַיַּגִּידוּ לוֹ אֵת כָּל הַקֹּרֹת אֹתָם לֵאמֹר

and~they(m)~will~Come To "Ya'aqov [*He restrains*]" Father~them(m) Land~ unto "Kena'an [*Lowered*]" and~ they(m)~will~make~Be.face.to.face to~ him At All the~Meet~ing(fp) At~ them(m) to~>~Say

and they came to "Ya'aqov [*He restrains*]" their father, unto the land of "Kena'an [*Lowered*]" and they told him all the meeting saying,

**42:30\*** דִּבֶּר הָאִישׁ אֲדֹנֵי הָאָרֶץ אִתָּנוּ קָשׁוֹת וַיִּתֵּן אֹתָנוּ כִּמְרַגְּלִים אֶת הָאָרֶץ

he~did~much~Speak the~Man Lord~s the~Land At~us Hard~s and~he~will~ Give At~us like~much~Tread.about~ ing(mp) At the~Land

and the man, the lord of the land, spoke to us hard and he gave us like spies of the land,

**42:31** וַנֹּאמֶר אֵלָיו כֵּנִים אֲנָחְנוּ לֹא הָיִינוּ מְרַגְּלִים

and~we~will~Say To~him Base~s We Not we~did~Exist much~Tread.about~ ing(mp)

and we said to him, we are bases, we do not exist as spies,

**42:32** שְׁנֵים עָשָׂר אֲנַחְנוּ אַחִים בְּנֵי אָבִינוּ הָאֶחָד אֵינֶנּוּ וְהַקָּטֹן הַיּוֹם אֶת אָבִינוּ בְּאֶרֶץ כְּנָעַן

Two Ten We Brother~s Son~s Father~us the~Unit Without~us and~ the~Small the~Day At Father~us in~ Land "Kena'an [*Lowered*]"

we are twelve brothers, sons of our father, the one is not with us and the small one is today with our father in the land of "Kena'an [*Lowered*]",

**42:33** וַיֹּאמֶר אֵלֵינוּ הָאִישׁ אֲדֹנֵי הָאָרֶץ בְּזֹאת אֵדַע כִּי כֵנִים אַתֶּם אֲחִיכֶם הָאֶחָד הַנִּיחוּ אִתִּי וְאֶת רַעֲבוֹן בָּתֵּיכֶם קְחוּ וָלֵכוּ

and~he~will~Say To~us the~Man Lord~s the~Land the~This i~will~ Know Given.that Base~s You(mp) Brother~you(mp) the~Unit !(mp)~ make~Rest At~me and~At Famine House~s~you(mp) !(mp)~Take and~ !(mp)~Walk

and the man, the lord of this land, said to us, I will know that you are bases, make one of your brothers rest with me, the one, and to the famine of your house, take and walk,

**42:34** וְהָבִיאוּ אֶת אֲחִיכֶם הַקָּטֹן אֵלַי וְאֵדְעָה כִּי לֹא מְרַגְּלִים אַתֶּם כִּי כֵנִים אַתֶּם אֶת אֲחִיכֶם אֶתֵּן לָכֶם וְאֶת הָאָרֶץ תִּסְחָרוּ

and~!(mp)~make~Come At Brother~ you(mp) the~Small To~me and~i~ will~Know~^ Given.that Not much~ Tread.about~ing(mp) You(mp) Given.that Base~s You(mp) At Brother~you(mp) i~will~Give to~ you(mp) and~At the~Land you(mp)~

and bring your small brother to me and I will know that you are not spies given that you are bases, I will give to you your brother and you will trade with the land,

will~Trade

**42:35** וַיְהִי הֵם מְרִיקִים שַׂקֵּיהֶם וְהִנֵּה אִישׁ צְרוֹר כַּסְפּוֹ בְּשַׂקּוֹ וַיִּרְאוּ
אֶת צְרֹרוֹת כַּסְפֵּיהֶם הֵמָּה וַאֲבִיהֶם וַיִּירָאוּ

and~he~will~Exist They(m) make~
Empty~ing(mp) Sack~s~them(m) and~
Look Man Bundle Silver~him in~
Sack~him and~they(m)~will~See At
Bundle~s Silver~s~them(m) They(m)
and~Father~them(m) and~they(m)~will~
Fear

and it came to pass they were
emptying their sacks and look, each
bundle of his silver was in him and
they saw the bundles of their silver,
they and their father and they
feared,

**42:36** וַיֹּאמֶר אֲלֵהֶם יַעֲקֹב אֲבִיהֶם אֹתִי שִׁכַּלְתֶּם יוֹסֵף אֵינֶנּוּ וְשִׁמְעוֹן
אֵינֶנּוּ וְאֶת בִּנְיָמִן תִּקָּחוּ עָלַי הָיוּ כֻלָּנָה

and~he~will~Say To~them(m) "Ya'aqov
[*He restrains*]" Father~them(m) At~
me you(mp)~will~much~Be.childless
"Yoseph [*Adding*]" Without~him and~
"Shimon [*Heard*]" Without~him and~
At "Binyamin [*Son of the right
hand*]" you(mp)~will~Take Upon~me
they~will~Exist All~them(f)

and "Ya'aqov [*He restrains*]", their
father, said to them, you will make
me be childless, "Yoseph [*Adding*]"
is not and "Shimon [*Heard*]" is not
and you will take "Binyamin [*Son
of the right hand*]", upon me all of
them exist,

**42:37** וַיֹּאמֶר רְאוּבֵן אֶל אָבִיו לֵאמֹר אֶת שְׁנֵי בָנַי תָּמִית אִם לֹא
אֲבִיאֶנּוּ אֵלֶיךָ תְּנָה אֹתוֹ עַל יָדִי וַאֲנִי אֲשִׁיבֶנּוּ אֵלֶיךָ

and~he~will~Say "Re'uven [*See a
son*]" To Father~him to~>>~Say At
Two Son~s~me you(ms)~will~make~
Die If Not i~will~make~Come~him
To~you(ms) !(ms)~Give~^ At~him
Upon Hand~me and~I i~will~make~
Turn.back~him To~you(ms)

and "Re'uven [*See a son*]" said to
his father saying, you will kill my
two sons if I will not bring him to
you, give him upon my hand and I
will return him to you,

**42:38** וַיֹּאמֶר לֹא יֵרֵד בְּנִי עִמָּכֶם כִּי אָחִיו מֵת וְהוּא לְבַדּוֹ נִשְׁאָר
וּקְרָאָהוּ אָסוֹן בַּדֶּרֶךְ אֲשֶׁר תֵּלְכוּ בָהּ וְהוֹרַדְתֶּם אֶת שֵׂיבָתִי
בְּיָגוֹן שְׁאוֹלָה

and~he~will~Say Not he~will~Go.down
Son~me With~you(mp) Given.that
Brother~him he~did~Die and~He to~
Separated.thing~him be~Remain~ing(ms)
and~he~did~Meet~him Harm in~the~
Road Which you(mp)~will~Walk in~
her and~you(mp)~will~make~Go.down
At Gray.headed~me in~Sorrow
Underworld~unto

and he said, my son will not go
down with you given that his
brother died and he remains by
himself and harm will meet him in
the road which you walk in and you
will bring down my gray head in
sorrow unto the underworld,

# Chapter 43

**43:1**

וְהָרָעָב כָּבֵד בָּאָרֶץ

and~the~Famine  Heavy  in~the~Land

and the famine was heavy in the land,

**43:2**

וַיְהִי כַּאֲשֶׁר כִּלּוּ לֶאֱכֹל אֶת הַשֶּׁבֶר אֲשֶׁר הֵבִיאוּ מִמִּצְרָיִם
וַיֹּאמֶר אֲלֵיהֶם אֲבִיהֶם שֻׁבוּ שִׁבְרוּ לָנוּ מְעַט אֹכֶל

and~he~will~Exist  like~Which  they~did~Finish  to~>~Eat  At  the~Barley  Which  they~did~make~Come  from~ "Mitsrayim [*Troubles*]"  and~he~will~Say  To~them(m)  Father~them(m)  !(mp)~Turn.back  !(mp)~Exchange  to~us  Small.amount  Foodstuff

and it came to pass, just as they finished eating the barley which they brought from "Mitsrayim [*Troubles*]" and their father said to them, turn back, exchange for us a small amount of foodstuff,

**43:3**

וַיֹּאמֶר אֵלָיו יְהוּדָה לֵאמֹר הָעֵד הֵעִד בָּנוּ הָאִישׁ לֵאמֹר לֹא
תִרְאוּ פָנַי בִּלְתִּי אֲחִיכֶם אִתְּכֶם

and~he~will~Say  To~him  "Yehudah [*Praised*]"  to~>~Say  >~make~ Wrap.around  he~did~make~Wrap.around  in~us  the~Man  to~>~Say  Not  you(mp)~will~See  Face~s~me  Except  Brother~you(mp)  At~you(mp)

and "Yehudah [*Praised*]" said to him saying, the man greatly warned us saying, you will not see my face except your brother be with you,

**43:4**

אִם יֶשְׁךָ מְשַׁלֵּחַ אֶת אָחִינוּ אִתָּנוּ נֵרְדָה וְנִשְׁבְּרָה לְךָ אֹכֶל

If  There.is~you(ms)  much~Send~ ing(ms)  At  Brother~us  At~us  we~ will~Go.down~^  and~we~will~ Exchange~^  to~you(ms)  Foodstuff

if you will send our brother with us, we will go down and we will exchange for you foodstuff,

**43:5**

וְאִם אֵינְךָ מְשַׁלֵּחַ לֹא נֵרֵד כִּי הָאִישׁ אָמַר אֵלֵינוּ לֹא תִרְאוּ פָנַי
בִּלְתִּי אֲחִיכֶם אִתְּכֶם

and~If  Without~you(ms)  much~Send~ ing(ms)  Not  we~will~Go.down  Given.that  the~Man  he~had~Say  To~ us  Not  you(mp)~will~See  Face~s~me  Except  Brother~you(mp)  At~you(mp)

and if you will not send, we will not go down given that the man had said to us, you will not see my face except your brother be with you,

**43:6**

וַיֹּאמֶר יִשְׂרָאֵל לָמָה הֲרֵעֹתֶם לִי לְהַגִּיד לָאִישׁ הַעוֹד לָכֶם אָח

and~he~will~Say  "Yisra'el [*He turns El*]"  to~What  you(mp)~did~make~ Be.dysfunctional  to~me  to~>~make~ Be.face.to.face  to~the~Man  the~ Yet.again  to~you(mp)  Brother

and "Yisra'el [*He turns El*]" said, why did you make me dysfunctional, telling to the man you had another brother,

**43:7** וַיֹּאמְרוּ שָׁאוֹל שָׁאַל הָאִישׁ לָנוּ וּלְמוֹלַדְתֵּנוּ לֵאמֹר הַעוֹד אֲבִיכֶם חַי הֲיֵשׁ לָכֶם אָח וַנַּגֶּד לוֹ עַל פִּי הַדְּבָרִים הָאֵלֶּה הֲיָדוֹעַ נֵדַע כִּי יֹאמַר הוֹרִידוּ אֶת אֲחִיכֶם

and~they(m)~will-Say >-Inquire he~did-Inquire the~Man to~us and~to~Kindred~us to~>-Say the~Yet.again Father~you(mp) Life the~There.is to~you(mp) Brother and~we~will~make~Be.face.to.face to~him Upon Mouth the~Word~s the~These the~>-Know we~will~Know Given.that he~will~Say !(mp)~make~Go.down At Brother~you(mp)

and they said, the man greatly inquired about us and about our kindred saying, is your father yet alive and is there to you a brother, and we told to him upon the mouth of these words, could we know that he would say, bring down your brother,

**43:8** וַיֹּאמֶר יְהוּדָה אֶל יִשְׂרָאֵל אָבִיו שִׁלְחָה הַנַּעַר אִתִּי וְנָקוּמָה וְנֵלֵכָה וְנִחְיֶה וְלֹא נָמוּת גַּם אֲנַחְנוּ גַם אַתָּה גַם טַפֵּנוּ

and~he~will~Say "Yehudah [Praised]" To "Yisra'el [He turns El]" Father~him !(ms)~Send~^ the~Young.man At~me and~we~will~Rise~^ and~we~will~Walk~^ and~we~will~Live~^ and~Not we~will~Die Also We Also You(ms) Also Children~us

and "Yehudah [Praised]" said to "Yisra'el [He turns El]" his father, send the young man with me and we will rise and we will walk and we will live and we will not die, also us, also you, also our children,

**43:9** אָנֹכִי אֶעֶרְבֶנּוּ מִיָּדִי תְּבַקְשֶׁנּוּ אִם לֹא הֲבִיאֹתִיו אֵלֶיךָ וְהִצַּגְתִּיו לְפָנֶיךָ וְחָטָאתִי לְךָ כָּל הַיָּמִים

I i~will~Barter~him from~Hand~me you(ms)~will~much~Search.out~him If Not i~did~make~Come~him To~you(ms) and~i~did~make~Set~him to~Face~s~you(ms) and~i~did~Err to~you(ms) All the~Day~s

I will barter him, from my hand you will search him out, if I do not bring him to you and I set him to your face then I will err to you all the days,

**43:10** כִּי לוּלֵא הִתְמַהְמָהְנוּ כִּי עַתָּה שַׁבְנוּ זֶה פַעֲמָיִם

Given.that Unless we~did~self~Linger Given.that Now we~did~Turn.back This Stroke.of.time~s2

for if we lingered, given that we now turned back this second time,

**43:11** וַיֹּאמֶר אֲלֵהֶם יִשְׂרָאֵל אֲבִיהֶם אִם כֵּן אֵפוֹא זֹאת עֲשׂוּ קְחוּ מִזִּמְרַת הָאָרֶץ בִּכְלֵיכֶם וְהוֹרִידוּ לָאִישׁ מִנְחָה מְעַט צֳרִי וּמְעַט דְּבַשׁ נְכֹאת וָלֹט בָּטְנִים וּשְׁקֵדִים

and~he~will~Say To~them(m) "Yisra'el [He turns El]" Father~them(m) If So Then This !(mp)~Do !(mp)~Take from~Choice.fruit the~Land in~

and "Yisra'el [He turns El]", their father, said to them, if it is so then this do, take from the choice fruit of the land in your instruments and

Instrument~you(mp)   and~!(mp)~make~
Go.down   to~the~Man   Donation
Small.amount   Balm   and~Small.amount
Honey   Spice   and~Myrrh   Pistachio
and~Almond

bring down to the man a donation
of a small amount of balm and a
small amount of honey, spice and
myrrh, pistachio and almond,

**43:12**   וְכֶסֶף מִשְׁנֶה קְחוּ בְיֶדְכֶם וְאֶת הַכֶּסֶף הַמּוּשָׁב בְּפִי אַמְתְּחֹתֵיכֶם
תָּשִׁיבוּ בְיֶדְכֶם אוּלַי מִשְׁגֶּה הוּא

and~Silver   Double   !(mp)~Take  in~
Hand~you(mp)   and~At   the~Silver
the~make.be~Turn.back~ing(ms)   in~
Mouth   Bag~s~you(mp)   you(mp)~will~
make~Turn.back   in~Hand~you(mp)
Possibly   Oversight   He

and take double the silver in your
hand and the returned silver in the
mouth of your bag you will return
in your hand, possibly he is an
oversight,

**43:13**   וְאֶת אֲחִיכֶם קָחוּ וְקוּמוּ שׁוּבוּ אֶל הָאִישׁ

and~At   Brother~you(mp)   !(mp)~Take
and~!(mp)~Rise   and~Turn.back   To
the~Man

and take your brother and rise and
turn back to the man,

**43:14**   וְאֵל שַׁדַּי יִתֵּן לָכֶם רַחֲמִים לִפְנֵי הָאִישׁ וְשִׁלַּח לָכֶם אֶת אֲחִיכֶם
אַחֵר וְאֶת בִּנְיָמִין וַאֲנִי כַּאֲשֶׁר שָׁכֹלְתִּי שָׁכָלְתִּי

and~Mighty.one   "Shaddai [*My
breasts*]"   he~will~Give   to~you(mp)
Bowels~s   to~the~Face~s   the~Man
and~he~did~much~Send   to~you(mp)   At
Brother~you(mp)   Other   and~At
"Binyamin [*Son of the right hand*]"
and~I   like~Which   i~did~Be.childless
i~did~Be.childless

and the mighty one of "Shaddai
[*My breasts*]" will give to you
bowels to the face of the man and
he will send to you your other
brother and "Binyamin [*Son of the
right hand*]" and just as I was
childless,

**43:15***   וַיִּקְחוּ הָאֲנָשִׁים אֶת הַמִּנְחָה הַזֹּאת וּמִשְׁנֶה כֶּסֶף לָקְחוּ בְיָדָם
וְאֶת בִּנְיָמִן וַיָּקֻמוּ וַיֵּרְדוּ מִצְרַיִם וַיַּעַמְדוּ לִפְנֵי יוֹסֵף

and~they(m)~will~Take   the~Man~s   At
the~Donation   the~This   and~Double
Silver   they~will~Take   in~Hand~
them(m)   and~At   "Binyamin [*Son of
the right hand*]"   and~they(m)~will~
Rise   and~they(m)~will~Go.down
"Mitsrayim [*Troubles*]"   and~they(m)~
will~Stand   to~Face~s   "Yoseph
[*Adding*]"

and the men took this donation and
double the silver they took in their
hand and "Binyamin [*Son of the
right hand*]", and they rose and they
went   down   unto   "Mitsrayim
[*Troubles*]" and they stood to the
face of "Yoseph [*Adding*]",

**43:16**   וַיַּרְא יוֹסֵף אִתָּם אֶת בִּנְיָמִין וַיֹּאמֶר לַאֲשֶׁר עַל בֵּיתוֹ הָבֵא אֶת
הָאֲנָשִׁים הַבָּיְתָה וּטְבֹחַ טֶבַח וְהָכֵן כִּי אִתִּי יֹאכְלוּ הָאֲנָשִׁים
בַּצָּהֳרָיִם

and~he~will~See "Yoseph [*Adding*]" At~them(m) At "Binyamin [*Son of the right hand*]" and~he~will~Say to~Which Upon House~him !(ms)~ make~Come At the~Man~s the~ House~unto and~!(ms)~Butcher Slaughtering and~!(ms)~make~Fixed Given.that At~me they(m)~will~Eat the~Man~s in~the~Shining~s2

and "Yoseph [*Adding*]" saw them with "Binyamin [*Son of the right hand*]" and he said to who was upon his house, bring the men unto the house and butcher a slaughtering and fix it given that the men will eat with me in noontime,

**43:17** וַיַּעַשׂ הָאִישׁ כַּאֲשֶׁר אָמַר יוֹסֵף וַיָּבֵא הָאִישׁ אֶת הָאֲנָשִׁים בֵּיתָה יוֹסֵף

and~he~will~Do the~Man like~Which he~did~Say "Yoseph [*Adding*]" and~ he~will~make~Come the~Man At the~Man~s House~unto "Yoseph [*Adding*]"

and the man did just as "Yoseph [*Adding*]" said and the man brought the men unto the house of "Yoseph [*Adding*]",

**43:18** * וַיִּירְאוּ הָאֲנָשִׁים כִּי הוּבְאוּ בֵּית יוֹסֵף וַיֹּאמְרוּ עַל דְּבַר הַכֶּסֶף הַשָּׁב בְּאַמְתְּחֹתֵינוּ בַּתְּחִלָּה אֲנַחְנוּ מוּבָאִים לְהִתְגֹּלֵל עָלֵינוּ וּלְהִתְנַפֵּל עָלֵינוּ וְלָקַחַת אֹתָנוּ לַעֲבָדִים וְאֶת חֲמֹרֵינוּ

and~they(m)~will~Fear the~Man~s Given.that they~did~make.be~Come House "Yoseph [*Adding*]" and~ they(m)~will~Say Upon Word the~ Silver the~Turn.back~ing(ms) in~Bag~ s~us in~the~First.time We make.be~ Come~ing(mp) to~>~self~Roll Upon~ us and~to~>~self~Fall Upon~us and~ to~>~Take At~us to~the~Servant~s and~At Donkey~s~us

and the men feared given that they were brought down unto the house of "Yoseph [*Adding*]" and they said, upon the matter of the returned silver in our bags the first time we were bringing we are being brought to roll upon us and to fall upon us and to take us for servants, and our donkeys,

**43:19** וַיִּגְּשׁוּ אֶל הָאִישׁ אֲשֶׁר עַל בֵּית יוֹסֵף וַיְדַבְּרוּ אֵלָיו פֶּתַח הַבָּיִת

and~they(m)~will~Draw.near To the~ Man Which Upon House "Yoseph [*Adding*]" and~they(m)~will~much~ Speak To~him Opening the~House

and they drew near to the man who was upon the house of "Yoseph [*Adding*]" and they spoke to him at the opening of the house,

**43:20** וַיֹּאמְרוּ בִּי אֲדֹנִי יָרֹד יָרַדְנוּ בַּתְּחִלָּה לִשְׁבָּר אֹכֶל

and~they(m)~will~Say Excuse.me Lord~me >~Go.down we~did~Go.down in~the~First.time to~>~Exchange Foodstuff

and they said, excuse me my lord, we quickly went down in the first time to exchange foodstuff,

**43:21** וַיְהִי כִּי בָאנוּ אֶל הַמָּלוֹן וַנִּפְתְּחָה אֶת אַמְתְּחֹתֵינוּ וְהִנֵּה כֶסֶף אִישׁ בְּפִי אַמְתַּחְתּוֹ כַּסְפֵּנוּ בְּמִשְׁקָלוֹ וַנָּשֶׁב אֹתוֹ בְּיָדֵנוּ

and~he~will~Exist  Given.that  we~did~
Come  To  the~Place.of.lodging  and~
we~will~Open~^  At  Bag~s~us  and~
Look  Silver  Man  in~Mouth  Bag~him
Silver~us  in~Weight~him  and~we~
will~make~Turn.back  At~him  in~
Hand~us  ▢

and it came to pass, that we came to
the place of lodging and we opened
our bags and look, the silver of
each was in the mouth of his bag,
our silver in his weight, and we
returned him in our hand,

**43:22** וְכֶסֶף אַחֵר הוֹרַדְנוּ בְיָדֵנוּ לִשְׁבָּר אֹכֶל לֹא יָדַעְנוּ מִי שָׂם כַּסְפֵּנוּ בְּאַמְתְּחֹתֵינוּ

and~Silver  Other  we~did~make~
Go.down  in~Hand~us  to~>~Exchange
Foodstuff  Not  we~did~Know  Who
he~did~Set.in.place  Silver~us  in~Bag~
s~us

and other silver we brought down
in our hand to exchange foodstuff,
we do not know who set in place
our silver in our bags,

**43:23** וַיֹּאמֶר שָׁלוֹם לָכֶם אַל תִּירָאוּ אֱלֹהֵיכֶם וֵאלֹהֵי אֲבִיכֶם נָתַן לָכֶם מַטְמוֹן בְּאַמְתְּחֹתֵיכֶם כַּסְפְּכֶם בָּא אֵלָי וַיּוֹצֵא אֲלֵהֶם אֶת שִׁמְעוֹן

and~he~will~Say  Completeness  to~
you(mp)  No  you(mp)~will~Fear
Power~s~you(mp)  and~Power~s
Father~you(mp)  he~did~Give  to~
you(mp)  Treasure  in~Bag~s~you(mp)
Silver~you(mp)  he~had~Come  To~me
and~he~will~make~Go.out  To~them(m)
At  "Shimon  [*Heard*]"

and he said, completeness to you,
you will not fear your powers and
the powers of your father gave to
you treasure in your bags, your
silver had come to me and he
brought out "Shimon [*Heard*]" to
them,

**43:24** וַיָּבֵא הָאִישׁ אֶת הָאֲנָשִׁים בֵּיתָה יוֹסֵף וַיִּתֵּן מַיִם וַיִּרְחֲצוּ רַגְלֵיהֶם וַיִּתֵּן מִסְפּוֹא לַחֲמֹרֵיהֶם

and~he~will~make~Come  the~Man  At
the~Man~s  House~unto  "Yoseph
[*Adding*]"  and~he~will~Give  Water~s2
and~they(m)~will~Wash  Foot~s~
them(m)  and~he~will~Give  Provender
to~Donkey~s~them(m)

and the man brought the men unto
the house of "Yoseph [*Adding*]"
and he gave water and they washed
their feet and he gave provender to
their donkeys,

**43:25** וַיָּכִינוּ אֶת הַמִּנְחָה עַד בּוֹא יוֹסֵף בַּצָּהֳרָיִם כִּי שָׁמְעוּ כִּי שָׁם יֹאכְלוּ לָחֶם

and~they(m)~will~make~Fixed  At  the~
Donation  Until  >~Come  "Yoseph
[*Adding*]"  in~the~Shining~s2  Given.that
they~did~Hear  Given.that  There
they(m)~will~Eat  Bread

and they fixed the donation until
"Yoseph [*Adding*]" came in the
noontime, given that they heard that
they will eat bread there,

**43:26** וַיָּבֹא יוֹסֵף הַבַּיְתָה וַיָּבִיאוּ לוֹ אֶת הַמִּנְחָה אֲשֶׁר בְּיָדָם הַבַּיְתָה

וַיִּשְׁתַּחֲווּ לוֹ אָרְצָה

and~he~will~Come "Yoseph [*Adding*]"
the~House~unto and~they(m)~will~
make~Come to~him At the~Donation
Which in~Hand~them(m) the~House~
unto and~they(m)~will~self~Bend.down
to~him Land~unto

and "Yoseph [*Adding*]" came unto
the house and they brought to him
the donation which was in their
hand unto the house, and they bent
themselves down unto the land to
him,

**43:27** וַיִּשְׁאַל לָהֶם לְשָׁלוֹם וַיֹּאמֶר הֲשָׁלוֹם אֲבִיכֶם הַזָּקֵן אֲשֶׁר
אֲמַרְתֶּם הַעוֹדֶנּוּ חָי

and~he~will~Inquire to~them(m) to~
Completeness and~he~will~Say ?~
Completeness Father~you(ms) the~
Beard Which you(mp)~did~Say ?~
Yet.again Life

and he inquired them about the
completeness, and he said, how is
the completeness of your father, the
bearded one which you said, is he
yet alive,

**43:28** וַיֹּאמְרוּ שָׁלוֹם לְעַבְדְּךָ לְאָבִינוּ עוֹדֶנּוּ חָי וַיִּקְּדוּ וישתחו
(וַיִּשְׁתַּחֲווּ)

and~they(m)~will~Say Completeness
to~Servant~you(ms) to~Father~us
Yet.again~him Life and~he~will~
Bow.the.head and~he~will~self~
Bend.down

and they said, completeness to your
servant, our father, he is yet alive,
and he bowed the head and he bent
himself down,

**43:29\*** וַיִּשָּׂא עֵינָיו וַיַּרְא אֶת בִּנְיָמִין אָחִיו בֶּן אִמּוֹ וַיֹּאמֶר הֲזֶה אֲחִיכֶם
הַקָּטֹן אֲשֶׁר אֲמַרְתֶּם אֵלָי וַיֹּאמַר אֱלֹהִים יָחְנְךָ בְּנִי

and~he~will~Lift.up Eye~s2~him and~
he~will~See At "Binyamin [*Son of
the right hand*]" Brother~him Son
Mother~him and~he~will~Say ?~This
Brother~you(mp) the~Small Which
you(mp)~did~Say To~me and~he~will~
Say "Elohiym [*Powers*]" he~will~
Show.beauty~you(ms) Son~me

and he lifted up his eyes and he saw
"Binyamin [*Son of the right hand*]"
his brother, the son of his mother
and he said, is this your brother, the
small one which you said to me,
and he said, "Elohiym [*Powers*]"
will show you beauty my son,

**43:30** וַיְמַהֵר יוֹסֵף כִּי נִכְמְרוּ רַחֲמָיו אֶל אָחִיו וַיְבַקֵּשׁ לִבְכּוֹת וַיָּבֹא
הַחַדְרָה וַיֵּבְךְּ שָׁמָּה

and~he~will~much~Hurry "Yoseph
[*Adding*]" Given.that they~will~be~
Burn.black Bowels~s~him To
Brother~him and~he~will~much~
Search.out to~>~Weep and~he~will~
Come the~Chamber~unto and~he~will~
Weep There~unto

and "Yoseph [*Adding*]" hurried
given that his bowels burned black
for his brother and he searched out
to weep and he came unto the
chamber and he wept unto there,

**43:31** וַיִּרְחַץ פָּנָיו וַיֵּצֵא וַיִּתְאַפַּק וַיֹּאמֶר שִׂימוּ לָחֶם

and~he~will~Wash  Face~s~him  and~ he~will~Go.out  and~he~will~self~ Hold.back  and~he~will~Say  !(mp)~ Set.in.place  Bread

and he washed his face and he went out and he held himself back and he said, set bread in place,

**43:32** וַיָּשִׂימוּ לוֹ לְבַדּוֹ וְלָהֶם לְבַדָּם וְלַמִּצְרִים הָאֹכְלִים אִתּוֹ לְבַדָּם כִּי לֹא יוּכְלוּן הַמִּצְרִים לֶאֱכֹל אֶת הָעִבְרִים לֶחֶם כִּי תוֹעֵבָה הִוא לְמִצְרָיִם

and~they(m)~will~Set.in.place  to~him to~Separated.thing~him  and~to~them(m) to~Separated.thing~them(m)  and~to~ "Mitsrayim [*Troubles*]"~s  the~Eat~ ing(mp)  At~him  to~Separated.thing~ them(m)  Given.that  Not  they(m)~will~ Be.able  the~"Mitsrayim [*Troubles*]"~s to~>~Eat  At  the~"Ever [*Cross over*]"~s  Bread  Given.that  Disgusting She  to~"Mitsrayim [*Troubles*]"

and they set a place for him by himself and for them by themselves and for the ones of "Mitsrayim [*Troubles*]" eating with him by themselves given that the ones of "Mitsrayim [*Troubles*]" were not able to eat bread with the ones of "Ever [*Cross over*]" given that she is disgusting to "Mitsrayim [*Troubles*]",

**43:33** וַיֵּשְׁבוּ לְפָנָיו הַבְּכֹר כִּבְכֹרָתוֹ וְהַצָּעִיר כִּצְעִרָתוֹ וַיִּתְמְהוּ הָאֲנָשִׁים אִישׁ אֶל רֵעֵהוּ

and~they(m)~will~Settle  to~Face~s~him the~Firstborn  like~Birthright~him  and~ the~Little.one  like~Youthfulness~him and~they(m)~will~Marvel  the~Man~s Man  To  Companion~him

and they settled to his face, the firstborn according to his birthright and the little one according to his youthfulness and the men marveled each to his companion,

**43:34\*** וַיִּשָּׂא מַשְׂאֹת מֵאֵת פָּנָיו אֲלֵהֶם וַתֵּרֶב מַשְׂאַת בִּנְיָמִן מִמַּשְׂאֹת כֻּלָּם חָמֵשׁ יָדוֹת וַיִּשְׁתּוּ וַיִּשְׁכְּרוּ עִמּוֹ

and~he~will~Lift.up  Uprising~s  from~ At  Face~s~him  To~them(m)  and~she~ will~Increase  Uprising  "Binyamin [*Son  of  the  right  hand*]"  from~ Uprising  All~them(m)  Five  Hand~s and~they(m)~will~Gulp  and~they(m)~ will~Be.drunk  With~him

and he lifted up the uprisings from his face to them, and the uprising of "Binyamin [*Son of the right hand*]" was increased more than the uprising of all of them, five hands, and they gulped and they were drunk with him,

# Chapter 44

**44:1\*** וַיְצַו אֶת אֲשֶׁר עַל בֵּיתוֹ לֵאמֹר מַלֵּא אֶת אַמְתְּחֹת הָאֲנָשִׁים אֹכֶל כַּאֲשֶׁר יוּכְלוּן שְׂאֵת וְשִׂים כֶּסֶף אִישׁ בְּפִי אַמְתַּחְתּוֹ

and~he~will~much~Direct  At  Which Upon  House~him  to~>~Say  !(ms)~ much~Fill  At  Bag~s  the~Man~s

and he directed the one who is upon his house saying, fill the bags of the men with foodstuff, just as they are

Foodstuff like~Which they(m)~will~
Be.able >~Lift.up and~!(ms)~
Set.in.place Silver Man in~Mouth
Bag~him

able to lift up and set in place the
silver of each in the mouth of his
bag,

**44:2** וְאֶת גְּבִיעִי גְּבִיעַ הַכֶּסֶף תָּשִׂים בְּפִי אַמְתַּחַת הַקָּטֹן וְאֵת כֶּסֶף
שִׁבְרוֹ וַיַּעַשׂ כִּדְבַר יוֹסֵף אֲשֶׁר דִּבֵּר

and~At Bowl~me Bowl the~Silver
you(mp)~will~Set.in.place in~Mouth
Bag the~Small and~At Silver
Barley~him and~he~will~Do like~Word
"Yoseph [Adding]" Which he~did~
much~Say

and my cup, the silver cup, you will
set in place in the mouth of the bag
of the small one and the silver of
his barley, and he did according to
the word of "Yoseph [Adding]"
which he said,

**44:3** הַבֹּקֶר אוֹר וְהָאֲנָשִׁים שֻׁלְּחוּ הֵמָּה וַחֲמֹרֵיהֶם

the~Morning Light and~the~Man~s
they~did~much.be~Send They(m) and~
Donkey~s~them(m)

the morning light and the men were
sent, they and their donkeys,

**44:4** הֵם יָצְאוּ אֶת הָעִיר לֹא הִרְחִיקוּ וְיוֹסֵף אָמַר לַאֲשֶׁר עַל בֵּיתוֹ
קוּם רְדֹף אַחֲרֵי הָאֲנָשִׁים וְהִשַּׂגְתָּם וְאָמַרְתָּ אֲלֵהֶם לָמָּה
שִׁלַּמְתֶּם רָעָה תַּחַת טוֹבָה

They(m) they~had~Go.out At the~City
Not they~did~make~Be.far and~
"Yoseph [Adding]" he~had~Say to~
Which Upon House~him !(ms)~Rise
!(ms)~Pursue After the~Man~s and~
you(ms)~did~make~Overtake~them(m)
and~you(ms)~did~Say To~them(m) to~
What you(mp)~did~much~
Make.restitution Dysfunctional Under
Functional

they had gone out of the city, they
were not far and "Yoseph
[Adding]" had said to who was
upon his house, rise, pursue after
the men and you will overtake them
and you will say to them why did
you make a restitution of
dysfunction in place of function,

**44:5** הֲלוֹא זֶה אֲשֶׁר יִשְׁתֶּה אֲדֹנִי בּוֹ וְהוּא נַחֵשׁ יְנַחֵשׁ בּוֹ הֲרֵעֹתֶם
אֲשֶׁר עֲשִׂיתֶם

?~Not This Which he~will~Gulp
Lord~me in~him and~He >~much~
Divine he~will~much~Divine in~him
you(mp)~did~make~Be.dysfunctional
Which you(mp)~did~Do

is not this which my lord gulps
with, and he greatly divines with,
you made dysfunction by what you
did,

**44:6** וַיַּשִּׂגֵם וַיְדַבֵּר אֲלֵהֶם אֶת הַדְּבָרִים הָאֵלֶּה

and~he~will~make~Overtake and~he~
will~much~Speak To~them(m) At
the~Word~s the~These

and he overtook and he spoke to
them these words,

**44:7** וַיֹּאמְרוּ אֵלָיו לָמָּה יְדַבֵּר אֲדֹנִי כַּדְּבָרִים הָאֵלֶּה חָלִילָה לַעֲבָדֶיךָ

# Mechanical Translation of Genesis

מֵעֲשׂוֹת כַּדָּבָר הַזֶּה

and~they(m)~will~Say To~him to~ What he~will~much~Speak Lord~me like~Word~s the~These Far.be.it to~ Servant~s~you(ms) from~>~Do like~ the~Word the~This

and they said to him, why does my lord speak according to these words, far be it for your servants to do in this manner,

**44:8** הֵן כֶּסֶף אֲשֶׁר מָצָאנוּ בְּפִי אַמְתְּחֹתֵינוּ הֱשִׁיבֹנוּ אֵלֶיךָ מֵאֶרֶץ כְּנָעַן וְאֵיךְ נִגְנֹב מִבֵּית אֲדֹנֶיךָ כֶּסֶף אוֹ זָהָב

Though Silver Which we~did~Find in~Mouth Bag~s~us we~did~make~ Turn.back To~you(ms) from~Land "Kena'an [Lowered]" and~Where we~ will~Steal from~House Lord~s~you(ms) Silver Or Gold

look, the silver which we found in the mouth of our bags we returned to you from the land of "Kena'an [Lowered]", why then would we steal silver or gold from the house of your lord,

**44:9** אֲשֶׁר יִמָּצֵא אִתּוֹ מֵעֲבָדֶיךָ וָמֵת וְגַם אֲנַחְנוּ נִהְיֶה לַאדֹנִי לַעֲבָדִים

Which he~will~be~Find At~him from~Servant~s~you(ms) and~he~did~ Die and~Also We we~will~Exist to~ Lord~me to~the~Servant~s

whoever be found with him out of your servants then he will die and we will also exist for my lord for servants,

**44:10** וַיֹּאמֶר גַּם עַתָּה כְדִבְרֵיכֶם כֶּן הוּא אֲשֶׁר יִמָּצֵא אִתּוֹ יִהְיֶה לִי עָבֶד וְאַתֶּם תִּהְיוּ נְקִיִּם

and~he~will~Say Also Now like~ Word~s~you(mp) So He Which he~ will~be~Find At~him he~will~Exist to~me Servant and~You(mp) you(mp)~will~Exist Innocent~s

and he said, let it be according to your words, so he who be found with him will exist for me a servant and you will exist as innocent ones,

**44:11** וַיְמַהֲרוּ וַיּוֹרִדוּ אִישׁ אֶת אַמְתַּחְתּוֹ אָרְצָה וַיִּפְתְּחוּ אִישׁ אַמְתַּחְתּוֹ

and~they(m)~will~much~Hurry and~ they(m)~will~make~Go.down Man At Bag~him Land~unto and~they(m)~will~ Open Man Bag~him

and they hurried and each brought down his bag unto the land and each opened his bag,

**44:12** וַיְחַפֵּשׂ בַּגָּדוֹל הֵחֵל וּבַקָּטֹן כִּלָּה וַיִּמָּצֵא הַגָּבִיעַ בְּאַמְתַּחַת בִּנְיָמִן

and~he~will~much~Search in~the~ Magnificent he~did~make~Pierce and~ in~the~Small he~did~much~Finish and~he~will~be~Find the~Bowl in~Bag "Binyamin [Son of the right hand]"

and he searched, he began with the magnificent one and with the small one he finished and the bowl was found in the bag of "Binyamin [Son of the right hand]",

**44:13\*** וַיִּקְרְעוּ שִׂמְלֹתָם וַיַּעֲמֹס אִישׁ עַל חֲמֹרוֹ וַיָּשֻׁבוּ הָעִירָה

and~they(m)~will~Tear Apparel~
them(m) and~he~will~Load Man
Upon Donkey~him and~they(m)~will~
Turn.back the~City~unto

and they tore their apparel in pieces
and each loaded upon his donkey
and they turned back unto the city,

**44:14** וַיָּבֹא יְהוּדָה וְאֶחָיו בֵּיתָה יוֹסֵף וְהוּא עוֹדֶנּוּ שָׁם וַיִּפְּלוּ לְפָנָיו
אָרְצָה

and~he~will~Come "Yehudah
[*Praised*]" and~Brother~s~him House~
unto "Yoseph [*Adding*]" and~He
Yet.again~him There and~they(m)~
will~Fall to~Face~s~him Land~unto

and "Yehudah [*Praised*]", and his
brothers, came unto the house of
"Yoseph [*Adding*]" and he was still
there and they fell to his face, unto
the land,

**44:15** וַיֹּאמֶר לָהֶם יוֹסֵף מָה הַמַּעֲשֶׂה הַזֶּה אֲשֶׁר עֲשִׂיתֶם הֲלוֹא
יְדַעְתֶּם כִּי נַחֵשׁ יְנַחֵשׁ אִישׁ אֲשֶׁר כָּמֹנִי

and~he~will~Say to~them(m) "Yoseph
[*Adding*]" What the~Work the~This
Which you(mp)~did~Do ?~Not
you(mp)~did~Know Given.that >~
much~Divine he~will~much~Divine
Man Which like~That.one~me

and "Yoseph [*Adding*]" said to
them, what is this work which you
did, did you not know that a man
such as one like me can greatly
divine,

**44:16** וַיֹּאמֶר יְהוּדָה מַה נֹּאמַר לַאדֹנִי מַה נְּדַבֵּר וּמַה נִּצְטַדָּק
הָאֱלֹהִים מָצָא אֶת עֲוֹן עֲבָדֶיךָ הִנֶּנּוּ עֲבָדִים לַאדֹנִי גַּם אֲנַחְנוּ
גַּם אֲשֶׁר נִמְצָא הַגָּבִיעַ בְּיָדוֹ

and~he~will~Say "Yehudah [*Praised*]"
What we~will~Say to~Lord~me What
we~will~much~Speak and~What we~
will~self~Be.correct the~"Elohiym
[*Powers*]" he~had~Find At Iniquity
Servant~s~you(ms) Look~us Servant~s
to~Lord~me Also We Also Which
he~did~be~Find the~Bowl in~Hand~
him

and "Yehudah [*Praised*]" said,
what will we say to my lord, what
will we speak and how will we
correct ourselves, the "Elohiym
[*Powers*]" has found the iniquity of
your servants, look at us, servants
to my lord, both us and the one
which the bowl is found in his
hand,

**44:17** וַיֹּאמֶר חָלִילָה לִּי מֵעֲשׂוֹת זֹאת הָאִישׁ אֲשֶׁר נִמְצָא הַגָּבִיעַ בְּיָדוֹ
הוּא יִהְיֶה לִּי עָבֶד וְאַתֶּם עֲלוּ לְשָׁלוֹם אֶל אֲבִיכֶם

and~he~will~Say Far.be.it to~me
from~>~Do This the~Man Which
he~did~be~Find the~Bowl in~Hand~
him He he~will~Exist to~me Servant
and~You(mp) !(mp)~Go.up to~
Completeness To Father~you(mp)

and he said, far be it for me to do
this, the man which the bowl has
been found in his hand, he will
exist for me a servant, and you, go
up to completeness to your father,

**44:18** וַיִּגַּשׁ אֵלָיו יְהוּדָה וַיֹּאמֶר בִּי אֲדֹנִי יְדַבֶּר נָא עַבְדְּךָ דָבָר בְּאָזְנֵי
אֲדֹנִי וְאַל יִחַר אַפְּךָ בְּעַבְדֶּךָ כִּי כָמוֹךָ כְּפַרְעֹה

and~he~will~Draw.near To~him "Yehudah [*Praised*]" and~he~will~Say Excuse.me Lord~me he~will~much~ Speak Please Servant~you(ms) Word in~Ear~s Lord~me and~No he~will~ Flare.up Nose~you(mp) in~Servant~ you(ms) Given.that like~That.one~ you(ms) like~"Paroh [*Great house*]"

and "Yehudah [*Praised*]" drew near to him and he said, excuse me my lord, please let your servant speak a word in the ears of my lord and do not let your nose flare up with your servant given that one like you is like "Paroh [*Great house*]",

**44:19** אֲדֹנִי שָׁאַל אֶת עֲבָדָיו לֵאמֹר הֲיֵשׁ לָכֶם אָב אוֹ אָח

Lord~me he~had~Inquire At Servant~ s~him to~>~Say ?~There.is to~ you(mp) Father Or Brother

my lord had inquired his servants saying, is there belonging to you a father or brother,

**44:20** וַנֹּאמֶר אֶל אֲדֹנִי יֶשׁ לָנוּ אָב זָקֵן וְיֶלֶד זְקֻנִים קָטָן וְאָחִיו מֵת וַיִּוָּתֵר הוּא לְבַדּוֹ לְאִמּוֹ וְאָבִיו אֲהֵבוֹ

and~we~will~Say To Lord~me There.is to~us Father Beard and~Boy Extreme.old.age~s Small and~Brother~ him he~had~Die and~he~will~be~ Reserve He to~Separated.thing~him to~Mother~him and~Father~him he~ had~Love~him

and we said to my lord, there is a father, a bearded one, and a boy of his extreme old age, a small one, and his brother had died and he was reserved by himself for his mother and his father has loved him,

**44:21** וַתֹּאמֶר אֶל עֲבָדֶיךָ הוֹרִדֻהוּ אֵלָי וְאָשִׂימָה עֵינִי עָלָיו

and~you(ms)~will~Say To Servant~s~ you(ms) !(mp)~make~Go.down~him To~me and~i~will~Set.in.place~^ Eye~ me Upon~him

and you said to your servants, bring him down to me and I will set in place my eye upon him,

**44:22** וַנֹּאמֶר אֶל אֲדֹנִי לֹא יוּכַל הַנַּעַר לַעֲזֹב אֶת אָבִיו וְעָזַב אֶת אָבִיו וָמֵת

and~we~will~Say To Lord~me Not he~will~Be.able the~Young.man to~>~ Leave At Father~him and~he~did~ Leave At Father~him and~he~did~Die

and we said to my lord, the young man will not be able to leave his father, then he will leave his father then he will die,

**44:23** וַתֹּאמֶר אֶל עֲבָדֶיךָ אִם לֹא יֵרֵד אֲחִיכֶם הַקָּטֹן אִתְּכֶם לֹא תֹסִפוּן לִרְאוֹת פָּנָי

and~you(ms)~will~Say To Servant~s~ you(ms) If Not he~will~Go.down Brother~you(mp) the~Small At~ you(mp) Not you(mp)~will~make~Add to~>~See Face~s~me

and you said to your servants, if your small brother will not go down with you, you will not again see my face,

**44:24** וַיְהִי כִּי עָלִינוּ אֶל עַבְדְּךָ אָבִי וַנַּגֶּד לוֹ אֵת דִּבְרֵי אֲדֹנִי

and~he~will~Exist Given.that we~did~

and it came to pass that we went up

Go.up  To  Servant~you(ms)  Father~me
and~we~will~make~Be.face.to.face  to~
him  At  Word~s  Lord~me

to your servant, my father, and we
told him the words of my lord,

**44:25**

וַיֹּאמֶר אָבִינוּ שֻׁבוּ שִׁבְרוּ לָנוּ מְעַט אֹכֶל

and~he~will~Say  Father~us  !(mp)~
Turn.back  !(mp)~Exchange  to~us
Small.amount  Foodstuff

and our father said, turn back,
exchange for us a small amount of
foodstuff,

**44:26**  וַנֹּאמֶר לֹא נוּכַל לָרֶדֶת אִם יֵשׁ אָחִינוּ הַקָּטֹן אִתָּנוּ וְיָרַדְנוּ כִּי
לֹא נוּכַל לִרְאוֹת פְּנֵי הָאִישׁ וְאָחִינוּ הַקָּטֹן אֵינֶנּוּ אִתָּנוּ

and~we~will~Say  Not  we~will~Be.able
to~>~Go.down  If  There.is  Brother~us
the~Small  At~us  we~will~Go.down
Given.that  Not  we~will~Be.able  to~>~
See  Face~s  the~Man  and~Brother~us
the~Small  Without~him  At~us

and we said, we will not be able to
go down, if our small brother is
with us, we will go down given that
we were not able to see the face of
the man as our small brother is not
with us,

**44:27**  וַיֹּאמֶר עַבְדְּךָ אָבִי אֵלֵינוּ אַתֶּם יְדַעְתֶּם כִּי שְׁנַיִם יָלְדָה לִי אִשְׁתִּי

and~he~will~Say  Servant~you(ms)
Father~me  To~us  You(mp)  you(mp)~
did~Know  Given.that  Two  she~did~
Bring.forth  to~me  Woman~me

and your servant, my father, said to
us, you know that my woman
brought forth for me two,

**44:28**  וַיֵּצֵא הָאֶחָד מֵאִתִּי וָאֹמַר אַךְ טָרֹף טֹרָף וְלֹא רְאִיתִיו עַד הֵנָּה

and~he~will~Go.out  the~Unit  from~At~
me  and~i~will~Say  Surely  >~
Tear.into.pieces  he~did~much.be~
Tear.into.pieces  and~Not  and~i~did~
See~him  Until  Thus.far

and the one went up from me and I
said, surely he was completely torn
into pieces and I will not see him
ever again,

**44:29**  וּלְקַחְתֶּם גַּם אֶת זֶה מֵעִם פָּנַי וְקָרָהוּ אָסוֹן וְהוֹרַדְתֶּם אֶת
שֵׂיבָתִי בְּרָעָה שְׁאֹלָה

and~you(mp)~did~Take  Also  At  This
from~With  Face~s~me  and~he~did~
Meet~him  Harm  and~you(mp)~did~
make~Go.down  At  Gray.headed~me
in~Dysfunctional  Underworld~unto

and you will take this one also from
my face and harm will meet him
and you will bring down my gray
head in dysfunction unto the
underworld,

**44:30**  וְעַתָּה כְּבֹאִי אֶל עַבְדְּךָ אָבִי וְהַנַּעַר אֵינֶנּוּ אִתָּנוּ וְנַפְשׁוֹ קְשׁוּרָה
בְנַפְשׁוֹ

and~Now  like~>~Come~me  To
Servant~you(ms)  Father~me  and~the~
Young.man  Without~us  At~us  and~
Being~him  Tie~ed(fs)  in~Being~him

and now, as I come to your servant,
my father, and the young man is not
with us, his being will be tied up in
his being,

**44:31**  וְהָיָה כִּרְאוֹתוֹ כִּי אֵין הַנַּעַר וָמֵת וְהוֹרִידוּ עֲבָדֶיךָ אֶת שֵׂיבַת

עַבְדְּךָ אָבִינוּ בְּיָגוֹן שְׁאֹלָה

and~he~did~Exist like~>~See~him
Given.that Without the~Young.man
and~he~did~Die and~we~did~make~
Go.down~him Servant~s~you(ms) At
Gray.headed Servant~you(ms) Father~
us in~Sorrow Underworld~unto

and it will come to pass, as he sees
that the young man is not, then he
will die and your servants will
bring down the gray head of your
servant, our father, in sorrow, unto
the underworld,

**44:32** כִּי עַבְדְּךָ עָרַב אֶת הַנַּעַר מֵעִם אָבִי לֵאמֹר אִם לֹא אֲבִיאֶנּוּ
אֵלֶיךָ וְחָטָאתִי לְאָבִי כָּל הַיָּמִים

Given.that Servant~you(ms) he~had~
Barter At the~Young.man from~With
Father~me to~>~Say If Not i~will~
make~Come~him To~you(ms) and~i~
did~Err to~Father~me All the~Day~s

given that your servant had bartered
the young man from my father
saying, if I do not bring him to you
then I will err to my father all the
days,

**44:33** וְעַתָּה יֵשֶׁב נָא עַבְדְּךָ תַּחַת הַנַּעַר עֶבֶד לַאדֹנִי וְהַנַּעַר יַעַל עִם
אֶחָיו

and~Now he~will~Settle Please
Servant~you(ms) Under the~Young.man
Servant to~Lord~me and~the~
Young.man he~will~Go.up With
Brother~s~him

and now, please, your servant will
settle in place of the young man,
the servant of my lord, and the
young man will go up with his
brothers,

**44:34** כִּי אֵיךְ אֶעֱלֶה אֶל אָבִי וְהַנַּעַר אֵינֶנּוּ אִתִּי פֶּן אֶרְאֶה בָרָע אֲשֶׁר
יִמְצָא אֶת אָבִי

Given.that Where i~will~Go.up To
Father~me and~the~Young.man
Without~him At~me Otherwise i~
will~See in~the~Dysfunctional Which
he~will~Find At Father~me

but how will I go up to my father
and the young man is not with me,
otherwise, I will see the
dysfunction which will find my
father,

# Chapter 45

**45:1** וְלֹא יָכֹל יוֹסֵף לְהִתְאַפֵּק לְכֹל הַנִּצָּבִים עָלָיו וַיִּקְרָא הוֹצִיאוּ כָל
אִישׁ מֵעָלָי וְלֹא עָמַד אִישׁ אִתּוֹ בְּהִתְוַדַּע יוֹסֵף אֶל אֶחָיו

and~Not he~did~Be.able "Yoseph
[*Adding*]" to~>~self~Hold.back to~All
the~be~Stand.erect~ing(mp) Upon~him
and~he~will~Call.out !(mp)~make~
Go.out All Man from~Upon~me
and~Not he~did~Stand Man At~him
in~>~self~Know "Yoseph [*Adding*]"
To Brother~s~him

and "Yoseph [*Adding*]" was not
able to hold himself back to all the
ones standing erect upon him and
he called out, make all the men go
out from upon me and a man did
not stand with him with "Yoseph
[*Adding*]" revealing himself to his
brothers,

**45:2** נַיִּתֵּן אֶת קֹלוֹ בִּבְכִי נַיִּשְׁמְעוּ מִצְרָיִם נַיִּשְׁמַע בֵּית פַּרְעֹה

and~he~will~Give At Voice~him in~
Weeping and~they(m)~will~Hear
"Mitsrayim [*Troubles*]" and~he~will~
Hear House "Paroh [*Great house*]"

and he gave his voice with weeping
and they heard the "Mitsrayim
[*Troubles*]" and the house of
"Paroh [*Great house*]" heard,

**45:3** נַיֹּאמֶר יוֹסֵף אֶל אֶחָיו אֲנִי יוֹסֵף הַעוֹד אָבִי חָי וְלֹא יָכְלוּ אֶחָיו
לַעֲנוֹת אֹתוֹ כִּי נִבְהֲלוּ מִפָּנָיו

and~he~will~Say "Yoseph [*Adding*]"
To Brother~s~him I "Yoseph
[*Adding*]" ?~Yet.again Father~me Life
and~Not they~did~Be.able Brother~s~
him to~>~Answer At~him Given.that
they~did~be~Stir from~Face~s~him

and "Yoseph [*Adding*]" said to his
brothers, I am "Yoseph [*Adding*]",
is my father yet alive, and his
brothers were not able to answer
him given that they were stirred
from his face,

**45:4** נַיֹּאמֶר יוֹסֵף אֶל אֶחָיו גְּשׁוּ נָא אֵלַי וַיִּגָּשׁוּ נַיֹּאמֶר אֲנִי יוֹסֵף
אֲחִיכֶם אֲשֶׁר מְכַרְתֶּם אֹתִי מִצְרָיְמָה

and~he~will~Say "Yoseph [*Adding*]"
To Brother~s~him !(mp)~Draw.near
Please To~me and~they(m)~will~
Draw.near and~he~will~Say I
"Yoseph [*Adding*]" Brother~you(mp)
Which you(mp)~did~Sell At~me
"Mitsrayim [*Troubles*]"~unto

and "Yoseph [*Adding*]" said to his
brothers, please draw near to me,
and they drew near and he said, I
am "Yoseph [*Adding*]" your brother
who you sold me unto "Mitsrayim
[*Troubles*]",

**45:5\*** וְעַתָּה אַל תֵּעָצְבוּ וְאַל יִחַר בְּעֵינֵיכֶם כִּי מְכַרְתֶּם אֹתִי הֵנָּה כִּי
לְמִחְיָה שְׁלָחַנִי אֱלֹהִים לִפְנֵיכֶם

and~Now No you(mp)~will~be~
Distress and~No he~will~Flare.up in~
Eye~s2~you(mp) Given.that you(mp)~
did~Sell At~me Thus.far Given.that
to~Reviving he~did~Send~me
"Elohiym [*Powers*]" to~Face~s~
you(mp)

and now you will not be distressed
and you will not flare up in your
eyes given that you sold me here,
given that "Elohiym [*Powers*]" sent
me to your face for a reviving,

**45:6** כִּי זֶה שְׁנָתַיִם הָרָעָב בְּקֶרֶב הָאָרֶץ וְעוֹד חָמֵשׁ שָׁנִים אֲשֶׁר אֵין
חָרִישׁ וְקָצִיר

Given.that This Year~s2 the~Hunger
in~Within the~Land and~Yet.again
Five Year~s Which Without Plowing
and~Harvest

given that these two years the
hunger is within the land and
another five years which is without
plowing and harvest,

**45:7** וַיִּשְׁלָחֵנִי אֱלֹהִים לִפְנֵיכֶם לָשׂוּם לָכֶם שְׁאֵרִית בָּאָרֶץ וּלְהַחֲיוֹת
לָכֶם לִפְלֵיטָה גְדֹלָה

and~he~will~Send~me "Elohiym

and "Elohiym [*Powers*]" sent me to

[*Powers*]" to~Face~s~you(mp) to~>~
Set.in.place to~you(mp) Remnant in~
the~Land and~to~>~make~Live to~
you(mp) to~Escape Magnificent

your face to set in place for you a
remnant in the land and to keep you
alive for a magnificent escape,

**45:8** וְעַתָּה לֹא אַתֶּם שְׁלַחְתֶּם אֹתִי הֵנָּה כִּי הָאֱלֹהִים וַיְשִׂימֵנִי לְאָב
לְפַרְעֹה וּלְאָדוֹן לְכָל בֵּיתוֹ וּמֹשֵׁל בְּכָל אֶרֶץ מִצְרָיִם

and~Now Not You(mp) you(mp)~did~
Send At~me Thus.far Given.that the~
"Elohiym [*Powers*]" and~he~will~
Set.in.place~me to~Father to~"Paroh
[*Great house*]" and~to~Lord to~All
House~him and~Regulate~ing(ms) in~
All Land "Mitsrayim [*Troubles*]"

and now, you will not send me this
far but the "Elohiym [*Powers*]",
and he set me in place as father to
"Paroh [*Great house*]" and as lord
to all his house and a regulator in
all the land of "Mitsrayim
[*Troubles*]",

**45:9** מַהֲרוּ וַעֲלוּ אֶל אָבִי וַאֲמַרְתֶּם אֵלָיו כֹּה אָמַר בִּנְךָ יוֹסֵף שָׂמַנִי
אֱלֹהִים לְאָדוֹן לְכָל מִצְרָיִם רְדָה אֵלַי אַל תַּעֲמֹד

!(mp)~much~Hurry and~!(mp)~Go.up
To Father~me and~you(mp)~did~Say
To~him In.this.way he~did~Say Son~
you(ms) "Yoseph [*Adding*]" he~did~
Set.in.place~me "Elohiym [*Powers*]"
to~Lord to~All "Mitsrayim
[*Troubles*]" !(ms)~Go.down~^ To~me
No you(ms)~will~Stand

hurry and go up to my father and
you will say to him in this way,
your son "Yoseph [*Adding*]" said
"Elohiym [*Powers*]" set me in place
for a lord to all "Mitsrayim
[*Troubles*]", go down to me, you
will not stand,

**45:10** וְיָשַׁבְתָּ בְאֶרֶץ גֹּשֶׁן וְהָיִיתָ קָרוֹב אֵלַי אַתָּה וּבָנֶיךָ וּבְנֵי בָנֶיךָ
וְצֹאנְךָ וּבְקָרְךָ וְכָל אֲשֶׁר לָךְ

and~you(ms)~did~Settle in~Land
"Goshen [*Draw near*]" and~you(ms)~
did~Exist Near To~me You(ms)
and~Son~s~you(ms) and~Son~s Son~s~
you(ms) and~Flocks~you(ms) and~
Cattle~you(ms) and~All Which to~
you(fs)

and you will settle in the land of
"Goshen [*Draw near*]" and you will
exist near to me, you and your sons
and the sons of your sons and your
flocks and your cattle and all which
belongs to you,

**45:11** וְכִלְכַּלְתִּי אֹתְךָ שָׁם כִּי עוֹד חָמֵשׁ שָׁנִים רָעָב פֶּן תִּוָּרֵשׁ אַתָּה
וּבֵיתְךָ וְכָל אֲשֶׁר לָךְ

and~i~did~much~Sustain At~you(ms)
There Given.that Yet.again Five
Year~s Hunger Otherwise you(ms)~
will~be~Inherit You(ms) and~House~
you(ms) and~All Which to~you(fs)

and I will sustain you there given
that another five years of hunger,
otherwise you will be inherited, you
and your house and all which
belongs to you,

**45:12** וְהִנֵּה עֵינֵיכֶם רֹאוֹת וְעֵינֵי אָחִי בִנְיָמִין כִּי פִי הַמְדַבֵּר אֲלֵיכֶם

and~Look Eye~s2~you(mp) See~ing(fp)

and look, your eyes are seeing and

and~Eye~s2 Brother~me "Binyamin [*Son of the right hand*]" Given.that Mouth~me much~Speak~ing(ms) To~you(mp)

the eyes of my brother "Binyamin [*Son of the right hand*]" given that my mouth is speaking to you,

**45:13** וְהִגַּדְתֶּם לְאָבִי אֶת כָּל כְּבוֹדִי בְּמִצְרַיִם וְאֵת כָּל אֲשֶׁר רְאִיתֶם וּמִהַרְתֶּם וְהוֹרַדְתֶּם אֶת אָבִי הֵנָּה

and~you(mp)~did~make~Be.face.to.face to~Father~me At All Honor~me in~ "Mitsrayim [*Troubles*]" and~At All Which you(mp)~did~See and~you(mp)~did~much~Hurry and~you(mp)~did~make~Go.down At Father~me Thus.far

and you will tell to my father all my honor in "Mitsrayim [*Troubles*]" and all which you saw and you will hurry and you will bring down my father here,

**45:14** וַיִּפֹּל עַל צַוְּארֵי בִנְיָמִן אָחִיו וַיֵּבְךְּ וּבִנְיָמִן בָּכָה עַל צַוָּארָיו

and~he~will~Fall Upon Back.of.the.neck~s "Binyamin [*Son of the right hand*]" Brother~him and~he~will~Weep and~"Binyamin [*Son of the right hand*]" he~did~Weep Upon Back.of.the.neck~s~him

and he fell upon the back of the neck of "Binyamin [*Son of the right hand*]" his brother and he wept and "Binyamin [*Son of the right hand*]" wept upon the back of his neck,

**45:15** וַיְנַשֵּׁק לְכָל אֶחָיו וַיֵּבְךְּ עֲלֵהֶם וְאַחֲרֵי כֵן דִּבְּרוּ אֶחָיו אִתּוֹ

and~he~will~much~Kiss to~All Brother~s~him and~he~will~Weep Upon~them(m) and~After So they~did~much~Speak Brother~s~him At~him

and he kissed all his brothers and he wept upon them and afterward his brothers spoke with him,

**45:16*** וְהַקֹּל נִשְׁמַע בֵּית פַּרְעֹה לֵאמֹר בָּאוּ אֲחֵי יוֹסֵף וַיִּיטַב בְּעֵינֵי פַּרְעֹה וּבְעֵינֵי עֲבָדָיו

and~the~Voice he~will~be~Hear House "Paroh [*Great house*]" to~>~Say they~did~Come Brother~s "Yoseph [*Adding*]" and~he~will~Do.well in~ Eye~s2 "Paroh [*Great house*]" and~ in~Eye~s2 Servant~s~him

and the voice was heard in the house of "Paroh [*Great house*]" saying, the brothers of "Yoseph [*Adding*]" came, and he was well in the eyes of "Paroh [*Great house*]" and in the eyes of his servants,

**45:17** וַיֹּאמֶר פַּרְעֹה אֶל יוֹסֵף אֱמֹר אֶל אַחֶיךָ זֹאת עֲשׂוּ טַעֲנוּ אֶת בְּעִירְכֶם וּלְכוּ בֹאוּ אַרְצָה כְּנָעַן

and~he~will~Say "Paroh [*Great house*]" To "Yoseph [*Adding*]" !(ms)~Say To Brother~s~you(ms) This !(mp)~Do !(mp)~Pack At Cattle~you(mp) and~ !(mp)~Walk !(mp)~Come Land~unto

and "Paroh [*Great house*]" said to "Yoseph [*Adding*]", say to your brothers, do this, pack your cattle and walk, come unto the land of "Kena'an [*Lowered*]",

"Kena'an   [*Lowered*]"

**45:18**   וּקְחוּ אֶת אֲבִיכֶם וְאֶת בָּתֵּיכֶם וּבֹאוּ אֵלָי וְאֶתְּנָה לָכֶם אֶת טוּב אֶרֶץ מִצְרַיִם וְאִכְלוּ אֶת חֵלֶב הָאָרֶץ

and~!(mp)~Take At Father~you(mp) and~At House~you(mp) and~!(mp)~Come To~me and~i~will~Give~^ to~you(mp) At Functional Land "Mitsrayim [*Troubles*]" and~!(mp)~Eat At Fat the~Land

and take your father and your house and come to me and I will give to you all the functional land of "Mitsrayim [*Troubles*]" and eat the fat of the land,

**45:19**   וְאַתָּה צֻוֵּיתָה זֹאת עֲשׂוּ קְחוּ לָכֶם מֵאֶרֶץ מִצְרַיִם עֲגָלוֹת לְטַפְּכֶם וְלִנְשֵׁיכֶם וּנְשָׂאתֶם אֶת אֲבִיכֶם וּבָאתֶם

and~You(ms) you(ms)~did~much.be~Direct~^ This !(mp)~Do !(mp)~Take to~you(mp) from~Land "Mitsrayim [*Troubles*]" Cart~s to~Children~you(mp) and~to~Woman~s~you(mp) and~you(mp)~did~Lift.up At Father~you(mp) and~you(mp)~did~Come

and you have been directed, do this, take for you from the land of "Mitsrayim [*Troubles*]" carts for your children and for your women and you will lift up your father and you will come,

**45:20**   וְעֵינְכֶם אַל תָּחֹס עַל כְּלֵיכֶם כִּי טוּב כָּל אֶרֶץ מִצְרַיִם לָכֶם הוּא

and~Eye~s2~you(mp) No you(ms)~will~Spare Upon Instrument~s~you(mp) Given.that Functional All Land "Mitsrayim [*Troubles*]" to~you(mp) He

and you will not spare your eyes upon your instruments given that the function of all the land of "Mitsrayim [*Troubles*]" belongs to you,

**45:21**   וַיַּעֲשׂוּ כֵן בְּנֵי יִשְׂרָאֵל וַיִּתֵּן לָהֶם יוֹסֵף עֲגָלוֹת עַל פִּי פַרְעֹה וַיִּתֵּן לָהֶם צֵדָה לַדָּרֶךְ

and~they(m)~will~Do So Son~s "Yisra'el [*He turns El*]" and~he~will~Give to~them(m) "Yoseph [*Adding*]" Cart~s Upon Mouth "Paroh [*Great house*]" and~he~will~Give to~them(m) Provisions to~the~Road

and the sons of "Yisra'el [*He turns El*]" did so and "Yoseph [*Adding*]" gave to them carts upon the mouth of "Paroh [*Great house*]" and he gave to them provisions for the road,

**45:22**   לְכֻלָּם נָתַן לָאִישׁ חֲלִפוֹת שְׂמָלֹת וּלְבִנְיָמִן נָתַן שְׁלֹשׁ מֵאוֹת כֶּסֶף וְחָמֵשׁ חֲלִפֹת שְׂמָלֹת

to~All~them(m) he~did~Give to~Man Replacement~s Apparel~s and~to~"Binyamin [*Son of the right hand*]" he~did~Give Three Hundred~s Silver and~Five Replacement~s Apparel~s

to all of them he gave to each a replacement of apparel and to "Binyamin [*Son of the right hand*]" he gave three hundred silver and five replacement apparel,

**45:23**   וּלְאָבִיו שָׁלַח כְּזֹאת עֲשָׂרָה חֲמֹרִים נֹשְׂאִים מִטּוּב מִצְרָיִם

וְעֶשֶׂר אֲתֹנֹת נֹשְׂאֹת בָּר וָלֶחֶם וּמָזוֹן לְאָבִיו לַדָּרֶךְ

and~to~Father~him he~did~Send like~ This Ten Donkey~s Lift.up~ing(mp) from~Functional "Mitsrayim [*Troubles*]" and~Ten She-donkey~s Lift.up~ing(fp) Grain and~Bread and~ Meat to~Father~him to~the~Road

and to his father he sent like this, ten donkeys lifting up from the functional of "Mitsrayim [*Troubles*]" and ten she donkeys lifting up grain and bread and meat for his father for the road,

**45:24**
וַיְשַׁלַּח אֶת אֶחָיו וַיֵּלֵכוּ וַיֹּאמֶר אֲלֵהֶם אַל תִּרְגְּזוּ בַּדָּרֶךְ

and~he~will~Send At Brother~s~him and~they(m)~will~Walk and~he~will~ Say To~them(m) No you(mp)~will~ Shake in~the~Road

and he sent his brothers and they walked and he said to them, you will not shake in the road,

**45:25**
וַיַּעֲלוּ מִמִּצְרָיִם וַיָּבֹאוּ אֶרֶץ כְּנַעַן אֶל יַעֲקֹב אֲבִיהֶם

and~they(m)~will~Go.up from~ "Mitsrayim [*Troubles*]" and~they(m)~ will~Come Land "Kena'an [*Lowered*]" To "Ya'aqov [*He restrains*]" Father~ them(m)

and they went up from "Mitsrayim [*Troubles*]" and they came to the land of "Kena'an [*Lowered*]", to "Ya'aqov [*He restrains*]" their father,

**45:26**
וַיַּגִּדוּ לוֹ לֵאמֹר עוֹד יוֹסֵף חַי וְכִי הוּא מֹשֵׁל בְּכָל אֶרֶץ מִצְרָיִם וַיָּפָג לִבּוֹ כִּי לֹא הֶאֱמִין לָהֶם

and~they(m)~will~make~Be.face.to.face to~him to~>~Say Yet.again "Yoseph [*Adding*]" Life and~Given.that He Regulate~ing(ms) in~All Land "Mitsrayim [*Troubles*]" and~he~will~ Be.numb Heart~him Given.that Not he~did~make~Firm to~them(m)

and they told to him saying, "Yoseph [*Adding*]" is still alive and given that he is regulator in all the land of "Mitsrayim [*Troubles*]", and his heart was numb given that he was not firm to them,

**45:27**
וַיְדַבְּרוּ אֵלָיו אֵת כָּל דִּבְרֵי יוֹסֵף אֲשֶׁר דִּבֶּר אֲלֵהֶם וַיַּרְא אֶת הָעֲגָלוֹת אֲשֶׁר שָׁלַח יוֹסֵף לָשֵׂאת אֹתוֹ וַתְּחִי רוּחַ יַעֲקֹב אֲבִיהֶם

and~they(m)~will~much~Speak To~him At All Word~s "Yoseph [*Adding*]" Which he~did~much~Speak To~ them(m) and~he~will~See At the~ Cart~s Which he~did~Send "Yoseph [*Adding*]" to~>~Lift.up At~him and~ she~will~Live Wind "Ya'aqov [*He restrains*]" Father~them(m)

and they spoke to him all the words of "Yoseph [*Adding*]" which he spoke to them and he saw the carts which "Yoseph [*Adding*]" sent to lift him up and the wind of "Ya'aqov [*He restrains*]", their father, lived,

**45:28**
וַיֹּאמֶר יִשְׂרָאֵל רַב עוֹד יוֹסֵף בְּנִי חָי אֵלְכָה וְאֶרְאֶנּוּ בְּטֶרֶם אָמוּת

and~he~will~Say "Yisra'el [*He turns El*]" Abundant Yet.again "Yoseph

and "Yisra'el [*He turns El*]" said, it is abundant, "Yoseph [*Adding*]" my

[*Adding*]" Son~me Life i~will~Walk~
^ and~i~will~See~him in~Before i~
will~Die

son is still alive, I will walk and I
will see him before I die,

# Chapter 46

**46:1** וַיִּסַּע יִשְׂרָאֵל וְכָל אֲשֶׁר לוֹ וַיָּבֹא בְּאֵרָה שָׁבַע וַיִּזְבַּח זְבָחִים
לֵאלֹהֵי אָבִיו יִצְחָק

and~he~will~Journey "Yisra'el [*He
turns El*]" and~All Which to~him
and~he~will~Come "B'er-Sheva [*Well
of oath*]"~unto and~he~will~Sacrifice
Thing.of.sacrifice~s to~Power~s Father~
him "Yits'hhaq [*He laughs*]"

and "Yisra'el [*He turns El*]"
journeyed and all which belonged
to him and he came unto "B'er-
Sheva [*Well of oath*]" and he
sacrificed things of sacrifice to the
powers of his father "Yits'hhaq [*He
laughs*]",

**46:2** וַיֹּאמֶר אֱלֹהִים לְיִשְׂרָאֵל בְּמַרְאֹת הַלַּיְלָה וַיֹּאמֶר יַעֲקֹב יַעֲקֹב
וַיֹּאמֶר הִנֵּנִי

and~he~will~Say "Elohiym [*Powers*]"
to~"Yisra'el [*He turns El*]" in~
Reflection the~Night and~he~will~Say
"Ya'aqov [*He restrains*]" "Ya'aqov
[*He restrains*]" and~he~will~Say
Look~me

and "Elohiym [*Powers*]" said to
"Yisra'el [*He turns El*]" in the
reflection of the night and he said,
"Ya'aqov [*He restrains*]", "Ya'aqov
[*He restrains*]", and he said, here
am I,

**46:3** וַיֹּאמֶר אָנֹכִי הָאֵל אֱלֹהֵי אָבִיךָ אַל תִּירָא מֵרְדָה מִצְרַיְמָה כִּי
לְגוֹי גָּדוֹל אֲשִׂימְךָ שָׁם

and~he~will~Say I the~Mighty.one
the~Power~s Father~you(ms) No
you(ms)~will~Fear from~>~Go.down
"Mitsrayim [*Troubles*]"~unto Given.that
to~Nation Magnificent i~will~
Set.in.place~you(ms) There

and he said, I am the mighty one,
the powers of your father, you will
not fear to go down unto
"Mitsrayim [*Troubles*]" given that I
will set you in place there for a
magnificent nation,

**46:4** אָנֹכִי אֵרֵד עִמְּךָ מִצְרַיְמָה וְאָנֹכִי אַעַלְךָ גַם עָלֹה וְיוֹסֵף יָשִׁית
יָדוֹ עַל עֵינֶיךָ

I i~will~Go.down With~you(ms)
"Mitsrayim [*Troubles*]"~unto and~I i~
will~make~Go.up~you(ms) Also >~
Go.up and~"Yoseph [*Adding*]" he~
will~Set.down Hand~him Upon Eye~
s2~you(ms)

I will go down with you unto
"Mitsrayim [*Troubles*]" and I will
bring you up, also go up, and
"Yoseph [*Adding*]" will set down
his hand upon your eyes,

**46:5** וַיָּקָם יַעֲקֹב מִבְּאֵר שָׁבַע וַיִּשְׂאוּ בְנֵי יִשְׂרָאֵל אֶת יַעֲקֹב אֲבִיהֶם

וְאֶת טַפָּם וְאֶת נְשֵׁיהֶם בָּעֲגָלוֹת אֲשֶׁר שָׁלַח פַּרְעֹה לָשֵׂאת אֹתוֹ

and~he~will~Rise "Ya'aqov [*He restrains*]" from~"B'er-Sheva [*Well of oath*]" and~they(m)~will~Lift.up Son~s "Yisra'el [*He turns El*]" At "Ya'aqov [*He restrains*]" Father~them(m) and~At Children~them(m) and~At Woman~s~them(m) in~the~Cart~s Which he~did~Send "Paroh [*Great house*]" to~>~Lift.up At~him

and "Ya'aqov [*He restrains*]" rose from "B'er-Sheva [*Well of oath*]" and the sons of "Yisra'el [*He turns El*]" lifted up "Ya'aqov [*He restrains*]" their father and their children and their women in the carts which "Paroh [*Great house*]" sent to lift him,

**46:6** וַיִּקְחוּ אֶת מִקְנֵיהֶם וְאֶת רְכוּשָׁם אֲשֶׁר רָכְשׁוּ בְּאֶרֶץ כְּנַעַן
וַיָּבֹאוּ מִצְרָיְמָה יַעֲקֹב וְכָל זַרְעוֹ אִתּוֹ

and~they(m)~will~Take At Livestock~s~them(m) and~At Goods~them(m) Which they~did~Accumulate in~Land "Kena'an [*Lowered*]" and~they(m)~will~Come "Mitsrayim [*Troubles*]"~unto "Ya'aqov [*He restrains*]" and~All Seed~him At~him □

and they took their livestocks and their goods which they accumulated in the land of "Kena'an [*Lowered*]" and "Ya'aqov [*He restrains*]" and all his seed came unto "Mitsrayim [*Troubles*]" with him,

**46:7** בָּנָיו וּבְנֵי בָנָיו אִתּוֹ בְּנֹתָיו וּבְנוֹת בָּנָיו וְכָל זַרְעוֹ הֵבִיא אִתּוֹ
מִצְרָיְמָה

Son~s~him and~Son~s Son~s~him At~him Daughter~s~him and~Daughter~s Son~s~him and~All Seed~him he~did~make~Come At~him "Mitsrayim [*Troubles*]"~unto

his sons and the sons of his sons with him, his daughters and the daughters of his sons and all his seeds he brought with him unto "Mitsrayim [*Troubles*]",

**46:8** וְאֵלֶּה שְׁמוֹת בְּנֵי יִשְׂרָאֵל הַבָּאִים מִצְרָיְמָה יַעֲקֹב וּבָנָיו בְּכֹר
יַעֲקֹב רְאוּבֵן

and~These Title~s Son~s "Yisra'el [*He turns El*]" the~Come~ing(mp) "Mitsrayim [*Troubles*]"~unto "Ya'aqov [*He restrains*]" and~Son~s~him Firstborn "Ya'aqov [*He restrains*]" "Re'uven [*See a son*]"

and these were the titles of the sons of "Yisra'el [*He turns El*]", the ones coming unto "Mitsrayim [*Troubles*]", "Ya'aqov [*He restrains*]" and his sons, the firstborn of "Ya'aqov [*He restrains*]" is "Re'uven [*See a son*]",

**46:9** וּבְנֵי רְאוּבֵן חֲנוֹךְ וּפַלּוּא וְחֶצְרֹן וְכַרְמִי

and~Son~s "Re'uven [*See a son*]" "Hhanokh [*Dedicated*]" and~"Palu [*Distinguished*]" and~"Hhetsron [*Surrounded by a wall*]" and~"Karmi [*My vineyard*]"

and the sons of "Re'uven [*See a son*]" were "Hhanokh [*Dedicated*]" and "Palu [*Distinguished*]" and "Hhetsron [*Surrounded by a wall*]" and "Karmi [*My vineyard*]",

**46:10** וּבְנֵי שִׁמְעוֹן יְמוּאֵל וְיָמִין וְאֹהַד וְיָכִין וְצֹחַר וְשָׁאוּל בֶּן הַכְּנַעֲנִית

and~Son~s "Shimon [*Heard*]" "Yemu'el [*Day of El*]" and~"Yamin [*Right hand*]" and~"Ohad [*Shouting*]" and~"Yakhin [*He will be firm*]" and~"Tsohhar [*White*]" and~"Sha'ul [*Unknown*]" Son "Kena'an [*Lowered*]"~s

and the sons of "Shimon [*Heard*]" were "Yemu'el [*Day of El*]" and "Yamin [*Right hand*]" and "Ohad [*Shouting*]" and "Yakhin [*He will be firm*]" and "Tsohhar [*White*]" and "Sha'ul [*Unknown*]", the son of ones of "Kena'an [*Lowered*]",

**46:11** וּבְנֵי לֵוִי גֵּרְשׁוֹן קְהָת וּמְרָרִי

and~Son~s "Lewi [*Joined*]" "Gershon [*Exile*]" "Qehat [*Assembly*]" and~ "Merari [*Bitter*]"

and the sons of "Lewi [*Joined*]" were "Gershon [*Exile*]", "Qehat [*Assembly*]" and "Merari [*Bitter*]",

**46:12\*** וּבְנֵי יְהוּדָה עֵר וְאוֹנָן וְשֵׁלָה וָפֶרֶץ וָזָרַח וַיָּמָת עֵר וְאוֹנָן בְּאֶרֶץ כְּנַעַן וַיִּהְיוּ בְנֵי פֶרֶץ חֶצְרֹן וְחָמוּל

and~Son~s "Yehudah [*Praised*]" "Eyr [*Awake*]" and~"Onan [*Strong*]" and~ "Sheylah [*Petition*]" and~"Perets [*Breach*]" and~"Zerahh [*Dawn*]" and~ he~will~Die "Eyr [*Awake*]" and~ "Onan [*Strong*]" in~Land "Kena'an [*Lowered*]" and~they(m)~will~Exist Son~s "Perets [*Breach*]" "Hhetsron [*Surrounded by a wall*]" and~ "Hhamul [*Compassion*]"

and the sons of "Yehudah [*Praised*]" were "Eyr [*Awake*]" and "Onan [*Strong*]" and "Sheylah [*Petition*]" and "Perets [*Breach*]" and "Zerahh [*Dawn*]" and "Eyr [*Awake*]" and "Onan [*Strong*]" died in the land of "Kena'an [*Lowered*]" and "Hhetsron [*Surrounded by a wall*]" and "Hhamul [*Compassion*]" existed as sons of "Perets [*Breach*]",

**46:13** וּבְנֵי יִשָּׂשכָר תּוֹלָע וּפֻוָּה וְיוֹב וְשִׁמְרוֹן

and~Son~s "Yis'sas'kar [*He will lift up the wage*]" "Tola [*Worm*]" and~ "Pu'ah [*Dispersion*]" and~"Yashuv [*He will return*]" and~"Shimron [*Watched*]"

and the sons of "Yis'sas'kar [*He will lift up the wage*]" were "Tola [*Worm*]" and "Pu'ah [*Dispersion*]" and "Yashuv [*He will return*]" and "Shimron [*Watched*]",

**46:14** וּבְנֵי זְבֻלוּן סֶרֶד וְאֵלוֹן וְיַחְלְאֵל

and~Son~s "Zevulun [*Residence*]" "Sered [*Remnant*]" and~"Eylon [*Strength*]" and~"Yahh'le'el [*El delays*]"

and the sons of "Zevulun [*Residence*]" were "Sered [*Remnant*]" and "Eylon [*Strength*]" and "Yahh'le'el [*El delays*]" ,

**46:15** אֵלֶּה בְּנֵי לֵאָה אֲשֶׁר יָלְדָה לְיַעֲקֹב בְּפַדַּן אֲרָם וְאֵת דִּינָה בִתּוֹ כָּל נֶפֶשׁ בָּנָיו וּבְנוֹתָיו שְׁלֹשִׁים וְשָׁלֹשׁ

These Son~s "Le'ah [*Weary*]" Which she~did~Bring.forth to~"Ya'aqov [*He*

These were the sons of "Le'ah [*Weary*]" who brought forth for

273

restrains]" in~"Padan-Aram [*Field palace*]" and~At "Dinah [*Judgement*]" Daughter~him All Being Son~s~him and~Daughter~s~him Three~s and~ Three

"Ya'aqov [*He restrains*]" in "Padan-Aram [*Field palace*]", and "Dinah [*Judgement*]" his daughter, all being his sons and his daughters, thirty three,

**46:16** וּבְנֵי גָד צִפְיוֹן וְחַגִּי שׁוּנִי וְאֶצְבֹּן עֵרִי וַאֲרוֹדִי וְאַרְאֵלִי

and~Son~s "Gad [*Fortune*]" "Tsiphyon [*Lookout*]" and~"Hhagi [*Festive*]" "Shuni [*Sleep*]" and~ "Etsbon [*I swell*]" "Eyriy [*My city*]" and~"Arodiy [*My roaming*]" and~ "Areliy [*Order of my El*]"

and the sons of "Gad [*Fortune*]" were "Tsiphyon [*Lookout*]" and "Hhagi [*Festive*]", "Shuni [*Sleep*]" and "Etsbon [*I swell*]", "Eyriy [*My city*]" and "Arodiy [*My roaming*]" and "Areliy [*Order of my El*]",

**46:17** וּבְנֵי אָשֵׁר יִמְנָה וְיִשְׁוָה וְיִשְׁוִי וּבְרִיעָה וְשֶׂרַח אֲחֹתָם וּבְנֵי בְרִיעָה חֶבֶר וּמַלְכִּיאֵל

and~Son~s "Asher [*Happy*]" "Yimnah [*Right*]" and~"Yishwah [*He resembles*]" and~"Yishwiy [*He resembles me*]" and~"Beri'ah [*With a companion*]" and~"Serahh [*Excess*]" Sister~them(m) and~Son~s "Beri'ah [*With a companion*]" "Hhever [*Companion*]" and~"Malki'el [*My king is El*]"

and the sons of "Asher [*Happy*]" were "Yimnah [*Right*]" and "Yishwah [*He resembles*]" and "Yishwiy [*He resembles me*]" and "Beri'ah [*With a companion*]" and "Serahh [*Excess*]" their sister, and the sons of "Beri'ah [*With a companion*]" were "Hhever [*Companion*]" and "Malki'el [*My king is El*]",

**46:18** אֵלֶּה בְּנֵי זִלְפָּה אֲשֶׁר נָתַן לָבָן לְלֵאָה בִּתּוֹ וַתֵּלֶד אֶת אֵלֶּה לְיַעֲקֹב שֵׁשׁ עֶשְׂרֵה נָפֶשׁ

These Son~s "Zilpah [*Trickling*]" Which he~did~Give "Lavan [*White*]" to~"Le'ah [*Weary*]" Daughter~him and~she~will~Bring.forth At These to~"Ya'aqov [*He restrains*]" Six Ten Being

these were the sons of "Zilpah [*Trickling*]" who "Lavan [*White*]" gave to "Le'ah [*Weary*]" his daughter and she brought forth these to "Ya'aqov [*He restrains*]", sixteen beings,

**46:19** בְּנֵי רָחֵל אֵשֶׁת יַעֲקֹב יוֹסֵף וּבִנְיָמִן

Son~s "Rahhel [*Ewe*]" Woman "Ya'aqov [*He restrains*]" "Yoseph [*Adding*]" and~"Binyamin [*Son of the right hand*]"

the sons of "Rahhel [*Ewe*]", the woman of "Ya'aqov [*He restrains*]", "Yoseph [*Adding*]" and "Binyamin [*Son of the right hand*]",

**46:20** וַיִּוָּלֵד לְיוֹסֵף בְּאֶרֶץ מִצְרַיִם אֲשֶׁר יָלְדָה לּוֹ אָסְנַת בַּת פּוֹטִי פֶרַע כֹּהֵן אֹן אֶת מְנַשֶּׁה וְאֶת אֶפְרָיִם

and~he~will~be~Bring.forth to~"Yoseph [*Adding*]" in~Land "Mitsrayim

and brought forth to "Yoseph [*Adding*]" in the land of "Mitsrayim

[*Troubles*]" Which she~did~Bring.forth to~him "Asnat [*Belonging to Nat*]" Daughter "Pothee-Phera [*He whom the Ra gave*]" Priest "On [*Vigor*]" At "Menasheh [*Causing to overlook*]" and~At "Ephrayim [*Double fruitfulness*]"

[*Troubles*]" who "Asnat [*Belonging to Nat*]", daughter of "Pothee-Phera [*He whom the Ra gave*]", priest of "On [*Vigor*]", brought forth to him, "Menasheh [*Causing to overlook*]" and "Ephrayim [*Double fruitfulness*]",

**46:21** וּבְנֵי בִנְיָמִן בֶּלַע וָבֶכֶר וְאַשְׁבֵּל גֵּרָא וְנַעֲמָן אֵחִי וָרֹאשׁ מֻפִּים וְחֻפִּים וָאָרְדְּ

and~Son~s "Binyamin [*Son of the right hand*]" "Bela [*Swallow*]" and~ "Bekher [*Young camel*]" and~ "Ashbeyl [*Fire flowing*]" "Gera [*Grain*]" and~"Na'aman [*Pleasantness*]" "Eyhhiy [*My brother*]" and~"Rosh [*Head*]" "Mupim [*Serpents*]" and~ "Hhupim [*Shores*]" and~"Ared [*I subdue*]"

and the sons of "Binyamin [*Son of the right hand*]" were "Bela [*Swallow*]" and "Bekher [*Young camel*]" and "Ashbeyl [*Fire flowing*]" and "Gera [*Grain*]" and "Na'aman [*Pleasantness*]", "Eyhhiy [*My brother*]" and "Rosh [*Head*]", "Mupim [*Serpents*]" and "Hhupim [*Shores*]" and "Ared [*I subdue*]",

**46:22** אֵלֶּה בְּנֵי רָחֵל אֲשֶׁר יֻלַּד לְיַעֲקֹב כָּל נֶפֶשׁ אַרְבָּעָה עָשָׂר

These Son~s "Rahhel [*Ewe*]" Which he~did~much~Bring.forth to~"Ya'aqov [*He restrains*]" All Being Four Ten

these were the sons of "Rahhel [*Ewe*]" who brought forth to "Ya'aqov [*He restrains*]", all being fourteen,

**46:23\*** וּבְנֵי דָן חֻשִׁים

and~Son~s "Dan [*Moderator*]" "Hhush [*Making haste*]"~s

and sons of "Dan [*Moderator*]" were the ones of "Hhush [*Making haste*]",

**46:24** וּבְנֵי נַפְתָּלִי יַחְצְאֵל וְגוּנִי וְיֵצֶר וְשִׁלֵּם

and~Son~s "Naphtali [*Wrestling*]" "Yahhtse'el [*El divides*]" and~"Guni [*My protection*]" and~"Yetser [*Forming*]" and~"Shilem [*Repaid*]"

and the sons of "Naphtali [*Wrestling*]" were "Yahhtse'el [*El divides*]" and "Guni [*My protection*]" and "Yetser [*Forming*]" and "Shilem [*Repaid*]",

**46:25** אֵלֶּה בְּנֵי בִלְהָה אֲשֶׁר נָתַן לָבָן לְרָחֵל בִּתּוֹ וַתֵּלֶד אֶת אֵלֶּה לְיַעֲקֹב כָּל נֶפֶשׁ שִׁבְעָה

These Son~s "Bilhah [*Wear out*]" Which he~did~Bring.forth "Lavan [*White*]" to~"Rahhel [*Ewe*]" Daughter~him and~she~will~Bring.forth At These to~"Ya'aqov [*He restrains*]" All Being Seven

These were the sons of "Bilhah [*Wear out*]" who "Lavan [*White*]" brought forth to "Rahhel [*Ewe*]", his daughter, and she brought forth these to "Ya'aqov [*He restrains*]", all being seven,

**46:26** כָּל הַנֶּפֶשׁ הַבָּאָה לְיַעֲקֹב מִצְרַיְמָה יֹצְאֵי יְרֵכוֹ מִלְּבַד נְשֵׁי בְנֵי יַעֲקֹב כָּל נֶפֶשׁ שִׁשִּׁים וָשֵׁשׁ

All the~Being the~Come~ing(fs) to~ "Ya'aqov [*He restrains*]" "Mitsrayim [*Troubles*]"~unto Go.out~ing(mp) Midsection~him from~to~Separated.thing Woman~s Son~s "Ya'aqov [*He restrains*]" All Being Six~s and~Six

all the beings, belonging to "Ya'aqov [*He restrains*]", coming out unto "Mitsrayim [*Troubles*]", going out of his midsection, besides the women of the sons of "Ya'aqov [*He restrains*]", all being sixty six,

**46:27** וּבְנֵי יוֹסֵף אֲשֶׁר יֻלַּד לוֹ בְמִצְרַיִם נֶפֶשׁ שְׁנָיִם כָּל הַנֶּפֶשׁ לְבֵית יַעֲקֹב הַבָּאָה מִצְרַיְמָה שִׁבְעִים

and~Son~s "Yoseph [*Adding*]" Which he~did~much.be~Bring.forth to~him in~"Mitsrayim [*Troubles*]" Being Two All the~Being to~House "Ya'aqov [*He restrains*]" the~Come~ing(fs) "Mitsrayim [*Troubles*]"~unto Seven~s

and the sons of "Yoseph [*Adding*]" who were brought forth to him in "Mitsrayim [*Troubles*]" were two beings, all the beings of the house of "Ya'aqov [*He restrains*]", the ones coming unto "Mitsrayim [*Troubles*]", seventy,

**46:28** וְאֶת יְהוּדָה שָׁלַח לְפָנָיו אֶל יוֹסֵף לְהוֹרֹת לְפָנָיו גֹּשְׁנָה וַיָּבֹאוּ אַרְצָה גֹּשֶׁן

and~At "Yehudah [*Praised*]" he~had~ Send to~Face~s~him To "Yoseph [*Adding*]" to~>~make~Throw to~Face~ s~him "Goshen [*Draw near*]"~unto and~they(m)~will~Come Land~unto "Goshen [*Draw near*]"

and he sent "Yehudah [*Praised*]" to his face, to "Yoseph [*Adding*]", to point to his face unto "Goshen [*Draw near*]" and they came unto the land of "Goshen [*Draw near*]",

**46:29** וַיֶּאְסֹר יוֹסֵף מֶרְכַּבְתּוֹ וַיַּעַל לִקְרַאת יִשְׂרָאֵל אָבִיו גֹּשְׁנָה וַיֵּרָא אֵלָיו וַיִּפֹּל עַל צַוָּארָיו וַיֵּבְךְּ עַל צַוָּארָיו עוֹד

and~he~will~Tie.up "Yoseph [*Adding*]" Chariot~him and~he~will~Go.up to~>~ Meet "Yisra'el [*He turns El*]" Father~him "Goshen [*Draw near*]"~ unto and~he~will~be~See To~him and~he~will~Fall Upon Back.of.the.neck~s~him and~he~will~ Weep Upon Back.of.the.neck~s~him Yet.again

and "Yoseph [*Adding*]" tied up his chariot and went up to meet "Yisra'el [*He turns El*]" his father, unto "Goshen [*Draw near*]", and he appeared to him and he fell upon the back of his neck and he wept upon the back of his neck yet again,

**46:30** וַיֹּאמֶר יִשְׂרָאֵל אֶל יוֹסֵף אָמוּתָה הַפָּעַם אַחֲרֵי רְאוֹתִי אֶת פָּנֶיךָ כִּי עוֹדְךָ חָי

and~he~will~Say "Yisra'el [*He turns El*]" To "Yoseph [*Adding*]" i~will~ Die~^ the~Stroke.of.time After >~

and "Yisra'el [*He turns El*]" said to "Yoseph [*Adding*]", I will die this time after seeing your face given

See~me  At  Face~s~you(ms)
Given.that  Yet.again~you(ms)  Life

that you are yet alive,

**46:31** נַיֹּאמֶר יוֹסֵף אֶל אֶחָיו וְאֶל בֵּית אָבִיו וְאַגִּידָה לְפַרְעֹה
וְאֹמְרָה אֵלָיו אַחַי וּבֵית אָבִי אֲשֶׁר בְּאֶרֶץ כְּנַעַן בָּאוּ אֵלָי

and~he~will~Say "Yoseph [Adding]"
To Brother~s~him and~To House
Father~him i~will~Go.up and~i~will~
make~Be.face.to.face~^ to~"Paroh [Great
house]" and~i~will~Say~^ To~him
Brother~s~me and~House Father~me
Which in~Land "Kena'an [Lowered]"
they~did~Come To~me

and "Yoseph [Adding]" said to his
brothers and to the house of his
father, I will go up and I will tell to
"Paroh [Great house]" and I will
say to him, my brothers and the
house of my father which was in
the land of "Kena'an [Lowered]"
came to me,

**46:32** וְהָאֲנָשִׁים רֹעֵי צֹאן כִּי אַנְשֵׁי מִקְנֶה הָיוּ וְצֹאנָם וּבְקָרָם וְכָל
אֲשֶׁר לָהֶם הֵבִיאוּ

and~the~Man~s See~ing(mp) Flocks
Given.that Man~s Livestock they~did~
Exist and~Flocks~them(m) and~Cattle~
them(m) and~All Which to~them(m)
they~did~make~Come

and the men are watchers of the
flock given that they exist as men
of the livestock and their flocks and
their cattle and they brought all
which belongs to them,

**46:33** וְהָיָה כִּי יִקְרָא לָכֶם פַּרְעֹה וְאָמַר מַה מַּעֲשֵׂיכֶם

and~he~did~Exist Given.that he~will~
Call.out to~you(mp) "Paroh [Great
house]" and~he~did~Say What Work~
s~you(mp)

and it will come to pass that "Paroh
[Great house]" will call you out,
and he will say, what is your work,

**46:34** וַאֲמַרְתֶּם אַנְשֵׁי מִקְנֶה הָיוּ עֲבָדֶיךָ מִנְּעוּרֵינוּ וְעַד עַתָּה גַּם אֲנַחְנוּ
גַּם אֲבֹתֵינוּ בַּעֲבוּר תֵּשְׁבוּ בְּאֶרֶץ גֹּשֶׁן כִּי תוֹעֲבַת מִצְרַיִם כָּל
רֹעֵה צֹאן

and~you(mp)~did~Say Man~s
Livestock they~did~Exist Servant~s~
you(ms) from~Young.age~s~us and~
Until Now Also We Also Father~s~
us in~On.account.of you(mp)~will~
Settle in~Land "Goshen [Draw
near]" Given.that Disgusting
"Mitsrayim [Troubles]" All Feed~
ing(ms) Flocks

and you will say, your servants
exist as men of livestock, from our
young age and until now, us and
also our fathers, so that you will
settle in the land of "Goshen [Draw
near]" given that the disgust of the
"Mitsrayim [Troubles]" is all
feeders of the flocks,

# Chapter 47

**47:1** וַיָּבֹא יוֹסֵף וַיַּגֵּד לְפַרְעֹה וַיֹּאמֶר אָבִי וְאַחַי וְצֹאנָם וּבְקָרָם וְכָל אֲשֶׁר לָהֶם בָּאוּ מֵאֶרֶץ כְּנָעַן וְהִנָּם בְּאֶרֶץ גֹּשֶׁן

and~he~will~Come "Yoseph [Adding]" and~he~will~make~Be.face.to.face to~ "Paroh [Great house]" and~he~will~Say Father~me and~Brother~s~me and~ Flocks~them(m) and~Cattle~them(m) and~All Which to~them(m) they~did~ Come from~Land "Kena'an [Lowered]" and~Look~them(m) in~ Land "Goshen [Draw near]"

and "Yoseph [Adding]" came and he told to "Paroh [Great house]", and he said, my father and my brothers and their flocks and their cattle and all which belonged to them came from the land of "Kena'an [Lowered]" and look at them in the land of "Goshen [Draw near]",

**47:2** וּמִקְצֵה אֶחָיו לָקַח חֲמִשָּׁה אֲנָשִׁים וַיַּצִּגֵם לִפְנֵי פַרְעֹה

and~from~Far.end Brother~s~him he~ did~Take Five Man~s and~he~will~ make~Set~them(m) to~Face~s "Paroh [Great house]"

and from the far end of his brothers he took five men and he presented them to the face of "Paroh [Great house]",

**47:3** וַיֹּאמֶר פַּרְעֹה אֶל אֶחָיו מַה מַּעֲשֵׂיכֶם וַיֹּאמְרוּ אֶל פַּרְעֹה רֹעֵה צֹאן עֲבָדֶיךָ גַּם אֲנַחְנוּ גַּם אֲבוֹתֵינוּ

and~he~will~Say "Paroh [Great house]" To Brother~s~him What Work~s~ you(mp) and~they(m)~will~Say To "Paroh [Great house]" Feed~ing(ms) Flocks Servant~s~you(ms) Also We Also Father~s~us

and "Paroh [Great house]" said to his brothers, what is your work, and they said to "Paroh [Great house]", your servants are feeders of the flocks, us and also our fathers,

**47:4** וַיֹּאמְרוּ אֶל פַּרְעֹה לָגוּר בָּאָרֶץ בָּאנוּ כִּי אֵין מִרְעֶה לַצֹּאן אֲשֶׁר לַעֲבָדֶיךָ כִּי כָבֵד הָרָעָב בְּאֶרֶץ כְּנָעַן וְעַתָּה יֵשְׁבוּ נָא עֲבָדֶיךָ בְּאֶרֶץ גֹּשֶׁן

and~they(m)~will~Say To "Paroh [Great house]" to~>~Sojourn in~the~ Land we~did~Come Given.that Without Pasture to~the~Flocks Which to~Servant~s~you(ms) Given.that Heavy the~Hunger in~Land "Kena'an [Lowered]" and~Now they(m)~will~ Settle Please Servant~s~you(ms) in~ Land "Goshen [Draw near]"

and they said to "Paroh [Great house]", to sojourn in the land have we come given that no pastures for the flocks which belong to your servants given that the hunger is heavy in the land of "Kena'an [Lowered]" and now, please, your servants will settle in the land of "Goshen [Draw near]",

**47:5** וַיֹּאמֶר פַּרְעֹה אֶל יוֹסֵף לֵאמֹר אָבִיךָ וְאַחֶיךָ בָּאוּ אֵלֶיךָ

and~he~will~Say "Paroh [Great house]"

and "Paroh [Great house]" said to

To "Yoseph [*Adding*]" to~>~Say
Father~you(ms) and~Brother~s~you(ms)
they~did~Come To~you(ms)

"Yoseph [*Adding*]" saying, your
father and your brothers came to
you,

**47:6** אֶרֶץ מִצְרַיִם לְפָנֶיךָ הִוא בְּמֵיטַב הָאָרֶץ הוֹשֵׁב אֶת אָבִיךָ וְאֶת
אַחֶיךָ יֵשְׁבוּ בְּאֶרֶץ גֹּשֶׁן וְאִם יָדַעְתָּ וְיֶשׁ בָּם אַנְשֵׁי חַיִל וְשַׂמְתָּם
שָׂרֵי מִקְנֶה עַל אֲשֶׁר לִי

Land "Mitsrayim [*Troubles*]" to~Face~
s~you(ms) She in~Best the~Land
!(ms)~make~Settle At Father~you(ms)
and~At Brother~s~you(ms) they(m)~
will~Settle in~Land "Goshen [*Draw
near*]" and~If you(ms)~did~Know
and~There.is in~them(m) Man~s Force
and~you(mp)~did~Set.in.place~them(m)
Noble~s Livestock Upon Which to~
me

the land of "Mitsrayim [*Troubles*]"
is to your face, she is in the best of
the land, your father and your
brothers will surely settle in the
land of "Goshen [*Draw near*]" and
if you know and there is in them
men of force then you will set them
in place as nobles of livestock upon
which belong to me,

**47:7** וַיָּבֵא יוֹסֵף אֶת יַעֲקֹב אָבִיו וַיַּעֲמִדֵהוּ לִפְנֵי פַרְעֹה וַיְבָרֶךְ יַעֲקֹב
אֶת פַּרְעֹה

and~he~will~make~Come "Yoseph
[*Adding*]" At "Ya'aqov [*He
restrains*]" Father~him and~he~will~
make~Stand~him to~Face~s "Paroh
[*Great house*]" and~he~will~much~
Kneel "Ya'aqov [*He restrains*]" At
"Paroh [*Great house*]"

and "Yoseph [*Adding*]" brought
"Ya'aqov [*He restrains*]" his father
and he stood him to the face of
"Paroh [*Great house*]" and
"Ya'aqov [*He restrains*]" respected
"Paroh [*Great house*]",

**47:8** וַיֹּאמֶר פַּרְעֹה אֶל יַעֲקֹב כַּמָּה יְמֵי שְׁנֵי חַיֶּיךָ

and~he~will~Say "Paroh [*Great house*]"
To "Ya'aqov [*He restrains*]" like~
What Day~s Year~s Life~s~you(ms)

and "Paroh [*Great house*]" said to
"Ya'aqov [*He restrains*]", how
many are the days of the years of
your life,

**47:9** וַיֹּאמֶר יַעֲקֹב אֶל פַּרְעֹה יְמֵי שְׁנֵי מְגוּרַי שְׁלֹשִׁים וּמְאַת שָׁנָה
מְעַט וְרָעִים הָיוּ יְמֵי שְׁנֵי חַיַּי וְלֹא הִשִּׂיגוּ אֶת יְמֵי שְׁנֵי חַיֵּי
אֲבֹתַי בִּימֵי מְגוּרֵיהֶם

and~he~will~Say "Ya'aqov [*He
restrains*]" To "Paroh [*Great house*]"
Day~s Year~s Pilgrimage~s~me
Three~s and~Hundred Year
Small.amount and~Dysfunctional~s
they~had~Exist Day~s Year~s Life~s~
me and~Not they~did~make~Overtake
At Day~s Year~s Life~s Father~s~
me in~Day~s Pilgrimage~s~them(m)

and "Ya'aqov [*He restrains*]" said
to "Paroh [*Great house*]", the days
of the years of my pilgrimage are a
hundred and thirty years, a small
and dysfunctional amount have the
days of the years of my life existed
and they did not overtake the days
of the years of the life of my father
in the days of their pilgrimage,

**47:10**

וַיְבָרֶךְ יַעֲקֹב אֶת פַּרְעֹה וַיֵּצֵא מִלִּפְנֵי פַרְעֹה

and~he~will~much~Kneel "Ya'aqov [He restrains]" At "Paroh [Great house]" and~he~will~Go.out from~to~Face~s "Paroh [Great house]"

and "Ya'aqov [He restrains]" respected "Paroh [Great house]" and he went out from the face of "Paroh [Great house]",

**47:11**

וַיּוֹשֵׁב יוֹסֵף אֶת אָבִיו וְאֶת אֶחָיו וַיִּתֵּן לָהֶם אֲחֻזָּה בְּאֶרֶץ מִצְרַיִם בְּמֵיטַב הָאָרֶץ בְּאֶרֶץ רַעְמְסֵס כַּאֲשֶׁר צִוָּה פַרְעֹה

and~he~will~make~Settle "Yoseph [Adding]" At Father~him and~At Brother~s~him and~he~will~Give to~them(m) Holdings in~Land "Mitsrayim [Troubles]" in~Best the~Land in~Land "Ra'meses [Child of the sun]" like~Which he~did~much~Direct "Paroh [Great house]"

and "Yoseph [Adding]" settled his father and his brothers and he gave to them holdings in the land of "Mitsrayim [Troubles]", in the best of the land, in the land of "Ra'meses [Child of the sun]" just as "Paroh [Great house]" directed,

**47:12**

וַיְכַלְכֵּל יוֹסֵף אֶת אָבִיו וְאֶת אֶחָיו וְאֵת כָּל בֵּית אָבִיו לֶחֶם לְפִי הַטָּף

and~he~will~Sustain "Yoseph [Adding]" At Father~him and~At Brother~s~him and~At All House Father~him Bread to~Mouth the~Children

and "Yoseph [Adding]" sustained his father and his brothers and all the house of his father, bread to the mouth of the children,

**47:13**

וְלֶחֶם אֵין בְּכָל הָאָרֶץ כִּי כָבֵד הָרָעָב מְאֹד וַתֵּלַהּ אֶרֶץ מִצְרַיִם וְאֶרֶץ כְּנַעַן מִפְּנֵי הָרָעָב

and~Bread Without in~All the~Land Given.that Heavy the~Hunger Many and~she~will~Faint Land "Mitsrayim [Troubles]" and~Land "Kena'an [Lowered]" from~Face~s the~Hunger

and bread was not in all the land given that the hunger was very heavy and the land of "Mitsrayim [Troubles]" was faint and the land of "Kena'an [Lowered]" from the face of the hunger,

**47:14**

וַיְלַקֵּט יוֹסֵף אֶת כָּל הַכֶּסֶף הַנִּמְצָא בְאֶרֶץ מִצְרַיִם וּבְאֶרֶץ כְּנַעַן בַּשֶּׁבֶר אֲשֶׁר הֵם שֹׁבְרִים וַיָּבֵא יוֹסֵף אֶת הַכֶּסֶף בֵּיתָה פַרְעֹה

and~he~will~much~Pick.up "Yoseph [Adding]" At All the~Silver the~be~Find~ing(ms) in~Land "Mitsrayim [Troubles]" and~in~Land "Kena'an [Lowered]" in~the~Barley Which They(m) Exchange~ing(mp) and~he~will~make~Come "Yoseph [Adding]" At the~Silver House~unto "Paroh [Great house]"

and "Yoseph [Adding]" picked up all the silver being found in the land of "Mitsrayim [Troubles]" and in the land of "Kena'an [Lowered]", with the barley which they were exchanging, and "Yoseph [Adding]" brought the silver unto the house of "Paroh [Great house]",

**47:15** וַיִּתֹּם הַכֶּסֶף מֵאֶרֶץ מִצְרַיִם וּמֵאֶרֶץ כְּנַעַן וַיָּבֹאוּ כָל מִצְרַיִם אֶל יוֹסֵף לֵאמֹר הָבָה לָּנוּ לֶחֶם וְלָמָּה נָמוּת נֶגְדֶּךָ כִּי אָפֵס כָּסֶף

and~he~will~Be.whole the~Silver from~Land "Mitsrayim [Troubles]" and~from~Land "Kena'an [Lowered]" and~they(m)~will~Come All "Mitsrayim [Troubles]" To "Yoseph [Adding]" to~>~Say !(ms)~Provide~^ to~us Bread and~to~What we~will~Die Opposite~you(ms) Given.that he~did~Come.to.an.end Silver

and the silver was whole from the land of "Mitsrayim [Troubles]" and from the land of "Kena'an [Lowered]" and all "Mitsrayim [Troubles]" came to "Yoseph [Adding]" saying, provide for us bread, why should we die opposite you given that the silver came to an end,

**47:16** וַיֹּאמֶר יוֹסֵף הָבוּ מִקְנֵיכֶם וְאֶתְּנָה לָכֶם בְּמִקְנֵיכֶם אִם אָפֵס כָּסֶף

and~he~will~Say "Yoseph [Adding]" !(mp)~Provide Livestock~you(mp) and~i~will~Give~^ to~you(mp) in~Livestock~you(mp) If he~did~Come.to.an.end Silver

and "Yoseph [Adding]" said, provide your livestock and I will give to you with your livestock if the silver came to an end,

**47:17** וַיָּבִיאוּ אֶת מִקְנֵיהֶם אֶל יוֹסֵף וַיִּתֵּן לָהֶם יוֹסֵף לֶחֶם בַּסּוּסִים וּבְמִקְנֵה הַצֹּאן וּבְמִקְנֵה הַבָּקָר וּבַחֲמֹרִים וַיְנַהֲלֵם בַּלֶּחֶם בְּכָל מִקְנֵהֶם בַּשָּׁנָה הַהִוא

and~they(m)~will~make~Come At Livestock~them(m) To "Yoseph [Adding]" and~he~will~Give to~them(m) "Yoseph [Adding]" Bread in~the~Horse~s and~in~Livestock the~Flocks and~in~Livestock the~Cattle and~in~the~Donkey~s and~he~will~much~Lead~them(m) in~the~Bread in~All Livestock~them(m) in~the~Year the~She

and they brought their livestock to "Yoseph [Adding]" and "Yoseph [Adding]" gave to them bread with the horses and with the livestock of the field and with the donkeys and he lead them in the bread with all their livestock in that year,

**47:18** וַתִּתֹּם הַשָּׁנָה הַהִוא וַיָּבֹאוּ אֵלָיו בַּשָּׁנָה הַשֵּׁנִית וַיֹּאמְרוּ לוֹ לֹא נְכַחֵד מֵאֲדֹנִי כִּי אִם תַּם הַכֶּסֶף וּמִקְנֵה הַבְּהֵמָה אֶל אֲדֹנִי לֹא נִשְׁאַר לִפְנֵי אֲדֹנִי בִּלְתִּי אִם גְּוִיָּתֵנוּ וְאַדְמָתֵנוּ

and~she~will~Be.whole the~Year the~She and~they(m)~will~Come To~him in~the~Year the~Second and~they(m)~will~Say to~him Not we~will~much~Keep.secret from~Lord~me Given.that If he~did~Be.whole the~Silver and~Livestock the~Beast To Lord~me Not we~did~be~Remain to~Face~s

and that year was whole and they came to him in the second year and they said to him, we will not keep secret from my lord that the silver has been whole and the livestock of the beast belong to my lord, we will not remain to the face of my lord except our body and our ground,

Lord~me   Except   If   Body~us   and~
Ground~us

**47:19** לָמָה נָמוּת לְעֵינֶיךָ גַּם אֲנַחְנוּ גַּם אַדְמָתֵנוּ קְנֵה אֹתָנוּ וְאֶת
אַדְמָתֵנוּ בַּלָּחֶם וְנִהְיֶה אֲנַחְנוּ וְאַדְמָתֵנוּ עֲבָדִים לְפַרְעֹה וְתֶן זֶרַע
וְנִחְיֶה וְלֹא נָמוּת וְהָאֲדָמָה לֹא תֵשָׁם

to~What   we~will~Die   to~Eye~s2~
you(ms)   Also   We   Also   Ground~us
!(ms)~Purchase   At~us   and~At
Ground~us   in~the~Bread   and~we~will~
Exist   We   and~Ground~us   Servant~s
to~"Paroh [*Great   house*]"   and~!(ms)~
Give   Seed   and~we~will~Live   and~Not
we~will~Die   and~the~Ground   Not
she~will~Desolate

why should we die to your eyes, us
and also our ground, purchase us
and our ground with bread and we
will exist, we and our ground will
be servants for "Paroh [*Great
house*]" and give seed and we will
live and we will not die and the
ground will not be desolate,

**47:20** וַיִּקֶן יוֹסֵף אֶת כָּל אַדְמַת מִצְרַיִם לְפַרְעֹה כִּי מָכְרוּ מִצְרַיִם
אִישׁ שָׂדֵהוּ כִּי חָזַק עֲלֵהֶם הָרָעָב וַתְּהִי הָאָרֶץ לְפַרְעֹה

and~he~will~Purchase   "Yoseph
[*Adding*]"   At   All   Ground   "Mitsrayim
[*Troubles*]"   to~"Paroh [*Great   house*]"
Given.that   they~did~Sell   "Mitsrayim
[*Troubles*]"   Man   Field~him   Given.that
he~did~Seize   Upon~them(m)   the~
Hunger   and~she~will~Exist   the~Land
to~"Paroh [*Great   house*]"

and "Yoseph [*Adding*]" purchased
all the ground of "Mitsrayim
[*Troubles*]" for "Paroh [*Great
house*]" given that "Mitsrayim
[*Troubles*]" sold each his field
given that the hunger seized upon
them and the land existed for
"Paroh [*Great house*]",

**47:21** וְאֶת הָעָם הֶעֱבִיר אֹתוֹ לֶעָרִים מִקְצֵה גְבוּל מִצְרַיִם וְעַד קָצֵהוּ

and~At   the~People   he~did~make~
Cross.over   At~him   to~City~s   from~
Far.end   Border   "Mitsrayim [*Troubles*]"
and~Until   Far.end~him

and he made the people cross over
to cities from the far end of the
border of "Mitsrayim [*Troubles*]"
and until his far end,

**47:22\*** רַק אַדְמַת הַכֹּהֲנִים לֹא קָנָה כִּי חֹק לַכֹּהֲנִים מֵאֵת פַּרְעֹה
וְאָכְלוּ אֶת חֻקָּם אֲשֶׁר נָתַן לָהֶם פַּרְעֹה עַל כֵּן לֹא מָכְרוּ אֶת
אַדְמָתָם

Only   Ground   the~Priest~s   Not   he~
did~Purchase   Given.that   Custom   to~
the~Priest~s   from~At   "Paroh [*Great
house*]"   and~they~did~Eat   At
Custom~them(m)   Which   he~did~Give
to~them(m)   "Paroh [*Great   house*]"
Upon   So   Not   they~did~Sell   At
Ground~them(m)

only the ground of the priests he did
not purchase given that the portion
for the priests is from "Paroh
[*Great house*]" and they ate their
portion which "Paroh [*Great
house*]" gave to them therefore,
they did not sell their ground,

**47:23** וַיֹּאמֶר יוֹסֵף אֶל הָעָם הֵן קָנִיתִי אֶתְכֶם הַיּוֹם וְאֶת אַדְמַתְכֶם

**282**

לְפַרְעֹה הֵא לָכֶם זֶרַע וּזְרַעְתֶּם אֶת הָאֲדָמָה

and~he~will~Say "Yoseph [Adding]"
To the~People Though i~did~Purchase
At~you(mp) the~Day and~At Ground~
you(mp) to~"Paroh [Great house]" Lo
to~you(mp) Seed and~you(mp)~did~
Sow At the~Ground

and "Yoseph [Adding]" said to the
people, though I purchased you
today and your ground for "Paroh
[Great house]", lo, to you is seed
and you will sow the ground,

**47:24** וְהָיָה בַּתְּבוּאֹת וּנְתַתֶּם חֲמִישִׁית לְפַרְעֹה וְאַרְבַּע הַיָּדֹת יִהְיֶה לָכֶם לְזֶרַע הַשָּׂדֶה וּלְאָכְלְכֶם וְלַאֲשֶׁר בְּבָתֵּיכֶם וְלֶאֱכֹל לְטַפְּכֶם

and~he~did~Exist in~the~Production
and~you(mp)~did~Give Fifth to~"Paroh
[Great house]" and~Four the~Hand~s
he~will~Exist to~you(mp) to~Seed
the~Field and~to~>~Eat~you(mp) and~
to~Which in~House~s~you(mp) and~
to~>~Eat to~Children~you(mp)

and it will come to pass in the
production and you will give a fifth
to "Paroh [Great house]" and four
of the hands will exist for you for
seed of the field and for you to eat
and to who is in your house and for
your children to eat,

**47:25** וַיֹּאמְרוּ הֶחֱיִתָנוּ נִמְצָא חֵן בְּעֵינֵי אֲדֹנִי וְהָיִינוּ עֲבָדִים לְפַרְעֹה

and~they(m)~will~Say you(ms)~did~
make~Live~us we~will~Find Beauty
in~Eye~s2 Lord~me and~we~did~Exist
Servant~s to~"Paroh [Great house]"

and they said, you made us live, we
will find beauty in the eyes of my
lord and we will exist as servants
for "Paroh [Great house]",

**47:26** וַיָּשֶׂם אֹתָהּ יוֹסֵף לְחֹק עַד הַיּוֹם הַזֶּה עַל אַדְמַת מִצְרַיִם לְפַרְעֹה לַחֹמֶשׁ רַק אַדְמַת הַכֹּהֲנִים לְבַדָּם לֹא הָיְתָה לְפַרְעֹה

and~he~did~Set.in.place At~her
"Yoseph [Adding]" to~Custom Until
the~Day the~This Upon Ground
"Mitsrayim [Troubles]" to~"Paroh
[Great house]" to~the~Fifth.part Only
Ground the~Priest~s to~
Separated.thing~them(m) Not she~did~
Exist to~"Paroh [Great house]"

and "Yoseph [Adding]" set her in
place for a custom until this day
concerning the ground of
"Mitsrayim [Troubles]" for "Paroh
[Great house]" for the fifth part,
only the ground of the priests is for
themselves and did not exist for
"Paroh [Great house]",

**47:27** וַיֵּשֶׁב יִשְׂרָאֵל בְּאֶרֶץ מִצְרַיִם בְּאֶרֶץ גֹּשֶׁן וַיֵּאָחֲזוּ בָהּ וַיִּפְרוּ וַיִּרְבּוּ מְאֹד

and~he~will~Settle "Yisra'el [He turns
El]" in~Land "Mitsrayim [Troubles]"
in~Land "Goshen [Draw near]" and~
they(m)~will~be~Hold in~her and~
they(m)~will~Reproduce and~they(m)~
will~Increase Many

and "Yisra'el [He turns El]" settled
in the land of "Mitsrayim
[Troubles]" in the land of "Goshen
[Draw near]" and they were held in
her and they reproduced and they
increased greatly,

**47:28** וַיְחִי יַעֲקֹב בְּאֶרֶץ מִצְרַיִם שְׁבַע עֶשְׂרֵה שָׁנָה וַיְהִי יְמֵי יַעֲקֹב שְׁנֵי חַיָּיו שֶׁבַע שָׁנִים וְאַרְבָּעִים וּמְאַת שָׁנָה

and~he~will~Exist "Ya'aqov [*He restrains*]" in~Land "Mitsrayim [*Troubles*]" Seven Ten Year and~he~will~Exist Day~s "Ya'aqov [*He restrains*]" Year~s Life~s~him Seven Year~s and~Four~s and~Hundred Year

and "Ya'aqov [*He restrains*]" existed in the land of "Mitsrayim [*Troubles*]" seventeen years and the days of "Ya'aqov [*He restrains*]", the years of his life, existed a hundred and forty seven years,

**47:29** וַיִּקְרְבוּ יְמֵי יִשְׂרָאֵל לָמוּת וַיִּקְרָא לִבְנוֹ לְיוֹסֵף וַיֹּאמֶר לוֹ אִם נָא מָצָאתִי חֵן בְּעֵינֶיךָ שִׂים נָא יָדְךָ תַּחַת יְרֵכִי וְעָשִׂיתָ עִמָּדִי חֶסֶד וֶאֱמֶת אַל נָא תִקְבְּרֵנִי בְּמִצְרָיִם

and~they(m)~will~Come.near Day~s "Yisra'el [*He turns El*]" to~>~Die and~he~will~Call.out to~Son~him to~ "Yoseph [*Adding*]" and~he~will~Say to~him If Please i~did~Find Beauty in~Eye~s2~you(ms) !(ms)~Set.in.place Please Hand~you(ms) Under Midsection~me and~you(ms)~did~Do By~me Kindness and~Truth No Please you(ms)~will~Bury~me in~ "Mitsrayim [*Troubles*]"

and the days of "Yisra'el [*He turns El*]" came near to die and he called out to his son, to "Yoseph [*Adding*]", and he said to him, please, if I found beauty in your eyes, please set in place your hand under my midsection and you will do by me kindness and truth, please, you will not bury me in "Mitsrayim [*Troubles*]",

**47:30** וְשָׁכַבְתִּי עִם אֲבֹתַי וּנְשָׂאתַנִי מִמִּצְרַיִם וּקְבַרְתַּנִי בִּקְבֻרָתָם וַיֹּאמַר אָנֹכִי אֶעֱשֶׂה כִדְבָרֶךָ

and~i~did~Lay.down With Father~s~me and~you(ms)~did~Lift.up~me from~ "Mitsrayim [*Troubles*]" and~you(ms)~did~Bury~me in~Burial.place~them(m) and~he~will~Say I i~will~Do like~ Word~you(ms)

and I will lay down with my fathers and you will lift me up from "Mitsrayim [*Troubles*]" and you will bury me in their burial place and he said, I will do like your word,

**47:31** וַיֹּאמֶר הִשָּׁבְעָה לִי וַיִּשָּׁבַע לוֹ וַיִּשְׁתַּחוּ יִשְׂרָאֵל עַל רֹאשׁ הַמִּטָּה

and~he~will~Say !(ms)~be~Swear~^ to~me and~he~will~be~Swear to~him and~he~will~self~Bend.down "Yisra'el [*He turns El*]" Upon Head the~Bed

and he said, be sworn to me and he was sworn to him and "Yisra'el [*He turns El*]" bent himself down upon the head of the bed,

# Chapter 48

**48:1** וַיְהִי אַחֲרֵי הַדְּבָרִים הָאֵלֶּה וַיֹּאמֶר לְיוֹסֵף הִנֵּה אָבִיךָ חֹלֶה וַיִּקַּח אֶת שְׁנֵי בָנָיו עִמּוֹ אֶת מְנַשֶּׁה וְאֶת אֶפְרָיִם

and~he~will~Exist After the~Word~s the~These and~he~will~Say to~

and it came to pass, after these words, and he said to "Yoseph

284

"Yoseph [*Adding*]" Look Father~ you(ms) Be.sick~ing(ms) and~he~will~ Take At Two Son~s~him With~him At "Menasheh [*Causing to overlook*]" and~At "Ephrayim [*Double fruitfulness*]"

[*Adding*]", look, your father is sick and he took his two sons with him, "Menasheh [*Causing to overlook*]" and "Ephrayim [*Double fruitfulness*]",

**48:2** וַיַּגֵּד לְיַעֲקֹב וַיֹּאמֶר הִנֵּה בִּנְךָ יוֹסֵף בָּא אֵלֶיךָ וַיִּתְחַזֵּק יִשְׂרָאֵל וַיֵּשֶׁב עַל הַמִּטָּה

and~he~will~make~Be.face.to.face to~ "Ya'aqov [*He restrains*]" and~he~ will~Say Look Son~you(ms) "Yoseph [*Adding*]" he~had~Come To~you(ms) and~he~will~self~Seize "Yisra'el [*He turns El*]" and~he~will~Settle Upon the~Bed

and he told "Ya'aqov [*He restrains*]" and he said, look, your son "Yoseph [*Adding*]" had come to you and "Yisra'el [*He turns El*]" strengthened himself and he settled upon the bed,

**48:3** וַיֹּאמֶר יַעֲקֹב אֶל יוֹסֵף אֵל שַׁדַּי נִרְאָה אֵלַי בְּלוּז בְּאֶרֶץ כְּנָעַן וַיְבָרֶךְ אֹתִי

and~he~will~Say "Ya'aqov [*He restrains*]" To "Yoseph [*Adding*]" Mighty.one "Shaddai [*My breasts*]" he~did~be~See To~me in~"Luz [*Almond*]" in~Land "Kena'an [*Lowered*]" and~he~will~much~Kneel At~me

and "Ya'aqov [*He restrains*]" said to "Yoseph [*Adding*]", the mighty one of "Shaddai [*My breasts*]" appeared to me in "Luz [*Almond*]", in the land of "Kena'an [*Lowered*]" and he respected me,

**48:4** וַיֹּאמֶר אֵלַי הִנְנִי מַפְרְךָ וְהִרְבִּיתִךָ וּנְתַתִּיךָ לִקְהַל עַמִּים וְנָתַתִּי אֶת הָאָרֶץ הַזֹּאת לְזַרְעֲךָ אַחֲרֶיךָ אֲחֻזַּת עוֹלָם

and~he~will~Say To~me Look~me make~Reproduce~ing(ms)~you(ms) and~ i~did~make~Increase~you(ms) and~i~ did~Give~you(ms) to~Assembled.flock People~s and~i~did~Give At the~ Land the~This to~Seed~you(ms) After~you(ms) Holdings Distant.time

and he said to me, here am I, making you reproduce and I will make you increase and I will give you for an assembled flock of peoples and I will give this land to your seed after you, a holdings for a distant time,

**48:5** וְעַתָּה שְׁנֵי בָנֶיךָ הַנּוֹלָדִים לְךָ בְּאֶרֶץ מִצְרַיִם עַד בֹּאִי אֵלֶיךָ מִצְרַיְמָה לִי הֵם אֶפְרַיִם וּמְנַשֶּׁה כִּרְאוּבֵן וְשִׁמְעוֹן יִהְיוּ לִי

and~Now Two Son~s~you(ms) be~ Bring.forth~ing(mp) to~you(ms) in~ Land "Mitsrayim [*Troubles*]" Until >~Come~me To~you(ms) "Mitsrayim [*Troubles*]"~unto to~me They(m) "Ephrayim [*Double fruitfulness*]" and~ "Menasheh [*Causing to overlook*]"

and now, your two sons are being brought forth to you in the land of "Mitsrayim [*Troubles*]" before I came to you unto "Mitsrayim [*Troubles*]", they belong to me, "Ephrayim [*Double fruitfulness*]" and "Menasheh [*Causing to*

like~"Re'uven [*See a son*]" and~ "Shimon [*Heard*]" they(m)~will~Exist to~me

overlook]", like "Re'uven [*See a son*]" and "Shimon [*Heard*]", they will belong to me,

**48:6** וּמוֹלַדְתְּךָ אֲשֶׁר הוֹלַדְתָּ אַחֲרֵיהֶם לְךָ יִהְיוּ עַל שֵׁם אֲחֵיהֶם יִקָּרְאוּ בְּנַחֲלָתָם

and~Kindred~you(ms) Which you(ms)~ did~make~Bring.forth After~them(m) to~you(ms) they(m)~will~Exist Upon Title Brother~s~them(m) they(m)~will~ be~Call.out in~Inheritance~them(m)

and your kindred which you caused to bring forth after them belong to you, they will exist in addition to the title of their brothers, they will be called out in their inheritance,

**48:7** וַאֲנִי בְּבֹאִי מִפַּדָּן מֵתָה עָלַי רָחֵל בְּאֶרֶץ כְּנַעַן בַּדֶּרֶךְ בְּעוֹד כִּבְרַת אֶרֶץ לָבֹא אֶפְרָתָה וָאֶקְבְּרֶהָ שָּׁם בְּדֶרֶךְ אֶפְרָת הִוא בֵּית לָחֶם

and~I in~>~Come~me from~"Padan [*Field*]" she~did~Die Upon~me "Rahhel [*Ewe*]" in~Land "Kena'an [*Lowered*]" in~the~Road in~Yet.again Short Land to~>~Come "Ephrat [*Fruitful*]"~unto and~i~will~Bury~her There in~Road "Ephrat [*Fruitful*]" She "Beyt-Lehhem [*House of bread*]"

and I, I came from "Padan [*Field*]", "Rahhel [*Ewe*]" died upon me in the land of "Kena'an [*Lowered*]", in the road while a short distance coming unto "Ephrat [*Fruitful*]" and I buried her there in the road of "Ephrat [*Fruitful*]", she is "Beyt-Lehhem [*House of bread*]",

**48:8** וַיַּרְא יִשְׂרָאֵל אֶת בְּנֵי יוֹסֵף וַיֹּאמֶר מִי אֵלֶּה

and~he~will~See "Yisra'el [*He turns El*]" At Son~s "Yoseph [*Adding*]" and~he~will~Say Who These

and "Yisra'el [*He turns El*]" saw the sons of "Yoseph [*Adding*]" and he said, who are these,

**48:9** וַיֹּאמֶר יוֹסֵף אֶל אָבִיו בָּנַי הֵם אֲשֶׁר נָתַן לִי אֱלֹהִים בָּזֶה וַיֹּאמַר קָחֶם נָא אֵלַי וַאֲבָרֲכֵם

and~he~will~Say "Yoseph [*Adding*]" To Father~him Son~s~me They(m) Which he~did~Give to~me "Elohiym [*Powers*]" in~This and~he~will~Say !(ms)~Take~them(m) Please To~me and~i~will~much~Kneel~them(m)

and "Yoseph [*Adding*]" said to his father, they are my sons which "Elohiym [*Powers*]" gave to me here, and he said, please take them to me and I will respect them,

**48:10** וְעֵינֵי יִשְׂרָאֵל כָּבְדוּ מִזֹּקֶן לֹא יוּכַל לִרְאוֹת וַיַּגֵּשׁ אֹתָם אֵלָיו וַיִּשַּׁק לָהֶם וַיְחַבֵּק לָהֶם

and~Eye~s2 "Yisra'el [*He turns El*]" they~did~Be.heavy from~Age Not he~ will~Be.able to~>~See and~he~will~ make~Draw.near At~them(m) To~him and~he~will~Kiss to~them(m) and~he~ will~much~Embrace to~them(m)

and the eyes of "Yisra'el [*He turns El*]" were heavy from age and he was not able to see and he drew them near to him and he kissed them and he embraced them,

**48:11** וַיֹּאמֶר יִשְׂרָאֵל אֶל יוֹסֵף רְאֹה פָנֶיךָ לֹא פִלָּלְתִּי וְהִנֵּה הֶרְאָה

אֹתִי אֱלֹהִים גַּם אֶת זַרְעֶךָ

| | |
|---|---|
| and~he~will~Say "Yisra'el [*He turns El*]" To "Yoseph [*Adding*]" >~See Face~s~you(ms) Not and~i~did~much~Plead and~Look he~did~make~See At~me "Elohiym [*Powers*]" Also At Seed~you(ms) | and "Yisra'el [*He turns El*]" said to "Yoseph [*Adding*]", not seeing your face and I pleaded and look, "Elohiym [*Powers*]" caused me to also see your seed, |

**48:12**     וַיּוֹצֵא יוֹסֵף אֹתָם מֵעִם בִּרְכָּיו וַיִּשְׁתַּחוּ לְאַפָּיו אָרְצָה

| | |
|---|---|
| and~he~will~make~Go.out "Yoseph [*Adding*]" At~them(m) from~With Knee~s~him and~he~will~self~Bend.down to~Nose~s~him Land~unto | and "Yoseph [*Adding*]" brought them out from by his knees and he bent himself down, his nose unto the land, |

**48:13**     וַיִּקַּח יוֹסֵף אֶת שְׁנֵיהֶם אֶת אֶפְרַיִם בִּימִינוֹ מִשְּׂמֹאל יִשְׂרָאֵל וְאֶת מְנַשֶּׁה בִשְׂמֹאלוֹ מִימִין יִשְׂרָאֵל וַיַּגֵּשׁ אֵלָיו

| | |
|---|---|
| and~he~will~Take "Yoseph [*Adding*]" At Two~them(m) At "Ephrayim [*Double fruitfulness*]" in~Right.hand~him from~Left.hand "Yisra'el [*He turns El*]" and~At "Menasheh [*Causing to overlook*]" in~Left.hand from~Right.hand "Yisra'el [*He turns El*]" and~he~will~make~Draw.near To~him | and "Yoseph [*Adding*]" took the two of them, "Ephrayim [*Double fruitfulness*]" in his right hand to the left hand of "Yisra'el [*He turns El*]" and "Menasheh [*Causing to overlook*]" in the left hand to the right hand of "Yisra'el [*He turns El*]" and he caused to draw near to him, |

**48:14**     וַיִּשְׁלַח יִשְׂרָאֵל אֶת יְמִינוֹ וַיָּשֶׁת עַל רֹאשׁ אֶפְרַיִם וְהוּא הַצָּעִיר וְאֶת שְׂמֹאלוֹ עַל רֹאשׁ מְנַשֶּׁה שִׂכֵּל אֶת יָדָיו כִּי מְנַשֶּׁה הַבְּכוֹר

| | |
|---|---|
| and~he~will~Send "Yisra'el [*He turns El*]" At Right.hand~him and~he~will~Set.down Upon Head "Ephrayim [*Double fruitfulness*]" and~He the~Little.one and~At Left.hand~him Upon Head "Menasheh [*Causing to overlook*]" he~did~much~Calculate At Hand~s2~him Given.that "Menasheh [*Causing to overlook*]" the~Firstborn | and "Yisra'el [*He turns El*]" sent his right hand and he set it down upon the head of "Ephrayim [*Double fruitfulness*]" and he was the little one and his left hand upon the head of "Menasheh [*Causing to overlook*]", he calculated his hands given that "Menasheh [*Causing to overlook*]" was the firstborn, |

**48:15**     וַיְבָרֶךְ אֶת יוֹסֵף וַיֹּאמַר הָאֱלֹהִים אֲשֶׁר הִתְהַלְּכוּ אֲבֹתַי לְפָנָיו אַבְרָהָם וְיִצְחָק הָאֱלֹהִים הָרֹעֶה אֹתִי מֵעוֹדִי עַד הַיּוֹם הַזֶּה

| | |
|---|---|
| and~he~will~much~Kneel At "Yoseph [*Adding*]" and~he~will~Say the~"Elohiym [*Powers*]" Which they~did~self~Walk Father~s~me to~Face~s~him "Avraham [*Father lifted*]" and~"Yits'hhaq [*He laughs*]" the~"Elohiym | and he respected "Yoseph [*Adding*]" and he said, the face of "Elohiym [*Powers*]" which my fathers, "Avraham [*Father lifted*]" and "Yits'hhaq [*He laughs*]", walked to, the "Elohiym [*Powers*]" |

[*Powers*]" the~Feed~ing(ms) At~me from~Yet.again~me Upon the~Day the~This

was the one feeding me all my life in addition to this day,

**48:16** הַמַּלְאָךְ הַגֹּאֵל אֹתִי מִכָּל רָע יְבָרֵךְ אֶת הַנְּעָרִים וְיִקָּרֵא בָהֶם שְׁמִי וְשֵׁם אֲבֹתַי אַבְרָהָם וְיִצְחָק וְיִדְגּוּ לָרֹב בְּקֶרֶב הָאָרֶץ

the~Messenger the~Redeem~ing(ms) At~me from~All Dysfunctional he~will~much~Kneel At the~Young.man~s and~he~will~be~Call.out in~them(m) Title~me and~Title Father~s~me "Avraham [*Father lifted*]" and~ "Yits'hhaq [*He laughs*]" and~they(m)~will~Amplify to~the~Abundance in~Within the~Land

the messenger redeeming me from all dysfunction will respect the young men and my title was called out in them, and the title of my fathers "Avraham [*Father lifted*]" and "Yits'hhaq [*He laughs*]" and they will amplify as an abundance within the land,

**48:17** וַיַּרְא יוֹסֵף כִּי יָשִׁית אָבִיו יַד יְמִינוֹ עַל רֹאשׁ אֶפְרַיִם וַיֵּרַע בְּעֵינָיו וַיִּתְמֹךְ יַד אָבִיו לְהָסִיר אֹתָהּ מֵעַל רֹאשׁ אֶפְרַיִם עַל רֹאשׁ מְנַשֶּׁה

and~he~will~See "Yoseph [*Adding*]" Given.that he~will~Set.down Father~him Hand Right.hand~him Upon Head "Ephrayim [*Double fruitfulness*]" and~he~will~Be.dysfunctional in~Eye~s2~him and~he~will~Uphold Hand Father~him to~>~make~Turn.aside At~her from~Upon Head "Ephrayim [*Double fruitfulness*]" Upon Head "Menasheh [*Causing to overlook*]"

and "Yoseph [*Adding*]" saw that his father set down the hand of his right hand upon the head of "Ephrayim [*Double fruitfulness*]" and he was dysfunctional in his eyes and he upheld the hand of his father to remove her from upon the head of "Ephrayim [*Double fruitfulness*]", upon the head of "Menasheh [*Causing to overlook*]",

**48:18** וַיֹּאמֶר יוֹסֵף אֶל אָבִיו לֹא כֵן אָבִי כִּי זֶה הַבְּכֹר שִׂים יְמִינְךָ עַל רֹאשׁוֹ

and~he~will~Say "Yoseph [*Adding*]" To Father~him Not So Father~me Given.that This the~Firstborn !(ms)~Set.in.place Right.hand~you(ms) Upon Head~him

and "Yoseph [*Adding*]" said to his father, not so my father given that this is the firstborn, set in place your right hand upon his head,

**48:19** וַיְמָאֵן אָבִיו וַיֹּאמֶר יָדַעְתִּי בְנִי יָדַעְתִּי גַּם הוּא יִהְיֶה לְעָם וְגַם הוּא יִגְדָּל וְאוּלָם אָחִיו הַקָּטֹן יִגְדַּל מִמֶּנּוּ וְזַרְעוֹ יִהְיֶה מְלֹא הַגּוֹיִם

and~he~will~much~Refuse Father~him and~he~will~Say i~did~Know Son~me i~did~Know Also He he~will~Exist to~People and~Also He he~will~Magnify and~But Brother~him the~

and his father refused and he said, I know my son, I know, he will also exist for a people and he will also magnify but, his small brother will magnify more than him and his

Small he~will~Magnify From~him and~Seed~him he~will~Exist Filling the~Nation~s

seed will exist as a filling of the nations,

**48:20** וַיְבָרֲכֵם בַּיּוֹם הַהוּא לֵאמוֹר בְּךָ יְבָרֵךְ יִשְׂרָאֵל לֵאמֹר יְשִׂמְךָ אֱלֹהִים כְּאֶפְרַיִם וְכִמְנַשֶּׁה וַיָּשֶׂם אֶת אֶפְרַיִם לִפְנֵי מְנַשֶּׁה

and~he~will~much~Kneel~them(m) in~ the~Day the~He to~>>~Say in~you(ms) he~will~much~Kneel "Yisra'el [*He turns El*]" to~>>~Say he~will~ Set.in.place~you(ms) "Elohiym [*Powers*]" like~"Ephrayim [*Double fruitfulness*]" and~like~"Menasheh [*Causing to overlook*]" and~he~will~ Set.in.place At "Ephrayim [*Double fruitfulness*]" to~Face~s "Menasheh [*Causing to overlook*]"

and he respected them in that day saying, in you "Yisra'el [*He turns El*]" will respect saying, "Elohiym [*Powers*]" will set you in place like "Ephrayim [*Double fruitfulness*]" and like "Menasheh [*Causing to overlook*]" and will set in place "Ephrayim [*Double fruitfulness*]" to the face of "Menasheh [*Causing to overlook*]",

**48:21** וַיֹּאמֶר יִשְׂרָאֵל אֶל יוֹסֵף הִנֵּה אָנֹכִי מֵת וְהָיָה אֱלֹהִים עִמָּכֶם וְהֵשִׁיב אֶתְכֶם אֶל אֶרֶץ אֲבֹתֵיכֶם

and~he~will~Say "Yisra'el [*He turns El*]" To "Yoseph [*Adding*]" Look I Die~ing(ms) and~he~did~Exist "Elohiym [*Powers*]" With~you(mp) and~he~did~make~Turn.back At~ you(mp) To Land Father~s~you(mp)

and "Yisra'el [*He turns El*]" said to "Yoseph [*Adding*]", look, I am dying and "Elohiym [*Powers*]" will exist with you and he will remove you to the land of your fathers,

**48:22** וַאֲנִי נָתַתִּי לְךָ שְׁכֶם אַחַד עַל אַחֶיךָ אֲשֶׁר לָקַחְתִּי מִיַּד הָאֱמֹרִי בְּחַרְבִּי וּבְקַשְׁתִּי

and~I i~did~Give to~you(ms) Shoulder Unit Upon Brother~s~ you(ms) Which i~did~Take from~ Hand the~"Emor [*Sayer*]"~of in~ Sword~me and~in~Bow~me

and I gave to you one shoulder in addition to your brothers which I took from the hand of the one of "Emor [*Sayer*]", with my sword and with my bow,

# Chapter 49

**49:1** וַיִּקְרָא יַעֲקֹב אֶל בָּנָיו וַיֹּאמֶר הֵאָסְפוּ וְאַגִּידָה לָכֶם אֵת אֲשֶׁר יִקְרָא אֶתְכֶם בְּאַחֲרִית הַיָּמִים

and~he~will~Call.out "Ya'aqov [*He restrains*]" To Son~s~him and~he~ will~Say !(mp)~be~Gather and~i~will~ make~Be.face.to.face~^ to~you(mp) At Which he~will~Meet At~you(mp) in~

and "Ya'aqov [*He restrains*]" called out to his sons and he said, be gathered and I will tell to you what will meet you in the end of the days,

End   the~Day~s

**49:2**

הִקָּבְצוּ וְשִׁמְעוּ בְּנֵי יַעֲקֹב וְשִׁמְעוּ אֶל יִשְׂרָאֵל אֲבִיכֶם

!(mp)~be~Gather.together   and~!(mp)~ Hear   Son~s   "Ya'aqov [*He restrains*]" and~!(mp)~Hear   To   "Yisra'el [*He turns El*]"   Father~you(mp)

be gathered together and hear, sons of "Ya'aqov [*He restrains*]", and hear "Yisra'el [*He turns El*]" your father,

**49:3**

רְאוּבֵן בְּכֹרִי אַתָּה כֹּחִי וְרֵאשִׁית אוֹנִי יֶתֶר שְׂאֵת וְיֶתֶר עָז

"Re'uven [*See a son*]"   Firstborn~me You(ms)   Strength~me   and~Summit Vigor~me   Remainder   Elevation   and~ Remainder   Strong

"Re'uven [*See a son*]", you are my firstborn, my strength and the summit of my vigor, the remainder of elevation and the remainder of the strong,

**49:4**

פַּחַז כַּמַּיִם אַל תּוֹתַר כִּי עָלִיתָ מִשְׁכְּבֵי אָבִיךָ אָז חִלַּלְתָּ יְצוּעִי עָלָה

Reckless   like~Water~s2   No   you(ms)~ will~make~Reserve   Given.that you(ms)~did~Go.up   Laying.place~s Father~you(ms)   At.that.time   you(ms)~ did~much~Pierce   Couch~me   he~had~ Go.up

reckless like water, you will not be reserved given that you went up to the laying place of your father, at that time you pierced, my couch had gone up,

**49:5**

שִׁמְעוֹן וְלֵוִי אַחִים כְּלֵי חָמָס מְכֵרֹתֵיהֶם

"Shimon [*Heard*]"   and~"Lewi [*Joined*]"   Brother~s   Instrument~s Violence   Cave~s~them(m)

"Shimon [*Heard*]" and "Lewi [*Joined*]" are brothers, instruments of violence are their caves,

**49:6**

בְּסֹדָם אַל תָּבֹא נַפְשִׁי בִּקְהָלָם אַל תֵּחַד כְּבֹדִי כִּי בְאַפָּם הָרְגוּ אִישׁ וּבִרְצֹנָם עִקְּרוּ שׁוֹר

in~Counsel~them(m)   No   you(ms)~will~ Come   Being~me   in~Assembled.flock~ them(m)   No   she~will~Unite   Honor~ me   Given.that   in~Nose~them(m)   they~ did~Kill   Man   and~in~Will~them(m) they~did~Pluck.up   Ox

in their council you will not come, my being is in their assembled flock, my honor will not unite given that in their nose they killed a man and their will they plucked up an ox,

**49:7**

אָרוּר אַפָּם כִּי עָז וְעֶבְרָתָם כִּי קָשָׁתָה אֲחַלְּקֵם בְּיַעֲקֹב וַאֲפִיצֵם בְּיִשְׂרָאֵל

Spit.upon~ed(ms)   Nose~them(m) Given.that   Strong   Wrath~them(m) Given.that   she~did~Be.hard   i~will~ much~Apportion~them(m)   in~"Ya'aqov [*He restrains*]"   and~i~will~make~ Scatter.abroad~them(m)   in~"Yisra'el [*He turns El*]"

spitted upon is their nose given that their wrath was strong, given that she was hard, I will apportion them in "Ya'aqov [*He restrains*]" and I will scatter them abroad in "Yisra'el [*He turns El*]",

**49:8** יְהוּדָה אַתָּה יוֹדוּךָ אַחֶיךָ יָדְךָ בְּעֹרֶף אֹיְבֶיךָ יִשְׁתַּחֲווּ לְךָ בְּנֵי אָבִיךָ

"Yehudah [*Praised*]" You(ms) they(m)~will~make~Throw.the.hand~ you(ms) Brother~s~you(ms) Hand~ you(ms) in~Neck Hostile~ing(ms) they(m)~will~self~Bend.down to~ you(ms) Son~s Father~you(ms)

"Yehudah [*Praised*]", your brothers will thank you, your hand is in the neck of the hostile ones, the sons of your father will bend themselves down to you,

**49:9** גּוּר אַרְיֵה יְהוּדָה מִטֶּרֶף בְּנִי עָלִיתָ כָּרַע רָבַץ כְּאַרְיֵה וּכְלָבִיא מִי יְקִימֶנּוּ

Whelp Lion "Yehudah [*Praised*]" from~Prey Son~me you(ms)~did~Go.up he~did~Stoop he~did~Stretch.out like~ Lion and~like~Lioness Who he~will~ make~Rise~him

a whelp of a lion is "Yehudah [*Praised*]", from the prey, my son, you went up, he stooped, he stretched out like a lion, like a lioness, who will make him rise,

**49:10** לֹא יָסוּר שֵׁבֶט מִיהוּדָה וּמְחֹקֵק מִבֵּין רַגְלָיו עַד כִּי יָבֹא שִׁילֹה וְלוֹ יִקְּהַת עַמִּים

Not he~will~Turn.aside Staff from~ "Yehudah [*Praised*]" and~much~ Inscribe~ing(ms) from~Between Foot~ s~him Until Given.that he~will~Come Tranquility and~to~him Obedience People~s

the staff will not turn aside from "Yehudah [*Praised*]" and the inscribing from between his feet until tranquility comes and to him is the obedience of the peoples,

**49:11** אֹסְרִי לַגֶּפֶן עִירֹה וְלַשֹּׂרֵקָה בְּנִי אֲתֹנוֹ כִּבֵּס בַּיַּיִן לְבֻשׁוֹ וּבְדַם עֲנָבִים סוּתֹה

Tie.up~ing(ms)~me to~Grapevine Colt~ him and~to~the~Choice.vine Son~me She-donkey~him he~did~much~ Tread.upon in~the~Wine Clothing~him and~in~Blood Grape~s Coat~him

tying me up to the grapevine of his colt, and to the choice vine, my son, his she-donkey, he treaded upon in the wine his clothing and in the blood of the grapes of his coat,

**49:12** חַכְלִילִי עֵינַיִם מִיָּיִן וּלְבֶן שִׁנַּיִם מֵחָלָב

Dull.red Eye~s2 from~Wine and~ White Tooth~s from~Fat

dull red are the eyes from wine, and white the teeth from fat,

**49:13** זְבוּלֻן לְחוֹף יַמִּים יִשְׁכֹּן וְהוּא לְחוֹף אֳנִיֹּת וְיַרְכָתוֹ עַל צִידֹן

"Zevulun [*Residence*]" to~Shore Water~s2 he~will~Dwell and~He to~ Shore Ship~s Hollow~him Upon "Tsidon [*Hunting*]"

"Zevulun [*Residence*]", to the shore of the water he will dwell and he is for the shore of ships, his hollow is upon "Tsidon [*Hunting*]",

**49:14** יִשָּׂשכָר חֲמֹר גָּרֶם רֹבֵץ בֵּין הַמִּשְׁפְּתָיִם

"Yis'sas'kar [*He will lift up the*

"Yis'sas'kar [*He will lift up*

wage]" Donkey Cartilage Stretch.out~ing(ms) Between the~Saddlebag~s

*the wage]"* is a donkey of cartilage, stretching out between the saddlebags,

**49:15** וַיַּרְא מְנֻחָה כִּי טוֹב וְאֶת הָאָרֶץ כִּי נָעֵמָה וַיֵּט שִׁכְמוֹ לִסְבֹּל וַיְהִי לְמַס עֹבֵד

and~he~will~See Place.of.rest Given.that Functional and~At the~Land Given.that she~did~Be.sweet and~he~will~Stretch Shoulder~him to~>~Carry and~he~will~Exist to~Task.work Serve~ing(ms)

and he saw the place of rest given that it was functional and the land given that she is sweet and he will stretch his shoulder to carry and he will exist for the task work of the server,

**49:16** דָּן יָדִין עַמּוֹ כְּאַחַד שִׁבְטֵי יִשְׂרָאֵל

"Dan [*Moderator*]" he~will~Moderate People~him like~Unit Staff~s "Yisra'el [*He turns El*]"

"Dan [*Moderator*]" will moderate his people like one of the staffs of "Yisra'el [*He turns El*]",

**49:17** יְהִי דָן נָחָשׁ עֲלֵי דֶרֶךְ שְׁפִיפֹן עֲלֵי אֹרַח הַנֹּשֵׁךְ עִקְּבֵי סוּס וַיִּפֹּל רֹכְבוֹ אָחוֹר

he~will~Exist "Dan [*Moderator*]" Serpent Upon Road Adder Upon Path the~Bite~ing(ms) Heel~s Horse and~he~will~Fall Ride~ing(ms)~him Back

"Dan [*Moderator*]" will exist as a serpent upon the road, an adder upon the path, the one biting the heels of a horse and his rider will fall back,

**49:18** לִישׁוּעָתְךָ קִוִּיתִי יְהֹוָה

to~Rescue~you(ms) i~did~much~Bound.up "YHWH [*He exists*]"

"YHWH [*He exists*]", I was bound up for your rescue,

**49:19** גָּד גְּדוּד יְגוּדֶנּוּ וְהוּא יָגֻד עָקֵב

"Gad [*Fortune*]" Band he~will~Invade~us and~He he~will~Invade Heel

"Gad [*Fortune*]" is a band, he will invade us and he will invade the heel,

**49:20** מֵאָשֵׁר שְׁמֵנָה לַחְמוֹ וְהוּא יִתֵּן מַעֲדַנֵּי מֶלֶךְ

from~"Asher [*Happy*]" Oil Bread~him and~He he~will~Give Tasty.food King

from "Asher [*Happy*]" is oil of his bread and he will give tasty food of the king,

**49:21** נַפְתָּלִי אַיָּלָה שְׁלֻחָה הַנֹּתֵן אִמְרֵי שָׁפֶר

"Naphtali [*Wrestling*]" Doe Send~ed(fs) the~Give~ing(ms) Statement~s Bright

"Naphtali [*Wrestling*]" is a doe sent, the giver of bright statements,

**49:22** בֵּן פֹּרָת יוֹסֵף בֵּן פֹּרָת עֲלֵי עָיִן בָּנוֹת צָעֲדָה עֲלֵי שׁוּר

Son Be.fruitful~ing(fs) "Yoseph

a son being fruitful is "Yoseph

[*Adding*]" Son Be.fruitful~ing(fs)
Upon Eye Daughter~s she~had~March
Upon Ox

[*Adding*]", a son being fruitful upon the eye, daughters had marched upon the ox,

**49:23**

וַיְמָרֲרֻהוּ וָרֹבּוּ וַיִּשְׂטְמֻהוּ בַּעֲלֵי חִצִּים

and~they(m)~will~Be.bitter~him and~they~did~Increase.in.number and~they(m)~will~Hold.a.grudge~him Master~s Arrow~s

and the masters of the arrows were bitter of him and they increased in number and they held a grudge of him,

**49:24**

וַתֵּשֶׁב בְּאֵיתָן קַשְׁתּוֹ וַיָּפֹזּוּ זְרֹעֵי יָדָיו מִידֵי אֲבִיר יַעֲקֹב מִשָּׁם רֹעֶה אֶבֶן יִשְׂרָאֵל

and~she~will~Settle in~Consistency Bow~him and~they(m)~will~Refine Arm~s Hand~s2~him from~Hand~s2 Valiant "Ya'aqov [*He restrains*]" from~There Feed~ing(ms) Stone "Yisra'el [*He turns El*]"

and his bow settled in consistency and they refined the arms of his hands, from the hands of the valiant of "Ya'aqov [*He restrains*]", from there are the feeders, the stone of "Yisra'el [*He turns El*]",

**49:25**

מֵאֵל אָבִיךָ וְיַעְזְרֶךָ וְאֵת שַׁדַּי וִיבָרֲכֶךָ בִּרְכֹת שָׁמַיִם מֵעָל בִּרְכֹת תְּהוֹם רֹבֶצֶת תָּחַת בִּרְכֹת שָׁדַיִם וָרָחַם

from~Mighty.one Father~you(ms) and~he~will~Help~you(ms) and~At "Shaddai [*My breasts*]" and~he~will~much~Kneel~you(ms) Present~s Sky~s2 from~Upon Present~s Deep.sea Stretch.out~ing(fs) Under Present~s Breast~s2 and~Bowels

from the mighty one of your father, he will help you, and with "Shaddai [*My breasts*]" he will respect you, presents of the sky from upon the presents of the deep sea stretching out underneath, presents of the breasts and bowels,

**49:26**

בִּרְכֹת אָבִיךָ גָּבְרוּ עַל בִּרְכֹת הוֹרַי עַד תַּאֲוַת גִּבְעֹת עוֹלָם תִּהְיֶין לְרֹאשׁ יוֹסֵף וּלְקָדְקֹד נְזִיר אֶחָיו

Present~s Father~you(ms) they~will~Overcome Upon Present~s Conceive~ing(mp)~me Until Yearning Knoll~s Distant.time they(f)~will~Exist to~Head "Yoseph [*Adding*]" and~to~Top.of.the.head Dedicated Brother~s~him

presents of your father will overcome upon the presents of my conceivers until the yearning of the knolls of a distant time, they will exist for a head of "Yoseph [*Adding*]" and to the top of the head, dedicated of his brothers,

**49:27**

בִּנְיָמִין זְאֵב יִטְרָף בַּבֹּקֶר יֹאכַל עַד וְלָעֶרֶב יְחַלֵּק שָׁלָל

"Binyamin [*Son of the right hand*]" Wolf he~will~Tear.into.pieces in~the~Morning he~will~Eat Until and~to~the~Evening he~will~Apportion Spoil

"Binyamin [*Son of the right hand*]" is a wolf, he will tear into pieces, in the morning he will eat again and to the evening he will apportion the spoil,

**49:28**

כָּל אֵלֶּה שִׁבְטֵי יִשְׂרָאֵל שְׁנֵים עָשָׂר וְזֹאת אֲשֶׁר דִּבֶּר לָהֶם

אֲבִיהֶם וַיְבָרֶךְ אוֹתָם אִישׁ אֲשֶׁר כְּבִרְכָתוֹ בֵּרַךְ אֹתָם

All These Staff~s "Yisra'el [*He turns El*]" Two Ten and~This Which he~did~much~Speak to~them(m) Father~them(m) and~he~will~much~Kneel At~them(m) Man Which like~Present~him he~did~much~Kneel At~them(m)

all these staffs of "Yisra'el [*He turns El*]" are twelve, and this which their father spoke to them, and he respected them, each who is like his present, he respected them,

**49:29** וַיְצַו אוֹתָם וַיֹּאמֶר אֲלֵהֶם אֲנִי נֶאֱסָף אֶל עַמִּי קִבְרוּ אֹתִי אֶל אֲבֹתָי אֶל הַמְּעָרָה אֲשֶׁר בִּשְׂדֵה עֶפְרוֹן הַחִתִּי

and~he~will~much~Direct At~them(m) and~he~will~Say To~them(m) I be~Gather~ing(ms) To People~me !(mp)~Bury At~me To Father~s~me To the~Cave Which in~Field "Ephron [*Powdery*]" the~"Hhet [*Shattered*]"~of

and he directed them and he said to them, I am being gathered to my people, bury me to my fathers, to the cave which is in the field of "Ephron [*Powdery*]" the one of "Hhet [*Shattered*]",

**49:30** בַּמְּעָרָה אֲשֶׁר בִּשְׂדֵה הַמַּכְפֵּלָה אֲשֶׁר עַל פְּנֵי מַמְרֵא בְּאֶרֶץ כְּנָעַן אֲשֶׁר קָנָה אַבְרָהָם אֶת הַשָּׂדֶה מֵאֵת עֶפְרֹן הַחִתִּי לַאֲחֻזַּת קָבֶר

in~the~Cave Which in~Field "Makhpelah [*Double*]" Which Upon Face~s "Mamre [*Bitter place*]" in~Land "Kena'an [*Lowered*]" Which he~did~Purchase "Avraham [*Father lifted*]" At the~Field from~At "Ephron [*Powdery*]" the~"Hhet [*Shattered*]"~of to~Holdings Grave

in the cave which is in the field of "Makhpelah [*Double*]" which is upon the face of "Mamre [*Bitter place*]" in the land of "Kena'an [*Lowered*]" which "Avraham [*Father lifted*]" purchased with the field from "Ephron [*Powdery*]" the one of "Hhet [*Shattered*]" for a holdings of a grave,

**49:31** שָׁמָּה קָבְרוּ אֶת אַבְרָהָם וְאֵת שָׂרָה אִשְׁתּוֹ שָׁמָּה קָבְרוּ אֶת יִצְחָק וְאֵת רִבְקָה אִשְׁתּוֹ וְשָׁמָּה קָבַרְתִּי אֶת לֵאָה

There~unto they~did~Bury At "Avraham [*Father lifted*]" and~At "Sarah [*Noblewoman*]" Woman~him There~unto they~did~Bury At "Yits'hhaq [*He laughs*]" and~At "Rivqah [*Ensnarer*]" Woman~him and~There~unto i~did~Bury At "Le'ah [*Weary*]"

unto there they buried "Avraham [*Father lifted*]" and "Sarah [*Noblewoman*]" his woman, unto there they buried "Yits'hhaq [*He laughs*]" and "Rivqah [*Ensnarer*]" his woman and unto there I buried "Le'ah [*Weary*]",

**49:32** מִקְנֵה הַשָּׂדֶה וְהַמְּעָרָה אֲשֶׁר בּוֹ מֵאֵת בְּנֵי חֵת

Livestock the~Field and~the~Cave Which in~him from~At Son~s "Hhet [*Shattered*]"

the livestock of the field and the cave which is in him from the sons of "Hhet [*Shattered*]",

**49:33** וַיְכַל יַעֲקֹב לְצַוֹּת אֶת בָּנָיו וַיֶּאֱסֹף רַגְלָיו אֶל הַמִּטָּה וַיִּגְוַע וַיֵּאָסֶף אֶל עַמָּיו

and~he~will~much~Finish "Ya'aqov [*He restrains*]" to~>~much~Direct At Son~s~him and~he~will~Gather Foot~ s~him To the~Bed and~he~will~ Expire and~he~will~be~Gather To People~s~him

and "Ya'aqov [*He restrains*]" finished directing his sons and he gathered his feet to the bed and he expired and he was gathered to his people,

# Chapter 50

**50:1** וַיִּפֹּל יוֹסֵף עַל פְּנֵי אָבִיו וַיֵּבְךְּ עָלָיו וַיִּשַּׁק לוֹ

and~he~will~Fall "Yoseph [*Adding*]" Upon Face~s Father~him and~he~ will~Weep Upon~him and~he~will~ Kiss to~him

and "Yoseph [*Adding*]" fell upon the face of his father and he wept upon him and he kissed him,

**50:2** וַיְצַו יוֹסֵף אֶת עֲבָדָיו אֶת הָרֹפְאִים לַחֲנֹט אֶת אָבִיו וַיַּחַנְטוּ הָרֹפְאִים אֶת יִשְׂרָאֵל

and~he~will~much~Direct "Yoseph [*Adding*]" At Servant~s~him At the~ Heal~ing(mp) to~>~Ripen At Father~ him and~they(m)~will~Ripen the~ Heal~ing(mp) At "Yisra'el [*He turns El*]"

and "Yoseph [*Adding*]" directed his servants, the healers, to ripen his father and the healers ripened "Yisra'el [*He turns El*]",

**50:3** וַיִּמְלְאוּ לוֹ אַרְבָּעִים יוֹם כִּי כֵּן יִמְלְאוּ יְמֵי הַחֲנֻטִים וַיִּבְכּוּ אֹתוֹ מִצְרַיִם שִׁבְעִים יוֹם

and~they(m)~will~Fill to~him Four~s Day Given.that So they(m)~will~Fill Day~s the~Ripen~ed(mp) and~they(m)~ will~Weep At~him "Mitsrayim [*Troubles*]" Seven~s Day

and the forty days were filled for him, for so will the days of the ripening be filled, and "Mitsrayim [*Troubles*]" wept for him for seventy days,

**50:4** וַיַּעַבְרוּ יְמֵי בְכִיתוֹ וַיְדַבֵּר יוֹסֵף אֶל בֵּית פַּרְעֹה לֵאמֹר אִם נָא מָצָאתִי חֵן בְּעֵינֵיכֶם דַּבְּרוּ נָא בְּאָזְנֵי פַרְעֹה לֵאמֹר

and~they(m)~will~Cross.over Day~s Time.of.weeping~him and~he~will~ much~Speak "Yoseph [*Adding*]" To House "Paroh [*Great house*]" to~>~ Say If Please i~did~Find Beauty in~Eye~s2~you(mp) !(mp)~much~Speak Please in~Ear~s "Paroh [*Great house*]"

and the days of the time of his weeping crossed over and "Yoseph [*Adding*]" spoke to the house of "Paroh [*Great house*]" saying, please, if I found beauty in your eyes, please speak in the ears of "Paroh [*Great house*]" saying,

to~>~Say

**50:5** אָבִי הִשְׁבִּיעַנִי לֵאמֹר הִנֵּה אָנֹכִי מֵת בְּקִבְרִי אֲשֶׁר כָּרִיתִי לִי בְּאֶרֶץ כְּנַעַן שָׁמָּה תִּקְבְּרֵנִי וְעַתָּה אֶעֱלֶה נָּא וְאֶקְבְּרָה אֶת אָבִי וְאָשׁוּבָה

| | |
|---|---|
| Father~me he~did~make~Swear~me to~>~Say Look I Die~ing(ms) in~ Grave~me Which i~did~Dig to~me in~Land "Kena'an [*Lowered*]" There~ unto you(ms)~will~Bury~me and~Now i~will~Go.up Please and~i~will~Bury~^ At Father~me and~i~will~Turn.back~^ | my father made me swear saying, look, I am dying in my grave which I dug for me in the land of "Kena'an [*Lowered*]", unto there you will bury me, and now, please, I will go up and I will bury my father and I will turn back, |

**50:6** וַיֹּאמֶר פַּרְעֹה עֲלֵה וּקְבֹר אֶת אָבִיךָ כַּאֲשֶׁר הִשְׁבִּיעֶךָ

| | |
|---|---|
| and~he~will~Say "Paroh [*Great house*]" !(ms)~Go.up and~!(ms)~Bury At Father~you(ms) like~Which he~did~ make~Swear~you(ms) | and "Paroh [*Great house*]" said, go up and bury your father just as he made you swear, |

**50:7** וַיַּעַל יוֹסֵף לִקְבֹּר אֶת אָבִיו וַיַּעֲלוּ אִתּוֹ כָּל עַבְדֵי פַרְעֹה זִקְנֵי בֵיתוֹ וְכֹל זִקְנֵי אֶרֶץ מִצְרָיִם

| | |
|---|---|
| and~he~will~Go.up "Yoseph [*Adding*]" to~>~Bury At Father~him and~ they(m)~will~Go.up At~him All Servant~s "Paroh [*Great house*]" Beard~s House~him and~All Beard~s Land "Mitsrayim [*Troubles*]" | and "Yoseph [*Adding*]" went up to bury his father and all the servants of "Paroh [*Great house*]" went up with him, the bearded ones of his house and all the bearded ones of the land of "Mitsrayim [*Troubles*]", |

**50:8** וְכֹל בֵּית יוֹסֵף וְאֶחָיו וּבֵית אָבִיו רַק טַפָּם וְצֹאנָם וּבְקָרָם עָזְבוּ בְּאֶרֶץ גֹּשֶׁן

| | |
|---|---|
| and~All House "Yoseph [*Adding*]" and~Brother~s~him and~House Father~ him Only Children~them(m) and~ Flocks~them(m) and~Cattle~them(m) they~did~Leave in~Land "Goshen [*Draw near*]" | and all the house of "Yoseph [*Adding*]" and his brothers and the house of his father, only their children and their flocks and their cattle were left in the land of "Goshen [*Draw near*]", |

**50:9** וַיַּעַל עִמּוֹ גַּם רֶכֶב גַּם פָּרָשִׁים וַיְהִי הַמַּחֲנֶה כָּבֵד מְאֹד

| | |
|---|---|
| and~he~will~Go.up With~him Also Rider Also Horseman~s and~he~will~ Exist the~Campsite Heavy Many | and the rider also went up with him, also the horsemen, and the campsite existed very heavy, |

**50:10** וַיָּבֹאוּ עַד גֹּרֶן הָאָטָד אֲשֶׁר בְּעֵבֶר הַיַּרְדֵּן וַיִּסְפְּדוּ שָׁם מִסְפֵּד גָּדוֹל וְכָבֵד מְאֹד וַיַּעַשׂ לְאָבִיו אֵבֶל שִׁבְעַת יָמִים

| | |
|---|---|
| and~they(m)~will~Come Until "Goren-Ha'atad [*Threshing floor of the* | and they came unto "Goren-Ha'atad [*Threshing floor of the brambles*]" |

brambles]" Which in~Other.side the~ "Yarden [Descender]" and~they(m)~ will~Lament There Lamenting Magnificent and~Heavy Many and~ he~will~Do to~Father~him Mourn Seven Day~s

which is on the other side of the "Yarden [Descender]", and they lamented there a magnificent and very heavy lamenting and he did a mourning to his father seven days,

**50:11** וַיַּרְא יוֹשֵׁב הָאָרֶץ הַכְּנַעֲנִי אֶת הָאֵבֶל בְּגֹרֶן הָאָטָד וַיֹּאמְרוּ אֵבֶל כָּבֵד זֶה לְמִצְרָיִם עַל כֵּן קָרָא שְׁמָהּ אָבֵל מִצְרַיִם אֲשֶׁר בְּעֵבֶר הַיַּרְדֵּן

and~he~will~See Settle~ing(ms) the~ Land the~"Kena'an [Lowered]"~of At the~Mourning in~"Goren-Ha'atad [Threshing floor of the brambles]" and~they(m)~will~Say Mourning Heavy This to~"Mitsrayim [Troubles]" Upon So he~did~Call.out Title~her "Aveyl-Mitsrayim [Mourning of Mitsrayim]" Which in~Other.side the~"Yarden [Descender]"

and the settlers of the land of the one of "Kena'an [Lowered]" saw the mourning in "Goren-Ha'atad [Threshing floor of the brambles]" and they said, this is a heavy mourning for "Mitsrayim [Troubles]", therefore, he called out her title "Aveyl-Mitsrayim [Mourning of Mitsrayim]" which is on the other side of the "Yarden [Descender]",

**50:12** וַיַּעֲשׂוּ בָנָיו לוֹ כֵּן כַּאֲשֶׁר צִוָּם

and~they(m)~will~Do Son~s~him to~ him So like~Which he~did~much~ Direct~them(m)

and his sons did to him so, just as he directed them,

**50:13** וַיִּשְׂאוּ אֹתוֹ בָנָיו אַרְצָה כְּנַעַן וַיִּקְבְּרוּ אֹתוֹ בִּמְעָרַת שְׂדֵה הַמַּכְפֵּלָה אֲשֶׁר קָנָה אַבְרָהָם אֶת הַשָּׂדֶה לַאֲחֻזַּת קֶבֶר מֵאֵת עֶפְרֹן הַחִתִּי עַל פְּנֵי מַמְרֵא

and~they(m)~will~Lift.up At~him Son~ s~him Land~unto "Kena'an [Lowered]" and~they(m)~will~Bury At~ him in~Cave Field the~"Makhpelah [Double]" Which he~did~Purchase "Avraham [Father lifted]" At the~ Field to~Holdings Grave from~At "Ephron [Powdery]" the~"Hhet [Shattered]"~of Upon Face~s "Mamre [Bitter place]"

and his sons lifted him up unto the land of "Kena'an [Lowered]" and they buried him in the cave of the field of the "Makhpelah [Double]", the field for holdings of a grave which "Avraham [Father lifted]" purchased, from "Ephron [Powdery]", the one of "Hhet [Shattered]", upon the face of "Mamre [Bitter place]",

**50:14** וַיָּשָׁב יוֹסֵף מִצְרַיְמָה הוּא וְאֶחָיו וְכָל הָעֹלִים אִתּוֹ לִקְבֹּר אֶת אָבִיו אַחֲרֵי קָבְרוֹ אֶת אָבִיו

and~he~will~Turn.back "Yoseph [Adding]" from~"Mitsrayim [Troubles]"~unto He and~Brother~s~

and "Yoseph [Adding]" turned back from unto "Mitsrayim [Troubles]", he and his brothers and all the ones

him and~All the~Go.up~ing(mp) At~
him to~>~Bury At Father~him After
>~Bury~him At Father~him

going up with him to bury his father
after he buried his father,

**50:15** וַיִּרְאוּ אֲחֵי יוֹסֵף כִּי מֵת אֲבִיהֶם וַיֹּאמְרוּ לוּ יִשְׂטְמֵנוּ יוֹסֵף
וְהָשֵׁב יָשִׁיב לָנוּ אֵת כָּל הָרָעָה אֲשֶׁר גָּמַלְנוּ אֹתוֹ

and~they(m)~will~See Brother~s
"Yoseph [Adding]" Given.that he~did~
Die Father~them(m) and~they(m)~will~
Say Would.that he~will~Hold.a.grudge~
us "Yoseph [Adding]" and~>~make~
Turn.back he~will~make~Turn.back to~
us At All the~Dysfunctional Which
we~did~Yield At~him

and the brothers of "Yoseph
[Adding]" saw that their father died
and they said, will "Yoseph
[Adding]" hold a grudge to us and
return to us all the dysfunction
which we yielded to him,

**50:16** וַיְצַוּוּ אֶל יוֹסֵף לֵאמֹר אָבִיךָ צִוָּה לִפְנֵי מוֹתוֹ לֵאמֹר

and~they(m)~will~much~Direct To
"Yoseph [Adding]" to~>~Say Father~
you(ms) he~had~much~Direct to~Face~
s Death~him to~>~Say

and directed "Yoseph [Adding]"
saying, your father had directed
before his death saying,

**50:17** כֹּה תֹאמְרוּ לְיוֹסֵף אָנָּא שָׂא נָא פֶּשַׁע אַחֶיךָ וְחַטָּאתָם כִּי רָעָה
גְמָלוּךָ וְעַתָּה שָׂא נָא לְפֶשַׁע עַבְדֵי אֱלֹהֵי אָבִיךָ וַיֵּבְךְ יוֹסֵף
בְּדַבְּרָם אֵלָיו

In.this.way you(mp)~will~Say to~
"Yoseph [Adding]" Please !(ms)~
Lift.up Please Revolution Brother~s~
you(ms) and~Error~them(m) Given.that
Dysfunctional they~did~Yield~you(ms)
and~Now !(ms)~Lift.up Please to~>~
Revolution Servant~s Power~s Father~
you(ms) and~he~will~Weep "Yoseph
[Adding]" in~>~much~Speak~them(m)
To~him

in this way you will say to "Yoseph
[Adding]", please lift up the
revolution of your brothers and
their error given that they yielded
you dysfunction and now please,
lift the revolution of your servants
of the powers of your father, and
"Yoseph [Adding]" wept in their
speaking to him,

**50:18** וַיֵּלְכוּ גַּם אֶחָיו וַיִּפְּלוּ לְפָנָיו וַיֹּאמְרוּ הִנֶּנּוּ לְךָ לַעֲבָדִים

and~they(m)~will~Walk Also Brother~
s~him and~they(m)~will~Fall to~Face~
s~him and~they(m)~will~Say Look~us
to~you(ms) to~Servant~s

and his brothers also walked and
they fell to his face and they said,
look, we belong to you for servants,

**50:19** וַיֹּאמֶר אֲלֵהֶם יוֹסֵף אַל תִּירָאוּ כִּי הֲתַחַת אֱלֹהִים אָנִי

and~he~will~Say To~them(m) "Yoseph
[Adding]" No you(mp)~will~Fear
Given.that the~Under "Elohiym
[Powers]" I

and "Yoseph [Adding]" said to
them, you will not fear given that I
am in the place of "Elohiym
[Powers]",

**50:20** וְאַתֶּם חֲשַׁבְתֶּם עָלַי רָעָה אֱלֹהִים חֲשָׁבָהּ לְטֹבָה לְמַעַן עֲשֹׂה כַּיּוֹם הַזֶּה לְהַחֲיֹת עַם רָב

and~You(mp) you(mp)~had~Think Upon~me Dysfunctional "Elohiym [*Powers*]" he~had~Think~her to~ Functional to~That >~Do like~the~ Day the~This to~>~make~Live People Abundant

and you had thought dysfunction upon me, "Elohiym [*Powers*]" had thought her for function, that it be done like this day, to make the people live abundantly,

**50:21** וְעַתָּה אַל תִּירָאוּ אָנֹכִי אֲכַלְכֵּל אֶתְכֶם וְאֶת טַפְּכֶם וַיְנַחֵם אוֹתָם וַיְדַבֵּר עַל לִבָּם

and~Now No you(mp)~will~Fear I i~will~much~Sustain At~you(mp) and~ At Children~you(mp) and~he~will~ Comfort At~them(m) and~he~will~ much~Speak Upon Heart~them(m)

and now, you will not fear, I will sustain you and your children, and he comforted them and he spoke upon their heart,

**50:22** וַיֵּשֶׁב יוֹסֵף בְּמִצְרַיִם הוּא וּבֵית אָבִיו וַיְחִי יוֹסֵף מֵאָה וָעֶשֶׂר שָׁנִים

and~he~will~Settle "Yoseph [*Adding*]" in~"Mitsrayim [*Troubles*]" He and~ House Father~him and~he~will~Live "Yoseph [*Adding*]" Hundred and~Ten Year~s

and "Yoseph [*Adding*]" settled in "Mitsrayim [*Troubles*]", he and the house of his father and "Yoseph [*Adding*]" lived a hundred and ten years,

**50:23** וַיַּרְא יוֹסֵף לְאֶפְרַיִם בְּנֵי שִׁלֵּשִׁים גַּם בְּנֵי מָכִיר בֶּן מְנַשֶּׁה יֻלְּדוּ עַל בִּרְכֵּי יוֹסֵף

and~he~will~See "Yoseph [*Adding*]" to~"Ephrayim [*Double fruitfulness*]" Son~s Third.generation~s Also Son~s "Makhir [*Sold*]" Son "Menasheh [*Causing to overlook*]" they~did~ much.be~Bring.forth Upon Knee~s "Yoseph [*Adding*]"

and "Yoseph [*Adding*]" saw the sons of the third generation belonging to "Ephrayim [*Double fruitfulness*]", also the sons of "Makhir [*Sold*]", the son of "Menasheh [*Causing to overlook*]", they were brought forth upon the knees of "Yoseph [*Adding*]",

**50:24** וַיֹּאמֶר יוֹסֵף אֶל אֶחָיו אָנֹכִי מֵת וֵאלֹהִים פָּקֹד יִפְקֹד אֶתְכֶם וְהֶעֱלָה אֶתְכֶם מִן הָאָרֶץ הַזֹּאת אֶל הָאָרֶץ אֲשֶׁר נִשְׁבַּע לְאַבְרָהָם לְיִצְחָק וּלְיַעֲקֹב

and~he~will~Say "Yoseph [*Adding*]" To Brother~s~him I Die~ing(ms) and~"Elohiym [*Powers*]" >~Visit he~ will~Visit At~you(mp) and~he~did~ make~Go.up At~you(mp) From the~ Land the~This To the~Land Which

and "Yoseph [*Adding*]" said to his brothers, I am dying and "Elohiym [*Powers*]" will surely visit you, and he will bring you up from this land to the land which he was sworn to "Avraham [*Father lifted*]", to

he~will~be~Swear to~"Avraham [*Father lifted*]" to~"Yits'hhaq [*He laughs*]" and~to~"Ya'aqov [*He restrains*]"

"Yits'hhaq [*He laughs*]" and to "Ya'aqov [*He restrains*]",

**50:25** נַיַּשְׁבַּע יוֹסֵף אֶת בְּנֵי יִשְׂרָאֵל לֵאמֹר פָּקֹד יִפְקֹד אֱלֹהִים אֶתְכֶם וְהַעֲלִתֶם אֶת עַצְמֹתַי מִזֶּה

and~he~will~make~Swear "Yoseph [*Adding*]" At Son~s "Yisra'el [*He turns El*]" to~>~Say >~Visit he~ will~Visit "Elohiym [*Powers*]" At~ you(mp) and~you(mp)~did~make~Go.up At Bone~s~me from~This

and "Yoseph [*Adding*]" caused the sons of "Yisra'el [*He turns El*]" to swear saying, "Elohiym [*Powers*]" will surely visit you and you will bring up my bones from this,

**50:26*** נַיָּמָת יוֹסֵף בֶּן מֵאָה וָעֶשֶׂר שָׁנִים וַיַּחַנְטוּ אֹתוֹ וַיִּישֶׂם בָּאָרוֹן בְּמִצְרָיִם

and~he~will~Die "Yoseph [*Adding*]" Son Hundred and~Ten Year~s and~ they(m)~will~Ripen At~him and~he~ will~much.be~Set.in.place in~the~Box in~"Mitsrayim [*Troubles*]"

and "Yoseph [*Adding*]" died, a son of a hundred and ten years, and they ripened him and he was set in place in the box in "Mitsrayim [*Troubles*]",

# Dictionary of Words and Names

## Words

**Abdomen:** The gut, the internal organs of the lower torso, the seat of the unconscious mind. Also, the seat of emotion. [masc] [AHLB: 1292-H (N)] [Strong's: 4577, 4578]

**Abundance:** An ample quantity of number (many) or plentiful supply of strength (great). [masc] [AHLB: 1439-J (N)] [Strong's: 7230]

**Abundant:** Great plenty or supply of numbers (many) or strength (great). From the idea of greatness in authority. e.g. One who is abundant in authority such as a master or teacher. Also, an archer as one abundant with arrows. [masc] [AHLB: 1439-A (N)] [Strong's: 7227, 7228, 7229]

**Accept:** To receive from the messenger what is given as a message. [AHLB: 1455-H (V)] [Strong's: 7521]

**Account of:** A telling of what occurred previously. Thus used in Hebrew as a rolling back around. [AHLB: 1058-B (N)] [Strong's: 1558]

**Accumulate:** To gather or pile up, especially little by little. [AHLB: 2772 (V)] [Strong's: 7408]

**Acquired:** What is accumulated in the sense of gathering to build a nest. What is obtained as one's own. Often used in the context of purchasing. [fem]

[AHLB: 1428-H (h¹)] [Strong's: 4736]

**Acquisition:** Something gained by purchase or exchange. [masc] [AHLB: 2360 (N)] [Strong's: 4943]

**Acquit:** To declare one innocent of a crime or oath. [AHLB: 1318-H (V)] [Strong's: 5343, 5352]

**Add:** An augmenting of something by increasing it in amount or supply. [AHLB: 1339-L (V)] [Strong's: 3254, 3255]

**Adder:** A species of viper, possibly an adder. [masc] [AHLB: 1477-B (bj)] [Strong's: 8207]

**Adhere:** To join or stick to someone or something. [AHLB: 2092 (V)] [Strong's: 1692, 1693]

**Advance:** To bring or move forward; to raise to a higher rank; to make progress. [AHLB: 2589 (V)] [Strong's: 6275]

**Affection:** A moderate feeling or emotion. A tender attachment or fondness. [fem] [AHLB: 1094-C (N¹)] [Strong's: 160]

**Afflict:** To oppress severely so as to cause persistent suffering or anguish in the sense of making dark. [AHLB: 1359-H (V)] [Strong's: 6031, 6033]

**Affliction:** The cause of persistent suffering, pain or distress.

[masc] [AHLB: 1359-A (f)] [Strong's: 6040, 6041]

**After:** A time to come beyond another event. [masc] [AHLB: 1181-C (N)] [Strong's: 310, 311]

**Age:** The part of existence extending from the beginning to any given time; a period of time marked by a central figure or prominent feature. [masc] [AHLB: 2132 (g)] [Strong's: 2207]

**Agree:** Two parties to be in concert or concurrence. [AHLB: 1022-J (V)] [Strong's: 225]

**All:** The whole of a group in the sense of being full of food. [masc] [AHLB: 1242-J (N)] [Strong's: 3605, 3606]

**Almond:** The nut or the tree. From the nut's shape like an open eye. [masc] [AHLB: 2872 (N)] [Strong's: 8247]

**Also:** In addition to. The idea of a gathering of objects or ideas. [AHLB: 1059-A (N)] [Strong's: 1571]

**Altar:** The place of sacrifice. [masc] [AHLB: 2117 (h)] [Strong's: 4196]

**Amber:** A fossil gum resin. [masc] [AHLB: **3003**] [Strong's: 916]

**Amplify:** To expand, multiply or increase. [AHLB: 1072-H (V)] [Strong's: 1711]

**Annoyance:** The act of disturbing or irritating. Something that is light in stature; considered worthless as compared with something of much greater value or importance. [fem] [AHLB: 1426-B (N$^1$)] [Strong's: 7045]

**Answer:** Something written or spoken in reply to a question. [AHLB: 1520-H (V)] [Strong's: 6030, 6032]

**Apart from:** At a little distance; away from in space or time; holding different opinions. [masc] [AHLB: **3004**] [Strong's: 1107]

**Apparel:** Something that clothes or adorns. As forming to the image of the body. [fem] [AHLB: 2489 (e$^1$)] [Strong's: 8071]

**Appearance:** What is seen or is in sight. [masc] [AHLB: 1438-H (a)] [Strong's: 4758]

**Appointed:** A fixed or officially set time such as a repetitive event or the seasons. A company or assembly of officially named persons. [masc] [AHLB: 1349-L (a)] [Strong's: 4150, 4151]

**Appointed time:** A fixed or officially set event, occasion or date. [fem] [AHLB: 1367-A (N)] [Strong's: 6256]

**Apportion:** To divide and mete out according to a plan among the appropriate recipients. [AHLB: 2167 (V)] [Strong's: 2505]

**Arm:** The human upper limb as representing power. [fem] [AHLB: 2139 (c)] [Strong's: 2220]

**Army:** A large organized group mustered together and armed for war or service. [masc] [AHLB: 1393-E (N)] [Strong's: 6635]

**Aroma:** A distinctive pervasive and usually pleasant or savory smell or odor. [fem] [AHLB: 1445-M (N)] [Strong's: 7381,

7382]

**Around:** On all sides; enclose so as to surround; in rotation or succession. [masc] [AHLB: 1324-B (b)] [Strong's: 5439]

**Arrange:** To set something in order or into a correct or suitable configuration, sequence or adjustment . [AHLB: 2576 (V)] [Strong's: 6186]

**Arrow:** A missile weapon shot from a bow having a pointed head, slender shaft and feathers as a butt. Used in Hebrew as dividing flesh. [masc] [AHLB: 1179-A (N)] [Strong's: 2671]

**Ash:** The solid residue left when material is thoroughly burned. [masc] [AHLB: 1388-C (N)] [Strong's: 665, 666]

**Ashamed:** Feeling shame, guilt or disgrace. i.e. To be dried up with shame. [AHLB: 1044-J (V)] [Strong's: 954]

**Assembled flock:** A large group, as a gathering of the flock of sheep to the shepherd. [masc] [AHLB: 1426-G (N)] [Strong's: 6951]

**At:** A function word to indicate presence or occurrence, a goal of an implied or indicated action, etc.. Commonly used as a grammatical tool to identify the direct object of a verb. [AHLB: 1022-A (N)] [Strong's: 853, 854, 3487]

**At that time:** A specified moment or time. [masc] [AHLB: 1007-A (N)] [Strong's: 227]

**At this point:** To indicate a specific moment or place in time. [masc] [AHLB: 1104-K (p)] [Strong's: 1988]

**Attach:** To bring one's self into an association with another; e.g.. have an attachment to another. [AHLB: 2219 (V)] [Strong's: 2836]

**Avenge:** To take vengeance for or on behalf of another; to gain satisfaction for a wrong by punishing the wrongdoer; e.g. to pursue and kill one who has murdered. [AHLB: 2433 (V)] [Strong's: 5358]

**Awake:** To bring sleep to an end; to not be in a state of sleeping. [AHLB: 1432-L (V)] [Strong's: 3364]

**Awe:** As shaking when in the presence of an awesome sight. Used once for the thigh (Job 40:17) as shaking in awe. [masc] [AHLB: 2598 (N)] [Strong's: 6343, 6344]

**Back:** The part of the body that is behind. To be in the rear of or behind something. [masc] [AHLB: 1181-C (c)] [Strong's: 268]

**Back of the neck:** The nape. Derived from the soreness of the neck when carrying a load or stress. [masc] [AHLB: 1411-D (g)] [Strong's: 6676, 6677]

**Backward:** With the back foremost; in a reverse or contrary way; i.e. To walk backward in the sense of being after oneself. [fem] [AHLB: 1181-C (cm[4])] [Strong's: 322]

**Bag:** A usually flexible container that may be closed for holding, storing, or carrying something; e.g. The mouth is spread apart to put something in or take something out.

[fem] [AHLB: 2362 (n$^2$)] [Strong's: 572]

**Bake:** To cook using dry heat, especially in an oven. The baking of something in an oven. [AHLB: 1017-H (V)] [Strong's: 644]

**Balm:** An aromatic preparation for a healing ointment. A salve rubbed and pressed into the skin. [masc] [AHLB: 1411-A (f)] [Strong's: 6875]

**Band:** A gathering of men for attacking or raiding. [com] [AHLB: 1050-B (d)] [Strong's: 1416]

**Barley:** A cereal grass used for food. As traded or sold. [masc] [AHLB: 2811 (N)] [Strong's: 7668]

**Barren:** Incapable of bearing children. Childless in the sense of being naked of children. [masc] [AHLB: 1365-B (bf)] [Strong's: 6185]

**Barter:** To exchange an item or service for another. [AHLB: 2573 (V)] [Strong's: 6148, 6149, 6151]

**Base:** The bottom or foundation which provides support. A person's home or family as being a base. A species of gnat. [masc] [AHLB: 1244-A (N)] [Strong's: 3653]

**Basket:** A receptacle made of interwoven materials such as reeds. [masc] [AHLB: 1334-A (N)] [Strong's: 5536]

**Battle:** A struggle between two armies. [fem] [AHLB: 2305 (h$^1$)] [Strong's: 4421]

**Be:** To exist or have breath. That which exists has breath. In Hebrew thought the breath is the character of someone or something. Just as a man has character, so do objects. [AHLB: 1097-J (V)] [Strong's: 1933, 1934]

**Be a whore:** A woman who practices promiscuous sexual behavior, especially for hire. As paid with food. [AHLB: 1152-H (V)] [Strong's: 2181]

**Be able:** To successfully prevail, overcome or endure. [AHLB: 1242-L (V)] [Strong's: 3201, 3202]

**Be abundant:** To be strong in might or numbers. From the abundant number of bones in the body. [AHLB: 2569 (V)] [Strong's: 6105]

**Be bitter:** One of the four basic taste sensations [AHLB: 1296-B (V)] [Strong's: 4843]

**Be childless:** To be without children through miscarriage, barrenness or loss of children. [AHLB: 2836 (V)] [Strong's: 7921]

**Be clean:** Free from dirt or pollution; unadulterated, pure. [AHLB: 1204-G (V)] [Strong's: 2891]

**Be correct:** To walk on the right path without losing the way. [AHLB: 2658 (V)] [Strong's: 6663]

**Be crafty:** The doing of a thing slyly or cunningly. [AHLB: 2404 (V)] [Strong's: 5230]

**Be drunk:** To be filled with intoxicating drink. [AHLB: 2839 (V)] [Strong's: 7937]

**Be dysfunctional:** Impaired or abnormal filling of purpose. To act wrongly by injuring or doing an evil action. [AHLB: 1460-B (V)] [Strong's: 4827, 7489]

**Be face to face:** To face another. Usually in the causative (hiphil or hophal) form meaning to tell, to give an account to another. [AHLB: 2372 (V)] [Strong's: 5046, 5047]

**Be far:** To be distant, a long way off. [AHLB: 2765 (V)] [Strong's: 7368]

**Be fruitful:** Abundantly productive. [AHLB: 1388-E (V)] [Strong's: 6500]

**Be hard:** Not easily penetrated; not easily yielding to pressure. [AHLB: 1435-H (V)] [Strong's: 7185]

**Be heavy:** To be great in weight, wealth or importance. [AHLB: 2246 (V)] [Strong's: 3513]

**Be hungry:** To have an urgent craving for food; famished. [AHLB: 2777 (V)] [Strong's: 7456]

**Be in misery:** A state of suffering and want due to poverty or affliction. [AHLB: 1232-D (V)] [Strong's: 3510]

**Be insubstantial:** Lacking in material nature; lacking firmness or solidity. To be light in weight. To curse or despise in the sense of making light. [AHLB: 1426-B (V)] [Strong's: 7043]

**Be numb:** Devoid of sensation or emotion. [AHLB: 1371-J (V)] [Strong's: 6313]

**Be old:** To be of an advanced age. [AHLB: 2132 (V)] [Strong's: 2204]

**Be rich:** To be wealthy. [AHLB: 2585 (V)] [Strong's: 6238]

**Be sad:** To be in a state of depression. [AHLB: 2130 (V)] [Strong's: 2196]

**Be small:** To have little size or slight dimensions; insignificant. [AHLB: 2703 (V)] [Strong's: 6994]

**Be strong:** Having or marked by great physical, moral or intellectual power. To be mentally astute, firm, obstinate or courageous. [AHLB: 1294-C (V)] [Strong's: 553]

**Be sweet:** One of the four basic taste sensations [AHLB: 2416 (V)] [Strong's: 5276]

**Be threefold:** Being three times as great or as many. [AHLB: 2847 (V)] [Strong's: 8027]

**Be unclean:** Morally or spiritually impure; dirty, filthy. [AHLB: 1197-E (V)] [Strong's: 2930]

**Be whole:** Free of wound or injury, defect or impairment, disease or deformity; mentally and emotionally sound. [AHLB: 1496-B (V)] [Strong's: 8552]

**Be zealous:** Filled with eagerness and ardent interest in pursuit of something. [AHLB: 1428-E (V)] [Strong's: 7065]

**Be.sick:** To be twisted through pain but may also mean to beseech through the idea of twisting. [AHLB: 1173-H (V)] [Strong's: 2470]

**Beard:** The hair that grows on a man's face. A long beard as a sign of old age and wisdom. An elder as a bearded one. [masc] [AHLB: 2132 (N)] [Strong's: 2205, 2206]

**Beast:** An animal as distinguished from man or a plant. A tall or large creature. [fem] [AHLB: 1036-G (N$^1$)] [Strong's: 929,

930]

**Beat:** To strike repeatedly; to drive or force by blows. [AHLB: 2623 (V)] [Strong's: 6470]

**Beautiful:** Generally pleasing. Possessing the qualities of loveliness. [masc] [AHLB: 1224-H (N)] [Strong's: 3303, 3304]

**Beauty:** The qualities in a person or thing that give pleasure to the senses or exalt the mind or spirit. As the beauty of the camp To give or show beauty, grace or mercy to another. [masc] [AHLB: 1175-A (N)] [Strong's: 2580]

**Bed:** A place for sleeping. Spread out sheet for sleeping. [fem] [AHLB: 1308-A (h$^1$)] [Strong's: 4296]

**Before:** What precedes another event. [masc] [AHLB: 2244 (N)] [Strong's: 2962]

**Behind:** In, to or toward the back .To be in back of, at the rear or following after something. [masc] [AHLB: 1181-C (j)] [Strong's: 314]

**Being:** The whole of a person, god or creature including the body, mind, emotion, character and inner parts. [fem] [AHLB: 2424 (N)] [Strong's: 5315]

**Belly:** The undersurface of an animal; the stomach and other digestive organs. [masc] [AHLB: 1054-A (j)] [Strong's: 1512]

**Bend down:** To turn from straight or even to curved; to make submissive, pay homage to another one by bowing low or getting on the knees with the face to the ground. [AHLB: 1468-H (V)] [Strong's: 7812]

**Bend the knee:** A kneeling down as a sign of respect to another. [masc] [AHLB: 2039 (n)] [Strong's: 86]

**Beqa:** A weight standard of measure equal to one-half shekel weight. [masc] [AHLB: 2034 (N)] [Strong's: 1235]

**Beside:** Being next to something in the sense of being in its shade. [masc] [AHLB: 1403-C (N)] [Strong's: 681]

**Best:** Excelling all others; most, largest; most productive or good, utility or satisfaction.. [masc] [AHLB: 1186-L (k)] [Strong's: 4315]

**Betray:** To lead astray; to deliver to an enemy by treachery; to reveal unintentionally. In the Aramaic this word means to "cast down." [AHLB: 1450-H (V)] [Strong's: 7411, 7412]

**Between:** In the time, space or interval that separates. As the wall is between the two sides of the tent. [masc] [AHLB: 1037-M (N)] [Strong's: 996, 997, 1143]

**Bind:** To make secure by tying; to confine, restrain or restrict as if with bonds. bind with a cord. [AHLB: 2572 (V)] [Strong's: 6123]

**Bind up:** To tie something. The tying of the tongue, silence. [AHLB: 1266-C (V)] [Strong's: 481]

**Bird:** A creature distinguished by a body covering of feathers and forelimbs modified as wings. [fem] [AHLB: 2685 (c)] [Strong's: 6833]

**Bird of prey:** A carnivorous bird that feeds on carrion or meat taken by hunting. [masc] [AHLB: 1354-M (N)] [Strong's: 5861]

**Birthing:** The act or process of bringing forth offspring from the womb. Total of the children born within an era. [fem] [AHLB: 1257-L (i³)] [Strong's: 8435]

**Birthright:** Rights, privileges or possessions to which a person is entitled by birth. The rights of the firstborn son (see Deut. 21:17). Also meaning the firstborn. [fem] [AHLB: 2016 (c¹)] [Strong's: 1062]

**Bite:** To seize especially with teeth or jaws; to sting, wound or pierce as with a fang. To give usury in the sense of a biting. [AHLB: 2441 (V)] [Strong's: 5391]

**Bitter:** A difficult taste or experience. In Isaiah 40:15 only, this word means "drop." [masc] [AHLB: 1296-A (N)] [Strong's: 4751, 4752]

**Blast:** To blow heavily. [AHLB: 2817 (V)] [Strong's: 7710]

**Blazing:** To burn brightly; to be conspicuously brilliant or resplendent. [masc] [AHLB: 1262-G (N)] [Strong's: 3858]

**Blindness:** Sightless; unquestioning, as having no regard to rational discrimination, guidance or restriction. As a shutting of the eyes. [masc] [AHLB: 3035 (N)] [Strong's: 5575]

**Blood:** The fluid that circulates through the heart and blood vessels with oxygen and nutrients to and carrying

waste from the cells of the body. [masc] [AHLB: 1082-A (N)] [Strong's: 1818]

**Blossom:** The flower of a seed plant. From its bright color and shape as like a spark. Also, an unknown bird of prey. [masc] [AHLB: 1317-A (N)] [Strong's: 5322]

**Body:** By extension, the physical form, either alive or dead; a corpse. [fem] [AHLB: 1052-A (f¹)] [Strong's: 1472]

**Boil:** To generate bubbles of vapor when heated. To cook a meat in water. Also meaning to ripen in the sense of being cooked. [AHLB: 2043 (V)] [Strong's: 1310]

**Bondwoman:** A female slave. One who is bound to another. [fem] [AHLB: 1013-A (N¹)] [Strong's: 519]

**Bone:** The hard tissue of which the skeleton is chiefly composed. As a numerous amount. [masc] [AHLB: 2569 (N)] [Strong's: 6106]

**Booth:** A temporary shelter; a small enclosure; dwelling place. [fem] [AHLB: 1333-J (N¹)] [Strong's: 5521]

**Border:** The outer edge of a region. [masc] [AHLB: 2049 (d)] [Strong's: 1366]

**Born:** Brought forth, as if by birth. [masc] [AHLB: 1257-L (b)] [Strong's: 3211]

**Bosom:** The human chest, especially the front side. [masc] [AHLB: 1163-M (N)] [Strong's: 2436]

**Bound up:** To be confined or hedged in together. To wait or to be held back in the sense of being bound up. [AHLB:

1419-J (V)] [Strong's: 6960]

**Bow:** A weapon made from a stiff branch to shoots arrows. A bow-shaped object such as a rainbow. [fem] [AHLB: 1435-A (N²)] [Strong's: 7198, 7199]

**Bow the head:** To lower the head as a sign of respect. [AHLB: 1418-B (V)] [Strong's: 6915]

**Bowels:** The large intestines as encompassed about by the torso. Compassion as coming from the bowels. Also, an unknown species of bird. [masc] [AHLB: 2762 (N)] [Strong's: 7356, 7358, 7359]

**Bowl:** A concave vessel especially for holding liquids. As with high sides. [masc] [AHLB: 2051 (b)] [Strong's: 1375]

**Box:** A rigid rectangular receptacle often with a cover. Any box-shaped object. [masc] [AHLB: 1020-H (j)] [Strong's: 727]

**Boy:** A male child from birth to puberty. [masc] [AHLB: 1257-L (N)] [Strong's: 3206]

**Bracelet:** An ornamental band or chain worn around the wrist. As the ends joined together. [masc] [AHLB: 2665 (b)] [Strong's: 6781]

**Bramble:** A rough, prickly vine or shrub. Thorn. [masc] [AHLB: 1432-J (N)] [Strong's: 6975]

**Branch:** A secondary shoot or stem arising from a main trunk or axis.. [masc] [AHLB: 2505 (b)] [Strong's: 8299]

**Breach:** A broken, ruptured or torn condition or area; a gap as in a wall made by battering. [masc] [AHLB: 2642 (N)] [Strong's: 6556]

**Bread:** Baked and leavened food primarily made of flour or meal. The kneading, or fighting, with bread dough. [masc] [AHLB: 2305 (N)] [Strong's: 3899, 3900, 3901]

**Bread cake:** Cakes baked on hot stones. [fem] [AHLB: 1348-A (N¹)] [Strong's: 5692]

**Break:** To throw something on the ground and break it by trampling. [AHLB: 1388-B (V)] [Strong's: 6565]

**Break out:** To be spread out wide or widespread. [AHLB: 2642 (V)] [Strong's: 6555]

**Breaking camp:** The packing up of camp for the purpose of beginning a journey. [masc] [AHLB: 2413 (a)] [Strong's: 4550, 4551]

**Breast:** Milk-producing glandular organs situated on the front part of the chest in the female; the fore part of the body between the neck and the abdomen. Also a goat-idol from the teats of the goat. [masc] [AHLB: 1464-A (N)] [Strong's: 7699, 7700]

**Breath:** Air inhaled or exhaled. The breath of man or god. The essence of life. [fem] [AHLB: 2443 (N¹)] [Strong's: 5396, 5397]

**Brick:** A building material typically rectangular and of moist clay hardened by heat. [fem] [AHLB: 2303 (N¹)] [Strong's: 3843]

**Bride price:** A payment given by or in behalf of a prospective husband to the bride's family. [masc] [AHLB: 1296-G (g)] [Strong's: 4119]

**Bright:** A radiating or reflective light. As cheerful. [masc]

[AHLB: 2869 (N)] [Strong's: 8233]

**Brimstone:** A rock of sulfur that burns. [fem] [AHLB: 2079 (N⁴)] [Strong's: 1614]

**Bring forth:** To issue out. To bring forth children, either by the woman who bears them or the man who fathered them. [AHLB: 1257-L (V)] [Strong's: 3205]

**Bronze:** An alloy of copper and tin. From its shine. [fem] [AHLB: 2395 (c²)] [Strong's: 5178]

**Brother:** A male who has the same parents as another or shares one parent with another. One who stands between the enemy and the family, a protector. The hearth of a fire used as a dividing wall that protects the family. [fem] [AHLB: 1008-A (N)] [Strong's: 251, 252, 254, 1889]

**Bruise:** An injury involving rupture of small blood vessels and discoloration without a skin break. The dark coloring of the skin caused by being hit or smashed. [masc] [AHLB: 2628 (N)] [Strong's: 6482]

**Build:** To construct a building, home or family. [AHLB: 1037-H (V)] [Strong's: 1124, 1129]

**Bull:** A male un-castrated bovine. [masc] [AHLB: 1388-A (N)] [Strong's: 6499]

**Bundle:** A group of things fastened together for convenient handling. Something that is bound up tightly. [masc] [AHLB: 1411-B (c)] [Strong's: 6872]

**Burial place:** The place of interment or deposit of a deceased body. [fem] [AHLB: 2696 (d¹)] [Strong's: 6900]

**Burn black:** To char wood in a fire. A passion that burns for another. [AHLB: 2266 (V)] [Strong's: 3648]

**Burst:** To break open, apart or into pieces out or through. [AHLB: 2811 (V)] [Strong's: 7665, 8406]

**Burst out:** To be larger, fuller, or more crowded. Break out or break forth as a blooming flower or the wings of a bird. [AHLB: 2636 (V)] [Strong's: 6524]

**Bury:** To dispose of by depositing in or as if in the earth. [AHLB: 2696 (V)] [Strong's: 6912]

**But:** On the contrary. An outcome desired in the sense of joining. [com] [AHLB: 1254-J (p)] [Strong's: 199]

**Butcher:** One who slaughters animals or dresses their flesh. [AHLB: 2227 (V)] [Strong's: 2873]

**By:** In proximity to. The sense of standing with another. [masc] [AHLB: 2550 (e)] [Strong's: 5978]

**Calculate:** To determine by mathematical deduction or practical judgement. To comprehend and carefully consider a path or course of action. [AHLB: 2477 (V)] [Strong's: 7919, 7920]

**Call out:** To raise one's voice or speak to someone loudly and with urgency. To call out, give, a name. Also, to "meet" in the sense of being called to a meeting and, through extension, an encounter by chance. In addition, to "read" in the sense of calling out the words written. [AHLB: 1434-E (V)] [Strong's: 7121, 7123]

**Camel:** Either of two ruminant mammals used as draft animals in the desert. The produce of the fields were tied in large bundles and transported on camels. [com] [AHLB: 2070 (N)] [Strong's: 1581]

**Camp:** Ground on which temporary shelters (as tents) are erected; a group of shelters erected on such ground. To stop for the night and pitch the tents. [AHLB: 1175-H (V)] [Strong's: 2583]

**Campsite:** A place suitable for or used as the location of a camp. The inhabitants of a camp. [masc] [AHLB: 1175-H (a)] [Strong's: 4264]

**Captain:** A military leader; the commander of a unit or a body of troops. The leader of a family, tribe or people as one who carries the burdens of the people. [masc] [AHLB: 1314-E (b)] [Strong's: 5387]

**Capture:** The act of catching, winning, or gaining control by force, stratagem, or guile. To take one away from his homeland as an involuntary prisoner. [AHLB: 1462-H (V)] [Strong's: 7617]

**Caravan:** A traveling company that follows a prescribed path. The Aramaic word means a road or path one travels. [fem] [AHLB: 1445-C (g$^1$ & N$^1$)] [Strong's: 735, 736]

**Carcass:** A dead body. [masc] [AHLB: 2593 (N)] [Strong's: 6297]

**Carry:** To transfer from one place to another; to transport as by vehicle. [AHLB: 2460 (V)] [Strong's: 5445, 5446]

**Cart:** A heavy, two-wheeled vehicle, animal-drawn, used for transporting freight or for farming. From its round wheels. [fem] [AHLB: 2524 (N$^1$)] [Strong's: 5699]

**Cartilage:** Translucent elastic tissue that lines the joints of the bony skeleton. [masc] [AHLB: 2084 (N)] [Strong's: 1634, 1635]

**Cast out:** To drive out, expel, thrust away. [AHLB: 2089 (V)] [Strong's: 1644]

**Cattle:** Domesticated bovine animals on a farm or ranch. Strong beasts used to break the soil with plows. [masc] [AHLB: 2035 (N)] [Strong's: 1165, 1241]

**Cave:** A natural underground chamber or series of chambers that open to the surface. A hole in the rock. [fem] [AHLB: 1250-A (k$^1$)] [Strong's: 4380, 4631]

**Cease:** To come to an end; to die out. Case from an activity for the purpose of rest or celebration. [AHLB: 2812 (V)] [Strong's: 7673]

**Cereal:** Relating to grain or plants that produce it. A plentiful crop. [masc] [AHLB: 1072-A (m)] [Strong's: 1715]

**Chain:** A series of links worn as an ornament or insignia in the sense of being spread over the neck. [masc] [AHLB: 2742 (b)] [Strong's: 7242]

**Chamber:** A bedroom; a natural or artificial enclosed space or cavity. Place surrounded by walls. An inner place as hidden or secret. [masc] [AHLB: 2150 (N)] [Strong's: 2315]

**Change:** To make different in some particular; to make radically different; exchange one thing for another. To repeat in the sense of a second time. [AHLB: 1474-H (V)] [Strong's: 8132, 8133, 8138]

**Charge:** A person or thing committed to the care of another. What is given to be watched over and protected. [fem] [AHLB: 2853 (h$^2$)] [Strong's: 4931]

**Chariot:** A two-wheeled horse-drawn battle car of ancient times used also in processions and races. [fem] [AHLB: 2769 (k$^1$)] [Strong's: 4818]

**Cheese:** A food consisting of the coagulated, compressed and usually ripened curd of milk separated from the whey. [fem] [AHLB: 1174-E (N$^1$)] [Strong's: 2529]

**Chestnut:** Probably the chestnut tree but uncertain. [masc] [AHLB: 2908 (j)] [Strong's: 6196]

**Chief:** Accorded highest rank or office; of greatest importance, significance, or influence. One who is yoked to another to lead and teach. [masc] [AHLB: 2001 (d)] [Strong's: 441]

**Child:** A young person, especially between infancy and youth. [masc] [AHLB: 1257-I (N)]

[Strong's: 2056]

**Children:** More than one child. [masc] [AHLB: 1201-A (N)] [Strong's: 2945]

**Chimney:** A vertical structure in a building and enclosing a flue or flues that carry off smoke. A hole in the roof where smoke escapes. [fem] [AHLB: 1439-C (d$^1$)] [Strong's: 699]

**Choice fruit:** Having qualities that appeal to a cultivated taste. As plucked from the tree or vine. [fem] [AHLB: 2124 (N$^1$)] [Strong's: 2173]

**Choice vine:** The best of the vine, the best grapes. [com] [AHLB: 2513 (g)] [Strong's: 8321]

**Choose:** To select freely and after consideration. [AHLB: 2012 (V)] [Strong's: 977]

**Chosen:** One who is the object of choice or of divine favor. [masc] [AHLB: 2012 (h)] [Strong's: 4005]

**Circumcise:** To cut off the foreskin of a male. A cutting of the front part of the male member. [AHLB: 1288-J (V)] [Strong's: 4135]

**Cistern:** An artificial reservoir for storing liquids and especially water. A hole, well or cistern that is dug out. A standard of measure. [masc] [AHLB: 1250-J (N)] [Strong's: 953, 2352, 2356, 3564, 3734]

**City:** An inhabited place of greater size, population, or importance than a town or village. [masc] [AHLB: 1526-M (N)] [Strong's: 5892]

**Cleave:** To divide by or as if by a cutting blow; to separate into distinct parts. break, cut or divide something in half. [AHLB: 2034 (V)] [Strong's: 1234]

**Clothe:** To cover with or as if with cloth or clothing; to provide with clothing; put on clothing. [AHLB: 2304 (V)] [Strong's: 3847, 3848]

**Clothing:** Garments in general. [masc] [AHLB: 2304 (d)] [Strong's: 3830, 3831]

**Cloud:** A visible mass of particles of water or ice in the form of fog, mist, or haze suspended usually at a considerable height in the air. [masc] [AHLB: 1359-B (N)] [Strong's: 6050, 6051]

**Cluster:** A number of similar things growing together or of things or persons collected or grouped closely together. A cluster of grapes from the vine or flowers from the plant. [masc] [AHLB: 2836 (nc)] [Strong's: 811]

**Coat:** An outer garment varying in length and style; the external growth on an animal. [masc] [AHLB: 1344-J (N)] [Strong's: 5497]

**Cold:** A condition of low temperature. [masc] [AHLB: 1434-A (N)] [Strong's: 7119, 7120]

**Collection:** An accumulation of objects or material. A collection of water (a pool, pond or sea) or horses (herd). [masc] [AHLB: 1419-J (h)] [Strong's: 4723]

**Colt:** A young male horse; a young untried person. As dark in color. [com] [AHLB: 1526-M (N)] [Strong's: 5895]

**Come:** To move toward something; approach; to reach a condition; fill a void by entering it. This can be understood as to come or to go. [AHLB: 1024-J (V)] [Strong's: 935]

**Come near:** To come close by or near to. [AHLB: 2729 (V)] [Strong's: 7126, 7127]

**Come to an end:** To cease. Conclude. [AHLB: 1383-C (V)] [Strong's: 656]

**Come up:** To rise up, as the sun does at the horizon. [AHLB: 2135 (V)] [Strong's: 2224]

**Comfort:** Consolation in time of trouble or worry. To give solace in time of difficulty or sorrow. [AHLB: 2392 (V)] [Strong's: 5162]

**Community:** A unified body of individuals; a group of people bound together. [masc] [AHLB: 1266-D (c)] [Strong's: 3816]

**Companion:** One that accompanies another. As a close companion. [masc] [AHLB: 1453-A (N)] [Strong's: 7453]

**Company:** A group of persons or things for carrying on a project or undertaking; company, as a group with a common testimony. May also mean a witness or testimony. [fem] [AHLB: 1349-A (N[1])] [Strong's: 5712, 5713]

**Compassionate:** Having or showing sympathetic consciousness of others' distress with a desire to alleviate it. [fem] [AHLB: 2171 (N[1])] [Strong's: 2551]

**Compel:** To drive or urge forcefully or irresistibly. A

pressing into an action or narrow place. [AHLB: 1018-J (V)] [Strong's: 213]

**Complete:** Having all necessary parts, elements or steps. A state of being whole or full. Left unaltered and whole in its original functional state without removing or adding to it. An offering or payment to make restitution. To finish. Used in Aramaic as a greeting expressing a desire for completeness to another. [masc] [AHLB: 2845 (N)] [Strong's: 8001, 8002, 8003]

**Completeness:** Something that has been finished or made whole. A state of being complete. Used in Aramaic as a greeting expressing a desire for completeness to another. [masc] [AHLB: 2845 (c)] [Strong's: 7965]

**Completion:** The act or process of completing. This can be in a positive sense or negative, such as in a failure. [fem] [AHLB: 1242-A (N$^1$)] [Strong's: 3617]

**Conceal:** To prevent disclosure or recognition of; to place out of sight. To completely cover over or hide. [AHLB: 1245-H (V)] [Strong's: 3680, 3780]

**Conceive:** To become pregnant with young. [AHLB: 1112-H (V)] [Strong's: 2029]

**Concerning:** Regarding. Marked interest or regard usually arising through a personal tie or relationship. A turning over and bringing together of a thought. [fem] [AHLB: 1004-J (N$^3$)] [Strong's: 182]

**Conclusion:** To come to an end.

The end of a time period or place or the end of something. The border of a country as its edges. [masc] [AHLB: 1432-A (N)] [Strong's: 7093]

**Concubine:** Cohabitation of persons not legally married; a woman living in a socially recognized state of being a mistress. [fem] [AHLB: **3048**] [Strong's: 6370]

**Confusion:** To bring to ruin; to make indistinct; to fail to differentiate from an often similar or related other. A barren place. Vanity as a state of waste. [masc] [AHLB: 1488-J (r)] [Strong's: 8414]

**Consent:** To give approval; to be in concord in opinion or sentiment; agreement as to action or opinion. A filling of a void in space or action. To be willing to go somewhere or do something. [AHLB: 1028-C (V)] [Strong's: 14]

**Consistency:** Agreement or harmony of parts or features; showing steady conformity to character, profession, belief, or custom. [masc] [AHLB: 1497-C (e)] [Strong's: 386]

**Consume:** To eat or drink; with the lips. [AHLB: 1339-H (V)] [Strong's: 5595]

**Contention:** An act or instance of striving or struggling against great difficulty or opposition. [fem] [AHLB: 1439-M (k$^1$)] [Strong's: 4808]

**Contribution:** What is given or supplied in common with others. [fem] [AHLB: 2451 (a$^1$)] [Strong's: 4978, 4979]

**Convict:** To find or prove to be guilty. [AHLB: 1238-L (V)]

[Strong's: 3198]

**Cord:** A long slender flexible material made of several strands woven or twisted together. Made of twisted fibers. [masc] [AHLB: 2650 (b)] [Strong's: 6616]

**Correct:** To make or set right. Conforming to fact, standard or truth. [masc] [AHLB: 2658 (b)] [Strong's: 6662]

**Correctness:** Conformity to fact, standard or truth. [fem] [AHLB: 2658 (N$^1$)] [Strong's: 6666]

**Couch:** An article of furniture for sitting or reclining. [masc] [AHLB: 1407-L (d)] [Strong's: 3326]

**Counsel:** Advice given especially as a result of consultation. A lawyer appointed to advise and represent in legal matters an individual client or public body. An assembly of persons who counsel another or a people. [masc] [AHLB: 1326-J (N)] [Strong's: 5475]

**Count:** To find the total number of units involved by naming the numbers in order up to and including. [AHLB: 2500 (V)] [Strong's: 5608]

**Couple:** To bind by joining or coupling together. [AHLB: 2143 (V)] [Strong's: 2266]

**Courageous:** Having or characterized by mental or moral strength to venture, persevere, and withstand danger, fear or difficulty. [masc] [AHLB: 2052 (ec)] [Strong's: 1368]

**Covenant:** A solemn and binding agreement between two or more parties especially for the performance of some action. Covenant is instituted through the sacrifice of a choice, fattened, animal that is cut in two pieces, and between which the parties of the covenant pass. If one party fails to meet the agreements of the covenant, then the other may do the same to them. (see Genesis 15:10,17 and Jeremiah 34:18-20) [fem] [AHLB: 1043-H (N$^4$)] [Strong's: 1285]

**Cover:** To afford protection or security; to hide from sight or knowledge. Cover over as with a lid. [AHLB: 2283 (V)] [Strong's: 3722]

**Covering:** Something that covers or conceals. A covering such as pitch or a monetary covering such as a bribe or ransom. A "village" as a covering. [masc] [AHLB: 2283 (g)] [Strong's: 3723, 3724]

**Cow:** The mature female of cattle. [fem] [AHLB: 1388-A (N$^1$)] [Strong's: 6510]

**Crash:** To break violently and noisily. [AHLB: 1461-H (V)] [Strong's: 7582, 7583]

**Crave:** To have a strong or inward desire for something. [AHLB: 2169 (V)] [Strong's: 2530]

**Craving:** A great desire or longing. [AHLB: 2277 (V)] [Strong's: 3700]

**Cremate:** To reduce a dead body to ashes by burning. [AHLB: 2512 (V)] [Strong's: 5635, 8313]

**Cremating:** The act of burning a dead body to ashes. [fem] [AHLB: 2512 (N$^1$)] [Strong's:

8316]

**Cross over:** To pass from one side to the other. To go across a river or through a land. [AHLB: 2520 (V)] [Strong's: 5674, 5675]

**Crossing:** A place or structure as on a street or over a river where pedestrians or vehicles pass from one side to the other. In the river for crossing. [masc] [AHLB: 2520 (a)] [Strong's: 4569]

**Crush:** To reduce to particles by pounding or grinding. Crush something to pieces. An oppression or struggle as crushing. [AHLB: 1455-B (V)] [Strong's: 7465, 7533, 7567]

**Cry:** To utter loudly; to shout; to shed tears, often noisily. A loud crying or calling out. [fem] [AHLB: 2679 (N$^1$)] [Strong's: 6818]

**Cry out:** To cry or call out loudly. [AHLB: 2679 (V)] [Strong's: 6817]

**Cup:** A drinking vessel . Also an unknown species of bird. [fem] [AHLB: 1245-J (N)] [Strong's: 3563]

**Custody:** Immediate charge and control exercised by a person or authority. A careful watching over as an office, guard or prison. [masc] [AHLB: 2853 (h)] [Strong's: 4929]

**Custom:** A usage or practice common to many or to a particular place or class or habitual with an individual. [masc] [AHLB: 1180-J (N)] [Strong's: 2706]

**Cut:** To penetrate with a sharp edged instrument. [AHLB: 2291 (V)] [Strong's: 3772]

**Cut in two:** To sever into two pieces or parts. [AHLB: 2047 (V)] [Strong's: 1334]

**Cut off:** To discontinue or terminate. To sever the tip or end. [AHLB: 2407 (V)] [Strong's: 5243]

**Cut piece:** A sacrificial animal that has been cut into pieces. [masc] [AHLB: 2047 (N)] [Strong's: 1335]

**Damage:** To bring to ruin by destruction. To destroy through disfigurement or corruption. [AHLB: 2830 (V)] [Strong's: 7843, 7844]

**Dark:** Devoid or partially devoid of light; not receiving, reflecting, transmitting, producing or radiating light. As the darkness of a moonless night. [fem] [AHLB: 2215 (N$^1$)] [Strong's: 2824, 2825]

**Darkness:** The state of being dark. As the darkness of a moonless night. [masc] [AHLB: 2215 (g)] [Strong's: 2822]

**Daughter:** A female having the relation of a child to parent. A village that resides outside of the city walls; as "the daughter of the city." [fem] [AHLB: 1037-A (N$^2$)] [Strong's: 1323]

**Daughter-in-law:** The wife of one's son. Bride of the son, as brought into the camp, in the sense of making the man complete. [fem] [AHLB: 1242-B (N$^1$)] [Strong's: 3618]

**Dawn:** To begin to grow light as the sun rises in the east. The place of the rising sun. [masc]

[AHLB: 2829 (N)] [Strong's: 7837]

**Day:** The time of light between one night and the next one. Usually in the context of daylight hours but may also refer to the entire day [masc] [AHLB: 1220-J (N)] [Strong's: 3117, 3118]

**Deal deceitfully:** To give as one's portion by a false impression. [AHLB: 1495-F (V)] [Strong's: 2048]

**Death:** A permanent cessation of all vital functions; the end of life. [masc] [AHLB: 1298-J (N)] [Strong's: 4192, 4193, 4194]

**Deceit:** The act or practice of not being honest. [fem] [AHLB: 1450-A (h¹)] [Strong's: 4820]

**Deceive:** To cause to accept as true or valid what is false or invalid. Can also mean usury in the sense of a deception. In the participle form can mean creditor in the sense of imposition. [AHLB: 1320-E (V)] [Strong's: 5377, 5378, 5383]

**Dedicated:** Devoted to the worship of God. [masc] [AHLB: 2390 (N)] [Strong's: 5139]

**Deep sea:** Extending far from some surface or area; in difficulty or distress. Deep and tumultuous water. A subterranean body of water. [fem] [AHLB: 1105-J (i)] [Strong's: 8415]

**Delay:** To stop, detain or hinder for a time. [AHLB: 1181-C (V)] [Strong's: 309]

**Delicacy:** The quality or state of being luxurious. Flavorful

meat. [masc] [AHLB: 2236 (a)] [Strong's: 4303]

**Delight:** A high degree of gratification. To desire something out of pleasure or necessity. [AHLB: 2191 (V)] [Strong's: 2654]

**Deliver:** To set free; to take and hand over to or leave for another. [AHLB: 2428 (V)] [Strong's: 5337, 5338]

**Deliver up:** To hand over to another. [AHLB: 2331 (V)] [Strong's: 4042]

**Deny:** To disclaim connection with or responsibility for. Withhold something from another or self as in a lie or submission. [AHLB: 2257 (V)] [Strong's: 3584]

**Depart early:** To go away or leave early; immediate obedience. Rise or go early in the sense of placing the load on the shoulders to depart. [AHLB: 2837 (V)] [Strong's: 7925]

**Deposit:** To place, especially for safekeeping or as a pledge. Something laid down. Sit down to rest or remain in place. [AHLB: 1307-L (V)] [Strong's: 3240]

**Deposited:** Valuables placed for safekeeping. Produce or other stores that are watched over. [masc] [AHLB: 2630 (j)] [Strong's: 6487]

**Desolate:** Devoid of inhabitants and visitors. [AHLB: 1473-B (V)] [Strong's: 8074, 8075]

**Despise:** To look down on with contempt or aversion. [AHLB: 1030-J (V)] [Strong's: 936]

**Destroy:** To ruin the structure,

organic existence, or condition of something. [AHLB: 2848 (V)] [Strong's: 8045, 8046]

**Dew:** Moisture condensed on the surfaces of cool bodies or objects, especially at night. [masc] [AHLB: 1196-A (N)] [Strong's: 2919, 2920]

**Die:** To pass from physical life; to pass out of existence. Come to an end through death. [AHLB: 1298-J (V)] [Strong's: 4191]

**Dig:** To break or loosen earth with an instrument or tool. To bargain in the sense of digging. [AHLB: 1250-H (V)] [Strong's: 3735, 3738, 3739]

**Dig out:** To dig something out of the ground. To dig into something as if searching. To confuse in the sense of being dug out. [AHLB: 2192 (V)] [Strong's: 2658, 2659]

**Dim:** Emitting a limited or insufficient amount of light; seen indistinctly or without clear outlines or details. . To be dark in the eyes or knowledge. [AHLB: 1235-B (V)] [Strong's: 3543]

**Diminish:** To make less or cause to appear less; to lessen the authority, dignity, or reputation of. Be lacking or to decrease. [AHLB: 2187 (V)] [Strong's: 2637]

**Dip:** To plunge or immerse momentarily or partially, as under the surface of a liquid, to moisten, cool, or coat. [AHLB: 2228 (V)] [Strong's: 2881]

**Direct:** To cause to turn, move, or point undeviatingly or to follow a straight course. Give instructions or orders for a path to be taken. [AHLB: 1397-H (V)] [Strong's: 6680]

**Directive:** Serving or intended to guide, govern, or influence; serving to point direction. [fem] [AHLB: 1397-H (h¹)] [Strong's: 4687]

**Discernment:** The quality of being able to grasp and comprehend what is obscure. An intimacy with a person, idea or concept. [fem] [AHLB: 1085-A (N²)] [Strong's: 1847]

**Disdain:** A feeling of contempt for what is beneath one; to look with scorn on. To treat something as spoiled or no longer of value. [AHLB: 1030-H (V)] [Strong's: 959]

**Disgrace:** A scorn, taunting or reproach as a piercing. [fem] [AHLB: 2208 (N¹)] [Strong's: 2781]

**Disgusting:** Something highly distasteful that arouses marked aversion in one. [fem] [AHLB: 2897 (g¹)] [Strong's: 8441]

**Dislocate:** To put out of place; to displace, as to dislocate a joint. Beheading by severing the neck.. [AHLB: 1430-L (V)] [Strong's: 3363]

**Dispute:** To engage in argument. Dispute or chide another in harassment or trial. [AHLB: 1439-M (V)] [Strong's: 7378]

**Distance:** Separation in space or time. A distant place or time. [masc] [AHLB: 2765 (c)] [Strong's: 7350]

**Distant:** Separated in space; situated at a great distance.

Something far off in the distance. [fem] [AHLB: 1104-E (N$^1$)] [Strong's: 1973]

**Distant time:** A time in the far past or future, as a time hidden from the present. [masc] [AHLB: 2544 (g)] [Strong's: 5769]

**Distress:** The state of being in great trouble, great physical or mental strain and stress. To be in pain from grief or heavy toil. [AHLB: 2566 (V)] [Strong's: 6087, 6088]

**Distressing pain:** Resulting from grief or heavy toil. This word can also mean an idol or image. [masc] [AHLB: 2566 (N)] [Strong's: 6089, 6091, 6092]

**Disturb:** To interfere with; to destroy tranquility; to throw into disorder. Agitate or trouble, as when stirring water. [AHLB: 2541 (V)] [Strong's: 5916]

**Divide:** To separate into two or more parts, areas or groups. To divide in half. [AHLB: 1179-H (V)] [Strong's: 2673]

**Divide apart:** To divide and separate. [AHLB: 2634 (V)] [Strong's: 6504]

**Divided part:** A part of a whole that was divided and separated. [masc] [AHLB: 2061 (N)] [Strong's: 1506]

**Divine:** Of relating to or proceeding directly from God. To know or experience something that shines out. [AHLB: 2395 (V)] [Strong's: 5172]

**Do:** To bring to pass; to bring about. To act or make something. [AHLB: 1360-H (V)] [Strong's: 6213]

**Do the marriage duty:** To perform the duty of the brother-in-law. When a brother dies, it is his brother's responsibility to marry his sister-in-law to provide his brother a child. [AHLB: 1036-L (V)] [Strong's: 2992]

**Do well:** To do something necessary to be done. be good, such as in being "functional." [AHLB: 1186-L (V)] [Strong's: 3190, 3191]

**Doe:** The adult female fallow deer. Feminine form of a strong one. [fem] [AHLB: 1012-M (N$^1$)] [Strong's: 355]

**Donation:** The act of making a gift; a free contribution. What is brought to another as a gift. [fem] [AHLB: 1307-A (h$^1$)] [Strong's: 4503, 4504]

**Donkey:** A male ass. [masc] [AHLB: 2175 (c)] [Strong's: 2543]

**Door:** A means of access; usually a swinging or sliding barrier by which an entry is closed and opened. [fem] [AHLB: 1081-A (N$^2$)] [Strong's: 1817]

**Double:** To make twice as great or as many. As a second or multiply by two. [masc] [AHLB: 1474-H (h)] [Strong's: 4932]

**Dove:** Any of numerous pigeons, especially a small wild one. [fem] [AHLB: 1221-J (N$^1$)] [Strong's: 3123]

**Dowry:** The money, goods, or estate that a woman brings to her husband in marriage. [masc] [AHLB: 2116 (N)] [Strong's: 2065]

**Draw:** To pull up or out of a

receptacle or place. To draw or pull something out. To prolong in the sense of drawing out time. To draw out a sound from a horn. [AHLB: 2358 (V)] [Strong's: 4900]

**Draw near:** To come close. [AHLB: 2379 (V)] [Strong's: 5066]

**Draw water:** To bringing up water from a well, usually using a rope and a bucket. [AHLB: 1477-D (V)] [Strong's: 7579]

**Dread:** Great fear, especially in the face of impending evil. [fem] [AHLB: 1183-A (N¹)] [Strong's: 2847]

**Dream:** A series of thoughts, images or emotions occurring during sleep. [masc] [AHLB: 2164 (c)] [Strong's: 2472]

**Drink:** To swallow liquid, whether of man or of the land. [AHLB: 1479-H (V)] [Strong's: 8248]

**Drinking:** The act of swallowing water or other liquid. The drinking of the land in the sense of its being watered or irrigated. [masc] [AHLB: 1479-H (a)] [Strong's: 4945]

**Drive:** To set or keep in motion; to press or force into an activity, course, or direction. [AHLB: 1302-G (V)] [Strong's: 5090]

**Drove:** A group of animals driven or moving in a body. Moved in the sense of being ordered or driven. [masc] [AHLB: 2530 (N)] [Strong's: 5739]

**Dry ground:** Land that has become dried, parched or void of water. [fem] [AHLB: 1044-L (N¹)] [Strong's: 3004]

**Dry out:** To be dried up as well as withered, ashamed or confused. [AHLB: 1044-L (V)] [Strong's: 3001]

**Dry up:** A dry wasteland. Also, a place that has been laid waste and made desolate. [AHLB: 2199 (V)] [Strong's: 2717, 2718]

**Dull red:** The color of blood and wine. [masc] [AHLB: 2158 (lbf)] [Strong's: 2447]

**Dwell:** To remain for a time; to live as a resident. Stay or sit in one location. [AHLB: 2838 (V)] [Strong's: 7931, 7932]

**Dysfunctional:** Impaired or abnormal action other than that for which a person or thing is intended. Something that does not function within its intended purpose. [c] [AHLB: 1460-A (N)] [Strong's: 7451, 7455]

**Ear:** The organ of hearing; so named from its broad shape. [fem] [AHLB: 1152-C (g)] [Strong's: 241]

**East:** The general direction of sunrise. As in front when facing the rising sun. Also, the ancient past as a distant time. [masc] [AHLB: 2698 (N)] [Strong's: 6924]

**East wind:** The wind that comes from the east. Toward the east as the origin of the east wind. [masc] [AHLB: 2698 (b)] [Strong's: 6921]

**Eastward:** Toward the east. Before another space or time; as the east is in front when facing the rising sun. [fem] [AHLB: 2698 (e¹)] [Strong's: 6926]

**Eat:** To take in food. A devouring

of a fire or a destruction. [AHLB: 1242-C (V)] [Strong's: 398, 399]

**Eight:** The number eight representing fullness from the sense of being fat or rich. [com] [AHLB: 2850 (c)] [Strong's: 8083, 8084]

**Elevation:** The height to which something is raised. [fem] [AHLB: 1323-A $(N^2)$] [Strong's: 7613]

**Emaciated:** Wasted away physically. [masc] [AHLB: 1088-A (N)] [Strong's: 1851]

**Embrace:** To clasp in the arms; to cherish or love; to take in or include in a larger group or whole. [AHLB: 2142 (V)] [Strong's: 2263]

**Emptiness:** Lack of contents which should be present. Void of contents or purpose. [masc] [AHLB: 1456-M (p)] [Strong's: 7387]

**Empty:** The lack of intelligence or significance in an action. An action or thought with no positive results. [masc] [AHLB: 1456-M (N)] [Strong's: 7385, 7386]

**Encounter:** A meeting between two hostile factions; to engage in conflict with. [AHLB: 2594 (V)] [Strong's: 6298]

**End:** A final point that marks the extent of something. The latter time as coming after everything else. [fem] [AHLB: 1181-C $(N^4)$] [Strong's: 319, 320]

**Endow:** To furnish with a dower or payment for a bride. Pay the price for a bride. Give a natural gift. [AHLB: 2116 (V)] [Strong's: 2064]

**Entwine:** To twist together or around; to become twisted. [AHLB: 2650 (V)] [Strong's: 6617]

**Err:** To miss the target, whether a literal target or a goal that is aimed for. See Judges 20:16. [AHLB: 1170-E (V)] [Strong's: 2398]

**Error:** An act or condition of ignorant or imprudent deviation from a code of behavior. A missing of the target in the sense of making a mistake. The sin offering which by transference becomes the sin. [fem] [AHLB: 1170-E $(N^1)$] [Strong's: 2401, 2402, 2403]

**Escape:** To get away, especially from confinement. [fem] [AHLB: 2609 $(b^1)$] [Strong's: 6413]

**Escaped one:** A person or animal that has gotten away. [masc] [AHLB: 2609 (b)] [Strong's: 6412]

**Eunuch:** A castrated man. As eunuchs were used as officers, may also mean an officer. [masc] [AHLB: 2510 (b)] [Strong's: 5631]

**Evening:** The latter part and close of the day and the early part of the night. Dark of the evening or dark-skinned people. Also the willow from its dark color. [masc] [AHLB: 2907 (N)] [Strong's: 6153, 6155]

**Ewe:** A female sheep. [fem] [AHLB: 2761 (N)] [Strong's: 7353]

**Ewe lamb:** A female lamb. [fem] [AHLB: 2273 $(N^1)$] [Strong's: 3535]

**Examine:** To inspect closely. Test, try or scrutinize. [AHLB: 2011 (V)] [Strong's: 974]

**Except:** With the exclusion of from the whole. The whole with the exception of one or more. [AHLB: 2021 (ef)] [Strong's: 1115]

**Exchange:** The act of giving or taking one thing in return for another. To buy or sell produce, usually grain. Bartering. [AHLB: 2811 (V)] [Strong's: 7666]

**Excuse me:** To exact neither punishment nor redress for one's self and interrupting. Used as an introduction for an entreaty or request. [masc] [AHLB: 1033-A (N)] [Strong's: 994]

**Exhale:** To give out a breath. To blow on a fire or the boiling water in a pot as an exhale. [AHLB: 2419 (V)] [Strong's: 5301]

**Exist:** To have real being whether material or spiritual. To have breath; that which exists has breath. In Hebrew thought the breath is the character of someone or something. Just as a man has character, so do objects. [AHLB: 1097-M (V)] [Strong's: 1961]

**Experienced:** Direct observation of or participation in events as a basis of knowledge. Something that is personally encountered, undergone or lived through in its use. [masc] [AHLB: 2178 (b)] [Strong's: 2593]

**Expire:** To breathe one's last breath; the last breath of death. [AHLB: 1062-J (V)] [Strong's: 1478]

**Expose:** To cause to be visible or open to public view. In the sense of uncovering. [masc] [AHLB: 2186 (ac)] [Strong's: 4286]

**Extreme old age:** A full and long life. [masc] [AHLB: 2132 (d)] [Strong's: 2208]

**Eye:** The organ of sight or vision that tears when a person weeps. A spring, just as an eye that weeps water out of the ground. [fem] [AHLB: 1359-M (N)] [Strong's: 5869, 5870]

**Face:** The front part of the human head; outward appearance. The face from its ability to turn or change shape. The presence of one through the sense of being in the face of. Always written in the idiomatic plural form. [masc] [AHLB: 1382-H (N)] [Strong's: 3942, 6440]

**Faint:** Lacking courage and spirit; weak, dizzy and likely to pass out. Lacking distinctness. [AHLB: 1258-H (V)] [Strong's: 3856]

**Fall:** To leave an erect position suddenly and involuntarily; to descend freely by the force of gravity. [AHLB: 2421 (V)] [Strong's: 5307, 5308]

**Fall upon:** To victimize another; to discover and claim an object. [AHLB: 1477-J (V)] [Strong's: 7779]

**Family:** A group of persons of common ancestry. A group of people joined together by certain convictions or common affiliation. [fem]

[AHLB: 2863 (h¹)] [Strong's: 4940]

**Family idol:** A household idol of a god, possibly believed to have a healing power. [masc] [AHLB: 1454-A (i)] [Strong's: 8655]

**Famine:** An extreme scarcity of food. [masc] [AHLB: 2777 (j)] [Strong's: 7459]

**Far be it:** Something least likely to happen. [fem] [AHLB: 1173-B (b¹)] [Strong's: 2486]

**Far end:** The most distant extremity of something; the end or edge. [masc] [AHLB: 1432-H (N)] [Strong's: 7097]

**Fat:** Animal tissue consisting of cells distended with greasy or oily matter; adipose tissue. The fat of an animal as the choicest part. Milk from its fat content. [masc] [AHLB: 2160 (N)] [Strong's: 2459, 2461]

**Father:** A man who has begotten a child. The father of the family provided the strength, support and structure to the household. The father fulfilled many functions for the family. He was the commander of the family army, provider of offspring to continue the family line, the priest and teacher. A father could have been of the immediate family or a lineage such as Jacob, who is the father of the Israelites. A father could have also been the patron of a profession or art. This word can also be fresh fruit (pronounced eyv), the father of the next generation of trees attached to the tree (pole). [masc] [AHLB: 1002-A (N)]

[Strong's: 1, 2, 3, 4]

**Father-in-law:** The father of one's wife or husband. [masc] [AHLB: 1174-A (N)] [Strong's: 2524]

**Fatten:** To make more substantial, fleshy or plump. fatten or fill up. The filling of the earth in Genesis 1 with sun, moon, plants, animals, etc. And the filling of man with life and the image of God. [AHLB: 1043-E (V)] [Strong's: 1254]

**Fault:** A lack, weakness or failing; a mistake; the responsibility for wrongdoing. Missing of the target. A faulty one is one who has missed the target. [masc] [AHLB: 1170-E (N)] [Strong's: 2399, 2400]

**Fear:** To be afraid of; a strong emotion caused by anticipation or awareness of danger. To dread what is terrible or revere what is respected. [AHLB: 1227-E (V)] [Strong's: 3372]

**Fearful:** Full of fear or dread. [masc] [AHLB: 1227-E (N)] [Strong's: 3373]

**Fearfulness:** Inclined to be afraid. [fem] [AHLB: 1227-E (N¹)] [Strong's: 3374]

**Fearing:** To be afraid or apprehensive. [masc] [AHLB: 1227-E (k)] [Strong's: 4172]

**Feast:** An elaborate meal often accompanied by a ceremony; a banquet. [masc] [AHLB: 1482-H (h)] [Strong's: 4960, 4961]

**Fed fat:** A member of the livestock that has been fed grains to fatten it for the slaughter. [masc] [AHLB: 1043-E (b)] [Strong's: 1277]

**Feed:** To give food to. Food for livestock. Provide feed or pasture to the flock. Commonly used in the participle form meaning a feeder or shepherd. [AHLB: 1453-H (V)] [Strong's: 7462]

**Feel:** To handle or touch in order to examine, test or explore some quality. Reach out with the hand to touch. [AHLB: 1297-J (V)] [Strong's: 3237]

**Female:** An individual that bears children. Designed with a hollow or groove into which a corresponding male part fits, as with a hole. [fem] [AHLB: 2430 (N$^1$)] [Strong's: 5347]

**Female owner:** A female master overseeing slaves or servants. [fem] [AHLB: 2052 (N$^2$)] [Strong's: 1404]

**Fence in:** A barrier intended to protect, prevent escape or intrusion, or to mark a boundary. To gather together and confine for protection. [AHLB: 2033 (V)] [Strong's: 1219]

**Few:** Small in number. [masc] [AHLB: 2680 (h)] [Strong's: 4213, 4705]

**Field:** An open land area free of trees and buildings. A level plot of ground. [masc] [AHLB: 1326-H (N)] [Strong's: 7704]

**Fifth:** The place of the numeral 'five' in order. Number 'five' in order. [masc] [AHLB: 2176 (bf)] [Strong's: 2549]

**Fifth part:** One portion from a division of five equal amounts. [masc] [AHLB: 2176 (g)] [Strong's: 2569, 2570]

**Fig:** An oblong or pear-shaped fruit from a tree of the fichus genus. A desirable and prolific fruit that must be searched for, as the fruit is green, thus blending in with the leaves and making it difficult to see. [fem] [AHLB: 1014-A (i)] [Strong's: 8384]

**Fill:** To put into as much as can be held or conveniently contained. To occupy the whole of with fruit, fat or other produce. [AHLB: 1288-E (V)] [Strong's: 4390, 4391, 4754]

**Filling:** An act or instance of filling; something used to fill a cavity, container, or depression. [masc] [AHLB: 1288-E (c)] [Strong's: 4393]

**Find:** To come upon, often accidentally; to meet with. Discover and secure through searching. [AHLB: 1294-E (V)] [Strong's: 4291, 4672]

**Finish:** To bring to an end; terminate. Complete an action, event. [AHLB: 1242-H (V)] [Strong's: 3615]

**Fire:** The phenomenon of combustion manifested by heat, light and flame. [fem] [AHLB: 1021-A (N)] [Strong's: 784, 785]

**Firm:** Securely or solidly fixed in place. Not subject to change or revision. To stand firm, as a support. [AHLB: 1290-C (V)] [Strong's: 539, 540]

**First:** The head of a time or position. [masc] [AHLB: 1458-D (ej)] [Strong's: 7223]

**First time:** From the idea of beginning the drilling process which is the most difficult and crucial part of drilling. [fem] [AHLB: 1173-A (i$^1$)] [Strong's: 8462]

**Firstborn:** The firstborn offspring, usually a son, of a man or animal. The prominent one. [masc] [AHLB: 2016 (c)] [Strong's: 1060]

**Firstborn female:** The firstborn daughter. The prominent one. [fem] [AHLB: 2016 (b$^1$)] [Strong's: 1067]

**Fish:** An aquatic animal. The act of trying to catch a fish. [masc] [AHLB: 1072-A (N)] [Strong's: 1709]

**Five:** Five in number from the number of fingers on a hand. [com] [AHLB: 2176 (N)] [Strong's: 2568, 2572]

**Fixed:** To set something firmly in place, either physically or with words. [AHLB: 1244-J (V)] [Strong's: 3559]

**Flare up:** To become suddenly excited or angry; to break out suddenly. Burn with a fierce anger. [AHLB: 1181-H (V)] [Strong's: 2734]

**Flee:** To run away often from danger or evil. To hurry toward a place of safety, to the standard for safety. Fleeing to any safe place such as a city or mountain. [AHLB: 1314-J (V)] [Strong's: 5127]

**Flee away:** To run away from. [AHLB: 2038 (V)] [Strong's: 1272]

**Flesh:** The soft parts of a human or animal, composed primarily of skeletal muscle. Skin and muscle or the whole of the person. Meat as food. [fem] [AHLB: 2025 (N)] [Strong's: 1154, 1320, 1321]

**Flocks:** Groups of birds or animals assembled or herded together. [fem] [AHLB: 1405-J (N)] [Strong's: 6629]

**Flood:** To cover with an overwhelming quantity or volume of water. [masc] [AHLB: 1035-J (a)] [Strong's: 3999]

**Floor:** The level base of a room, barn or threshing floor. [masc] [AHLB: 2085 (g)] [Strong's: 1637]

**Flour:** Finely ground meal of grain largely freed from bran. [fem] [AHLB: 1334-J (N$^2$)] [Strong's: 5560]

**Flutter:** To flap the wings rapidly. To move with quick wavering or flapping motions. Shake as a bird in the nest. [AHLB: 2763 (V)] [Strong's: 7363]

**Fly:** To move in or pass through the air with wings. Soar in the air. [AHLB: 1362-J (V)] [Strong's: 5774]

**Flyer:** A flying creature such as a bird or insect. [masc] [AHLB: 1362-J (N)] [Strong's: 5775, 5776]

**Following:** To go, proceed or come after. Being next in order or time. Subsequent to. As the river follows the path of its banks. [fem] [AHLB: 1479-J (i$^1$)] [Strong's: 8669]

**Folly:** Lack of good sense or prudence and foresight. In the sense of fading away. [fem] [AHLB: 2369 (N$^1$)] [Strong's: 5039]

**Food:** Something that nourishes, sustains, or supplies. For giving sustenance and making one whole. [fem] [AHLB: 1242-C (N$^1$)] [Strong's: 402]

**Foodstuff:** A substance with food value; the raw material of food before or after processing. For giving sustenance and making one whole. [masc] [AHLB: 1242-C (g)] [Strong's: 400]

**Foolish:** To be arrogantly confident. [AHLB: 2275 (V)] [Strong's: 3688, 5528]

**Foot:** The terminal part of the leg upon which the human or animal stands. [fem] [AHLB: 2749 (N)] [Strong's: 7271, 7272]

**Force:** The pressure exerted to make a piercing. [masc] [AHLB: 1173-M (N)] [Strong's: 2428, 2429]

**Forearm:** The part of the arm between the elbow and the wrist. A linear standard of measure equal to the length of the forearm. [fem] [AHLB: 1013-A (N$^1$)] [Strong's: 520]

**Foreign:** Situated outside one's own country. Alien in character. A strange person, place or thing as being unrecognized. [masc] [AHLB: 2406 (N)] [Strong's: 5235, 5236]

**Foreigner:** A person belonging to or owing allegiance to a foreign country. One who is not known. [masc] [AHLB: 2406 (f)] [Strong's: 5237]

**Foreskin:** A fold of skin that covers the end of the penis. [fem] [AHLB: 2577 (N$^1$)] [Strong's: 6190]

**Forget:** To lose remembrance of; to cease remembering or noticing. In Aramaic, to "find." [AHLB: 2835 (V)] [Strong's: 7911, 7912]

**Fortune:** A store of material possessions. Also, the coriander seed. [masc] [AHLB: 1050-A (N)] [Strong's: 1407, 1409]

**Four:** Four in number from the four sides of a square. [com] [AHLB: 2744 (n)] [Strong's: 702, 703, 705]

**Fourth:** Fourth in numeric order. [masc] [AHLB: 2744 (bf)] [Strong's: 7243, 7244]

**Fragment:** A part broken off, detached, or incomplete. The removal of a piece resulting in a hole. [fem] [AHLB: 1390-A (N)] [Strong's: 6595]

**Freely:** Having no restrictions. To work or do an action without wages or without cause. [masc] [AHLB: 1175-A (p)] [Strong's: 2600]

**Fresh Wine:** Newly pressed wine. [masc] [AHLB: 1458-L (ic)] [Strong's: 8492]

**From:** A function word indicating a starting point or origin. In the sense of the plant coming out of the seed. [com] [AHLB: 1290-A (h)] [Strong's: 4480, 4481]

**Full:** Containing as much or as many as is possible or normal. [masc] [AHLB: 1288-E (N)] [Strong's: 4392]

**Functional:** Fulfilling the action for which a person or thing is specially fitted or used, or for which a thing exists. Something that functions within its intended purpose. [com] [AHLB: 1186-J (N)] [Strong's: 2896, 2898]

**Furnace:** An enclosed structure in which heat is produced. [masc] [AHLB: 2251 (em)]

[Strong's: 3536]

**Fury:** Intense, disordered, and often destructive rage. An intense heat from anger. [fem] [AHLB: 1174-A (N$^1$)] [Strong's: 2528, 2534]

**Game:** Animals being pursued or taken in hunting. The produce of the hunt. [masc] [AHLB: 1395-M (N)] [Strong's: 6718]

**Garden:** A plot of ground where crops are grown. A place for growing crops, and often surrounded by a rock wall or hedge to protect it from grazing animals. [com] [AHLB: 1060-A (N)] [Strong's: 1588]

**Garment:** An article of clothing. Garments for covering. [masc] [AHLB: 2004 (N)] [Strong's: 899]

**Gate:** The opening in a wall or fence through which livestock or people pass. Can be the gatekeeper. Also sha'ar, a unit of measurement. [masc] [AHLB: 2862 (N)] [Strong's: 8179, 8651, 8652]

**Gather:** To bring together; to accumulate and place in readiness.. [AHLB: 1339-C (V)] [Strong's: 622]

**Gather together:** To come or bring into a group, mass or unit. [AHLB: 2695 (V)] [Strong's: 6908]

**Generation:** A body of living beings constituting a single step in the line of descent from an ancestor. Generation as a circle of time. [masc] [AHLB: 1089-J (N)] [Strong's: 1755]

**Gentle:** Free from harshness, sternness, or violence. To act softly. A charmer. [masc] [AHLB: 1009-A (N)] [Strong's: 328]

**Gift:** To endow with some power, quality, or attribute; the act, power or right of giving. What is given. [masc] [AHLB: 2451 (a)] [Strong's: 4976]

**Girl:** A young, unmarried woman. [fem] [AHLB: 1257-L (N$^1$)] [Strong's: 3207]

**Give:** To make a present; to grant or bestow by formal action. Present as a gift. [AHLB: 2451 (V)] [Strong's: 5414]

**Give a tenth:** To tithe; a tenth part of something given voluntarily for the support of a religious establishment. [AHLB: 2563 (V)] [Strong's: 6237]

**Give milk:** To provide nourishment to the young by the female. [AHLB: 1058-J (V)] [Strong's: 5763]

**Given that:** Prone or disposed to according to what preceded. A reference to the previous or following context. In the sense of a burning knowledge. [AHLB: 1240-A (N)] [Strong's: 3588]

**Glow:** To shine with an intense light. Be or give off light; to be bright. [AHLB: 1020-J (V)] [Strong's: 215]

**Go around:** To be completely around something. [AHLB: 1324-B (V)] [Strong's: 5437]

**Go down:** To go or come lower from a higher place. [AHLB: 1441-L (V)] [Strong's: 3381]

**Go left:** To choose the left hand or path. [AHLB: **3036**] [Strong's: 8041]

**Go out:** To go, come or issue forth. [AHLB: 1392-L (V)] [Strong's: 3318, 3319]

**Go Right:** To choose, turn or go to the right hand. [AHLB: 1290-L (V)] [Strong's: 541, 3231]

**Go up:** To go, come or bring higher. [AHLB: 1357-H (V)] [Strong's: 5924, 5927]

**Goat:** Related to the sheep but of lighter build and with backwardly arching horns, a short tail, and usually straight hair. From its thick hair used to make tents. [masc] [AHLB: 2494 (b)] [Strong's: 8163]

**Gold:** A malleable yellow metallic element that is used especially in coins, jewelry, and dentures. A precious metal. [masc] [AHLB: 1140-G (N)] [Strong's: 1722, 2091]

**Goods:** Something that has economic utility or satisfies an economic want; personal property having intrinsic value but usually excluding money, securities and negotiable instruments. As collected substances. [masc] [AHLB: 2772 (d)] [Strong's: 7399]

**Gopher:** Wood from an unknown tree. [masc] [AHLB: 2079 (N)] [Strong's: 1613]

**Governor:** An official elected or appointed to act as ruler, chief executive, or nominal head of a political unit. One who has dominion over another; also a rule or law as a master. [masc] [AHLB: 2843 (b)] [Strong's: 7989, 7990]

**Grain:** A seed or fruit of a cereal grass. The grain and the field as a place for growing grain. In Aramaic this word means a "field" as the place of grain. [masc] [AHLB: 1043-A (N)] [Strong's: 1250, 1251]

**Grain flour:** Usually finely ground seeds of wheat. [masc] [AHLB: 2711 (N)] [Strong's: 7058]

**Grape:** A smooth-skinned juicy greenish white to deep red or purple berry grown on a vine and eaten dried or fresh as a fruit or fermented to produce wine. [masc] [AHLB: 2555 (N)] [Strong's: 6025]

**Grapevine:** A woody vine that usually climbs by tendrils and produces fruits that are grapes. [masc] [AHLB: 2078 (N)] [Strong's: 1612]

**Grapple:** A hand-to-hand struggle. Rolling around in the dust when wrestling. [AHLB: 1042-C (V)] [Strong's: 79]

**Grass:** Herbage suitable or used for grazing animals. Young green sprouts. [masc] [AHLB: 1090-E (N)] [Strong's: 1877, 1883]

**Grave:** An excavation for the burial of a body. Meriting serious consideration. [masc] [AHLB: 2696 (N)] [Strong's: 6913]

**Gray headed:** One who has gray hair from old age; an old man. [fem] [AHLB: 1324-M (N¹)] [Strong's: 7872]

**Great tree:** The strongest of the woods. [masc] [AHLB: 1012-A (j)] [Strong's: 436, 437]

**Green:** A color somewhat less yellow than that of fresh growing grass and of that part of the spectrum between blue and yellow. The color of grasses and herbs as thin. [masc] [AHLB: 1456-L (N)] [Strong's: 3418, 3419]

**Grief:** Deep and poignant distress caused by or as if by bereavement. As an exchange. [fem] [AHLB: 1296-J (N¹)] [Strong's: 4786]

**Grope:** To feel about blindly or uncertainly in search of something. A groping around in the darkness to find something. [AHLB: 1297-B (V)] [Strong's: 4959]

**Ground:** The surface of the earth. From its red color. [fem] [AHLB: 1082-C (N¹)] [Strong's: 127]

**Guard:** The act or duty of protecting or defending. To watch over or guard in the sense of preserving or protecting. [AHLB: 2853 (V)] [Strong's: 8104]

**Guide:** One who leads or directs another in his way. [AHLB: 1307-H (V)] [Strong's: 5148]

**Guilt:** The fact of having committed a breach of conduct especially violating law and involving a penalty; the state of one who has committed an offense, especially consciously. [masc] [AHLB: 1473-C (N)] [Strong's: 817, 818]

**Gulp:** To swallow hurriedly or greedily or in one swallow. [AHLB: 1482-H (V)] [Strong's: 8354, 8355]

**Gust:** A sudden brief rush of wind. The strong blowing of a wind. The wind of a bird's wing when taking flight.

[AHLB: 2440 (V)] [Strong's: 5380]

**Guzzle:** To drink greedily, continually, or habitually. A drinking of water as from a pond. [AHLB: 1059-E (V)] [Strong's: 1572]

**Hair:** The covering of filaments on a human head or the body of an animal. [masc] [AHLB: 2494 (N)] [Strong's: 8177, 8181]

**Hand:** The terminal, functional part of the forelimb when modified in humans as a grasping organ. Hand with the ability to work, throw and give thanks. [fem] [AHLB: 1211-A (N)] [Strong's: 3027, 3028, 3197]

**Handful:** As much of or as many as the hand can grasp. [masc] [AHLB: 2714 (g)] [Strong's: 7062]

**Hang:** To suspend with no support from below. [AHLB: 1495-H (V)] [Strong's: 8518]

**Happiness:** A state of well-being and contentment. One who is happy is one whose life is lived straightly. [masc] [AHLB: 1480-C (g)] [Strong's: 837]

**Happy:** Enjoying well-being and contentment. One who is happy is one whose life is lived straightly. [AHLB: 1480-C (V)] [Strong's: 833]

**Hard:** Not easily penetrated; resistant to stress; firm; lacking in responsiveness. [masc] [AHLB: 1435-H (N)] [Strong's: 7186]

**Hardship:** Privation; suffering; something that causes or entails suffering or privation.

[masc] [AHLB: 2566 (j)] [Strong's: 6093]

**Harm:** Physical or mental damage; injury. The pain from the thorn. [masc] [AHLB: 1336-C (c)] [Strong's: 611]

**Harp:** A plucked stringed musical instrument; [masc] [AHLB: 2270 (ec)] [Strong's: 3658]

**Harvest:** The season for gathering agricultural crops; reap. Time when the plants are severed from their roots to be used for seed or food. [masc] [AHLB: 2727 (b)] [Strong's: 7105]

**Hate:** Intense hostility and aversion usually deriving from fear, anger, or sense of injury; extreme dislike or antipathy; [AHLB: 1336-E (V)] [Strong's: 8130, 8131]

**Hazel:** A light brown to strong yellowish brown color; small trees or shrubs bearing nuts enclosed in a leafy involucres. [masc] [AHLB: 1260-J (N)] [Strong's: 3869]

**He:** The male who is neither speaker nor hearer. As one looked toward. [masc] [AHLB: 1093-J (N)] [Strong's: 1931, 1932]

**Head:** The top of the body. A person in authority or role of leader. The top, beginning or first of something. [masc] [AHLB: 1458-D (N)] [Strong's: 7217, 7218, 7389]

**Head of grain:** The cluster of seeds of grain plants. Also, meaning a flood that gives water to the soil for growing crops. [masc] [AHLB: 2806 (ec)] [Strong's: 7641]

**Headrest:** A support for the head.

Place where the head is laid. [fem] [AHLB: 1458-D (k¹)] [Strong's: 4763]

**Heal:** To restore to health or wholeness. [AHLB: 1454-E (V)] [Strong's: 7495]

**Hear:** To perceive or apprehend by the ear; to listen to with attention. To listen or to pay attention with ensuing obedience. [AHLB: 2851 (V)] [Strong's: 8085, 8086]

**Heart:** Literally, the vital organ which pumps blood, but, also seen as the seat of thought and emotion; the mind. [masc] [AHLB: 1255-A (N)] [Strong's: 1079, 3820, 3821]

**Heat:** Natural body warmth, as well as the time of estrous when animals mate. Conception from an animal's mating or through the heat of passion. [AHLB: 1174-L (V)] [Strong's: 3179]

**Heavy:** Having great weight. Something that is weighty. May also be grief or sadness in the sense of heaviness. This word is also used for the liver as the heaviest of the organs. [fem] [AHLB: 2246 (N)] [Strong's: 3515, 3516]

**Heel:** What is restrained when taking a step forward. [masc] [AHLB: 2571 (N)] [Strong's: 6119, 6120]

**He-goat:** A male goat. [masc] [AHLB: 1504-M (N)] [Strong's: 8495]

**Heifer:** A young cow, especially one that has not had a calf. [fem] [AHLB: 2524 (N¹)] [Strong's: 5697]

**Height:** The highest part or most advanced point; the condition of being tall or high. In the sense of being raised up. [fem] [AHLB: 1427-J (N$^1$)] [Strong's: 6967]

**Heir:** One who inherits or is entitled to inherit property. [masc] [AHLB: 1313-M (N)] [Strong's: 5209]

**Help:** To give assistance or support to. [AHLB: 2535 (V)] [Strong's: 5826]

**Helper:** One that helps. Who comes to assist with a trouble or burden. [masc] [AHLB: 2535 (N)] [Strong's: 5828]

**Herb:** The grasses and plants of the field used for their medicinal, savory, or aromatic qualities. [fem] [AHLB: 2561 (N)] [Strong's: 6211, 6212]

**Here:** In or at this place. [masc] [AHLB: 1374-A (N)] [Strong's: 6311]

**Hhomer:** A dry standard of measurement equal to 65 Imperial gallons. [masc] [AHLB: 2175 (g)] [Strong's: 2563]

**Hide:** To put out of sight; to conceal from view; to keep secret. Hide or conceal. [AHLB: 2516 (V)] [Strong's: 5641, 5642, 8368]

**High:** Advanced toward the acme or culmination. [masc] [AHLB: 1048-H (c)] [Strong's: 1364]

**Hill:** A rounded natural elevation of land lower than a mountain. [masc] [AHLB: 1112-A (N)] [Strong's: 2022]

**Hip:** Each side of the trunk formed by the lateral parts of the pelvis and upper part of the femur (thigh bone) together with the fleshy parts

covering them. [masc] [AHLB: 1320-H (N)] [Strong's: 5384]

**Hire:** Payment for labor or personal services; to engage the personal service of another. [AHLB: 2479 (V)] [Strong's: 7936]

**Hit:** To deliver a blow by action. To strike with the hand. To clap, kill or harm. [AHLB: 1310-H (V)] [Strong's: 5221]

**Hold:** To have possession or ownership of; to keep in restraint; to have or maintain in one's grasp. Grab something and keep hold of it. Also, one's holdings. [AHLB: 1168-C (V)] [Strong's: 270]

**Hold a grudge:** Be unwilling to give in or admit to. [AHLB: 2474 (V)] [Strong's: 7852]

**Hold back:** To hinder the progress or achievement of; restrain, as the banks of a river hold back the water. [AHLB: 1387-C (V)] [Strong's: 662]

**Hold up:** To continue in the same condition without failing or losing effectiveness or force. Be a support or aid for strength or rest. [AHLB: 2492 (V)] [Strong's: 5582, 5583]

**Holdings:** Property owned. [fem] [AHLB: 1168-C (N$^1$)] [Strong's: 272]

**Hollow:** What is of a concave shape such as a saddle or pasture in a valley. Also, may mean the sheep of the pasture. [masc] [AHLB: 1250-A (N)] [Strong's: 3733]

**Hollow:** The hollow of the loins between the legs. [fem] [AHLB: 1448-L (N$^1$)] [Strong's: 3410, 3411]

**Honey:** A sweet material elaborated out of the nectar of flowers in the honey sac of various bees. Also, dates as a thick, sticky and sweet food. [masc] [AHLB: 2094 (N)] [Strong's: 1706]

**Honor:** A showing of merited respect. To regard or treat with respect. To consider something as heavy in the sense of respect. [masc] [AHLB: 2246 (c)] [Strong's: 3519]

**Horn:** One of a pair of bony processes that arise from the head of many animals and used as a wind instrument. The horns of an animal or a musical instrument in the shape of a horn. [fem] [AHLB: 2732 (N)] [Strong's: 7161, 7162]

**Horse:** A domesticated animal used as a beast of burden, a draft animal or for riding. From its turning around in play. [masc] [AHLB: 1337-J (N)] [Strong's: 5483]

**Horseman:** One that rides a horse. From the spreading of the legs to ride. Also the dung of the cattle as spread out flat. [masc] [AHLB: 2644 (N)] [Strong's: 6569, 6571]

**Hostile:** Marked by especially overt antagonism. To be hostile to another as an enemy. [AHLB: 1002-M (V)] [Strong's: 340, 341]

**Hostility:** Conflict, opposition, or resistance; overt acts of warfare. [fem] [AHLB: 1002-M (N[1])] [Strong's: 342]

**Hot:** Having a relatively high temperature; eager; fresh; peppery. Also, meaning a father-in-law in the sense of being hot. [masc] [AHLB: 1174-A (N)] [Strong's: 2525, 2527]

**Hot spring:** A spring with water above body temperature. [masc] [AHLB: 1220-B (N)] [Strong's: 3222]

**House:** The structure or the family, as a household that resides within the house. May also mean within. [masc] [AHLB: 1045-M (N)] [Strong's: 1004, 1005]

**How long:** An unknown duration of time. [masc] [AHLB: 1298-A (f)] [Strong's: 4970]

**Human:** Of, relating to, or characteristic of man. The first man. From the reddish skin as coming from the reddish ground. Also, used for all of mankind as the descendants of the first man. [masc] [AHLB: 1082-C (N)] [Strong's: 120]

**Hundred:** A specific number but also a large amount without any reference to a specific number. [fem] [AHLB: 1277-A (N[1])] [Strong's: 3967, 3969]

**Hunger:** A craving or urgent need for food. [masc] [AHLB: 2777 (N)] [Strong's: 7457, 7458]

**Hunt:** To attempt to find something with the intent to capture. Hunt in the sense of laying in ambush. [AHLB: 1395-J (V)] [Strong's: 6679]

**Hunter:** One who searches for something. Lays in ambush. [masc] [AHLB: 1395-M (N)] [Strong's: 6719]

**Hurl:** To throw down with

violence. The area which a bow can be shot from a central point. [AHLB: 1192-H (V)] [Strong's: 2909]

**Hurry:** To carry or cause to go with haste. [AHLB: 1296-G (V)] [Strong's: 4116, 4117]

**I:** A person aware of possessing a personal identity in self-reference. [com] [Strong's: 576, 589, 595]

**Ice:** Frozen water. Cold ice, frost or crystals. [masc] [AHLB: 2730 (N)] [Strong's: 7140]

**If:** Allowing that; on condition that. A desire to bind two ideas together. [AHLB: 1013-M (N)] [Strong's: 518]

**Image:** A reproduction or imitation of the form of a person or thing. The form of something as a shadow of the original. [masc] [AHLB: 2663 (N)] [Strong's: 6754, 6755]

**Imitate:** To follow as a model, pattern or example. [AHLB: 1499-B (V)] [Strong's: 8591]

**In front:** Before or opposite to something. [masc] [AHLB: 2403 (g)] [Strong's: 5227]

**In this way:** To do something in a certain manner; a reference to the previous or following context. [AHLB: 1235-A (N)] [Strong's: 3541, 3542, 3602]

**Increase:** To become progressively greater; to multiply by the production of young. An abundance of number, strength or authority. [AHLB: 1439-H (V)] [Strong's: 7235, 7236]

**Increase in number:** To become progressively greater; to multiply by the production of young. Multiply. Also,

meaning "to shoot" from the abundant arrows of the archer. [AHLB: 1439-B (V)] [Strong's: 7231, 7232]

**Indeed:** Without any question. [masc] [AHLB: 1290-C (op)] [Strong's: 552]

**Inflame:** To excite to excessive or uncontrollable action or feeling. [AHLB: 2104 (V)] [Strong's: 1814, 1815]

**Inherit:** To come into possession of or receive especially as a right or divine portion. To receive from an ancestor at his death. To take possession, either by seizing or through inheritance. [AHLB: 1458-L (V)] [Strong's: 3423]

**Inheritance:** The acquisition of a possession from past generations. [fem] [AHLB: 2391 (N$^1$)] [Strong's: 5159]

**Iniquity:** Gross injustice; wickedness. The result of twisted actions. [masc] [AHLB: 1512-A (m)] [Strong's: 5771]

**In-law:** One related by marriage. [masc] [AHLB: 2224 (N)] [Strong's: 2860]

**Innocence:** Freedom from guilt or sin through being unacquainted with evil. A state of innocence as an infant. [masc] [AHLB: 1318-A (fj)] [Strong's: 5356]

**Innocent:** Free from guilt or sin. A state of innocence as an infant. [masc] [AHLB: 1318-A (f)] [Strong's: 5355]

**Inquire:** To ask about. To search into. Seek to understand what is not known. [AHLB: 1472-D (V)] [Strong's: 7592, 7593]

**Inscribe:** To write, engrave or

print as a lasting record. A decree or custom. [AHLB: 1180-B (V)] [Strong's: 2710]

**Instrument:** A utensil or implement. A means whereby something is achieved, performed, or furthered. For carrying or storing various materials. [masc] [AHLB: 1242-A (f)] [Strong's: 3627]

**Intercede:** To intervene between parties to reconcile differences. Supplicate on the behalf of another. [AHLB: 2910 (V)] [Strong's: 6279]

**Interpret:** To explain or tell the meaning of. [AHLB: 2653 (V)] [Strong's: 6590, 6622]

**Interpretation:** The act or result of interpreting. [masc] [AHLB: 2653 (ej)] [Strong's: 6623]

**Invade:** To enter for conquest or plunder. The slicing through of a band of men. [AHLB: 1050-J (V)] [Strong's: 1464]

**Invention:** A product of the imagination. Designing or planning of inventions or plans. [fem] [AHLB: 2213 (a$^1$)] [Strong's: 4284]

**Iron:** A heavy element that readily rusts, is the most used of metals and is vital to bodily processes. [masc] [AHLB: **3005**| [Strong's: 1270, 6523]

**Island:** A tract of land surrounded by water. As the destination of a ship. [masc] [AHLB: 1014-A (f)] [Strong's: 336, 339]

**Jar:** A sudden and unexpected shake; a wide-mouthed container. [masc] [AHLB: 1234-A (N)] [Strong's: 3537]

**Join:** To put or bring together to form a unit. A joining together of people. Also, the joining together through debt as the lender or borrower. [AHLB: 1259-J (V)] [Strong's: 3867]

**Journey:** Travel or passage from one place to another. To break camp and begin a journey. [AHLB: 2413 (V)] [Strong's: 5265]

**Joy:** A state of felicity or happiness. [fem] [AHLB: 2487 (N$^1$)] [Strong's: 8057]

**Judge:** A public official authorized to decide questions brought before a court. To rule over cases of dispute or wrongdoing. [AHLB: 2864 (V)] [Strong's: 8199, 8200]

**Judgement:** A pronounced opinion. [masc] [AHLB: 2864 (h)] [Strong's: 4941]

**Keep back:** To hold something back or restrain. [AHLB: 2182 (V)] [Strong's: 2820]

**Keep secret:** To refrain from disclosing information. [AHLB: 2255 (V)] [Strong's: 3582]

**Keep silent:** To hold in peace or be silent. [AHLB: 2211 (V)] [Strong's: 2790]

**Keep watch:** To be on the look-out for danger or opportunity. [AHLB: 1408-H (V)] [Strong's: 6822]

**Kill:** To deprive of life; to slaughter. [AHLB: 1440-F (V)] [Strong's: 2026]

**Kind:** A category of creature that comes from its own kind as a firm rule. [masc] [AHLB: 1290-M (N)] [Strong's: 4327]

**Kindness:** Of a sympathetic nature; quality or state of

being sympathetic. In the sense of bowing the neck to another as a sign of kindness. [masc] [AHLB: 2181 (N)] [Strong's: 2617]

**Kindred:** A group of related individuals. [fem] [AHLB: 1257-L (a²)] [Strong's: 4138]

**King:** The male ruler of a nation or city state. In Aramaic this word can mean "council." [masc] [AHLB: 2340 (N)] [Strong's: 4428, 4430, 4431]

**Kingdom place:** The area under the control of a king. [fem] [AHLB: 2340 (a¹)] [Strong's: 4467]

**Kiss:** To touch together as when kissing with the lips or in battle with weapons. [AHLB: 2445 (V)] [Strong's: 5401]

**Knead:** To work and press dough. Knead dough for bread. [AHLB: 1274-J (V)] [Strong's: 3888]

**Knee:** The joint between the femur and tibia of the leg. [AHLB: 2039 (N)] [Strong's: 1290, 1291]

**Kneel:** To bend the knee, to kneel in homage or to drink water. Frequently meaning to kneel in homage before another presenting a gift (often translated as bless). [AHLB: 2039 (V)] [Strong's: 1288, 1289]

**Knife:** A cutting instrument consisting of a sharp blade and handle. What is used for preparing and eating food. [fem] [AHLB: 1242-C (a²)] [Strong's: 3979]

**Knock:** To strike something with a sharp blow. [AHLB: 2109 (V)] [Strong's: 1849]

**Knoll:** A small round hill. [fem] [AHLB: 2051 (N¹)] [Strong's: 1389]

**Know:** To have an intimate relationship with another person. An idea or an experience. [AHLB: 1085-L (V)] [Strong's: 3045, 3046]

**Labor:** To exert one's power of body or mind, especially with painful or strenuous effort. A labor that causes grief, pain or weariness. A laborer as one who toils. [com] [AHLB: 2551 (N)] [Strong's: 5999, 6001]

**Lace:** A cord or string used to draw the edges of shoes or a garment together, as twisted around the foot for attaching sandals. [masc] [AHLB: 2509 (c)] [Strong's: 8288]

**Ladder:** Used to raise up. A structure for climbing up or down. [masc] [AHLB: 1334-J (p)] [Strong's: 5551]

**Lament:** To mourn aloud; wail. [AHLB: 2495 (V)] [Strong's: 5594]

**Lamenting:** The act of mourning. [masc] [AHLB: 2495 (h)] [Strong's: 4553]

**Land:** The solid part of the earth's surface. Whole of the earth or a region. [fem] [AHLB: 1455-C (N)] [Strong's: 772, 776, 778]

**Last night:** The previous night or a time past. [masc] [AHLB: 1297-C (N)] [Strong's: 570]

**Later:** At a time following. [fem] [AHLB: 1181-A (a)] [Strong's: 4279]

**Laugh:** To show mirth, joy, or scorn with a smile and chuckle or explosive sound.

[AHLB: 2660 (V)] [Strong's: 6711]

**Laughter:** The sound of or as of laughing. [masc] [AHLB: 2660 (c)] [Strong's: 6712]

**Lay down:** To give up; to lie down for copulation, rest or sleep. [AHLB: 2834 (V)] [Strong's: 7901]

**Laying place:** The location one lays for rest or sleep. [masc] [AHLB: 2834 (h)] [Strong's: 4903, 4904]

**Lead:** To guide on a way, especially by going in advance. The flock directed to the pasture at the end of the journey. [AHLB: 1311-G (V)] [Strong's: 5095]

**Leaf:** Foliage of a tree or plant. As high in the tree. [masc] [AHLB: 1357-H (N)] [Strong's: 5929]

**Lean:** To cast one's weight to one side for support. Lean on something for rest or support. [AHLB: 2861 (V)] [Strong's: 8172]

**Leave:** To go away from or to neglect. [AHLB: 2532 (V)] [Strong's: 5800]

**Left hand:** The left hand, side or direction. [masc] [AHLB: 3036] [Strong's: 8040]

**Length:** A measured distance or dimension. [masc] [AHLB: 1448-C (g)] [Strong's: 753]

**Lentil:** A leguminous plant with flattened edible seeds. [fem] [AHLB: 2531 (N)] [Strong's: 5742]

**Let alone:** To be left behind by those who leave. [AHLB: 2401 (V)] [Strong's: 5203]

**Level valley:** A depression in the earth's surface between ranges of mountains. Wide level valley as a division between mountains ranges. [fem] [AHLB: 2034 (e$^1$)] [Strong's: 1236, 1237]

**Lie:** To stay at rest in a horizontal position. [AHLB: 2879 (V)] [Strong's: 8266]

**Life:** The quality that distinguishes a vital and functional being from a dead body. Literally the stomach, the organ that holds food (see Job 38:39) in the sense of being full of life when the stomach is filled. Also, used idiomatically of living creatures, especially in conjunction with land, ground or field. [fem] [AHLB: 1171-A (N)] [Strong's: 2416, 2417]

**Lift up:** To lift up a burden or load and carry it. To lift up camp and begin a journey. [AHLB: 1314-E (V)] [Strong's: 4984, 5375, 5376]

**Light:** The illumination from the sun, moon, stars, fire, candle or other source. [com] [AHLB: 1020-J (N)] [Strong's: 216, 217]

**Likeness:** Copy; resemblance. The quality or state of being like something or someone else. As a son from the blood of his father resembles his father. [fem] [AHLB: 1082-H (N$^3$)] [Strong's: 1823]

**Limp:** To walk lamely, especially favoring one leg; to go unsteadily; to proceed with difficulty or slowly. From damage to the ridge of the hip. [AHLB: 2664 (V)] [Strong's: 6760]

**Linen:** Fabric made of flax and

noted for its strength, coolness and luster. A white cloth. Marble from its whiteness. [masc] [AHLB: 1481-A (N)] [Strong's: 7893, 8336]

**Linger:** To be slow in parting or in quitting something. [masc] [AHLB: 1281-B (N)] [Strong's: 4102]

**Lion:** A large carnivorous chiefly nocturnal cat. A feared animal. [masc] [AHLB: 1442-H (b)] [Strong's: 738, 744]

**Lioness:** A female lion. [fem] [AHLB: 1255-E (b)] [Strong's: 3833]

**Lip:** The rim or edge of something. Language as spoken from the lips. [fem] [AHLB: 1339-A (N¹)] [Strong's: 8193]

**Listen:** To pay attention to sound; to hear with thoughtful attention and obedience. [AHLB: 1152-C (V)] [Strong's: 238, 239]

**Little one:** Small in size or extent. Something or someone that is smaller, younger or less significant. [masc] [AHLB: 2680 (b)] [Strong's: 2191, 2192, 6810]

**Live:** To be alive and continue alive. Have life within. The revival of life gained from food or other necessity. [AHLB: 1171-H (V)] [Strong's: 2418, 2421, 2425]

**Livestock:** Animals kept or raised for use or pleasure. What is purchased or possessed. [masc] [AHLB: 1428-H (h)] [Strong's: 4735]

**Lo:** To draw attention to something important. [masc]

[AHLB: 1093-A (N)] [Strong's: 1887, 1888]

**Load:** That which is put on a person or pack animal to be carried. [AHLB: 2552 (V)] [Strong's: 6006]

**Loathe:** To dislike greatly and often with disgust. Consider something cut off. [AHLB: 1432-J (V)] [Strong's: 6973]

**Loin covering:** A sash or belt that encircles the waist. [fem] [AHLB: 2147 (c¹)] [Strong's: 2290]

**Loins:** The pubic region; the generative organs. In the sense of the next generation being drawn out of the loins. [fem] [AHLB: 2166 (N)] [Strong's: 2504, 2783]

**Look:** To ascertain by the use of one's eyes. [masc] [AHLB: 1106-H (e)] [Strong's: 2009]

**Look down:** To look out and down as through a window. [AHLB: 2877 (V)] [Strong's: 8259]

**Look with respect:** To look upon with high regard. [AHLB: 1476-H (V)] [Strong's: 8159]

**Lord:** The ruler as the foundation to the community. [masc] [AHLB: 1083-C (c)] [Strong's: 113]

**Lost:** One who has departed from the correct path or way. [masc] [AHLB: 2799 (N)] [Strong's: 7562, 7563]

**Love:** Strong affection for another arising from personal ties. To provide and protect that which is given as a privilege. An intimacy of action and emotion. [AHLB: 1094-C (V)] [Strong's: 157]

**Luminary:** That which gives off

light. [masc] [AHLB: 1020-J (a)] [Strong's: 3974]

**Magician:** One who performs tricks of illusion and sleight of hand. Writes magical circles and lines. [masc] [AHLB: 2203 (qp)] [Strong's: 2748, 2749]

**Magnificent:** Something with increased size, power or authority. [masc] [AHLB: 2054 (c)] [Strong's: 1419]

**Magnified:** An increased significance or size. [masc] [AHLB: 2054 (N)] [Strong's: 1432]

**Magnify:** To increase in size or one's position of honor. [AHLB: 2054 (V)] [Strong's: 1431]

**Maid:** An unmarried young woman . As joined to a mistress. [fem] [AHLB: 2863 (e¹)] [Strong's: 8198]

**Make a vow:** To promise solemnly. Make an agreement where one promises an action if the other reciprocates with another action. [AHLB: 2385 (V)] [Strong's: 5087]

**Make bricks:** To shape moist clay or earth into blocks for construction purposes. Can also mean to be "white." [AHLB: 2303 (V)] [Strong's: 3835]

**Make restitution:** To restore or make right through action, payment or restoration to a rightful owner. [AHLB: 2845 (V)] [Strong's: 7999, 8000]

**Male:** Being the gender who begets offspring. One who acts and speaks for the family. In Aramaic this word means "ram." [masc] [AHLB: 2121 (N)] [Strong's: 1798, 2145]

**Male goat:** [masc] [AHLB: 2587 (d)] [Strong's: 6259, 6260]

**Male kid:** A young goat. [masc] [AHLB: 1510-A (f)] [Strong's: 1423]

**Man:** An adult male human. As mortal. Also, used to mean "each" in the sense of an individual. [masc] [AHLB: 2003 (b)] [Strong's: 376, 377]

**Mandrakes:** A plant boiled as an aphrodisiac. [masc] [AHLB: 1073-N (o)] [Strong's: 1736]

**Many:** A large but indefinite number. An abundance of things (many, much, great), actions (complete, wholly, strong, quick) or character (very). [masc] [AHLB: 1004-J (k)] [Strong's: 3966]

**March:** To move along steadily, usually with a rhythmic stride and in step with others. [AHLB: 2676 (V)] [Strong's: 6805]

**Marry:** To join as husband and wife. [AHLB: 2027 (V)] [Strong's: 1166]

**Marsh Grass:** The tall grasses that line a marsh as a wall. [masc] [AHLB: 1008-A (r)] [Strong's: 260]

**Marvel:** Something that causes wonder or astonishment. To see or perceive a full sight, such as a wonder or miracle. [AHLB: 1496-H (V)] [Strong's: 8539]

**Master:** Having chief authority; a workman qualified to teach apprentices. [masc] [AHLB: 2027 (N)] [Strong's: 1167, 1169]

**Mature:** Having completed natural growth and

development. An upright and correct nature. [masc] [AHLB: 1496-A (N)] [Strong's: 8535]

**Meat:** Solid food as distinguished from drink; flesh; a meal. [masc] [AHLB: 1152-J (a)] [Strong's: 4202, 4203]

**Meditate:** To engage in contemplation. A sweeping away in thought. [AHLB: 1330-J (V)] [Strong's: 7742]

**Meet:** To come into the presence of. Go to meet another or a chance encounter. [AHLB: 1434-H (V)] [Strong's: 7122, 7125, 7136]

**Messenger:** One who bears a message or runs an errand. Walks for another. [masc] [AHLB: 1264-D (a)] [Strong's: 4397, 4398]

**Midsection:** The lower abdomen and back. [fem] [AHLB: 1448-L (N)] [Strong's: 3409]

**Midst:** The center or middle of the whole. [masc] [AHLB: 1494-J (N)] [Strong's: 8432]

**Mighty one:** One who holds authority over others, such as a judge, chief or god. In the sense of being yoked to one another. [masc] [AHLB: 1012-A (N)] [Strong's: 410]

**Mimic:** To imitate another person's speech as an interpretation or in scorn. [AHLB: 1271-J (V)] [Strong's: 3887]

**Mind:** Literally, the heart which pumps blood, but also seen as the seat of thought and emotion. [masc] [AHLB: 1255-B (N)] [Strong's: 3824, 3825]

**Minister:** To give aid or service.

Be in service to another. [AHLB: 2884 (V)] [Strong's: 8334]

**Mist:** A vapor or fine spray. [masc] [AHLB: 1004-A (N)] [Strong's: 108]

**Mix:** To combine in one mass. Mix up. [AHLB: 1035-B (V)] [Strong's: 1101]

**Moderate:** To rule over quarrels or other conflicts. [AHLB: 1083-M (V)] [Strong's: 1777, 1778]

**Moist:** Slightly or moderately wet. [masc] [AHLB: 1261-A (N)] [Strong's: 3892, 3893]

**Mold:** To give shape to. Press or squeeze, as when pressing clay into a shape to form a vessel. [AHLB: 1411-L (V)] [Strong's: 3334, 3335]

**Monument:** A lasting evidence, reminder, or example of someone or something. As standing tall and firm. [fem] [AHLB: 2426 (a¹)] [Strong's: 4676]

**Moon:** The earth's only known satellite that reflects the sun's light. Also, a month as a counting of time by the cycles of the moon. [masc] [AHLB: 1445-L (N)] [Strong's: 3391, 3393, 3394]

**Moreover:** In addition to what has been said. [AHLB: 1017-A (N)] [Strong's: 637, 638]

**Morning:** The time from sunrise to noon. Breaking of daylight. [masc] [AHLB: 2035 (g)] [Strong's: 1242]

**Mortal man:** Subject to death. As mortal. [masc] [AHLB: 1298-A (N)] [Strong's: 4962]

**Mortar:** A thick and slimy soil used to join bricks or for making bricks. A dry standard of measurement equal to 65 Imperial gallons. [masc] [AHLB: 2175 (g)] [Strong's: 2563]

**Mother:** A female parent. Maternal tenderness or affection. One whose arms hold the family together through her work and love. One who fulfills the role of a mother. [fem] [AHLB: 1013-A (N)] [Strong's: 517]

**Mound:** An artificial hill or bank of earth or stones. Something such as rocks or a spring out of the ground. [masc] [AHLB: 1058-A (N)] [Strong's: 1530, 1531]

**Mount:** To increase in amount or extent; to get up on something above the level of the ground. [masc] [AHLB: 1112-B (N)] [Strong's: 2042]

**Mourn:** To feel or express grief or sorrow. [AHLB: 1035-C (V)] [Strong's: 56]

**Mourning:** A flowing of tears. Also, a meadow as a weeping ground. [com] [AHLB: 1035-C (N)] [Strong's: 57, 58, 60]

**Mouth:** The opening through which food enters the body. [masc] [AHLB: 1373-A (N)] [Strong's: 6310]

**Multiple:** Involving more than one. [masc] [AHLB: 2569 (d)] [Strong's: 6099]

**Multitude:** A great number of people. Loud group. [masc] [AHLB: 1105-A (j)] [Strong's: 1995]

**Myriad:** A great abundance in numbers. [fem] [AHLB: 1439-B (N¹)] [Strong's: 7233]

**Myrrh:** An aromatic gum resin obtained from a tree and having a bitter slightly pungent taste. [masc] [AHLB: 1262-J (N)] [Strong's: 3910]

**Naked:** Without clothes in the sense of bare skin. [masc] [AHLB: 1365-A (ecp)] [Strong's: 5903]

**Nakedness:** The shame of one being naked. Idiomatic for sexual relations. In the Aramaic this word means dishonor in the sense of being naked. [fem] [AHLB: 1365-K (N¹)] [Strong's: 6172, 6173]

**Narrow:** Of slender width. A narrow, tight place or situation. An enemy or adversary as one who closes in with pressure. [masc] [AHLB: 1411-A (N)] [Strong's: 6862]

**Nation:** A community of people of one or more nationalities and having a more or less defined territory and government. The people of a nation as the back, or body. [masc] [AHLB: 1052-A (f)] [Strong's: 1471]

**Near:** Close to; at or within a short distance from. Also, a kin, as a near relative. [masc] [AHLB: 2729 (c)] [Strong's: 7138]

**Neck:** The part of a person that connects the head with the body. [masc] [AHLB: 2580 (N)] [Strong's: 6203]

**Nest:** A bed or receptacle prepared by a bird for its eggs and young. The stall of an animal as a nest. [masc] [AHLB: 1428-A (N)] [Strong's: 7064]

**Net:** An open-meshed fabric twisted, knotted, or woven at regular intervals. Also, a thicket as an interwoven network of thorns. [masc] [AHLB: 2459 (N)] [Strong's: 5442, 7638]

**Nevertheless:** In spite of that. A flowing of certainty. [AHLB: 1035-C (N)] [Strong's: 61]

**New moon:** The moon phase when its dark side is toward the earth; the thin crescent moon. first crescent of the moon as the renewal of the moon, the first day of the month. Also, a month as the interval between crescents. [masc] [AHLB: 2151 (g)] [Strong's: 2320]

**Night:** The time from dusk to dawn; night time hours associated with darkness and sleep. [com] [AHLB: 1265-M (N)] [Strong's: 3915]

**Nine:** Nine in number. The total number of hours in an ancient day or night. [com] [AHLB: 1476-A (i)] [Strong's: 8672, 8673]

**No:** The negative of an alternative choice. To be without; to not be. [masc] [AHLB: 1254-A (N)] [Strong's: 408, 409, 3809]

**Noble:** Possessing outstanding qualities or properties. Of high birth or exalted rank. One who has authority. May also mean "heavy" from the weight of responsibility on one in authority. [masc] [AHLB: 1342-A (N)] [Strong's: 5620, 8269]

**Nod:** A quick downward motion of the head. To shake or wag out of pity, sorrow or wandering. [AHLB: 1303-J

(V)] [Strong's: 5110, 5111]

**North:** From the North Star which is watched for direction. [fem] [AHLB: 1408-A (j)] [Strong's: 6828]

**Nose:** The organ bearing the nostrils on the anterior of the face. Literally, the nostril but also meaning the nose, especially when in the plural. This word can also mean anger because of the flaring of the nostrils when angry. [masc] [AHLB: 1017-A (N)] [Strong's: 639]

**Not:** A function word to stand for the negative. As being without. [AHLB: 1254-J (N)] [Strong's: 3808]

**Nothing:** Not any thing. [fem] [AHLB: 1289-D (d$^1$)] [Strong's: 3972]

**Nourishment:** Food; nutriment. For giving sustenance and making one whole. [masc] [AHLB: 1242-C (a)] [Strong's: 3978]

**Now:** At the present time or moment. [masc] [AHLB: 1367-H (N)] [Strong's: 6258]

**Nude:** Without clothes in the sense of bare skin. [masc] [AHLB: 1365-A (cp)] [Strong's: 6174]

**Number:** A sum of units. Counting as a recording. [masc] [AHLB: 2500 (h)] [Strong's: 4557]

**Oak:** The tough durable wood of the oak tree. Strongest of the woods. [fem] [AHLB: 1012-A (N$^1$)] [Strong's: 424, 427]

**Oath:** Something corroborated by a vow. A binding agreement, including the curse for violating the oath. [fem]

[AHLB: 1012-A (N¹)]
[Strong's: 423]

**Obedience:** Submission to the will of another. In the sense of being restrained. [fem] [AHLB: 1419-L (N¹)] [Strong's: 3349]

**Occupation:** The principal business of one's life. [fem] [AHLB: 1264-D (k¹)] [Strong's: 4399]

**Oil:** An unctuous combustible substance that is liquid, is not water-soluble, and leaves a greasy stain. Usually olive oil and used as a medicinal ointment. Also, meaning fat or rich. [masc] [AHLB: 2850 (N)] [Strong's: 8081, 8082]

**Old age:** One up in years. [fem] [AHLB: 2132 (e¹)] [Strong's: 2209]

**Olive:** The fruit or the tree. Fruit used for food and a source of oil. [masc] [AHLB: 1160-M (N)] [Strong's: 2132]

**On account of:** As a crossing over from one idea to another. [masc] [AHLB: 2520 (d)] [Strong's: 5668, 5669]

**One of the flock:** A member of a flock of sheep or goats. [masc] [AHLB: 1327-A (N)] [Strong's: 2089, 7716]

**Only:** A single instance or thing and nothing more or different. [AHLB: 1456-A (N)] [Strong's: 7535]

**Open:** Having no confining barrier. To open up as opening a gate or door. [AHLB: 2649 (V)] [Strong's: 6605, 6606]

**Open up:** To make available or accessible. Open the eyes or ears. [AHLB: 2631 (V)]

[Strong's: 6491]

**Opening:** Something that is open, as an entrance or opening of a tent, house or city. [masc] [AHLB: 2649 (N)] [Strong's: 6607, 6608]

**Opposite:** Something in front of and pronounced. Also a story as being told face to face. [masc] [AHLB: 2372 (N)] [Strong's: 5048, 5049]

**Or:** An alternative or optional desire. [AHLB: 1006-A (N)] [Strong's: 176]

**Ornament:** Something that lends grace and beauty. Precious ornaments probably with gems. [fem] [AHLB: 2329 (m¹)] [Strong's: 4030]

**Other:** One that remains of two or more. A time, person or thing that follows after. [masc] [AHLB: 1181-C (N)] [Strong's: 312, 317]

**Other side:** As being across from this side. [masc] [AHLB: 2520 (N)] [Strong's: 5676]

**Otherwise:** In a different manner or way.. As a turning toward another direction. [AHLB: 1382-A (N)] [Strong's: 6435]

**Outcry:** A vehement protest; a loud cry. [fem] [AHLB: 2131 (N)] [Strong's: 2201]

**Outside:** A place or region beyond an enclosure or barrier. [masc] [AHLB: 1179-J (N)] [Strong's: 2351]

**Oven:** A chamber used for baking, heating or drying. As a lamp for cooking. [masc] [AHLB: 1319-J (i)] [Strong's: 8574]

**Overcome:** To get the better of. Be successful in strength or authority. [AHLB: 2052 (V)] [Strong's: 1396]

**Overlook:** To unintentionaly look past, forget. [AHLB: 1320-H (V)] [Strong's: 5382]

**Overseer:** One who carefully watches over; a superintendent. [masc] [AHLB: 2630 (b)] [Strong's: 6496]

**Oversight:** Watchful and responsible care. [fem] [AHLB: 1463-A (h¹)] [Strong's: 4870]

**Overtake:** To catch up with. Also, to remove in the sense of taking over. [AHLB: 2410 (V)] [Strong's: 5253, 5381]

**Overturn:** To turn something over or upside down, as if pouring out its contents. [AHLB: 1379-F (V)] [Strong's: 2015]

**Overturning:** The act of turning something over. [fem] [AHLB: 1379-F (N¹)] [Strong's: 2018]

**Owner:** Possessor of an article or property. [masc] [AHLB: 2052 (b)] [Strong's: 1376]

**Ox:** A domestic bovine animal used for pulling heavy loads. [masc] [AHLB: 1480-J (N)] [Strong's: 7794, 8450]

**Pack:** A bundle arranged for carrying. [AHLB: 2237 (V)] [Strong's: 2943]

**Palm:** A tropical tree with fan-shaped leaves. Part of the hand between the base of the fingers and the wrist. Also, the sole of the foot; another palm-shaped object such as a spoon. [fem] [AHLB: 1247-A (N)] [Strong's: 3709, 3710]

**Parcel:** A section or portion of land that has been purchased or aquired. [fem] [AHLB:

2167 (N¹)] [Strong's: 2513]

**Parching heat:** To shrivel or toast with intense heat. [masc] [AHLB: 2199 (g)] [Strong's: 2721]

**Part:** To separate. Part the lips to open the mouth. [AHLB: 1386-H (V)] [Strong's: 6475]

**Partner:** One that shares. A close companion. [masc] [AHLB: 1453-A (k)] [Strong's: 4828]

**Pass over:** To pass through, by or over something. Also, to change in the sense of going to another one, side or thought. [AHLB: 2165 (V)] [Strong's: 2498, 2499]

**Pasture:** A place of feeding or grazing. [masc] [AHLB: 1453-H (h)] [Strong's: 4829]

**Path:** The road or route one travels. [masc] [AHLB: 1445-C (g)] [Strong's: 734]

**Payment:** Something that is paid. [fem] [AHLB: 2479 (ac²)] [Strong's: 4909]

**Peel:** The skin or rind of a fruit; to strip off an outer layer. [AHLB: 2626 (V)] [Strong's: 6478]

**Peel off:** To strip off an outer layer. spread apart. To invade in the sense of spreading out for an attack. Also, to strip off clothing in the sense of spreading the garment for removal. [AHLB: 2646 (V)] [Strong's: 6584]

**People:** Human beings. [masc] [AHLB: 1358-A (N)] [Strong's: 5971, 5972]

**Perform:** To do a great action out of a judgement. [AHLB: 1380-E (V)] [Strong's: 6381]

**Pick up:** To take hold of and lift up. To gather together.

[AHLB: 2320 (V)] [Strong's: 3950]

**Pierce:** To run into or through as with a pointed weapon or tool. Pierce a hole through. Also, meaning common in the sense of taking something set apart for a special function and using for common purposes. [AHLB: 1173-B (V)] [Strong's: 2490]

**Pierce through:** To make a hole by puncturing or penetrating. To curse in the sense of piercing through. [AHLB: 2430 (V)] [Strong's: 5344]

**Pierced:** Having holes. [masc] [AHLB: 1173-B (N)] [Strong's: 2491]

**Pile up:** To heap something up in a mound. [AHLB: 2656 (V)] [Strong's: 6651]

**Pilgrimage:** A journey of a pilgrim; the course of life on earth. One who travels in a strange land. The pilgrimage or the dwelling place of a stranger. [masc] [AHLB: 1066-J (d)] [Strong's: 4033]

**Pistachio:** A greenish-yellow nut from a small tree of the same name. From its belly shape. [masc] [AHLB: 2015 (g)] [Strong's: 992]

**Pitch tent:** To set up camp. By extension, can also mean a distant shining, such as the moon. [AHLB: 1104-C (V)] [Strong's: 166, 167]

**Place:** An indefinite region or expanse; a particular part of a surface or body. A place one rises up to. [masc] [AHLB: 1427-J (a)] [Strong's: 4725]

**Place of lodging:** An establishment for lodging and entertaining travelers. A place for spending the night. [masc] [AHLB: 1267-J (a)] [Strong's: 4411]

**Place of rest:** A location where there is freedom from activity or labor; a place for resting or lodging. [fem] [AHLB: 1307-J (k$^1$)] [Strong's: 4496]

**Plague:** An epidemic disease causing high mortality. An epidemic or other sore or illness as a touch from God. [masc] [AHLB: 2376 (N)] [Strong's: 5061]

**Plant:** To put or set into the ground for growth. Establish plants in the sense of setting into place in the soil. [AHLB: 2398 (V)] [Strong's: 5193]

**Plead:** To entreat or appeal earnestly. Fall to the ground to plead a cause to one in authority. An action to prevent a judgement. [AHLB: 1380-B (V)] [Strong's: 6419]

**Pleasant:** Having qualities that tend to give pleasure. An object of desire. [fem] [AHLB: 2169 (N$^1$)] [Strong's: 2532]

**Please:** A pleading or request for something. To make another happy or gratified. [AHLB: 1300-A (N)] [Strong's: 577, 4994]

**Pleasure:** A state of gratification. [com] [AHLB: 2528 (N)] [Strong's: 5730]

**Plenty:** A full or more than adequate supply. What is full, satisfied or abundant . [masc] [AHLB: 2461 (N)] [Strong's: 7647, 7649]

**Plot:** To devise a plan of action, usually with evil intent.

[AHLB: 1151-B (V)] [Strong's: 2161]

**Pluck away:** To take off something or someone by force through picking off, robbing or plundering. [AHLB: 2059 (V)] [Strong's: 1497]

**Pluck up:** To pull or dig out the roots. [AHLB: 2905 (V)] [Strong's: 6131, 6132]

**Plunder:** To commit robbery or looting. [AHLB: 1030-B (V)] [Strong's: 962]

**Poplar:** A tree with white bark. [fem] [AHLB: 2303 (e¹)] [Strong's: 3839]

**Portion:** An individual's part or share of something. The portions dispersed out. [masc] [AHLB: 2167 (N)] [Strong's: 2506]

**Possession:** Something owned, occupied or controlled. The goods and wealth acquired as the acquiring of materials for building a nest. [masc] [AHLB: 1428-B (b)] [Strong's: 7075]

**Possibly:** Being within the limits of ability, capacity, or realization. A possible outcome. To desire what you are without in the sense of joining. [com] [AHLB: 1254-J (f)] [Strong's: 194]

**Post:** The place at which a soldier is stationed. As standing tall and firm. A garrison. [masc] [AHLB: 2426 (b)] [Strong's: 5333]

**Posterity:** The offspring of a progenitor to the furthest generation. Continuation through the next generation. [masc] [AHLB: 2402 (N)]

[Strong's: 5220]

**Pour:** To cause to flow in a stream. To give full expression to. [AHLB: 2412 (V)] [Strong's: 5258, 5259, 5260]

**Pour down:** To pour molten metal. [AHLB: 1410-L (V)] [Strong's: 3251, 3332]

**Pour out:** To let flow a liquid including the blood of an animal in sacrifice or a man. [AHLB: 2865 (V)] [Strong's: 8210]

**Pouring:** A liquid poured out as an offering or the pouring of a molten metal to form images. [masc] [AHLB: 2412 (N)] [Strong's: 5261, 5262]

**Powder:** Matter in a fine particulate state. An abundant amount of powdery substance as dust or ash. [masc] [AHLB: 2565 (N)] [Strong's: 6083]

**Power:** Possession of control, authority, or influence over others; physical might. The power or might of one who rules or teaches. One who yokes with another. Often applies to rulers or a god. [masc] [AHLB: 1012-H (c)] [Strong's: 430, 433]

**Precipitate:** To rain. [AHLB: 2336 (V)] [Strong's: 4305]

**Pregnancy:** The quality of containing unborn young within the body. From the mound of the belly. [masc] [AHLB: 1112-H (j)] [Strong's: 2032]

**Pregnant:** Containing unborn young within the body. [fem] [AHLB: 1112-H (N¹)] [Strong's: 2030]

**Prepare:** To make ready

beforehand. Be ready. [AHLB: 2587 (V)] [Strong's: 6257]

**Present:** A gift given to another on bended knee and in respect. Also a pool of water as a place where one kneels down to drink from. [fem] [AHLB: 2039 (N¹)] [Strong's: 1293, 1295]

**Press:** Pressure or pushing action. [AHLB: 2470 (V)] [Strong's: 7818]

**Press hard:** To push or urge another into an action. [AHLB: 2629 (V)] [Strong's: 6484]

**Prey:** An animal taken as food by a predator. The meat that is torn by the predator. [masc] [AHLB: 2245 (N)] [Strong's: 2964, 2965]

**Priest:** One authorized to perform the sacred rites as a mediatory agent between man and God. The base which supports the people. [masc] [AHLB: 1244-G (g)] [Strong's: 3548]

**Prison:** A place of confinement. [masc] [AHLB: 1342-G (N)] [Strong's: 5470]

**Prisoner:** One who is bound or confined. [masc] [AHLB: 1342-C (b)] [Strong's: 615, 616]

**Produce:** Agricultural products, especially fresh fruits and vegetables. The harvested product of a crop. [masc] [AHLB: 1388-H (f)] [Strong's: 6529]

**Production:** Total output of a commodity or an industry. An increase of produce, usually of fruit in the sense of filling. [fem] [AHLB: 1024-J (i¹)]

[Strong's: 8393]

**Profit:** A valuable return; to derive benefit. The taking of money or something of value through force in the sense of cutting. [masc] [AHLB: 2031 (N)] [Strong's: 1215]

**Prolong:** To lengthen or delay. [AHLB: 1448-C (V)] [Strong's: 748, 749]

**Prophet:** One gifted with more than ordinary spiritual and moral insight. who brings forth the inner fruit. [masc] [AHLB: 1301-E (b)] [Strong's: 5029, 5030]

**Prosper:** To succeed. Move forward in distance, position or in thriving. [AHLB: 2662 (V)] [Strong's: 6743, 6744]

**Prostitute:** Devoted to corrupt purposes. A female prostitute set aside for a special purpose. [fem] [AHLB: 2700 (N¹)] [Strong's: 6948]

**Prostitution:** As paid with food. [masc] [AHLB: 1152-B (d)] [Strong's: 2183]

**Provender:** Dry food for domestic animals. A gathering of food. [masc] [AHLB: 1339-E (hc)] [Strong's: 4554]

**Provide:** To give what is due. Also to grant or allow permission. [AHLB: 1094-L (V)] [Strong's: 3051, 3052]

**Provide food:** Supply nourishment. [AHLB: 2315 (V)] [Strong's: 3938]

**Provisions:** A stock of needed materials. The produce of the hunt. Also, used for "food" in general. [fem] [AHLB: 1395-M (N¹)] [Strong's: 6720]

**Purchase:** Something owned, occupied or controlled. The

goods and wealth acquired as the acquiring of materials for building a nest. [AHLB: 1428-H (V)] [Strong's: 7066, 7069]

**Pure:** Unmixed with any other matter. Someone or something that is free of impurities. This can be a metal such as gold or animals. [masc] [AHLB: 1204-G (c)] [Strong's: 2889, 2890]

**Pursue:** To follow in order to overtake, capture, kill, or defeat. Pursue in chase or persecution. [AHLB: 2755 (V)] [Strong's: 7291]

**Put:** To set or fix anything in place. To establish or appoint. [AHLB: 1335-L (V)] [Strong's: 3455]

**Qeshiytah:** A unit of value, money. [fem] [AHLB: 2739 (b[1])] [Strong's: 7192]

**Quarrel:** A ground of dispute or complaint. A clash between sides. [AHLB: 2562 (V)] [Strong's: 6229]

**Quiver:** A case for holding or carrying arrows. As hung over the shoulder. [masc] [AHLB: 1495-A (f)] [Strong's: 8522]

**Rafter:** The beams which the roof of the house sits on. [fem] [AHLB: 1434-J (N[1])] [Strong's: 6982]

**Raiment:** Clothing; garments. [fem] [AHLB: 1245-A (N[3])] [Strong's: 3682]

**Rain shower:** The rain of the skies. In Aramaic this word means the "body." [masc] [AHLB: 2090 (N)] [Strong's: 1653, 1655]

**Raise:** To lift something up. [AHLB: 1450-J (V)]

[Strong's: 7311, 7313]

**Raven:** A glossy black bird. As black in color. [masc] [AHLB: 2907 (g)] [Strong's: 6158]

**Reach:** To touch or grasp; to get up to or as far as. Come together in meeting by chance. To give or place as a meeting. [AHLB: 2592 (V)] [Strong's: 6293]

**Rebel:** To oppose or disobey one in authority or control. [AHLB: 2352 (V)] [Strong's: 4775]

**Rebuke:** To criticize sharply. [AHLB: 2076 (V)] [Strong's: 1605]

**Reckless:** Marked by lack of proper caution. [masc] [AHLB: 2599 (N)] [Strong's: 6349]

**Reckon:** To appoint, assign, count or number a set of things or people. [AHLB: 1290-H (V)] [Strong's: 4483, 4487]

**Recognize:** To acknowledge or take notice of in some definite way. [AHLB: 2406 (V)] [Strong's: 5234]

**Red:** Of the color red. Ruddy; florid. [masc] [AHLB: 1082-C (c)] [Strong's: 122]

**Redeem:** To buy back. Restore one to his original position or avenge his death. In the participle form this verb means "avenger," as it is the role of the nearest relative to buy back one in slavery or avenge his murder. [AHLB: 1058-D (V)] [Strong's: 1350]

**Reed-pipe:** A wind instrument made of reeds. Related to lust through the heavy breathing of passion. [masc] [AHLB:

2523 (o)] [Strong's: 5748]

**Refine:** To reduce to a pure state. [AHLB: 1375-B (V)] [Strong's: 6338, 6339]

**Reflection:** The return of light or sound waves from a surface; production of an image as by a mirror. [fem] [AHLB: 1438-A (a$^1$)] [Strong's: 4759]

**Refuse:** To express one's self as being unwilling to accept. [AHLB: 1290-D (V)] [Strong's: 3985]

**Regulate:** To govern or correct according to rule. Rule over a dominion. To bring order, method, or uniformity to. To compare one thing to another in the sense of a rule of measurement, often as a proverb or parable. [AHLB: 2359 (V)] [Strong's: 4910, 4911]

**Regulation:** An authoritative rule dealing with details or procedure. The power and authority of one to regulate and control over another. [fem] [AHLB: 2359 (k$^1$)] [Strong's: 4475]

**Reign:** To rule over a kingdom as king or queen. [AHLB: 2340 (V)] [Strong's: 4427]

**Relate:** To have a relationship with another through marriage. [AHLB: 2224 (V)] [Strong's: 2859]

**Remain:** To continue unchanged; to stay behind. [AHLB: 1480-D (V)] [Strong's: 7604]

**Remainder:** A remaining group, part or trace. [masc] [AHLB: 1480-L (N)] [Strong's: 3499]

**Remember:** To bring to mind or think of again. Remember in thought as a memorial or mention through speech. To act or speak on behalf of another. [AHLB: 2121 (V)] [Strong's: 2142]

**Remnant:** A usually small part, member, or trace remaining. [fem] [AHLB: 1480-D (N$^4$)] [Strong's: 7611]

**Remove the cover:** Usually to be exposed from the removal of clothing. To reveal something by exposing it. [AHLB: 1357-H (V)] [Strong's: 1540, 1541]

**Replacement:** That which takes the place of , especially as a substitute or successor. In the sense of passing through one thing to another. [fem] [AHLB: 2165 (b$^1$)] [Strong's: 2487]

**Report:** An account or statement of an event or happening. What is heard. [masc] [AHLB: 2851 (N)] [Strong's: 8088]

**Reproduce:** To produce new individuals of the same kind. Be abundant in fruit. [AHLB: 1388-H (V)] [Strong's: 6509]

**Rescue:** To free from confinement, danger, or evil. A deliverance or freedom from a trouble. [fem] [AHLB: 1476-L (d$^1$)] [Strong's: 3444]

**Reserve:** To set aside; to retain or hold over to a future time or place. Leave behind a remainder. [AHLB: 1480-L (V)] [Strong's: 3498]

**Reside:** To dwell permanently or continuously. [AHLB: 2118 (V)] [Strong's: 2082]

**Rest:** Freedom from activity or labor. To rest from trouble or labor. [AHLB: 1307-J (V)] [Strong's: 5117]

**Resting place:** Location where a person or object is free from activity or labor. [masc] [AHLB: 1307-J (a)] [Strong's: 4494]

**Restrain:** To prevent from doing. Hold back, in the sense of grabbing the heel. [AHLB: 2571 (V)] [Strong's: 6117]

**Restrict:** To confine within bounds. Hold back or prevent someone or something. [AHLB: 1242-E (V)] [Strong's: 3607]

**Reviving:** Restoring to consciousness or life. [fem] [AHLB: 1171-H (h¹)] [Strong's: 4241]

**Revolution:** A sudden, radical or complete change. [masc] [AHLB: 2647 (N)] [Strong's: 6588]

**Rib:** Any of the paired bony or cartilaginous bones that stiffen the walls of the thorax and protect the organs beneath. As roasted over the fire. A ridge of a hill from its similar shape to the ribs. [fem] [AHLB: 2664 (N)] [Strong's: 5967, 6763]

**Riches:** Wealth. The possessions that make one wealthy. [masc] [AHLB: 2585 (N)] [Strong's: 6239]

**Ride:** To sit and travel in any conveyance. To sit astride an animal, wagon or chariot.. [AHLB: 2769 (V)] [Strong's: 7392]

**Rider:** The one traveling in a conveyance chariot or its rider or a rider of a horse or wagon. The top millstone as supported on top of the bottom millstone. [masc]

[AHLB: 2769 (N)] [Strong's: 7393, 7395]

**Right hand:** The right hand or the direction of the right hand. [fem] [AHLB: 1290-L (b)] [Strong's: 3225]

**Ring:** A circular band worn as an ornament. [masc] [AHLB: 2388 (N)] [Strong's: 5141]

**Ripen:** To bring to completeness or perfection. Give off the fragrance of the fruit as it ripens. To add spices to a body for embalming. [AHLB: 2177 (V)] [Strong's: 2590]

**Rise:** To assume an upright position. Raise or rise up. Also, in the sense of continuing or establishing something. [AHLB: 1427-J (V)] [Strong's: 6965, 6966]

**Rising:** A rising of smoke from a burnt offering. Captivity in the sense of placing a yoke on the captives. [fem] [AHLB: 1357-J (N¹)] [Strong's: 1473, 5930]

**River:** A natural stream of water of considerable volume. The life-giving water that washes over the soil. [masc] [AHLB: 1319-G (N)] [Strong's: 5103, 5104]

**Road:** A route or path for travel. Road that is walked, as well as the path or manner of life. [masc] [AHLB: 2112 (N)] [Strong's: 1870]

**Roam:** To wander around restlessly. [AHLB: 1441-J (V)] [Strong's: 7300]

**Robe:** A long flowing outer garment. Wide garment. [fem] [AHLB: 1089-C (N²)] [Strong's: 155]

**Rod:** A slender bar of wood or

metal. [masc] [AHLB: 1426-A (a)] [Strong's: 4731]

**Roll:** A written document that may be wrapped round on itself. [AHLB: 1058-B (V)] [Strong's: 1556, 5953]

**Roof covering:** Material used for a top or covering of a building. What covers something. [masc] [AHLB: 1245-H (h)] [Strong's: 4372]

**Round about:** A circuitous way or route. [AHLB: 1349-A (N)] [Strong's: 1157]

**Roundness:** Cylindrical; something as a circle, globe or ring that is round. A round thing or place. A coin as a round piece of gold or silver. A round loaf of bread. The plain, as a round piece of land. [fem] [AHLB: 2258 (e)] [Strong's: 3603]

**Ruddy:** Having a healthy reddish color. [masc] [AHLB: 1082-C (jf)] [Strong's: 132]

**Rule:** To exert control, direction, or influence over, especially by curbing or restraining. by walking among the subjects. [AHLB: 1441-H (V)] [Strong's: 7287]

**Run:** To go faster than a walk. [AHLB: 1455-J (V)] [Strong's: 7323]

**Sack:** The plundering of a captured town. A usually rectangular bag of paper, canvas. [masc] [AHLB: 1341-A (N)] [Strong's: 8242]

**Sacrifice:** An act of offering to deity something precious. To kill an animal for an offering. [AHLB: 2117 (V)] [Strong's: 1684, 2076]

**Saddle:** A shaped mounted support on which an object can travel. To bind up with a saddle. [AHLB: 2144 (V)] [Strong's: 2280]

**Saddlebag:** One of a pair of covered pouches laid behind the saddle. For carrying items. [masc] [AHLB: 2870 (h)] [Strong's: 4942]

**Safely:** A state or place of safety. [masc] [AHLB: 2013 (N)] [Strong's: 983]

**Salt:** An ingredient that gives savor, piquancy, or zest to food. Also, mariners from their sailing on the seas (pronounced ma-lahh). Also, old rags or clothes, probably from their saltiness from the body (pronounced ma-lahh). [masc] [AHLB: 2338 (N)] [Strong's: 4416, 4417, 4418, 4419]

**Sand:** Loose granular material from the disintegration of rocks and consisting of particles not as fine as silt and used in mortar. Sand is used as an abrasive ingredient for drilling by placing it in the hole being drilled. [masc] [AHLB: 1173-J (N)] [Strong's: 2344]

**Sandal:** A shoe consisting of a sole strapped to the foot. [fem] [AHLB: 2415 (N)] [Strong's: 5275]

**Say:** To speak chains of words that form sentences. [AHLB: 1288-C (V)] [Strong's: 559, 560]

**Scarlet:** Any of various bright reds. The color of the gums. [masc] [AHLB: 1474-A (f)] [Strong's: 8144]

**Scatter:** To fling away heedlessly.

To separate and go in various directions. [AHLB: 2422 (V)] [Strong's: 5310]

**Scatter abroad:** To sow, cast or fling widely. [AHLB: 1386-J (V)] [Strong's: 6327]

**Scratch:** Also, to plow in the sense of scratching a line in the soil. This word can also mean "to hold in peace" or be silent. [AHLB: 2211 (V)] [Strong's: 2790]

**Scroll:** A roll as of papyrus, leather or parchment for writing a document. Document or record written on a sheet of skin or papyrus and rolled up. This word can also mean a "census" in the sense of recording numbers (pronounced se-phar). In Aramaic this word can also mean a scribe, as one who writes a scroll (pronounced sa-phar). [masc] [AHLB: 2500 (N)] [Strong's: 5609, 5610, 5612, 5613]

**Sea:** A large body of water. Also, the direction of the great sea (Mediterranean), the west. [masc] [AHLB: 1220-A (N)] [Strong's: 3220, 3221]

**Se'ah:** A dry standard of measure equal to 1/3 ephah. [fem] [AHLB: 1323-A (N¹)] [Strong's: 5429]

**Search:** To look thoroughly in an effort to find or discover something. [AHLB: 2189 (V)] [Strong's: 2664]

**Search out:** To search until the object of the search is found. [AHLB: 2036 (V)] [Strong's: 1245]

**Seat:** A special chair of one in eminence. Usually a throne or seat of authority. [masc] [AHLB: 1245-E (e)] [Strong's: 3678, 3764]

**Second:** As second in numeric order. [com] [AHLB: 1474-H (f)] [Strong's: 8145]

**See:** To take notice or perceive something or someone. To see visions. [AHLB: 1438-H (V)] [Strong's: 7200, 7202, 7207, 7212]

**Seed:** The grains or ripened ovules of plants used for sowing. As scattered in the field to produce a crop. The singular word can be used for one or more. Also, the descendants of an individual, either male or female. [masc] [AHLB: 2137 (N)] [Strong's: 2233, 2234]

**Seeing as:** In the degree that. Sense of paying attention. [AHLB: 1359-L (N)] [Strong's: 3282]

**Seek:** To look for or search for something or for answers. [AHLB: 2114 (V)] [Strong's: 1875]

**Seethe:** To boil a soup or boil with pride. [AHLB: 1142-J (V)] [Strong's: 2102, 2103]

**Seize:** To possess or take by force. Grab hold tightly. To refrain or support by grabbing hold. [AHLB: 2152 (V)] [Strong's: 2388]

**Seize hold:** To take hold of something by force. [AHLB: 2899 (V)] [Strong's: 8610]

**Sell:** To give up property to another for money or another valuable compensation. [AHLB: 2337 (V)] [Strong's: 4376]

**Send:** To cause to go; to direct,

order, or request to go. [AHLB: 2842 (V)] [Strong's: 7971, 7972]

**Separate:** To set or keep apart. Divide or separate something. [AHLB: 2005 (V)] [Strong's: 914]

**Separated thing:** Someone or something separated from the whole, often meaning "alone." This may also be a branch as separated from the tree (as well as a staff made from a branch). Linen cloth fibers which are divided. A lie or liar, as what causes a separation through careless words, lying, or bragging. [masc] [AHLB: 1027-A (N)] [Strong's: 905, 906, 907]

**Serpent:** A noxious reptile that hisses, creeps and bites, often venomously; devil; snake. [masc] [AHLB: 2395 (N)] [Strong's: 5175]

**Servant:** One who provides a service to another, as a slave or hired hand. [masc] [AHLB: 2518 (N)] [Strong's: 5649, 5650, 5652]

**Serve:** To provide a service to another, as a servant or slave or to work at a profession. [AHLB: 2518 (V)] [Strong's: 5647, 5648]

**Service:** Labor provided by a servant or slave. [fem] [AHLB: 2518 (c$^1$)] [Strong's: 5656]

**Set:** To put something in a place. [AHLB: 1394-L (V)] [Strong's: 3322]

**Set apart:** To put someone or something apart for a special purpose. [AHLB: 2700 (V)] [Strong's: 6942]

**Set down:** To cause to sit down. Set or lay down. [AHLB: 1482-M (V)] [Strong's: 7896]

**Set in place:** To set anything in a place. [AHLB: 1335-J (V)] [Strong's: 7760, 7761]

**Set-aside:** To reserve or put aside something in the sense of keeping in the shadow. [AHLB: 1403-C (V)] [Strong's: 680]

**Settle:** To stay in a dwelling place for the night or for long periods of time. Also to sit down. [AHLB: 1462-L (V)] [Strong's: 3427, 3488]

**Settling:** The place of settling as a temporary dwelling. [masc] [AHLB: 1462-L (a)] [Strong's: 4186]

**Seven:** Seven in number. [com] [AHLB: 2808 (N)] [Strong's: 7651, 7657]

**Seventh:** The seventh in numeric order. [masc] [AHLB: 2808 (bf)] [Strong's: 7637]

**Seventh time:** A sequence of events ending with the seventh. [fem] [AHLB: 2808 (e$^2$)] [Strong's: 7659]

**Sew together:** To join two pieces of cloth with stitches of thread. [AHLB: 2900 (V)] [Strong's: 8609]

**Sha'ar:** A standard of measure. [masc] [AHLB: 2862 (N)] [Strong's: 8180]

**Shadow:** The dark figure cast on a surface by a body intercepting the rays from a light source. [masc] [AHLB: 1403-A (N)] [Strong's: 6738]

**Shake:** To tremble in fear or anger. [AHLB: 2748 (V)] [Strong's: 7264, 7265]

**Shape:** The outline of an

individual. [masc] [AHLB: 1503-D (g)] [Strong's: 8389]

**Sharpen:** To hone in the sense of narrowing the blade edge by using a whetstone or hammer. To narrow the eyes in the sense of looking sharply, as in squinting. [AHLB: 2309 (V)] [Strong's: 3913]

**Shave:** To cut off the hair from the face or another part of the body. [AHLB: 2065 (V)] [Strong's: 1548]

**She:** The female who is neither the speaker nor the one addressed. As one looked toward. [fem] [AHLB: 1093-J (N)] [Strong's: 1931, 1932]

**Sheaf:** Stalks and ears of a cereal grass bound together. A sheaf of grain that is bound. [masc] [AHLB: 1266-C (d)] [Strong's: 485]

**Shear:** To cut or clip wool or hair from something. [AHLB: 1053-B (V)] [Strong's: 1494]

**She-donkey:** A female donkey. As used as a gift. [fem] [AHLB: 1497-C (c)] [Strong's: 860]

**Sheep:** A mammal related to the goat domesticated for its flesh and wool. [masc] [AHLB: 2273 (N)] [Strong's: 3532, 3775]

**Sheet:** A broad piece of cloth or metal. As hammered out flat. [masc] [AHLB: 2797 (b)] [Strong's: 7549]

**She-goat:** A female goat. [fem] [AHLB: 1513-A (N)] [Strong's: 5795, 5796]

**Sheqel:** A chief Hebrew weight standard of measurement. [masc] [AHLB: 2874 (N)] [Strong's: 8255, 8625]

**Shield:** A broad piece of defensive armor carried on the arm. A protective structure. Wall of protection. [masc] [AHLB: 1060-A (a)] [Strong's: 4043]

**Shine:** To emit rays of light. Shine brightly. To shine or cause another to shine through one's actions or words. [AHLB: 1104-B (V)] [Strong's: 1984]

**Shining:** Emitting or reflecting light. From the glistening of olive oil. Something that shines brightly. Also, noon as the brightest part of the day. [fem] [AHLB: 1411-G (g)] [Strong's: 2096, 6672]

**Ship:** A large sea-going vessel. As searching through the sea for a distant shore. [masc] [AHLB: 1014-A (f¹)] [Strong's: 591]

**Shoham:** An unknown, precious stone. [masc] [AHLB: 1473-G (g)] [Strong's: 7718]

**Shore:** The land bordering a body of water. A place covered. [masc] [AHLB: 1178-J (N)] [Strong's: 2348]

**Short:** Having little length. A brief distance. [fem] [AHLB: 2250 (e¹)] [Strong's: 3530]

**Shoulder:** Capacity for bearing a task or blame. The shoulders as the place where loads are placed. [masc] [AHLB: 2837 (N)] [Strong's: 7926]

**Show beauty:** As the beauty of the camp itself. To give or show beauty, grace or mercy to another. [AHLB: 1175-B (V)] [Strong's: 2589, 2603, 2604]

**Shrub:** A low-growing, usually severally stemmed bush or woody plant, as used for making booths. [masc] [AHLB: 1330-M (N)] [Strong's: 7880]

**Shut:** To close an opening. To block or close an opening. [AHLB: 2467 (V)] [Strong's: 5462, 5463, 5534]

**Shut up:** To stop by halting or closing. [AHLB: 2515 (V)] [Strong's: 5640]

**Side:** An area next to something. [masc] [AHLB: 1395-A (N)] [Strong's: 6654, 6655]

**Sign:** The motion, gesture, or mark representing an agreement between two parties. A wondrous or miraculous sign. [fem] [AHLB: 1022-J (N)] [Strong's: 226, 852]

**Signet:** A seal used officially to give personal authority to a document. A signature ring or cylinder with the owner's seal that is pressed into clay to show ownership. [masc] [AHLB: 2223 (g)] [Strong's: 2368]

**Signet ring:** The finger ring with the mark of the owner that is sunk into a lump of clay as a seal. [fem] [AHLB: 2229 (N$^2$)] [Strong's: 2885]

**Silver:** A soft metal capable of a high degree of polish used for coinage, implements and ornaments. Desired, valuable metal. [masc] [AHLB: 2277 (N)] [Strong's: 3701, 3702]

**Since:** From a time in the past until now, in the sense of being on the heel of something else. [AHLB: 2571 (N)] [Strong's: 6118]

**Sinew:** A tendon. [masc] [AHLB: 1050-M (N)] [Strong's: 1517]

**Sister:** A female person having the same parents as another person. [fem] [AHLB: 1008-A (N$^3$)] [Strong's: 269]

**Six:** Six in number. [com] [AHLB: 1481-A (N)] [Strong's: 8337, 8346, 8353, 8361]

**Sixth:** The sixth in numeric order. [com] [AHLB: 1481-A (ef)] [Strong's: 8345]

**Skin:** The integument covering men or animals, as well as leather made from animal skins. The husk of a seed. [masc] [AHLB: 1365-J (N)] [Strong's: 5784, 5785]

**Skin bag:** Used for holding cheese, water or any other liquid. [fem] [AHLB: 1174-A (N$^2$)] [Strong's: 2573]

**Sky:** The upper atmosphere that constitutes an apparent great vault or arch over the earth. Place of the winds. [masc] [AHLB: 1473-A (N)] [Strong's: 8064, 8065]

**Slander:** Speaking evil of another (usually done quietly). [fem] [AHLB: 1071-A (N$^1$)] [Strong's: 1681]

**Slaughtering:** The act of slaughtering, the meat of the slaughter or one who slaughters. Also an executioner as one who slaughters. [masc] [AHLB: 2227 (N)] [Strong's: 2874, 2876, 2877]

**Slay:** To strike, beat or kill. [AHLB: 2823 (V)] [Strong's: 7819, 7820]

**Sleep:** To rest in a state of suspended consciousness. [AHLB: 1474-L (V)] [Strong's: 3462]

**Slick:** The portions dispersed out. [masc] [AHLB: 2167 (N)] [Strong's: 2509]

**Slip away:** To get away through deliverance or escape. [AHLB: 2339 (V)] [Strong's: 4422]

**Small:** Someone or something that is not very large in size, importance, age or significance. [masc] [AHLB: 2703 (N)] [Strong's: 6996]

**Small amount:** Something that is few or small in size or amount. [masc] [AHLB: 2347 (N)] [Strong's: 4592]

**Smear:** To overspread with oil as a treatment or a sign of authority. [AHLB: 2357 (V)] [Strong's: 4886]

**Smell:** The odor or scent of a thing. As carried on the wind. To be "refreshed", as when taking in a deep breath. [AHLB: 1445-J (V)] [Strong's: 7304, 7306]

**Smoke:** The gaseous products of combustion. [masc] [AHLB: 2583 (N)] [Strong's: 6226, 6227]

**Smoldering:** To burn sluggishly without flame. The smoke of the burning incense or fat. [masc] [AHLB: 2705 (ec)] [Strong's: 7008]

**Smooth:** Having an even, continuous surface. This word can also mean "flattery" in the sense of being slippery [fem] [AHLB: 2167 (N$^1$)] [Strong's: 2513, 2514]

**Snap:** To make a sudden closing; break suddenly with a sharp sound. Snap and splinter a piece of wood. Also, to lash out in anger as a splintering. [AHLB: 2726 (V)] [Strong's: 7107, 7108]

**Snooze:** To take a nap. [fem] [AHLB: 1474-A (N$^1$)] [Strong's: 8139, 8142]

**So:** In a manner or way indicated or suggested. What comes before or after another event. In the sense of being a base or a firm standing. [AHLB: 1244-A (N)] [Strong's: 3651, 3652]

**Sojourn:** To stay as a temporary resident. Travel in a strange land. Also, the extended meaning of "to be afraid" of a stranger. [AHLB: 1066-J (V)] [Strong's: 1481]

**Sojourner:** One who stays temporarily. Travels from place to place. [masc] [AHLB: 1462-L (i)] [Strong's: 8453]

**Solitary:** Separated from the whole of the unit (see Psalm 68:7 [6]). [masc] [AHLB: 1165-L (b)] [Strong's: 3173]

**Son:** A male offspring. One who continues the family line. This can be the son of the father or a later male descendant. [masc] [AHLB: 1037-A (N)] [Strong's: 1121, 1123, 1247, 1248]

**Song:** The act or art of singing. [fem] [AHLB: 1480-M (N)] [Strong's: 7892]

**Sorrow:** Deep distress and regret. [masc] [AHLB: 1210-A (j)] [Strong's: 3015]

**South country:** An region of land to the south of another area. [masc] [AHLB: 2371 (N)] [Strong's: 5045]

**Sow:** To spread seeds on the ground. [AHLB: 2137 (V)]

[Strong's: 2232]

**Spare:** To forbear to destroy, punish, or harm; give asylum. Give refuge to another. [AHLB: 1176-J (V)] [Strong's: 2347]

**Speak:** A careful arrangement of words or commands said orally. [AHLB: 2093 (V)] [Strong's: 1696]

**Speckled:** The spots marking sheep and goats. [masc] [AHLB: 2431 (c)] [Strong's: 5348]

**Speech:** The chain of words when speaking. [fem] [AHLB: 1288-C (N[1])] [Strong's: 565]

**Spice:** Various aromatic vegetable products used to season or flavor foods. [fem] [AHLB: 1310-E (c$^2$)] [Strong's: 5219]

**Spit upon:** To eject saliva on another. [AHLB: 1457-C (V)] [Strong's: 779]

**Split:** To divide lengthwise. [AHLB: 2606 (V)] [Strong's: 6385, 6386]

**Spoil:** Plunder taken from an enemy in war or robbery. To impair the quality or effect of. [masc] [AHLB: 1472-B (N)] [Strong's: 7998]

**Spot:** A small area visibly different from the surrounding area. To be covered with spots. [AHLB: 1196-E (V)] [Strong's: 2921]

**Spotted:** An animal with white spots which appear as hailstones. [masc] [AHLB: 2037 (c)] [Strong's: 1261]

**Spread wide:** When in the piel form meaning to urge one to take action or entice. [AHLB: 1390-H (V)] [Strong's: 6601]

**Spring:** A source of water issuing from the ground. As the eye of the ground. [masc] [AHLB: 1359-M (a)] [Strong's: 4599]

**Spring up:** To grow up as a plant. [AHLB: 2666 (V)] [Strong's: 6779]

**Sprout:** To send up or out new growth, as of a plant. Sprout green sprouts. [AHLB: 1090-E (V)] [Strong's: 1876]

**Staff:** A walking stick made from the branch of a tree. Also, a tribe as a branch of the family. [masc] [AHLB: 2805 (N)] [Strong's: 7625, 7626]

**Stagger:** To reel from side to side. Wag or shake back and forth or up and down. Also, a wandering as staggering about. [AHLB: 1322-J (V)] [Strong's: 5128]

**Stalk:** The main stem and support of a plant. [masc] [AHLB: 1428-H (N)] [Strong's: 3657, 3661, 7070]

**Stand:** To rise, raise or set in a place. [AHLB: 2550 (V)] [Strong's: 5975, 5976]

**Stand erect:** Vertical in position. Standing upright. To stand erect. To set in place. [AHLB: 2426 (V)] [Strong's: 5324]

**Star:** A natural luminous body visible in the night sky. [masc] [AHLB: 1232-B (g)] [Strong's: 3556]

**Stare:** A careful looking, a close inspection. [AHLB: 2367 (V)] [Strong's: 5027]

**Statement:** A single declaration or remark. [masc] [AHLB: 1288-C (N)] [Strong's: 561]

**Stave:** A branch used as a staff. Also, a tribe as a branch of the family. [masc] [AHLB: 1285-H (N)] [Strong's: 4294]

**Stay the night:** To remain or stay all night. [AHLB: 1267-J (V)] [Strong's: 3885]

**Steal:** To wrongfully take the property of another; rob. [AHLB: 2073 (V)] [Strong's: 1589]

**Sterile:** Failing to produce or incapable of producing offspring, fruit or spores. Being without children in the sense of being plucked of fruit. [masc] [AHLB: 2905 (N)] [Strong's: 6135]

**Stew:** Fish or meat cooked with vegetables. To become agitated or worried. [masc] [AHLB: 2386 (b)] [Strong's: 5138]

**Stink:** To emit a bad odor or be loathsome. [AHLB: 1044-D (V)] [Strong's: 887, 888]

**Stir:** To disturb the quiet of; agitate. [AHLB: 1035-G (V)] [Strong's: 926, 927]

**Stone:** A piece of rock, often in the context of building material. [fem] [AHLB: 1037-C (N)] [Strong's: 68, 69]

**Stoop:** To bend the body forward and downward while bending the knees. Stoop or crouch down by bending or getting on the knees. [AHLB: 2290 (V)] [Strong's: 3766]

**Stop:** To cause to cease. Stop from occurring in the sense of halting, shutting or restraining. [AHLB: 2570 (V)] [Strong's: 6113]

**Stranger:** A foreigner; a person or thing unknown or with whom one is unacquainted. [masc] [AHLB: 1066-A (N)] [Strong's: 1616]

**Straw:** Stalks of grain after threshing; dry, stalky plant residue. When more permanent structures were built, they were constructed of stones and bricks made of clay and straw; replacing the tent panels as the main component of construction for dwellings. [masc] [AHLB: 1037-A (i)] [Strong's: 8401]

**Stream:** A body of running water; any body of flowing water. [masc] [AHLB: 1227-D (N)] [Strong's: 2975]

**Street:** A thoroughfare, especially in a city, town or village wider than an alley. As wide. [fem] [AHLB: 2759 (c)] [Strong's: 7339]

**Strength:** The quality or state of being strong. [masc] [AHLB: 1238-J (N)] [Strong's: 3581]

**Stretch:** To extend in length. Stretch out something. [AHLB: 1308-H (V)] [Strong's: 5186]

**Stretch out:** To lie, stretch out as to rest. [AHLB: 2745 (V)] [Strong's: 7257]

**Strife:** Bitter, sometimes violent conflict or dissension. [masc] [AHLB: 1439-M (N)] [Strong's: 7379]

**Strip:** To remove clothing, covering, or surface matter from. As peeled. [fem] [AHLB: 2626 (N[1])] [Strong's: 6479]

**Striped:** Having stripes or streaks. As appearing to be whipped with a cord. [masc] [AHLB: 2572 (c)] [Strong's: 6124]

**Striped bruise:** Marks made by ropes binding the wrist or lashes with a rope. [fem] [AHLB: 2143 (d[1])] [Strong's:

2250]

**Stroke of time:** A continual beating of time, one moment after the other. Also, a moment in time. [fem] [AHLB: 2623 (N)] [Strong's: 6471]

**Strong:** Having or marked by great physical strength. [masc] [AHLB: 1352-A (N)] [Strong's: 5794]

**Strong One:** Anyone or thing that functions with strength like an ox. This can be a ram or stag (as strong leaders), chief, pillar (as the strong support of a building), or oak tree (one of the strongest of the woods) [masc] [AHLB: 1012-M (N)] [Strong's: 352, 353, 354]

**Subdue:** To conquer and bring into subjection; bring under control. Place the foot on the land in the sense of subduing it. Also, to place one's foot into another nation in the sense of subduing it. [AHLB: 2251 (V)] [Strong's: 3533]

**Submerge:** To hide by burying or to cover. [AHLB: 2234 (V)] [Strong's: 2934]

**Subside:** Become quiet or less. To calm down or set down. [AHLB: 1471-B (V)] [Strong's: 7918]

**Substance:** A fundamental or characteristic part or quality. Any standing thing or person. [masc] [AHLB: 1427-L (d)] [Strong's: 3351]

**Subtle:** Difficult to understand or distinguish. In craftiness or prudence. [masc] [AHLB: 2908 (d)] [Strong's: 6175]

**Suckle:** To give milk to from the breast or udder. [AHLB:

1318-L (V)] [Strong's: 3243]

**Summer:** The season between spring and autumn. [masc] [AHLB: 1432-M (N)] [Strong's: 7007, 7019]

**Summit:** The head, top or beginning of a place, such as a river or mountain, or a time, such as an event. The point at which something starts; origin, principal, foremost, source. [fem] [AHLB: 1458-D (N$^4$)] [Strong's: 7225]

**Sun:** The luminous body around which the earth revolves and from which it receives heat and light. [fem] [AHLB: 2854 (N)] [Strong's: 8121, 8122]

**Support:** To uphold or defend; to hold up or serve as a foundation or prop for. [AHLB: 2488 (V)] [Strong's: 5564]

**Sure:** Safe from danger or harm; marked by or given to feelings of confident certainty. What is firm. [fem] [AHLB: 1290-C (N$^1$)] [Strong's: 545, 546, 548]

**Surely:** In a sure manner. To be firm in something. [masc] [AHLB: 1244-C (N)] [Strong's: 389, 403]

**Sustain:** To provide what is needed to make someone or something whole or complete. [AHLB: 1242-J (V)] [Strong's: 3557]

**Swallow:** To pass through the mouth and move into the esophagus to the stomach. [AHLB: 2020 (V)] [Strong's: 1104]

**Swarm:** To move, as a large mass of creatures. [AHLB: 2881 (V)] [Strong's: 8317]

**Swarmer:** The creature(s) of a large swarm. [masc] [AHLB: 2881 (N)] [Strong's: 8318]

**Swear:** To make or take an oath. [AHLB: 2808 (V)] [Strong's: 7650]

**Swearing:** The act of taking an oath. [fem] [AHLB: 2808 (d$^1$)] [Strong's: 7621]

**Sweat:** To excrete moisture in visible quantities through the pores of the skin. [fem] [AHLB: 1154-A (N$^1$)] [Strong's: 2188]

**Sweet:** Pleasing to the taste. Not sour, bitter or salty. Something that smells pleasing. [masc] [AHLB: 1310-B (bc)] [Strong's: 5207, 5208]

**Swimmer:** The fish of the waters. [fem] [AHLB: 1072-A (N$^1$)] [Strong's: 1710]

**Sword:** A weapon with a long blade for cutting or thrusting. [fem] [AHLB: 2199 (N)] [Strong's: 2719]

**Take:** To receive what is given or to gain possession by seizing. [AHLB: 2319 (V)] [Strong's: 3947]

**Take a fifth:** To separate out one equal portion out of five. [AHLB: 2176 (V)] [Strong's: 2567]

**Take upon:** The placing of a yoke on the shoulders to perform work or undertake a task. [AHLB: 1012-L (V)] [Strong's: 2974]

**Talk:** To deliver or express in spoken words. [AHLB: 1288-B (V)] [Strong's: 4448, 4449]

**Tamarisk:** The tree or a grove of desert shrubs and trees with masses of minute flowers. .

[masc] [AHLB: 1472-C (N)] [Strong's: 815]

**Tambourine:** A shallow, one-headed drum with looses disks at the sides played by shaking, striking with the hand, or rubbing with the thumb. [masc] [AHLB: 1500-J (N)] [Strong's: 8596]

**Taniyn:** A large unknown sea animal. [masc] [AHLB: 1497-A (s)] [Strong's: 8577]

**Tar:** A dark and thick liquid that floats to the surface of water and is used as a waterproof covering for boats. In Aramaic this word means "wine," probably from the dark and thick wine that floats to the surface of the wine vat. [masc] [AHLB: 2175 (N)] [Strong's: 2561, 2562, 2564]

**Task work:** A forced labor or service. [masc] [AHLB: 1291-A (N)] [Strong's: 4522, 4523]

**Tasty food:** Having a marked and pleasing flavor. As a pleasurable thing. [masc] [AHLB: 2528 (a)] [Strong's: 4574]

**Teaching:** Acquired knowledge or skills that mark the direction one is to take in life. A straight direction. Knowledge passed from one person to another. [fem] [AHLB: 1227-H (i$^1$)] [Strong's: 8451]

**Tear:** To rip into pieces. [AHLB: 2734 (V)] [Strong's: 7167]

**Tear away:** To remove reluctantly. [AHLB: 2643 (V)] [Strong's: 6561, 6562]

**Tear into pieces:** To tear into pieces as a predator does to its prey. To rip a cloth into pieces. [AHLB: 2245 (V)]

[Strong's: 2963]

**Ten:** Ten in number. [com] [AHLB: 2563 (N)] [Strong's: 6235, 6236, 6240, 6242, 6243]

**Tender:** Having a soft or yielding texture; easily broken, cut, or damaged. From the tenderness of the loins. [masc] [AHLB: 1448-A (N)] [Strong's: 7390]

**Tent:** The black, goat hair dwelling of the nomad. The shining light of the campfire next to the tent in the distance is a guide for those returning home late, just as a star is used as a guide. [masc] [AHLB: 1104-C (g)] [Strong's: 168]

**Tenth:** The tenth in order. [masc] [AHLB: 2563 (bf)] [Strong's: 6224]

**Tenth one:** That which occupies the tenth position in a sequence. [masc] [AHLB: 2563 (c)] [Strong's: 6218]

**Tenth part:** One portion of a whole divided into ten equal portions. [masc] [AHLB: 2563 (a)] [Strong's: 4643]

**Terminate:** To stop or refrain from continuing an action. [AHLB: 2148 (V)] [Strong's: 2308]

**Terror:** A state of intense fear. [fem] [AHLB: 1220-C (N¹)] [Strong's: 367]

**Test:** A critical examination, observation, or evaluation; trial. [AHLB: 1314-H (V)] [Strong's: 5254]

**That:** The person, thing, or idea indicated, mentioned, or understood from the situation. A close watching. [masc] [AHLB: 1359-A (a)]

[Strong's: 4616]

**That one:** Being the person, thing, or idea specified, mentioned, or understood. [AHLB: 1282-A (N)] [Strong's: 1119, 3644, 3926]

**Then:** An inquiry of a time or place. [AHLB: 1374-C (N)] [Strong's: 645]

**There:** Used to identify another place. [AHLB: 1473-A (N)] [Strong's: 8033, 8536]

**There is:** Something that exists. [masc] [AHLB: 1228-A (N)] [Strong's: 786, 3426]

**These:** The persons, things, or ideas present or near in place, time, or thought or just mentioned. A grammatical tool used to identify something specific in the sense of looking toward a sight. [AHLB: 1104-A (N)] [Strong's: 411, 412, 428, 429, 459, 479]

**They(f):** Those ones. As ones looked toward. [fem] [AHLB: 1093-J (N)] [Strong's: 2007, 3860]

**They(m):** As ones looked toward. [masc] [AHLB: 1093-J (N)] [Strong's: 1992, 1994]

**Thin:** Not dense in distribution; not well-fleshed. [masc] [AHLB: 1456-A (N)] [Strong's: 7534]

**Thing of sacrifice:** An animal killed for an offering. [masc] [AHLB: 2117 (N)] [Strong's: 1685, 2077]

**Think:** To plan or design a course of action, item or invention. [AHLB: 2213 (V)] [Strong's: 2803, 2804]

**Third:** The third within the order. [masc] [AHLB: 2847 (bf)]

[Strong's: 7992, 8523]

**Third generation:** The third increment within the sequence. [masc] [AHLB: 2847 (e)] [Strong's: 8029]

**This:** A person, thing, or idea present or near in place, time, or thought or just mentioned. As prominent or pointed out. [AHLB: 1143-A (N)] [Strong's: 1454, 1668, 1768, 1791, 1797, 1836, 2063, 2088, 2090, 2097, 2098]

**This one:** The one nearer or more immediately under observation or discussion. [fem] [AHLB: 1260-F (N¹)] [Strong's: 1976]

**Thistle:** A prickly plant used by the shepherd to build a corral around the flock at night. [masc] [AHLB: 1089-A (l)] [Strong's: 1863]

**Though:** However; nevertheless. In spite of the fact of. A possible or desired location. To bring attention to an event. [masc] [AHLB: 1106-A (N)] [Strong's: 581, 2004, 2005, 2006, 3861]

**Thought:** The forming of ideas in the mind. [masc] [AHLB: 1411-L (N)] [Strong's: 3336]

**Thousand:** Ten times one hundred in amount or number. [masc] [AHLB: 2001 (N)] [Strong's: 505, 506]

**Thread:** A filament of fibers twisted together by spinning and used for sewing or tying items together. [masc] [AHLB: 1170-J (N)] [Strong's: 2339]

**Three:** A total of three in number or amount. [com] [AHLB: 2847 (c)] [Strong's: 7969,

7970]

**Three days ago:** An idiom for the past. [masc] [AHLB: 2847 (eqp)] [Strong's: 8032]

**Throw:** To propel through the air by a forward motion. throw straight. To drizzle as a throwing down of water. Also, to teach in the sense of throwing or pointing a finger in a straight line as the direction one is to walk. [AHLB: 1227-H (V)] [Strong's: 3384]

**Throw out:** To remove from a place, usually in a sudden or unexpected manner. Cast out, down or away. [AHLB: 2844 (V)] [Strong's: 7993]

**Throw the hand:** To stretch out the hand to grab, as well as to show praise or confession. [AHLB: 1211-H (V)] [Strong's: 1911, 3029, 3034]

**Thrust:** To push or drive with force a pole into the ground, such as when setting up the tent. To blow the trumpet in the sense of throwing out the sound. [AHLB: 2902 (V)] [Strong's: 8628]

**Thus far:** The point beyond which something has not yet proceeded. [masc] [AHLB: 1106-H (N)] [Strong's: 2008]

**Tie:** To fasten, attach, or close by means of a line, ribbon, or cord. Tie around. To "conspire" in the sense of tying up. [AHLB: 2740 (V)] [Strong's: 7194]

**Tie up:** To wrap or fasten. [AHLB: 1342-C (V)] [Strong's: 631]

**Time:** The measured or measurable period during

which an action, process or condition exists or continues. A counting or reckoning of time. [masc] [AHLB: 1290-H (g)] [Strong's: 4489]

**Time of weeping:** A period of sadness or mourning. [fem] [AHLB: 1034-A (N$^4$)] [Strong's: 1068]

**Tired:** Drained of strength and energy; fatigued. [masc] [AHLB: 1362-M (N)] [Strong's: 5889]

**Title:** The name of an individual is more than an identifier but descriptive of his character (which is the breath in Hebrew thought). The character of an individual or place. [masc] [AHLB: 1473-A (N)] [Strong's: 8034, 8036]

**To:** Used as a function word to indicate movement or an action or condition suggestive of progress toward a place, person, or thing reached. A moving to or toward something to be with it, as the ox moves toward a destination. [AHLB: 1104-A (N)] [Strong's: 413]

**Together:** In or into one place, mass, collection, or group. [masc] [AHLB: 1165-L (N)] [Strong's: 3162]

**Toil:** To work hard and long. [masc] [AHLB: 1062-L (b)] [Strong's: 3018, 3019]

**Token:** Something given as a promise as an exchange. [masc] [AHLB: 2573 (j)] [Strong's: 6162]

**Tomorrow:** On or for the day after today. [fem] [AHLB: 1181-A (a$^2$)] [Strong's: 4283]

**Tongue:** A fleshy moveable process on the floor of the mouth used in speaking and eating. The tongue for speaking. Also, language as a tongue. [masc] [AHLB: 2325 (c)] [Strong's: 3956]

**Tooth:** Hard bony appendages on the jaws used for chewing and mastication of food and forming of sounds when talking. [com] [AHLB: 1474-A (N)] [Strong's: 8127, 8128]

**Top of the head:** The crown of the head. [masc] [AHLB: 1418-A (lc)] [Strong's: 6936]

**Torch:** A burning stick of resinous wood. Also, lightning as a torch in the night sky. [masc] [AHLB: 2317 (b)] [Strong's: 3940]

**Torn:** Pulled apart. Flesh that is torn. [fem] [AHLB: 2245 (N$^1$)] [Strong's: 2966]

**Toss:** To heave or fling about; to throw with a quick, light, or careless motion. Be thrown about or wander around as nodding the head. [AHLB: 1303-B (V)] [Strong's: 5074, 5075]

**Touch:** To lay hands upon; to touch or strike. To be touched by a plague. [AHLB: 2376 (V)] [Strong's: 5060]

**Tower:** A structure higher than its diameter and high relative to its surroundings. Place of great size. [masc] [AHLB: 2054 (h)] [Strong's: 4026]

**Trade:** The business of buying and selling or bartering commodities. To go about as a merchant trading goods. In Psalm 38:11 this word is used for the beating of the heart in the sense of going about to and fro. [AHLB: 2473 (V)] [Strong's: 5503]

**Trance:** A state of partly suspended animation or inability to function. A deep sleep or unconsciousness. [fem] [AHLB: 2754 (i$^1$)] [Strong's: 8639]

**Tranquility:** A state of rest. [masc] [AHLB: 1472-H (V)] [Strong's: 7886]

**Tread:** To trample under foot. [AHLB: 2775 (V)] [Strong's: 7429, 7430]

**Tread about:** Usually in the sense of spying. To be on foot walking through a foreign land. Also, to trample another with the tongue. [AHLB: 2749 (V)] [Strong's: 7270, 8637]

**Tread upon:** To step or walk on. [AHLB: 2249 (V)] [Strong's: 3526]

**Treader:** A creature that crawls or creeps on something. [masc] [AHLB: 2775 (N)] [Strong's: 7431]

**Treasure:** Wealth hoarded up or stored. What is hidden. [masc] [AHLB: 2234 (ac)] [Strong's: 4301]

**Tree:** A woody perennial plant with a supporting stem or trunk and multiple branches. tree or the wood from the tree. The singular word is used for one or more. [masc] [AHLB: 1363-A (N)] [Strong's: 636, 6086]

**Tremble:** To shake involuntarily; shiver. [AHLB: 2201 (V)] [Strong's: 2729]

**Trembling:** Shaking involuntarily, shivering. [fem] [AHLB: 2201 (N$^1$)] [Strong's: 2731]

**Trembling in fear:** Also, to be in fear, as if broken. [masc] [AHLB: 1183-A (N)] [Strong's: 2844]

**Tribe:** A social group consisting of numerous families, clans or generations together. A family lineage as bound together. [fem] [AHLB: 1013-J (N$^1$)] [Strong's: 523, 524]

**Trouble:** To agitate mentally or spiritually; worry; disturb. [fem] [AHLB: 1411-A (N$^1$)] [Strong's: 6869]

**Trough:** A long, shallow often V-shaped receptacle for the drinking water or food of domestic animals. [masc] [AHLB: 1446-G (N)] [Strong's: 7298]

**Truth:** The state of being the case. Fact. What is firm. Accurately so. [fem] [AHLB: 1290-C (N$^2$)] [Strong's: 571]

**Tunic:** A simple slip-on garment with or without sleeves. [fem] [AHLB: 2298 (c$^2$)] [Strong's: 3801]

**Turn:** To rotate or revolve. To face another direction. turn the face or to turn directions. To turn something back or away. [AHLB: 1382-H (V)] [Strong's: 6437]

**Turn aside:** To change the location, position, station, or residence of. To remove. [AHLB: 1342-J (V)] [Strong's: 5493, 7787]

**Turn away:** To deviate from the correct path toward another direction. [AHLB: 1342-H (V)] [Strong's: 8280]

**Turn back:** To return to a previous place or state.

[AHLB: 1462-J (V)] [Strong's: 7725, 8421]

**Turn over:** To turn aside in fainting or hiding. [AHLB: 2537 (V)] [Strong's: 5848]

**Turtledove:** A small wild pigeon. [fem] [AHLB: 1503-J (N)] [Strong's: 8449]

**Twilight:** The light from the sky between full night and sunrise; or between sunset and full night. [fem] [AHLB: 2543 (N$^1$)] [Strong's: 5939]

**Twin:** Born with one other or as a pair at birth. [masc] [AHLB: 1496-D (c)] [Strong's: 8380]

**Twist:** A winding or wrapping together; entwined in pain or joy. [AHLB: 1173-J (V)] [Strong's: 2342]

**Two:** From the two major changes of the seasons. A doubling of one. [com] [AHLB: 1474-H (N)] [Strong's: 8147, 8578, 8648]

**Unaware:** Without design, attention, preparation, or premeditation. [masc] [AHLB: 1035-A (f)] [Strong's: 1097]

**Uncircumcised:** A male with a foreskin. [masc] [AHLB: 2577 (N)] [Strong's: 6189]

**Uncover:** To remove the covering. [AHLB: 1365-H (V)] [Strong's: 6168]

**Under:** Beneath. Below or underneath. Also, to be underneath in the sense of being in place of something else. [masc] [AHLB: 2892 (N)] [Strong's: 8478, 8479]

**Understand:** To grasp the meaning of. [AHLB: 1037-M (V)] [Strong's: 995]

**Underworld:** The place of the dead as an unknown place. [com] [AHLB: 1472-D (c)] [Strong's: 7585]

**Unfilled:** Empty. As an empty box that needs to be filled. [masc] [AHLB: 1028-J (r)] [Strong's: 922]

**Unit:** A single quantity regarded as a whole. Unit within the whole, a unified group. [masc] [AHLB: 1165-C (N)] [Strong's: 259]

**Unite:** To put together to form a single unit. [AHLB: 1165-L (V)] [Strong's: 3161]

**Unleavened bread:** A hard and flat bread or cake made without yeast. As a food that can be sucked on. [fem] [AHLB: 1294-B (N$^1$)] [Strong's: 4682]

**Unless:** Except on the condition that. [masc] [AHLB: 1254-B (o)] [Strong's: 3884]

**Until:** A repetition of time either definite or indefinite. The conclusion of a determinate period of time. Another time; once more. [AHLB: 1349-A (N)] [Strong's: 5703, 5704, 5705]

**Uphold:** To give support or to steady. [AHLB: 2895 (V)] [Strong's: 8551]

**Upon:** To be on or over in the sense of the yoke that is placed on the neck of the ox. [AHLB: 1357-A (N)] [Strong's: 5921, 5922]

**Upper:** Higher than the others. [masc] [AHLB: 1357-A (fj)] [Strong's: 5945, 5946]

**Uprising:** Violence in defiance of something. Something that is lifted up such as a burden, gift or flame. [fem] [AHLB:

1314-E (a²)] [Strong's: 4864]

**Upward:** In a direction from lower to higher. [masc] [AHLB: 1357-A (a)] [Strong's: 4605]

**Utterance:** An oral or written statement. [masc] [AHLB: 1312-D (N)] [Strong's: 5002]

**Valiant:** Possessing or acting with bravery or boldness. The mighty power of a bird in flight. Anything or anyone of great mental or physical strength. [masc] [AHLB: 1043-C (b)] [Strong's: 46, 47]

**Valley:** An elongated depression between ranges of hills or mountains. As deep. Obscure, in the sense of dark. [masc] [AHLB: 2553 (N)] [Strong's: 6010, 6012]

**Veil:** To cover, provide, obscure, or conceal with or as if with a cloth. [masc] [AHLB: 2678 (b)] [Strong's: 6809]

**Vessel:** A container for holding an variety of items. [fem] [AHLB: 1028-A (i)] [Strong's: 8392]

**Vigor:** Active bodily or mental strength or force. The power within the belly or loins for reproduction or creative work. [masc] [AHLB: 1014-J (N)] [Strong's: 202]

**Village:** A settlement usually larger than a hamlet and smaller than a town. [fem] [AHLB: 1204-M (N¹)] [Strong's: 2918]

**Vineyard:** A planting of grapevines. [masc] [AHLB: 2288 (N)] [Strong's: 3754]

**Violence:** Exertion of physical force so as to injure or abuse. A violent shaking. [masc]

[AHLB: 2172 (N)] [Strong's: 2555]

**Virgin:** An unmarried young woman who is absolutely chaste. [fem] [AHLB: 2045 (d¹)] [Strong's: 1330]

**Vision:** Something seen in a dream, trance, or ecstasy. [fem] [AHLB: 1168-H (a¹)] [Strong's: 4236]

**Visit:** To meet with another for the purpose of assisting, inspecting or oversee. [AHLB: 2630 (V)] [Strong's: 6485]

**Visualize:** To see or form a mental image of. Dream dreams. [AHLB: 2164 (V)] [Strong's: 2492]

**Voice:** The faculty of utterance. Sound of the shepherd, musical instrument, the wind, thunder, etc. [masc] [AHLB: 1426-J (N)] [Strong's: 6963]

**Vow:** To promise solemnly. [masc] [AHLB: 2385 (N)] [Strong's: 5088]

**Wadi:** The bed or valley of a stream in the Middle East. A choice piece of land desired in an inheritance because of its fertility. [masc] [AHLB: 2391 (N)] [Strong's: 5158]

**Wage:** The reward or price paid for one's labor. [masc] [AHLB: 2479 (N)] [Strong's: 7938, 7939]

**Waist:** The slender part of the body above the hips. Also, an unknown animal, probably from its slender size. [masc] [AHLB: 2363 (N)] [Strong's: 4975]

**Walk:** To move along on foot. Walk a journey. Also, customs as a lifestyle that is walked or lived. [AHLB: 1264-F (V)] [Strong's: 1946, 1980, 1981]

**Wall:** A high thick masonry structure forming an enclosure for defense or protection. What is bored through by the enemy to enter a city. An army, militia or wealth as a wall of protection. [masc] [AHLB: 1173-M (N)] [Strong's: 2426]

**Wander:** To go astray due to deception or influence. [AHLB: 1499-H (V)] [Strong's: 8582]

**Wash:** To cleanse by the application of liquid as water. In Aramaic this word means "trust." [AHLB: 2764 (V)] [Strong's: 7364, 7365]

**Wasteland:** Barren or uncultivated land. [fem] [AHLB: 2199 (N$^1$)] [Strong's: 2723, 2724]

**Watch:** To keep vigil. To keep someone or something under close observation. To expect. [AHLB: 1359-B (V)] [Strong's: 6049]

**Water:** Liquid that descends from the sky as rain, forms streams, lakes and seas, and is a major constituent of all living matter. From the water of the sea, as an unknown place; but, used for all water. [masc] [AHLB: 1281-A (N)] [Strong's: 4325, 7890]

**Watering trough:** A trench for bringing water into the village. A place for domestic animals to quench thirst. [fem] [AHLB: 1479-J (N$^2$)] [Strong's: 8268]

**We:** I and the rest of a group. [com] [Strong's: 580, 586, 587, 5168]

**Weak:** One who dangles the head in poverty or hunger. [masc] [AHLB: 1081-A (N)] [Strong's: 1800]

**Wear Out:** To make useless, especially by long or hard usage. [AHLB: 1035-H (V)] [Strong's: 1086, 1089]

**Weary:** Exhausted in strength, endurance, vigor or freshness. [AHLB: 1258-D (V)] [Strong's: 3811]

**Week:** A period of time consisting of seven days or seven years. [masc] [AHLB: 2808 (d)] [Strong's: 7620]

**Weep:** To express deep sorrow, especially by shedding tears. [AHLB: 1034-H (V)] [Strong's: 1058]

**Weeping:** The act of expressing sorrow by shedding tears. [masc] [AHLB: 1034-A (f)] [Strong's: 1065]

**Weigh:** To ascertain the heaviness of by a balance or scale. Weigh out, usually of silver for payment. [AHLB: 2874 (V)] [Strong's: 8254]

**Weight:** The amount a thing weighs. Relative heaviness. [masc] [AHLB: 2874 (h)] [Strong's: 4948]

**Well:** A dug-out hole, usually a well or cistern. [fem] [AHLB: 1250-D (N)] [Strong's: 875]

**What:** Interrogative expressing inquiry about the identity, nature, or value of an object. Something that is unknown; can also be why, when or how. [AHLB: 1281-A (N)] [Strong's: 3964, 4100, 4101]

**Wheat:** A cereal grain that yields

a fine white flour, the chief ingredient of bread. In the sense of ripening on the stalk. [fem] [AHLB: 2177 (e¹)] [Strong's: 2406, 2591]

**Whelp:** Usually a young lion. [masc] [AHLB: 1066-J (N)] [Strong's: 1482, 1484]

**Where:** At, in, or to what place. Also, an unknown species of animal. [AHLB: 1010-A (N)] [Strong's: 335, 346, 349, 351, 375]

**Wherever:** Anywhere at all. A search for a person, place or time. [masc] [AHLB: 1014-A (N)] [Strong's: 575]

**Which:** Or who, what or that. As a rope attaches two objects together, this word links the action of the sentence to the one doing the action. [AHLB: 1480-C (N)] [Strong's: 834]

**White:** Free from color. [com] [AHLB: 2303 (N)] [Strong's: 3836]

**White bread:** Made with bleached flour. [masc] [AHLB: 1181-J (f)] [Strong's: 2355, 2751]

**Who:** What or which person or persons. Someone that is unknown. [masc] [AHLB: 1286-A (N)] [Strong's: 4310]

**Whole:** Free of wound or injury; free of defect or impairment; having all its proper parts or components. [masc] [AHLB: 1496-B (b)] [Strong's: 8549]

**Why:** For what cause, purpose or reason for which. [masc] [AHLB: 1085-J (a)] [Strong's: 4069]

**Wide:** Having great extent or breadth. [masc] [AHLB: 2759 (N)] [Strong's: 7338, 7342]

**Widen:** To make wide, large or roomy. [AHLB: 2759 (V)] [Strong's: 7337]

**Widow:** A woman who has lost her husband by death. As bound in grief. [fem] [AHLB: 1266-C (m¹)] [Strong's: 490]

**Widowhood:** The quality of being a widow. As bound in grief. [fem] [AHLB: 1266-C (m³)] [Strong's: 491]

**Width:** Largeness of extent or scope. From the width of a road. [masc] [AHLB: 2759 (g)] [Strong's: 7341]

**Wild ass:** A wild animal as prolific. [masc] [AHLB: 1388-E (N)] [Strong's: 6501]

**Wilderness:** A tract or region uncultivated and uninhabited by human beings. Place of order, a sanctuary. [masc] [AHLB: 2093 (h)] [Strong's: 4057]

**Will:** Used to express determination, insistence, persistence, or willfulness. One's desire. From instructions that are written on potsherds. [masc] [AHLB: 1455-H (j)] [Strong's: 7522]

**Wind:** A natural movement of air; breath. The wind of man or god. The breath. A space between in the sense of a wind between. [fem] [AHLB: 1445-J (N)] [Strong's: 7305, 7307]

**Window:** A hole in the wall that admits light and a view of the other side.. [com] [AHLB: 1173-A (j)] [Strong's: 2474]

**Wine:** Fermented juice of fresh grapes. From the mire in the wine. [masc] [AHLB: 1221-M (N)] [Strong's: 3196]

**Wing:** An appendage that allows an animal, bird or insect to fly. Also, the wings of a garment. [fem] [AHLB: 2269 (N)] [Strong's: 3671]

**Winter:** The season between summer and spring. Time of the piercing cold and relative bleakness. [masc] [AHLB: 2208 (g)] [Strong's: 2779]

**Wipe away:** To remove by drying or sweeping away through rubbing. To polish in the sense of a vigorous rubbing; erase. [AHLB: 1284-H (V)] [Strong's: 4229]

**Wise:** Characterized by deep understanding. Also, a wise man. [masc] [AHLB: 2159 (N)] [Strong's: 2450]

**With:** Through the idea of being together in a group. [masc] [AHLB: 1358-M (N)] [Strong's: 5868, 5973, 5974]

**Withdraw:** To take back or away; to turn away or move back. [AHLB: 1163-E (V)] [Strong's: 2244]

**Wither:** To become dry and sapless; to shrivel. [AHLB: 2671 (V)] [Strong's: 6798]

**Withhold:** To hold back from action. [AHLB: 2343 (V)] [Strong's: 4513]

**Within:** In the sense of being close or in the interior of. An approaching. [AHLB: 2729 (N)] [Strong's: 7130, 7131]

**Without:** A lacking of something or the inability to do or have something. The search for a place of unknown origin. [masc] [AHLB: 1014-M (N)] [Strong's: 369, 370, 371]

**Witness:** Attestation of a fact or event; one who gives evidence. [fem] [AHLB: 1349-A (N)] [Strong's: 5707]

**Wolf:** A yellowish colored animal. [masc] [AHLB: 1140-D (N)] [Strong's: 2061]

**Woman:** An adult female person. As mortal. [fem] [AHLB: 2003 (b¹)] [Strong's: 802]

**Womb:** An organ where something is generated or grows before birth. [fem] [AHLB: 2015 (N)] [Strong's: 990]

**Word:** An arrangement of words, ideas or concepts to form sentences. A plague as a thing. [masc] [AHLB: 2093 (N)] [Strong's: 1697, 1698]

**Work:** Activity where one exerts strength or faculties to do or perform something. A work or action. [masc] [AHLB: 1360-H (a)] [Strong's: 4639]

**Would that:** In the sense of joining. A yearning for certain direction or action. [AHLB: 1254-J (N)] [Strong's: 3863]

**Wrap:** To envelop and secure for transport or storage. Also, meaning to faint. [AHLB: 2547 (V)] [Strong's: 5968]

**Wrap around:** [AHLB: 1349-J (V)] [Strong's: 5749]

**Wrath:** Strong vengeful anger. As crossing over from peace. [fem] [AHLB: 2520 (N¹)] [Strong's: 5678, 5679]

**Wrestle:** To contend by grappling with to throw one's opponent off balance. [masc] [AHLB: 3034] [Strong's: 5319]

**Wrist:** The joint between the hand and arm. Also, a garment with sleeves that reaches to the wrist. [masc] [AHLB: 1383-A (N)] [Strong's: 6446, 6447]

**Yard:** The grounds of a building or group of buildings. villages outside of the larger cities, as "the yard of the city." A courtyard as outside the house. [masc] [AHLB: 2197 (N)] [Strong's: 2691]

**Year:** The period of around 365 solar days. In the sense of repeating. [fem] [AHLB: 1474-A (N$^1$)] [Strong's: 8140, 8141]

**Yearning:** To long persistently, wistfully, or sadly. What is desired, whether good or bad. [fem] [AHLB: 1005-J (i$^1$)] [Strong's: 8378]

**Yesterday:** On the day last past. A time that is before. [masc] [AHLB: 1288-J (i)] [Strong's: 8543]

**Yet again:** A repeating of something. [masc] [AHLB: 1349-J (N)] [Strong's: 5750, 5751]

**Yield:** To produce or be productive. [AHLB: 2070 (V)] [Strong's: 1580]

**Yoke:** A wooden bar or frame by which two draft animals are joined at the heads or necks for working together. [masc] [AHLB: 1357-J (N)] [Strong's: 5923]

**You(fs):** Pronoun, second person, feminine singular [fem] [Strong's: 859]

**You(mp):** Pronoun, second person, masculine plural [masc] [Strong's: ?]

**You(ms):** Pronoun, second person, masculine singular [masc] [Strong's: 607, 608]

**Young age:** A young person. [fem] [AHLB: 2418 (d)] [Strong's: 5271]

**Young maiden:** A young female of marriageable age or newly married as at the prime age for work. [fem] [AHLB: 1357-A (p$^1$)] [Strong's: 5959]

**Young man:** A male that has moved from youth to young adulthood. [masc] [AHLB: 2418 (N)] [Strong's: 5288, 5289]

**Young pigeon:** A young featherless bird as plucked. [masc] [AHLB: 2059 (g)] [Strong's: 1469]

**Young woman:** A female that has moved from youth to young adulthood [fem] [AHLB: 2418 (N$^1$)] [Strong's: 5291]

**Youthfulness:** Young acting no matter the age. [fem] [AHLB: 2680 (b$^1$)] [Strong's: 6812]

# Prefixes, Suffixes and Conjugations

**!(fp)~:** Feminine plural imperative verb.

**!(fs)~:** Feminine singular imperative verb.

**!(mp)~:** Masculine plural imperative verb.

**!(ms)~:** Masculine singular imperative verb.

**?~:** The interrogative hey converting the sentence into a question.

**~&:** Paragogic Nun; added to the ordinary forms of words, to express additional emphasis, or some change in the sense.

**~^:** Paragogic Hey; added to the ordinary forms of words, to express additional emphasis, or some change in the sense.

**~ed(fp):** Feminine plural verb passive participle denoting an action (such as baked).

**~ed(fs):** Feminine singular verb passive participle denoting an action (such as baked).

**~ed(mp):** Masculine plural verb passive participle denoting an action (such as baked).

**~ed(ms):** Masculine singular verb passive participle denoting an action (such as baked).

**~her:** Third person feminine singular pronoun (her) also used as a possessive pronoun (of him or his).

**~him:** Third person masculine singular pronoun (him) also used as a possessive pronoun (of him or his).

**~ing(fp):** Feminine plural verb participle denoting an action (such as baking) or one of action (such as a baker).

**~ing(fs):** Feminine singular verb participle denoting an action (such as baking) or one of action (such as a baker).

**~ing(mp):** Masculine plural verb participle denoting an action (such as baking) or one of action (such as a baker).

**~ing(ms):** Masculine singular verb participle denoting an action (such as baking) or one of action (such as a baker).

**~me:** First person common singular pronoun (me), also used as a possessive pronoun (of me or my).

**~of:** Identifies the noun as possessive.

**~s:** Identifies the noun as a quantitative or qualitative plural.

**~s2:** Identifies the noun as a dual plural.

**~them(f):** Third person feminine plural pronoun (them) also used as a possessive pronoun (of them or their).

**~them(m):** Third person masculine plural pronoun (them) also used as a possessive pronoun (of them or their).

**~unto:** Directional Hey; implies movement toward the location identified in the word this suffix is attached to.

**~us:** First person common plural pronoun (we), also used as a possessive pronoun (of us or our).

**~you(fp):** Second person feminine plural pronoun (you), also used as a possessive pronoun

369

(of you or your).

~**you(fs):** Second person feminine singular pronoun (you), alsoused as a possessive pronoun (of you or your).

~**you(mp):** Second person masculine plural pronoun (you), also used as a possessive pronoun (of you or your).

~**you(ms):** Second person masculine singular pronoun (you), also used as a possessive pronoun (of you or your).

>~: Identifies the verb as infinitive.

**and**~: The conjunction meaning and. Often used as the vav consecutive meaning that when prefixed to a verb it will usually reverse the tense of the verb.

**be**~: Identifies the verb as a Niphal (passive).

**did**~: Identifies the verb as perfect tense.

**from**~: A preposition meaning from.

**had**~: Identifies the verb as past perfect.

**he**~: Identifies the subject of the verb as third person masculine singular.

i~: Identifies the subject of the verb as first person common singular.

**in**~: A preposition meaning in or with.

**like**~: A preposition meaning like.

**make be**~: Identifies the verb as a Hophal (passive causative).

**make**~: Identifies the verb as a

Hiphil (active causative).

**much be**~: Identifies the verb as a Pual (passive intensive).

**much**~: Identifies the verb as a Piel (active intensive).

**self**~: Identifies the verb as Hitpael (reflexive).

**she**~: Identifies the subject of the verb as third person feminine singular.

**the**~: The definite article meaning "the".

**they(f)**~: Identifies the subject of the verb as third person feminine singular.

**they(m)**~: Identifies the subject of the verb as third person masculine plural.

**they**~: Identifies the subject of the verb as third person common plural.

**to**~: A preposition meaning to or for.

**we**~: Identifies the subject of the verb as first person common plural.

**which**~: A preposition meaning which or who.

**will**~: Identifies the verb as imperfect tense.

**you(fp)**~: Identifies the subject of the verb as third person masculine plural.

**you(fs)**~: Identifies the subject of the verb as second person feminine singular.

**you(mp)**~: Identifies the subject of the verb as second person masculine plural.

**you(ms)**~: Identifies the subject of the verb as second person masculine singular.

# Names

**Adah** [*Ornament*]: [Strong's: 5711]

**Adbe'el** [*Grief of El*]: [Strong's: 110]

**Admah** [*Red ground*]: Or Adamah [Strong's: 126]

**Adonai** [*My lords*]: [Strong's: 136]

**Adulam** [*Witness of the people*]: [Strong's: 5726]

**Ahalivamah** [*Tent of the high place*]: [Strong's: 173]

**Ahhuzat** [*Holdings*]: [Strong's: 276]

**Akad** [*Jar*]: Can also mean spark. The actual meaning is uncertain. [Strong's: 390]

**Akhbor** [*Mouse*]: [Strong's: 5907]

**Almodad** [*El of measure*]: The origins of modad is uncertain. [Strong's: 486]

**Alon-Bakhut** [*Oak of weeping*]: [Strong's: 439]

**Alwah** [*Wicked*]: [Strong's: 5933]

**Alwan** [*Tall*]: [Strong's: 5935]

**Amaleq** [*People gathered*]: [Strong's: 6002, 6003]

**Amon** [*Tribe*]: [Strong's: 5983]

**Amraphel** [*Speaker of judgement*]: Can also mean One that speaks of secrets, Sayer of darkness or Fall of the sayer. [Strong's: 569]

**Anah** [*Answer*]: [Strong's: 6034]

**Anam** [*Affliction of water*]: [Strong's: 6047]

**Aner** [*Answer*]: Meaning and origin are uncertain. [Strong's: 6063]

**Aqan** [*Sharp sighted*]: [Strong's: 6130]

**Aram** [*Palace*]: From a root meaning a high place such as used for building palaces and forts. [Strong's: 758]

**Aram-Nahhara'im** [*Palace of two rivers*]: [Strong's: 763]

**Aran** [*Joyous*]: [Strong's: 765]

**Araq** [*Gnawing*]: [Strong's: 6208]

**Ararat** [*Curse*]: meaning uncertain [Strong's: 780]

**Ared** [*I subdue*]: Can also mean I go down. [Strong's: 714]

**Areliy** [*Order of my El*]: [Strong's: 692]

**Arodiy** [*My roaming*]: [Strong's: 722]

**Arpakhshad** [*I will fail the breast*]: The meaning of the word rapak is uncertain. [Strong's: 775]

**Arwad** [*I will preside over*]: [Strong's: 721]

**Aryokh** [*Tall*]: From a root meaning long. [Strong's: 746]

**Ashbeyl** [*Fire flowing*]: Can also mean Fire of Bel. [Strong's: 788]

**Asher** [*Happy*]: [Strong's: 836]

**Ashkanaz** [*Fire spread*]: [Strong's: 813]

**Ashterot-Qaraniym** [*Growths of two horns*]: [Strong's: 6255]

**Ashur** [*Step*]: [Strong's: 804]

**Asnat** [*Belonging to Nat*]: [Strong's: 621]

**Aveyl-Mitsrayim** [*Mourning of Mitsrayim*]: [Strong's: 67]

**Avida** [*My father knows*]: [Strong's: 28]

**Aviyma'el** [*My father is from El*]: [Strong's: 39]

**Aviymelekh** [*My father is king*]: Can also mean Father of the king [Strong's: 40]

**Avraham** [*Father lifted*]: [Strong's: 85]

**Avram** [*Father raised*]: [Strong's: 87]

**Awit** [*Crooked*]: [Strong's: 5762]

**Ay** [*Heap of ruins*]: [Strong's: 5857]

**Ayah** [*Falcon*]: [Strong's: 345]

**Ba'al-Hhanan** [*Master of beauty*]: Can also mean Ba'al is Beauty [Strong's: 1177]

**Basmat** [*Spice*]: [Strong's: 1315]

**Batsrah** [*Sheepfold*]: [Strong's: 1224]

**Bavel** [*Confusion*]: From a root meaning to mix up. [Strong's: 894]

**Bedad** [*Solitary*]: [Strong's: 911]

**Be'eri** [*My well*]: [Strong's: 882]

**Be'er-Lahhiy-Ro'iy** [*Well for the living seeing me*]: [Strong's: 883]

**Bekher** [*Young camel*]: [Strong's: 1071]

**Bela** [*Swallow*]: [Strong's: 1106]

**Ben-Amiy** [*Son of my people*]: [Strong's: 1151]

**Ben-Oni** [*Son of my sorrow*]: [Strong's: 1126]

**Be'or** [*Burning*]: [Strong's: 1160]

**Bera** [*With dysfunction*]: Can also mean With shouting, Son of evil, A well or Declaring. Meaning and origin are uncertain. [Strong's: 1298]

**Bered** [*Hail*]: [Strong's: 1260]

**Beri'ah** [*With a companion*]: [Strong's: 1283]

**B'er-Sheva** [*Well of oath*]: [Strong's: 884]

**Betu'el** [*Destruction of El*]: [Strong's: 1328]

**Beyt-El** [*House of El*]: [Strong's: 1008]

**Beyt-Lehhem** [*House of bread*]: [Strong's: 1035]

**Bilhah** [*Wear out*]: [Strong's: 1090]

**Bilhan** [*Worn out*]: [Strong's: 1092]

**Binyamin** [*Son of the right hand*]: [Strong's: 1144]

**Birsha** [*With wickedness*]: [Strong's: 1306]

**Buz** [*Despise*]: [Strong's: 938]

**Dameseq** [*Blood sack*]: [Strong's: 1834]

**Dan** [*Moderator*]: [Strong's: 1835]

**Dedan** [*Friendship*]: Can also mean breasts or judge from the root DN. [Strong's: 1719]

**Devorah** [*Bee*]: [Strong's: 1683]

**Dinah** [*Judgement*]: [Strong's: 1783]

**Dinhavah** [*Give judgement*]: [Strong's: 1838]

**Diqlah** [*Palm grove*]: Meaning and origin are uncertain. [Strong's: 1853]

**Dishan** [*Thresher*]: [Strong's: 1789]

**Dishon** [*Threshing*]: [Strong's: 1787]

**Dodan** [*Passion*]: Can also mean friendship, breast or judge from the root DN. [Strong's: 1721]

**Dotan** [*Well*]: [Strong's: 1886]

**Dumah** [*Silence*]: [Strong's: 1746]

**Eden** [*Pleasure*]: [Strong's: 5731]

**Edom** [*Red*]: [Strong's: 123]

**Elam** [*Ancient*]: [Strong's: 5867]

**Elasar** [*El is noble*]: Can also mean Mighty one is chastiser or Revolting from mighty one. [Strong's: 495]

**El-Beyt-El** [*El of Beyt El*]: [Strong's: 416]

**Elda'ah** [*El knows*]: [Strong's: 420]

**El-Elohey-Yisra'el** [*El of the powers of Yisra'el*]: [Strong's: 415]

**Eliezer** [*My El is a helper*]: Can also mean Mighty one of help [Strong's: 461]

**Eliphaz** [*My El is pure gold*]: [Strong's: 464]

**Elishah** [*El of help*]: Meaning of the word shah is uncertain. [Strong's: 473]

**Elohiym** [*Powers*]: [Strong's: 430]

**El-Ra'iy** [*El seeing me*]: [Strong's: n/a]

**Emor** [*Sayer*]: [Strong's: 567]

**Enosh** [*Man*]: [Strong's: 583]

**Epher** [*Calf*]: [Strong's: 6081]

**Ephrat** [*Fruitful*]: [Strong's: 672]

**Ephrayim** [*Double fruitfulness*]: [Strong's: 669]

**Ephron** [*Powdery*]: [Strong's: 6085]

**Erekh** [*long*]: [Strong's: 751]

**Esav** [*Doing*]: [Strong's: 6215]

**Eseq** [*Quarrel*]: [Strong's: 6230]

**Eshban** [*Fire of understanding*]: [Strong's: 790]

**Eshkol** [*Cluster*]: [Strong's: 812]

**Etsbon** [*I swell*]: [Strong's: 675]

**Ever** [*Cross over*]: [Strong's: 5677, 5680]

**Eyhhiy** [*My brother*]: [Strong's: 278]

**Eylah** [*Oak*]: [Strong's: 425]

**Eylon** [*Strength*]: [Strong's: 356]

**Eyl-Paran** [*Post of decoration*]: The word Eyl can also mean ram, hart, tree, lintel, oak, mighty or strength. [Strong's: 364]

**Eym** [*Terror*]: [Strong's: 368]

**Eynayim** [*Double spring*]: [Strong's: 5879]

**Eyn-Mishpat** [*Eye of judgement*]: Can also mean Spring of judgement. [Strong's: 5880]

**Eyphah** [*Darkness*]: [Strong's: 5891]

**Eyr** [*Awake*]: [Strong's: 6147]

**Eyriy** [*My city*]: [Strong's: 6179]

**Eytser** [*Restraint*]: [Strong's: 687]

**Eyval** [*Stone*]: [Strong's: 5858]

**Gad** [*Fortune*]: [Strong's: 1410]

**Gahham** [*Burning*]: [Strong's: 1514]

**Galeyd** [*Mound of witness*]: [Strong's: 1567]

**Gatam** [*Burnt valley*]: [Strong's: 1609]

**Gera** [*Grain*]: [Strong's: 1617]

**Gerar** [*Chew*]: [Strong's: 1642]

**Gershon** [*Exile*]: [Strong's: 1648]

**Getar** [*Fear*]: Can also mean The vale of trial or searching. [Strong's: 1666]

**Ghamorah** [*Rebellion*]: Can also mean submersion. [Strong's: 6017]

**Ghaza** [*Strong*]: [Strong's: 5804]

**Ghir** [*City*]: [Strong's: 5893]

**Gil'ad** [*Mound of witness*]: [Strong's: 1568]

**Girgash** [*Stranger on clods*]: Can also mean dwelling on clay soil. [Strong's: 1622]

**Giyhhon** [*Burst*]: [Strong's: 1521]

**Gomer** [*Complete*]: [Strong's: 1586]

**Goren-Ha'atad** [*Threshing floor of the brambles*]: [Strong's: 329]

**Goshen** [*Draw near*]: [Strong's: 1657]

**Goyim** [*Nations*]: [Strong's: 1471]

**Guni** [*My protection*]: [Strong's: 1476]

**Hadad** [*The beloved*]: [Strong's: 1908]

**Hadar** [*Honor*]: [Strong's: 1924]

**Hadoram** [*Honor*]: [Strong's: 1913]

**Hagar** [*Stranger*]: Meaning and origin are uncertain. [Strong's: 1904]

**Ham** [*Roar*]: From a root meaning the roar of the sea. [Strong's: 1990]

**Hamitspah** [*Watchtower*]: [Strong's: 4709]

**Haran** [*Hill country*]: [Strong's: 2039]

**Hevel** [*Empty*]: [Strong's: 1893]

**Heymam** [*Exterminating*]: [Strong's: 1967]

**Hhadar** [*Chamber*]: [Strong's: 2316]

**Hhagi** [*Festive*]: may also mean my feast. [Strong's: 2291]

**Hham** [*Hot*]: [Strong's: 2526]

**Hhamat** [*Fortress*]: Can also mean heat, anger or wall. [Strong's: 2577]

**Hhamor** [*Donkey*]: [Strong's: 2544]

**Hhamul** [*Compassion*]: [Strong's: 2538]

**Hhanokh** [*Dedicated*]: [Strong's: 2585]

**Hharan** [*Burning*]: [Strong's: 2771]

**Hhatsarmawet** [*Yard of death*]: [Strong's: 2700]

**Hhats'tson-Tamar** [*Dividing the palm tree*]: [Strong's: 2688]

**Hhawah** [*Living*]: [Strong's: 2332]

**Hhawilah** [*Twisting*]: May have the meaning of suffers pain from the idea of twisting. [Strong's: 2341]

**Hhazo** [*Vision*]: [Strong's: 2375]

**Hhemdan** [*Desirable*]: [Strong's: 2533]

**Hhet** [*Shattered*]: [Strong's: 2845, 2850]

**Hhetsron** [*Surrounded by a wall*]: [Strong's: 2696]

**Hhever** [*Companion*]: [Strong's: 2268]

**Hhevron** [*Company*]: [Strong's: 2275]

**Hhideqel** [*Rapid*]: [Strong's: 2313]

**Hhiw** [*Village*]: [Strong's: 2340]

**Hhiyrah** [*Bleached white*]: [Strong's: 2437]

**Hhor** [*Cave Dweller*]: [Strong's: 2752]

**Hhoriy** [*Cave dweller*]: [Strong's: 2753]

**Hhovah** [*Hiding place*]: From a root meaning bosom as a place of refuge. [Strong's: 2327]

**Hhul** [*Twist*]: [Strong's: 2343]

**Hhupim** [*Shores*]: [Strong's: 2650]

**Hhush** [*Making haste*]: [Strong's: 2366]

**Hhusham** [*Haste*]: [Strong's: 2367]

**Irad** [*Wild donkey*]: [Strong's: 5897]

**Iyram** [*Their city*]: [Strong's: 5902]

**Kadesh** [*Set apart*]: [Strong's: 6946]

**Kalahh** [*Old age*]: [Strong's: 3625]

**Kalneh** [*Consummation*]: [Strong's: 3641]

**Kaphtor** [*Knob*]: [Strong's: 3732]

**Karmi** [*My vineyard*]: [Strong's: 3756]

**Kasluhh** [*Fortified*]: Can also mean hopes of life. Meaning and origin are uncertain. [Strong's: 3695]

**Kedarla'omer** [*Attack for sheaves*]: [Strong's: 3540]

**Kena'an** [*Lowered*]: [Strong's: 3667, 3669]

**Keran** [*Lyre*]: [Strong's: 3763]

**Keruv** [*Sword*]: [Strong's: 3742]

**Kesad** [*Clod breaker*]: Appears to be the prefix K meaning like and the root SD meaning level field - like a level field. [Strong's: 3777, 3778]

**Keziv** [*False*]: [Strong's: 3580]

**Kit** [*Bruiser*]: Can also mean breaking or bruising. Meaning and origin are uncertain. [Strong's: 3794]

**Kush** [*Black*]: [Strong's: 3568]

**Lamekh** [*Powerful*]: Can also mean suffering. Meaning and origin are uncertain. [Strong's: 3929]

**Lavan** [*White*]: [Strong's: 3837]

**Le'ah** [*Weary*]: [Strong's: 3812]

**Lehav** [*Flame*]: [Strong's: 3853]

**Lesha** [*Fissure*]: [Strong's: 3962]

**Lethush** [*Sharpened*]: [Strong's: 3912]

**Le'um** [*Peoples*]: [Strong's: 3817]

**Lewi** [*Joined*]: [Strong's: 3878]

**Loth** [*Covering*]: [Strong's: 3876]

**Lothan** [*Covering*]: [Strong's: 3877]

**Lud** [*Birth*]: Can also mean nativity or generation. [Strong's: 3865, 3866]

**Luz** [*Almond*]: [Strong's: 3870]

**Ma'akhah** [*Cursing*]: [Strong's: 4601]

**Maday** [*Measure*]: Can also mean measure, judging, habit or covering. [Strong's: 4074]

**Magdi'eyl** [*Prince of El*]: [Strong's: 4025]

**Magog** [*Roof*]: [Strong's: 4031]

**Mahalalel** [*Praise of El*]: [Strong's: 4111]

**Mahhalat** [*Stringed instrument*]: [Strong's: 4257]

**Mahhanayim** [*Two camps*]: [Strong's: 4266]

**Makhir** [*Sold*]: [Strong's: 4353]

**Makhpelah** [*Double*]: [Strong's: 4375]

**Malki'el** [*My king is El*]: [Strong's: 4439]

**Malkiy-Tsedeq** [*King of righteousness*]: Can also mean My king is Tsedeq or My king is righteousness. [Strong's: 4442]

**Mamre** [*Bitter place*]: Can also mean rebellious. From a root meaning bitter. [Strong's: 4471]

**Manahhat** [*Rest*]: [Strong's: 4506]

**Masa** [*Burden*]: [Strong's: 4854]

**Mash** [*Drawn out*]: [Strong's: 4851]

**Masreyqah** [*Choice vine*]: [Strong's: 4957]

**Mathreyd** [*Driven*]: [Strong's: 4308]

**Medan** [*Quarrel*]: [Strong's: 4091]

**Meheythaveyl** [*Favored of El*]: [Strong's: 4105]

**Mehhuya'el** [*Who proclaims El*]: [Strong's: 4232]

**Menasheh** [*Causing to overlook*]: [Strong's: 4519]

**Merari** [*Bitter*]: [Strong's: 4847]

**Mesha** [*Storm*]: [Strong's: 4852]

**Meshek** [*Draw out*]: [Strong's: 4902]

**Metusha'el [*His death asks*]:** Can also mean Their death asks. [Strong's: 4967]

**Metushelahh [*His death sends*]:** Can also be Their death sends. [Strong's: 4968]

**Mey-Zahav [*Water of gold*]:** [Strong's: 4314]

**Midian [*Strife*]:** [Strong's: 4080]

**Migdal-Eyder [*Tower of the flock*]:** [Strong's: 4029]

**Milkah [*Queen*]:** [Strong's: 4435]

**Mishma [*Hearing*]:** [Strong's: 4927]

**Mitsrayim [*Troubles*]:** [Strong's: 4713, 4714]

**Mivsam [*Sweet odor*]:** [Strong's: 4017]

**Mivtsar [*Fortress*]:** [Strong's: 4014]

**Miz'zah [*Faint*]:** Or may mean fear. [Strong's: 4199]

**Mo'av [*From father*]:** [Strong's: 4124]

**Moreh [*Teacher*]:** Can also mean rain. [Strong's: 4176]

**Moriyah [*Appearance of Yah*]:** Can also mean seen of Yah, chosen of Yah, seeing Yah [Strong's: 4232]

**Mupim [*Serpents*]:** [Strong's: 4649]

**Na'amah [*Sweet*]:** [Strong's: 5279]

**Na'aman [*Pleasantness*]:** [Strong's: 5283]

**Nahhat [*Rest*]:** [Strong's: 5184]

**Nahhor [*Snorting*]:** [Strong's: 5152]

**Naphish [*Refreshed*]:** [Strong's: 5305]

**Naphtali [*Wrestling*]:** [Strong's: 5321]

**Naphtuhh [*Opening*]:** [Strong's: 5320]

**Nephilim [*Fallen ones*]:** [Strong's: 5303]

**Nevayot [*Flourishings*]:** [Strong's: 5032]

**Nimrod [*Rebellion*]:** [Strong's: 5248]

**Ninweh [*Agreeable*]:** Can also mean handsome. Meaning and origin are uncertain. [Strong's: 5210]

**No'ahh [*Rest*]:** [Strong's: 5146]

**Nod [*Wander*]:** [Strong's: 5113]

**Ohad [*Shouting*]:** [Strong's: 161]

**Omar [*Speaker*]:** [Strong's: 201]

**On [*Vigor*]:** [Strong's: 204]

**Onam [*Vigorous*]:** [Strong's: 208]

**Onan [*Strong*]:** [Strong's: 209]

**Ophir [*Reduced to ashes*]:** From a root meaning ashes, dust or powder. [Strong's: 211]

**Padan [*Field*]:** [Strong's: 6307]

**Padan-Aram [*Field palace*]:** [Strong's: 6307]

**Palu [*Distinguished*]:** [Strong's: 6396]

**Paran [*Decoration*]:** [Strong's: 6290]

**Paroh [*Great house*]:** [Strong's: 6547]

**Patros [*Mouthful of dough*]:** Can also mean persuasion of ruin. [Strong's: 6255]

**Pa'u [*Screaming*]:** [Strong's: 6464]

**Peleg [*Half*]:** [Strong's: 6389]

**Peleshet [*Immigrant*]:** [Strong's: 6430]

**Peni'el [*Face of El*]:** [Strong's: 6439]

**Perat [*Break*]:** [Strong's: 6578]

**Perets [*Breach*]:** [Strong's: 6557]

**Perez [*Peasant*]:** Meaning one who dwells in a village. [Strong's: 6522]

**Pikhol [*Face of all*]:** [Strong's: 6369]

376

**Pildash** [*Bean thresher*]: [Strong's: 6394]

**Pinon** [*Darkness*]: [Strong's: 6373]

**Pishon** [*Scatter*]: [Strong's: 6376]

**Pothee-Phera** [*He whom the Ra gave*]: [Strong's: 6319]

**Potiphar** [*Belonging to the sun*]: [Strong's: 6318]

**Pu'ah** [*Dispersion*]: [Strong's: 6312]

**Puth** [*Bow*]: Meaning and origin are uncertain. [Strong's: 6316]

**Qadmon** [*Ancient one*]: Can also mean Easterner. [Strong's: 6935]

**Qayin** [*Acquired*]: [Strong's: 7014, 7017, 8423]

**Qedar** [*Dark*]: [Strong's: 6938]

**Qedmah** [*Original*]: [Strong's: 6929]

**Qehat** [*Assembly*]: [Strong's: 6955]

**Qemu'el** [*Raised of El*]: [Strong's: 7055]

**Qeniz** [*Hunter*]: [Strong's: 7073, 7074]

**Qethurah** [*Incense*]: [Strong's: 6989]

**Qeynan** [*Possession*]: [Strong's: 7018]

**Qiryat-Arba** [*City of four*]: [Strong's: 7153]

**Qorahh** [*Bald*]: [Strong's: 7141]

**Rahhel** [*Ewe*]: [Strong's: 7354]

**Ramah** [*Mane of a horse*]: [Strong's: 7484]

**Ra'meses** [*Child of the sun*]: [Strong's: 7486]

**Rapha** [*Heal*]: [Strong's: 7497]

**Rehhovot** [*Wide streets*]: [Strong's: 7344]

**Rehhovot-Ghir** [*Wide streets of the city*]: [Strong's: 7344, 5892]

**Resen** [*Halter*]: [Strong's: 7449]

**Re'u** [*Companion*]: [Strong's: 7466]

**Re'u'el** [*Companion of El*]: [Strong's: 7467]

**Re'umah** [*Lifted up*]: [Strong's: 7208]

**Re'uven** [*See a son*]: [Strong's: 7205]

**Riphat** [*Health*]: Can also mean remedy, medicine, release or pardon. [Strong's: 7384]

**Rivqah** [*Ensnarer*]: [Strong's: 7259]

**Rosh** [*Head*]: [Strong's: 7220]

**Samlah** [*Garment*]: [Strong's: 8072]

**Sarah** [*Noblewoman*]: [Strong's: 8297]

**Sarai** [*Princess*]: From a root meaning to turn the head. [Strong's: 8283]

**Savtah** [*Go about*]: [Strong's: 5454]

**Savteka** [*Lead around*]: [Strong's: 5455]

**Sedom** [*Secret*]: Can also mean burning or cement. Meaning and origin are uncertain. [Strong's: 5467]

**Se'iyr** [*Hairy*]: [Strong's: 8165]

**Sephar** [*Numbering*]: [Strong's: 5611]

**Serahh** [*Excess*]: [Strong's: 8294]

**Sered** [*Remnant*]: [Strong's: 5624]

**Serug** [*Branch*]: From a root meaning to be intertwined. [Strong's: 8286]

**Seva** [*Drunkard*]: [Strong's: 5434]

**Shaddai** [*My breasts*]: [Strong's: 7706]

**Shalem** [*Complete*]: [Strong's: 8004]

**Sham'mah** [*Desolate*]: [Strong's: 8048]

**Sha'ul** [*Unknown*]: [Strong's: 7586]

**Shaweh** [*Plain*]: [Strong's: 7740]

**Shaweh-Qiryatayim** [*Plain of cities*]: [Strong's: 7741]

**Shekhem** [*Shoulder*]: [Strong's: 7927]

**Shelahh** [*Sent*]: [Strong's: 7974]

**Sheleph** [*Pull*]: [Strong's: 8026]

**Shem** [*Character*]: [Strong's: 8035]

**Shemever** [*Character of wing*]: Can also mean lofty flight. [Strong's: 8038]

**Shepho** [*Bare place*]: [Strong's: 8195]

**Shet** [*Buttocks*]: [Strong's: 8352]

**Sheva** [*Seven*]: [Strong's: 7614]

**Sheylah** [*Petition*]: [Strong's: 7956]

**Shilem** [*Repaid*]: [Strong's: 8006]

**Shimon** [*Heard*]: [Strong's: 8095]

**Shimron** [*Watched*]: [Strong's: 8110]

**Shinar** [*Country of two rivers*]: Can also mean sleeps [Strong's: 8152]

**Shinav** [*Teeth of father*]: Can also mean Changing father or Splendour of father. [Strong's: 8134]

**Shivah** [*Oath*]: [Strong's: 7656]

**Shoval** [*Leg*]: [Strong's: 7732]

**Shu'a** [*Wealthy*]: [Strong's: 7770]

**Shu'ahh** [*Sinking*]: [Strong's: 7744]

**Shuni** [*Sleep*]: May also mean my sleep. [Strong's: 7764]

**Shur** [*Caravan*]: [Strong's: 7793]

**Sidim** [*Fields*]: [Strong's: 7708]

**Sin** [*Thorn*]: [Strong's: 5513]

**Sithnah** [*Accusation*]: [Strong's: 7856]

**Sukot** [*Booths*]: [Strong's: 5523]

**Tahhash** [*Badger*]: [Strong's: 8477]

**Tamar** [*Palm tree*]: [Strong's: 8559]

**Tarshish** [*Contemplate*]: [Strong's: 8659]

**Terahh** [*Station*]: [Strong's: 8646]

**Teyma** [*Wonder*]: Can also mean Desert. [Strong's: 8485]

**Teyman** [*South*]: [Strong's: 8487, 8489]

**Thevahh** [*Slaughtering*]: [Strong's: 2875]

**Tidal** [*Breaker of the yoke*]: Meaning and origin are uncertain. [Strong's: 8413]

**Timna** [*Withhold*]: [Strong's: 8555]

**Timnat** [*Portion*]: [Strong's: 8553]

**Tiras** [*Breaking*]: Meaning and origin are uncertain. [Strong's: 8494]

**Togarmah** [*Gnaw a bone*]: [Strong's: 8425]

**Tola** [*Worm*]: [Strong's: 8439]

**Tsaphnat-Paneyahh** [*Treasury of the rest*]: [Strong's: 6847]

**Tsemar** [*Woolen*]: [Strong's: 6786]

**Tsepho** [*Watcher*]: [Strong's: 6825]

**Tseviim** [*Gazelles*]: [Strong's: 6636]

**Tsidon** [*Hunting*]: [Strong's: 6721]

**Tsilah** [*Shadow*]: [Strong's: 6741]

**Tsiphyon** [*Lookout*]: [Strong's: 6837]

**Tsiv'ghon** [*Colored*]: [Strong's: 6649]

**Tso'ar** [*Tiny*]: Meaning insignificant. [Strong's: 6820]

**Tsohhar** [*White*]: [Strong's: 6714]

**Tuval** [*Flow*]: [Strong's: 8422]

**Tuval-Qayin** [*Flow of acquiring*]: [Strong's: 8423]

**Ur** [*Light*]: [Strong's: 218]

**Uts** [*Counsel*]: [Strong's: 5780]

**Uval** [*Round*]: [Strong's: 5745]

**Uzal** [*Waver*]: [Strong's: 187]

**Ya'aqov** [*He restrains*]: [Strong's: 3290]

**Yaboq** [*Emptying*]: [Strong's: 2999]

**Yahh'le'el**] [*El delays*]: [Strong's: 3177]

**Yahhtse'el** [*El divides*]: [Strong's: 3183]

**Yakhin** [*He will be firm*]: [Strong's: 3199]

**Yalam** [*He is concealed*]: [Strong's: 3281]

**Yamin** [*Right hand*]: [Strong's: 3226]

**Yaphet** [*Wonder*]: [Strong's: 3315]

**Yaq'shan** [*Snarer*]: [Strong's: 3370]

**Yaqthan** [*He is small*]: [Strong's: 3355]

**Yarden** [*Descender*]: [Strong's: 3383]

**Yared** [*Descend*]: [Strong's: 3382]

**Yashuv** [*He will return*]: [Strong's: 3102]

**Yaval** [*Watercourse*]: [Strong's: 2989]

**Yawan** [*Wine*]: Closely related to the Hebrew word yayin meaning wine. [Strong's: 3120]

**Yegar-Sa'haduta** [*Fear of a witness*]: [Strong's: 3026]

**Yehudah** [*Praised*]: [Strong's: 3063]

**Yehudit** [*Praised*]: [Strong's: 3067]

**Yemu'el** [*Day of El*]: [Strong's: 3223]

**Yerahh** [*Moon*]: [Strong's: 3392]

**Yetet** [*Nail*]: [Strong's: 3509]

**Yethur** [*He rows*]: [Strong's: 3195]

**Yetser** [*Forming*]: [Strong's: 3337]

**Ye'ush** [*He will assemble*]: [Strong's: 3274]

**Yevus** [*He threshes*]: [Strong's: 2983]

**YHWH** [*He exists*]: The actual pronunciation of this name is not certain. [Strong's: 3068]

**YHWH-Yireh** [*YHWH will see*]: [Strong's: 3070]

**Yidlap** [*He will drip*]: [Strong's: 3044]

**Yimnah** [*Right*]: [Strong's: 3232]

**Yish'baq** [*He will leave alone*]: [Strong's: 3435]

**Yishma'el** [*El will listen*]: [Strong's: 3458]

**Yishwah** [*He resembles*]: [Strong's: 3438]

**Yishwiy** [*He resembles me*]: [Strong's: 3440]

**Yiskah** [*He covers*]: [Strong's: 3252]

**Yisra'el** [*He turns El*]: [Strong's: 3478]

**Yis'sas'kar** [*He will lift up the wage*]: [Strong's: 3485]

**Yitran** [*Remainder*]: [Strong's: 3506]

**Yits'hhaq** [*He laughs*]: [Strong's: 3327]

**Yoseph** [*Adding*]: [Strong's: 3130]

**Yovav** [*Howler*]: [Strong's: 2980]

**Yuval** [*Creek*]: [Strong's: 3106]

**Za'awan** [*Trembling*]: [Strong's: 2190]

**Zerahh** [*Dawn*]: [Strong's: 2226]

Zevulun [*Residence*]: [Strong's: 2074]

Zilpah [*Trickling*]: [Strong's: 2153]

Zimran [*Musician*]: [Strong's: 2175]

Zuz [*Creature*]: [Strong's: 2104]

# Concordance of Words and Names

## Words

**Abdomen (2):** 15:4, 25:23

**Abundance (5):** 16:10, 27:28, 30:30, 32:13, 48:16

**Abundant (13):** 6:5, 7:11, 13:6, 21:34, 24:25, 25:23, 26:14, 30:43, 33:9, 36:7, 37:34, 45:28, 50:20

**Accept (1):** 33:10

**Account of (3):** 12:13, 30:27, 39:5

**Accumulate (5):** 12:5, 31:18 (2), 36:6, 46:6

**Acquired (4):** 17:12, 17:13, 17:23, 17:27

**Acquisition (1):** 15:2

**Acquit (1):** 24:8

**Acquit (1):** 24:41

**Add (14):** 4:2, 4:12, 8:10, 8:12, 8:21 (2), 18:29, 25:1, 30:24, 37:5, 37:8, 38:5, 38:26, 44:23

**Adhere (4):** 2:24, 19:19, 31:23, 34:3

**Advance (2):** 12:8, 26:22

**Adder (1):** 49:17

**Affection (1):** 29:20

**Afflict (5):** 15:13, 16:6, 16:9, 31:50, 34:2

**Affliction (4):** 16:11, 29:32, 31:42, 41:52

**After (85):** 5:4, 5:7, 5:10, 5:13, 5:16, 5:19, 5:22, 5:26, 5:30, 6:4, 9:9, 9:28, 10:1, 10:18, 10:32, 11:10, 11:11, 11:13, 11:15, 11:17, 11:19, 11:21, 11:23, 11:25, 13:14, 14:17, 15:1, 15:14, 16:13, 17:7 (2), 17:8, 17:9, 17:10, 17:19, 18:5, 18:10, 18:12, 18:19, 19:6, 19:17, 19:26, 22:1, 22:13, 22:20, 23:19, 24:5, 24:8, 24:36, 24:39, 24:55, 24:61, 24:67, 25:11, 25:26, 26:18, 30:21, 31:23, 31:36, 32:19, 32:20, 32:21 (2), 33:7, 35:5, 35:12, 37:17, 38:30, 39:7, 40:1, 41:3, 41:6, 41:19, 41:23, 41:27, 41:30, 41:31, 41:39, 44:4, 45:15, 46:30, 48:1, 48:4, 48:6, 50:14

**Age (1):** 48:10

**Agree (3):** 34:15, 34:22, 34:23

**All (342):** 1:21 (2), 1:25, 1:26 (2), 1:28, 1:29 (3), 1:30 (4), 1:31, 2:1, 2:2, 2:3, 2:5 (2), 2:6, 2:9, 2:11, 2:13, 2:16, 2:19 (3), 2:20 (2), 3:1 (2), 3:14 (3), 3:17, 3:20, 4:14, 4:15 (2), 4:21, 4:22, 5:5, 5:8, 5:11, 5:14, 5:17, 5:20, 5:23, 5:27, 5:31, 6:2, 6:5 (2), 6:12, 6:13, 6:17 (2), 6:19 (3), 6:20 (2), 6:21, 6:22, 7:1, 7:2, 7:3, 7:4, 7:5, 7:8, 7:11, 7:14 (6), 7:15, 7:16, 7:19 (2), 7:21 (3), 7:22 (2), 7:23, 8:1 (2), 8:9, 8:17 (3), 8:19 (4), 8:20 (2), 8:21, 8:22, 9:2 (4), 9:3 (2), 9:5, 9:10 (4), 9:11, 9:12, 9:15 (3), 9:16 (2), 9:17, 9:19, 9:29, 10:21, 10:29, 11:1, 11:4, 11:6 (2), 11:8, 11:9 (2), 12:3, 12:5, 12:20, 13:1, 13:9, 13:10 (2), 13:11, 13:15, 14:3, 14:7, 14:11 (2), 14:16, 14:20, 14:23, 15:10, 16:12 (3), 17:8, 17:10, 17:12 (2), 17:23 (3), 17:27, 18:18, 18:25, 18:26, 18:28, 19:4, 19:12, 19:17, 19:25 (2), 19:28, 19:31, 20:7, 20:8 (2), 20:13, 20:16 (2), 20:18, 21:6, 21:12, 21:22, 22:18, 23:10, 23:17 (2), 23:18, 24:1, 24:2, 24:10, 24:20, 24:36, 24:66, 25:4, 25:5, 25:18, 25:25, 26:3, 26:4 (2), 26:11, 26:15, 27:33, 27:37, 28:14, 28:15, 28:22, 29:3, 29:8, 29:13, 29:22, 30:32 (3), 30:33, 30:35 (3), 30:40, 30:41, 31:1 (2), 31:6, 31:8 (2), 31:12 (2), 31:16 (2), 31:18 (2), 31:21, 31:34, 31:37 (2), 31:43, 32:11 (2), 32:20, 33:8, 33:11, 33:13, 34:15, 34:19, 34:22, 34:23, 34:24 (3), 34:25, 34:29 (3), 35:2, 35:4, 35:6, 36:6 (3), 37:3, 37:4, 37:35 (2), 39:3, 39:4, 39:5 (2), 39:6, 39:8, 39:22 (2), 39:23, 40:17, 40:20, 41:8 (2), 41:19, 41:29, 41:30, 41:35, 41:37, 41:39, 41:40, 41:41, 41:43, 41:44, 41:46, 41:48, 41:51 (2), 41:54 (2), 41:55 (2), 41:56 (2), 41:57 (2), 42:6, 42:11, 42:29, 42:36, 43:9, 43:34, 44:32, 45:1 (2), 45:8 (2), 45:9, 45:10, 45:11, 45:13 (2), 45:15, 45:20, 45:22, 45:26, 45:27, 46:1, 46:6, 46:7, 46:15, 46:22, 46:25, 46:26 (2), 46:27, 46:32, 46:34, 47:1, 47:12, 47:13, 47:14, 47:15, 47:17, 47:20, 48:16, 49:28, 50:7 (2), 50:8, 50:14, 50:15

**Almond (1):** 43:11

**Also (94):** 3:6, 3:22, 4:4, 4:22, 4:26, 6:3, 6:4, 7:3, 10:21, 13:5, 13:16, 14:7, 14:16 (2), 15:14, 16:13, 17:16, 19:21, 19:34, 19:35, 19:38, 20:4, 20:5, 20:6 (2), 20:12, 21:13, 21:26 (2), 22:20, 22:24, 24:14, 24:19, 24:25 (3), 24:44 (2), 24:46 (2), 26:21, 27:31, 27:33, 27:34, 27:38, 27:45, 29:27, 29:30 (2), 29:33, 30:3, 30:6, 30:8, 30:15, 30:30, 31:15, 32:7, 32:19, 32:20 (3), 32:21, 33:7, 35:17, 37:7, 38:10, 38:11, 38:22, 38:24, 40:15, 42:22, 42:28, 43:8 (2), 43:8, 44:9, 44:10, 44:16 (2), 44:29, 46:4, 46:34 (2), 47:3 (2), 47:19 (2), 48:11, 48:19 (2), 50:9 (2), 50:18, 50:23

**381**

Altar (13): 8:20 (2), 12:7, 12:8, 13:4, 13:18, 22:9 (2), 26:25, 33:20, 35:1, 35:3, 35:7
Amber (1): 2:12
Amplify (1): 48:16
Annoyance (2): 27:12, 27:13
Answer (19): 18:27, 23:5, 23:10, 23:14, 24:50, 27:37, 27:39, 30:33, 31:14, 31:31, 31:36, 31:43, 34:13, 35:3, 40:18, 41:16 (2), 42:22, 45:3
Apart from (3): 14:24, 41:16, 41:44
Apparel (7): 9:23, 35:2, 37:34, 41:14, 44:13, 45:22 (2)
Appearance (11): 2:9, 12:11, 24:16, 26:7, 29:17, 39:6, 41:2, 41:3, 41:4 (2), 41:21
Appointed (4): 1:14, 17:21, 18:14, 21:2
Appointed time (10): 8:11, 18:10, 18:14, 21:22, 24:11 (2), 29:7, 31:10, 38:1, 38:27
Apportion (3): 14:15, 49:7, 49:27
Arm (1): 49:24
Army (4): 2:1, 21:22, 21:32, 26:26
Arom (4): 8:21, 27:27 (3)
Around (3): 23:17, 35:5, 41:48
Arrange (2): 14:8, 22:9
Arrow (1): 49:23
Ash (1): 18:27
Ashamed (1): 2:25
Assembled flock (4): 28:3, 35:11, 48:4, 49:6
At (1147): 1:1 (2), 1:4, 1:7, 1:16 (4), 1:17, 1:21 (3), 1:22 (2), 1:25 (3), 1:27 (3), 1:28 (2), 1:29 (2), 1:30, 1:31, 2:3 (2), 2:5, 2:6, 2:7, 2:8, 2:10, 2:11, 2:13, 2:15, 2:19, 2:22, 2:24 (2), 3:8, 3:10, 3:18, 3:23, 3:24 (4), 4:1 (3), 4:2 (2), 4:11 (2), 4:12, 4:14, 4:15, 4:17 (2), 4:18 (4), 4:20, 4:22, 4:25 (2), 4:26, 5:1, 5:2 (2), 5:3, 5:4, 5:6, 5:7, 5:9, 5:10, 5:12, 5:13, 5:15, 5:16, 5:18, 5:19, 5:21, 5:22 (2), 5:24 (2), 5:25, 5:26, 5:29, 5:30, 5:32 (3), 6:2, 6:6, 6:7, 6:9, 6:10 (3), 6:12 (2), 6:13, 6:14 (2), 6:15, 6:17, 6:18 (3), 6:19, 6:22, 7:1, 7:4, 7:7, 7:9, 7:13, 7:16, 7:17, 7:23 (2), 8:1 (4), 8:6, 8:7, 8:8 (2), 8:9, 8:10, 8:12, 8:13, 8:16, 8:17 (2), 8:18, 8:21 (3), 9:1 (3), 9:3, 9:5 (2), 9:6, 9:8, 9:9 (3), 9:10 (3), 9:11 (2), 9:12, 9:13, 9:15, 9:22, 9:23 (2), 9:24, 10:8, 10:11 (3), 10:12, 10:13 (4), 10:14 (3), 10:15 (2), 10:16 (3), 10:17 (3), 10:18 (3), 10:24 (2), 10:26 (4), 10:27 (3), 10:28 (3), 10:29 (3), 11:5 (2), 11:8, 11:10, 11:11, 11:12, 11:13, 11:14, 11:15, 11:16, 11:17, 11:18, 11:19, 11:20, 11:21, 11:22, 11:23, 11:24, 11:25, 11:26 (3), 11:27 (4), 11:31 (4), 12:4, 12:5 (4), 12:7, 12:12 (3), 12:14, 12:15 (2), 12:17 (2), 12:19, 12:20 (3),

13:5, 13:6, 13:10 (4), 13:11, 13:15, 13:16 (2), 14:2 (2), 14:4, 14:5 (4), 14:6, 14:7 (2), 14:8, 14:9 (2), 14:11 (2), 14:12 (2), 14:14, 14:16 (4), 14:17 (3), 14:23, 14:24, 15:3, 15:5 (2), 15:7, 15:10 (3), 15:11, 15:13, 15:14, 15:18 (2), 15:19 (3), 15:20 (3), 15:21 (4), 16:3 (2), 16:10, 16:16, 17:2, 17:3, 17:4, 17:5, 17:6, 17:7, 17:8 (2), 17:9, 17:11, 17:14 (2), 17:15, 17:16, 17:19 (3), 17:20 (3), 17:21 (2), 17:22, 17:23 (5), 17:27 (2), 18:7, 18:19 (3), 18:28, 19:5, 19:8, 19:10 (3), 19:11, 19:13 (2), 19:14, 19:15 (2), 19:17, 19:19, 19:21, 19:24, 19:25 (3), 19:27, 19:29 (4), 19:32, 19:33 (2), 19:34, 19:35, 20:2, 20:6, 20:8, 20:10, 20:13, 20:14, 20:16 (2), 20:17 (2), 21:1, 21:2, 21:3, 21:4 (2), 21:5, 21:8, 21:9, 21:10, 21:13, 21:14, 21:15, 21:16, 21:17 (2), 21:18 (2), 21:19 (3), 21:20, 21:25, 21:26, 21:28, 21:30 (2), 22:1, 22:2 (3), 22:3 (4), 22:4 (2), 22:6 (3), 22:9 (4), 22:10 (3), 22:12 (2), 22:13 (2), 22:16 (3), 22:17 (2), 22:21 (3), 22:22 (5), 22:23, 22:24 (4), 23:5, 23:6 (2), 23:8 (3), 23:9, 23:10, 23:13, 23:15, 23:16, 23:19, 23:20, 24:1, 24:5, 24:6, 24:7, 24:8, 24:9, 24:14, 24:30 (3), 24:32, 24:35, 24:36, 24:40, 24:47, 24:48 (2), 24:49, 24:52, 24:55, 24:56, 24:57, 24:59 (4), 24:60 (2), 24:61, 24:64 (2), 24:66, 24:67, 25:2 (6), 25:3 (2), 25:5, 25:9, 25:10, 25:11, 25:19, 25:20, 25:22, 25:26, 25:28 (2), 25:31, 25:33, 25:34, 26:3 (2), 26:4 (2), 26:8, 26:10, 26:11, 26:14, 26:18, 26:24 (2), 26:27 (2), 26:31, 26:33, 26:34 (2), 27:1, 27:6, 27:8, 27:9, 27:15 (3), 27:16, 27:17 (2), 27:27, 27:30 (2), 27:34, 27:36, 27:37, 27:40, 27:41 (2), 27:42, 27:45, 28:1, 28:3, 28:4 (3), 28:5, 28:6 (3), 28:9, 28:15, 28:18 (2), 28:19, 29:3 (3), 29:5, 29:8, 29:10 (4), 29:11, 29:13 (2), 29:18, 29:19 (2), 29:20, 29:21, 29:22, 29:23 (2), 29:24, 29:27, 29:28, 29:29, 29:30, 29:31, 29:33, 29:35, 30:4, 30:9 (2), 30:11, 30:13, 30:14, 30:15 (2), 30:20 (2), 30:21, 30:22 (2), 30:23, 30:24, 30:25, 30:26 (4), 30:29 (3), 30:30, 30:33, 30:35 (2), 30:36, 30:38, 30:41, 31:1 (3), 31:2, 31:5, 31:6, 31:7, 31:9, 31:12, 31:15, 31:17 (2), 31:18 (2), 31:19 (2), 31:20, 31:21 (2), 31:23 (2), 31:25 (3), 31:26 (2), 31:27, 31:30, 31:31, 31:32, 31:34 (2), 31:35, 31:37, 31:41, 31:42 (2), 31:50, 31:52 (3), 32:1, 32:5, 32:8 (4), 32:11 (2), 32:12, 32:13,

32:18, 32:20 (4), 32:23 (4), 32:24 (2), 32:30, 32:32, 32:33, 33:1, 33:2 (5), 33:5 (4), 33:11, 33:15, 33:18, 33:19, 34:2 (3), 34:3, 34:4, 34:5 (2), 34:6, 34:7, 34:8 (2), 34:9 (2), 34:10, 34:12, 34:13 (3), 34:14, 34:16 (3), 34:17, 34:21 (4), 34:22, 34:23, 34:26 (3), 34:28 (5), 34:29 (4), 34:30, 34:31, 35:2, 35:3, 35:4 (3), 35:9, 35:10, 35:12 (2), 35:13, 35:14, 35:15 (2), 35:22, 35:29, 36:2 (3), 36:3, 36:4 (2), 36:5 (3), 36:6 (7), 36:7, 36:12, 36:14 (3), 36:24 (2), 36:35, 37:2 (4), 37:3, 37:4 (2), 37:5, 37:8, 37:9, 37:11, 37:12, 37:14 (2), 37:16, 37:18 (2), 37:22 (2), 37:23 (3), 37:24, 37:26 (2), 37:28 (3), 37:29, 37:31 (2), 37:32, 37:35, 37:36, 38:1, 38:3, 38:4, 38:5 (2), 38:8, 38:10, 38:20, 38:21, 39:2, 39:3, 39:4, 39:5 (2), 39:6, 39:7, 39:8, 39:9, 39:19, 39:20, 39:21, 39:22 (2), 39:23 (2), 40:3, 40:4 (3), 40:6, 40:7 (2), 40:8, 40:9, 40:11 (3), 40:13, 40:14, 40:15, 40:17, 40:19 (3), 40:20 (3), 40:21, 40:22, 40:23, 41:4, 41:7, 41:8 (4), 41:9 (2), 41:10 (3), 41:12 (2), 41:13 (2), 41:14, 41:15 (2), 41:16 (2), 41:20, 41:24, 41:25, 41:28, 41:30, 41:34, 41:35, 41:39 (2), 41:41, 41:42 (3), 41:43 (2), 41:44 (2), 41:45, 41:48, 41:51 (3), 41:52, 41:56, 42:4 (2), 42:7 (2), 42:8, 42:9 (2), 42:13, 42:16 (2), 42:17, 42:18, 42:20, 42:22, 42:24 (3), 42:25, 42:26, 42:27 (2), 42:29 (2), 42:30 (3), 42:32, 42:33 (2), 42:34 (3), 42:35, 42:36 (2), 42:37 (2), 42:38, 43:2, 43:3, 43:4 (2), 43:5, 43:7, 43:8, 43:12, 43:13, 43:14 (2), 43:15 (2), 43:16 (4), 43:17, 43:18 (2), 43:21 (2), 43:23, 43:24, 43:25, 43:26, 43:29, 43:32 (2), 43:34, 44:1 (2), 44:2 (2), 44:4, 44:6, 44:9, 44:10, 44:11, 44:16, 44:19, 44:22 (2), 44:23, 44:24, 44:26 (2), 44:28, 44:29 (2), 44:30, 44:31, 44:32, 44:34 (2), 45:1, 45:2, 45:3, 45:4, 45:5, 45:8, 45:11, 45:13 (3), 45:15, 45:17, 45:18 (4), 45:19, 45:24, 45:27 (3), 46:5 (4), 46:6 (3), 46:7 (2), 46:15, 46:18, 46:20 (2), 46:25, 46:28, 46:30, 47:6 (2), 47:7 (2), 47:9, 47:10, 47:11 (2), 47:12 (3), 47:14 (2), 47:17, 47:19 (2), 47:20, 47:21 (2), 47:22 (3), 47:23 (3), 47:26, 48:1 (3), 48:3, 48:4, 48:8, 48:10, 48:11 (2), 48:12, 48:13 (3), 48:14 (3), 48:15 (2), 48:16 (2), 48:17, 48:20, 48:21, 49:1 (2), 49:15, 49:25, 49:28 (2), 49:29 (2), 49:30 (2), 49:31 (5), 49:32, 49:33, 50:2 (4), 50:3, 50:5, 50:6, 50:7 (2), 50:11,

50:13 (4), 50:14 (3), 50:15 (2), 50:21 (3), 50:24 (2), 50:25 (3), 50:26

**At that time (6):** 4:26, 12:6, 13:7, 24:41, 39:5, 49:4

**At this point (1):** 16:13

**Attach (1):** 34:8

**Avenge (2):** 4:15, 4:24

**Awake (5):** 9:24, 28:16, 41:4, 41:7, 41:21

**Awe (2):** 31:42, 31:53

**Back (1):** 49:17

**Back of the neck (8):** 27:16, 27:40, 33:4, 41:42, 45:14 (2), 46:29 (2)

**Backward (2):** 9:23 (2)

**Bag (15):** 42:27, 42:28, 43:12, 43:18, 43:21 (2), 43:22, 43:23, 44:1 (2), 44:2, 44:8, 44:11 (2), 44:12

**Bake (9):** 19:3, 40:1, 40:2, 40:5, 40:16, 40:17, 40:20, 40:22, 41:10

**Balm (2):** 37:25, 43:11

**Band (1):** 49:19

**Barley (7):** 42:1, 42:2, 42:19, 42:26, 43:2, 44:2, 47:14

**Barren (1):** 15:2

**Barter (2):** 43:9, 44:32

**Base (7):** 40:13, 41:13, 42:11, 42:19, 42:31, 42:33, 42:34

**Basket (4):** 40:16, 40:17 (2), 40:18

**Battle (2):** 14:2, 14:8

**Be (1):** 27:29

**Be a whore (3):** 34:31, 38:15, 38:24

**Be able (22):** 13:6, 13:16, 15:5, 19:19, 19:22, 24:50, 29:8, 30:8, 31:35, 32:26, 32:29, 34:14, 36:7, 37:4, 43:32, 44:1, 44:22, 44:26 (2), 45:1, 45:3, 48:10

**Be abundant (1):** 26:16

**Be bitter (1):** 49:23

**Be childless (5):** 27:45, 31:38, 42:36, 43:14 (2)

**Be clean (1):** 35:2

**Be correct (2):** 38:26, 44:16

**Be crafty (1):** 37:18

**Be drunk (2):** 9:21, 43:34

**Be dysfunctional (9):** 19:7, 19:9, 21:11, 21:12, 31:7, 38:10, 43:6, 44:5, 48:17

**Be face to face (37):** 3:11, 9:22, 12:18, 14:13, 21:26, 22:20, 24:23, 24:28, 24:49 (2), 26:32, 27:42, 29:12 (2), 29:15, 31:20, 31:22, 31:27, 32:6, 32:30, 33:12, 37:5, 37:16, 38:13, 38:24, 41:24, 41:25, 42:29, 43:6, 43:7, 44:24, 45:13, 45:26, 46:31, 47:1, 48:2, 49:1

**Be far (2):** 21:16, 44:4

**Be fruitful (2):** 49:22 (2)

**Be hard (3):** 35:16, 35:17, 49:7

**Be heavy (3):** 18:20, 34:19, 48:10

**Be hungry (1):** 41:55

**Be in misery (1):** 34:25

Be insubstantial (6): 8:8, 8:11, 8:21, 12:3, 16:4, 16:5

Be numb (1): 45:26

Be old (5): 18:13, 19:31, 24:1, 27:1, 27:2

Be rich (1): 14:23

Be sad (1): 40:6

Be small (1): 32:11

Be strong (1): 25:23

Be sweet (1): 49:15

Be threefold (3): 15:9 (3)

Be unclean (3): 34:5, 34:13, 34:27

Be whole (3): 47:15, 47:18 (2)

Be zealous (3): 26:14, 30:1, 37:11

Be sick (1): 48:1

Beard (10): 18:11, 18:12, 19:4, 24:2, 25:8, 35:29, 43:27, 44:20, 50:7 (2)

Beast (21): 1:24, 1:25, 1:26, 2:20, 3:14, 6:7, 6:20, 7:2 (2), 7:8 (2), 7:14, 7:21, 7:23, 8:1, 8:17, 8:20, 9:10, 34:23, 36:6, 47:18

Beat (1): 41:8

Beautiful (9): 12:11, 12:14, 29:17 (2), 39:6 (2), 41:2, 41:4, 41:18

Beauty (14): 6:8, 18:3, 19:19, 30:27, 32:6, 33:8, 33:10, 33:15, 34:11, 39:4, 39:21, 47:25, 47:29, 50:4

Bed (3): 47:31, 48:2, 49:33

Before (10): 2:5 (2), 19:4, 24:15, 24:45, 27:4, 27:33, 37:18, 41:50, 45:28

Behind (2): 33:2 (2)

Being (43): 1:20, 1:21, 1:24, 1:30, 2:7, 2:19, 9:4, 9:5 (2), 9:10, 9:12, 9:15, 9:16, 12:5, 12:13, 14:21, 17:14, 19:17, 19:19, 19:20, 23:8, 27:4, 27:19, 27:25, 27:31, 32:31, 34:3, 34:8, 35:18, 36:6, 37:21, 42:21, 44:30 (2), 46:15, 46:18, 46:22, 46:25, 46:26 (2), 46:27 (2), 49:6

Belly (1): 3:14

Bend down (23): 18:2, 19:1, 22:5, 23:7, 23:12, 24:26, 24:48, 24:52, 27:29 (2), 33:3, 33:6, 33:7 (2), 37:7, 37:9, 37:10, 42:6, 43:26, 43:28, 47:31, 48:12, 49:8

Bend the knee (1): 41:43

Beq (1): 24:22

Beside (5): 39:10, 39:15, 39:16, 39:18, 41:3

Best (2): 47:6, 47:11

Betray (1): 29:25

Between (76): 1:4 (2), 1:6, 1:7 (2), 1:14 (2), 1:18 (2), 3:15 (4), 9:12 (3), 9:13 (2), 9:15 (3), 9:16 (2), 9:17 (2), 10:12 (2), 13:3 (2), 13:7 (2), 13:8 (4), 15:17, 16:5 (2), 16:14 (2), 17:2 (2), 17:7 (3), 17:10 (3), 17:11 (2), 20:1 (2), 23:15 (2), 26:28 (3), 30:36 (2), 31:37, 31:44 (2), 31:48 (2), 31:49 (2), 31:50 (2), 31:51 (2), 31:53, 32:17 (2), 42:23, 49:10, 49:14

Bind (1): 22:9

Bind up (1): 37:7

Bird (2): 7:14, 15:10

Bird of prey (1): 15:11

Birthing (13): 2:4, 5:1, 6:9, 10:1, 10:32, 11:10, 11:27, 25:12, 25:13, 25:19, 36:1, 36:9, 37:2

Birthright (6): 25:31, 25:32, 25:33, 25:34, 27:36, 43:33

Bite (1): 49:17

Bitter (1): 27:34

Black (4): 30:32, 30:33, 30:35, 30:40

Blast (3): 41:6, 41:23, 41:27

Blazing (1): 3:24

Blindness (1): 19:11

Blood (11): 4:10, 4:11, 9:4, 9:5, 9:6 (2), 37:22, 37:26, 37:31, 42:22, 49:11

Blossom (1): 40:10

Body (1): 47:18

Boil (1): 40:10

Bondwoman (7): 20:17, 21:10 (2), 21:12, 21:13, 30:3, 31:33

Bone (7): 2:23 (2), 7:13, 17:23, 17:26, 29:14, 50:25

Booth (1): 33:17

Border (3): 10:19, 23:17, 47:21

Born (5): 14:14, 17:12, 17:13, 17:23, 17:27

Bosom (1): 16:5

Bound up (2): 1:9, 49:18

Bow (8): 9:13, 9:14, 9:16, 21:16, 21:20, 27:3, 48:22, 49:24

Bow the head (3): 24:26, 24:48, 43:28

Bowels (6): 20:18, 29:31, 30:22, 43:14, 43:30, 49:25

Bowl (5): 44:2 (2), 44:12, 44:16, 44:17

Box (1): 50:26

Boy (19): 4:23, 21:8, 21:14, 21:15, 21:16, 30:26, 32:23, 33:1, 33:2 (2), 33:5 (2), 33:6, 33:7, 33:13, 33:14, 37:30, 42:22, 44:20

Bracelet (3): 24:22, 24:30, 24:47

Bramble (1): 3:18

Branch (3): 40:10, 40:12, 38:29

Bread (24): 3:19, 14:18, 18:5, 21:14, 25:34, 27:17, 28:20, 31:54 (2), 37:25, 39:6, 41:54, 41:55, 43:25, 43:31, 43:32, 45:23, 47:12, 47:13, 47:15, 47:17 (2), 47:19, 49:20

Bread cake (1): 18:6

Break (1): 17:14

Break out (4): 28:14, 30:30, 30:43, 38:29

Breaking camp (1): 13:3

Breast (1): 49:25

Breath (2): 2:7, 7:22

Brick (2): 11:3 (2)

Bride price (1): 34:12

Bright (1): 49:21

Brimstone (1): 19:24

**Bring forth (170):** 3:16, 4:1, 4:2, 4:17, 4:18 (4), 4:20, 4:22, 4:25, 4:26, 5:3, 5:4 (2), 5:6, 5:7 (2), 5:9, 5:10 (2), 5:12, 5:13 (2), 5:15, 5:16 (2), 5:18, 5:19 (2), 5:21, 5:22 (2), 5:25, 5:26 (2), 5:28, 5:30 (2), 5:32, 6:1, 6:4, 6:10, 10:1, 10:8, 10:13, 10:15, 10:21, 10:24 (2), 10:25, 10:26, 11:10, 11:11 (2), 11:12, 11:13 (2), 11:14, 11:15 (2), 11:16, 11:17 (2), 11:18, 11:19 (2), 11:20, 11:21 (2), 11:22, 11:23 (2), 11:24, 11:25 (2), 11:26, 11:27 (2), 16:1, 16:2, 16:11, 16:15 (2), 16:16, 17:17 (2), 17:19, 17:20, 17:21, 18:13, 19:37, 19:38, 20:17, 21:2, 21:3 (2), 21:5, 21:7, 21:9, 22:20, 22:23 (2), 22:24, 24:15, 24:24, 24:36, 24:47, 25:2, 25:3, 25:12, 25:19, 25:24, 25:26, 29:32, 29:33, 29:34 (2), 29:35 (2), 30:1, 30:3, 30:5, 30:7, 30:9, 30:10, 30:12, 30:17, 30:19, 30:20, 30:21, 30:23, 30:25, 30:39, 31:8 (2), 31:43, 34:1, 35:16 (2), 35:17 (2), 35:26, 36:4 (2), 36:5 (2), 36:12, 36:14, 38:3, 38:4, 38:5 (2), 38:28 (2), 40:20, 41:50 (2), 44:27, 46:15, 46:18, 46:20 (2), 46:22, 46:25 (2), 46:27, 48:5, 48:6, 50:23

**Bronze (1):** 4:22

**Brother (178):** 4:2, 4:8 (2), 4:9 (2), 4:10, 4:11, 4:21, 9:5, 9:22, 9:25, 10:21, 10:25, 12:5, 13:8, 13:11, 14:12, 14:13 (2), 14:14, 14:16, 16:12, 19:7, 20:5, 20:13, 20:16, 22:20, 22:21, 22:23, 24:15, 24:27, 24:29, 24:48, 24:53, 24:55, 25:18, 25:26, 26:31, 27:6, 27:11, 27:23, 27:29, 27:30, 27:35, 27:37, 27:40, 27:41, 27:42, 27:43, 27:44, 27:45, 28:2, 28:5, 29:4, 29:10 (3), 29:12, 29:15, 31:23, 31:25, 31:32, 31:37 (2), 31:46, 31:54, 32:4, 32:7, 32:12, 32:14, 32:18, 33:3, 33:9, 34:11, 34:25, 35:1, 35:7, 36:6, 37:2, 37:4 (2), 37:5, 37:8, 37:9, 37:10 (2), 37:11, 37:12, 37:13, 37:14, 37:16, 37:17, 37:19, 37:23, 37:26 (2), 37:27 (2), 37:30, 38:1, 38:8 (2), 38:9 (2), 38:11, 38:29, 38:30, 42:3, 42:4 (2), 42:6, 42:7, 42:8, 42:13, 42:15, 42:16, 42:19, 42:20, 42:21 (2), 42:28 (2), 42:32, 42:33, 42:34 (2), 42:38, 43:3, 43:4, 43:5, 43:6, 43:7 (2), 43:13, 43:14, 43:29 (2), 43:30, 44:14, 44:19, 44:20, 44:23, 44:26 (2), 44:33, 45:1, 45:3 (2), 45:4 (2), 45:12, 45:14, 45:15 (2), 45:16, 45:17, 45:24, 46:31 (2), 47:1, 47:2, 47:3, 47:5, 47:6, 47:11, 47:12, 48:6, 48:19, 48:22, 49:5, 49:8, 49:26, 50:8, 50:14, 50:15, 50:17, 50:18, 50:24

**Bruise (1):** 4:23

**Build (16):** 2:22, 4:17, 8:20, 10:11, 11:4, 11:5, 11:8, 12:7, 12:8, 13:18, 16:2, 22:9, 26:25, 30:3, 33:17, 35:7

**Bull (1):** 32:16

**Bundle (2):** 42:35 (2)

**Burial place (3):** 35:20 (2), 47:30

**Burn black (1):** 43:30

**Burst (1):** 19:9

**Burst out (1):** 40:10

**Bury (28):** 15:15, 23:4, 23:6 (2), 23:8, 23:11, 23:13, 23:15, 23:19, 25:9, 25:10, 35:8, 35:19, 35:29, 47:29, 47:30, 48:7, 49:29, 49:31 (2), 49:31, 50:5 (2), 50:6, 50:7, 50:13, 50:14 (2)

**But (2):** 28:19, 48:19

**Butcher (1):** 43:16

**By (14):** 3:12, 19:19, 20:9, 20:13, 21:23, 28:20, 29:19, 29:27, 31:5, 31:7, 31:32, 35:3, 40:14, 47:29

**Calculate (2):** 3:6, 48:14

**Call out (110):** 1:5 (2), 1:8, 1:10 (2), 2:19 (2), 2:20, 2:23, 3:9, 3:20, 4:17, 4:25, 4:26 (2), 5:2, 5:3, 5:29, 11:9, 12:8, 12:18, 13:4, 16:11, 16:13, 16:14, 16:15, 17:5, 17:15, 17:19, 19:5, 19:22, 19:37, 19:38, 20:8, 20:9, 21:3, 21:12, 21:17, 21:31, 22:11, 22:14, 22:15, 24:57, 24:58, 25:25, 25:26, 25:30, 26:9, 26:18 (2), 26:20, 26:21, 26:22, 26:25, 26:33, 27:1, 27:36, 27:42, 28:1, 28:19, 29:32, 29:33, 29:34, 29:35, 30:6, 30:8, 30:11, 30:13, 30:18, 30:20, 30:21, 30:24, 31:4, 31:47 (2), 31:48, 31:54, 32:3, 32:31, 33:17, 33:20, 35:7, 35:8, 35:10 (2), 35:15, 35:18 (2), 38:3, 38:4, 38:5, 38:29, 38:30, 39:14 (2), 39:15, 39:18, 41:8, 41:14, 41:43, 41:45, 41:51, 41:52, 45:1, 46:33, 47:29, 48:6, 48:16, 49:1, 50:11

**Camel (25):** 12:16, 24:10 (2), 24:11, 24:14, 24:19, 24:20, 24:22, 24:30, 24:31, 24:32 (2), 24:35, 24:44, 24:46 (2), 24:61, 24:63, 24:64, 30:43, 31:17, 31:34, 32:8, 32:16, 37:25

**Camp (2):** 26:17, 33:18

**Campsite (8):** 32:3, 32:8, 32:9 (2), 32:11, 32:22, 33:8, 50:9

**Captain (4):** 17:20, 23:6, 25:16, 34:2

**Capture (3):** 14:14, 31:26, 34:29

**Caravan (1):** 37:25

**Carcass (1):** 15:11

**Carry (1):** 49:15

**Cart (4):** 45:19, 45:21, 45:27, 46:5

**Cartilage (1):** 49:14

**Cast out (3):** 3:24, 4:14, 21:10

**Cattle (18):** 12:16, 13:5, 18:7 (2), 18:8, 20:14, 21:27, 24:35, 26:14, 32:8, 33:13,

34:28, 45:10, 45:17, 46:32, 47:1, 47:17, 50:8

Cave (12): 19:30, 23:9, 23:11, 23:17, 23:19, 23:20, 25:9, 49:5, 49:29, 49:30, 49:32, 50:13

Cease (3): 2:2, 2:3, 8:22

Cereal (2): 27:28, 27:37

Chain (1): 41:42

Chamber (1): 43:30

Change (1): 41:32

Charge (1): 26:5

Chariot (2): 41:43, 46:29

Cheese (1): 18:8

Chestnut (1): 30:37

Chief (43): 36:15 (5), 36:16 (4), 36:17 (5), 36:18 (4), 36:19, 36:21, 36:29 (5), 36:30 (5), 36:40 (4), 36:41 (3), 36:42 (3), 36:43 (3)

Child (1): 11:30

Children (8): 34:29, 43:8, 45:19, 46:5, 47:12, 47:24, 50:8, 50:21

Chimney (2): 7:11, 8:2

Choice fruit (1): 43:11

Choice vine (1): 49:11

Choose (2): 6:2, 13:11

Chosen (1): 23:6

Circumcise (16): 17:10, 17:12, 17:13 (2), 17:14, 17:23, 17:24, 17:25, 17:26, 17:27, 21:4, 34:15, 34:17, 34:22 (2), 34:24

Cistern (9): 37:20, 37:22, 37:24 (2), 37:28, 37:29 (2), 40:15, 41:14

City (48): 4:17 (2), 10:12, 11:4, 11:5, 11:8, 13:12, 18:24, 18:26, 18:28, 19:4, 19:12, 19:14, 19:15, 19:16, 19:20, 19:21, 19:22, 19:25 (2), 19:29 (2), 23:10, 23:18, 24:10, 24:11, 24:13, 26:33, 28:19, 33:18 (2), 34:20 (2), 34:24 (2), 34:25, 34:27, 34:28, 35:5, 36:32, 36:35, 36:39, 41:35, 41:48 (2), 44:4, 44:13, 47:21

Cleave (2): 7:11, 22:3

Clothe (6): 3:21, 27:15, 27:16, 28:20, 38:19, 41:42

Clothing (1): 49:11

Cloud (4): 9:13, 9:14 (2), 9:16

Cluster (1): 40:10

Coat (1): 49:11

Cold (1): 8:22

Collection (1): 1:10

Colt (2): 32:16, 49:11

Come (216): 2:19, 2:22, 4:3, 4:4, 6:4, 6:13, 6:17, 6:18, 6:19, 6:20, 7:1, 7:7, 7:9, 7:13, 7:15, 7:16 (2), 8:9, 8:11, 10:19 (2), 10:30, 11:31, 12:5, 12:11, 12:14, 13:10, 13:18, 14:5, 14:7, 14:13, 15:12, 15:15, 15:17, 16:2, 16:4, 16:8, 18:11, 18:19, 18:21, 19:1, 19:3, 19:5, 19:8, 19:9, 19:10, 19:22, 19:23, 19:31, 19:33, 19:34, 20:3, 20:9, 20:13, 22:9, 23:2, 23:10, 23:18, 24:1, 24:30, 24:31, 24:32, 24:41, 24:42, 24:62 (2), 24:63, 24:67, 25:18, 25:29, 26:10, 26:27, 26:32, 27:4, 27:5, 27:7, 27:10, 27:12, 27:14, 27:18, 27:25, 27:30, 27:31, 27:33 (2), 27:35, 28:11, 29:6, 29:9, 29:13, 29:21, 29:23 (2), 29:30, 30:3, 30:4, 30:14, 30:16 (2), 30:33, 30:38 (2), 31:18, 31:24, 31:33 (2), 31:39, 32:7, 32:9, 32:12, 32:14, 33:1, 33:11, 33:14, 33:18 (2), 34:5, 34:7, 34:20, 34:25, 34:27, 35:6, 35:9, 35:16, 35:27, 37:2, 37:10 (2), 37:14, 37:19, 37:23, 37:25, 37:28, 37:30, 37:32, 38:2, 38:8, 38:9, 38:16 (2), 38:18, 39:11, 39:14 (2), 39:16, 39:17 (2), 40:6, 41:14, 41:21 (2), 41:29, 41:35, 41:50, 41:54, 41:57, 42:5 (2), 42:6, 42:7, 42:9, 42:10, 42:12, 42:15, 42:19, 42:20, 42:21, 42:29, 42:34, 42:37, 43:2, 43:9, 43:16, 43:17, 43:18 (2), 43:21, 43:23, 43:24, 43:25, 43:26 (2), 43:30, 44:14, 44:30, 44:32, 45:16, 45:17, 45:18, 45:19, 45:25, 46:1, 46:6, 46:7, 46:8, 46:26, 46:27, 46:28, 46:31, 46:32, 47:1 (2), 47:4, 47:5, 47:7, 47:14, 47:15, 47:17, 47:18, 48:2, 48:5, 48:7 (2), 49:6, 49:10, 50:10

Come near (5): 12:11, 20:4, 27:41, 37:18, 47:29

Come to an end (2): 47:15, 47:16

Come up (1): 32:32

Comfort (9): 5:29, 6:6, 6:7, 24:67, 27:42, 37:35 (2), 38:12, 50:21

Community (4): 25:23 (3), 27:29

Companion (6): 11:3, 11:7, 15:10, 38:12, 38:20, 43:33

Company (1): 21:30

Compassionate (1): 19:16

Compel (1): 19:15

Complete (4): 15:16, 26:29, 26:31, 34:21

Completeness (13): 15:15, 28:21, 29:6 (2), 37:4, 37:14 (2), 41:16, 43:23, 43:27 (2), 43:28, 44:17

Completion (1): 18:21

Conceal (8): 7:19, 7:20, 9:23, 18:17, 24:65, 37:26, 38:14, 38:15

Conceive (21): 4:1, 4:17, 16:4 (2), 16:5, 19:36, 21:2, 25:21, 29:32, 29:33, 29:34, 29:35, 30:5, 30:7, 30:17, 30:19, 30:23, 38:3, 38:4, 38:18, 49:26

Concerning (3): 21:11, 21:25, 26:32

Conclusion (5): 4:3, 6:13, 8:6, 16:3, 41:1

Concubine (4): 22:24, 25:6, 35:22, 36:12

Confusion (1): 1:2

**Consent (2):** 24:5, 24:8
**Consistency (1):** 49:24
**Consume (4):** 18:23, 18:24, 19:15, 19:17
**Contention (1):** 13:8
**Contribution (1):** 25:6
**Convict (6):** 20:16, 21:25, 24:14, 24:44, 31:37, 31:42
**Cord (2):** 38:18, 38:25
**Correct (10):** 6:9, 7:1, 18:23, 18:24 (2), 18:25 (2), 18:26, 18:28, 20:4
**Correctness (3):** 15:6, 18:19, 30:33
**Couch (1):** 49:4
**Counsel (1):** 49:6
**Count (13):** 15:5 (2), 16:10, 24:66, 29:13, 32:13, 37:9, 37:10, 40:8, 40:9, 41:8, 41:12, 41:49
**Couple (1):** 14:3
**Courageous (4):** 6:4, 10:8, 10:9 (2)
**Covenant (27):** 6:18, 9:9, 9:11, 9:12, 9:13, 9:15, 9:16, 9:17, 14:13, 15:18, 17:2, 17:4, 17:7 (2), 17:9, 17:10, 17:11, 17:13 (2), 17:14, 17:19 (2), 17:21, 21:27, 21:32, 26:28, 31:44
**Cover (2):** 6:14, 32:21
**Covering (1):** 6:14
**Cow (12):** 32:16, 41:2, 41:3 (2), 41:4 (2), 41:18, 41:19, 41:20 (2), 41:26, 41:27
**Crash (1):** 24:21
**Crave (2):** 2:9, 3:6
**Craving (2):** 31:30 (2)
**Cremate (2):** 11:3, 38:24
**Cremating (1):** 11:3
**Cross over (24):** 8:1, 12:6, 15:17, 18:3, 18:5 (2), 23:16, 30:32, 31:21, 31:52 (2), 32:11, 32:17, 32:22, 32:23, 32:24 (2), 32:32, 33:3, 33:14, 37:28, 41:46, 47:21, 50:4
**Crossing (1):** 32:23
**Crush (1):** 25:22
**Cry (2):** 19:13, 27:34
**Cry out (3):** 4:10, 27:34, 41:55
**Cup (5):** 40:11 (3), 40:13, 40:21
**Custody (6):** 40:3, 40:4, 40:7, 41:10, 42:17, 42:19
**Custom (4):** 26:5, 47:22 (2), 47:26
**Cut (8):** 9:11, 15:18, 17:14, 21:27, 21:32, 26:28, 31:44, 41:36
**Cut in two (2):** 15:10 (2)
**Cut off (1):** 17:11
**Cut piece (1):** 15:10
**Damage (15):** 6:11, 6:12 (2), 6:13, 6:17, 9:11, 9:15, 13:10, 18:28 (2), 19:13 (2), 19:14, 19:29, 38:9
**Dark (1):** 15:12
**Darkness (4):** 1:2, 1:4, 1:5, 1:18
**Daughter (110):** 5:4, 5:7, 5:10, 5:13, 5:16, 5:19, 5:22, 5:26, 5:30, 6:1, 6:2, 6:4,

11:11, 11:13, 11:15, 11:17, 11:19, 11:21, 11:23, 11:25, 11:29, 17:17, 19:8, 19:12, 19:14, 19:15, 19:16, 19:30 (2), 19:36, 20:12 (2), 24:3, 24:13, 24:23, 24:24, 24:37, 24:47 (2), 24:48, 25:20, 26:34 (2), 27:46 (3), 28:1, 28:2, 28:6, 28:8, 28:9, 29:6, 29:10, 29:16, 29:18, 29:23, 29:24, 29:28, 29:29, 30:13, 30:21, 31:26, 31:28, 31:31, 31:41, 31:43 (3), 31:50 (2), 32:1, 34:1 (2), 34:3, 34:5, 34:7, 34:8, 34:9 (2), 34:16 (2), 34:17, 34:19, 34:21 (2), 36:2 (4), 36:3, 36:6, 36:14 (2), 36:18, 36:25, 36:39 (2), 37:35, 38:2, 38:12, 41:45, 41:50, 46:7 (2), 46:15 (2), 46:18, 46:20, 46:25, 49:22
**Daughter-in-law (4):** 11:31, 38:11, 38:16, 38:24
**Dawn (3):** 19:15, 32:25, 32:27
**Day (152):** 1:5 (2), 1:8, 1:13, 1:14 (2), 1:16, 1:18, 1:19, 1:23, 1:31, 2:2 (2), 2:3, 2:4, 2:17, 3:5, 3:8, 3:14, 3:17, 4:3, 4:14, 5:1, 5:2, 5:4, 5:5, 5:8, 5:11, 5:14, 5:17, 5:20, 5:23, 5:27, 5:31, 6:3, 6:4, 6:5, 7:4 (2), 7:10, 7:11 (2), 7:12, 7:13, 7:17, 7:24, 8:3, 8:4, 8:6, 8:10, 8:12, 8:14, 8:22 (2), 9:29, 10:25, 11:32, 14:1, 15:18, 17:12, 17:23, 17:26, 18:1, 18:11, 19:37, 19:38, 21:4, 21:8, 21:26, 21:34, 22:4, 22:14, 24:1, 24:12, 24:42, 24:55, 25:7, 25:24, 25:31, 25:33, 26:1, 26:8, 26:15, 26:18, 26:32, 26:33, 27:2, 27:41, 27:44, 27:45, 29:7, 29:14, 29:20, 29:21, 30:14, 30:32, 30:33, 30:35, 30:36, 31:22, 31:23, 31:39, 31:40, 31:43, 31:48, 32:33, 33:13, 33:16, 34:25, 35:3, 35:20, 35:28, 35:29, 37:34, 38:12, 39:10 (2), 39:11, 40:4, 40:7, 40:12, 40:13, 40:18, 40:19, 40:20 (2), 41:1, 41:9, 42:13, 42:17, 42:18, 42:32, 43:9, 44:32, 47:8, 47:9 (4), 47:23, 47:26, 47:28, 47:29, 48:15, 48:20, 49:1, 50:3 (3), 50:4, 50:10, 50:20
**Deal deceitfully (1):** 31:7
**Death (7):** 21:16, 25:11, 26:18, 27:2, 27:7, 27:10, 50:16
**Deceit (2):** 27:35, 34:13
**Deceive (1):** 3:13
**Dedicated (1):** 49:26
**Deep sea (4):** 1:2, 7:11, 8:2, 49:25
**Delay (3):** 24:56, 32:5, 34:19
**Delicacy (6):** 27:4, 27:7, 27:9, 27:14, 27:17, 27:31
**Delight (1):** 34:19
**Deliver (6):** 31:9, 31:16, 32:12, 32:31, 37:21, 37:22
**Deliver up (1):** 14:20
**Deny (1):** 18:15

**387**

**Depart early (8):** 19:2, 19:27, 20:8, 21:14, 22:3, 26:31, 28:18, 32:1
**Deposit (1):** 2:15
**Deposited (1):** 41:36
**Desolate (1):** 47:19
**Despise (1):** 38:23
**Destroy (1):** 34:30
**Dew (2):** 27:28, 27:39
**Die (78):** 2:17 (2), 3:3, 3:4 (2), 5:5, 5:8, 5:11, 5:14, 5:17, 5:20, 5:27, 5:31, 7:22, 9:29, 11:28, 11:32, 18:25, 19:19, 20:3, 20:7 (2), 23:2, 23:3, 23:4, 23:6 (2), 23:8, 23:11, 23:13, 23:15, 25:8, 25:17, 25:32, 26:9, 26:11 (2), 27:4, 30:1, 33:13, 35:8, 35:18, 35:19, 35:29, 36:33, 36:34, 36:35, 36:36, 36:37, 36:38, 36:39, 37:18, 38:7, 38:10, 38:11, 38:12, 42:2, 42:20, 42:37, 42:38, 43:8, 44:9, 44:20, 44:22, 44:31, 45:28, 46:12, 46:30, 47:15, 47:19 (2), 47:29, 48:7, 48:21, 50:5, 50:15, 50:24, 50:26
**Dig (2):** 26:25, 50:5
**Dig out (8):** 21:30, 26:15, 26:18 (2), 26:19, 26:21, 26:22, 26:32
**Dim (1):** 27:1
**Diminish (3):** 8:3, 8:5, 18:28
**Dip (1):** 37:31
**Direct (27):** 2:16, 3:11, 3:17, 6:22, 7:5, 7:9, 7:16, 12:20, 18:19, 21:4, 26:11, 27:8, 28:1, 28:6, 32:5, 32:18, 32:20, 42:25, 44:1, 45:19, 47:11, 49:29, 49:33, 50:2, 50:12, 50:16 (2)
**Directive (1):** 26:5
**Discernment (3):** 2:9, 2:17, 3:22
**Disdain (1):** 25:34
**Disgrace (2):** 30:23, 34:14
**Disgusting (2):** 43:32, 46:34
**Dislocate (1):** 32:26
**Dispute (4):** 26:20, 26:21, 26:22, 31:36
**Distance (2):** 22:4, 37:18
**Distant (2):** 19:9, 35:21
**Distant time (13):** 3:22, 6:3, 6:4, 9:12, 9:16, 13:15, 17:7, 17:8, 17:13, 17:19, 21:33, 48:4, 49:26
**Distress (3):** 6:6, 34:7, 45:5
**Distressing pain (1):** 3:16
**Disturb (1):** 34:30
**Divide (2):** 32:8, 33:1
**Divide apart (9):** 2:10, 10:5, 10:32, 13:9, 13:11, 13:14, 25:23, 30:40, 15:17
**Divine (5):** 30:27, 44:5 (2), 44:15 (2)
**Do (155):** 1:7, 1:11, 1:12, 1:16, 1:25, 1:26, 1:31, 2:2 (2), 2:3, 2:4, 2:18, 3:1, 3:7, 3:13, 3:14, 3:21, 4:10, 5:1, 6:6, 6:7, 6:14 (2), 6:15, 6:16 (2), 6:22 (2), 7:4, 7:5, 8:6, 8:21, 9:6, 9:24, 11:4, 11:6 (2), 12:2, 12:5, 12:18, 13:4, 14:2, 16:6, 18:5,

18:6, 18:7, 18:8, 18:17, 18:19, 18:21, 18:25 (2), 18:29, 18:30, 18:31, 18:32, 19:3, 19:8 (2), 19:19, 19:22, 20:5, 20:6, 20:9 (3), 20:10, 20:13, 21:1, 21:6, 21:8, 21:22, 21:23 (2), 21:26, 22:12, 22:16, 24:12, 24:14, 24:49, 24:66, 26:10, 26:29 (2), 26:30, 27:4, 27:7, 27:9, 27:14, 27:17, 27:19, 27:31, 27:37, 27:45, 28:15, 29:22, 29:25, 29:26, 29:28, 30:30, 30:31, 31:1, 31:12, 31:16, 31:26, 31:28, 31:29, 31:43, 31:46, 32:11, 33:17, 34:7 (2), 34:14, 34:19, 34:31, 35:1, 35:3, 37:3, 38:10, 39:3, 39:9, 39:11, 39:19, 39:22 (2), 39:23, 40:14, 40:15, 40:20, 41:25, 41:28, 41:32, 41:34, 41:47, 41:55, 42:18, 42:20, 42:25, 42:28, 43:11, 43:17, 44:2, 44:5, 44:7, 44:15, 44:17, 45:17, 45:19, 45:21, 47:29, 47:30, 50:10, 50:12, 50:20
**Do the marriage duty (1):** 38:8
**Do well (11):** 4:7 (2), 12:13, 12:16, 32:10, 32:13 (2), 34:18, 40:14, 41:37, 45:16
**Doe (1):** 49:21
**Donation (12):** 4:3, 4:4, 4:5, 32:14, 32:19, 32:21, 32:22, 33:10, 43:11, 43:15, 43:25, 43:26
**Donkey (17):** 12:16, 22:3, 22:5, 24:35, 30:43, 32:6, 34:28, 36:24, 42:26, 42:27, 43:18, 43:24, 44:3, 44:13, 45:23, 47:17, 49:14
**Door (3):** 19:6, 19:9, 19:10
**Double (3):** 41:43, 43:12, 43:15
**Dove (5):** 8:8, 8:9, 8:10, 8:11, 8:12
**Dowry (1):** 30:20
**Draw (1):** 37:28
**Draw near (20):** 18:23, 19:9 (2), 27:21, 27:22, 27:25 (2), 27:26, 27:27, 29:10, 33:3, 33:6, 33:7 (2), 43:19, 44:18, 45:4 (2), 48:10, 48:13
**Draw water (8):** 24:11, 24:13, 24:19, 24:20 (2), 24:43, 24:44, 24:45
**Dread (1):** 35:5
**Dream (34):** 20:3, 20:6, 31:10, 31:11, 31:24, 37:5, 37:6, 37:8, 37:9 (2), 37:10, 37:19, 37:20, 40:5 (3), 40:8, 40:9 (2), 40:16, 41:7, 41:8, 41:11 (2), 41:12 (2), 41:15 (2), 41:17, 41:22, 41:25, 41:26, 41:32, 42:9
**Drink (27):** 2:6, 2:10, 19:32, 19:33, 19:34, 19:35, 21:19, 24:14, 24:18, 24:19, 24:43, 24:45, 24:46 (2), 29:2, 29:3, 29:7, 29:8, 29:10, 40:1, 40:2, 40:9, 40:13, 40:20, 40:21, 40:23, 41:9
**Drinking (3):** 13:10, 40:5, 40:21
**Drive (2):** 31:18, 31:26
**Drove (10):** 29:2 (2), 29:3, 29:8, 30:40, 32:17 (4), 32:20
**Dry ground (2):** 1:9, 1:10

**Dry out (2):** 8:7, 8:14

**Dry up (2):** 8:13 (2)

**Dull red (1):** 49:12

**Dwell (8):** 3:24, 9:27, 14:13, 16:12, 25:18, 26:2, 35:22, 49:13

**Dysfunctional (38):** 2:9, 2:17, 3:5, 3:22, 6:5 (2), 8:21, 13:13, 19:19, 24:50, 26:29, 28:8, 31:24, 31:29 (2), 31:49, 31:52, 37:2, 37:20, 37:33, 38:7, 39:9, 40:7, 41:3, 41:4, 41:19 (2), 41:20, 41:21, 41:27, 44:4, 44:29, 44:34, 47:9, 48:16, 50:15, 50:17, 50:20

**Ear (7):** 20:8, 23:10, 23:13, 23:16, 35:4, 44:18, 50:4

**East (12):** 2:8, 3:24, 10:30, 11:2, 12:8 (2), 13:11, 13:14, 25:6 (2), 28:14, 29:1

**East wind (3):** 41:6, 41:23, 41:27

**Eastward (2):** 2:14, 4:16

**Eat (66):** 2:16 (2), 2:17 (2), 3:1, 3:2, 3:3, 3:5, 3:6 (2), 3:11 (2), 3:12, 3:13, 3:14, 3:17 (3), 3:18, 3:19, 3:22, 6:21, 9:4, 14:24, 18:8, 19:3, 24:33 (2), 24:54, 25:34, 26:30, 27:4, 27:7, 27:10, 27:19, 27:25 (2), 27:31, 27:33, 28:20, 31:15 (2), 31:38, 31:40, 31:46, 31:54 (2), 32:33, 37:20, 37:25, 37:33, 39:6, 40:17, 40:19, 41:4, 41:20, 43:2, 43:16, 43:25, 43:32 (2), 45:18, 47:22, 47:24 (2), 49:27

**Eight (16):** 5:4, 5:7, 5:10, 5:13, 5:16, 5:17, 5:19, 5:25, 5:26, 5:28, 14:14, 16:16, 17:12, 21:4, 22:23, 35:28

**Elevation (1):** 49:3

**Emaciated (4):** 41:3, 41:4, 41:6, 41:7

**Embrace (3):** 29:13, 33:4, 48:10

**Emptiness (1):** 31:42

**Empty (4):** 14:14, 37:24, 41:27, 42:35

**Encounter (2):** 32:18, 33:8

**End (1):** 49:1

**Endow (1):** 30:20

**Entwine (1):** 30:8

**Err (7):** 20:9, 31:39, 39:9, 40:1, 42:22, 43:9, 44:32

**Error (6):** 4:7, 13:13, 18:20, 20:9, 31:36, 50:17

**Escape (2):** 32:9, 45:7

**Escaped one (1):** 14:13

**Eunuch (4):** 37:36, 39:1, 40:2, 40:7

**Evening (13):** 1:5, 1:8, 1:13, 1:19, 1:23, 1:31, 8:11, 19:1, 24:11, 24:63, 29:23, 30:16, 49:27

**Ewe (2):** 31:38, 32:15

**Ewe lamb (3):** 21:28, 21:29, 21:30

**Examine (2):** 42:15, 42:16

**Except (8):** 3:11, 4:15, 19:21, 21:26, 38:9, 43:3, 43:5, 47:18

**Exchange (14):** 41:56, 41:57, 42:2, 42:3, 42:5, 42:6, 42:7, 42:10, 43:2, 43:4, 43:20, 43:22, 44:25, 47:14

**Excuse me (2):** 43:20, 44:18

**Exhale (1):** 2:7

**Exist (318):** 1:2, 1:3 (2), 1:5 (2), 1:6 (2), 1:7, 1:8 (2), 1:9, 1:11, 1:13 (2), 1:14 (2), 1:15 (2), 1:19 (2), 1:23 (2), 1:24, 1:29, 1:30, 1:31 (2), 2:5, 2:7, 2:10, 2:18, 2:24, 2:25, 3:1, 3:5, 3:20, 3:22, 4:2 (2), 4:3, 4:8 (2), 4:12, 4:14 (2), 4:17, 4:20, 4:21, 5:4, 5:5, 5:8, 5:11, 5:14, 5:17, 5:20, 5:23, 5:27, 5:31, 5:32, 6:1, 6:3, 6:4, 6:9, 6:19, 6:21, 7:6, 7:10 (2), 7:12, 7:17, 8:5, 8:6, 8:13, 9:2, 9:3, 9:11, 9:13, 9:14, 9:15, 9:16, 9:18, 9:25, 9:26, 9:27, 9:28, 9:29, 10:8, 10:9, 10:10, 10:19, 10:30, 11:1, 11:2, 11:3 (2), 11:11, 11:30, 11:32, 12:2, 12:10, 12:11, 12:12, 12:14, 12:16, 13:3, 13:5, 13:6, 13:7, 13:8, 14:1, 15:1, 15:5, 15:12, 15:13, 15:17 (2), 16:12, 17:1 (2), 17:4, 17:5, 17:7, 17:8, 17:11, 17:13, 17:16 (2), 18:11, 18:12, 18:18 (2), 18:25, 19:14, 19:17, 19:26, 19:29, 19:34, 20:12, 20:13, 21:20 (2), 21:22, 21:30, 22:1, 22:20, 23:1, 24:14, 24:15, 24:22, 24:30, 24:41, 24:43, 24:51, 24:52, 24:60, 24:67, 25:3, 25:11, 25:20, 25:27, 26:1 (2), 26:3, 26:8, 26:14, 26:28 (2), 26:32, 26:34, 26:35, 27:1, 27:12, 27:23, 27:30 (2), 27:33, 27:39, 27:40, 28:3, 28:14, 28:21, 28:22, 29:10, 29:13, 29:17, 29:20, 29:23, 29:25, 30:25, 30:29, 30:30, 30:32, 30:34, 30:41, 30:42, 30:43, 31:3, 31:5, 31:8 (2), 31:10, 31:40, 31:42, 31:44, 32:6, 32:9, 32:11, 33:9, 34:5, 34:10, 34:15, 34:16, 34:22, 34:25 (2), 35:3, 35:5, 35:10, 35:11, 35:16, 35:17, 35:18, 35:22 (2), 35:28, 36:7, 36:11, 36:12, 36:13, 36:14, 36:22, 37:2, 37:20, 37:23, 37:27, 38:1, 38:5, 38:7, 38:9 (2), 38:21, 38:22, 38:23, 38:24, 38:27, 38:28, 38:29, 39:2 (3), 39:5 (2), 39:6, 39:7, 39:10 (2), 39:11, 39:13, 39:15, 39:18, 39:19, 39:20, 39:21, 39:22, 40:1, 40:4, 40:13, 40:20, 41:1, 41:8, 41:13 (2), 41:27, 41:36 (2), 41:40, 41:48, 41:53, 41:54 (2), 41:56, 42:5, 42:11, 42:31, 42:35, 42:36, 43:2, 43:21, 44:9, 44:10 (2), 44:17, 44:24, 44:31, 45:10, 46:12, 46:32, 46:33, 46:34, 47:9, 47:19, 47:20, 47:24 (2), 47:25, 47:26, 47:28 (2), 48:1, 48:5, 48:6, 48:19 (2), 48:21, 49:15, 49:17, 49:26, 50:9

**Experienced (1):** 14:14

**Expire (6):** 6:17, 7:21, 25:8, 25:17, 35:29, 49:33

**Expose (1):** 30:37

**Extreme old age (4):** 21:2, 21:7, 37:3, 44:20

**Eye (80):** 3:5, 3:6, 3:7, 6:8, 13:10, 13:14, 16:4, 16:5, 16:6, 16:7 (2), 18:2, 18:3, 19:8, 19:14, 19:19, 20:15, 20:16, 21:11, 21:12, 21:19, 22:4, 22:13, 23:11, 23:18, 24:13, 24:16, 24:29, 24:30, 24:42, 24:43, 24:45, 24:63, 24:64, 27:1, 27:12, 28:8, 29:17, 29:20, 30:27, 30:41, 31:10, 31:12, 31:35, 31:40, 32:6, 33:1, 33:5, 33:8, 33:10, 33:15, 34:11, 34:18 (2), 37:25, 38:7, 38:10, 39:4, 39:7, 39:21, 41:37 (2), 42:24, 43:29, 44:21, 45:5, 45:12 (2), 45:16 (2), 45:20, 46:4, 47:19, 47:25, 47:29, 48:10, 48:17, 49:12, 49:22, 50:4

**Face (140):** 1:2 (2), 1:20, 1:29, 2:6, 3:8, 4:5, 4:6, 4:14 (2), 4:16, 6:1, 6:7, 6:11, 6:13 (2), 7:1, 7:3, 7:4, 7:7, 7:18, 7:23, 8:8, 8:9, 8:13, 9:23, 10:9 (2), 11:4, 11:8, 11:9, 11:28, 13:9, 13:10, 16:6, 16:8, 16:12, 17:1, 17:3, 17:17, 17:18, 18:8, 18:16, 18:22, 19:13, 19:21, 19:27, 19:28 (2), 20:15, 23:3, 23:4, 23:8, 23:12, 23:17, 23:19, 24:7, 24:12, 24:33, 24:40, 24:51, 25:9, 25:18 (2), 27:7 (2), 27:10, 27:20, 27:30, 27:46, 29:26, 30:30, 30:33, 30:40, 31:2, 31:5, 31:21, 31:35, 32:4, 32:17, 32:18, 32:21 (4), 32:22, 32:31 (2), 33:3, 33:10 (2), 33:14 (2), 33:18, 34:10, 34:21, 35:1, 35:7, 36:6, 36:7, 36:31, 38:15, 40:7, 40:9, 41:31, 41:43, 41:46 (2), 41:56, 43:3, 43:5, 43:9, 43:14, 43:15, 43:31, 43:33, 44:14, 44:23, 44:26, 44:29, 45:3, 45:5, 45:7, 46:28 (2), 46:30, 47:2, 47:6, 47:7, 47:10, 47:13, 47:18, 48:11, 48:15, 48:20, 49:30, 50:1, 50:13, 50:16, 50:18

**Faint (1):** 47:13

**Fall (18):** 2:21, 4:5, 4:6, 14:10, 15:12 (2), 17:3, 17:17, 24:64, 25:18, 33:4, 43:18, 44:14, 45:14, 46:29, 49:17, 50:1, 50:18

**Fall upon (2):** 3:15 (2)

**Family (12):** 8:19, 10:5, 10:18, 10:20, 10:31, 10:32, 12:3, 24:38, 24:40, 24:41, 28:14, 36:40

**Family idol (3):** 31:19, 31:34, 31:35

**Famine (3):** 42:19, 42:33, 43:1

**Far be it (4):** 18:25 (2), 44:7, 44:17

**Far end (6):** 8:3, 19:4, 23:9, 47:2, 47:21 (2)

**Fat (4):** 4:4, 18:8, 45:18, 49:12

**Father (208):** 2:24, 4:20, 4:21, 9:18, 9:22 (2), 9:23 (2), 10:21, 11:28, 11:29 (2), 12:1, 15:15, 17:4, 17:5, 19:31, 19:32 (2), 19:33 (2), 19:34 (2), 19:35, 19:36, 19:37, 19:38, 20:12, 20:13, 22:7 (2), 22:21, 24:7, 24:23, 24:38, 24:40, 26:3, 26:15 (2), 26:18 (2), 26:24, 27:6, 27:9, 27:10, 27:12, 27:14, 27:18 (2), 27:19, 27:22, 27:26, 27:30, 27:31 (2), 27:31, 27:32, 27:34 (3), 27:38 (3), 27:39, 27:41 (2), 28:2, 28:7, 28:8, 28:13, 28:21, 29:9, 29:12 (2), 31:1 (2), 31:3, 31:5 (2), 31:6, 31:7, 31:9, 31:14, 31:16, 31:18, 31:19, 31:29, 31:30, 31:35, 31:42, 31:53 (2), 32:10 (2), 33:19, 34:4, 34:6, 34:11, 34:13, 34:19, 35:18, 35:22, 35:27, 36:9, 36:24, 36:43, 37:1, 37:2 (2), 37:4, 37:10 (2), 37:11, 37:12, 37:22, 37:32, 37:35, 38:11 (2), 41:51, 42:13, 42:29, 42:32 (2), 42:35, 42:36, 42:37, 43:2, 43:7, 43:8, 43:11, 43:23, 43:27, 43:28, 44:17, 44:19, 44:20 (2), 44:22 (2), 44:24, 44:25, 44:27, 44:30, 44:31, 44:32 (2), 44:34 (2), 45:3, 45:8, 45:9, 45:13 (2), 45:18, 45:19, 45:23 (2), 45:25, 45:27, 46:1, 46:3, 46:5, 46:29, 46:31 (2), 46:34, 47:1, 47:3, 47:5, 47:6, 47:7, 47:9, 47:11, 47:12 (2), 47:30, 48:1, 48:9, 48:15, 48:16, 48:17 (2), 48:18 (2), 48:19, 48:21, 49:2, 49:4, 49:8, 49:25, 49:26, 49:28, 49:29, 50:1, 50:2, 50:5 (2), 50:6, 50:7, 50:8, 50:10, 50:14 (2), 50:15, 50:16, 50:17, 50:22

**Father-in-law (2):** 38:13, 38:25

**Fatten (11):** 1:1, 1:21, 1:27 (3), 2:3, 2:4, 5:1, 5:2 (2), 6:7

**Fault (2):** 20:6, 41:9

**Fear (21):** 3:10, 15:1, 18:15, 19:30, 20:8, 21:17, 26:7, 26:24, 28:17 (2), 31:31, 32:8, 32:12, 35:17, 42:18, 42:35, 43:18, 43:23, 46:3, 50:19, 50:21

**Fearful (1):** 22:12

**Fearfulness (1):** 20:11

**Fearing (1):** 9:2

**Feast (5):** 19:3, 21:8, 26:30, 29:22, 40:20

**Fed fat (6):** 41:2, 41:4, 41:5, 41:7, 41:18, 41:20

**Feed (22):** 4:2, 13:7 (2), 13:8 (2), 26:20 (2), 29:7, 29:9, 30:31, 30:36, 36:24, 37:2, 37:12, 37:13, 37:16, 41:2, 41:18, 46:34, 47:3, 48:15, 49:24

**Feel (1):** 27:12

**Female (6):** 1:27, 5:2, 6:19, 7:3, 7:9, 7:16

**Female owner (3):** 16:4, 16:8, 16:9

**Fence in (1):** 11:6

**Few (2):** 19:20 (2)

**Field (48):** 2:5 (2), 2:19, 2:20, 3:1, 3:14, 3:18, 4:8, 14:7, 23:9, 23:11, 23:13, 23:17 (3), 23:19, 23:20, 24:63, 24:65, 25:9, 25:10, 25:27, 25:29, 27:3, 27:5, 27:27, 29:2, 30:14, 30:16, 31:4, 32:4,

33:19, 34:5, 34:7, 34:28, 36:35, 37:7, 37:15, 39:5, 41:48, 47:20, 47:24, 49:29, 49:30 (2), 49:32, 50:13 (2)

**Fifth (3):** 1:23, 30:17, 47:24

**Fifth part (1):** 47:26

**Fig (1):** 3:7

**Fill (16):** 1:22, 1:28, 6:11, 6:13, 9:1, 21:19, 24:16, 25:24, 26:15, 29:21, 29:27, 29:28, 42:25, 44:1, 50:3 (2)

**Filling (1):** 48:19

**Find (56):** 2:20, 4:14, 4:15, 6:8, 8:9, 11:2, 16:7, 18:3, 18:26, 18:28, 18:29, 18:30 (2), 18:31, 18:32, 19:11, 19:15, 19:19, 26:12, 26:19, 26:32, 27:20, 30:14, 30:27, 31:32, 31:33, 31:34, 31:35, 31:37, 32:6, 32:20, 33:8, 33:10, 33:15, 34:11, 36:24, 37:15, 37:17, 37:32, 38:20, 38:22, 38:23, 39:4, 41:38, 44:8, 44:9, 44:10, 44:12, 44:16 (2), 44:17, 44:34, 47:14, 47:25, 47:29, 50:4

**Finish (17):** 2:1, 2:2, 6:16, 17:22, 18:33, 21:15, 24:15, 24:19 (2), 24:22, 24:45, 27:30, 41:30, 41:53, 43:2, 44:12, 49:33

**Fire (4):** 15:17, 19:24, 22:6, 22:7

**Firm (3):** 15:6, 42:20, 45:26

**First (10):** 8:13, 13:4, 25:25, 26:1, 28:19, 32:18, 33:2, 38:28, 40:13, 41:20

**First time (4):** 13:3, 41:21, 43:18, 43:20

**Firstborn (15):** 10:15, 22:21, 25:13, 27:19, 27:32, 35:23, 36:15, 38:6, 38:7, 41:51, 43:33, 46:8, 48:14, 48:18, 49:3

**Firstborn female (6):** 4:4, 19:31, 19:33, 19:34, 19:37, 29:26

**Fish (1):** 9:2

**Five (34):** 5:6, 5:10, 5:11, 5:15, 5:17, 5:21, 5:23, 5:30 (2), 5:32, 6:15, 7:20, 7:24, 8:3, 9:28, 9:29, 11:11, 11:12, 11:32, 12:4, 14:9, 18:24 (2), 18:26, 18:28 (4), 25:7, 43:34, 45:6, 45:11, 45:22, 47:2

**Fixed (3):** 41:32, 43:16, 43:25

**Flare up (11):** 4:5, 4:6, 18:30, 18:32, 30:2, 31:35, 31:36, 34:7, 39:19, 44:18, 45:5

**Flee (7):** 14:10 (2), 19:20, 39:12, 39:13, 39:15, 39:18

**Flee away (9):** 16:6, 16:8, 27:43, 31:20, 31:21, 31:22, 31:27, 35:1, 35:7

**Flesh (33):** 2:21, 2:23 (2), 2:24, 6:3, 6:12, 6:13, 6:17, 6:19, 7:15, 7:16, 7:21, 8:17, 9:4, 9:11, 9:15 (2), 9:16, 9:17, 17:11, 17:13, 17:14, 17:23, 17:24, 17:25, 29:14, 37:27, 40:19, 41:2, 41:3, 41:4, 41:18, 41:19

**Flocks (63):** 4:2, 4:4, 12:16, 13:5, 20:14, 21:27, 21:28, 24:35, 26:14, 27:9, 29:2, 29:3, 29:6, 29:7, 29:8, 29:9, 29:10 (2), 30:31, 30:32, 30:36, 30:38 (2), 30:39 (2), 30:40 (2), 30:40, 30:41 (2), 30:42,

30:43, 31:4, 31:8 (2), 31:10 (2), 31:12, 31:19, 31:38, 31:41, 31:43 (2), 32:6, 32:8, 33:13 (2), 34:28, 37:2, 37:12, 37:14, 38:12, 38:13, 38:17, 45:10, 46:32 (2), 46:34, 47:1, 47:3, 47:4, 47:17, 50:8

**Flood (12):** 6:17, 7:6, 7:7, 7:10, 7:17, 9:11 (2), 9:15, 9:28, 10:1, 10:32, 11:10

**Flour (1):** 18:6

**Flutter (1):** 1:2

**Fly (1):** 1:20

**Flyer (22):** 1:20, 1:21, 1:22, 1:26, 1:28, 1:30, 2:19, 2:20, 6:7, 6:20, 7:3, 7:8, 7:14, 7:21, 7:23, 8:17, 8:19, 8:20, 9:2, 9:10, 40:17, 40:19

**Following (2):** 3:16, 4:7

**Folly (1):** 34:7

**Food (4):** 1:29, 1:30, 6:21, 9:3

**Foodstuff (15):** 14:11, 41:35 (2), 41:36, 41:48 (3), 42:7, 42:10, 43:2, 43:4, 43:20, 43:22, 44:1, 44:25

**Foolish (1):** 31:28

**Foot (13):** 8:9, 18:4, 19:2, 24:32 (2), 29:1, 30:30, 33:14 (2), 41:44, 43:24, 49:10, 49:33

**Force (2):** 34:29, 47:6

**Forearm (5):** 6:15 (3), 6:16, 7:20

**Foreign (4):** 17:12, 17:27, 35:2, 35:4

**Foreigner (1):** 31:15

**Foreskin (6):** 17:11, 17:14, 17:23, 17:24, 17:25, 34:14

**Forget (3):** 27:45, 40:23, 41:30

**Fortune (1):** 30:11

**Four (30):** 2:10, 5:13, 7:4 (2), 7:12 (2), 7:17, 8:6, 11:13, 11:15, 11:16, 11:17, 14:5, 14:9, 15:13, 18:28, 18:29 (2), 23:15, 23:16, 25:20, 26:34, 31:41, 32:7, 32:16, 33:1, 46:22, 47:24, 47:28, 50:3

**Fourth (3):** 1:19, 2:14, 15:16

**Fragment (1):** 18:5

**Freely (1):** 29:15

**Fresh Wine (2):** 27:28, 27:37

**From (75):** 2:6, 2:7, 2:9, 2:17 (2), 2:19, 2:22, 3:3, 3:5, 3:11 (2), 3:12, 3:17 (2), 3:19, 3:22, 4:10, 4:11, 5:29, 6:20, 7:2, 7:8 (3), 7:23, 8:2, 8:10, 8:16, 8:19, 9:18, 9:21, 10:11, 13:14, 16:2, 17:6, 17:16 (2), 19:12, 19:14, 19:24, 21:15, 21:17, 22:11, 22:12, 22:15, 23:6 (2), 23:13, 25:29, 25:30, 26:16, 27:45, 29:2, 30:2, 30:3, 30:16, 31:13, 32:14, 33:15, 34:7, 35:11, 37:28, 38:17, 38:26, 39:9 (2), 40:14, 40:17, 41:2, 41:3, 41:14, 41:18, 41:40, 48:19, 50:24

**Full (3):** 23:9, 41:7, 41:22

**Functional (45):** 1:4, 1:10, 1:12, 1:18, 1:21, 1:25, 1:31, 2:9 (2), 2:12, 2:17, 2:18, 3:5, 3:6, 3:22, 6:2, 15:15, 16:6, 18:7, 19:8,

20:15, 24:10, 24:16, 24:50, 25:8, 26:7, 26:29, 27:9, 29:19, 30:20, 31:24, 31:29, 40:16, 41:5, 41:22, 41:24, 41:26 (2), 41:35, 44:4, 45:18, 45:20, 45:23, 49:15, 50:20

**Furnace (1):** 19:28

**Fury (1):** 27:44

**Game (9):** 25:27, 25:28, 27:5, 27:7, 27:19, 27:25, 27:30, 27:31, 27:33

**Garden (14):** 2:8, 2:9, 2:10, 2:15, 2:16, 3:1, 3:2, 3:3, 3:8 (2), 3:10, 3:23, 3:24, 13:10

**Garment (14):** 24:53, 27:15, 27:27, 28:20, 37:29, 38:14, 38:19, 39:12 (2), 39:13, 39:15, 39:16, 39:18, 41:42

**Gate (9):** 19:1, 22:17, 23:10, 23:18, 24:60, 28:17, 34:20, 34:24 (2)

**Gather (15):** 6:21, 25:8, 25:17, 29:3, 29:7, 29:8, 29:22, 30:23, 34:30, 35:29, 42:17, 49:1, 49:29, 49:33 (2)

**Gather together (3):** 41:35, 41:48, 49:2

**Generation (7):** 6:9, 7:1, 9:12, 15:16, 17:7, 17:9, 17:12

**Gentle (1):** 33:14

**Gift (1):** 34:12

**Girl (1):** 34:4

**Give (149):** 1:17, 1:29, 3:6, 3:12 (2), 4:12, 9:2, 9:3, 9:12, 9:13, 12:7, 13:15, 13:17, 14:20, 14:21, 15:2, 15:3, 15:7, 15:10, 15:18, 16:3, 16:5, 17:2, 17:5, 17:6, 17:8, 17:16, 17:20, 18:7, 18:8, 20:6, 20:14, 20:16, 21:14, 21:27, 23:4, 23:9 (2), 23:11 (3), 23:13, 24:7, 24:32, 24:35, 24:36, 24:41, 24:53 (2), 25:5, 25:6, 25:34, 26:3, 26:4, 27:17, 27:28, 27:37, 28:4 (2), 28:13, 28:20, 28:22, 29:19 (2), 29:24, 29:26, 29:27, 29:28, 29:29, 29:33, 30:4, 30:6, 30:9, 30:14, 30:18 (2), 30:26, 30:28, 30:31 (2), 30:35, 30:40, 31:7, 31:9, 32:17, 34:8, 34:9, 34:11, 34:12 (2), 34:14, 34:16, 34:21, 35:4, 35:12 (3), 38:9, 38:14, 38:16, 38:17, 38:18 (2), 38:26, 38:28, 39:4, 39:8, 39:20, 39:21, 39:22, 40:3, 40:11, 40:13, 40:21, 41:10, 41:41, 41:42, 41:43, 41:45, 41:48 (2), 42:25, 42:27, 42:30, 42:34, 42:37, 43:14, 43:23, 43:24 (2), 45:2, 45:18, 45:21 (2), 45:22 (2), 46:18, 47:11, 47:16, 47:17, 47:19, 47:22, 47:24, 48:4 (2), 48:9, 48:22, 49:20, 49:21

**Give a tenth (2):** 28:22 (2)

**Give milk (1):** 33:13

**Given that (290):** 1:4, 1:10, 1:12, 1:18, 1:21, 1:25, 2:3, 2:5, 2:17, 2:23, 3:1, 3:5 (2), 3:6 (2), 3:7, 3:10, 3:11, 3:14, 3:17, 3:19 (2), 3:20, 4:12, 4:23, 4:24, 4:25 (2), 5:24, 6:1, 6:2, 6:5, 6:6, 6:7 (2), 6:12,

6:13, 7:1, 7:4, 8:9, 8:11, 8:21, 9:6, 10:25, 11:9, 12:10, 12:11, 12:12, 12:14, 12:18, 13:6, 13:8, 13:10, 13:15, 13:17, 14:14, 15:4, 15:8, 15:13, 15:16, 16:4, 16:5, 16:11, 16:13, 17:5, 17:15, 18:5, 18:15 (2), 18:19, 18:20 (2), 19:2, 19:8, 19:13 (2), 19:14, 19:22, 19:30, 20:6, 20:7 (2), 20:9, 20:10, 20:11, 20:18, 21:7, 21:10, 21:12, 21:13, 21:16, 21:17, 21:18, 21:30 (2), 21:31, 22:12 (2), 22:16, 22:17, 24:4, 24:14, 24:41, 25:21, 25:28, 25:30, 26:3, 26:7 (2), 26:8, 26:9, 26:13, 26:16, 26:20, 26:22, 26:24, 26:28, 27:1, 27:20, 27:23, 27:36, 28:6, 28:8, 28:11, 28:15, 28:17, 29:2, 29:9, 29:12 (2), 29:15, 29:21, 29:31, 29:32 (3), 29:33 (2), 29:34, 30:1, 30:9, 30:13, 30:16, 30:20, 30:26, 30:30, 30:33, 31:5, 31:6, 31:12, 31:15, 31:16, 31:20, 31:22, 31:30, 31:31 (2), 31:32, 31:35 (2), 31:36, 31:37, 31:42, 31:49, 32:11, 32:12, 32:18, 32:21, 32:26, 32:27 (2), 32:29 (2), 32:31, 32:33, 33:10, 33:11 (2), 33:13, 34:5, 34:7, 34:14, 34:19, 35:7, 35:10, 35:17, 35:18, 36:7, 37:3, 37:4, 37:17, 37:26, 37:27, 37:35, 38:9, 38:11, 38:14 (2), 38:15, 38:16 (3), 38:26, 39:3, 39:6, 39:9, 39:13, 39:15, 40:14, 40:15 (2), 40:16, 41:21, 41:31, 41:32, 41:49 (2), 41:51, 41:52, 41:57, 42:1, 42:2, 42:4, 42:5, 42:12, 42:15, 42:16, 42:23 (2), 42:33, 42:34 (2), 42:38, 43:5, 43:7, 43:10 (2), 43:16, 43:18, 43:21, 43:25 (2), 43:30, 43:32 (2), 44:15, 44:18, 44:24, 44:26, 44:27, 44:31, 44:32, 44:34, 45:3, 45:5 (2), 45:6, 45:8, 45:11, 45:12, 45:20, 45:26 (2), 46:3, 46:30, 46:32, 46:33, 46:34, 47:4 (2), 47:13, 47:15, 47:18, 47:20 (2), 47:22, 48:14, 48:17, 48:18, 49:4, 49:6, 49:7 (2), 49:10, 49:15 (2), 50:3, 50:15, 50:17, 50:19

**Glow (2):** 1:15, 1:17

**Go around (5):** 2:11, 2:13, 19:4, 37:7, 42:24

**Go down (39):** 11:5, 11:7, 12:10, 15:11, 18:21, 24:16, 24:18, 24:45, 24:46, 26:2, 28:12, 37:25, 37:35, 38:1, 39:1 (2), 42:2, 42:3, 42:38 (2), 43:4, 43:5, 43:7, 43:11, 43:15, 43:20 (2), 43:22, 44:11, 44:21, 44:23, 44:26 (2), 44:29, 44:31, 45:9, 45:13, 46:3, 46:4

**Go left (1):** 13:9

**Go out (79):** 1:12, 1:24, 2:10, 4:16, 8:7 (2), 8:16, 8:17, 8:18, 8:19, 9:10, 9:18, 10:11, 10:14, 11:31, 12:4, 12:5, 14:8, 14:17, 14:18, 15:4, 15:5, 15:7, 15:14, 17:6, 19:5, 19:6, 19:8, 19:12, 19:14 (2),

19:16, 19:17, 19:23, 24:5, 24:11, 24:13, 24:15, 24:43, 24:45, 24:50, 24:53, 24:63, 25:25, 25:26, 27:3, 27:30 (2), 28:10, 30:16, 31:13, 31:33, 34:1, 34:6, 34:24 (2), 34:26, 35:11, 35:18, 38:24, 38:25, 38:28, 38:29, 38:30, 39:12, 39:15, 40:14, 41:45, 41:46, 42:15, 42:28, 43:23, 43:31, 44:4, 44:28, 45:1, 46:26, 47:10, 48:12

**Go Right (1):** 13:9

**Go up (51):** 2:6, 8:20, 13:1, 17:22, 19:15, 19:28, 19:30, 22:2, 22:13, 24:16, 26:23, 28:12, 31:10, 31:12, 32:25, 32:27, 35:1, 35:3, 35:13, 37:28, 38:12, 38:13, 40:10, 41:2, 41:3, 41:5, 41:18, 41:19, 41:22, 41:27, 44:17, 44:24, 44:33, 44:34, 45:9, 45:25, 46:4 (2), 46:29, 46:31, 49:4 (2), 49:9, 50:5, 50:6, 50:7 (2), 50:9, 50:14, 50:24, 50:25

**Goat (1):** 37:31

**Gold (9):** 2:11, 2:12, 13:2, 24:22 (2), 24:35, 24:53, 41:42, 44:8

**Goods (11):** 12:5, 13:6, 14:11, 14:12, 14:16 (2), 14:21, 15:14, 31:18, 36:7, 46:6

**Gopher (1):** 6:14

**Governor (1):** 42:6

**Grain (5):** 41:35, 41:49, 42:3, 42:25, 45:23

**Grain flour (1):** 18:6

**Grape (3):** 40:10, 40:11, 49:11

**Grapevine (3):** 40:9, 40:10, 49:11

**Grapple (2):** 32:25, 32:26

**Grass (2):** 1:11, 1:12

**Grave (8):** 23:4, 23:6 (2), 23:9, 23:20, 49:30, 50:5, 50:13

**Gray headed (5):** 15:15, 25:8, 42:38, 44:29, 44:31

**Great tree (5):** 12:6, 13:18, 14:13, 18:1, 35:8

**Green (2):** 1:30, 9:3

**Grief (1):** 26:35

**Grope (4):** 27:21, 27:22, 31:34, 31:37

**Ground (43):** 1:25, 2:5, 2:6, 2:7, 2:9, 2:19, 3:17, 3:19, 3:23, 4:2, 4:3, 4:10, 4:11, 4:12, 4:14, 5:29, 6:1, 6:7, 6:20, 7:4, 7:8, 7:23, 8:8, 8:13, 8:21, 9:2, 9:20, 12:3, 19:25, 28:14, 28:15, 47:18, 47:19 (4), 47:20, 47:22 (2), 47:23 (2), 47:26 (2)

**Guard (15):** 2:15, 3:24, 4:9, 17:9, 17:10, 18:19, 24:6, 26:5, 28:15, 28:20, 30:31, 31:24, 31:29, 37:11, 41:35

**Guide (2):** 24:27, 24:48

**Guilt (2):** 26:10, 42:21

**Gulp (17):** 9:21, 24:14 (2), 24:18, 24:19, 24:22, 24:44, 24:46 (2), 24:54, 25:34, 26:30, 27:25, 30:38 (2), 43:34, 44:5

**Gust (1):** 15:11

**Guzzle (1):** 24:17

**Hair (3):** 25:25, 27:11, 27:23

**Hand (95):** 3:22, 4:11, 5:29, 8:9, 9:2, 9:5 (3), 14:20, 14:22, 16:6, 16:9, 16:12 (2), 19:10, 19:16 (3), 21:18, 21:30, 22:6, 22:10, 22:12, 24:2, 24:9, 24:10, 24:18, 24:22, 24:30, 24:47, 25:26, 27:16, 27:17, 27:22 (2), 27:23 (2), 30:35, 31:29, 31:39, 32:12 (2), 32:14, 32:17, 33:10, 33:19, 34:21, 35:4, 37:21, 37:22 (2), 37:27, 38:18, 38:20 (2), 38:28 (2), 38:29, 38:30, 39:1, 39:3, 39:4, 39:6, 39:8, 39:12, 39:13, 39:22, 39:23, 40:11, 40:13, 41:35, 41:42 (2), 41:44, 42:37, 43:9, 43:12 (2), 43:15, 43:21, 43:22, 43:26, 43:34, 44:16, 44:17, 46:4, 47:24, 47:29, 48:14, 48:17 (2), 48:22, 49:8, 49:24 (2)

**Handful (1):** 41:47

**Hang (3):** 40:19, 40:22, 41:13

**Happiness (1):** 30:13

**Happy (1):** 30:13

**Hard (2):** 42:7, 42:30

**Hardship (3):** 3:16, 3:17, 5:29

**Harm (3):** 42:4, 42:38, 44:29

**Harp (2):** 4:21, 31:27

**Harvest (3):** 8:22, 30:14, 45:6

**Hate (7):** 24:60, 26:27, 29:31, 29:33, 37:4, 37:5, 37:8

**Hazel (1):** 30:37

**He (124):** 2:11, 2:13, 2:14 (2), 2:19, 3:6, 3:15, 3:16, 4:4, 4:20, 4:21, 4:26, 6:3, 9:3, 9:18, 10:8, 10:9, 10:21, 13:1, 14:3, 14:7, 14:12, 14:13, 14:15, 14:17, 14:18, 15:2, 15:4, 15:18, 16:12, 17:12, 18:1, 18:8, 18:10, 19:30, 19:33, 19:35, 19:37, 19:38, 20:5 (2), 20:7, 20:13, 20:16, 21:13, 21:17, 21:22, 21:31, 22:14, 24:7, 24:15, 24:54, 24:62, 24:65, 25:29, 26:12, 26:24, 26:32, 27:31, 27:33, 28:11, 28:19, 29:12 (2), 30:16, 30:33, 30:35, 31:16, 31:20, 31:21, 31:43, 32:3, 32:14, 32:19, 32:22 (2), 32:23, 32:32, 33:3, 33:16, 34:19, 35:6, 36:1, 36:8, 36:19, 36:24, 36:43, 37:2, 37:3, 37:27, 38:11, 38:12, 39:3, 39:6, 39:22, 39:23, 41:11, 41:25, 41:26, 41:28, 41:31 (2), 42:6 (2), 42:14, 42:27, 42:38, 43:12, 44:5, 44:10, 44:14, 44:17, 44:20, 45:20, 45:26, 48:14, 48:19 (2), 48:20, 49:13, 49:19, 49:20, 50:14, 50:22

**Head (20):** 2:10, 3:15, 8:5, 11:4, 28:12, 28:18, 40:13, 40:16, 40:17, 40:19, 40:20 (2), 47:31, 48:14 (2), 48:17 (3), 48:18, 49:26

**Head of grain (10):** 41:5, 41:6, 41:7 (2), 41:22, 41:23, 41:24 (2), 41:26, 41:27

**Headrest (2):** 28:11, 28:18

**Heal (3):** 20:17, 50:2 (2)

**Hear (62):** 3:8, 3:10, 3:17, 4:23, 11:7, 14:14, 16:2, 16:11, 17:20, 18:10, 21:6, 21:12, 21:17 (2), 21:26, 22:18, 23:6, 23:8, 23:11, 23:13, 23:15, 23:16, 24:30, 24:52, 26:5, 27:5, 27:6, 27:8, 27:13, 27:34, 27:43, 28:7, 29:13, 29:33, 30:6, 30:17, 30:22, 31:1, 34:5, 34:7, 34:17, 34:24, 35:22, 37:6, 37:17, 37:21, 37:27, 39:10, 39:15, 39:19, 41:15 (2), 42:2, 42:21, 42:22, 42:23, 43:25, 45:2 (2), 45:16, 49:2 (2)

**Heart (13):** 6:5, 6:6, 8:21 (2), 17:17, 18:5, 24:45, 27:41, 31:20, 34:3, 42:28, 45:26, 50:21

**Heat (5):** 30:38, 30:39, 30:41 (2), 31:10

**Heavy (9):** 12:10, 13:2, 41:31, 43:1, 47:4, 47:13, 50:9, 50:10, 50:11

**Heel (4):** 3:15, 25:26, 49:17, 49:19

**He-goat (2):** 30:35, 32:15

**Heifer (1):** 15:9

**Height (1):** 6:15

**Heir (1):** 21:23

**Help (1):** 49:25

**Helper (2):** 2:18, 2:20

**Herb (7):** 1:11, 1:12, 1:29, 1:30, 2:5, 3:18, 9:3

**Here (3):** 19:12, 22:5, 40:15

**Hide (2):** 4:14, 31:49

**High (1):** 7:19

**Hill (20):** 7:19, 7:20, 8:4, 8:5, 10:30, 12:8, 14:10, 19:17, 19:19, 19:30, 22:2, 22:14, 31:21, 31:23, 31:25 (2), 31:54 (2), 36:8, 36:9

**Hip (2):** 32:33 (2)

**Hire (2):** 30:16 (2)

**Hit (12):** 4:15, 8:21, 14:5, 14:7, 14:15, 14:17, 19:11, 32:9, 32:12, 34:30, 36:35, 37:21

**Hold (4):** 22:13, 25:26, 34:10, 47:27

**Hold a grudge (3):** 27:41, 49:23, 50:15

**Hold back (2):** 43:31, 45:1

**Hold up (1):** 18:5

**Holdings (9):** 17:8, 23:4, 23:9, 23:20, 36:43, 47:11, 48:4, 49:30, 50:13

**Hollow (2):** 31:34, 49:13

**Honey (1):** 43:11

**Honor (3):** 31:1, 45:13, 49:6

**Horn (1):** 22:13

**Horse (2):** 47:17, 49:17

**Horseman (1):** 50:9

**Hostile (2):** 22:17, 49:8

**Hostility (1):** 3:15

**Hot (2):** 8:22, 18:1

**Hot spring (1):** 36:24

**House (109):** 6:14, 7:1, 12:1, 12:15, 12:17, 14:14, 15:2, 15:3, 17:12, 17:13, 17:23 (2), 17:27 (2), 18:19, 19:2, 19:3, 19:4, 19:10, 19:11, 20:13, 20:18, 24:2, 24:7,

24:23, 24:27, 24:28, 24:31, 24:32, 24:38, 24:40, 27:15, 28:2, 28:17, 28:21, 28:22, 29:13, 30:30, 31:14, 31:30, 31:37, 31:41, 33:17, 34:19, 34:26, 34:29, 34:30, 35:2, 36:6, 38:11 (2), 39:2, 39:4, 39:5 (3), 39:8, 39:9, 39:11 (3), 39:14, 39:16, 39:20 (2), 39:21, 39:22 (2), 39:23, 40:3 (2), 40:5, 40:7, 40:14, 41:10, 41:40, 41:51, 42:19 (2), 42:33, 43:16 (2), 43:17, 43:18, 43:19 (2), 43:24, 43:26 (2), 44:1, 44:4, 44:8, 44:14, 45:2, 45:8, 45:11, 45:16, 45:18, 46:27, 46:31 (2), 47:12, 47:14, 47:24, 50:4, 50:7, 50:8 (2), 50:22

**How long (1):** 30:30

**Human (53):** 1:26, 1:27, 2:5, 2:7 (2), 2:8, 2:15, 2:16, 2:18, 2:19 (2), 2:20 (2), 2:21, 2:22 (2), 2:23, 2:25, 3:8, 3:9, 3:12, 3:17, 3:20, 3:21, 3:22, 3:24, 4:1, 4:25, 5:1 (2), 5:2, 5:3, 5:4, 5:5, 6:1, 6:2, 6:3, 6:4, 6:5, 6:6, 6:7 (2), 7:21, 7:23, 8:21 (2), 9:5 (2), 9:6 (3), 11:5, 16:12

**Hundred (64):** 5:3, 5:4, 5:5, 5:6, 5:7, 5:8, 5:10, 5:11, 5:13, 5:14, 5:16, 5:17, 5:18, 5:19, 5:20, 5:22, 5:23, 5:25, 5:26, 5:27, 5:28, 5:30, 5:31, 5:32, 6:3, 6:15, 7:6, 7:11, 7:24, 8:3, 8:13, 9:28, 9:29, 11:10, 11:11, 11:13, 11:15, 11:17, 11:19, 11:21, 11:23, 11:25, 11:32, 14:14, 15:13, 17:17, 21:5, 23:1, 23:15, 23:16, 25:7, 25:17, 26:12, 32:7, 32:15 (2), 33:1, 33:19, 35:28, 45:22, 47:9, 47:28, 50:22, 50:26

**Hunger (23):** 12:10 (2), 26:1 (2), 41:27, 41:30 (2), 41:31, 41:36 (2), 41:50, 41:54 (2), 41:56 (2), 41:57, 42:5, 45:6, 45:11, 47:4, 47:13 (2), 47:20

**Hunt (3):** 27:3, 27:5, 27:33

**Hunter (2):** 10:9 (2)

**Hurl (1):** 21:16

**Hurry (13):** 18:6 (2), 18:7, 19:22, 24:18, 24:20, 24:46, 27:20, 41:32, 43:30, 44:11, 45:9, 45:13

**I (97):** 3:10, 4:9, 6:17, 7:4, 9:9, 9:12, 14:23, 15:1, 15:2, 15:7, 15:14, 16:5, 16:8, 17:1, 17:4, 18:13, 18:17 (2), 18:27, 19:19, 20:6 (2), 21:24, 21:26, 22:5, 23:4, 24:3, 24:13, 24:24, 24:27, 24:31, 24:34, 24:37, 24:42, 24:43, 24:45, 25:22, 25:30, 25:32, 26:24 (2), 27:8, 27:11, 27:19, 27:24, 27:32, 27:34, 27:38, 28:13, 28:15, 28:16, 28:20, 29:33, 30:1, 30:2, 30:3, 30:30, 31:5, 31:13, 31:38, 31:39, 31:44, 31:52, 32:12, 33:14, 34:30 (2), 35:11, 37:10, 37:16, 37:30 (2), 38:17, 38:25, 40:16, 41:9, 41:11, 41:15, 41:44, 42:18, 42:37, 43:9, 43:14, 45:3,

45:4, 46:3, 46:4 (2), 47:30, 48:7, 48:21, 48:22, 49:29, 50:5, 50:19, 50:21, 50:24

**Ice (1):** 31:40

**If (76):** 4:7 (2), 13:9 (2), 13:16, 14:23 (2), 15:4, 15:5, 17:17, 18:3, 18:21, 18:26, 18:28, 18:30, 20:7, 21:23, 23:8, 23:13, 24:8, 24:19, 24:21, 24:33, 24:38, 24:41, 24:42, 24:49 (2), 25:22, 26:29, 27:21, 27:46, 28:15, 28:17, 28:20, 30:1, 30:27, 30:31, 31:8 (2), 31:50 (2), 31:52 (2), 32:9, 32:27, 32:29, 33:10, 34:15, 34:17, 35:10, 37:8, 37:32, 38:9, 38:17, 39:6, 39:9, 40:14, 42:15 (2), 42:16, 42:19, 42:37, 43:4, 43:5, 43:9, 43:11, 44:23, 44:26, 44:32, 47:6, 47:16, 47:18 (2), 47:29, 50:4

**Image (5):** 1:26, 1:27 (2), 5:3, 9:6

**Imitate (1):** 27:12

**In front (2):** 25:21, 30:38

**In this way (10):** 15:5, 22:5, 24:30, 31:8 (2), 31:37, 32:5 (2), 45:9, 50:17

**Increase (29):** 1:22 (2), 1:28, 3:16 (2), 7:17, 7:18, 8:17, 9:1, 9:7 (2), 15:1, 16:10 (2), 17:2, 17:20, 21:20, 22:17 (2), 26:4, 26:24, 28:3, 34:12, 35:11, 38:12, 41:49, 43:34, 47:27, 48:4

**Increase in number (3):** 6:1, 18:20, 49:23

**Indeed (1):** 18:13

**Inflame (1):** 31:36

**Inherit (10):** 15:3, 15:4 (2), 15:7, 15:8, 21:10, 22:17, 24:60, 28:4, 45:11

**Inheritance (2):** 31:14, 48:6

**Iniquity (4):** 4:13, 15:16, 19:15, 44:16

**In-law (3):** 19:12, 19:14 (2)

**Innocence (1):** 20:5

**Innocent (2):** 24:41, 44:10

**Inquire (13):** 24:47, 24:57, 26:7, 32:18, 32:30 (2), 37:15, 38:21, 40:7, 43:7 (2), 43:27, 44:19

**Inscribe (1):** 49:10

**Instrument (9):** 24:53 (2), 27:3, 31:37 (2), 42:25, 43:11, 45:20, 49:5

**Intercede (2):** 25:21 (2)

**Interpret (9):** 40:8, 40:16, 40:22, 41:8, 41:12 (2), 41:13, 41:15 (2)

**Interpretation (5):** 40:5, 40:8, 40:12, 40:18, 41:11

**Invade (2):** 49:19 (2)

**Invention (1):** 6:5

**Iron (1):** 4:22

**Island (1):** 10:5

**Jar (9):** 24:14, 24:15, 24:16, 24:17, 24:18, 24:20, 24:43, 24:45, 24:46

**Join (1):** 29:34

**Journey (10):** 11:2, 12:9 (2), 33:12, 33:17, 35:5, 35:16, 35:21, 37:17, 46:1

**Joy (1):** 31:27

**Judge (5):** 16:5, 18:25, 19:9 (2), 31:53

**Judgement (3):** 18:19, 18:25, 40:13

**Keep back (4):** 20:6, 22:12, 22:16, 39:9

**Keep secret (1):** 47:18

**Keep silent (2):** 24:21, 34:5

**Keep watch (1):** 31:49

**Kill (16):** 4:8, 4:14, 4:15, 4:23, 4:25, 12:12, 20:4, 20:11, 26:7, 27:41, 27:42, 34:25, 34:26, 37:20, 37:26, 49:6

**Kind (17):** 1:11, 1:12 (2), 1:21 (2), 1:24 (2), 1:25 (3), 6:20 (3), 7:14 (4)

**Kindness (11):** 19:19, 20:13, 21:23, 24:12, 24:14, 24:27, 24:49, 32:11, 39:21, 40:14, 47:29

**Kindred (9):** 11:28, 12:1, 24:4, 24:7, 31:3, 31:13, 32:10, 43:7, 48:6

**King (41):** 14:1 (4), 14:2 (5), 14:5, 14:8 (5), 14:9 (5), 14:10, 14:17 (3), 14:18, 14:21, 14:22, 17:6, 17:16, 20:2, 26:1, 26:8, 35:11, 36:31 (2), 39:20, 40:1 (2), 40:5, 41:46, 49:20

**Kingdom place (2):** 10:10, 20:9

**Kiss (11):** 27:26, 27:27, 29:11, 29:13, 31:28, 32:1, 33:4, 41:40, 45:15, 48:10, 50:1

**Knead (1):** 18:6

**Knee (3):** 30:3, 48:12, 50:23

**Kneel (73):** 1:22, 1:28, 2:3, 5:2, 9:1, 9:26, 12:2, 12:3 (3), 14:19 (2), 14:20, 17:16 (2), 17:20, 18:18, 22:17 (2), 22:18, 24:1, 24:11, 24:27, 24:31, 24:35, 24:48, 24:60, 25:11, 26:3, 26:4, 26:12, 26:24, 26:29, 27:4, 27:7, 27:10, 27:19, 27:23, 27:25, 27:27 (2), 27:29 (2), 27:30, 27:31, 27:33 (2), 27:34, 27:38, 27:41, 28:1, 28:3, 28:6 (2), 28:14, 30:27, 30:30, 32:1, 32:27, 32:30, 35:9, 39:5, 47:7, 47:10, 48:3, 48:9, 48:15, 48:16, 48:20 (2), 49:25, 49:28 (2)

**Knife (2):** 22:6, 22:10

**Knock (1):** 33:13

**Knoll (1):** 49:26

**Know (57):** 3:5 (2), 3:7, 4:1, 4:9, 4:17, 4:25, 8:11, 9:24, 12:11, 15:8, 15:13 (2), 18:19, 18:21, 19:5, 19:8, 19:33, 19:35, 20:6, 20:7, 21:26, 22:12, 24:14, 24:16, 24:21, 25:27, 27:2, 28:16, 29:5 (2), 30:26, 30:29, 31:6, 31:32, 33:13, 38:9, 38:16, 38:26, 38:27, 39:6, 39:8, 41:21, 41:31, 41:39, 42:23, 42:33, 42:34, 43:7 (2), 43:22, 44:15, 44:27, 45:1, 47:6, 48:19 (2)

**Labor (1):** 41:51

**Lace (1):** 14:23

**Ladder (1):** 28:12

**Lament (2):** 23:2, 50:10

**Lamenting (1):** 50:10

Land (311): 1:1, 1:2, 1:10, 1:11 (2), 1:12, 1:15, 1:17, 1:20, 1:22, 1:24 (2), 1:25, 1:26 (2), 1:28 (2), 1:29, 1:30 (2), 2:1, 2:4 (2), 2:5 (2), 2:6, 2:11, 2:12, 2:13, 4:12, 4:14, 4:16, 6:4, 6:5, 6:6, 6:11 (2), 6:12 (2), 6:13 (2), 6:17 (2), 7:3, 7:4, 7:6, 7:10, 7:12, 7:14, 7:17 (2), 7:18, 7:19, 7:21 (2), 7:23, 7:24, 8:1, 8:3, 8:7, 8:9, 8:11, 8:13, 8:14, 8:17 (3), 8:19, 8:22, 9:1, 9:2, 9:7, 9:10 (2), 9:11, 9:13, 9:14, 9:16, 9:17, 9:19, 10:5, 10:8, 10:10, 10:11, 10:20, 10:25, 10:31, 10:32, 11:1, 11:2, 11:4, 11:8, 11:9 (2), 11:28, 11:31, 12:1 (2), 12:5 (2), 12:6 (2), 12:7, 12:10 (2), 13:6, 13:7, 13:9, 13:10, 13:12, 13:15, 13:16 (2), 13:17, 14:19, 14:22, 15:7, 15:13, 15:18, 16:3, 17:8 (2), 18:2, 18:18, 18:25, 19:1, 19:23, 19:28 (2), 19:31 (2), 20:1, 20:15, 21:21, 21:23, 21:32, 21:34, 22:2, 22:18, 23:2, 23:7, 23:12, 23:13, 23:15, 23:19, 24:3, 24:4, 24:5 (2), 24:7 (2), 24:37, 24:52, 24:62, 25:6, 26:1, 26:2, 26:3 (2), 26:4 (2), 26:12, 26:22, 27:28, 27:39, 27:46, 28:4, 28:12, 28:13, 28:14, 29:1, 30:25, 31:3, 31:13 (2), 31:18, 32:4, 32:10, 33:3, 33:18, 34:1, 34:2, 34:10, 34:21 (2), 34:30, 35:6, 35:12 (2), 35:16, 35:22, 36:5, 36:6 (2), 36:7, 36:16, 36:17, 36:20, 36:21, 36:30, 36:31, 36:34, 36:43, 37:1 (2), 37:10, 38:9, 40:15, 41:19, 41:29, 41:30 (2), 41:31, 41:33, 41:34 (2), 41:36 (3), 41:41, 41:43, 41:44, 41:45, 41:46, 41:47, 41:48, 41:52, 41:53, 41:54 (2), 41:55, 41:56 (2), 41:57 (2), 42:5, 42:6 (3), 42:7, 42:9, 42:12, 42:13, 42:29, 42:30 (2), 42:32, 42:33, 42:34, 43:1, 43:11, 43:26, 44:8, 44:11, 44:14, 45:6, 45:7, 45:8, 45:10, 45:17, 45:18 (2), 45:19, 45:20, 45:25, 45:26, 46:6, 46:12, 46:20, 46:28, 46:31, 46:34, 47:1 (2), 47:4 (3), 47:6 (3), 47:11 (3), 47:13 (3), 47:14 (2), 47:15 (2), 47:20, 47:27 (2), 47:28, 48:3, 48:4, 48:5, 48:7 (2), 48:12, 48:16, 48:21, 49:15, 49:30, 50:5, 50:7, 50:8, 50:11, 50:13, 50:24 (2)

Last night (3): 19:34, 31:29, 31:42
Later (1): 30:33
Laugh (11): 17:17, 18:12, 18:13, 18:15 (2), 19:14, 21:6, 21:9, 26:8, 39:14, 39:17
Laughter (1): 21:6
Lay down (21): 19:4, 19:32, 19:33 (2), 19:34 (2), 19:35 (2), 26:10, 28:11, 28:13, 30:15, 30:16, 34:2, 34:7, 35:22, 39:7, 39:10, 39:12, 39:14, 47:30
Laying place (1): 49:4

Lead (2): 33:14, 47:17
Leaf (2): 3:7, 8:11
Lean (1): 18:4
Leave (11): 2:24, 24:27, 28:15, 39:6, 39:12, 39:13, 39:15, 39:18, 44:22 (2), 50:8
Left hand (6): 13:9, 14:15, 24:49, 48:13 (2), 48:14
Length (2): 6:15, 13:17
Lentil (1): 25:34
Let alone (1): 31:28
Level valley (1): 11:2
Lie (1): 21:23
Life (66): 1:20, 1:21, 1:24 (2), 1:25, 1:28, 1:30 (2), 2:7 (2), 2:9, 2:19 (2), 2:20, 3:1, 3:14 (2), 3:17, 3:20, 3:22, 3:24, 6:17, 6:19, 7:11, 7:14, 7:15, 7:21, 7:22, 8:1, 8:17, 8:19, 8:21, 9:2, 9:3, 9:5, 9:10 (3), 9:12, 9:15, 9:16, 18:10, 18:14, 23:1 (2), 25:6, 25:7 (2), 26:19, 27:46 (2), 37:20, 37:33, 42:15, 42:16, 43:7, 43:27, 43:28, 45:3, 45:26, 45:28, 46:30, 47:8, 47:9 (2), 47:28
Lift up (49): 4:7, 4:13, 7:17, 13:6, 13:10, 13:11, 13:14, 18:2, 18:24, 18:26, 19:21, 20:1, 21:16, 21:18, 22:4, 22:13, 24:63, 24:64, 27:3, 27:38, 29:1, 29:11, 31:10, 31:12, 31:17, 32:21, 33:1, 33:5, 36:7, 37:25 (2), 39:7, 40:13, 40:19, 40:20, 42:26, 43:29, 43:34, 44:1, 45:19, 45:23 (2), 45:27, 46:5 (2), 47:30, 50:13, 50:17 (2)
Light (7): 1:3 (2), 1:4 (2), 1:5, 1:18, 44:3
Likeness (3): 1:26, 5:1, 5:3
Limp (1): 32:32
Linen (1): 41:42
Linger (2): 19:16, 43:10
Lion (2): 49:9 (2)
Lioness (1): 49:9
Lip (8): 11:1, 11:6, 11:7 (2), 11:9, 22:17, 41:3, 41:17
Listen (1): 4:23
Little one (8): 19:31, 19:34, 19:35, 19:38, 25:23, 29:26, 43:33, 48:14
Live (56): 3:22, 5:3, 5:5, 5:6, 5:7, 5:9, 5:10, 5:12, 5:13, 5:15, 5:16, 5:18, 5:19, 5:21, 5:25, 5:26, 5:28, 5:30, 6:19, 6:20, 7:3, 11:12, 11:13, 11:14, 11:15, 11:16, 11:17, 11:18, 11:19, 11:20, 11:21, 11:22, 11:23, 11:24, 11:25, 11:26, 12:12, 12:13, 17:18, 19:19, 19:20, 19:32, 19:34, 20:7, 25:17, 27:40, 31:32, 42:2, 42:18, 43:8, 45:7, 45:27, 47:19, 47:25, 50:20, 50:22
Livestock (29): 4:20, 13:2, 13:7 (2), 23:18, 26:14 (2), 29:7, 30:29, 31:9, 31:18 (2), 33:17, 34:5, 34:23, 36:6, 36:7, 46:6,

46:32, 46:34, 47:6, 47:16 (2), 47:17 (4), 47:18, 49:32

**Lo (1):** 47:23

**Load (1):** 44:13

**Loathe (1):** 27:46

**Loin covering (1):** 3:7

**Loins (1):** 35:11

**Look (126):** 1:29, 1:31, 6:12, 6:13, 6:17, 8:11, 8:13, 9:9, 12:11, 12:19, 15:3, 15:4, 15:12, 15:17, 16:2, 16:6, 16:11, 16:14, 17:4, 17:20, 18:2, 18:9, 18:10, 18:27, 18:31, 19:2, 19:8, 19:19, 19:20, 19:21, 19:28, 20:3, 20:15, 20:16 (2), 22:1, 22:7 (2), 22:11, 22:13, 22:20, 24:13, 24:15, 24:30, 24:43, 24:45, 24:51, 24:63, 25:24, 25:32, 26:8, 26:9, 27:1, 27:2, 27:6, 27:18, 27:36, 27:39, 27:42, 28:12 (2), 28:13, 28:15, 29:2 (2), 29:6, 29:25, 30:3, 31:2, 31:10, 31:11, 31:51 (2), 32:19, 32:21, 33:1, 34:21, 37:7 (3), 37:9 (2), 37:13, 37:15, 37:19, 37:25, 37:29, 38:13, 38:23, 38:24, 38:27, 38:29, 40:6, 40:9, 40:16, 41:1, 41:2, 41:3, 41:5, 41:6, 41:7, 41:17, 41:18, 41:19, 41:22, 41:23, 41:29, 42:2, 42:13, 42:15, 42:22, 42:27, 42:28, 42:35, 43:21, 44:16, 45:12, 46:2, 47:1, 48:1, 48:2, 48:4, 48:11, 48:21, 50:5, 50:18

**Look down (3):** 18:16, 19:28, 26:8

**Look with respect (2):** 4:4, 4:5

**Lord (74):** 18:12, 19:2, 19:18 23:6, 23:11, 23:15, 24:9, 24:10 (2), 24:12 (2), 24:14, 24:18, 24:27 (3), 24:35, 24:36 (2), 24:37, 24:39, 24:42, 24:44, 24:48 (2), 24:49, 24:51, 24:54, 24:56, 24:65, 31:35, 32:5, 32:6, 32:19, 33:8, 33:13, 33:14 (2), 33:15, 39:2, 39:3, 39:7, 39:8 (2), 39:16, 39:19, 39:20, 40:1, 40:7, 42:10, 42:30, 42:33, 43:20, 44:5, 44:7, 44:8, 44:9, 44:16 (2), 44:18 (2), 44:19, 44:20, 44:22, 44:24, 44:33, 45:8, 45:9, 47:18 (3), 47:25

**Lost (3):** 18:23, 18:25 (2)

**Love (14):** 22:2, 24:67, 25:28 (2), 27:4, 27:9, 27:14, 29:18, 29:30, 29:32, 34:3, 37:3, 37:4, 44:20

**Luminary (5):** 1:14, 1:15, 1:16 (3)

**Magician (2):** 41:8, 41:24

**Magnificent (33):** 1:16 (2), 1:21, 4:13, 10:12, 10:21, 12:2, 12:17, 15:12, 15:14, 15:18, 17:20, 18:18, 19:11, 20:9, 21:8, 21:18, 27:1, 27:15, 27:33, 27:34, 27:42, 29:2, 29:7, 29:16, 39:9 (2), 39:14, 41:29, 44:12, 45:7, 46:3, 50:10

**Magnified (1):** 26:13

**Magnify (14):** 12:2, 19:13, 19:19, 21:8, 21:20, 24:35, 25:27, 26:13 (2), 38:11, 38:14, 41:40, 48:19 (2)

**Maid (28):** 12:16, 16:1, 16:2, 16:3, 16:5, 16:6, 16:8, 20:14, 24:35, 25:12, 29:24 (2), 29:29 (2), 30:4, 30:7, 30:9, 30:10, 30:12, 30:18, 30:43, 32:6, 32:23, 33:1, 33:2, 33:6, 35:25, 35:26

**Make a vow (2):** 28:20, 31:13

**Make bricks (1):** 11:3

**Make restitution (1):** 44:4

**Male (14):** 1:27, 5:2, 6:19, 7:3, 7:9, 7:16, 17:10, 17:12, 17:14, 17:23, 34:15, 34:22, 34:24, 34:25

**Male goat (2):** 31:10, 31:12

**Male kid (5):** 27:9, 27:16, 38:17, 38:20, 38:23

**Man (159):** 2:23, 2:24, 3:6, 3:16, 4:1, 4:23, 6:4, 6:9, 7:2 (2), 9:5, 9:20, 10:5, 11:3, 11:7, 12:20, 13:8, 13:11, 13:13, 13:16, 14:24, 15:10, 16:3, 17:23, 17:27, 18:2, 18:16, 18:22, 19:4 (2), 19:5, 19:8 (2), 19:9, 19:10, 19:11, 19:12, 19:16, 19:31, 20:7, 20:8, 23:6, 24:13, 24:16, 24:21, 24:22, 24:26, 24:29, 24:30 (2), 24:32 (2), 24:54, 24:58, 24:59, 24:61, 24:65, 25:27 (3), 26:7 (2), 26:11, 26:13, 26:31, 27:11 (2), 29:19, 29:22, 29:32, 29:34, 30:15, 30:18, 30:20, 30:43, 31:49, 31:50, 32:7, 32:25, 32:29, 33:1, 34:7, 34:14, 34:20, 34:21, 34:22, 34:25, 37:15 (2), 37:17, 37:19, 37:28, 38:1, 38:2, 38:21, 38:22, 38:25, 39:1, 39:2, 39:11 (2), 39:14 (2), 40:5 (2), 41:11, 41:12, 41:33, 41:38, 41:44, 42:11, 42:13, 42:21, 42:25, 42:28, 42:30, 42:33, 42:35, 43:3, 43:5, 43:6, 43:7, 43:11, 43:13, 43:14, 43:15, 43:16 (2), 43:17 (3), 43:18, 43:19, 43:21, 43:24 (2), 43:33 (2), 44:1 (2), 44:3, 44:4, 44:11 (2), 44:13, 44:15, 44:17, 44:26, 45:1 (2), 45:22, 46:32 (2), 46:34, 47:2, 47:6, 47:20, 49:6, 49:28

**Mandrakes (5):** 30:14 (2), 30:15 (2), 30:16

**Many (38):** 1:31, 4:5, 7:18, 7:19 (2), 12:14, 13:2, 13:13, 15:1, 17:2 (2), 17:6 (2), 17:20 (2), 18:20, 19:3, 19:9, 20:8, 21:11, 24:16, 24:35, 26:13, 26:16, 27:33, 27:34, 30:43 (2), 32:8, 34:7, 34:12, 41:19, 41:31, 41:49, 47:13, 47:27, 50:9, 50:10

**March (1):** 49:22

**Marry (1):** 20:3

**Marsh Grass (2):** 41:2, 41:18

**Marvel (1):** 43:33

**Master (4):** 14:13, 20:3, 37:19, 49:23

**Mature (4):** 6:9, 20:5, 20:6, 25:27

**Meat (1):** 45:23
**Meditate (1):** 24:63
**Meet (19):** 14:17, 15:10, 18:2, 19:1, 21:33, 24:12, 24:17, 24:65, 27:20, 29:13, 30:16, 32:7, 33:4, 42:4, 42:29, 42:38, 44:29, 46:29, 49:1
**Messenger (17):** 16:7, 16:9, 16:10, 16:11, 19:1, 19:15, 21:17, 22:11, 22:15, 24:7, 24:40, 28:12, 31:11, 32:2, 32:4, 32:7, 48:16
**Midsection (9):** 24:2, 24:9, 32:26 (2), 32:32, 32:33 (2), 46:26, 47:29
**Midst (17):** 1:6, 2:9, 3:3, 3:8, 9:21, 15:10, 18:24, 18:26, 19:29, 23:6, 23:9, 23:10, 35:2, 37:7, 40:20, 41:48, 42:5
**Mighty one (16):** 14:18, 14:19, 14:20, 14:22, 17:1, 21:33, 28:3, 31:13, 31:29, 35:1, 35:3, 35:11, 43:14, 46:3, 48:3, 49:25
**Mimic (1):** 42:23
**Mind (3):** 20:5, 20:6, 31:26
**Minister (2):** 39:4, 40:4
**Mist (1):** 2:6
**Mix (2):** 11:7, 11:9
**Moderate (4):** 6:3, 15:14, 30:6, 49:16
**Moist (1):** 30:37
**Mold (4):** 2:7, 2:8, 2:19, 32:8
**Monument (11):** 28:18, 28:22, 31:13, 31:45, 31:51, 31:52 (2), 35:14 (2), 35:20 (2)
**Moon (1):** 37:9
**Moreover (4):** 3:1, 18:13, 18:23, 40:16
**Morning (19):** 1:5, 1:8, 1:13, 1:19, 1:23, 1:31, 19:27, 20:8, 21:14, 22:3, 24:54, 26:31, 28:18, 29:25, 32:1, 40:6, 41:8, 44:3, 49:27
**Mortal man (1):** 34:30
**Mortar (1):** 11:3
**Mother (26):** 2:24, 3:20, 20:12, 21:21, 24:28, 24:53, 24:55, 24:67 (2), 27:11, 27:13, 27:14 (2), 27:29, 28:2 (2), 28:5, 28:7, 29:10 (3), 30:14, 32:12, 37:10, 43:29, 44:20
**Mound (7):** 31:46 (2), 31:48, 31:51, 31:52 (3)
**Mount (1):** 14:6
**Mourn (2):** 37:34, 50:10
**Mourning (4):** 27:41, 37:35, 50:11 (2)
**Mouth (21):** 4:11, 8:11, 24:57, 25:28, 29:2, 29:3 (2), 29:8, 29:10, 34:26, 41:40, 42:27, 43:7, 43:12, 43:21, 44:1, 44:2, 44:8, 45:12, 45:21, 47:12
**Multiple (1):** 18:18
**Multitude (2):** 17:4, 17:5
**Myriad (1):** 24:60
**Myrrh (2):** 37:25, 43:11
**Naked (3):** 3:7, 3:10, 3:11
**Nakedness (5):** 9:22, 9:23 (2), 42:9, 42:12
**Narrow (1):** 14:20

**Nation (25):** 10:5 (2), 10:20, 10:31, 10:32 (2), 12:2, 15:14, 17:4, 17:5, 17:6, 17:16, 17:20, 18:18 (2), 20:4, 21:13, 21:18, 22:18, 25:23, 26:4, 35:11 (2), 46:3, 48:19
**Near (2):** 19:20, 45:10
**Neck (1):** 49:8
**Nest (1):** 6:14
**Net (1):** 22:13
**Nevertheless (2):** 17:19, 42:21
**New moon (11):** 7:11 (2), 8:4 (2), 8:5 (2), 8:13, 8:14 (2), 29:14, 38:24
**Night (25):** 1:5, 1:14, 1:16, 1:18, 7:4, 7:12, 8:22, 14:15, 19:5, 19:33, 19:34, 19:35, 20:3, 26:24, 30:15, 30:16, 31:24, 31:39, 31:40, 32:14, 32:22, 32:23, 40:5, 41:11, 46:2
**Nine (19):** 5:5, 5:8, 5:9, 5:11, 5:14, 5:17, 5:20, 5:27 (2), 5:30, 9:29, 11:19, 11:24, 11:25, 17:1 (2), 17:17, 17:24 (2)
**No (39):** 13:8, 15:1, 18:3, 18:30, 18:32, 19:7, 19:8, 19:17 (2), 19:18, 21:12, 21:16, 21:17, 22:12 (2), 24:56, 26:2, 26:24, 31:35, 33:10, 35:17, 37:22 (2), 37:27, 42:22, 43:23, 44:18, 45:5 (2), 45:9, 45:20, 45:24, 46:3, 47:29, 49:4, 49:6 (2), 50:19, 50:21
**Noble (25):** 12:15, 21:22, 21:32, 26:26, 37:36, 39:1, 39:21, 39:22, 39:23, 40:2 (2), 40:3, 40:4, 40:9, 40:16, 40:20 (2), 40:21, 40:22, 40:23, 41:9, 41:10 (2), 41:12, 47:6
**Nod (2):** 4:12, 4:14
**North (2):** 13:14, 28:14
**Nose (14):** 2:7, 3:19, 7:22, 18:24, 19:1, 24:47, 27:45, 30:2, 39:19, 42:6, 44:18, 48:12, 49:6, 49:7
**Not (212):** 2:5, 2:17, 2:18, 2:20, 2:25, 3:1, 3:3 (2), 3:4, 3:17, 4:5, 4:7 (2), 4:9, 4:12, 6:3, 7:2, 8:9, 8:12, 8:21 (2), 8:22, 9:4, 9:11 (2), 9:15, 9:23, 11:6, 11:7, 12:18, 13:6 (2), 13:9, 14:23, 15:3, 15:4, 15:10, 15:13, 15:16, 16:1, 16:10, 17:5, 17:12, 17:14, 17:15, 18:15 (2), 18:21, 18:24, 18:25, 18:28, 18:29, 18:30, 18:31, 18:32, 19:2, 19:8, 19:19, 19:20, 19:22, 19:33, 19:35, 20:4, 20:5, 20:6, 20:9, 20:12, 21:10, 21:26 (3), 22:12, 22:16, 23:6, 23:11, 24:3, 24:5, 24:8 (2), 24:16, 24:21, 24:27, 24:33, 24:37, 24:38, 24:39, 24:41, 24:49, 24:50, 26:22, 26:29, 27:2, 27:12, 27:21, 27:23, 27:36, 28:1, 28:6, 28:15, 28:16, 29:7, 29:8, 29:25, 29:26, 30:1, 30:31, 30:40, 30:42, 31:7, 31:15, 31:27, 31:28, 31:32 (2), 31:33, 31:34, 31:35 (2), 31:38 (2), 31:39, 31:52 (2), 32:13, 32:26, 32:27,

32:29, 32:33, 34:7, 34:14, 34:17, 34:19, 34:23, 35:5, 35:10, 36:7, 37:4, 37:13, 37:21, 37:32, 38:9, 38:14, 38:16, 38:20, 38:21, 38:22 (2), 38:23, 38:26 (2), 39:6, 39:8, 39:9, 39:10, 40:8, 40:15, 40:23, 41:19, 41:21, 41:31, 41:36, 41:44, 42:2, 42:4, 42:8, 42:10, 42:11, 42:12, 42:16, 42:20, 42:21, 42:22 (2), 42:23, 42:31, 42:34, 42:37, 42:38, 43:3, 43:5 (2), 43:8, 43:9, 43:22, 43:32, 44:4, 44:5, 44:15, 44:22, 44:23 (2), 44:26 (2), 44:28, 44:32, 45:1 (2), 45:3, 45:8, 45:26, 47:9, 47:18 (2), 47:19 (2), 47:22 (2), 47:26, 48:10, 48:11, 48:18, 49:10

**Nothing (6):** 22:12, 30:31, 39:6, 39:9, 39:23, 40:15

**Nourishment (4):** 2:9, 3:6, 6:21, 40:17

**Now (40):** 3:22, 4:11, 11:6, 12:19, 19:9, 20:7, 21:23, 22:12, 24:49, 26:22, 26:29, 27:3, 27:8, 27:36, 27:43, 29:32, 29:34, 30:30, 31:13, 31:16, 31:28, 31:30, 31:42, 31:44, 32:5, 32:11, 37:20, 41:33, 43:10, 44:10, 44:30, 44:33, 45:5, 45:8, 46:34, 47:4, 48:5, 50:5, 50:17, 50:21

**Nude (1):** 2:25

**Number (2):** 34:30, 41:49

**Oak (1):** 35:4

**Oath (3):** 24:41 (2), 26:28

**Obedience (1):** 49:10

**Occupation (5):** 2:2 (2), 2:3, 33:14, 39:11

**Oil (5):** 27:28, 27:39, 28:18, 35:14, 49:20

**Old age (1):** 24:36

**Olive (1):** 8:11

**On account of (15):** 3:17, 8:21, 12:13, 12:16, 18:26, 18:29, 18:31, 18:32, 21:30, 26:24, 27:4, 27:10, 27:19, 27:31, 46:34

**One of the flock (4):** 22:7, 22:8, 30:32 (2)

**Only (10):** 6:5, 14:24, 19:8, 20:11, 24:8, 26:29, 41:40, 47:22, 47:26, 50:8

**Open (9):** 7:11, 8:6, 24:32, 29:31, 30:22, 41:56, 42:27, 43:21, 44:11

**Open up (3):** 3:5, 3:7, 21:19

**Opening (10):** 4:7, 6:16, 18:1, 18:2, 18:10, 19:6, 19:11 (2), 38:14, 43:19

**Opposite (7):** 2:18, 2:20, 21:16 (2), 31:32, 31:37, 47:15

**Or (6):** 24:49, 24:50, 24:55, 31:43, 44:8, 44:19

**Ornament (1):** 24:53

**Other (15):** 4:25, 8:10, 8:12, 17:21, 26:21, 26:22, 29:19, 29:27, 29:30, 30:24, 37:9, 41:3, 41:19, 43:14, 43:22

**Other side (2):** 50:10, 50:11

**Otherwise (17):** 3:3, 3:22, 11:4, 19:15, 19:17, 19:19, 24:6, 26:7, 26:9, 31:24, 31:31, 32:12, 38:11, 38:23, 42:4, 44:34, 45:11

**Outcry (2):** 18:20, 18:21

**Outside (12):** 6:14, 9:22, 15:5, 19:16, 19:17, 24:11, 24:29, 24:31, 39:12, 39:13, 39:15, 39:18

**Oven (1):** 15:17

**Overcome (5):** 7:18, 7:19, 7:20, 7:24, 49:26

**Overlook (1):** 41:51

**Overseer (1):** 41:34

**Oversight (1):** 43:12

**Overtake (4):** 31:25, 44:4, 44:6, 47:9

**Overturn (4):** 3:24, 19:21, 19:25, 19:29

**Overturning (1):** 19:29

**Owner (2):** 27:29, 27:37

**Ox (3):** 32:6, 49:6, 49:22

**Pack (1):** 45:17

**Palm (9):** 8:9, 20:5, 31:42, 32:26 (2), 32:33 (2), 40:11, 40:21

**Parcel (1):** 33:19

**Parching heat (1):** 31:40

**Part (1):** 4:11

**Partner (1):** 26:26

**Pass over (4):** 31:7, 31:41, 35:2, 41:14

**Pasture (1):** 47:4

**Path (2):** 18:11, 49:17

**Payment (3):** 29:15, 31:7, 31:41

**Peel (2):** 30:37, 30:38

**Peel off (1):** 37:23

**People (33):** 11:6, 14:16, 17:14, 17:16, 19:4, 23:7, 23:11, 23:12, 23:13, 25:8, 25:17, 26:10, 26:11, 27:29, 28:3, 32:8, 33:15, 34:16, 34:22, 35:6, 35:29, 41:40, 41:55, 42:6, 47:21, 47:23, 48:4, 48:19, 49:10, 49:16, 49:29, 49:33, 50:20

**Perform (1):** 18:14

**Pick up (2):** 31:46, 47:14

**Pierce (8):** 4:26, 6:1, 9:20, 10:8, 11:6, 41:54, 44:12, 49:4

**Pierce through (1):** 30:28

**Pierced (1):** 34:27

**Pile up (2):** 41:35, 41:49

**Pilgrimage (6):** 17:8, 28:4, 36:7, 37:1, 47:9 (2)

**Pistachio (1):** 43:11

**Pitch tent (2):** 13:12, 13:18

**Place (47):** 1:9, 12:6, 13:3, 13:4, 13:14, 18:24, 18:26, 18:33, 19:12, 19:13, 19:14, 19:27, 20:11, 20:13, 21:31, 22:3, 22:4, 22:9, 22:14, 24:23, 24:25, 24:31, 26:7 (2), 28:11 (3), 28:16, 28:17, 28:19, 29:3, 29:22, 29:26, 30:25, 32:1, 32:3, 32:31, 33:17, 35:7, 35:13, 35:14, 35:15, 36:40, 38:21, 38:22, 39:20, 40:3

**Place of lodging (2):** 42:27, 43:21

**Place of rest (1):** 49:15

**Plague (1):** 12:17

**Plant (3):** 2:8, 9:20, 21:33

**Plead (3):** 20:7, 20:17, 48:11

Pleasant (1): 27:15

Please (75): 12:11, 12:13, 13:8, 13:9, 13:14, 15:5, 16:2 (2), 18:3 (2), 18:4, 18:21, 18:27, 18:30, 18:31, 18:32, 19:2 (2), 19:7, 19:8 (2), 19:18, 19:19, 19:20 (2), 22:2, 24:2, 24:12, 24:14, 24:17, 24:23, 24:42, 24:43, 24:45, 25:30, 26:28, 27:2, 27:3, 27:9, 27:19, 27:21, 27:26, 30:14, 30:27, 31:12, 32:12, 32:30, 33:10 (2), 33:11, 33:14, 33:15, 34:8, 37:6, 37:14, 37:16, 37:32, 38:16, 38:25, 40:8, 40:14, 44:18, 44:33, 45:4, 47:4, 47:29 (2), 47:29, 48:9, 50:4 (2), 50:5, 50:17 (3)

Pleasure (1): 18:12

Plenty (8): 25:8, 35:29, 41:29, 41:30, 41:31, 41:34, 41:47, 41:53

Plot (1): 11:6

Plowing (1): 45:6

Pluck away (2): 21:25, 31:31

Pluck up (1): 49:6

Plunder (2): 34:27, 34:29

Poplar (1): 30:37

Portion (3): 14:24 (2), 31:14

Possession (3): 31:18, 34:23, 36:6

Possibly (12): 16:2, 18:24, 18:28, 18:29, 18:30, 18:31, 18:32, 24:5, 24:39, 27:12, 32:21, 43:12

Post (1): 19:26

Posterity (1): 21:23

Pour (1): 35:14

Pour down (2): 28:18, 35:14

Pour out (3): 9:6 (2), 37:22

Pouring (1): 35:14

Powder (9): 2:7, 3:14, 3:19 (2), 13:16 (2), 18:27, 26:15, 28:14

Power (31): 9:26, 24:3 (2), 24:7, 24:12, 24:27, 24:42, 24:48, 26:24, 27:20, 28:13 (2), 30:8, 31:5, 31:29, 31:30, 31:32, 31:42 (2), 31:53 (3), 32:10 (2), 35:2, 35:4, 43:23 (2), 46:1, 46:3, 50:17

Precipitate (3): 2:5, 7:4, 19:24

Pregnancy (1): 3:16

Pregnant (3): 16:11, 38:24, 38:25

Present (16): 12:2, 27:12, 27:35, 27:36 (2), 27:38, 27:41, 28:4, 33:11, 39:5, 49:25 (3), 49:26 (2), 49:28

Press (1): 40:11

Press hard (3): 19:3, 19:9, 33:11

Prey (2): 8:11, 49:9

Priest (7): 14:18, 41:45, 41:50, 46:20, 47:22 (2), 47:26

Prison (8): 39:20 (2), 39:21, 39:22 (2), 39:23, 40:3, 40:5

Prisoner (1): 39:22

Produce (9): 1:11 (2), 1:12, 1:29, 3:2, 3:3, 3:6, 4:3, 30:2

Production (1): 47:24

Profit (1): 37:26

Prolong (1): 26:8

Prophet (1): 20:7

Prosper (7): 24:21, 24:40, 24:42, 24:56, 39:2, 39:3, 39:23

Prostitute (3): 38:21 (2), 38:22

Prostitution (1): 38:24

Provender (4): 24:25, 24:32, 42:27, 43:24

Provide (8): 11:3, 11:4, 11:7, 29:21, 30:1, 38:16, 47:15, 47:16

Provide food (1): 25:30

Provisions (3): 27:3, 42:25, 45:21

Purchase (12): 4:1, 14:19, 14:22, 25:10, 33:19, 39:1, 47:19, 47:20, 47:22, 47:23, 49:30, 50:13

Pure (6): 7:2 (2), 7:8 (2), 8:20 (2)

Pursue (5): 14:14, 14:15, 31:23, 35:5, 44:4

Put (1): 24:33

Qeshiytah (1): 33:19

Quarrel (1): 26:20

Quiver (1): 27:3

Rafter (1): 19:8

Raiment (1): 20:16

Rain shower (2): 7:12, 8:2

Raise (5): 7:17, 14:22, 31:45, 39:18, 41:44

Raven (1): 8:7

Reach (3): 23:8, 28:11, 32:2

Rebel (1): 14:4

Rebuke (1): 37:10

Reckless (1): 49:4

Reckon (2): 13:16 (2)

Recognize (10): 27:23, 31:32, 37:32, 37:33, 38:25, 38:26, 42:7 (2), 42:8 (2)

Red (2): 25:30 (2)

Redeem (1): 48:16

Reed-pipe (1): 4:21

Refine (1): 49:24

Reflection (1): 46:2

Refuse (3): 37:35, 39:8, 48:19

Regulate (8): 1:18, 3:16, 4:7, 24:2, 37:8 (2), 45:8, 45:26

Regulation (2): 1:16 (2)

Reign (12): 36:31 (2), 36:32, 36:33, 36:34, 36:35, 36:36, 36:37, 36:38, 36:39, 37:8 (2)

Relate (1): 34:9

Remain (5): 7:23, 14:10, 32:9, 42:38, 47:18

Remainder (2): 49:3 (2)

Remember (10): 8:1, 9:15, 9:16, 19:29, 30:22, 40:14 (2), 40:23, 41:9, 42:9

Remnant (1): 45:7

Remove the cover (2): 9:21, 35:7

Replacement (2): 45:22 (2)

Report (1): 29:13

Reproduce (13): 1:22, 1:28, 8:17, 9:1, 9:7, 17:6, 17:20, 26:22, 28:3, 35:11, 41:52, 47:27, 48:4

**Rescue (1):** 49:18
**Reserve (4):** 30:36, 32:25, 44:20, 49:4
**Reside (1):** 30:20
**Rest (4):** 8:4, 19:16, 39:16, 42:33
**Resting place (1):** 8:9
**Restrain (1):** 27:36
**Restrict (2):** 8:2, 23:6
**Reviving (1):** 45:5
**Revolution (3):** 31:36, 50:17 (2)
**Rib (2):** 2:21, 2:22
**Riches (1):** 31:16
**Ride (3):** 24:61, 41:43, 49:17
**Rider (1):** 50:9
**Right hand (7):** 13:9, 24:49, 48:13 (2), 48:14, 48:17, 48:18
**Ring (4):** 24:22, 24:30, 24:47, 35:4
**Ripen (4):** 50:2 (2), 50:3, 50:26
**Rise (52):** 4:8, 6:18, 9:9, 9:11, 9:17, 13:17, 17:7, 17:19, 17:21, 18:16, 19:1, 19:14, 19:15, 19:33, 19:35 (2), 21:18, 21:32, 22:3, 22:19, 23:3, 23:7, 23:17, 23:20, 24:10, 24:54, 24:61, 25:34, 26:3, 27:19, 27:31, 27:43, 28:2, 31:13, 31:17, 31:21, 31:35, 32:23, 35:1, 35:3, 37:7, 37:35, 38:8, 38:19, 39:15, 41:30, 43:8, 43:13, 43:15, 44:4, 46:5, 49:9
**Rising (7):** 8:20, 22:2, 22:3, 22:6, 22:7, 22:8, 22:13
**River (9):** 2:10, 2:13, 2:14 (2), 15:18 (3), 31:21, 36:37
**Road (31):** 3:24, 6:12, 16:7, 18:19, 19:2, 19:31, 24:21, 24:27, 24:40, 24:42, 24:48, 24:56, 28:20, 30:36, 31:23, 31:35, 32:2, 33:16, 35:3, 35:19, 38:14, 38:16, 38:21, 42:25, 42:38, 45:21, 45:23, 45:24, 48:7 (2), 49:17
**Roam (1):** 27:40
**Robe (1):** 25:25
**Rod (7):** 30:37 (2), 30:38, 30:39, 30:41 (2), 32:11
**Roll (4):** 29:3, 29:8, 29:10, 43:18
**Roof covering (1):** 8:13
**Round about (4):** 7:16, 20:7, 20:18, 26:8
**Roundness (7):** 13:10, 13:11, 13:12, 19:17, 19:25, 19:28, 19:29
**Ruddy (1):** 25:25
**Rule (2):** 1:26, 1:28
**Run (10):** 18:2, 18:7, 24:17, 24:20, 24:28, 24:29, 29:12, 29:13, 33:4, 41:14
**Sack (5):** 37:34, 42:25, 42:27, 42:35 (2)
**Sacrifice (2):** 31:54, 46:1
**Saddle (1):** 22:3
**Saddlebag (1):** 49:14
**Safely (1):** 34:25
**Salt (2):** 14:3, 19:26
**Sand (3):** 22:17, 32:13, 41:49
**Sandal (1):** 14:23

**Say (608):** 1:3, 1:6, 1:9, 1:11, 1:14, 1:20, 1:22, 1:24, 1:26, 1:28, 1:29, 2:16, 2:18, 2:23, 3:1 (2), 3:2, 3:3, 3:4, 3:9, 3:10, 3:11, 3:12, 3:13 (2), 3:14, 3:16, 3:17 (2), 3:22, 4:1, 4:6, 4:8, 4:9 (2), 4:10, 4:13, 4:15, 4:23, 5:29, 6:3, 6:7, 6:13, 7:1, 8:15, 8:21, 9:1, 9:8 (2), 9:12, 9:17, 9:25, 9:26, 10:9, 11:3, 11:4, 11:6, 12:1, 12:7, 12:11, 12:12, 12:13, 12:18, 12:19, 13:8, 13:14, 14:19, 14:21, 14:22, 14:23, 15:1, 15:2, 15:3, 15:4, 15:5 (2), 15:7, 15:8, 15:9, 15:13, 15:18, 16:2, 16:5, 16:6, 16:8 (2), 16:9, 16:10, 16:11, 16:13, 17:1, 17:3, 17:9, 17:15, 17:17, 17:18, 17:19, 18:3, 18:5 (2), 18:6, 18:9 (2), 18:10, 18:12, 18:13 (2), 18:15 (2), 18:17, 18:20, 18:23, 18:26, 18:27, 18:28, 18:29 (2), 18:30 (2), 18:31 (2), 18:32 (2), 19:2 (2), 19:5, 19:7, 19:9 (2), 19:12, 19:14, 19:15, 19:17, 19:18, 19:21, 19:31, 19:34, 20:2, 20:3, 20:4, 20:5 (2), 20:6, 20:9, 20:10, 20:11 (2), 20:13 (2), 20:15, 20:16, 21:1, 21:6, 21:7, 21:10, 21:12 (2), 21:16, 21:17, 21:22 (2), 21:24, 21:26, 21:29, 21:30, 22:1 (2), 22:2 (2), 22:3, 22:5, 22:7 (4), 22:8, 22:9, 22:11 (2), 22:12, 22:14, 22:16, 22:20, 23:3, 23:5, 23:8, 23:10, 23:13, 23:14, 24:2, 24:5, 24:6, 24:7, 24:12, 24:14 (2), 24:17, 24:18, 24:19, 24:23, 24:24, 24:25, 24:27, 24:30, 24:31, 24:33 (2), 24:34, 24:37, 24:39, 24:40, 24:42, 24:43, 24:44, 24:45, 24:46, 24:47 (2), 24:50, 24:54, 24:55, 24:56, 24:57, 24:58 (2), 24:60, 24:65 (2), 25:22, 25:23, 25:30, 25:31, 25:32, 25:33, 26:2 (2), 26:7 (2), 26:9 (4), 26:10, 26:11, 26:16, 26:20, 26:22, 26:24, 26:27, 26:28 (2), 26:32, 27:1 (2), 27:2, 27:6 (3), 27:11, 27:13, 27:18 (2), 27:19, 27:20 (2), 27:21, 27:22, 27:24 (2), 27:25, 27:26, 27:27, 27:31, 27:32 (2), 27:33, 27:34, 27:35, 27:36 (2), 27:37, 27:38, 27:39, 27:41, 27:42, 27:46, 28:1, 28:6, 28:13, 28:16, 28:17, 28:20, 29:4 (2), 29:5 (2), 29:6 (2), 29:7, 29:8, 29:14, 29:15, 29:18, 29:19, 29:21, 29:25, 29:26, 29:32, 29:33, 29:34, 29:35, 30:1, 30:2, 30:3, 30:6, 30:8, 30:11, 30:13, 30:14, 30:15 (2), 30:16, 30:18, 30:20, 30:23, 30:24, 30:25, 30:27, 30:28, 30:29, 30:31 (2), 30:34, 31:1, 31:3, 31:5, 31:8 (2), 31:11 (2), 31:12, 31:14, 31:16, 31:24, 31:26, 31:29 (2), 31:31 (2), 31:35, 31:36, 31:43, 31:46, 31:48, 31:49, 31:51, 32:3, 32:5 (3), 32:7, 32:9, 32:10 (2), 32:13, 32:17,

**401**

32:18 (2), 32:19, 32:20, 32:21 (2),
32:27 (2), 32:28 (2), 32:29 (2), 32:30
(2), 33:5 (2), 33:8 (2), 33:9, 33:10,
33:12, 33:13, 33:15 (2), 34:4 (2), 34:8,
34:11 (2), 34:12, 34:14, 34:20, 34:30,
34:31, 35:1, 35:2, 35:10, 35:11, 35:17,
37:6, 37:8, 37:9, 37:10, 37:13 (2),
37:14, 37:15, 37:16, 37:17 (2), 37:19,
37:20, 37:21, 37:22, 37:26, 37:30,
37:32, 37:33, 37:35, 38:8, 38:11 (2),
38:13, 38:16 (2), 38:17 (2), 38:18 (2),
38:21 (2), 38:22 (2), 38:23, 38:24 (2),
38:25 (2), 38:26, 38:28, 38:29, 39:7,
39:8, 39:12, 39:14 (2), 39:17, 39:19,
40:7, 40:8 (2), 40:9, 40:12, 40:16,
40:18, 41:9, 41:15 (2), 41:16, 41:24,
41:25, 41:38, 41:39, 41:41, 41:44,
41:54, 41:55 (2), 42:1, 42:2, 42:4, 42:7
(2), 42:9, 42:10, 42:12, 42:13, 42:14
(2), 42:18, 42:21, 42:22 (3), 42:28 (2),
42:29, 42:31, 42:33, 42:36, 42:37 (2),
42:38, 43:2, 43:3 (3), 43:5, 43:6, 43:7
(3), 43:8, 43:11, 43:16, 43:17, 43:18,
43:20, 43:23, 43:27 (2), 43:28, 43:29
(3), 43:31, 44:1, 44:2, 44:4 (2), 44:7,
44:10, 44:15, 44:16 (2), 44:17, 44:18,
44:19, 44:20, 44:21, 44:22, 44:23,
44:25, 44:26, 44:27, 44:28, 44:32, 45:3,
45:4 (2), 45:9 (2), 45:16, 45:17 (2),
45:24, 45:26, 45:28, 46:2 (3), 46:3,
46:30, 46:31 (2), 46:33, 46:34, 47:1,
47:3 (2), 47:4, 47:5 (2), 47:8, 47:9,
47:15, 47:16, 47:18, 47:23, 47:25,
47:29, 47:30, 47:31, 48:1, 48:2, 48:3,
48:4, 48:8, 48:9 (2), 48:11, 48:15,
48:18, 48:19, 48:20 (2), 48:21, 49:1,
49:29, 50:4 (2), 50:5, 50:6, 50:11,
50:15, 50:16 (2), 50:17, 50:18, 50:19,
50:24, 50:25

**Scarlet (2):** 38:28, 38:30

**Scatter (1):** 9:19

**Scatter abroad (5):** 10:18, 11:4, 11:8, 11:9, 49:7

**Scratch (1):** 4:22

**Scroll (1):** 5:1

**Sea (12):** 1:10, 1:22, 1:26, 1:28, 9:2, 12:8, 13:14, 14:3, 22:17, 28:14, 32:13, 41:49

**Se'ah (1):** 18:6

**Search (2):** 31:35, 44:12

**Search out (5):** 31:39, 37:15, 37:16, 43:9, 43:30

**Seat (1):** 41:40

**Second (13):** 1:8, 2:13, 4:19, 6:16, 7:11, 8:14, 22:15, 30:7, 30:12, 32:20, 41:5, 41:52, 47:18

**See (141):** 1:4, 1:9, 1:10, 1:12, 1:18, 1:21, 1:25, 1:31, 2:19, 3:6, 6:2, 6:5, 6:12, 7:1,
8:5, 8:8, 8:13, 9:14, 9:16, 9:22, 9:23,
11:5, 12:1, 12:7 (2), 12:12, 12:14,
12:15, 13:10, 13:14, 13:15, 16:4, 16:5,
16:13 (2), 17:1, 18:1, 18:2 (2), 18:21,
19:1, 19:28, 20:10, 21:9, 21:16, 21:19,
22:4, 22:8, 22:13, 22:14, 24:30, 24:63,
24:64, 26:2, 26:8, 26:24, 26:28 (2),
27:1, 27:27, 28:6, 28:8, 29:2, 29:10,
29:31, 29:32, 30:1, 30:9, 31:2, 31:5,
31:10, 31:12 (2), 31:42, 31:43, 31:50,
32:3, 32:21, 32:26, 32:31, 33:1, 33:5,
33:10 (2), 34:1, 34:2, 35:1, 35:9, 37:4,
37:14, 37:18, 37:20, 37:25, 38:2, 38:14,
38:15, 39:3, 39:13, 39:14, 39:23, 40:6,
40:16, 41:19, 41:22, 41:28, 41:33,
41:41, 42:1 (2), 42:7, 42:9, 42:12,
42:21, 42:27, 42:35, 43:3, 43:5, 43:16,
43:29, 44:23, 44:26, 44:28, 44:31,
44:34, 45:12, 45:13, 45:27, 45:28,
46:29, 46:30, 46:32, 48:3, 48:8, 48:10,
48:11 (2), 48:17, 49:15, 50:11, 50:15,
50:23

**Seed (59):** 1:11 (2), 1:12 (2), 1:29 (2), 3:15
(2), 4:25, 7:3, 8:22, 9:9, 12:7, 13:15,
13:16 (2), 15:3, 15:5, 15:13, 15:18,
16:10, 17:7 (2), 17:8, 17:9, 17:10,
17:12, 17:19, 19:32, 19:34, 21:12,
21:13, 22:17 (2), 22:18, 24:7, 24:60,
26:3, 26:4 (3), 26:24, 28:4, 28:13, 28:14
(2), 32:13, 35:12, 38:8, 38:9 (2), 46:6,
46:7, 47:19, 47:23, 47:24, 48:4, 48:11,
48:19

**Seeing as (1):** 22:16

**Seek (5):** 9:5 (3), 25:22, 42:22

**Seethe (1):** 25:29

**Seize (6):** 19:16, 21:18, 41:56, 41:57, 47:20, 48:2

**Seize hold (2):** 4:21, 39:12

**Sell (10):** 25:31, 25:33, 31:15, 37:27, 37:28, 37:36, 45:4, 45:5, 47:20, 47:22

**Send (66):** 3:22, 3:23, 8:7, 8:8, 8:9, 8:10,
8:12, 12:20, 18:16, 19:10, 19:13, 19:29,
20:2, 21:14, 22:10, 22:12, 24:7, 24:40,
24:54, 24:56, 24:59, 25:6, 26:27, 26:29,
26:31, 27:42, 27:45, 28:5, 28:6, 30:25,
31:4, 31:27, 31:42, 32:4, 32:6, 32:19,
32:27 (2), 37:13, 37:14, 37:22, 37:32,
38:17 (2), 38:20, 38:23, 38:25, 41:8,
41:14, 42:4, 42:16, 43:4, 43:5, 43:8,
43:14, 44:3, 45:5, 45:7, 45:8, 45:23,
45:24, 45:27, 46:5, 46:28, 48:14, 49:21

**Separate (5):** 1:4, 1:6, 1:7, 1:14, 1:18

**Separated thing (14):** 2:18, 21:28, 21:29,
26:1, 30:40, 32:17, 32:25, 42:38, 43:32
(3), 44:20, 46:26, 47:26

**Serpent (6):** 3:1, 3:2, 3:4, 3:13, 3:14, 49:17

**Servant (88):** 9:25 (2), 9:26, 9:27, 12:16, 14:15, 18:3, 18:5, 19:2, 19:19, 20:8, 20:14, 21:25, 24:2, 24:5, 24:9, 24:10, 24:14, 24:17, 24:34, 24:35, 24:52, 24:53, 24:59, 24:61, 24:65 (2), 24:66, 26:15, 26:19, 26:24, 26:25, 26:32, 27:37, 30:43, 32:5, 32:6, 32:11, 32:17 (2), 32:19, 32:21, 33:5, 33:14, 39:17, 39:19, 40:20 (2), 41:10, 41:12, 41:37, 41:38, 42:10, 42:11, 42:13, 43:18, 43:28, 44:7, 44:9 (2), 44:10, 44:16 (2), 44:17, 44:18 (2), 44:19, 44:21, 44:23, 44:24, 44:27, 44:30, 44:31 (2), 44:32, 44:33 (2), 45:16, 46:34, 47:3, 47:4 (2), 47:19, 47:25, 50:2, 50:7, 50:17, 50:18

**Serve (23):** 2:5, 2:15, 3:23, 4:2, 4:12, 14:4, 15:13, 15:14, 25:23, 27:29, 27:40, 29:15, 29:18, 29:20, 29:25, 29:27, 29:30, 30:26 (2), 30:29, 31:6, 31:41, 49:15

**Service (3):** 26:14, 29:27, 30:26

**Set (4):** 30:38, 33:15, 43:9, 47:2

**Set apart (1):** 2:3

**Set down (8):** 3:15, 4:25, 30:40 (2), 41:33, 46:4, 48:14, 48:17

**Set in place (47):** 2:8, 4:15, 6:16, 9:23, 13:16, 21:13, 21:14, 21:18, 22:6, 22:9, 24:2, 24:9, 24:47, 27:37, 28:11, 28:18 (2), 28:22, 30:36, 30:41, 30:42, 31:21, 31:34, 31:37, 32:13, 32:17, 33:2, 37:34, 40:15, 41:42, 43:22, 43:31, 43:32, 44:1, 44:2, 44:21, 45:7, 45:8, 45:9, 46:3, 47:6, 47:26, 47:29, 48:18, 48:20 (2), 50:26

**Set-aside (1):** 27:36

**Settle (70):** 4:16, 4:20, 11:2, 11:31, 13:6 (2), 13:7, 13:12 (2), 13:18, 14:7, 14:12, 16:3, 18:1, 19:1, 19:25, 19:29, 19:30 (3), 20:1, 20:15, 21:16 (2), 21:20, 21:21, 22:5, 22:19, 23:10, 24:3, 24:37, 24:55, 24:62, 25:11, 25:27, 26:6, 26:17, 27:19, 27:44, 29:14, 29:19, 31:34, 34:10, 34:16, 34:21, 34:22, 34:23, 34:30, 35:1, 36:7, 36:8, 36:20, 37:1, 37:25, 38:11 (2), 38:14, 43:33, 44:33, 45:10, 46:34, 47:4, 47:6 (2), 47:11, 47:27, 48:2, 49:24, 50:11, 50:22

**Settling (3):** 10:30, 27:39, 36:43

**Seven (70):** 4:24 (2), 5:7, 5:12, 5:25, 5:26, 5:31 (3), 7:2 (2), 7:3 (2), 7:4, 7:10, 7:11, 8:4, 8:10, 8:12, 8:14, 11:21, 11:26, 12:4, 21:28, 21:29, 21:30, 23:1, 25:7, 25:17, 29:18, 29:20, 29:27, 29:30, 31:23, 33:3, 37:2, 41:2, 41:3, 41:4, 41:5, 41:6, 41:7, 41:18, 41:19, 41:20, 41:22, 41:23, 41:24, 41:26 (4), 41:27 (4), 41:29, 41:30, 41:34, 41:36, 41:47, 41:48,

41:53, 41:54, 46:25, 46:27, 47:28 (2), 50:3, 50:10

**Seventh (4):** 2:2 (2), 2:3, 8:4

**Seventh time (2):** 4:15, 4:24

**Sew together (1):** 3:7

**Sha'ar (1):** 26:12

**Shadow (1):** 19:8

**Shake (1):** 45:24

**Shape (4):** 29:17, 39:6, 41:18, 41:19

**Sharpen (1):** 4:22

**Shave (1):** 41:14

**She (58):** 2:12, 3:12, 3:20, 4:22, 7:2, 10:11, 10:12, 12:14, 12:18, 12:19, 14:2, 14:8, 17:14, 19:20 (2), 19:38, 20:2, 20:3, 20:5 (3), 20:12, 22:20, 22:24, 23:2, 23:15, 23:19, 24:44, 25:21, 26:7 (2), 26:9 (2), 26:12, 27:38, 29:2, 29:9, 29:25, 32:19, 34:14, 35:6, 35:19, 35:20, 35:22, 35:27, 37:32, 38:1, 38:14, 38:16, 38:21, 38:25 (2), 40:10, 43:32, 47:6, 47:17, 47:18, 48:7

**Sheaf (4):** 37:7 (4)

**Shear (3):** 31:19, 38:12, 38:13

**She-donkey (4):** 12:16, 32:16, 45:23, 49:11

**Sheep (4):** 30:32, 30:33, 30:35, 30:40

**Sheet (9):** 1:6, 1:7 (3), 1:8, 1:14, 1:15, 1:17, 1:20

**She-goat (11):** 15:9, 27:9, 27:16, 30:32, 30:33, 30:35, 31:38, 32:15, 37:31, 38:17, 38:20

**Sheqel (2):** 23:15, 23:16

**Shield (1):** 15:1

**Shine (1):** 12:15

**Shining (3):** 6:16, 43:16, 43:25

**Ship (1):** 49:13

**Shoham (1):** 2:12

**Shore (2):** 49:13 (2)

**Short (2):** 35:16, 48:7

**Shoulder (6):** 9:23, 21:14, 24:15, 24:45, 48:22, 49:15

**Show beauty (4):** 33:5, 33:11, 42:21, 43:29

**Shrub (2):** 2:5, 21:15

**Shut (5):** 2:21, 7:16, 8:2, 19:6, 19:10

**Shut up (2):** 26:15, 26:18

**Side (1):** 6:16

**Sign (6):** 1:14, 4:15, 9:12, 9:13, 9:17, 17:11

**Signet (2):** 38:18, 38:25

**Signet ring (1):** 41:42

**Silver (41):** 13:2, 17:12, 17:13, 17:23, 17:27, 20:16, 23:9, 23:13, 23:15, 23:16 (2), 24:35, 24:53, 31:15, 37:28, 42:25, 42:27, 42:28, 42:35 (2), 43:12 (2), 43:15, 43:18, 43:21 (2), 43:22 (2), 43:23, 44:1, 44:2 (2), 44:8 (2), 45:22, 47:14 (2), 47:15 (2), 47:16, 47:18

**Since (2):** 22:18, 26:5

**Sinew (2):** 32:33 (2)

**Sister (24):** 4:22, 12:13, 12:19, 20:2, 20:5, 20:12, 24:30 (2), 24:59, 24:60, 25:20, 26:7, 26:9, 28:9, 29:13, 30:1, 30:8, 34:13, 34:14, 34:27, 34:31, 36:3, 36:22, 46:17

**Six (16):** 5:15, 5:18, 5:20, 5:21, 5:23, 5:27, 7:6, 7:11, 8:13, 16:16, 25:26, 30:20, 31:41, 46:18, 46:26 (2)

**Sixth (2):** 1:31, 30:19

**Skin (2):** 3:21, 27:16

**Skin bag (3):** 21:14, 21:15, 21:19

**Sky (41):** 1:1, 1:8, 1:9, 1:14, 1:15, 1:17, 1:20, 1:26, 1:28, 1:30, 2:1, 2:4 (2), 2:19, 2:20, 6:7, 6:17, 7:3, 7:11, 7:19, 7:23, 8:2 (2), 9:2, 11:4, 14:19, 14:22, 15:5, 19:24, 21:17, 22:11, 22:15, 22:17, 24:3, 24:7, 26:4, 27:28, 27:39, 28:12, 28:17, 49:25

**Slander (1):** 37:2

**Slaughtering (7):** 37:36, 39:1, 40:3, 40:4, 41:10, 41:12, 43:16

**Slay (2):** 22:10, 37:31

**Sleep (2):** 2:21, 41:5

**Slick (1):** 27:11

**Slip away (5):** 19:17 (2), 19:19, 19:20, 19:22

**Small (20):** 1:16, 9:24, 19:11, 27:15, 27:42, 29:16, 29:18, 42:13, 42:15, 42:20, 42:32, 42:34, 43:29, 44:2, 44:12, 44:20, 44:23, 44:26 (2), 48:19

**Small amount (11):** 18:4, 24:17, 24:43, 26:10, 30:15, 30:30, 43:2, 43:11 (2), 44:25, 47:9

**Smear (1):** 31:13

**Smell (2):** 8:21, 27:27

**Smoke (1):** 15:17

**Smoldering (2):** 19:28 (2)

**Smooth (1):** 27:16

**Snap (2):** 40:2, 41:10

**Snooze (2):** 28:16, 31:40

**So (52):** 1:7, 1:9, 1:11, 1:15, 1:24, 1:30, 2:24, 4:15, 6:4, 6:22, 10:9, 11:9, 15:14, 16:14, 18:5 (2), 19:8, 19:22, 20:6, 21:31, 23:19, 25:22, 25:26, 25:30, 26:33, 29:26, 29:28, 29:34, 29:35, 30:6, 30:15, 31:48, 32:21, 32:33, 33:10, 33:17, 34:7, 38:26, 41:13, 41:31, 42:20, 42:21, 42:25, 43:11, 44:10, 45:15, 45:21, 47:22, 48:18, 50:3, 50:11, 50:12

**Sojourn (9):** 12:10, 19:9, 20:1, 21:23, 21:34, 26:3, 32:5, 35:27, 47:4

**Sojourner (1):** 23:4

**Solitary (3):** 22:2, 22:12, 22:16

**Son (365):** 3:16, 4:17, 4:25, 4:26, 5:4, 5:7, 5:10, 5:13, 5:16, 5:19, 5:22, 5:26, 5:28, 5:30, 5:32, 6:2, 6:4, 6:10, 6:18 (2), 7:6, 7:7 (2), 7:13 (2), 8:16 (2), 8:18 (2), 9:1, 9:8, 9:18, 9:19, 9:24, 10:1 (2), 10:2, 10:3, 10:4, 10:6, 10:7 (2), 10:20, 10:21, 10:22, 10:23, 10:25, 10:29, 10:31, 10:32, 11:5, 11:10, 11:11, 11:13, 11:15, 11:17, 11:19, 11:21, 11:23, 11:25, 11:31 (5), 12:4, 12:5, 14:12, 15:2, 15:3, 16:11, 16:15 (2), 16:16, 17:1, 17:12 (2), 17:16, 17:17, 17:19, 17:23, 17:24, 17:25 (2), 17:26, 17:27, 18:7, 18:8, 18:10, 18:14, 18:19, 19:12, 19:37, 19:38 (2), 21:2, 21:3, 21:4 (2), 21:5 (2), 21:7 (2), 21:9, 21:10 (3), 21:11, 21:13, 22:2, 22:3, 22:6, 22:7, 22:8, 22:9, 22:10, 22:12, 22:13, 22:16, 22:20, 23:3, 23:5, 23:7, 23:8, 23:10 (2), 23:11, 23:16, 23:18, 23:20, 24:3, 24:4, 24:5, 24:6, 24:7, 24:8, 24:15, 24:24, 24:36, 24:37, 24:38, 24:40, 24:44, 24:47, 24:48, 24:51, 25:3, 25:4 (2), 25:6 (2), 25:9 (2), 25:10, 25:11, 25:12, 25:13, 25:16, 25:19, 25:20, 25:22, 25:26, 26:34, 27:1 (2), 27:5, 27:6, 27:8, 27:13, 27:15 (2), 27:17, 27:18, 27:20 (2), 27:21 (2), 27:24, 27:25, 27:26, 27:27, 27:29, 27:31, 27:32, 27:37, 27:42 (2), 27:43, 28:5, 28:9, 29:1, 29:5, 29:12, 29:13, 29:32, 29:33, 29:34 (2), 29:35, 30:1, 30:5, 30:6, 30:7, 30:10, 30:12, 30:14, 30:15 (2), 30:16, 30:17, 30:19, 30:20, 30:23, 30:24, 30:35, 31:1, 31:16, 31:17, 31:28, 31:43 (3), 32:1, 32:12, 32:16, 32:33, 33:19, 34:2, 34:5, 34:7, 34:8, 34:13, 34:18, 34:20, 34:24, 34:25, 34:26, 34:27, 35:5, 35:17, 35:22, 35:23, 35:24, 35:25, 35:26 (2), 35:29, 36:5, 36:6, 36:10 (3), 36:11, 36:12 (2), 36:13 (2), 36:14, 36:15 (2), 36:16, 36:17 (3), 36:18, 36:19, 36:20, 36:21, 36:22, 36:23, 36:24, 36:25, 36:26, 36:27, 36:28, 36:31, 36:32, 36:33, 36:35, 36:38, 36:39, 37:2 (3), 37:3 (2), 37:32, 37:33, 37:34, 37:35 (2), 38:3, 38:4, 38:5, 38:11, 38:26, 41:46, 41:50, 42:1, 42:5, 42:11, 42:13, 42:32, 42:37, 42:38, 43:29 (2), 45:9, 45:10 (3), 45:21, 45:28, 46:5, 46:7 (4), 46:8 (2), 46:9, 46:10 (2), 46:11, 46:12 (2), 46:13, 46:14, 46:15 (2), 46:16, 46:17 (2), 46:18, 46:19, 46:21, 46:22, 46:23, 46:24, 46:25, 46:26, 46:27, 47:29, 48:1, 48:2, 48:5, 48:8, 48:9, 48:19, 49:1, 49:2, 49:8, 49:9, 49:11, 49:22 (2), 49:32, 49:33, 50:12, 50:13, 50:23 (3), 50:25, 50:26

**Song (1):** 31:27

**Sorrow (2):** 42:38, 44:31

**South country (7):** 12:9, 13:1, 13:3, 13:14, 20:1, 24:62, 28:14

**Sow (6):** 1:11, 1:12, 1:29 (2), 26:12, 47:23

**Spare (1):** 45:20

**404**

**Speak (71):** 8:15, 12:4, 16:13, 17:3, 17:22, 17:23, 18:19, 18:27, 18:29, 18:30, 18:31, 18:32, 18:33, 19:14, 19:21, 20:8, 21:1, 21:2, 23:3, 23:8, 23:13, 23:16, 24:7, 24:15, 24:30, 24:33 (2), 24:45, 24:50, 24:51, 27:5, 27:6, 27:19, 28:15, 29:9, 31:24, 31:29, 32:20, 34:3, 34:6, 34:8, 34:13, 34:20, 35:13, 35:14, 35:15, 37:4, 39:10, 39:17, 39:19, 41:9, 41:17, 41:28, 42:7, 42:14, 42:24, 42:30, 43:19, 44:6, 44:7, 44:16, 44:18, 45:12, 45:15, 45:27 (2), 49:28, 50:4 (2), 50:17, 50:21

**Speckled (9):** 30:32 (2), 30:33, 30:35, 30:39, 31:8 (2), 31:10, 31:12

**Speech (1):** 4:23

**Spice (2):** 37:25, 43:11

**Spit upon (9):** 3:14, 3:17, 4:11, 5:29, 9:25, 12:3, 27:29 (2), 49:7

**Split (1):** 10:25

**Spoil (1):** 49:27

**Spot (6):** 30:32 (2), 30:33, 30:35 (2), 30:39

**Spotted (2):** 31:10, 31:12

**Spread wide (1):** 9:27

**Spring (2):** 7:11, 8:2

**Spring up (6):** 2:5, 2:9, 3:18, 19:25, 41:6, 41:23

**Sprout (1):** 1:11

**Staff (3):** 49:10, 49:16, 49:28

**Stagger (2):** 4:12, 4:14

**Stalk (2):** 41:5, 41:22

**Stand (16):** 18:8, 18:22, 19:17, 19:27, 24:30, 24:31, 29:35, 30:9, 41:1, 41:3, 41:17, 41:46, 43:15, 45:1, 45:9, 47:7

**Stand erect (12):** 18:2, 21:28, 21:29, 24:13, 24:43, 28:12, 28:13, 33:20, 35:14, 35:20, 37:7, 45:1

**Star (5):** 1:16, 15:5, 22:17, 26:4, 37:9

**Stare (3):** 15:5, 19:17, 19:26

**Statement (1):** 49:21

**Stave (2):** 38:18, 38:25

**Stay the night (9):** 19:2 (2), 24:23, 24:25, 24:54, 28:11, 31:54, 32:14, 32:22

**Steal (12):** 30:33, 31:19, 31:20, 31:26, 31:27, 31:30, 31:32, 31:39 (2), 40:15 (2), 44:8

**Sterile (3):** 11:30, 25:21, 29:31

**Stew (2):** 25:29, 25:34

**Stink (1):** 34:30

**Stir (1):** 45:3

**Stone (15):** 2:12, 11:3, 28:11, 28:18, 28:22, 29:2, 29:3 (2), 29:8, 29:10, 31:45, 31:46 (2), 35:14, 49:24

**Stoop (1):** 49:9

**Stop (3):** 16:2, 20:18 (2)

**Stranger (2):** 15:13, 23:4

**Straw (2):** 24:25, 24:32

**Stream (6):** 41:1, 41:2, 41:3 (2), 41:17, 41:18

**Street (1):** 19:2

**Strength (3):** 4:12, 31:6, 49:3

**Stretch (9):** 12:8, 24:14, 26:25, 33:19, 35:21, 38:1, 38:16, 39:21, 49:15

**Stretch out (5):** 4:7, 29:2, 49:9, 49:14, 49:25

**Strife (1):** 13:7

**Strip (1):** 30:37

**Striped (7):** 30:35, 30:39, 30:40, 31:8 (2), 31:10, 31:12

**Striped bruise (1):** 4:23

**Stroke of time (10):** 2:23, 18:32, 27:36, 29:34, 29:35, 30:20, 33:3, 41:32, 43:10, 46:30

**Strong (2):** 49:3, 49:7

**Strong One (5):** 15:9, 22:13 (2), 31:38, 32:15

**Subdue (1):** 1:28

**Submerge (1):** 35:4

**Subside (1):** 8:1

**Substance (2):** 7:4, 7:23

**Subtle (1):** 3:1

**Suckle (4):** 21:7, 24:59, 32:16, 35:8

**Summer (1):** 8:22

**Summit (3):** 1:1, 10:10, 49:3

**Sun (6):** 15:12, 15:17, 19:23, 28:11, 32:32, 37:9

**Support (1):** 27:37

**Sure (1):** 20:12

**Surely (15):** 7:23, 9:4, 9:5, 18:32, 20:12, 23:13, 26:9, 27:13, 27:30, 28:16, 29:14, 34:15, 34:22, 34:23, 44:28

**Sustain (3):** 45:11, 47:12, 50:21

**Swallow (2):** 41:7, 41:24

**Swarm (5):** 1:20, 1:21, 7:21, 8:17, 9:7

**Swarmer (2):** 1:20, 7:21

**Swear (19):** 21:23, 21:24, 21:31, 22:16, 24:3, 24:7, 24:9, 24:37, 25:33 (2), 26:3, 26:31, 31:53, 47:31 (2), 50:5, 50:6, 50:24, 50:25

**Swearing (2):** 24:8, 26:3

**Sweat (1):** 3:19

**Sweet (1):** 8:21

**Swimmer (2):** 1:26, 1:28

**Sword (6):** 3:24, 27:40, 31:26, 34:25, 34:26, 48:22

**Take (142):** 2:15, 2:21, 2:22, 2:23, 3:6, 3:19, 3:22, 3:23, 4:11, 4:19, 5:24, 6:2, 6:21, 7:2, 8:9, 8:20, 9:23, 11:29, 11:31, 12:5, 12:15, 12:19 (2), 14:11, 14:12, 14:21, 14:23, 14:24, 15:9, 15:10, 16:3, 17:23, 18:4, 18:5, 18:7, 18:8, 19:14, 19:15, 20:2, 20:3, 20:14, 21:14, 21:21, 21:27, 21:30, 22:2, 22:3, 22:6 (2), 22:10, 22:13, 23:13, 24:3, 24:4, 24:7 (2), 24:10, 24:22, 24:37, 24:38, 24:40, 24:48, 24:51, 24:61, 24:65, 24:67, 25:1, 25:20, 26:34, 27:9, 27:13, 27:14, 27:15, 27:35, 27:36 (2), 27:45, 27:46, 28:1, 28:2, 28:6 (2), 28:9, 28:11, 28:18,

29:23, 30:9, 30:15 (2), 30:37, 31:1, 31:23, 31:32, 31:34, 31:45, 31:46, 31:50, 32:14, 32:23, 32:24, 33:10, 33:11 (2), 34:2, 34:4, 34:9, 34:16, 34:17, 34:21, 34:25, 34:26, 34:28, 36:2, 36:6, 37:24, 37:31, 38:2, 38:6, 38:20, 38:23, 38:28, 39:20, 40:11, 42:16, 42:24, 42:33, 42:36, 43:11, 43:12, 43:13, 43:15 (2), 43:18, 44:29, 45:18, 45:19, 46:6, 47:2, 48:1, 48:9, 48:13, 48:22

**Take a fifth (1):** 41:34
**Take upon (2):** 18:27, 18:31
**Talk (1):** 21:7
**Tamarisk (1):** 21:33
**Tambourine (1):** 31:27
**Taniyn (1):** 1:21
**Tar (2):** 11:3, 14:10
**Task work (1):** 49:15
**Tasty food (1):** 49:20
**Teaching (1):** 26:5
**Tear (3):** 37:29, 37:34, 44:13
**Tear away (1):** 27:40
**Tear into pieces (5):** 37:33 (2), 44:28 (2), 49:27
**Ten (51):** 5:8, 5:10, 5:14, 6:3, 7:11, 7:20, 8:4, 8:14, 11:24, 11:25, 14:4 (2), 14:5, 14:14, 16:3, 17:20, 17:25, 18:31 (2), 18:32 (2), 23:1, 24:10, 24:22, 25:16, 31:7, 31:38, 31:41 (3), 32:15 (2), 32:16 (3), 32:23, 35:22, 37:2, 37:9, 37:28, 42:3, 42:13, 42:32, 45:23 (2), 46:18, 46:22, 47:28, 49:28, 50:22, 50:26
**Tender (3):** 18:7, 29:17, 33:13
**Tent (23):** 4:20, 9:21, 9:27, 12:8, 13:3, 13:5, 18:1, 18:2, 18:6, 18:9, 18:10, 24:67, 25:27, 26:25, 31:25, 31:33 (5), 31:34, 33:19, 35:21
**Tenth (2):** 8:5 (2)
**Tenth one (1):** 24:55
**Tenth part (1):** 14:20
**Terminate (3):** 11:8, 18:11, 41:49
**Terror (1):** 15:12
**Test (1):** 22:1
**That (7):** 12:13, 18:19 (2), 18:24, 27:25, 37:22, 50:20
**That one (7):** 9:26, 9:27, 19:15, 34:15, 41:39, 44:15, 44:18
**Then (3):** 27:33, 27:37, 43:11
**There (102):** 2:8, 2:10, 2:11, 2:12, 3:23, 10:14, 11:2, 11:7, 11:8, 11:9 (2), 11:31, 12:7, 12:8 (2), 12:10, 13:3, 13:4 (2), 13:14, 13:18, 14:10, 18:16, 18:22, 18:28, 18:29, 18:30 (2), 18:31, 18:32, 19:20 (2), 19:22 (2), 19:27, 20:1, 20:13, 21:17, 21:31, 21:33, 22:2, 22:9, 23:13, 24:5, 24:6, 24:7, 24:8, 25:10, 26:8, 26:17 (2), 26:19, 26:20, 26:22, 26:23,

26:25 (3), 27:9, 27:45, 28:2, 28:6, 28:11, 29:2, 29:3, 30:32, 31:13 (2), 31:46, 32:14, 32:30, 33:19, 33:20, 35:1 (2), 35:3, 35:7 (2), 35:15, 35:27, 38:2, 39:1, 39:11, 39:20, 39:22, 40:3, 41:12, 42:2 (2), 42:26, 43:25, 43:30, 44:14, 45:11, 46:3, 48:7, 49:24, 49:31 (3), 50:5, 50:10
**There is (21):** 18:24, 23:8, 24:23, 24:42, 24:49, 28:16, 31:29, 33:9, 33:11, 39:4, 39:5 (2), 39:8, 42:1, 42:2, 43:4, 43:7, 44:19, 44:20, 44:26, 47:6
**These (94):** 2:4, 6:9, 9:19 (2), 10:1, 10:5, 10:20, 10:29, 10:31, 10:32 (2), 11:10, 11:27, 14:3, 15:1, 15:10, 15:17, 19:8, 19:25, 20:8, 21:29, 22:1, 22:20, 22:23, 24:28, 25:4, 25:7, 25:12, 25:13, 25:16 (2), 25:17, 25:19, 26:3, 26:4, 27:46, 29:13, 31:43, 32:18, 33:5, 34:21, 35:26, 36:1, 36:5, 36:9, 36:10, 36:12, 36:13 (2), 36:14, 36:15, 36:16 (2), 36:17 (3), 36:18 (2), 36:19 (2), 36:20, 36:21, 36:23, 36:24, 36:25, 36:26, 36:27, 36:28, 36:29, 36:30, 36:31, 36:40, 36:43, 37:2, 38:25 (2), 39:7, 39:17, 39:19, 40:1, 41:35, 43:7, 44:6, 44:7, 46:8, 46:15, 46:18 (2), 46:22, 46:25 (2), 48:1, 48:8, 49:28
**They(f) (6):** 6:2, 33:6, 41:19, 41:26 (2), 41:27
**They(m) (21):** 3:7, 6:4, 7:14, 14:13, 14:24, 25:16, 34:21, 34:22, 34:23, 37:16, 40:12, 40:18, 42:8, 42:23, 42:35 (2), 44:3, 44:4, 47:14, 48:5, 48:9
**Thin (5):** 41:19, 41:20, 41:23, 41:24, 41:27
**Thing of sacrifice (2):** 31:54, 46:1
**Think (5):** 15:6, 31:15, 38:15, 50:20 (2)
**Third (9):** 1:13, 2:14, 6:16, 22:4, 31:22, 32:20, 34:25, 40:20, 42:18
**Third generation (1):** 50:23
**This (138):** 2:23 (3), 3:13, 3:14, 5:1, 5:29, 6:15, 7:1, 7:11, 7:13, 9:12, 9:17, 11:6, 12:7, 12:12, 12:18, 15:4, 15:7, 15:18, 16:8, 17:10, 17:21, 17:23, 17:26, 18:13, 18:25, 19:13, 19:14, 19:20, 19:21, 20:5, 20:6, 20:10, 20:11, 20:13, 21:10 (2), 21:26, 21:30, 22:16, 24:5, 24:7, 24:8, 24:9, 24:58, 25:22, 25:30, 25:32, 26:3, 26:10, 26:11, 26:33, 27:20, 27:21, 27:24, 27:36, 28:15, 28:16, 28:17 (3), 28:20, 28:22, 29:25, 29:27 (2), 29:28, 29:33, 30:31, 31:1, 31:13, 31:38, 31:41, 31:48, 31:51, 31:52 (4), 32:3, 32:11, 32:20, 32:30, 32:33, 33:8, 33:15, 34:4, 34:14, 34:15, 34:22, 35:17, 37:6, 37:10, 37:17, 37:22, 37:32, 38:21, 38:22, 38:23, 38:28, 39:9 (2), 39:11, 40:12,

40:14, 40:18, 41:38, 41:39, 42:15 (2), 42:18, 42:21, 42:28, 42:33, 43:10, 43:11, 43:15, 43:29, 44:5, 44:7, 44:15, 44:17, 44:29, 45:6, 45:17, 45:19, 45:23, 47:26, 48:4, 48:9, 48:15, 48:18, 49:28, 50:11, 50:20, 50:24, 50:25

**This one (2):** 24:65, 37:19

**Thistle (1):** 3:18

**Though (12):** 3:22, 4:14, 11:6, 15:3, 19:34, 27:11, 27:37, 29:7, 30:34, 39:8, 44:8, 47:23

**Thought (2):** 6:5, 8:21

**Thousand (2):** 20:16, 24:60

**Thread (1):** 14:23

**Three (47):** 5:3, 5:5, 5:16, 5:22, 5:23, 6:10, 6:15 (2), 7:13, 9:19, 9:28, 11:12, 11:13, 11:14, 11:15, 11:16, 11:17, 11:18, 11:20, 11:22, 14:4, 14:14, 17:25, 18:2, 18:6, 18:30 (2), 25:17, 29:2, 29:34, 30:36, 32:16, 38:24, 40:10, 40:12 (2), 40:13, 40:16, 40:18 (2), 40:19, 41:46, 42:17, 45:22, 46:15 (2), 47:9

**Three days ago (2):** 31:2, 31:5

**Throw (2):** 31:51, 46:28

**Throw out (4):** 21:15, 37:20, 37:22, 37:24

**Throw the hand (2):** 29:35, 49:8

**Thrust (2):** 31:25 (2)

**Thus far (8):** 15:16 (2), 21:23, 21:29, 44:28, 45:5, 45:8, 45:13

**Tie (4):** 30:41, 30:42, 38:28, 44:30

**Tie up (9):** 39:20 (2), 40:3, 40:5, 42:16, 42:19, 42:24, 46:29, 49:11

**Time (2):** 31:7, 31:41

**Time of weeping (1):** 50:4

**Tired (2):** 25:29, 25:30

**Title (112):** 2:11, 2:13, 2:14, 2:19, 2:20, 3:20, 4:17 (2), 4:19 (2), 4:21, 4:25, 4:26 (2), 5:2, 5:3, 5:29, 6:4, 10:25 (2), 11:4, 11:9, 11:29 (2), 12:2, 12:8, 13:4, 16:1, 16:11, 16:13, 16:15, 17:5 (2), 17:15 (2), 17:19, 19:22, 19:37, 19:38, 21:3, 21:33, 22:14, 22:24, 24:29, 25:1, 25:13 (2), 25:16, 25:25, 25:26, 25:30, 26:18 (2), 26:21, 26:22, 26:25, 26:33, 27:36, 28:19 (2), 29:16 (2), 29:32, 29:33, 29:34, 29:35, 30:6, 30:8, 30:11, 30:13, 30:18, 30:20, 30:21, 30:24, 31:48, 32:3, 32:28, 32:29, 32:30 (2), 32:31, 33:17, 35:8, 35:10 (4), 35:15, 35:18, 36:10, 36:32, 36:35, 36:39 (2), 36:40 (2), 38:1, 38:2, 38:3, 38:4, 38:5, 38:6, 38:29, 38:30, 41:45, 41:51, 41:52, 46:8, 48:6, 48:16 (2), 50:11

**To (476):** 1:9, 2:19, 2:22, 3:1, 3:2, 3:4, 3:9, 3:14, 3:16 (2), 3:19 (2), 4:4 (2), 4:5 (2), 4:6, 4:7, 4:8 (2), 4:9, 4:10, 4:13, 6:4, 6:6, 6:16, 6:18, 6:19, 6:20, 6:21, 7:1, 7:7, 7:9 (2), 7:13, 7:15 (2), 8:9 (4), 8:11,

8:12, 8:15, 8:21, 9:8 (2), 9:17, 11:3, 12:1 (2), 12:4, 12:7 (2), 12:11, 12:15, 13:4, 13:8, 13:14, 14:3, 14:7, 14:17, 14:18, 14:21, 14:22 (2), 15:1, 15:4, 15:7, 15:9, 15:15, 16:2 (2), 16:4, 16:5, 16:6, 16:9, 16:11, 16:13, 17:1 (2), 17:9, 17:15, 17:18, 18:1, 18:6, 18:7 (2), 18:9, 18:10, 18:13, 18:14, 18:21, 18:27, 18:29, 18:31, 18:33, 19:2, 19:3 (2), 19:5 (3), 19:6, 19:8, 19:10, 19:12, 19:14, 19:18, 19:21, 19:27, 19:31, 19:34, 20:2, 20:3, 20:4, 20:6 (2), 20:10, 20:13, 20:17, 21:12 (2), 21:14, 21:17, 21:22, 21:29, 21:32, 22:1, 22:2 (2), 22:3, 22:5 (2), 22:7, 22:9, 22:11, 22:12, 22:15, 22:19 (2), 23:3, 23:13, 23:14, 23:16, 23:19, 24:2, 24:4 (2), 24:5 (3), 24:6, 24:10 (2), 24:11, 24:14, 24:20 (2), 24:24, 24:25, 24:29 (2), 24:30 (2), 24:38 (2), 24:39, 24:40, 24:41, 24:42, 24:43, 24:44, 24:45 (2), 24:50, 24:56, 24:58, 24:65, 25:6, 25:8, 25:9 (2), 25:17, 25:30, 26:1, 26:2 (2), 26:9, 26:16, 26:24, 26:26, 26:27 (2), 27:1 (2), 27:5, 27:6 (2), 27:9, 27:11, 27:18, 27:19 (2), 27:20, 27:21, 27:22, 27:26, 27:38, 27:39, 27:42, 27:43, 27:46, 28:1, 28:5, 28:7 (2), 28:9, 28:15, 28:21, 29:13, 29:21 (2), 29:23 (2), 29:25, 29:30, 29:34, 30:1, 30:3, 30:4, 30:14 (2), 30:16, 30:17, 30:22, 30:25 (2), 30:27, 30:29, 30:39, 30:40, 31:3 (2), 31:4, 31:5, 31:11, 31:13, 31:16, 31:18, 31:24 (2), 31:29, 31:35, 31:39, 31:43, 31:52 (2), 32:4, 32:7 (3), 32:9, 32:10, 32:17, 32:20, 32:28, 32:31, 33:13, 33:14, 34:4, 34:6, 34:11 (3), 34:12, 34:14, 34:17, 34:20 (2), 34:24 (2), 34:30 (2), 35:1 (2), 35:2 (2), 35:4, 35:7, 35:9, 35:27, 35:29, 36:6, 37:2, 37:6, 37:10 (2), 37:13 (2), 37:18, 37:19, 37:22 (3), 37:23, 37:26, 37:29, 37:30, 37:32, 37:35, 37:36, 38:2, 38:8, 38:9, 38:16 (4), 38:18, 38:22, 38:25, 39:7, 39:8, 39:10 (2), 39:14, 39:16, 39:17 (2), 39:19, 39:20, 39:21, 40:3, 40:6, 40:8 (2), 40:11, 40:14, 40:16, 41:14, 41:15, 41:17, 41:21 (2), 41:24, 41:25, 41:28, 41:32, 41:38, 41:39, 41:41, 41:44, 41:55 (2), 41:57, 42:7 (2), 42:9, 42:10, 42:12, 42:14 (2), 42:17, 42:18, 42:20, 42:21 (3), 42:22, 42:24 (2), 42:25, 42:28 (2), 42:29, 42:31, 42:33, 42:34, 42:36, 42:37 (3), 43:2, 43:3, 43:5, 43:8, 43:9, 43:11, 43:13, 43:19 (2), 43:21, 43:23 (2), 43:29, 43:30, 43:33, 44:4, 44:6, 44:7, 44:8, 44:17, 44:18, 44:20, 44:21 (2),

44:22, 44:23, 44:24, 44:27, 44:30, 44:32, 44:34, 45:1, 45:3, 45:4 (2), 45:9 (3), 45:10, 45:12, 45:17 (2), 45:18, 45:24, 45:25, 45:27 (2), 46:28, 46:29, 46:30, 46:31 (4), 47:3 (2), 47:4, 47:5 (2), 47:8, 47:9, 47:15, 47:17, 47:18 (2), 47:23, 48:2, 48:3 (2), 48:4, 48:5, 48:9 (2), 48:10, 48:11, 48:13, 48:18, 48:21 (2), 49:1, 49:2, 49:29 (4), 49:33 (2), 50:4, 50:16, 50:17, 50:19, 50:24 (2)

**Together (6):** 13:6 (2), 22:6, 22:8, 22:19, 36:7

**Toil (1):** 31:42

**Token (3):** 38:17, 38:18, 38:20

**Tomorrow (1):** 19:34

**Tongue (3):** 10:5, 10:20, 10:31

**Tooth (1):** 49:12

**Top of the head (1):** 49:26

**Torch (1):** 15:17

**Torn (1):** 31:39

**Toss (1):** 31:40

**Touch (8):** 3:3, 12:17, 20:6, 26:11, 26:29, 28:12, 32:26, 32:33

**Tower (2):** 11:4, 11:5

**Trade (5):** 23:16, 34:10, 34:21, 37:28, 42:34

**Trance (2):** 2:21, 15:12

**Tranquility (1):** 49:10

**Tread (10):** 1:21, 1:26, 1:28, 1:30, 7:8, 7:14, 7:21, 8:17, 8:19, 9:2

**Tread about (7):** 42:9, 42:11, 42:14, 42:16, 42:30, 42:31, 42:34

**Tread upon (1):** 49:11

**Treader (10):** 1:24, 1:25, 1:26, 6:7, 6:20, 7:14, 7:23, 8:17, 8:19, 9:3

**Treasure (1):** 43:23

**Tree (30):** 1:11, 1:12, 1:29 (2), 2:9 (3), 2:16, 2:17, 3:1, 3:2, 3:3, 3:6 (2), 3:8, 3:11, 3:12, 3:17, 3:22, 3:24, 6:14, 18:4, 18:8, 22:3, 22:6, 22:7, 22:9 (2), 23:17, 40:19

**Tremble (2):** 27:33, 42:28

**Trembling (1):** 27:33

**Trembling in fear (1):** 9:2

**Tribe (1):** 25:16

**Trouble (3):** 35:3, 42:21 (2)

**Trough (2):** 30:38, 30:41

**Truth (6):** 24:27, 24:48, 24:49, 32:11, 42:16, 47:29

**Tunic (9):** 3:21, 37:3, 37:23 (2), 37:31 (2), 37:32 (2), 37:33

**Turn (4):** 18:22, 24:31, 24:49, 24:63

**Turn aside (11):** 8:13, 19:2, 19:3, 30:32, 30:35, 35:2, 38:14, 38:19, 41:42, 48:17, 49:10

**Turn away (1):** 32:29

**Turn back (69):** 3:19 (2), 8:3 (2), 8:7, 8:9, 8:12, 14:7, 14:16 (2), 14:17, 15:16, 16:9, 18:10 (2), 18:14, 18:33, 20:7 (2),

20:14, 21:32, 22:5, 22:19, 24:5 (2), 24:6, 24:8, 26:18, 27:44, 27:45, 28:15, 28:21, 29:3, 30:31, 31:3, 31:13, 32:1, 32:7, 32:10, 33:16, 34:10, 37:14, 37:22, 37:29, 37:30, 38:22, 38:29, 40:13, 40:21, 41:13, 42:24, 42:25, 42:28, 42:37, 43:2, 43:10, 43:12 (2), 43:13, 43:18, 43:21, 44:8, 44:13, 44:25, 48:21, 50:5, 50:14, 50:15 (2)

**Turn over (2):** 30:42 (2)

**Turtledove (1):** 15:9

**Twilight (1):** 15:17

**Twin (2):** 25:24, 38:27

**Twist (2):** 8:10, 8:12

**Two (63):** 1:16, 2:25, 3:7, 4:19, 5:8, 5:18, 5:20, 5:26, 5:28, 6:19, 6:20, 7:2, 7:9 (2), 7:15 (2), 9:22, 9:23, 10:25, 11:20, 14:4, 17:20, 19:1, 19:8, 19:15, 19:16, 19:30 (2), 19:36, 21:27, 21:31, 22:3, 22:6, 22:8, 24:22, 25:16, 25:23 (2), 27:9, 27:45, 29:16, 31:33, 31:37, 31:41, 32:8, 32:11, 32:23 (2), 33:1, 34:25, 35:22, 40:2, 40:5, 41:50, 42:13, 42:32, 42:37, 44:27, 46:27, 48:1, 48:5, 48:13, 49:28

**Unaware (1):** 31:20

**Uncircumcised (1):** 17:14

**Uncover (1):** 24:20

**Under (32):** 1:7, 1:9, 2:21, 4:25, 6:16, 6:17, 7:19, 16:9, 18:4, 18:8, 21:15, 22:13, 24:2, 24:9, 30:2, 30:15, 35:4, 35:8 (2), 36:33, 36:34, 36:35, 36:36, 36:37, 36:38, 36:39, 41:35, 44:4, 44:33, 47:29, 49:25, 50:19

**Understand (2):** 41:33, 41:39

**Underworld (4):** 37:35, 42:38, 44:29, 44:31

**Unfilled (1):** 1:2

**Unit (47):** 1:5, 1:9, 2:11, 2:21, 2:24, 3:22, 4:19, 8:5, 8:13 (2), 10:25, 11:1 (2), 11:6 (2), 19:9, 21:15, 22:2, 26:10, 27:38, 27:44, 27:45, 29:20, 32:9, 32:23, 33:13, 34:16, 34:22, 37:9, 37:20, 40:5, 41:5, 41:11, 41:22, 41:25, 41:26, 42:11, 42:13 (2), 42:16, 42:19, 42:27, 42:32, 42:33, 44:28, 48:22, 49:16

**Unite (1):** 49:6

**Unleavened bread (1):** 19:3

**Unless (2):** 31:42, 43:10

**Until (65):** 3:19, 6:7 (3), 7:23 (3), 8:5, 8:7, 10:19 (2), 11:31, 12:6 (2), 13:3 (2), 13:12, 13:15, 14:6, 14:14, 14:15, 14:23, 15:16, 15:18, 19:4, 19:11, 19:22, 19:37, 19:38, 22:5, 24:19, 24:33, 25:18, 26:13, 26:33, 27:33, 27:34, 27:44, 27:45, 28:15, 29:8, 31:24, 31:29, 32:5, 32:25, 32:33, 33:3 (2), 33:14, 34:5, 38:1, 38:11, 38:17, 39:16, 41:49, 43:25,

44:28, 46:34, 47:21, 47:26, 48:5, 49:10, 49:26, 49:27, 50:10

**Uphold (1):** 48:17

**Upon (307):** 1:2 (2), 1:7, 1:11, 1:15, 1:17, 1:20 (2), 1:26, 1:28, 1:29, 1:30, 2:5, 2:16, 2:21, 2:24, 3:14, 4:14, 6:1, 6:7, 6:12, 6:17, 7:3, 7:4 (2), 7:6, 7:8, 7:10, 7:12, 7:14, 7:17 (2), 7:18 (2), 7:19, 7:21 (2), 7:23, 7:24, 8:1, 8:3, 8:4, 8:7, 8:8, 8:9, 8:11, 8:13, 8:17 (2), 8:19, 9:2 (2), 9:14, 9:16, 9:17, 9:23, 10:9, 11:4, 11:8, 11:9 (2), 11:28, 12:17, 12:20, 13:9, 13:11, 14:6, 14:15, 15:11, 15:12 (2), 16:5, 16:7 (2), 16:12, 16:14, 17:3, 17:17, 17:22, 18:2, 18:3, 18:5 (2), 18:8, 18:16, 18:19 (2), 19:4, 19:8, 19:16, 19:17, 19:22, 19:23, 19:24 (2), 19:28 (2), 19:31, 20:3, 20:6, 20:9 (2), 20:11, 20:18, 21:11, 21:12 (2), 21:14, 21:25, 21:31, 22:2, 22:6, 22:9, 22:17, 23:3, 23:19, 24:9, 24:13, 24:15, 24:18, 24:22, 24:30 (3), 24:42, 24:43, 24:45, 24:46, 24:47 (2), 24:49 (2), 24:61, 24:64, 25:6, 25:9, 25:18 (2), 25:30, 26:7, 26:9, 26:10, 26:21, 26:22, 26:32, 26:33, 27:12, 27:13, 27:16 (2), 27:39, 27:40 (2), 27:41, 28:6, 28:9, 28:13 (2), 28:18, 29:2 (2), 29:3 (2), 29:8, 29:10, 29:34, 29:35, 30:3, 30:6, 30:28, 30:33, 30:37, 30:40, 31:10, 31:12, 31:17, 31:20, 31:34, 31:46, 31:48, 31:50, 32:12, 32:22, 32:32, 32:33 (2), 33:1 (3), 33:4, 33:10, 33:13, 33:17, 34:3, 34:12, 34:25, 34:27, 34:30, 35:5, 35:13, 35:14 (2), 35:20, 37:8 (3), 37:23, 37:34, 38:12, 38:14 (2), 38:19, 38:21, 38:26, 38:28, 38:29, 38:30, 39:4, 39:5, 40:2 (3), 40:11, 40:13, 40:16, 40:17, 40:19 (3), 40:21 (2), 41:1, 41:3, 41:10, 41:13, 41:15, 41:17, 41:32, 41:33, 41:34, 41:40 (2), 41:41, 41:42 (3), 41:43, 41:45, 41:56, 42:6, 42:21 (2), 42:24, 42:26, 42:36, 42:37, 43:7, 43:16, 43:18 (3), 43:19, 44:1, 44:4, 44:13, 44:21, 45:1 (2), 45:14 (2), 45:15, 45:20, 45:21, 46:4, 46:29 (2), 47:6, 47:20, 47:22, 47:26, 47:31, 48:2, 48:6, 48:7, 48:14 (2), 48:15, 48:17 (3), 48:18, 48:22, 49:13, 49:17 (2), 49:22 (2), 49:25, 49:26, 49:30, 50:1 (2), 50:11, 50:13, 50:20, 50:21, 50:23

**Upper (5):** 14:18, 14:19, 14:20, 14:22, 40:17

**Uprising (5):** 43:34 (5)

**Upward (3):** 6:16, 7:20, 22:9

**Utterance (1):** 22:16

**Valiant (1):** 49:24

**Valley (6):** 14:3, 14:8, 14:10, 14:17 (2), 37:14

**Veil (3):** 24:65, 38:14, 38:19

**Vessel (26):** 6:14 (2), 6:15, 6:16 (2), 6:18, 6:19, 7:1, 7:7, 7:9, 7:13, 7:15, 7:17, 7:18, 7:23, 8:1, 8:4, 8:6, 8:9 (2), 8:10, 8:13, 8:16, 8:19, 9:10, 9:18

**Vigor (1):** 49:3

**Village (1):** 25:16

**Vineyard (1):** 9:20

**Violence (4):** 6:11, 6:13, 16:5, 49:5

**Virgin (1):** 24:16

**Vision (1):** 15:1

**Visit (9):** 21:1, 39:4, 39:5, 40:4, 41:34, 50:24 (2), 50:25 (2)

**Visualize (14):** 28:12, 37:5, 37:6, 37:9 (2), 37:10, 40:5, 40:8, 41:1, 41:5, 41:11 (2), 41:15, 42:9

**Voice (25):** 3:8, 3:10, 3:17, 4:10, 4:23, 16:2, 21:12, 21:16, 21:17 (2), 22:18, 26:5, 27:8, 27:13, 27:22 (2), 27:38, 27:43, 29:11, 30:6, 39:14, 39:15, 39:18, 45:2, 45:16

**Vow (2):** 28:20, 31:13

**Wadi (3):** 26:17, 26:19, 32:24

**Wage (7):** 15:1, 30:18, 30:28, 30:32, 30:33, 31:8 (2)

**Waist (1):** 37:34

**Walk (121):** 2:14, 3:8, 3:14, 5:22, 5:24, 6:9, 7:18, 8:3, 8:5, 9:23, 11:31, 12:1, 12:4 (2), 12:5, 12:9, 12:19, 13:3, 13:5, 13:17, 14:11, 14:12, 14:24, 15:2, 16:8, 17:1, 18:16, 18:22, 18:33, 19:2, 19:32, 21:14, 21:16, 21:19, 22:2, 22:3, 22:5, 22:6, 22:8, 22:13, 22:19, 24:4, 24:5, 24:8, 24:10 (2), 24:38, 24:39, 24:40, 24:42, 24:51, 24:55, 24:56, 24:58 (2), 24:61 (2), 24:65, 25:22, 25:32, 25:34, 26:1, 26:13 (2), 26:16, 26:17, 26:26, 26:31, 27:5, 27:9, 27:13, 27:14, 28:2, 28:5, 28:7, 28:9, 28:10, 28:15, 28:20, 29:1, 29:7, 30:14, 30:25, 30:26, 31:19, 31:30 (2), 31:44, 32:1, 32:2, 32:7, 32:18, 32:20, 32:21, 33:12 (2), 34:17, 35:3, 35:22, 36:6, 37:12, 37:13, 37:14, 37:17 (2), 37:20, 37:25, 37:27, 38:11, 38:19, 41:55, 42:19, 42:26, 42:33, 42:38, 43:8, 45:17, 45:24, 45:28, 48:15, 50:18

**Wander (3):** 20:13, 21:14, 37:15

**Wash (5):** 18:4, 19:2, 24:32, 43:24, 43:31

**Wasteland (1):** 7:22

**Watch (1):** 9:14

**Water (55):** 1:2, 1:6 (3), 1:7 (2), 1:9, 1:10, 1:20, 1:21, 1:22, 6:17, 7:6, 7:7, 7:10, 7:17, 7:18 (2), 7:19, 7:20, 7:24, 8:1, 8:3 (2), 8:5, 8:7, 8:8, 8:9, 8:11, 8:13, 9:11, 9:15, 16:7, 18:4, 21:14, 21:15, 21:19

(2), 21:25, 24:11, 24:13 (2), 24:17, 24:32, 24:43 (2), 26:18, 26:19, 26:20, 26:32, 30:38, 37:24, 43:24, 49:4, 49:13

**Watering trough (2):** 24:20, 30:38

**We (18):** 13:8, 19:13, 29:4, 37:7, 42:11 (2), 42:13, 42:21, 42:31, 42:32, 43:8, 43:18, 44:9, 44:16, 46:34, 47:3, 47:19 (2)

**Weak (1):** 41:19

**Wear Out (1):** 18:12

**Weary (1):** 19:11

**Week (2):** 29:27, 29:28

**Weep (16):** 21:16, 23:2, 27:38, 29:11, 33:4, 37:35, 42:24, 43:30 (2), 45:14 (2), 45:15, 46:29, 50:1, 50:3, 50:17

**Weeping (1):** 45:2

**Weigh (1):** 23:16

**Weight (3):** 24:22 (2), 43:21

**Well (23):** 14:10 (2), 16:14, 21:19, 21:25, 21:30, 24:11, 24:20, 26:15, 26:18, 26:19, 26:20, 26:21, 26:22, 26:25, 26:32, 29:2 (3), 29:3 (2), 29:8, 29:10

**What (63):** 2:19, 3:13, 4:6 (2), 4:10, 12:18 (2), 12:19, 15:2, 15:8, 18:13, 20:9 (2), 20:10, 21:17, 21:29, 23:15, 24:31, 25:22, 25:32, 26:10, 27:20, 27:37, 27:45, 27:46, 28:17, 29:15, 29:25 (2), 30:31, 31:26, 31:27, 31:30, 31:32, 31:36 (2), 31:37, 31:43, 32:28, 32:30, 33:15, 37:10, 37:15, 37:20, 37:26, 38:16, 38:18, 38:29, 39:8, 42:1, 42:28, 43:6, 44:4, 44:7, 44:15, 44:16 (3), 46:33, 47:3, 47:8, 47:15, 47:19

**Wheat (1):** 30:14

**Whelp (1):** 49:9

**Where (12):** 3:9, 4:9, 16:8, 18:9, 19:5, 22:7, 26:9, 37:16, 38:21, 39:9, 44:8, 44:34

**Wherever (3):** 16:8, 32:18, 37:30

**Which (411):** 1:7 (2), 1:11, 1:12, 1:21, 1:29 (2), 1:30, 1:31, 2:2 (2), 2:3, 2:8, 2:11, 2:19, 2:22, 3:1, 3:3, 3:11, 3:12, 3:17, 3:23, 4:11, 5:5, 5:29, 6:2, 6:4 (2), 6:7, 6:15, 6:17 (2), 6:21, 6:22, 7:2, 7:4, 7:5, 7:8 (2), 7:9, 7:15, 7:16, 7:19, 7:22 (2), 7:23 (2), 8:1, 8:6, 8:17, 8:21, 9:2, 9:3, 9:10, 9:12 (2), 9:15, 9:16, 9:17 (2), 9:24, 10:14, 11:5, 11:6, 11:7, 12:1, 12:4, 12:5 (2), 12:11, 12:20, 13:1, 13:3, 13:4, 13:14, 13:15, 13:16, 13:18, 14:5, 14:6, 14:15, 14:17, 14:20, 14:23, 14:24 (2), 15:4, 15:7, 15:14, 15:17, 16:15, 17:10, 17:12, 17:14, 17:21, 17:23, 18:5, 18:8, 18:17, 18:19 (2), 18:24, 18:33, 19:5, 19:8, 19:11, 19:12, 19:19, 19:21, 19:27, 19:29, 20:3, 20:7, 20:9, 20:13 (3), 20:16, 21:1 (2), 21:2, 21:3, 21:4, 21:9, 21:12, 21:17, 21:22, 21:23 (2), 21:25, 21:29, 22:2 (2), 22:3, 22:9, 22:14,

22:16, 22:17, 22:18, 23:9 (2), 23:11, 23:16, 23:17 (5), 23:20, 24:2, 24:3 (2), 24:5, 24:7 (3), 24:14, 24:15, 24:22, 24:24, 24:27, 24:32, 24:36, 24:37, 24:40, 24:42, 24:44, 24:47, 24:48, 24:51, 24:52, 24:54, 24:66, 25:5, 25:6, 25:7, 25:9, 25:10, 25:12, 25:18, 26:1, 26:2, 26:3, 26:5, 26:15, 26:18 (2), 26:29 (2), 26:32, 27:4, 27:8, 27:9, 27:10, 27:14, 27:15, 27:17, 27:19, 27:27, 27:30, 27:40, 27:41, 27:44, 27:45, 28:4, 28:13, 28:15 (3), 28:18, 28:20, 28:22 (2), 29:8, 29:9, 29:10, 29:27, 30:2, 30:18, 30:25, 30:26 (2), 30:29 (2), 30:30, 30:33, 30:35, 30:37, 30:38 (2), 31:1 (2), 31:12, 31:13 (2), 31:16 (2), 31:18 (2), 31:19, 31:21, 31:32, 31:43 (2), 31:49, 31:51, 32:3, 32:8, 32:11, 32:13, 32:24, 32:32, 32:33, 33:5, 33:8, 33:9, 33:11, 33:14 (2), 33:15, 33:18, 33:19, 34:1, 34:11, 34:12, 34:13, 34:14, 34:22, 34:27, 34:28 (2), 34:29, 35:2 (2), 35:3, 35:4 (3), 35:5, 35:6 (2), 35:12, 35:13, 35:14, 35:15, 35:26, 35:27, 36:5, 36:6, 36:24, 36:31, 37:6, 37:10, 37:22, 37:23 (2), 38:10, 38:14, 38:18 (2), 38:25, 38:30, 39:1, 39:3, 39:5 (2), 39:6 (2), 39:8, 39:9, 39:17, 39:19, 39:20, 39:22 (2), 39:23 (2), 40:3, 40:5 (2), 40:7, 40:13, 40:14, 40:22, 41:13, 41:21, 41:25, 41:28 (2), 41:36, 41:38, 41:43, 41:48 (2), 41:50, 41:53, 41:54, 41:55, 41:56, 42:9, 42:14, 42:21, 42:38, 43:2 (2), 43:14, 43:16, 43:17, 43:19, 43:26, 43:27, 43:29, 44:1 (2), 44:2, 44:4, 44:5 (2), 44:8, 44:9, 44:10, 44:15 (2), 44:16, 44:17, 44:34, 45:4, 45:6, 45:10, 45:11, 45:13, 45:27 (2), 46:1, 46:5, 46:6, 46:15, 46:18, 46:20, 46:22, 46:25, 46:27, 46:31, 46:32, 47:1, 47:4, 47:6, 47:11, 47:14, 47:22, 47:24, 48:6, 48:9, 48:15, 48:22, 49:1, 49:28 (2), 49:29, 49:30 (3), 49:32, 50:5, 50:6, 50:10, 50:11, 50:12, 50:13, 50:15, 50:24

**White (4):** 30:35, 30:37 (2), 49:12

**White bread (1):** 40:16

**Who (18):** 3:11, 19:12, 21:7, 21:26, 24:23, 24:47, 24:65, 27:18, 27:32, 27:33, 32:18 (2), 33:5, 33:8, 38:25, 43:22, 48:8, 49:9

**Whole (1):** 17:1

**Why (2):** 26:27, 40:7

**Wide (1):** 34:21

**Widen (1):** 26:22

**Widow (1):** 38:11

**Widowhood (2):** 38:14, 38:19

**Width (2):** 6:15, 13:17

**Wild ass (1):** 16:12

**Wilderness (7):** 14:6, 16:7, 21:14, 21:20, 21:21, 36:24, 37:22

**Will (1):** 49:6

**Wind (12):** 1:2, 3:8, 6:3, 6:17, 7:15, 7:22, 8:1, 26:35, 32:17, 41:8, 41:38, 45:27

**Window (2):** 8:6, 26:8

**Wine (10):** 9:21, 9:24, 14:18, 19:32, 19:33, 19:34, 19:35, 27:25, 49:11, 49:12

**Wing (2):** 1:21, 7:14

**Winter (1):** 8:22

**Wipe away (4):** 6:7, 7:4, 7:23 (2)

**Wise (3):** 41:8, 41:33, 41:39

**With (83):** 3:6, 13:1, 13:14, 18:16, 18:23, 18:25, 19:30, 19:32, 19:34, 19:35, 21:10 (2), 21:22, 21:23 (2), 22:5, 23:4 (2), 24:12, 24:14, 24:25, 24:27, 24:54, 24:58, 25:11, 26:3, 26:16, 26:20 (2), 26:28 (2), 26:29 (2), 27:44, 28:15, 29:6, 29:9 (2), 29:14, 29:25, 29:30, 30:8, 30:15, 30:16, 31:2, 31:3, 31:23, 31:24, 31:29 (2), 31:31, 31:32, 31:38, 31:50, 32:5, 32:7, 32:10, 32:13, 32:25, 32:26, 32:29 (2), 33:1, 33:15, 35:2, 35:4, 35:6, 39:7, 39:10, 39:12, 39:14, 41:32, 42:38, 43:34, 44:29, 44:32, 44:33, 46:4, 47:30, 48:1, 48:12, 48:21, 50:9

**Withdraw (3):** 3:8, 3:10, 31:27

**Wither (1):** 41:23

**Withhold (1):** 30:2

**Within (8):** 18:12, 18:24, 24:3, 25:22, 41:21 (2), 45:6, 48:16

**Without (39):** 2:5, 5:24, 7:8, 11:30, 19:31, 20:7, 20:11, 28:17, 29:4, 30:1, 30:33, 31:2, 31:5, 31:50, 37:24, 37:29, 37:30, 39:9, 39:11, 39:23, 40:8, 41:8, 41:15, 41:24, 41:39, 41:49, 42:7, 42:13, 42:32, 42:36 (2), 43:5, 44:26, 44:30, 44:31, 44:34, 45:6, 47:4, 47:13

**Witness (5):** 31:44, 31:48, 31:50, 31:52 (2)

**Wolf (1):** 49:27

**Woman (152):** 2:22, 2:23, 2:24, 2:25, 3:1, 3:2, 3:4, 3:6, 3:8, 3:12, 3:13 (2), 3:15, 3:16, 3:17, 3:20, 3:21, 4:1, 4:17, 4:19, 4:23 (2), 4:25, 6:2, 6:18 (2), 7:2 (2), 7:7 (2), 7:13 (2), 8:16 (2), 8:18 (2), 11:29 (3), 11:31, 12:5, 12:11 (2), 12:12, 12:14, 12:15, 12:17, 12:18, 12:19 (2), 12:20, 13:1, 14:16, 16:1, 16:3 (2), 17:15, 17:19, 18:9, 18:10, 18:11, 19:15, 19:16, 19:26, 20:2, 20:3, 20:7, 20:11, 20:12, 20:14, 20:17, 20:18, 21:21, 23:19, 24:3, 24:4, 24:5, 24:7, 24:8, 24:15, 24:36, 24:37, 24:38, 24:39, 24:40, 24:44, 24:51, 24:67, 25:1, 25:10, 25:20, 25:21 (2), 26:7 (2), 26:8, 26:9, 26:10, 26:11, 26:34, 27:46, 28:1, 28:2, 28:6 (2), 28:9 (2), 29:21, 29:28, 30:4,

30:9, 30:26, 31:17, 31:35, 31:50, 32:23, 33:5, 34:4, 34:8, 34:12, 34:21, 34:29, 36:2, 36:6, 36:10 (2), 36:12, 36:13, 36:14, 36:17, 36:18 (2), 36:39, 37:2, 38:6, 38:8, 38:9, 38:12, 38:14, 38:20, 39:7, 39:8, 39:9, 39:19, 41:45, 44:27, 45:19, 46:5, 46:19, 46:26, 49:31 (2)

**Womb (4):** 25:23, 25:24, 30:2, 38:27

**Word (61):** 11:1, 12:17, 15:1 (2), 15:4, 18:14, 18:25, 19:8, 19:21, 19:22, 20:8, 20:10, 20:11, 20:18, 21:11, 21:26, 22:1, 22:16, 22:20, 24:9, 24:28, 24:30, 24:33, 24:50, 24:52, 24:66, 27:34, 27:42, 29:13, 30:31, 30:34, 31:1, 32:20, 34:14, 34:18, 34:19, 37:8, 37:11, 37:14, 39:7, 39:17, 39:19 (2), 40:1, 41:28, 41:32, 41:37, 42:16, 42:20, 43:7, 43:18, 44:2, 44:6, 44:7 (2), 44:10, 44:18, 44:24, 45:27, 47:30, 48:1

**Work (6):** 5:29, 20:9, 40:17, 44:15, 46:33, 47:3

**Would that (4):** 17:18, 23:13, 30:34, 50:15

**Wrap (1):** 38:14

**Wrap around (2):** 43:3 (2)

**Wrath (1):** 49:7

**Wrestle (1):** 30:8

**Wrist (3):** 37:3, 37:23, 37:32

**Yard (1):** 25:16

**Year (1):** 1:14

**Year (160):** 5:3, 5:4, 5:5 (2), 5:6 (2), 5:7 (2), 5:8 (2), 5:9, 5:10 (2), 5:11 (2), 5:12, 5:13 (2), 5:14 (2), 5:15 (2), 5:16 (2), 5:17 (2), 5:18 (2), 5:19, 5:20 (2), 5:21, 5:22, 5:23 (2), 5:25 (2), 5:26 (2), 5:27 (2), 5:28 (2), 5:30 (2), 5:31 (2), 5:32, 6:3, 7:6, 7:11 (2), 8:13, 9:28 (2), 9:29 (2), 11:10 (2), 11:11, 11:12, 11:13 (2), 11:14, 11:15 (2), 11:16, 11:17 (2), 11:18, 11:19 (2), 11:20, 11:21 (2), 11:22, 11:23, 11:24, 11:25 (2), 11:26, 11:32 (2), 12:4 (2), 14:4 (2), 14:5, 15:13, 16:3, 16:16 (2), 17:1 (2), 17:17 (2), 17:21, 17:24, 17:25, 21:5, 23:1 (4), 25:7 (4), 25:17 (4), 25:20, 25:26, 26:12, 26:34, 29:18, 29:20, 29:27, 29:30, 31:38, 31:41 (3), 35:28 (2), 37:2, 41:1, 41:26 (2), 41:27 (2), 41:29, 41:30, 41:34, 41:35, 41:36, 41:46, 41:47, 41:48, 41:50, 41:53, 41:54, 45:6 (2), 45:11, 47:8, 47:9 (4), 47:17, 47:18 (2), 47:28 (4), 50:22, 50:26

**Yearning (2):** 3:6, 49:26

**Yesterday (2):** 31:2, 31:5

**Yet again (55):** 4:25, 7:4, 8:10, 8:12 (2), 8:21 (2), 8:22, 9:11 (2), 9:15, 17:5, 18:22, 18:29, 19:12, 24:20, 25:6, 29:7, 29:9, 29:27, 29:30, 29:33, 29:34, 29:35, 30:7,

30:19, 31:14, 32:29, 35:9, 35:10, 35:16, 35:20, 37:5, 37:8, 37:9 (2), 38:4, 38:5, 38:26, 40:13, 40:19, 43:6, 43:7, 43:27, 43:28, 44:14, 45:3, 45:6, 45:11, 45:26, 45:28, 46:29, 46:30, 48:7, 48:15

**Yield (4):** 21:8 (2), 50:15, 50:17

**Yoke (1):** 27:40

**You(fs) (7):** 12:11, 12:13, 24:23, 24:47, 24:60, 31:6, 39:9

**You(mp) (15):** 29:4, 42:9, 42:14, 42:16 (2), 42:19 (2), 42:33, 42:34 (2), 44:10, 44:17, 44:27, 45:8, 50:20

**You(ms) (48):** 3:11, 3:14, 3:15, 3:19, 4:7, 4:11, 6:18, 6:21, 7:1, 8:16, 9:7, 13:14, 13:15, 15:15, 16:13, 17:9 (2), 20:7, 21:22, 21:26, 22:12, 23:6, 23:13, 24:44, 26:27, 26:29, 27:18, 27:21, 27:24, 27:32, 28:13, 29:14, 29:15, 30:26, 30:29, 31:43, 31:44, 31:52, 32:13, 32:18, 38:23, 41:40, 43:8, 45:10, 45:11, 45:19, 49:3, 49:8

**Young age (2):** 8:21, 46:34

**Young maiden (1):** 24:43

**Young man (27):** 14:24, 18:7, 19:4, 21:12, 21:17 (2), 21:18, 21:19, 21:20, 22:3, 22:5 (2), 22:12, 22:19, 25:27, 34:19, 37:2, 41:12, 43:8, 44:22, 44:30, 44:31, 44:32, 44:33 (2), 44:34, 48:16

**Young pigeon (1):** 15:9

**Young woman (9):** 24:14, 24:16, 24:28, 24:55, 24:57, 24:61, 34:3 (2), 34:12

**Youthfulness (1):** 43:33

# Prefixes, Suffixes and Conjugations

!(fp)~ (2)

!(fs)~ (16)

!(mp)~ (102)

!(ms)~ (172)

?~ (46)

~& (14)

~^ (61)

~ed(fp) (5)

~ed(fs) (8)

~ed(mp) (6)

~ed(ms) (23)

~her (270)

~him (1171)

~ing(fp) (20)

~ing(fs) (39)

~ing(mp) (81)

~ing(ms) (205)

~me (660)

~of (95)

~s (1584)

~s2 (203)

~them(f) (26)

~them(m) (335)

~unto (135)

~us (147)

~you(fp) (3)

~you(fs) (73)

~you(mp) (150)

~you(ms) (497)

>~ (494)

and~ (4132)

be~ (206)

did~ (990)

from~ (360)

had~ (91)

he~ (2144)

i~ (380)

in~ (823)

like~ (146)

make be~ (19)

make~ (486)

much be~ (18)

much~ (310)

self~ (63)

she~ (371)

the~ (1774)

they(f)~ (28)

they(m)~ (363)

they~ (162)

to~ (1362)

we~ (122)

which~ (1)

will~ (2801)

you(fp)~ (1)

you(fs)~ (11)

you(mp)~ (89)

you(ms)~(218

# Name

Adah [*Ornament*] (8): 4:19, 4:20, 4:23, 36:2, 36:4, 36:10, 36:12, 36:16

Adbe'el [*Grief of El*] (1): 25:13

Admah [*Red ground*] (3): 10:19, 14:2, 14:8

Adonai [*My lords*] (8): 15:2, 15:8, 18:3, 18:27, 18:30, 18:31, 18:32, 20:4

Adulam [*Witness of the people*] (3): 38:1, 38:12, 38:20

Ahalivamah [*Tent of the high place*] (7): 36:2, 36:5, 36:14, 36:18 (2), 36:25, 36:41

Ahhuzat [*Holdings*] (1): 26:26

Akad [*Jar*] (1): 10:10

Akhbor [*Mouse*] (2): 36:38, 36:39

Almodad [*El of measure*] (1): 10:26

Alon-Bakhut [*Oak of weeping*] (1): 35:8

Alwah [*Wicked*] (1): 36:40

Alwan [*Tall*] (1): 36:23

Amaleq [*People gathered*] (3): 14:7, 36:12, 36:16

Amon [*Tribe*] (1): 19:38

Amraphel [*Speaker of judgement*] (2): 14:1, 14:9

Anah [*Answer*] (9): 36:2, 36:14, 36:18, 36:20, 36:24 (2), 36:25 (2), 36:29

Anam [*Affliction of water*] (1): 10:13

Aner [*Answer*] (2): 14:13, 14:24

Aqan [*Sharp sighted*] (1): 36:27

Aram [*Palace*] (8): 10:22, 10:23, 22:21, 25:20 (2), 28:5, 31:20, 31:24

Aram-Nahhara'im [*Palace of two rivers*] (1): 24:10

Aran [*Joyous*] (1): 36:28

Araq [*Gnawing*] (1): 10:17

Ararat [*Curse*] (1): 8:4

Ared [*I subdue*] (1): 46:21

Areliy [*Order of my El*] (1): 46:16

Arodiy [*My roaming*] (1): 46:16

Arpakhshad [*I will fail the breast*] (6): 10:22, 10:24, 11:10, 11:11, 11:12, 11:13

Arwad [*I will preside over*] (1): 10:18

Aryokh [*Tall*] (2): 14:1, 14:9

Ashbeyl [*Fire flowing*] (1): 46:21

Asher [*Happy*] (4): 30:13, 35:26, 46:17, 49:20

Ashkanaz [*Fire spread*] (1): 10:3

Ashterot-Qaraniym [*Growths of two horns*] (1): 14:5

Ashur [*Step*] (5): 2:14, 10:11, 10:22, 25:3, 25:18

Asnat [*Belonging to Nat*] (3): 41:45, 41:50, 46:20

Aveyl-Mitsrayim [*Mourning of Mitsrayim*] (1): 50:11

Avida [*My father knows*] (1): 25:4

Aviyma'el [*My father is from El*] (1): 10:28

Aviymelekh [*My father is king*] (24): 20:2, 20:3, 20:4, 20:8, 20:9, 20:10, 20:14, 20:15, 20:17, 20:18, 21:22, 21:25 (2), 21:26, 21:27, 21:29, 21:32, 26:1, 26:8, 26:9, 26:10, 26:11, 26:16, 26:26

Avraham [*Father lifted*] (133): 17:5, 17:9, 17:15, 17:17, 17:18, 17:22, 17:23 (2), 17:24, 17:26, 18:6, 18:7, 18:11, 18:13, 18:16, 18:17, 18:18, 18:19, 18:22, 18:23, 18:27, 18:33 (2), 19:27, 19:29, 20:1, 20:2, 20:9, 20:10, 20:11, 20:14, 20:17, 20:18, 21:2, 21:3, 21:4, 21:5, 21:7, 21:8, 21:9, 21:10, 21:11, 21:12, 21:14, 21:22, 21:24, 21:25, 21:27, 21:28, 21:29, 21:34, 22:1 (2), 22:3, 22:4, 22:5, 22:6, 22:7, 22:8, 22:9, 22:10, 22:11 (2), 22:13 (2), 22:14, 22:15, 22:19 (2), 22:20, 22:23, 23:2, 23:3, 23:5, 23:7, 23:10, 23:12, 23:14, 23:16 (2), 23:18, 23:19, 23:20, 24:1 (2), 24:2, 24:6, 24:9, 24:12 (2), 24:15, 24:27, 24:34, 24:42, 24:48, 24:52, 24:59, 25:1, 25:5, 25:6 (2), 25:7, 25:8, 25:10 (2), 25:11, 25:12 (2), 25:19 (2), 26:1, 26:3, 26:5, 26:15, 26:18 (2), 26:24 (2), 28:4 (2), 28:9, 28:13, 31:42, 31:53, 32:10, 35:12, 35:27, 48:15, 48:16, 49:30, 49:31, 50:13, 50:24

Avram [*Father raised*] (59): 11:26, 11:27, 11:29 (2), 11:31 (2), 12:1, 12:4 (2), 12:5, 12:6, 12:7, 12:9, 12:10, 12:14, 12:16, 12:17, 12:18, 13:1, 13:2, 13:4, 13:5, 13:7, 13:8, 13:12, 13:14, 13:18, 14:12, 14:13 (2), 14:14, 14:19, 14:21, 14:22, 14:23, 15:1 (2), 15:2, 15:3, 15:11, 15:12, 15:13, 15:18, 16:1, 16:2 (2), 16:3 (3), 16:5, 16:6, 16:15 (2), 16:16 (2), 17:1 (2), 17:3, 17:5

Awit [*Crooked*] (1): 36:35

Ay [*Heap of ruins*] (2): 12:8, 13:3

Ayah [*Falcon*] (1): 36:24

Ba'al-Hhanan [*Master of beauty*] (2): 36:38, 36:39

Basmat [*Spice*] (6): 26:34, 36:3, 36:4, 36:10, 36:13, 36:17

Batsrah [*Sheepfold*] (1): 36:33

Bavel [*Confusion*] (2): 10:10, 11:9

Bedad [*Solitary*] (1): 36:35

Be'eri [*My well*] (1): 26:34

Be'er-Lahhiy-Ro'iy [*Well for the living seeing me*] (3): 16:14, 24:62, 25:11

Bekher [*Young camel*] (1): 46:21

414

**Bela** [*Swallow*] (5): 14:2, 14:8, 36:32, 36:33, 46:21

**Ben-Amiy** [*Son of my people*] (1): 19:38

**Ben-Oni** [*Son of my sorrow*] (1): 35:18

**Be'or** [*Burning*] (1): 36:32

**Bera** [*With dysfunction*] (1): 14:2

**Bered** [*Hail*] (1): 16:14

**Beri'ah** [*With a companion*] (2): 46:17 (2)

**B'er-Sheva** [*Well of oath*] (11): 21:14, 21:31, 21:32, 21:33, 22:19 (2), 26:23, 26:33, 28:10, 46:1, 46:5

**Betu'el** [*Destruction of El*] (9): 22:22, 22:23, 24:15, 24:24, 24:47, 24:50, 25:20, 28:2, 28:5

**Beyt-El** [*House of El*] (12): 12:8 (2), 13:3 (2), 28:19, 31:13, 35:1, 35:3, 35:6, 35:8, 35:15, 35:16

**Beyt-Lehhem** [*House of bread*] (2): 35:19, 48:7

**Bilhah** [*Wear out*] (9): 29:29, 30:3, 30:4, 30:5, 30:7, 35:22, 35:25, 37:2, 46:25

**Bilhan** [*Worn out*] (1): 36:27

**Binyamin** [*Son of the right hand*] (17): 35:18, 35:24, 42:4, 42:36, 43:14, 43:15, 43:16, 43:29, 43:34, 44:12, 45:12, 45:14 (2), 45:22, 46:19, 46:21, 49:27

**Birsha** [*With wickedness*] (1): 14:2

**Buz** [*Despise*] (1): 22:21

**Dameseq** [*Blood sack*] (2): 14:15, 15:2

**Dan** [*Moderator*] (6): 14:14, 30:6, 35:25, 46:23, 49:16, 49:17

**Dedan** [*Friendship*] (3): 10:7, 25:3 (2)

**Devorah** [*Bee*] (1): 35:8

**Dinah** [*Judgement*] (8): 30:21, 34:1, 34:3, 34:5, 34:13, 34:25, 34:26, 46:15

**Dinhavah** [*Give judgement*] (1): 36:32

**Diqlah** [*Palm grove*] (1): 10:27

**Dishan** [*Thresher*] (4): 36:21, 36:26, 36:28, 36:30

**Dishon** [*Threshing*] (3): 36:21, 36:25, 36:30

**Dodan** [*Passion*] (1): 10:4

**Dotan** [*Well*] (2): 37:17 (2)

**Dumah** [*Silence*] (1): 25:14

**Eden** [*Pleasure*] (6): 2:8, 2:10, 2:15, 3:23, 3:24, 4:16

**Edom** [*Red*] (13): 25:30, 32:4, 36:1, 36:8, 36:9, 36:16, 36:17, 36:19, 36:21, 36:31, 36:32, 36:43 (2)

**Elam** [*Ancient*] (3): 10:22, 14:1, 14:9

**Elasar** [*El is noble*] (2): 14:1, 14:9

**El-Beyt-El** [*El of Beyt El*] (1): 35:7

**Elda'ah** [*El knows*] (1): 25:4

**El-Elohey-Yisra'el** [*El of the powers of Yisra'el*] (1): 33:20

**Eliezer** [*My El is a helper*] (1): 15:2

**Eliphaz** [*My El is pure gold*] (7): 36:4, 36:10, 36:11, 36:12 (2), 36:15, 36:16

**Elishah** [*El of help*] (1): 10:4

**Elohiym** [*Powers*] (187): 1:1, 1:2, 1:3, 1:4 (2), 1:5, 1:6, 1:7, 1:8, 1:9, 1:10 (2), 1:11, 1:12, 1:14, 1:16, 1:17, 1:18, 1:20, 1:21 (2), 1:22, 1:24, 1:25 (2), 1:26, 1:27 (2), 1:28 (2), 1:29, 1:31, 2:2, 2:3 (2), 2:4, 2:5, 2:7, 2:8, 2:9, 2:15, 2:16, 2:18, 2:19, 2:21, 2:22, 3:1 (2), 3:3, 3:5 (2), 3:8 (2), 3:9, 3:13, 3:14, 3:21, 3:22, 3:23, 4:25, 5:1 (2), 5:22, 5:24 (2), 6:2, 6:4, 6:9, 6:11, 6:12, 6:13, 6:22, 7:9, 7:16, 8:1 (2), 8:15, 9:1, 9:6, 9:8, 9:12, 9:16, 9:17, 9:27, 17:3, 17:7, 17:8, 17:9, 17:15, 17:18, 17:19, 17:22, 17:23, 19:29 (2), 20:3, 20:6, 20:11, 20:13, 20:17 (2), 21:2, 21:4, 21:6, 21:12, 21:17 (3), 21:19, 21:20, 21:22, 21:23, 22:1, 22:3, 22:8, 22:9, 22:12, 23:6, 25:11, 27:28, 28:4, 28:12, 28:17, 28:20, 28:21, 28:22, 30:2, 30:6, 30:17, 30:18, 30:20, 30:22 (2), 30:23, 31:7, 31:9, 31:11, 31:16 (2), 31:24, 31:42, 31:50, 32:2, 32:3, 32:29, 32:31, 33:5, 33:10, 33:11, 35:1, 35:5, 35:7, 35:9, 35:10, 35:11, 35:13, 35:15, 39:9, 40:8, 41:16, 41:25, 41:28, 41:32 (2), 41:38, 41:39, 41:51, 41:52, 42:18, 42:28, 43:29, 44:16, 45:5, 45:7, 45:8, 45:9, 46:2, 48:9, 48:11, 48:15 (2), 48:20, 48:21, 50:19, 50:20, 50:24, 50:25

**El-Ra'iy** [*El seeing me*] (1): 16:13

**Emor** [*Sayer*] (6): 10:16, 14:7, 14:13, 15:16, 15:21, 48:22

**Enosh** [*Man*] (6): 4:26, 5:6, 5:7, 5:9, 5:10, 5:11

**Epher** [*Calf*] (1): 25:4

**Ephrat** [*Fruitful*] (4): 35:16, 35:19, 48:7 (2)

**Ephrayim** [*Double fruitfulness*] (11): 41:52, 46:20, 48:1, 48:5, 48:13, 48:14, 48:17 (2), 48:20 (2), 50:23

**Ephron** [*Powdery*] (12): 23:8, 23:10 (2), 23:13, 23:14, 23:16 (2), 23:17, 25:9, 49:29, 49:30, 50:13

**Erekh** [*long*] (1): 10:10

**Esav** [*Doing*] (76): 25:25, 25:26, 25:27, 25:28, 25:29, 25:30, 25:32, 25:34 (2), 26:34, 27:1, 27:5 (2), 27:6, 27:11, 27:15, 27:19, 27:21, 27:22, 27:23, 27:24, 27:30, 27:32, 27:34, 27:37, 27:38 (2), 27:41 (2), 27:42 (2), 28:5, 28:6, 28:8, 28:9, 32:4, 32:5, 32:7, 32:9, 32:12, 32:14, 32:18, 32:19, 32:20, 33:1, 33:4, 33:9, 33:15, 33:16, 35:1, 35:29, 36:1, 36:2, 36:4, 36:5, 36:6, 36:8 (2), 36:9, 36:10 (3), 36:12 (2), 36:13, 36:14 (2), 36:15 (2), 36:17 (2), 36:18 (2), 36:19, 36:40, 36:43

**Eseq** [*Quarrel*] (1): 26:20

Eshban [*Fire of understanding*] (1): 36:26

Eshkol [*Cluster*] (2): 14:13, 14:24

Etsbon [*I swell*] (1): 46:16

Ever [*Cross over*] (13): 10:21, 10:24, 10:25, 11:14, 11:15, 11:16, 11:17, 14:13, 39:14, 39:17, 40:15, 41:12, 43:32

Eyhhiy [*My brother*] (1): 46:21

Eylah [*Oak*] (1): 36:41

Eylon [*Strength*] (3): 26:34, 36:2, 46:14

Eyl-Paran [*Post of decoration*] (1): 14:6

Eym [*Terror*] (1): 14:5

Eynayim [*Double spring*] (2): 38:14, 38:21

Eyn-Mishpat [*Eye of judgement*] (1): 14:7

Eyphah [*Darkness*] (1): 25:4

Eyr [*Awake*] (5): 38:3, 38:6, 38:7, 46:12 (2)

Eyriy [*My city*] (1): 46:16

Eytser [*Restraint*] (3): 36:21, 36:27, 36:30

Eyval [*Stone*] (1): 36:23

Gad [*Fortune*] (4): 30:11, 35:26, 46:16, 49:19

Gahham [*Burning*] (1): 22:24

Galeyd [*Mound of witness*] (2): 31:47, 31:48

Gatam [*Burnt valley*] (2): 36:11, 36:16

Gera [*Grain*] (1): 46:21

Gerar [*Chew*] (8): 10:19, 20:1, 20:2, 26:1, 26:6, 26:17, 26:20, 26:26

Gershon [*Exile*] (1): 46:11

Getar [*Fear*] (1): 10:23

Ghamorah [*Rebellion*] (9): 10:19, 13:10, 14:2, 14:8, 14:10, 14:11, 18:20, 19:24, 19:28

Ghaza [*Strong*] (1): 10:19

Gil'ad [*Mound of witness*] (4): 31:21, 31:23, 31:25, 37:25

Girgash [*Stranger on clods*] (2): 10:16, 15:21

Giyhhon [*Burst*] (1): 2:13

Gomer [*Complete*] (2): 10:2, 10:3

Goren-Ha'atad [*Threshing floor of the brambles*] (2): 50:10, 50:11

Goshen [*Draw near*] (10): 45:10, 46:28 (2), 46:29, 46:34, 47:1, 47:4, 47:6, 47:27, 50:8

Goyim [*Nations*] (2): 14:1, 14:9

Guni [*My protection*] (1): 46:24

Hadad [*The beloved*] (2): 36:35, 36:36

Hadar [*Honor*] (1): 36:39

Hadoram [*Honor*] (1): 10:27

Hagar [*Stranger*] (12): 16:1, 16:3, 16:4, 16:8, 16:15 (2), 16:16, 21:9, 21:14, 21:17 (2), 25:12

Ham [*Roar*] (1): 14:5

Hamitspah [*Watchtower*] (1): 31:49

Haran [*Hill country*] (6): 11:26, 11:27 (2), 11:28, 11:29, 11:31

Hevel [*Empty*] (8): 4:2 (2), 4:4 (2), 4:8 (2), 4:9, 4:25

Heymam [*Exterminating*] (1): 36:22

Hhadar [*Chamber*] (1): 25:15

Hhagi [*Festive*] (1): 46:16

Hham [*Hot*] (9): 5:32, 6:10, 7:13, 9:18 (2), 9:22, 10:1, 10:6, 10:20

Hhamat [*Fortress*] (1): 10:18

Hhamor [*Donkey*] (11): 33:19, 34:2, 34:4, 34:6, 34:8, 34:13, 34:18 (2), 34:20, 34:24, 34:26

Hhamul [*Compassion*] (1): 46:12

Hhanokh [*Dedicated*] (11): 4:17 (2), 4:18, 5:18, 5:19, 5:21, 5:22, 5:23, 5:24, 25:4, 46:9

Hharan [*Burning*] (7): 11:31, 11:32, 12:4, 12:5, 27:43, 28:10, 29:4

Hhatsarmawet [*Yard of death*] (1): 10:26

Hhats'tson-Tamar [*Dividing the palm tree*] (1): 14:7

Hhawah [*Living*] (2): 3:20, 4:1

Hhawilah [*Twisting*] (4): 2:11, 10:7, 10:29, 25:18

Hhazo [*Vision*] (1): 22:22

Hhemdan [*Desirable*] (1): 36:26

Hhet [*Shattered*] (22): 10:15, 15:20, 23:3, 23:5, 23:7, 23:10 (3), 23:16, 23:18, 23:20, 25:9, 25:10, 26:34 (2), 27:46 (2), 36:2, 49:29, 49:30, 49:32, 50:13

Hhetsron [*Surrounded by a wall*] (2): 46:9, 46:12

Hhever [*Companion*] (1): 46:17

Hhevron [*Company*] (5): 13:18, 23:2, 23:19, 35:27, 37:14

Hhideqel [*Rapid*] (1): 2:14

Hhiw [*Village*] (3): 10:17, 34:2, 36:2

Hhiyrah [*Bleached white*] (2): 38:1, 38:12

Hhor [*Cave Dweller*] (5): 14:6, 36:20, 36:21, 36:29, 36:30

Hhoriy [*Cave dweller*] (1): 36:22

Hhovah [*Hiding place*] (1): 14:15

Hhul [*Twist*] (1): 10:23

Hhupim [*Shores*] (1): 46:21

Hhush [*Making haste*] (1): 46:23

Hhusham [*Haste*] (2): 36:34, 36:35

Irad [*Wild donkey*] (2): 4:18 (2)

Iyram [*Their city*] (1): 36:43

Kadesh [*Set apart*] (3): 14:7, 16:14, 20:1

Kalahh [*Old age*] (2): 10:11, 10:12

Kalneh [*Consummation*] (1): 10:10

Kaphtor [*Knob*] (1): 10:14

Karmi [*My vineyard*] (1): 46:9

Kasluhh [*Fortified*] (1): 10:14

Kedarla'omer [*Attack for sheaves*] (5): 14:1, 14:4, 14:5, 14:9, 14:17

Kena'an [*Lowered*] (57): 9:18, 9:22, 9:25, 9:26, 9:27, 10:6, 10:15, 10:18, 10:19, 11:31, 12:5 (2), 12:6, 13:7, 13:12, 15:21, 16:3, 17:8, 23:2, 23:19, 24:3,

24:37, 28:1, 28:6, 28:8, 31:18, 33:18, 34:30, 35:6, 36:2, 36:5, 36:6, 37:1, 38:2, 42:5, 42:7, 42:13, 42:29, 42:32, 44:8, 45:17, 45:25, 46:6, 46:10, 46:12, 46:31, 47:1, 47:4, 47:13, 47:14, 47:15, 48:3, 48:7, 49:30, 50:5, 50:11, 50:13

**Keran** [*Lyre*] (1): 36:26

**Keruv** [*Sword*] (1): 3:24

**Kesad** [*Clod breaker*] (4): 11:28, 11:31, 15:7, 22:22

**Keziv** [*False*] (1): 38:5

**Kit** [*Bruiser*] (1): 10:4

**Kush** [*Black*] (4): 2:13, 10:6, 10:7, 10:8

**Lamekh** [*Powerful*] (10): 4:18, 4:19, 4:23 (2), 4:24, 5:25, 5:26, 5:28, 5:30, 5:31

**Lavan** [*White*] (54): 24:29 (2), 24:50, 25:20, 27:43, 28:2, 28:5, 29:5, 29:10 (3), 29:13 (2), 29:14, 29:15, 29:16, 29:19, 29:21, 29:22, 29:24, 29:25, 29:26, 29:29, 30:25, 30:27, 30:34, 30:36, 30:40 (2), 30:42, 31:1, 31:2, 31:12, 31:19, 31:20, 31:22, 31:24, 31:25 (2), 31:26, 31:31, 31:33, 31:34, 31:36 (2), 31:43, 31:47, 31:48, 31:51, 32:1 (2), 32:5, 46:18, 46:25

**Le'ah** [*Weary*] (33): 29:16, 29:17, 29:23, 29:24, 29:25, 29:30, 29:31, 29:32, 30:9, 30:10, 30:11, 30:12, 30:13, 30:14 (2), 30:16, 30:17, 30:18, 30:19, 30:20, 31:4, 31:14, 31:33 (2), 33:1, 33:2, 33:7, 34:1, 35:23, 35:26, 46:15, 46:18, 49:31

**Lehav** [*Flame*] (1): 10:13

**Lesha** [*Fissure*] (1): 10:19

**Lethush** [*Sharpened*] (1): 25:3

**Le'um** [*Peoples*] (1): 25:3

**Lewi** [*Joined*] (6): 29:34, 34:25, 34:30, 35:23, 46:11, 49:5

**Loth** [*Covering*] (30): 11:27, 11:31, 12:4, 12:5, 13:1, 13:5, 13:7, 13:8, 13:10, 13:11 (2), 13:12, 13:14, 14:12, 14:16, 19:1 (2), 19:5, 19:6, 19:9, 19:10, 19:12, 19:14, 19:15, 19:18, 19:23, 19:29 (2), 19:30, 19:36

**Lothan** [*Covering*] (4): 36:20, 36:22 (2), 36:29

**Lud** [*Birth*] (2): 10:13, 10:22

**Luz** [*Almond*] (3): 28:19, 35:6, 48:3

**Ma'akhah** [*Cursing*] (1): 22:24

**Maday** [*Measure*] (1): 10:2

**Magdi'eyl** [*Prince of El*] (1): 36:43

**Magog** [*Roof*] (1): 10:2

**Mahalalel** [*Praise of El*] (5): 5:12, 5:13, 5:15, 5:16, 5:17

**Mahhalat** [*Stringed instrument*] (1): 28:9

**Mahhanayim** [*Two camps*] (1): 32:3

**Makhir** [*Sold*] (1): 50:23

**Makhpelah** [*Double*] (6): 23:9, 23:17, 23:19, 25:9, 49:30, 50:13

**Malki'el** [*My king is El*] (1): 46:17

**Malkiy-Tsedeq** [*King of righteousness*] (1): 14:18

**Mamre** [*Bitter place*] (10): 13:18, 14:13, 14:24, 18:1, 23:17, 23:19, 25:9, 35:27, 49:30, 50:13

**Manahhat** [*Rest*] (1): 36:23

**Masa** [*Burden*] (1): 25:14

**Mash** [*Drawn out*] (1): 10:23

**Masreyqah** [*Choice vine*] (1): 36:36

**Mathreyd** [*Driven*] (1): 36:39

**Medan** [*Quarrel*] (1): 25:2

**Meheythaveyl** [*Favored of El*] (1): 36:39

**Mehhuya'el** [*Who proclaims El*] (2): 4:18 (2)

**Menasheh** [*Causing to overlook*] (11): 41:51, 46:20, 48:1, 48:5, 48:13, 48:14 (2), 48:17, 48:20 (2), 50:23

**Merari** [*Bitter*] (1): 46:11

**Mesha** [*Storm*] (1): 10:30

**Meshek** [*Draw out*] (1): 10:2

**Metusha'el** [*His death asks*] (2): 4:18 (2)

**Metushelahh** [*His death sends*] (5): 5:21, 5:22, 5:25, 5:26, 5:27

**Mey-Zahav** [*Water of gold*] (1): 36:39

**Midian** [*Strife*] (5): 25:2, 25:4, 36:35, 37:28, 37:36

**Migdal-Eyder** [*Tower of the flock*] (1): 35:21

**Milkah** [*Queen*] (7): 11:29 (2), 22:20, 22:23, 24:15, 24:24, 24:47

**Mishma** [*Hearing*] (1): 25:14

**Mitsrayim** [*Troubles*] (99): 10:6, 10:13, 12:10, 12:11, 12:12, 12:14 (2), 13:1, 13:10, 15:18, 16:1, 16:3, 21:9, 21:21, 25:12, 25:18, 26:2, 37:25, 37:28, 37:36, 39:1 (2), 39:2, 39:5, 40:1 (2), 40:5, 41:8, 41:19, 41:29, 41:30, 41:33, 41:34, 41:36, 41:41, 41:43, 41:44, 41:45, 41:46 (2), 41:48, 41:53, 41:54, 41:55 (2), 41:56 (2), 41:57, 42:1, 42:2, 42:3, 43:2, 43:15, 43:32 (3), 45:2, 45:4, 45:8, 45:9, 45:13, 45:18, 45:19, 45:20, 45:23, 45:25, 45:26, 46:3, 46:4, 46:6, 46:7, 46:8, 46:20, 46:26, 46:27 (2), 46:34, 47:6, 47:11, 47:13, 47:14, 47:15 (2), 47:20 (2), 47:21, 47:26, 47:27, 47:28, 47:29, 47:30, 48:5 (2), 50:3, 50:7, 50:11, 50:14, 50:22, 50:26

**Mivsam** [*Sweet odor*] (1): 25:13

**Mivtsar** [*Fortress*] (1): 36:42

**Miz'zah** [*Faint*] (2): 36:13, 36:17

**Mo'av** [*From father*] (3): 19:37 (2), 36:35

**Moreh** [*Teacher*] (1): 12:6

**Moriyah** [*Appearance of Yah*] (1): 22:2

Mupim [*Serpents*] (1): 46:21

Na'amah [*Sweet*] (1): 4:22

Na'aman [*Pleasantness*] (1): 46:21

Nahhat [*Rest*] (2): 36:13, 36:17

Nahhor [*Snorting*] (16): 11:22, 11:23, 11:24, 11:25, 11:26, 11:27, 11:29 (2), 22:20, 22:23, 24:10, 24:15, 24:24, 24:47, 29:5, 31:53

Naphish [*Refreshed*] (1): 25:15

Naphtali [*Wrestling*] (4): 30:8, 35:25, 46:24, 49:21

Naphtuhh [*Opening*] (1): 10:13

Nephilim [*Fallen ones*] (1): 6:4

Nevayot [*Flourishings*] (3): 25:13, 28:9, 36:3

Nimrod [*Rebellion*] (2): 10:8, 10:9

Ninweh [*Agreeable*] (2): 10:11, 10:12

No'ahh [*Rest*] (41): 5:29, 5:30, 5:32 (2), 6:8, 6:9 (3), 6:10, 6:13, 6:22, 7:1, 7:5, 7:6, 7:7, 7:9 (2), 7:11, 7:13 (3), 7:15, 7:23, 8:1, 8:6, 8:11, 8:13, 8:15, 8:18, 8:20, 9:1, 9:8, 9:17, 9:18, 9:19, 9:20, 9:24, 9:28, 9:29, 10:1, 10:32

Nod [*Wander*] (1): 4:16

Ohad [*Shouting*] (1): 46:10

Omar [*Speaker*] (2): 36:11, 36:15

On [*Vigor*] (3): 41:45, 41:50, 46:20

Onam [*Vigorous*] (1): 36:23

Onan [*Strong*] (5): 38:4, 38:8, 38:9, 46:12 (2)

Ophir [*Reduced to ashes*] (1): 10:29

Padan [*Field* ] (1): 48:7

Padan-Aram [*Field palace*] (10): 25:20, 28:2, 28:5, 28:6, 28:7, 31:18, 33:18, 35:9, 35:26, 46:15

Palu [*Distinguished*] (1): 46:9

Paran [*Decoration*] (1): 21:21

Paroh [*Great house*] (94): 12:15 (3), 12:17, 12:18, 12:20, 37:36, 39:1, 40:2, 40:7, 40:11 (3), 40:13 (2), 40:14, 40:17, 40:19, 40:20, 40:21, 41:1, 41:4, 41:7, 41:8 (2), 41:9, 41:10, 41:14 (2), 41:15, 41:16 (2), 41:17, 41:25 (3), 41:28 (2), 41:32, 41:33, 41:34, 41:35, 41:37, 41:38, 41:39, 41:41, 41:42, 41:44 (2), 41:45, 41:46 (2), 41:55 (2), 42:15, 42:16, 44:18, 45:2, 45:8, 45:16 (2), 45:17, 45:21, 46:5, 46:31, 46:33, 47:1, 47:2, 47:3 (2), 47:4, 47:5, 47:7 (2), 47:8, 47:9, 47:10 (2), 47:11, 47:14, 47:19, 47:20 (2), 47:22 (2), 47:23, 47:24, 47:25, 47:26 (2), 50:4 (2), 50:6, 50:7

Patros [*Mouthful of dough*] (1): 10:14

Pa'u [*Screaming*] (1): 36:39

Peleg [*Half*] (5): 10:25, 11:16, 11:17, 11:18, 11:19

Peleshet [*Immigrant*] (8): 10:14, 21:32, 21:34, 26:1, 26:8, 26:14, 26:15, 26:18

Peni'el [*Face of El*] (2): 32:31, 32:32

Perat [*Break*] (2): 2:14, 15:18

Perets [*Breach*] (3): 38:29, 46:12 (2)

Perez [*Peasant*] (3): 13:7, 15:20, 34:30

Pikhol [*Face of all*] (3): 21:22, 21:32, 26:26

Pildash [*Bean thresher*] (1): 22:22

Pinon [*Darkness*] (1): 36:41

Pishon [*Scatter*] (1): 2:11

Pothee-Phera [*He whom the Ra gave*] (3): 41:45, 41:50, 46:20

Potiphar [*Belonging to the sun*] (2): 37:36, 39:1

Pu'ah [*Dispersion*] (1): 46:13

Puth [*Bow*] (1): 10:6

Qadmon [*Ancient one*] (1): 15:19

Qayin [*Acquired*] (17): 4:1, 4:2, 4:3, 4:5 (2), 4:6, 4:8 (2), 4:9, 4:13, 4:15 (2), 4:16, 4:17, 4:24, 4:25, 15:19

Qedar [*Dark*] (1): 25:13

Qedmah [*Original*] (1): 25:15

Qehat [*Assembly*] (1): 46:11

Qemu'el [*Raised of El*] (1): 22:21

Qeniz [*Hunter*] (4): 15:19, 36:11, 36:15, 36:42

Qethurah [*Incense*] (2): 25:1, 25:4

Qeynan [*Possession*] (5): 5:9, 5:10, 5:12, 5:13, 5:14

Qiryat-Arba [*City of four*] (2): 23:2, 35:27

Qorahh [*Bald*] (4): 36:5, 36:14, 36:16, 36:18

Rahhel [*Ewe*] (44): 29:6, 29:9, 29:10, 29:11, 29:12, 29:16, 29:17, 29:18 (2), 29:20, 29:25, 29:28, 29:29, 29:30 (2), 29:31, 30:1 (2), 30:2, 30:6, 30:7, 30:8, 30:14, 30:15, 30:22, 30:25, 31:4, 31:14, 31:19, 31:32, 31:33, 31:34, 33:1, 33:2, 33:7, 35:16, 35:19, 35:20, 35:24, 35:25, 46:19, 46:22, 46:25, 48:7

Ramah [*Mane of a horse*] (2): 10:7 (2)

Ra'meses [*Child of the sun*] (1): 47:11

Rapha [*Heal*] (2): 14:5, 15:20

Rehhovot [*Wide streets*] (2): 26:22, 36:37

Rehhovot-Ghir [*Wide streets of the city*] (1): 10:11

Resen [*Halter*] (1): 10:12

Re'u [*Companion*] (4): 11:18, 11:19, 11:20, 11:21

Re'u'el [*Companion of El*] (5): 36:4, 36:10, 36:13, 36:17 (2)

Re'umah [*Lifted up*] (1): 22:24

Re'uven [*See a son*] (13): 29:32, 30:14, 35:22, 35:23, 37:21, 37:22, 37:29, 42:22, 42:37, 46:8, 46:9, 48:5, 49:3

Riphat [*Health*] (1): 10:3

Rivqah [*Ensnarer*] (30): 22:23, 24:15, 24:29, 24:30, 24:45, 24:51, 24:53,

24:58, 24:59, 24:60, 24:61 (2), 24:64, 24:67, 25:20, 25:21, 25:28, 26:7, 26:8, 26:35, 27:5, 27:6, 27:11, 27:15, 27:42, 27:46, 28:5, 29:12, 35:8, 49:31

**Rosh** [*Head*] (1): 46:21

**Samlah** [*Garment*] (2): 36:36, 36:37

**Sarah** [*Noblewoman*] (37): 17:15, 17:17, 17:19, 17:21, 18:6, 18:9, 18:10 (2), 18:11 (2), 18:12, 18:13, 18:14, 18:15, 20:2 (2), 20:14, 20:16, 20:18, 21:1 (2), 21:2, 21:3, 21:6, 21:7, 21:9, 21:12, 23:1 (2), 23:2 (2), 23:19, 24:36, 24:67, 25:10, 25:12, 49:31

**Sarai** [*Princess*] (17): 11:29, 11:30, 11:31, 12:5, 12:11, 12:17, 16:1, 16:2 (2), 16:3, 16:5, 16:6 (2), 16:8 (2), 17:15 (2)

**Savtah** [*Go about*] (1): 10:7

**Savteka** [*Lead around*] (1): 10:7

**Sedom** [*Secret*] (21): 10:19, 13:10, 13:12, 13:13, 14:2, 14:8, 14:10, 14:11, 14:12, 14:17, 14:21, 14:22, 18:16, 18:20, 18:22, 18:26, 19:1 (2), 19:4, 19:24, 19:28

**Se'iyr** [*Hairy*] (9): 14:6, 32:4, 33:14, 33:16, 36:8, 36:9, 36:20, 36:21, 36:30

**Sephar** [*Numbering*] (1): 10:30

**Serahh** [*Excess*] (1): 46:17

**Sered** [*Remnant*] (1): 46:14

**Serug** [*Branch*] (4): 11:20, 11:21, 11:22, 11:23

**Seva** [*Drunkard*] (1): 10:7

**Shaddai** [*My breasts*] (6): 17:1, 28:3, 35:11, 43:14, 48:3, 49:25

**Shalem** [*Complete*] (2): 14:18, 33:18

**Sham'mah** [*Desolate*] (2): 36:13, 36:17

**Sha'ul** [*Unknown*] (3): 36:37, 36:38, 46:10

**Shaweh** [*Plain*] (1): 14:17

**Shaweh-Qiryatayim** [*Plain of cities*] (1): 14:5

**Shekhem** [*Shoulder*] (18): 12:6, 33:18, 33:19, 34:2, 34:4, 34:6, 34:8, 34:11, 34:13, 34:18, 34:20, 34:24, 34:26 (2), 35:4, 37:12, 37:13, 37:14

**Shelahh** [*Sent*] (6): 10:24 (2), 11:12, 11:13, 11:14, 11:15

**Sheleph** [*Pull*] (1): 10:26

**Shem** [*Character*] (14): 5:32, 6:10, 7:13, 9:18, 9:23, 9:26, 9:27, 10:1, 10:21, 10:22, 10:31, 11:10 (2), 11:11

**Shemever** [*Character of wing*] (1): 14:2

**Shepho** [*Bare place*] (1): 36:23

**Shet** [*Buttocks*] (7): 4:25, 4:26, 5:3, 5:4, 5:6, 5:7, 5:8

**Sheva** [*Seven*] (3): 10:7, 10:28, 25:3

**Sheylah** [*Petition*] (5): 38:5, 38:11, 38:14, 38:26, 46:12

**Shilem** [*Repaid*] (1): 46:24

**Shimon** [*Heard*] (10): 29:33, 34:25, 34:30, 35:23, 42:24, 42:36, 43:23, 46:10, 48:5, 49:5

**Shimron** [*Watched*] (1): 46:13

**Shinar** [*Country of two rivers*] (4): 10:10, 11:2, 14:1, 14:9

**Shinav** [*Teeth of father*] (1): 14:2

**Shivah** [*Oath*] (1): 26:33

**Shoval** [*Leg*] (3): 36:20, 36:23, 36:29

**Shu'a** [*Wealthy*] (2): 38:2, 38:12

**Shu'ahh** [*Sinking*] (1): 25:2

**Shuni** [*Sleep*] (1): 46:16

**Shur** [*Caravan*] (3): 16:7, 20:1, 25:18

**Sidim** [*Fields*] (3): 14:3, 14:8, 14:10

**Sin** [*Thorn*] (1): 10:17

**Sithnah** [*Accusation*] (1): 26:21

**Sukot** [*Booths*] (2): 33:17 (2)

**Tahhash** [*Badger*] (1): 22:24

**Tamar** [*Palm tree*] (5): 38:6, 38:11 (2), 38:13, 38:24

**Tarshish** [*Contemplate*] (1): 10:4

**Terahh** [*Station*] (9): 11:24, 11:25, 11:26, 11:27 (2), 11:28, 11:31, 11:32 (2)

**Teyma** [*Wonder*] (1): 25:15

**Teyman** [*South*] (4): 36:11, 36:15, 36:34, 36:42

**Thevahh** [*Slaughtering*] (1): 22:24

**Tidal** [*Breaker of the yoke*] (2): 14:1, 14:9

**Timna** [*Withhold*] (3): 36:12, 36:22, 36:40

**Timnat** [*Portion*] (3): 38:12, 38:13, 38:14

**Tiras** [*Breaking*] (1): 10:2

**Togarmah** [*Gnaw a bone*] (1): 10:3

**Tola** [*Worm*] (1): 46:13

**Tsaphnat-Paneyahh** [*Treasury of the rest*] (1): 41:45

**Tsemar** [*Woolen*] (1): 10:18

**Tsepho** [*Watcher*] (2): 36:11, 36:15

**Tseviim** [*Gazelles*] (3): 10:19, 14:2, 14:8

**Tsidon** [*Hunting*] (3): 10:15, 10:19, 49:13

**Tsilah** [*Shadow*] (3): 4:19, 4:22, 4:23

**Tsiphyon** [*Lookout*] (1): 46:16

**Tsiv'ghon** [*Colored*] (6): 36:2, 36:14, 36:20, 36:24 (2), 36:29

**Tso'ar** [*Tiny*] (7): 13:10, 14:2, 14:8, 19:22, 19:23, 19:30 (2)

**Tsohhar** [*White*] (3): 23:8, 25:9, 46:10

**Tuval** [*Flow*] (1): 10:2

**Tuval-Qayin** [*Flow of acquiring*] (2): 4:22 (2)

**Ur** [*Light*] (3): 11:28, 11:31, 15:7

**Uts** [*Counsel*] (3): 10:23, 22:21, 36:28

**Uval** [*Round*] (1): 10:28

**Uzal** [*Waver*] (1): 10:27

**Ya'aqov** [*He restrains*] (180): 25:26, 25:27, 25:28, 25:29, 25:30, 25:31, 25:33 (2), 25:34, 27:6, 27:11, 27:15, 27:17, 27:19, 27:21, 27:22 (2), 27:30 (2), 27:36,

27:41 (2), 27:42, 27:46, 28:1, 28:5 (2),
28:6, 28:7, 28:10, 28:16, 28:18, 28:20,
29:1, 29:4, 29:10 (2), 29:11, 29:12,
29:13, 29:15, 29:18, 29:20, 29:21,
29:28, 30:1 (2), 30:2, 30:4, 30:5, 30:7,
30:9, 30:10, 30:12, 30:16, 30:17, 30:19,
30:25, 30:31, 30:36 (2), 30:37, 30:40,
30:41, 30:42, 31:1, 31:2, 31:3, 31:4,
31:11, 31:17, 31:20, 31:22, 31:24, 31:25
(2), 31:26, 31:29, 31:31, 31:32, 31:33,
31:36 (2), 31:43, 31:45, 31:46, 31:47,
31:51, 31:53, 31:54, 32:2, 32:3, 32:4,
32:5, 32:7, 32:8, 32:10, 32:19, 32:21,
32:25, 32:26, 32:28, 32:29, 32:30,
32:31, 32:33, 33:1, 33:10, 33:17, 33:18,
34:1, 34:3, 34:5 (2), 34:6, 34:7 (2),
34:13, 34:19, 34:25, 34:27, 34:30, 35:1,
35:2, 35:4 (2), 35:5, 35:6, 35:9, 35:10
(2), 35:14, 35:15, 35:20, 35:22, 35:23,
35:26, 35:27, 35:29, 36:6, 37:1, 37:2,
37:34, 42:1 (2), 42:4, 42:29, 42:36,
45:25, 45:27, 46:2 (2), 46:5 (2), 46:6,
46:8 (2), 46:15, 46:18, 46:19, 46:22,
46:25, 46:26 (2), 46:27, 47:7 (2), 47:8,
47:9, 47:10, 47:28 (2), 48:2, 48:3, 49:1,
49:2, 49:7, 49:24, 49:33, 50:24

**Yaboq** [*Emptying*] **(1):** 32:23
**Yahh'le'el** [*El delays*] **(1):** 46:14
**Vahhtse'el** [*El divides*] **(1):** 46:24
**Yakhin** [*He will be firm*] **(1):** 46:10
**Yalam** [*He is concealed*] **(3):** 36:5, 36:14,
    36:18
**Yamin** [*Right hand*] **(1):** 46:10
**Yaphet** [*Wonder*] **(9):** 5:32, 6:10, 7:13, 9:18,
    9:23, 9:27, 10:1, 10:2, 10:21
**Yaq'shan** [*Snarer*] **(2):** 25:2, 25:3
**Yaqthan** [*He is small*] **(3):** 10:25, 10:26,
    10:29
**Yarden** [*Descender*] **(5):** 13:10, 13:11,
    32:11, 50:10, 50:11
**Yared** [*Descend*] **(5):** 5:15, 5:16, 5:18, 5:19,
    5:20
**Yashuv** [*He will return*] **(1):** 46:13
**Yaval** [*Watercourse*] **(1):** 4:20
**Yawan** [*Wine*] **(2):** 10:2, 10:4
**Yegar-Sa'haduta** [*Fear of a witness*] **(1):**
    31:47
**Yehudah** [*Praised*] **(28):** 29:35, 35:23,
    37:26, 38:1, 38:2, 38:6, 38:7, 38:8,
    38:11, 38:12 (2), 38:15, 38:20, 38:22,
    38:23, 38:24 (2), 38:26, 43:3, 43:8,
    44:14, 44:16, 44:18, 46:12, 46:28, 49:8,
    49:9, 49:10
**Yehudit** [*Praised*] **(1):** 26:34
**Yemu'el** [*Day of El*] **(1):** 46:10
**Yerahh** [*Moon*] **(1):** 10:26
**Yetet** [*Nail*] **(1):** 36:40

**Yethur** [*He rows*] **(1):** 25:15
**Yetser** [*Forming*] **(1):** 46:24
**Ye'ush** [*He will assemble*] **(3):** 36:5, 36:14,
    36:18
**Yevus** [*He threshes*] **(2):** 10:16, 15:21
**YHWH** [*He exists*] **(165):** 2:4, 2:5, 2:7, 2:8,
    2:9, 2:15, 2:16, 2:18, 2:19, 2:21, 2:22,
    3:1, 3:8 (2), 3:9, 3:13, 3:14, 3:21, 3:22,
    3:23, 4:1, 4:3, 4:4, 4:6, 4:9, 4:13, 4:15
    (2), 4:16, 4:26, 5:29, 6:3, 6:5, 6:6, 6:7,
    6:8, 7:1, 7:5, 7:16, 8:20, 8:21 (2), 9:26,
    10:9 (2), 11:5, 11:6, 11:8, 11:9 (2),
    12:1, 12:4, 12:7 (2), 12:8 (2), 12:17,
    13:4, 13:10 (2), 13:13, 13:14, 13:18,
    14:22, 15:1, 15:2, 15:4, 15:6, 15:7, 15:8,
    15:18, 16:2, 16:5, 16:7, 16:9, 16:10,
    16:11 (2), 16:13, 17:1, 18:1, 18:13,
    18:14, 18:17, 18:19 (2), 18:20, 18:22,
    18:26, 18:33, 19:13 (2), 19:14, 19:16,
    19:24 (2), 19:27, 20:18, 21:1 (2), 21:33,
    22:11, 22:14, 22:15, 22:16, 24:1, 24:3,
    24:7, 24:12, 24:21, 24:26, 24:27 (2),
    24:31, 24:35, 24:40, 24:42, 24:44, 24:48
    (2), 24:50, 24:51, 24:52, 24:56, 25:21
    (2), 25:22, 25:23, 26:2, 26:12, 26:22,
    26:24, 26:25, 26:28, 26:29, 27:7, 27:20,
    27:27, 28:13 (2), 28:16, 28:20, 28:21,
    29:31, 29:32, 29:33, 29:35, 30:24,
    30:27, 30:30, 31:3, 31:49, 32:10, 38:7
    (2), 38:10, 39:2, 39:3 (2), 39:5 (2),
    39:21, 39:23 (2), 49:18
**YHWH-Yireh** [*YHWH will see*] **(1):** 22:14
**Yidlap** [*He will drip*] **(1):** 22:22
**Yimnah** [*Right*] **(1):** 46:17
**Yish'baq** [*He will leave alone*] **(1):** 25:2
**Yishma'el** [*El will listen*] **(21):** 16:11, 16:15,
    16:16, 17:18, 17:20, 17:23, 17:25,
    17:26, 25:9, 25:12, 25:13 (2), 25:16,
    25:17, 28:9 (2), 36:3, 37:25, 37:27,
    37:28, 39:1
**Yishwah** [*He resembles*] **(1):** 46:17
**Yishwiy** [*He resembles me*] **(1):** 46:17
**Yiskah** [*He covers*] **(1):** 11:29
**Yisra'el** [*He turns El*] **(42):** 32:29, 32:33,
    34:7, 35:10 (2), 35:21, 35:22 (2), 36:31,
    37:3, 37:13, 42:5, 43:6, 43:8, 43:11,
    45:21, 45:28, 46:1, 46:2, 46:5, 46:8,
    46:29, 46:30, 47:27, 47:29, 47:31, 48:2,
    48:8, 48:10, 48:11, 48:13 (2), 48:14,
    48:20, 48:21, 49:2, 49:7, 49:16, 49:24,
    49:28, 50:2, 50:25
**Yis'sas'kar** [*He will lift up the wage*] **(4):**
    30:18, 35:23, 46:13, 49:14
**Yitran** [*Remainder*] **(1):** 36:26
**Yits'hhaq** [*He laughs*] **(80):** 17:19, 17:21,
    21:3, 21:4, 21:5, 21:8, 21:10, 21:12,
    22:2, 22:3, 22:6, 22:7, 22:9, 24:4, 24:14,

24:62, 24:63, 24:64, 24:66, 24:67 (2), 25:5, 25:6, 25:9, 25:11 (2), 25:19 (2), 25:20, 25:21, 25:26, 25:28, 26:1, 26:6, 26:8, 26:9 (2), 26:12, 26:16, 26:17, 26:18, 26:19, 26:20, 26:25, 26:27, 26:31, 26:32, 26:35, 27:1, 27:5, 27:20, 27:21, 27:22, 27:26, 27:30 (2), 27:32, 27:33, 27:37, 27:39, 27:46, 28:1, 28:5, 28:6, 28:8, 28:13, 31:18, 31:42, 31:53, 32:10, 35:12, 35:27 (2), 35:28, 35:29, 46:1, 48:15, 48:16, 49:31, 50:24

Yoseph [*Adding*] (156): 30:24, 30:25, 33:2, 33:7, 35:24, 37:2 (2), 37:3, 37:5, 37:13, 37:17, 37:23 (2), 37:28 (3), 37:29, 37:31, 37:33, 39:1, 39:2, 39:4, 39:5, 39:6 (2), 39:7, 39:10, 39:20, 39:21, 39:22, 40:3, 40:4, 40:6, 40:8, 40:9, 40:12, 40:16, 40:18, 40:22, 40:23, 41:14, 41:15, 41:16, 41:17, 41:25, 41:39, 41:41, 41:42, 41:44, 41:45 (2), 41:46 (2), 41:49, 41:50, 41:51, 41:54, 41:55, 41:56, 41:57, 42:3, 42:4, 42:6 (2), 42:7, 42:8, 42:9, 42:14, 42:18, 42:23, 42:25, 42:36, 43:15, 43:16, 43:17 (2), 43:18, 43:19, 43:24, 43:25, 43:26, 43:30, 44:2, 44:4, 44:14, 44:15, 45:1 (2), 45:3 (2), 45:4 (2), 45:9, 45:16, 45:17, 45:21, 45:26, 45:27 (2), 45:28, 46:4, 46:19, 46:20, 46:27, 46:28, 46:29, 46:30, 46:31, 47:1, 47:5, 47:7, 47:11, 47:12 (3), 47:15, 47:16, 47:17 (2), 47:20, 47:23, 47:26, 47:29, 48:1, 48:2, 48:3, 48:8, 48:9, 48:11, 48:12, 48:13, 48:15, 48:17, 48:18, 48:21, 49:22, 49:26, 50:1, 50:2, 50:4, 50:7, 50:8, 50:14, 50:15 (2), 50:16, 50:17 (2), 50:19, 50:22 (2), 50:23 (2), 50:24, 50:25, 50:26

Yovav [*Howler*] (3): 10:29, 36:33, 36:34

Yuval [*Creek*] (1): 4:21

Za'awan [*Trembling*] (1): 36:27

Zerahh [*Dawn*] (5): 36:13, 36:17, 36:33, 38:30, 46:12

Zevulun [*Residence*] (4): 30:20, 35:23, 46:14, 49:13

Zilpah [*Trickling*] (7): 29:24, 30:9, 30:10, 30:12, 35:26, 37:2, 46:18

Zimran [*Musician*] (1): 25:2

Zuz [*Creature*] (1): 14:5

# *Appendixes*

## Appendix A: Verb Translations

**be~Change:** repeat
**be~Kneel:** be respected
**be~see:** appear
**be~Seek~ing:** require
**make~Add:** again
**make~Be.face.to.face:** tell
**make~Boil:** ripen
**make~Came:** bring
**make~Damage:** destroy
**make~Die:** kill
**make~Go.down:** bring down
**make~Go.out:** bring out
**make~Go.up:** brought up
**make~Mimic:** interpret
**make~Pass.over:** change
**make~Pierce:** begin
**make~Remember:** mention
**make~Rest:** leave
**make~Run:** quickly brought
**make~See:** show
**make~Set:** present
**make~Suckle~ing(fs):** nurse
**make~Throw:** point
**make~Throw.the.hand:** thank
**make~Turn.aside:** remove
**make~Turn.back:** return

**make~Turn.over:** feeble
**make~Visit:** set over
**make~Wrap.around:** warn
**much.be~Tie~ing(fp):** robust
**much~Be.unclean:** defile
**much~Be.zealous:** envious
**much~Bring.forth~ing(fs):** midwife
**much~Count:** recount
**much~Err:** reconcile
**much~Fill:** fulfill
**much~Kneel:** respect
**much~Laugh:** mock
**much~Live:** keep alive
**much~Pass.over:** change
**much~Send:** send off
**much~Shine:** commend
**much~Steal:** steal away
**much~Tread.about:** spy
**self~Be.crafty:** act craftily
**self~Kneel:** respect self
**self~Know:** reveal self
**self~Recognize:** make self unrecognizable
**self~See:** look at self
**self~Show.beauty:** beseech
**self~Sieze:** strengthen self

# Appendix B: Phrase Translations

**Add Yet.again:** continue
**After So:** afterward
**Also Now:** let it be
**and~But:** but
**from~Distant to~:** beyond
**from~Facing:** opposite
**from~Outside to~the~City:** outside the city
**from~to~Separated.thing:** besides
**from~to~Upward:** upward
**from~Tomorrow:** the next day
**from~Under to~:** under
**from~Upon to~:** upon
**from~Upward to~:** upon
**from~With:** from
**from~Without:** from where
**from~Yet.again~me:** all my life
**Given.that If:** except, instead, unless
**Given.that Seeing.as Which:** seeing that
**Given.that So:** since
**Given.that Unless:** for if
**Given.that Upon:** because
**Given.that Upon So:** since
**If Not:** or not
**in~Before:** before
**in~This:** here
**in~What:** how
**in~Which:** whereas
**in~which~Also:** whereas
**in~Yet.again:** while, within

**Life:** alive
**Life~s:** life
**like~from~:** about
**like~Small.amount:** might have
**like~That.one:** as
**like~the~Word the~This:** in this manner
**like~What:** how many
**like~Which:** just as
**Look~me:** here am I
**Moreover Because:** really (as a question)
**Nose~s2:** nostrils
**Seventh.time~s2:** sevenfold
**Shining~s2:** noontime
**Short Land:** short distance
**Since Which:** because
**Sky~s2:** sky
**So Given.that:** because
**Stroke.of.time~s2:** second time
**Thus.far:** here
**to~say:** saying
**to~So:** because of this
**to~What:** why
**Until Given.that:** until
**Until Thus.far:** ever again, yet
**Upon So:** therefore
**Upon Word:** because of
**Water~s2:** water
**What Thus.far:** what is this
**Without This Given.that:** this is nothing but

**Yesterday Three.days.ago:**
previously

# Appendix C: Alternative Translations

**After:** afterward, behind
**Also:** both, should
**Also Sure:** indeed
**and:** as, that, then
**and~he~will~Exist:** and it came to pass
**Appointed:** appointed one, appointed place, appointed time
**At:** to, with
**Company:** witness
**Do:** make
**Do.well:** Go.well
**Except:** not
**Exist:** was
**Face~s:** face
**from:** at, kinds, more than, out of, rather than, to
**Given.that:** but, given, that
**He:** that, it
**I:** me
**If:** or, that
**in:** with
**Life:** living
**like:** according to, as, at, such as
**Look:** here
**make:** cause
**Man:** each
**Many:** great, greatly, much, much more, very
**Midst:** middle
**Mighty.one:** might
**Mold:** distress
**Moreover:** also

**much:** many
**No:** not
**Nose:** anger
**Not:** no, nothing
**Nothing:** anything
**On.account.of:** so that
**Only:** at all
**Opposite:** in the face of
**Other:** another
**s2:** two
**Second:** second time
**See:** watch
**Separated.thing:** self
**She:** that
**Small.amount:** small thing
**So:** should
**Stroke.of.time:** time
**Surely:** only
**the~Day:** today
**the~Night:** tonight
**There.is:** is, will
**Though:** look
**to:** about, as, at, for, belong to, by, has
**To:** at, by
**to~Face~s:** before
**to~me:** I have
**to~That:** so that, that
**Unaware:** not
**Under:** in place of, underneath
**Unit:** one
**Unit~s:** few
**Until:** again, as far as, also, before, concerning, unto

**Upon:** about, above, because, in addition to
**What:** how
**Where:** how, why
**Which:** because, because of what, how, such as, that, what, when, where, who, whoever, whose

**With:** by
**Without:** not, not with, where
**Word:** matter, thing
**Yet.again:** again, also, another, still, while, yet

# Appendix D: Idioms

**a son of thirty years:** thirty years old

**bearded one:** aged

**beauty in the eyes:** accepted

**bone of the day:** noontime

**eye:** spring

**face fell:** sad

**functional in the eye:** pleases

**lift up your face:** accept you

**nose:** anger

**nose flare up:** be very angry

**one shoulder:** in agreement

**sea:** west

**uncover the nakedness:** sexual relations

## Appendix E: Pronunciations for transliterated words and names

**a:** as the "a" in father.
**ai:** as the "ai" in aisle.
**e:** as the "e" in egg.
**ey:** as the "ey" in grey.
**gh:** as the "g" in rug.
**hh:** as the "ch" in the name Bach.
**i:** as the "ee" in knee.
**iy:** as the "ee" in knee.

**kh:** as the "ch" in the name Bach.
**o:** as the "o" in bone.
**th:** as a "t" but differentiates between the letter tav and thet.
**ts:** as the "ts" in pots.
**u:** as the "u" in tune.

# Appendix F: Verse Notes

**1:3** The phrase "the~Day the~Seventh," as seen in verse 2, is translated as "the seventh day," but the phrase "Day the~Seventh," as seen in this verse, should be translated as "day of the seventh." The prefix "the," before the word "Day," may have accidentally been dropped by a scribe and is therefore added into the RMT in order to make the same phrases of verse 2 and 3 coincide.

**2:9** The singular word "tree" may imply a "tree" or "trees." The context of this and following verses do not specify if there is one tree or a forest of trees. Compare this with 2:16.

**4:3** The phrase "from~conclusion" is usually followed by a number of years or days to identify the end of that time frame, such as in 8:6 where it states "at the conclusion of the forty days." In 4:3 it appears that either a period of days or years is missing or this verse is prophetic of the end of days.

**4:8** The conversation between Qayin and Hevel is missing from the text. The phrase "let us go into the plain" is from the Greek Septuagint. The Septuagint may have been translated from a Hebrew text with the conversation intact or the translators may have supplied it to clarify the text.

**4:26** The phrase "call out in the title" may also be translated as "met with the title."

**6:11** The grammar of the MT "and~she~will~be~Fill the~Land Violence" requires the translation "the land of violence was filled" unlike most translations which read "the land was filled with violence." If the latter is the correct translation, the Hebrew is missing the word "at" or "with." Also see verse 13.

**9:2** The grammar of the phrase "in~All Which she~will~Tread the~Ground" identifies "the~Ground" as the subject of the verb,

429

requiring the translation "in all which the ground will tread." The standard translation of this phrase is "and everything that treads upon the ground" where "the ground" is identified as the object of the verb, contrary to the Hebrew grammar of the verse. It is probable that the Hebrew is in error and should read "in~All Which Tread~ing(mp) Upon the~Ground" allowing the translation "in all which tread upon the ground."

**9:21** All modern translations have "his tent" but the Hebrew spelling of this word should be translated as "her tent." The Hebrew spelling may be in error but, in the modern Bedouin culture, which is very similar to the ancient Hebrew culture, the family tent is owned by the wife. Therefore, it is possible that the Hebrew text may use the word "her tent" in reference to this cultural context.

**9:22** The phrase "nakedness of the father" is an idiom for "sexual relations with the wife of the father" as seen in Leviticus 18:8. Also, the phrase "uncover the nakedness" is another idiom for "sexual relations." The common interpretation of this verse is that Hham saw his father naked; however this is not a wrongful act. The idiomatic phrasing of this verse means that Hham had sexual relations with his mother. This type of relationship is forbidden and is the reason why Kena'an, the product of this union, is cursed in verse 25.

**10:11** The construction of the sentence identifies Ashur as the subject of the verb "go out" and would be translated as "Ashur went out." If however, the original meaning of the phrase was "he went out to Ashur," (where the "he" is Nimrod) the word "to" should have preceded the word Ashur.

**11:29** The subject of the verb "took" is probably incorrectly written as third person singular (he~), as the subjects of the verb is identified as Avram and Nahhor. The subject of the verb should probably be third person plural (they~).

**12:8** All modern translations have "his tent" but the Hebrew spelling of this word should be translated as "her tent." The

Hebrew spelling may be in error but, in the modern Bedouin culture, which is very similar to the Ancient Hebrew culture, the family tent is owned by the wife. Therefore, it is possible that the Hebrew text may use the word "her tent" in reference to this cultural context. The phrase "he called out in the title" may also be translated as "he met with the title."

**12:15** The word "to" appears to be missing before the word "House."

**13:3** All modern translations have "his tent" but the Hebrew spelling of this word should be translated as "her tent." The Hebrew spelling may be in error but, in the modern Bedouin culture, which is very similar to the Ancient Hebrew culture, the family tent is owned by the wife. Therefore, it is possible that the Hebrew text may use the word "her tent" in reference to this cultural context.

**13:4** The phrase "call out in the title" may also be translated as "met with the title."

**14:23** The first part of the verse is in the positive while the final sentence is in the negative. The word "not" appears to be missing from the first part of the verse three times as the context requires it to also be in the negative.

**15:2** The Hebrew text has the names listed as "Dameseq Eliezer" which requires the translation "Dameseq of Eliezer" or as a compound name - "Dameseq-Eliezer." If the standard translation of "Eliezer of Damascus" is correct then the names must be reversed to "Eliezer Dameseq."

**17:16** The verb "i~did~Give" should be translated as "I gave" but the context indicates that this verb should have been written as "i~will~Give" and would then be translated as "I will give."

**18:1** The text in the Hebrew translated in the MT as "and~He Sit~ing(ms) Opening the~Tent like~Hot the~Day" does not contextually make sense. The Hebrew may be in error and may have originally been written as "and~He Sit~ing(ms) in~Opening the~Tent in~Hot the~Day".

**18:3** The name "Adonai" may be translated as the name "Adonai [*my lords*]" or as "my lords." Context supports both translations as there are three men before Avraham allowing for the "my lords" translation but, the three uses of the pronoun "you" in the singular implies that he is speaking to one individual supporting the translation of the name "Adonai [*my lords*]".

**18:10** The prefix "in," or other clarifying word, is missing from the word "opening."

**19:4** The phrase "they~did~be~Surround" implies that the men of Sedom were surrounded. As the context of the verse is the men of Sedom surrounding the house of Loth it appears that the phrase should read "they~did~Surround." The phrase "and~the~Door he~did~Shut" should read "and~at the~door he~did~shut" (compare with 19:10).

**20:2** The Hebrew of this verse appears to be missing some text. It appears this verse should read something like "and Avraham said to Sarah his woman [missing text, possibly - say you are my brother] [missing text, possibly - and he said to Aviymelek the king of Gerar] she is my sister and Aviymelekh the king of Gerar sent [missing text, possibly - his servant] and he took Sarah (See 20:5)

**20:6** Most translations have something like "and it was I who kept you from sinning against me" implying the sin of Aviymelekh. The Hebrew however implies it is the sin (fault) of Avraham.

**23:10** The word "Gate" is missing the prefix "to."

**25:30** The phrase "the~red" appears twice and is probably an accidental repeat by a scribe.

**26:15** The phrase "and~they(m)~will~much~Fill~them(m) Powder" is missing a preposition and should probably read "and~they(m)~will~much~Fill~them(m) With Powder" or "and~they(m)~will~much~Fill~them(m) in~Powder."

**26:23** The phrase "from~There 'B'er.Sheva [*Pit of oath*]'" is missing the word or prefix "to."

**26:25** The phrase "he called out in the title" may also be translated as "he met with the title."

**26:28** The phrase Between~s~us is written twice in the Hebrew. In one case the word between is written in the masculine plural and the other is in the feminine plural. It would appear that one of these was accidentally added to the text.

**26:29** The phrase "like~Which," meaning "just as," implies the phrase before is similar in meaning to the phrase after. If the phrase after the "like~Which" is positive then the phrase before must also be positive but, the phrase is negative. The probable solution is that the word "Not" is missing prior to the verb "you(ms)~will~Do."

**27:28** The sentence "and~he~will~Give to~you(ms) the~'Elohiym [*Powers*]' from~Dew the~Sky~s2" may also be translated as "and he gave to you the powers from the dew of the sky."

**29:24** The word Maid (final word of the verse) appears to be missing the prefix "to~" (see 29:29 for a comparison).

**29:34** The word "he~did~call.out" is probably an error for "she~did~call.out" as Le'ah called out the names of the other three children (see 29:32, 29:33 and 29:35).

**30:11** The phrase "in~Fortune" is in error for "he~did~come Fortune."

**31:4** The phrase "the~Field To Flocks~him" should be translated as "the field to his flocks" but may have originally been written as "To the~Field Flocks~him" which would be translated as "to the field of his flock" which better fits the context of the sentence structure.

**31:21** The word "Upon" or "To" appears to be missing from the word "hill."

**32:1** This verse is the first verse of chapter 32 in Hebrew Bibles but in English Bibles this verse is the last verse (55) of chapter 31. For the remainder of this chapter the verse numbers in English Bibles will be one number lower. For instance, verse 32:5 in the Hebrew Bible will be 32:4 in English Bibles.

**32:31** The verse appears to be missing the phrase "he~did~say" prior to "i~did~see."

**33:18** The verse appears to be missing one or two prepositions. There are several possible translations for this verse depending on where the preposition or prepositions are placed. One possible translation is "and Ya'aqov came *to* Shalem, a city of Shekhem." Another possible translation is "and Ya'aqov came *in* completeness *to* the city of Shekhem" (the word Shalem would be a noun rather than a proper name). Another is "and Ya'aqov of Shalem came *to* the city of Shekhem" (nowhere does the text suggest that Ya'aqov is from Shalem which would invalidate this translation).

**35:1** The word "To," the prefix "to" or the suffix "unto" appears to be missing from the name "Beyt El."

**35:3** The word "To," the prefix "to" or the suffix "unto" appears to missing from the name "Beyt El."

**35:21** All modern translations have "his tent" but the Hebrew spelling of this word should be translated as "her tent." The Hebrew spelling may be in error but, in the modern Bedouin culture, which is very similar to the Ancient Hebrew culture, the family tent is owned by the wife. Therefore, it is possible that the Hebrew text may use the word "her tent" in reference to this cultural context.

**35:27** The word "To," the prefix "to" or the suffix "unto" appears to be missing from the name "Mamre" and "Qiryat Arbahh."

**36:24** The list of the sons of Tsiv'on begin with "and" unlike any other list of names. Either the "and" was accidentally added to the beginning of the list of names or there is suppose to be a name preceding this first "and."

**36:26** The Hebrew text identifies this name as Dishan  but is probably written in error and should be Dishon. Compare the names of the sons of Dishan from Genesis 36:28 and 1 Chronicles 1:42 and the names of the sons of Dishon from Genesis 36:26 and 1 Chronicles 1:41 (although, in the Genesis account the first son is Hhemdan but in the Chronicles account it is Amram. In the middle (paleo) Hebrew script the letters used to write each of these names are similar in appearance and are easy to juxtapose.)

**37:21** The phrase "Not we~will~make~Hit~him Being" would literally be translated as "we will not hit him, a being" and makes no grammatical sense. The phrase may have originally been written as "Not we~will~make~Hit Being~him" meaning "we will not hit his being."

**39:2** The Hebrew word for "lord" is written in the plural, possibly in reference to the great power (often emphasised by plurality) that Potiphar holds. This is also found in verses 3, 7, 8, 19 and 20.

**40:1** The Hebrew word for "lord" is written in the plural, possibly in reference to the great power (often emphasised by plurality) that the King holds. Also in verse 7.

**40:4** The context of the story implies that Yoseph was placed in charge over the drinker and the baker. The structure of the sentence as written should be translated as "and the noble of the slaughterers visited Yoseph with them." The verb "visit" is written in the text as simple-active (Visit) but should be in the causative-active (make~Visit) which would then be translated as "and the noble of the slaughterers set Yoseph over them."

**41:39** An alternate reading would be "and Paroh said to Yoseph, after Elohiym..." It is not certain if the word "After" is part of what Paroh said or if it comes before the words of Paroh.

**41:40** The phrase, from the RMT, "upon your mouth he will kiss all my people" could be also be translated as "and by the words of your mouth will all my people be touched" or "and by your edge (of the sword) will all my people be armed."

**42:19** The phrase "!(mp)~make~Come Barley Famine House~s~you(mp)" appears to be missing the prefix "to~" before the word "Famine."

**42:25** Most translations have "with grain" but the word "with" is not in the Hebrew text. Either this word is missing from the text or the word grain is in the construct state - instruments of grain.

**42:30** The Hebrew word for "lord" is written in the plural, possibly in reference to the great power (often emphasised by plurality) that Yoseph holds. Also in verse 33.

**43:14** The word "i-did-Be.childless" is written twice, probably a scribal error.

**43:15** The phrase "and~they(m)~will~Go.down 'Mitsrayim [*Troubles*]'" should read "and Mitsrayim went down." However, the context implies the sons went down to Mitsrayim therefore, the suffix "unto" or the prefix "to" is missing from the word Mitsrayim which would then read "and they went down unto Mitsrayim."

**43:18** The RMT for "they~did~make.be~Come House 'Yoseph [*Adding*]'" should read "and they were brought down house of

Yoseph." The word house appears to be missing the suffix "unto" or the prefix "to" so that it would read "and they were brought down unto the house of Yoseph." The phrase "and~to~>~Take At~us to~the~Servant~s" can be translated as "and to take us to the servants" or "and take us for servants."

**43:29** The grammar of the phrase "and~he~will~Say 'Elohiym [*Powers*]' he~will~Show.beauty~you(ms) Son~me" can also be translated as "and Elohiym said, he will show you beauty my son."

**43:34** The beginning of this verse reads differently in the *Biblia Hebraica Stuttgartensia* which would be translated in the MT as "and~he~will~Lift.up Uprising~s from~At Uprising Uprising~s". In the RMT this would be translated as "and he lifted up the uprisings from the uprising of the uprisings."

**44:1** The three nouns "Bag~s the~Man~s Foodstuff" should grammatically be translated as "the bags of the men of the foodstuff" but, apparently a word, such as "With," is missing before the word "Foodstuff."

**44:13** The phrase "and~he~will~Load Man," would be translated as "and a man loaded" but context dictates that the phrase should read as "and~they(m)~will~Load Man" which would then be translated as "and each loaded" (compare with 44:11).

**45:5** The verb "he~will~Flare.up" appears to be an error as the context implies that it should be "you(mp)~will~Flare.up."

**45:16** The prefix "in" appears to be missing before the word "house."

**46:12** The subject of the verb "and~he~will~die" is identified as Eyr and Onan therefore, the verb should be written as "and~they~will~die."

**46:23** It is uncertain if the descendant of Dan identified here is named Hhushim (a plural name due to the "im" suffix) or are the descendants of Hhush (plural in number). Because the verse begins with "and the sons" (plural) it would appear that it is the descendants of Hhush but, the total number of children born to Bilhah are seven (see vs. 25) and Hushim would be only one of these.

**47:22** The Hebrew word translated as "Custom" in the MT is hhoq meaning custom (see vs. 26) but may have been miswritten for the word hheleq meaning a portion (see 31:14).

**50:26** Even this verse will end with a comma as the first verse of the next book (Shemot/Exodus) begins with "and these are the names..." implying a continuation of this verse.

# *Bibliography*

Jeff A. Benner, <u>Ancient Hebrew Lexicon of the Bible</u>, (Virtual Bookworm, College Station, Tx. 2005)

Benjamin Davidson, <u>The Analytical Hebrew and Chaldee Lexicon</u>, (London, Samuel Bagster)

<u>Gesenius' Hebrew Grammar</u>, (London, Oxford Press, 2nd English Ed. 1910)

<u>The American Standard Version of the Holy Bible</u>

<u>The Holy Bible, King James Version</u>

<u>Jewish Publication Society of America Version, 1917 Edition</u>

<u>Biblia Hebraica Leningradensia</u>

<u>Biblia Hebraica Stutgartensia</u>

_**Notes**_

Jeff A. Benner

Jeff A. Benner

Printed in the United States
83850LV00002BB/1/A